Style

Manual

An official guide to the form and style
of Federal Government publishing | **2016**

Keeping America Informed | OFFICIAL | DIGITAL | SECURE

gpostyle@gpo.gov

Production and Distribution Notes

This publication was typeset electronically using Helvetica and Minion Pro typefaces. It was printed using vegetable oil-based ink on recycled paper containing 30% post consumer waste.

The GPO STYLE MANUAL will be distributed to libraries in the Federal Depository Library Program. To find a depository library near you, please go to the Federal depository library directory at http://catalog.gpo.gov/fdlpdir/public.jsp.

The electronic text of this publication is available for public use free of charge at https://www.govinfo.gov/gpo-style-manual.

Library of Congress Cataloging-in-Publication Data

Names: United States. Government Publishing Office, author.
Title: Style manual : an official guide to the form and style of federal
    government publications / U.S. Government Publishing Office.
Other titles: Official guide to the form and style of federal government
    publications | Also known as: GPO style manual
Description: 2016; official U.S. Government edition. | Washington, DC : U.S.
    Government Publishing Office, 2016. | Includes index.
Identifiers: LCCN 2016055634| ISBN 9780160936029 (cloth) | ISBN 0160936020
    (cloth) | ISBN 9780160936012 (paper) | ISBN 0160936012 (paper)
Subjects: LCSH: Printing—United States—Style manuals. | Printing,
    Public—United States—Handbooks, manuals, etc. | Publishers and
    publishing—United States—Handbooks, manuals, etc. | Authorship—Style
    manuals. | Editing—Handbooks, manuals, etc.
Classification: LCC Z253 .U58 2016 | DDC 808/.02—dc23 | SUDOC GP 1.23/4:ST
    9/2016
LC record available at https://lccn.loc.gov/2016055634

Use of ISBN Prefix

AUTHENTICATED
U.S. GOVERNMENT
INFORMATION
GPO

This is the official U.S. Government edition of this publication and is herein identified to certify its authenticity. ISBN 978–0–16–093601–2 is for U.S. Government Publishing Office official editions only. The Superintendent of Documents of the U.S. Government Publishing Office requests that any reprinted edition be labeled clearly as a copy of the authentic work, and that a new ISBN be assigned.

For sale by the Superintendent of Documents, U.S. Government Publishing Office
Internet: bookstore.gpo.gov Phone: toll free (866) 512-1800; DC area (202) 512-1800
Fax: (202) 512-2104 Mail: Stop IDCC, Washington, DC 20402-0001

ISBN 978-0-16-093601-2 (Paper)

THE UNITED STATES GOVERNMENT PUBLISHING OFFICE STYLE MANUAL
IS PUBLISHED UNDER THE DIRECTION AND AUTHORITY OF

THE DIRECTOR OF THE UNITED STATES GOVERNMENT PUBLISHING OFFICE
Davita E. Vance-Cooks

———

———

Previous printings of the GPO STYLE MANUAL: 1894, 1898, 1900, 1903, 1908, 1909, 1911, 1912, 1914, 1917, 1922, 1923, 1924, 1926, 1928, 1929, 1933, 1934, 1935, 1937, 1939, 1945, 1953, 1959, 1962, 1967, 1973, 1984, 2000, 2008

EXTRACT FROM THE PUBLIC PRINTING LAW

(TITLE 44, U.S.C.)

§ 1105. Form and style of work for departments

The Director of the Government Publishing Office shall determine the form and style in which the printing or binding ordered by a department is executed, and the material and the size of type used, having proper regard to economy, workmanship, and the purposes for which the work is needed.

(Pub. L. 90–620, Oct. 22, 1968, 82 Stat. 1261; Pub. L. 113–235, div. H, title I, § 1301(c)(1), Dec. 16, 2014, 128 Stat. 2537.)

HISTORICAL AND REVISION NOTES

Based on 44 U.S. Code, 1964 ed., § 216 (Jan. 12, 1895, ch. 23, § 51, 28 Stat. 608).

AMENDMENTS

2014—Pub. L. 113–235 substituted "Director of the Government Publishing Office" for "Public Printer".

About This Manual

The GPO STYLE MANUAL, as it is popularly known, is issued under the authority of section 1105 of title 44 of the U.S. Code, which requires the Director of the GPO to "determine the form and style in which the printing . . . ordered by a department is executed, . . . having proper regard to economy, workmanship, and the purposes for which the work is needed." The MANUAL is prepared by the GPO Style Board, composed of proofreading, printing, and Government documents specialists from within GPO, where all congressional publications and many other key Government documents are prepared.

The first GPO STYLE MANUAL appeared in 1894. It was developed originally as a printer's stylebook to standardize word and type treatment, and it remains so today. Through successive editions, however, the MANUAL has come to be widely recognized by writers and editors both within and outside the Federal Government as one of the most useful resources in the editorial arsenal. And now in the 21st century, writers and editors are using the MANUAL in the preparation of the informational content of Government publications that appear in digital formats.

Writers and editors whose disciplines have taught them aspects of style different from those found in the GPO STYLE MANUAL will appreciate the difficulty of establishing a single standard. Users of this MANUAL should consider it instead as a general guide. Its rules cannot be regarded as rigid, for the printed word assumes many shapes and variations in final presentation, and usage changes over time as language evolves. Periodically the MANUAL is updated, as this edition has been, to eliminate obsolete standards, update form and usage, and adjust the guidance for document preparation and appearance to current custom.

Comments and suggestions from users of the GPO STYLE MANUAL are welcomed. All such correspondence may be emailed to the GPO Style Board at gpostyle@gpo.gov.

A digital version of this MANUAL appears on GPO's **govinfo** at https://www.govinfo.gov/gpo-style-manual. Revisions and updates are made to the online version of this MANUAL periodically. Accordingly, that document rather than the printed edition should be consulted as the most up-to-date version available.

For the purposes of the GPO STYLE MANUAL, examples provided throughout both the printed and digital versions are to be given the same weight as the enumerated rules.

Acknowledgments

The GPO Style Board would like to thank the following people for assistance in the production of this edition of the GPO STYLE MANUAL:

Special thanks go to Michael M. Shelton, Program Analyst, Office of Policy, National Park Service, and Member of the U.S. Board on Geographic Names, for his wealth of knowledge, special consultation, and research during the entire revision process of this MANUAL. He has, indeed, been a true friend to the Board.

M. Michael Abramson, past Chair of the GPO Style Board, who acted as an adviser to the present Style Board.

Elizabeth Appel, Bureau of Indian Affairs, U.S. Department of the Interior, for advice on the issue of capitalization of "Tribe" and "Tribal."

Douglas Caldwell, Geospatial Research Laboratory, U.S. Army Engineer Research and Development Center and Jacqueline Nolan, Geography and Map Division, Library of Congress, for information on acronyms and cartographic names.

The offices of Indiana Senators Dan Coats and Joe Donnelly and Indiana Governor Mike Pence for information regarding the demonym "Hoosier."

Rachel R. Creviston, Chief of Staff, Office of the Secretary of the Senate; Matthew P. McGowan, Senate Committee on Rules and Administration; and Corey Plank, Lead Cartographer—Remote Sensing, Bureau of Land Management, for consulting on the issue regarding compass directional abbreviations.

Linda Crown, Administrative Specialist, Office of Weights and Measures, National Institute of Standards and Technology, for information on terms of measures.

Robert W. Dahl, Cadastral Surveyor, U.S. Department of the Interior, Bureau of Land Management, Minerals & Realty Management Directorate, Division of Lands, Realty & Cadastral Survey (WO–350), for his contribution of the Principal Meridians and Base Lines of the United States tables, Chapter 18.

Cynthia L. Etkin, Program Planning Specialist, Office of the Superintendent of Documents, Government Publishing Office, for her assistance in the production of this MANUAL.

Dean Gardei, Brand and Web Manager, Government Publishing Office, for the design of the cover and title page.

Solange A. Garvey, Foreign Affairs Officer and Leo Dillon, Office of the Geographer and Global Issues, U.S. Department of State; and Trent Palmer, Executive Secretary for Foreign Names, U.S. Board on Geographic Names, for information on foreign countries and terms.

Jeremy Gelb, IT Specialist, Government Publishing Office, for technical assistance in the production of this MANUAL.

Christine Jones, Editorial Team Lead, Information Design and Publishing Staff, National Center for Health Statistics, Centers for Disease Control and Prevention, for information on medical eponyms.

Library Services & Content Management Staff, including Patricia A. Duplantis, Systems Librarian; Laurie B. Hall, Chief and Acting Superintendent of Documents; James M. Mauldin, Manager, Office of Archival Management; and Kelly M. Seifert, Strategic Communications Coordinator, for their feedback and support.

Christine McMahon, Program Planner, Programs, Strategy and Technology, Government Publishing Office, for her contribution in updating the GPO's Digital Information Initiatives.

James Moore, Gibbs & Cox, Inc., for information regarding technical abbreviations.

Kirk Petri and Jon Quandt, Lead Program Planners, Programs, Strategy and Technology, and John Foley and Jiang (John) Zheng, IT Specialists, Information Technology, Government Publishing Office, for their contributions in updating the information technology acronyms and initialisms section in the abbreviations and letter symbols chapter.

Kathleen Swiatek, IT Specialist, IT Product Support, for Bill language assistance.

Marcia Thompson, Chief, Congressional Record Index Office, Government Publishing Office, for revisions to the pages relating to the Congressional Record Index.

Louis Yost, Executive Secretary and Jennifer Runyon, Staff, U.S. Board on Geographic Names, for help on a variety of names and geographic issues.

Employees of the Production Planning and Control Division, Government Publishing Office, for their contributions during the preproduction/production process.

Employees of the Proof and Copy Markup Section, Government Publishing Office, for their constant contributions to the GPO Style Manual.

Current users who have contributed many ideas and suggestions that were incorporated into this edition of the GPO Style Manual.

GPO's Digital Information Initiatives

In the digital age, GPO is responsible for providing public access to the digital versions of many of the official documents it prints, as well as—to the greatest extent possible—the digital versions of Government publications that are not printed but are otherwise made available on other Federal websites. GPO recognizes that a Federal author today often begins the content creation process at a computer, and frequently publishes the final document to the web without creating a print version that will make its way to a user's hands or a library's shelves.

GPO Access

To accommodate this transition in Federal publishing strategies while preserving GPO's core responsibility for ensuring public access to Government publications, Congress enacted Public Law 103–40, the Government Printing Office Electronic Information Access Enhancement Act of 1993, which required GPO to establish access to key Government publications in digital format and provide a system of storage to ensure permanent public access to the information they contain. Opened to the public in 1994, the resulting website, GPO Access, was GPO's entrance into the digital age. In 2003, the National Archives and Records Administration formally recognized GPO as an affiliate archive for the digital content on the GPO Access site. GPO Access operated for 15 years before it was retired following the introduction of GPO's Federal Digital System (FDsys).

Federal Digital System (FDsys)

To meet continued public demand for access to digital Government publications, provide for an increased range of search and retrieval options, and ensure the preservation of official Government information content in the 21st century, GPO embarked on the construction of a more comprehensive online capability, called the Federal Digital System, or FDsys, available at www.fdsys.gov.

FDsys was launched as a beta website in 2009 and permanently replaced GPO Access in 2011. FDsys provides free access to hundreds of thousands of official Federal Government publications in digital format from all three branches of the Federal Government, including congressional bills, the Congressional Record, the Federal Register, the Compilation of Presidential Documents, the U.S. Code, the Code of Federal Regulations, and opinions from more than 100 Federal courts. In 2016, GPO reached a milestone of two billion retrievals of digital Government information from FDsys (the equivalent of nine retrievals per second over seven years of operation).

govinfo beta website

In February 2016, GPO launched the next generation of digital public access, **govinfo** (at www.govinfo.gov) as a public beta website to eventually replace the FDsys public website. **govinfo** is a redesign of FDsys featuring a modern, easy-to-use look and feel that syncs with the need of today's Government information users for quick and effective digital access across a variety of digital platforms. It was developed with a focus on implementing feedback from users and improving overall search and access to FDsys content. The redesigned, mobile-friendly website incorporates state-of-the-art innovative technologies and includes several new features for an overall enhanced user experience. **govinfo** is the new front door to accessing the same official, preserved content that GPO has made available through *GPO Access* and FDsys for more than two decades.

The key new features of **govinfo** include the capability to link related content, new ways to browse content, a new open-source search engine, enhancements to the search filters, and more options for sharing pages and content on social media.

Digital preservation

Content in FDsys and **govinfo** is preserved to ensure permanent availability in electronic form. As a preservation repository, GPO follows archival system standards to ensure long-term preservation and access to digital content. GPO's digital stewardship vision is to operate a standards-based preservation repository and to implement user-friendly, responsive, and innovative technologies to ensure that all archived content information can be obtained, rendered, used, and understood by the designated community into the future.

In 2015, GPO began pursuing certification of its flagship system as a Trustworthy Digital Repository for Government information under ISO 16363: Audit and Certification of Trustworthy Digital Repositories.

Authentication of digital documents

The increasing use of documents in digital format poses a special challenge in verifying authenticity, because digital technology makes such documents easy to alter or copy in unauthorized or illegitimate ways. GPO assures users that the publications available from GPO websites are as official and authentic as publications that have been printed by GPO for many years. GPO digital systems operate with established trust relationships between all parties in digital transactions. A visible digital signature, viewed as the GPO Seal of Authenticity signified by an eagle, verifies document integrity and authenticity on GPO online Federal documents. The visible digital signature on PDF documents on FDsys and **govinfo** signifies a guarantee that the information in the document is official, authentic, and secure.

XML bulk data repository

Since the launch of FDsys, GPO has worked with partners in the legislative and executive branches to expand the availability of Government information content in support of an open and transparent government. One such effort involves making content available in machine-readable Extensible Markup Language (XML) format for bulk download. The effort began in 2009 and has grown to nine collections now available through GPO's bulk data repository at www.gpo.gov/fdsys/bulkdata. The repository features data collections including text, summary, and status information for bills introduced in the House of Representatives and the Senate, the annual official and unofficial digital versions of the Code of Federal Regulations, the Federal Register, the U.S. Government Manual, and the Public Papers of the Presidents of the United States.

Information available on GPO's XML bulk data repository helps maximize the ways this data can be used or repurposed by users. Making information available in XML permits data to be reused and repurposed for mobile web applications, data mashups, and other analytical tools by third-party providers, contributing to efforts supporting openness and transparency in government.

Catalog of U.S. Government Publications (CGP)

GPO is responsible for creating a catalog and index for all public documents published by the Federal Government that are not confidential in character. This work serves libraries and the public nationwide and enables people to locate desired Government publications in all formats. The public interface for accessing these cataloging records is the Catalog of U.S. Government Publications (CGP), which is available in digital format at http://catalog.gpo. gov. Using the CGP, anyone can freely access descriptive information for historical and current Government publications as well as digital links to their full content. Print versions of U.S. Government publications may be found by contacting a Federal depository library: https://catalog.gpo.gov/ fdlpdir/FDLPdir.jsp.

Ben's Guide to the U.S. Government

Ben's Guide, available at http://bensguide.gpo.gov, provides learning tools for K–12 students, parents, and educators. The site provides age-specific explanations about how the Federal Government works, explains the use of the primary source materials available on FDsys and **govinfo**, and explains GPO's role in the Federal Government.

Online U.S. Government Bookstore

Government information users may also locate and order publications available for sale in both print and digital—including eBook—formats through GPO's Publication and Information Sales Program. Orders may be placed online securely at https://bookstore.gpo.gov.

Applicability of the GPO Style Manual to digital publications

The rules of grammar, spelling, punctuation, and related matters, as stated in this Manual, will serve well when preparing documents for digital access. Most of the documents on FDsys and **govinfo** are derived from databases used in the printing of Government publications. As the availability of Government publications in digital formats continues to grow, the rules as stated in this Manual will continue to be GPO's standard for all document preparation, whether for conventional printing or digital access.

Contents

Chapter		Page
	About This Manual	v
	GPO's Digital Information Initiatives	ix
1.	Advice to Authors and Editors	1
2.	General Instructions	7
3.	Capitalization Rules	27
4.	Capitalization Examples	45
5.	Spelling	81
6.	Compounding Rules	97
7.	Compounding Examples	111
8.	Punctuation	193
9.	Abbreviations and Letter Symbols	221
	Standard word abbreviations	238
	Standard letter symbols for units of measure	248
	Standard Latin abbreviations	252
	Information technology acronyms and initialisms	256
10.	Signs and Symbols	263
11.	Italic	269
12.	Numerals	273
13.	Tabular Work	285
14.	Leaderwork	303
15.	Footnotes, Indexes, Contents, and Outlines	307
16.	Datelines, Addresses, and Signatures	313
17.	Useful Tables	325
	U.S. Presidents and Vice Presidents	325
	State Populations and Their Capitals	326
	Principal Foreign Countries	327
	Demonyms: Names of Nationalities	337
	Currency	339
	Metric and U.S. Measures	345
	Common Measures and Their Metric Equivalents	346
	Measurement Conversion	347
18.	Geologic Terms and Geographic Divisions	349
19.	Congressional Record	377
	Congressional Record Index	413
20.	Reports and Hearings	425
	Index	441

1. Advice to Authors and Editors

The GPO STYLE MANUAL is intended to facilitate the production of Government publications. Careful observance of the following suggestions will aid in expediting your publication and reduce costs.

1.1. Making changes after submission of copy delays the production of the publication and adds to the expense of the work; therefore, copy must be carefully edited before being submitted to the Government Publishing Office.

1.2. Legible copy, not faint reproductions, must be furnished.

1.3. Copy should be on one side only with each sheet numbered consecutively. If both sides of copy are to be used, a duplicate set of copy must be furnished.

1.4. To avoid unnecessary expense, it is advisable to have each page begin with a new paragraph.

1.5. Proper names, signatures, figures, foreign words, and technical terms should be written plainly.

1.6. Chemical symbols, such as Al, Cl, Tl are sometimes mistaken for A1, C1, T1. Editors must indicate whether the second character is a letter or a figure.

1.7. Footnote reference marks in text and tables should be arranged consecutively from left to right across each page of copy.

1.8. Photographs, drawings, and legends being used for illustrations should be placed in the manuscript where they are to appear in the publication. They should be on individual sheets, as they are handled separately during typesetting.

1.9. If a publication is composed of several parts, a scheme of the desired arrangement must accompany the first installment of copy.

1.10. To reduce the possibility of costly blank pages, avoid use of new odd pages and halftitles whenever possible. Generally these refinements should be limited to quality bookwork.

1.11.   Samples should be furnished if possible. They should be plainly marked showing the desired type, size of type page, illustrations if any, paper, trim, lettering, and binding.

1.12.   In looseleaf or perforated-on-fold work, indicate folio sequence, including blank pages, by circling in blue. Begin with first text page (title). Do not folio separate covers or dividers.

1.13.   Indicate on copy if separate or self-cover. When reverse printing in whole or in part is required, indicate if solid or tone.

1.14.   Avoid use of oversize fold-ins wherever possible. This can be done by splitting a would-be fold-in and arranging the material to appear as facing pages in the text. Where fold-ins are numerous and cannot be split, consider folding and inserting these into an envelope pasted to the inside back cover.

1.15.   Every effort should be made to keep complete jobs of over 4 pages to signatures (folded units) of 8, 12, 16, 24, or 32 pages. Where possible, avoid having more than two blank pages at the end.

1.16.   Indicate alternative choice of paper on the requisition. Where possible, confine choice of paper to general use items carried in inventory as shown in the GPO Paper Catalogue (https://www.gpo.gov/pdfs/customers/GPOPaperCatalogue0614.pdf).

1.17.   If nonstandard trim sizes and/or type areas are used, indicate head and back margins. Otherwise, GPO will determine the margins.

1.18.   Customers should submit copy for running heads and indicate the numbering sequence for folios, including the preliminary pages.

1.19.   Corrections should be made on first proofs returned, as later proofs are intended for verification only. All corrections must be indicated on the "R" (revise) set of proofs, and only that set should be returned to GPO.

1.20.   Corrections should be marked in the margins of a proof opposite the indicated errors, not by writing over the print or between the lines. All queries on proofs must be answered or no change will be made.

1.21. The following GPO publications relate to material included in this MANUAL.

Government Paper Specification Standards

The purpose of these standards is to achieve compliance with relevant statutes regarding printing papers; address environmental, workplace safety, and paper longevity issues; and achieve maximum savings in the Government's paper purchases. 2011 (https://www.gpo.gov/pdfs/customers/sfas/vol12/vol_12.pdf).

GPO Paper Samples

This publication is a supplement to Government Paper Specification Standards. It includes samples of papers used by GPO. Used as a planning aid and guide in selecting an adequate grade, weight, and color of paper for a job of printing. 2011.

1.22.   Corrections made to proofs should be indicated as follows:

⊙	Insert period	*rom.*	Roman type
⋀	Insert comma	*caps.*	Caps—used in margin
:	Insert colon	≡	Caps—used in text
;	Insert semicolon	*c+sc*	Caps & small caps—used in margin
?	Insert question mark	≝	Caps & small caps—used in text
!	Insert exclamation mark	*l.c.*	Lowercase—used in margin
=/	Insert hyphen	/	Used in text to show deletion or substitution
∜	Insert apostrophe		
⩔⩔	Insert quotation marks	ℯ	Delete
⊥N	Insert 1-en dash	ℨ	Delete and close up
⊥M	Insert 1-em dash	*w.f.*	Wrong font
#	Insert space	⌒	Close up
ld>	Insert ( ) points of space	⊐	Move right
shill	Insert shilling	⊏	Move left
⋁	Superior	⊓	Move up
⋀	Inferior	⊔	Move down
(/)	Parentheses	‖	Align vertically
[/]	Brackets	⹀	Align horizontally
☐	Indent 1 em	⊐⊏	Center horizontally
☐☐	Indent 2 ems	⊔⊓	Center vertically
¶	Paragraph	*eq.#*	Equalize space—used in margin
no ¶	No paragraph	ⱱⱱⱱ	Equalize space—used in text
tr	Transpose [1]—used in margin	....	Let it stand—used in text
∽	Transpose [2]—used in text	*stet.*	Let it stand—used in margin
sp	Spell out	⊗	Letter(s) not clear
ital	Italic—used in margin	*run over*	Carry over to next line
____	Italic—used in text	*run back*	Carry back to preceding line
b.f.	Boldface—used in margin	*out, see copy*	Something omitted—see copy
〜〜〜	Boldface—used in text	ℐ/?	Question to author to delete [3]
s.c.	Small caps—used in margin	⋀	Caret—General indicator used to mark position of error.
≡	Small caps—used in text		

[1] In lieu of the traditional mark "tr" used to indicate letter or number transpositions, the striking out of the incorrect letters or numbers and the placement of the correct matter in the margin of the proof is the preferred method of indicating transposition corrections.

[2] Corrections involving more than two characters should be marked by striking out the entire word or number and placing the correct form in the margin. This mark should be reserved to show transposition of words.

[3] The form of any query carried should be such that an answer may be given simply by crossing out the complete query if a negative decision is made or the right-hand (question mark) portion to indicate an affirmative answer.

TYPOGRAPHICAL ERRORS   *reset 8pt. C & SC*

It does not appear that the earliest printers had any method of correcting errors before the form was on the press. The learned The learned correctors of the first two centuries of printing were not proofreaders in our sense, they were rather what we should term office editors. Their labors were chiefly to see that the proof corresponded to the copy, but that the printed page was correct in its latinity—that the words were there, and that the sense was right. They cared but little about orthography, bad letters, or purely printer's errors, and when the text seemed to them wrong they consulted fresh authorities or altered it on their own responsibility. Good proofs, in the modern sense, were impossible until professional readers were employed, men who had first a printer's education, and then spent many years in the correction of proof. The orthography of English, which for the past century has undergone little change, was very fluctuating until after the publication of Johnson's Dictionary, and capitals, which have been used with considerable regularity for the past 80 years, were previously used on the miss or hit plan. The approach to regularity, so far as we have, may be attributed to the growth of a class of professional proofreaders, and it is to them that we owe the correctness of modern printing. More errors have been found in the Bible than in any other one work. For many generations it was frequently the case that Bibles were brought out stealthily, from fear of governmental interference. They were frequently printed from imperfect texts, and were often modified to meet the views of those who published them. The story is related that a certain woman in Germany, who was the wife of a printer, and had become disgusted with the continual assertions of the superiority of man over woman which she had heard, hurried into the composing room while her husband was at supper and altered a sentence in the Bible, which he was printing, so that it read Narr instead of Herr, thus making the verse read "And he shall be thy fool" instead of "and he shall be thy lord." The word not was omitted by Barker, the king's printer in England in 1632, in printing the seventh commandment. He was fined £3,000 on this account.

NOTE.—The system of marking proofs can be made easier by the use of an imaginary vertical line through the center of the type area. The placement of corrections in the left-hand margin for those errors found in the left-hand portion of the proof and in the right-hand margin for right-side errors prevents overcrowding of marks and facilitates corrections.

2. General Instructions

Job planning

2.1.   New publications are evaluated by application specialists who review their requirements and design the necessary formats. Each format is made to conform exactly to the copy's specifications for page dimensions, line length, indentions, typefaces, etc. Upon completion, sample pages are produced and submitted to the customer. At this time, customer agencies are requested to indicate precise details of any style changes because this set of pages serves as a guide for the copy preparer, the beginning of actual production.

2.2.   Changes in the needs of the library community have led to a move toward uniform treatment of the component parts of publications. In developing standards to guide publishers of Government documents, consideration has been given to the changing needs of those who seek to produce, reference, index, abstract, store, search, and retrieve data. Certain identifying elements will be printed on all publications in accordance with this MANUAL and with standards developed by the American National Standards Institute (ANSI).

Publications such as books and pamphlets should contain:
(a)   Title and other title information;
(b)   Name of department issuing or creating the publication;
(c)   Name of author(s) and editor(s) (department or individual);
(d)   Date of issuance;
(e)   Availability (publisher, printer, or other source and address);
(f)   Superintendent of Documents classification and stock numbers, if applicable; and
(g)   International Standard Book Number (ISBN).

(See ANSI Standard Z39.15, Title Leaves of a Book.)

Reports of a scientific or technical nature should contain:
(a) Title and other title information;
(b) Report number;
(c) Author(s);
(d) Performing organization;
(e) Sponsoring department;
(f) Date of issuance;
(g) Type of report and period covered;
(h) Availability (publisher, printer, or other source and address); and
(i) Superintendent of Documents classification and stock numbers if applicable.

(See ANSI/NISO Standard Z39.18—2005 (R2010), Scientific and Technical Reports—Preparation, Presentation, and Preservation.)

Journals, magazines, periodicals, and similar publications should contain:
(a) Title and other title information;
(b) Volume and issue numbers;
(c) Date of issue;
(d) Publishing or sponsoring department;
(e) Availability (publisher, printer, or other source and address);
(f) International Standard Serial Number; and
(g) Superintendent of Documents classification and stock numbers if applicable.

(See ANSI Standard Z39.1, American Standard Reference Data and Arrangement of Periodicals.)

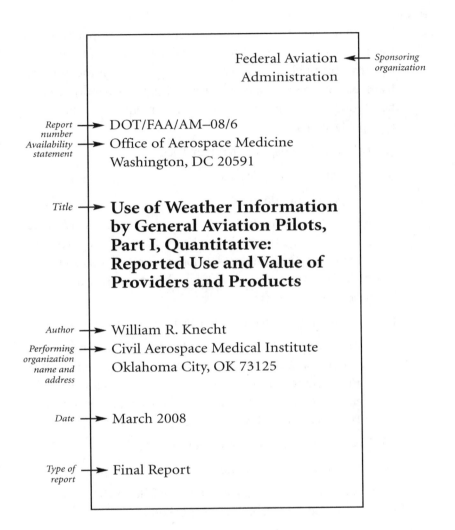

Federal Aviation *Sponsoring organization*
Administration

Report number → DOT/FAA/AM–08/6

Availability statement → Office of Aerospace Medicine
Washington, DC 20591

Title → **Use of Weather Information by General Aviation Pilots, Part I, Quantitative: Reported Use and Value of Providers and Products**

Author → William R. Knecht

Performing organization name and address → Civil Aerospace Medical Institute
Oklahoma City, OK 73125

Date → March 2008

Type of report → Final Report

Notes:

(1) This sample report cover is reduced in size.

(2) In this sample, items are justified left. Other cover designs and typefaces are acceptable.

(3) This sample page was prepared according to the guidelines of the American National Standards Institute, www.ansi.org. Users of ANSI standards are cautioned that all standards are reviewed periodically and subject to revision.

Makeup

2.3.   The design and makeup of a publication is the responsibility of the publisher. However, when the following elements occur in Government publications, they generally appear in the sequence listed below. The designation "new odd page" generally refers to bookwork and is not required in most pamphlet- and magazine-type publications.

(a) *False title* (frontispiece, if any, on back).

(b) *Frontispiece*, faces title page.

(c) *Title page* (new odd page).

(d) *Back of title*, blank, but frequently carries such useful bibliographic information as list of board members, congressional resolution authorizing publication, note of editions and printings, GPO imprint if departmental imprint appears on title page, sales notice, etc.

(e) *Letter of transmittal* (new odd page).

(f) *Foreword* (new odd page), differs from a preface in that it is an introductory note written as an endorsement by a person other than the author. An introduction differs from a foreword or a preface in that it is the initial part of the text; if the book is divided into chapters, it should be the first chapter.

(g) *Preface* (new odd page), by author.

(h) *Acknowledgments* (new odd page), if not part of preface.

(i) *Contents* (new odd page), immediately followed by list of illustrations and list of tables, as parts of contents.

(j) *Halftitle*, new odd page preceding first page of text.

(k) *Text*, begins with page 1 (if halftitle is used, begins with p. 3).

(l) *Glossary* (new odd page).

(m) *Bibliography* (new odd page).

(n) *Appendix* (new odd page).

(o) *Index* (new odd page).

2.4. Preliminary pages use small-cap Roman numerals. Pages in the back of the book (index, etc.), use lowercase Roman numerals.

2.5. Booklets of 32 pages or less can be printed more economically with a self-cover. A table of contents, title page, foreword, preface, etc., is not usually necessary with so few pages. If some of this preliminary matter is necessary, it is more practical to combine them (e.g., contents on cover; or contents, title, and foreword on cover 2).

2.6. Widow lines (lines less than full width of measure) at top of pages are to be avoided, if possible, but are permitted if absolutely necessary to maintain uniform makeup and page depth. Rewording to fill the line is a preferred alternative.

2.7. Paragraphs may start on the last line of a page whenever necessary. If it is found necessary to make a short page, the facing page should be of approximate equal depth.

2.8. A blank space or sink of 6 picas should be placed at the head of each new odd or even page of 46-pica or greater depth; pages with a depth of from 36 to 45 picas, inclusive, will carry a 5-pica sink; pages less than 36 picas, 4 picas.

2.9. When centered top folios are used, the folio on a new page is set 2 points smaller than the top folios, centered at the bottom, and enclosed in parentheses.

2.10. When running heads with top folios are used, running heads are included in overall page depth. However, first pages of chapters and other pages with bottom folios do not include the folios as part of the overall page depth.

2.11. Jobs that have bottom folios will align them in the margin, including those on preliminary pages. If at all possible, avoid use of running heads in conjunction with bottom folios.

2.12. Contents, list of illustrations, preface, or any other matter that makes a page in itself will retain normal 6-pica sink.

2.13. Footnote references are repeated in boxheads or in continued lines over tables, unless special orders are given not to do so.

2.14.   When a table continues, its headnote is repeated without the word *Continued.*

2.15.   A landscape or broadside table that continues from an even to an odd page must be positioned to read through the center (gutter) of the publication when its size is not sufficient to fill both pages.

2.16.   A broadside table of less than page width will center on the page.

2.17.   Centerheads, whether in boldface, caps, caps and small caps, small caps, or italic, should have more space above than below. Uniform spacing should be maintained throughout the page.

2.18.   In making up a page of two or more columns, text preceding a page-width illustration will be divided equally into the appropriate number of columns above the illustration.

2.19.   All backstrips should read down (from top to bottom).

Copy preparation

2.20.   At the beginning of each job the proper formats must be plainly marked. New Odd or New Page, Preliminary, Cover, Title, or Back Title should also be plainly indicated.

2.21.   Copy preparers must mark those things not readily understood when reading the manuscript. They must also mark the correct element identifier code for each data element, as well as indicate other matters of style necessary to give the publication good typographic appearance.

2.22.   Preparers must indicate the proper subformat at the beginning of each extension, verify folios, and plainly indicate references, footnotes, cut-ins, etc.

2.23.   Quoted or extract matter and lists should be set smaller than text with space above and below. Quotation marks at the beginning and end of paragraphs should be omitted. If the same type size is used, quoted matter should be indented 2 ems on both sides with space top and bottom, and initial and closing quotes should be omitted.

2.24.   In congressional hearings, the name of the interrogator or witness who continues speaking is repeated following a head set in boldface, a paragraph enclosed in parentheses, or a paragraph enclosed in brackets.

In a head set in boldface, the title "Mr." is not used, and "the Honorable" preceding a name is shortened to "Hon." Street addresses are also deleted. Example: "Statement of Hon. John P. Blank, Member, American Bar Association, Washington, DC".

2.25. Paragraph or section numbers (or letters) followed by figures or letters in parentheses will close up, as "section 7(B)(1)(*a*)," "paragraph 23(*a*)," "paragraph b(7)," "paragraph (*a*)(2)"; *but* "section 9(a) (*1*) and (*2*)", "section 7 *a* and *b*". In case of an unavoidable break, division will be made after elements in parentheses, and no hyphen is used.

Capitalization
2.26. The customer should indicate use of capital and lowercase letters.

Datelines, addresses, and signatures
2.27. Copy preparers must mark caps, small caps, italic, abbreviations, indentions, and line breaks where necessary. (For more detailed instructions, see Chapter 16 "Datelines, Addresses, and Signatures.")

Decimals and common fractions
2.28. In figure columns containing both decimals and common fractions, such decimals and/or fractions will not be aligned. The columns will be set flush right.

"Et cetera," "etc.," and "and so forth"
2.29. In printing a speaker's language, the words *and so forth* or *et cetera* are preferred, but in "FIC & punc." matter *etc.* is acceptable. If a quoted extract is set in type smaller than that of the preceding text and the speaker has summed up the remainder of the quotation with the words *and so forth* or *et cetera*, these words should be placed at the beginning of the next line, flush and lowercase, and an em dash should be used at the end of the extract.

Folioing and stamping copy

2.30. Folios should be placed in the upper right corner, preferably half an inch from the top.

Headings

2.31. The element identifier codes to be used for all headings must be marked. Caps, caps and small caps, small caps, caps and lowercase, sentence case, or italic must be prepared. (See rule 3.53.)

Pickup

2.32. The jacket number of a job from which matter is to be picked up must be indicated. New matter and pickup matter should conform in style.

Sidenotes and cut-in notes

2.33. Sidenotes and cut-in notes are set each line flush left and ragged right, unless otherwise prepared, and are always set solid. Sidenotes are usually set in 6 point, 4½ picas wide. Footnotes to sidenotes and text should be set 21½ picas.

SEC. 920. Abuse of the rule.	An alleged violation of the rule relating to admission to the floor presents a question of privilege (III, 2624, 2625; VI, 579), but not a higher question of privilege than an election case (III, 2626). In one case where an ex-Member was abusing the privilege . . . .

Signs, symbols, etc.

2.34. All signs, symbols, dashes, superiors, etc., must be clearly marked. Names of Greek letters must be indicated, as they are frequently mistaken for italic letters or symbols.

2.35. Some typesetting systems produce characters that look the same as figures. A lowercase l resembles a figure 1 and a capital O looks like a figure 0. Questionable characters will be printed as figures unless otherwise marked.

Letters illustrating shape and form

2.36. Use the same font for text and capital letters that convey shape and form, e.g., U-shape(d), A-frame, T-bone, and I-beam.

2.37. Plurals are formed by adding an apostrophe and the letter *s* to letters illustrating shape and form, such as T's and Y's. *Golf tee(s)* should be spelled, as shape is not indicated.

2.38. A capital letter is used in *U-boat, V–8,* and other expressions which have no reference to shape or form.

Fol. lit. and FIC & punc.

2.39. After submittal to GPO, manuscript copy is stamped "Fol. lit." or "FIC & punc." The difference between these two typesetting instructions is explained thus:

Copy is followed when stamped "Fol. lit." (follow literally). Copy authorized to be marked "Fol. lit." must be thoroughly prepared by the requisitioning agency as to capitalization, punctuation (including compounding), abbreviations, signs, symbols, figures, and italic. Such copy, including even obvious errors, will be followed. The lack of preparation on copy so designated will, in itself, constitute preparation. "Fol. lit." does not include size and style of type or spacing.

Obvious errors are corrected in copy marked "FIC & punc." (follow, including capitalization and punctuation).

2.40. Bill copy will be followed as supplied and treated as "FIC & punc." (See rule 2.39.) This data is transmitted to the GPO with formatting codes in place, requiring minimal copy preparation.

2.41. Copy preparer's instructions, which accompany each job, are written to cover the general style and certain peculiarities or deviations from style. These instructions must be followed.

Abbreviations

2.42. In marking abbreviations to be spelled, preparers must show what the spelled form should be, unless the abbreviations are common. An unfamiliar abbreviation, with spelled-out form unavailable, will not be changed.

Type composition

2.43. Operators and revisers must study carefully the rules governing composition.

2.44. In correcting pickup matter, the operator must indicate plainly on the proof what portion, if any, was actually reset.

2.45. Every precaution must be taken to prevent the soiling of proofs, as it is necessary for the reviser to see clearly every mark on the margin of a proof after it has been corrected.

2.46. Queries intended for the author are not to be corrected. Such queries, however, are not to be carried on jobs going directly to press.

Leading and spacing

2.47. Spacing of text is governed by the leading, narrow spacing being more desirable in solid than in leaded matter.

2.48. Solid matter (text) is defined as those lines set without horizontal space between them. Leaded text is defined as lines separated by 1 or 2 points of space.

2.49. A single justified word space will be used between sentences (key one space when typing). This applies to all types of composition.

2.50. Center or flush heads set in caps, caps and small caps, small caps, or boldface are keyed with regular justified spaces between words.

2.51. Centerheads are set apart from the text by the use of spacing. More space is always inserted above a heading than below. In 10-point type, the spacing would be 10 points over and 8 points under a heading; in 8- and 6-point type, the spacing would be 8 points above and 6 points below.

2.52. Unless otherwise marked, flush heads are separated from text by 4 points of space above and 2 points of space below in solid matter, and by 6 points of space above and 4 points of space below in leaded matter.

2.53. Full-measure numbered or lettered paragraphs and quoted extracts are not separated by space from adjoining matter.

2.54. Extracts that are set off from the text by smaller type or are indented on both sides or indented 3 ems on the left side (courtwork only) are separated by 6 points of space in leaded matter and by 4 points of space in solid matter.

2.55. Extracts set solid in leaded matter are separated from the text by 6 points.

2.56. Flush lines following extracts are separated by 6 points of space in leaded matter and by 4 points in solid matter.

2.57. Footnotes and legends are leaded if the text is leaded, and are solid if the text is solid.

2.58. Leaderwork is separated from text by 4 points above and 4 points below.

Indents

2.59. In measures less than 30 picas, the paragraph indent is 1 em. Paragraph indents in cut-in matter are 3 ems, overs are 2 ems. Datelines and signatures are indented in multiples of 2 ems. Addresses are set flush left.

2.60. In measures 30 picas or wider, the paragraph indent is 2 ems. Paragraph indents in cut-in matter are 6 ems, overs are 4 ems. Datelines and signatures are indented in multiples of 2 ems. Addresses are set flush left.

2.61. In measures less than 30 picas, overruns in hanging indents are 1 em more than the first line. To avoid conflict with an indent that follows, such as a subentry or paragraph, the overrun indent is made 1 em more than the following line.

2.62. In measures 30 picas or wider, overruns in hanging indents are 2 ems more than the first line. To avoid conflict with an indent that follows, such as a subentry or paragraph, the overrun indent is made 2 ems more than the following line.

2.63. Indents of matter set in smaller type should be the same, in points, as that of adjoining main-text indented matter.

2.64. Two-line centerheads are centered, but heads of three or more lines are set with a hanging indent.

2.65. Overs in flush heads are indented 2 ems in measures less than 30 picas, and 3 ems in wider measures.

Legends for illustrations

2.66. It is preferred that legends and explanatory data consisting of one or two lines are set centered, while those with more than two lines are set with a hanging indent. Legends are set full measure regardless of the width of the illustration. Paragraph style is acceptable.

2.67. Legend lines for illustrations that appear broad or turn page (landscape) should be printed to read up; an even-page legend should be on the inside margin and an odd-page legend on the outside margin.

2.68. Unless otherwise indicated, legends for illustrations are set in 8-point roman, sentence case.

2.69. Periods are used after legends and explanatory remarks beneath illustrations. However, legends without descriptive language do not use a period. (See rule 8.116.)

2.70. At the beginning of a legend or standing alone, *Figure* preceding the identifying number or letter is set in caps and small caps and is not abbreviated.

        Figure 5, *not* Fig. 5   Figure A, *not* Fig. A

2.71. If a chart carries both a legend and footnotes, the legend is placed above the chart.

2.72. Letter symbols used in legends for illustrations are set in lowercase italic without periods.

Proofreading

2.73. All special instructions, layouts, and style sheets must be included with the first installment of each job.

2.74. If the proofreader detects inconsistent or erroneous statements, it is their responsibility to query them.

2.75. All queries appearing on the copy must be carried to the author's set of proofs.

2.76. Proofs that are illegible or are in any manner defective must be called to the attention of the deskperson.

2.77. The manner in which correction marks are made on a proof is of considerable importance. Straggling, unsymmetrical characters, disconnected marks placed in the margin above or below the lines to which they relate, irregular lines leading from an incorrect letter or word to a correction, large marks, marks made with a blunt pencil, indistinct marks, and frequent use of the eraser to obliterate marks hastily or incorrectly made are faults to be avoided. The transposition mark should not be used in little-known words or in figures. It is better to cancel the letters or figures and write them in the margin in the order in which they are to appear.

2.78. In reading proof of wide tables, the proofreader should place the correction as near as possible to the error.

2.79. To assure proper placement of footnotes, the proofreader and reviser must draw a ring around footnote references on the proofs, then check off each corresponding footnote number.

2.80. Proofreaders must not make important changes in indents or tables without consulting the referee.

2.81. Follow the marks of the copy preparer, as they are in a position to know more about the peculiarities of a job than one who reads but a small portion of it.

2.82. Any proposed deviation from the prepared manuscript must be queried to the referee.

2.83. All instructions on copy must be carried on proof by readers.

2.84. Folios of copy must be run by the proofreader and marked on the proof.

2.85. All instructions, comments, and extraneous notes on both copy and proofs that are not intended to be set as part of the text must be circled.

Revising galley proofs

2.86.   The importance of revising proofs cannot be overemphasized. Although a reviser is not expected to read proof, it is not enough to follow the marks found on the proof. The reviser should detect errors and inconsistencies and must see that all corrections have been properly made and that words or lines have not been transposed or eliminated in making the corrections.

2.87.   A reviser must not remodel the punctuation of the proofreaders or make any important changes. If an important change should be made, the reviser must submit the proposed change to the supervisor for a decision.

2.88.   In the body of the work, new pages must be properly indicated on the proof. (For new-page information, see rule 2.3 "Makeup.")

2.89.   All instructions and queries on proofs must be transferred to the revised set of proofs.

Revising page proofs

2.90.   Page revising requires great diligence and care. The reviser must see that the rules governing the instructions of previous workers have been followed.

2.91.   The reviser is responsible for marking all bleed and off-center pages.

2.92.   A blank page must be indicated at the bottom of the preceding page.

2.93.   Special care must be exercised in revising corrected matter. If it appears that a correction has not been made, the reviser should carefully examine each line on the page to see if the correction was inserted in the wrong place.

2.94.   The following rules must be carefully observed:

(a) See that the proof is clean and clear; request another if necessary.

(b) Verify that the galley proofs are in order and that the data on the galleys runs in properly to facilitate continuous makeup.

(c) Make sure that different sets of proofs of the same job are correctly marked in series ("R," "2R," "3R," etc.); where a sheet is stamped "Another proof," carry the same designating "R" on the corresponding clean proof. Advance the "R," "2R," "3R," etc., on each set of page proofs returned from the originating office.

(d) Run the page folios, make sure they are consecutive and that the running heads, if used, are correct. Check connection pages. Verify correct sequence for footnote references and placement. It is imperative that footnotes appear or begin on the same page as their reference, unless style dictates that all footnotes are to appear together in one location.

(e) Watch for dropouts, doublets, and transpositions.

(f) Legend lines of full-page illustrations that appear broad should be printed to read up—the even-page legend on the binding or inside margin and the odd-page legend on the outside margin.

(g) If a footnote is eliminated, do not renumber the footnotes; change footnote to read "Footnote eliminated."

2.95. If a footnote is added in proof, use the preceding number with a superior letter added, as [15a].

2.96. If a table (with or without footnotes) ends a page that has footnotes to the text, the text footnotes fall at the bottom of the page, with a 50-point rule above them. (See rule 13.76.)

Press revising

2.97. Press revising calls for the exercise of utmost care. The press reviser must be thoroughly familiar with the style and makeup of Government publications. They are required to OK all forms that go to press—bookwork, covers, jobwork, etc.—and must see that all queries are answered. Knowledge of the bindery operations required to complete a book or job and familiarity with all types of imposition, folds, etc., is helpful. The reviser must be capable of ascertaining the proper head, back, and side margins for all work, to ensure proper trimming of the completed job.

2.98. Although speed is essential when forms reach the press reviser, accuracy is still paramount and must not be sacrificed.

Signature marks, etc.

2.99. Unless otherwise indicated, signature marks are set in 6-point lowercase and indented 3 ems.

2.100. Figures indicating the year should follow the jacket number in signature marks:

125–327—16——4   116–529—16—vol. 1——3
116–529—16—pt. 5——3

2.101. When the allmark (○) and signature or the imprint and signature appear on same page, the signature line is placed below the allmark or imprint. (See rule 2.113.)

2.102. The allmark is placed below the page, bulletin, or circular number but above the signature line, if both appear on the same page.

2.103. Imprints and signature lines appearing on short pages of text are placed at the bottom of the page.

2.104. On a congressional job reprinted because of a change, the House and Senate have approved the following styles:

House of Representatives: Senate:
  ★17–234—16——2   17–235—16——2 ★(Star Print)

2.105. The following forms are used for signature marks in House and Senate documents and reports printed on session jackets:

H. Doc. 73, 16–1——2   S. Doc. 57, 16–1——2
S. Doc. 57, 16–2, pt. 1——2   S. Doc. 57, 16–2, vol. 1——2
H. Rept. 120, 16–2——8   S. Rept. 100, 16–2——9

2.106. In a document or report printed on other than a session jacket, use the jacket number, year, and signature number only, omitting the document or report number. (See rule 2.100.)

2.107. For pasters or foldouts, the jacket number, the year, and the page to be faced by the paster or foldout are used as follows (note punctuation):

> 12–344——16 (Face p. 10)

2.108. On a paster or foldout facing an even page, the marks are placed on the lower right-hand side; on a paster or foldout facing an odd page, the marks are placed on the lower left-hand side.

2.109. If more than one paster or foldout faces the same page, they are numbered as follows:

> 12–344——16 (Face p. 19) No. 1
> 12–344——16 (Face p. 19) No. 2

2.110. When a paster or foldout follows the text, the allmark is placed on the last page of the text and never on the paster or foldout.

Imprints

2.111. Unless otherwise stipulated, the GPO imprint must appear on all printed matter, with the exception of certain classified work.

2.112. The full GPO imprint is used on the title page of a congressional speech.

2.113. The imprint and allmark are not used together on any page; if one is used, the other is omitted.

2.114. The imprint is not used on a halftitle or on any page of a cover, with the exception of congressional hearings.

2.115. If there is a title page, the imprint is placed on the title page; but if there is no title page, or if the title page is entirely an illustration, the imprint is placed on the last page of the text 4 ems from flush right and below the bottom folio.

2.116. The GPO logo is used only on GPO publications. If it is printed on page II, the full imprint is used on the title page; if it is printed on the title page, use the half imprint only, thus—Washington : 2016.

Imprint variations

2.117.   This is one style of an imprint that can appear on the title page.

> For sale by the Superintendent of Documents, U.S. Government Publishing Office
> • Internet: bookstore.gpo.gov • Phone: Toll Free 866–512–1800
> • DC area 202–512–1800 • Fax: 202–512–2104
> • Mail: Stop SSOP, Washington, DC 20402–0001
> • www.govinfo.gov

2.118.   In the event that a title page is not used, the imprint is printed on the last page and positioned flush left below the text.

> For sale by the Superintendent of Documents, U.S. Government Publishing Office
> • Internet: bookstore.gpo.gov • Phone: toll free 866–512–1800
> • DC area 202–512–1800 • Fax: 202–512–2250
> • Mail: Stop SSOP, Washington, DC 20402–0001
> • www.govinfo.gov

2.119.   Outside-purchase publications are identified by the GPO logo at the beginning of the imprint line. These lines are positioned 4 ems from the right margin.

> GPO   U.S. GOVERNMENT PUBLISHING OFFICE: 2016—456–789

2.120.   Publications purchased outside that are reprinted by the GPO use an em dash in lieu of the GPO logo.

> —U.S. GOVERNMENT PUBLISHING OFFICE: 2016—456–789

2.121.   Jobs set on outside purchase but printed by the GPO use an asterisk in lieu of the GPO logo.

> *U.S. GOVERNMENT PUBLISHING OFFICE: 2016—456–789

2.122.   Publications produced from camera copy supplied to the GPO are identified by *cc* printed at the end of the line.

> U.S. GOVERNMENT PUBLISHING OFFICE: 2016—123–456–cc

Reprints

2.123.   To aid bibliographic identification of reprints or revisions, the dates of the original edition and of reprint or revision should be supplied by the author on the title page or in some other suitable place. Thus:

First edition July 2000	Original edition May 2000
Reprinted July 2005	Reprinted May 2005
First printed June 2000	Revised July 2007
Revised June 2005	

2.124.   The year in the imprint on cover, title page, or elsewhere is not changed from that in the original print, nor are the signatures changed, unless other revisions are necessary.

Sales notices

2.125.   The use of sales notices is discouraged.

2.126.   If there is a cover but no title page, the sales notice is printed on the cover. Unless otherwise indicated, if there is a title page, with or without a cover, the sales notice is printed at the bottom of the title page below a cross rule. If there is no cover or title page, any sales notice is printed at the end of the text, below the imprint, and the two are separated by a cross rule.

Franking

2.127.   The franking (mailing) privilege on covers for Government publications should be at least 1⅛ inches from the trim.

Bibliographies or references

2.128.   There are many styles available to bibliographers, for there are many classes of documents.

A Government bulletin citation, according to one authority, would be treated as follows:

Author's name (if the article is signed); title of article (in quotation marks); the publication (usually in italic), with correct references to volume, number, series, pages, date, and publisher (U.S. Govt. Pub. Off.).

Therefore the example would read:

> U.S. Department of the Interior, "Highlights in history of forest and re-
> lated natural resource conservation," *Conservation Bulletin*, No. 41 (serial
> number not italic), Washington, U.S. Dept. of the Interior (*or* U.S. Govt. Pub.
> Off.), 1997. 1 p. (*or* p. 1).

Another Government periodical citation would read as follows:

> Kirwan, Patrick S., "New Qualified Plug-in Electric Drive Motor Vehicle
> Credit," *Internal Revenue Bulletin*, No. 2009-48, pp. 713–717 (November 30,
> 2009), Internal Revenue Service.

Clarity may be maintained by capitalizing each word in book titles,
with only the first word in the title of articles.

Other examples are:

> Preston W. Slosson, *The Great Crusade And After: 1914–1928* (New York:
> Macmillan, 1930)
> Edward B. Rosa, "The economic importance of the scientific work of the
> government," *J. Wash. Acad. Sci.* 10, 342 (1920)

or:

> Preston W. Slosson, The Great Crusade and After: 1914–1928 (New York:
> Macmillan, 1930)
> Edward B. Rosa, "The Economic Importance of the Scientific Work of the
> Government," J. Wash. Acad. Sci. 10, 342 (1920)

Note in this that the principal words in both book titles and titles
of articles are capitalized. Consistency is more important in bibliographic style than the style itself.

The science of bibliography is covered in many texts, and the following references are available for study:

> The Chicago Manual of Style, University of Chicago Press, Chicago, 2010
> (www.chicagomanualofstyle.org/home.html).
> Words Into Type, Prentice-Hall, New York, 1974.

3. Capitalization Rules
(See also Chapter 4 "Capitalization Examples" and Chapter 9 "Abbreviations and Letter Symbols")

3.1. It is impossible to give rules that will cover every conceivable problem in capitalization, but, by considering the purpose to be served and the underlying principles, it is possible to attain a considerable degree of uniformity. The list of approved forms given in chapter 4 will serve as a guide. Obviously such a list cannot be complete. The correct usage with respect to any term not included can be determined by analogy or by application of the rules.

Historic or documentary accuracy

3.2. Where historic, documentary, technical, or scientific accuracy is required, capitalization and other features of style of the original text should be followed.

Proper names

3.3. Proper names are capitalized.

Rome	John Macadam	Italy
Brussels	Macadam family	Anglo-Saxon

Derivatives of proper names

3.4. Derivatives of proper names used with a proper meaning are capitalized.

Roman (of Rome)	Johannean	Italian

3.5. Derivatives of proper names used with acquired independent common meaning, or no longer identified with such names, are set lowercased. Since this depends upon general and long-continued usage, a more definite and all-inclusive rule cannot be formulated in advance.

roman (type)	macadam (crushed rock)	italicize
brussels sprouts	watt (electric unit)	anglicize
venetian blinds	plaster of paris	pasteurize

Common nouns and adjectives in proper names

3.6. A common noun or adjective forming an essential part of a proper name is capitalized; the common noun used alone as a substitute for the name of a place or thing is not capitalized.

> Massachusetts Avenue; the avenue
> Washington Monument; the monument
> Statue of Liberty; the statue
> Hoover Dam; the dam
> Boston Light; the light
> Modoc National Forest; the national forest
> Panama Canal; the canal
> Soldiers' Home in Holyoke; the soldiers' home
> Johnson House (hotel); Johnson house (residence)
> Crow Reservation; the reservation
> Cape of Good Hope; the cape
> Jersey City
> Washington City
> *but* city of Washington; the city
> Cook County; the county
> Great Lakes; the lakes
> Lake of the Woods; the lake
> North Platte River; the river
> Lower California
> *but* lower Mississippi
> Charles the First; Charles I
> Seventeenth Census; the 1960 census

3.7. If a common noun or adjective forming an essential part of a name becomes separated from the rest of the name by an intervening common noun or adjective, the entire expression is no longer a proper noun and is therefore not capitalized.

> Union Station: union passenger station
> Eastern States: eastern farming States
> United States popularly elected government

3.8. A common noun used alone as a well-known short form of a specific proper name is capitalized.

> the Capitol building in Washington, DC; *but* State capitol building
> the Channel (English Channel)
> the Chunnel (tunnel below English Channel)
> the District (District of Columbia)

3.9.   The plural form of a common noun capitalized as part of a proper name is also capitalized.

> Seventh and I Streets
> Lakes Erie and Ontario
> Potomac and James Rivers
> State and Treasury Departments
> British, French, and United States Governments
> Presidents Washington and Adams

3.10.   A common noun used with a date, number, or letter, merely to denote time or sequence, or for the purpose of reference, record, or temporary convenience, does not form a proper name and is therefore not capitalized. (See also rule 3.39.)

abstract B	figure 7	room A722
amendment 5	first district (not	rule 8
apartment 2	congressional)	schedule K
appendix C	flight 007	section 3
article 1	graph 8	signature 4
book II	group 7	spring 1926
chapter III	mile 7.5	station 27
chart B	page 2	table 4
class I	paragraph 4	title IV
collection 6	part I	volume X
column 2	phase 3	ward 2
drawing 6	plate IV	
exhibit D	region 3	

3.11.   The following terms are lowercased, even with a name or number.

aqueduct	irrigation project	shipway
breakwater	jetty	slip
buoy	levee	spillway
chute	lock	turnpike
dike	pier	watershed
dock	reclamation project	weir
drydock	ship canal	wharf

Definite article in proper place names

3.12.   To achieve greater distinction or to adhere to the authorized form, the word *the* (or its equivalent in a foreign language) is capitalized when used as a part of an official name or title. When such name or title is used adjectively, *the* is not capitalized, nor is *the* supplied at any time when not in copy.

> *British Consul* v. *The Mermaid* (title of legal case)
> The Dalles (OR); The Weirs (NH); *but* the Dalles region; the Weirs streets
> The Hague; *but* the Hague Court; the Second Hague Conference
> El Salvador; Las Cruces; L'Esterel
> The National Mall; The Mall (Washington, DC only)
> The Gambia
> *but* the Congo, the Sudan, the Netherlands

3.13.   Rule 3.12 does not apply in references to newspapers, periodicals, vessels, airships, trains, firm names, etc.

> the Washington Post   the U–3
> the Times   the *Los Angeles*
> the Atlantic Monthly   the Hotel Roanoke
> the *Mermaid*   the National Photo Co.

Particles in names of persons

3.14.   In foreign names such particles as *d', da, de, della, den, du, van,* and *von* are capitalized unless preceded by a forename or title. Individual usage, if ascertainable, should be followed.

> Da Ponte; Cardinal da Ponte
> Den Uyl; Johannes den Uyl; Prime Minister den Uyl
> Du Pont; E.I. du Pont de Nemours & Co.
> Van Rensselaer; Stephen van Rensselaer
> Von Braun; Dr. Wernher von Braun
> *but* d'Orbigny; Alcide d'Orbigny; de la Madrid; Miguel de la Madrid

3.15.   In anglicized names such particles are usually capitalized, even if preceded by a forename or title, but individual usage, if ascertainable, should be followed.

> Justice Van Devanter; Reginald De Koven
> Thomas De Quincey; William De Morgan
> Henry van Dyke (his usage)
> Samuel F. Du Pont (his usage); Irénée du Pont

3.16.   If copy is not clear as to the form of such a name (for example, *La Forge* or *Laforge*), the two-word form should be used.

3.17.   In names set in capitals, *de, von*, etc., are also capitalized.

Names of organized bodies

3.18.   The full names of existing or proposed organized bodies and their shortened names are capitalized; other substitutes, which are most often regarded as common nouns, are capitalized only in certain specified instances to indicate preeminence or distinction.

National governmental units:

U.S. Congress: 114th Congress; the Congress; Congress; the Senate; the House; Committee of the Whole, the Committee; *but* committee (all other congressional committees)

Department of Agriculture: the Department; Division of Publications, the Division; similarly all major departmental units; *but* legislative, executive, and judicial departments

Bureau of the Census: the Census Bureau, the Bureau; *but* the agency

Environmental Protection Agency: the Agency

Geological Survey: the Survey

Government Publishing Office: the Publishing Office, the Office

American Embassy, British Embassy: the Embassy; *but* the consulate; the consulate general

Treasury of the United States: General Treasury; National Treasury; Public Treasury; the Treasury; Treasury notes; New York Subtreasury, the subtreasury

Department of Defense: Military Establishment; Armed Forces; All-Volunteer Forces; *but* armed services

U.S. Army: the Army; All-Volunteer Army; the Infantry; 81st Regiment; Army Establishment; the Army Band; Army officer; Regular Army officer; Reserve officer; Volunteer officer; *but* army shoe; Grant's army; Robinson's brigade; the brigade; the corps; the regiment; infantryman

U.S. Navy: the Navy; the Marine Corps; Navy (Naval) Establishment; Navy officer; *but* naval shipyard; naval officer; naval station

U.S. Air Force: the Air Force

U.S. Coast Guard: the Coast Guard

French Ministry of Foreign Affairs; the Ministry; French Army; British Navy

American Indian and Alaska Native federally recognized entities:

Shawnee Tribe, the Tribe; Cherokee Nation, the Nation; Alturas Indian Rancheria, the Rancheria; Cahuilla Band of Indians, the Band; Takotna Village, the Village; Akiak Native Community, the Community

International organizations:

United Nations: the Council; the Assembly; the Secretariat

Permanent Court of Arbitration: the Court; the Tribunal (only in the proceed-
ings of a specific arbitration tribunal)
Hague Peace Conference of 1907: the Hague Conference; the Peace Conference;
the Conference
Common-noun substitutes:
Virginia General Assembly: the assembly
California State Highway Commission: Highway Commission of California;
the highway commission; the commission
Montgomery County Board of Health: the Board of Health, Montgomery
County; the board of health; the board
Common Council of the City of Pittsburgh: the common council; the council
Buffalo Consumers' League: the consumers' league; the league
Republican Party: the party
Southern Railroad Co.: the Southern Railroad; Southern Co.; Southern Road;
the railroad company; the company
Riggs National Bank: the Riggs Bank; the bank
Metropolitan Club: the club
Yale School of Law: Yale University School of Law; School of Law, Yale Uni-
versity; school of law

3.19. The names of members and adherents of organized bodies are capitalized to distinguish them from the same words used merely in a
descriptive sense.

a Representative (U.S.)	a Shriner	a Boy Scout
a Republican	a Socialist	a Knight (K.C., K.P., etc.)
an Elk	an Odd Fellow	
a Federalist	a Democrat	

Names of countries, domains, and administrative divisions

3.20. The official designations of countries, national domains, and their
principal administrative divisions are capitalized only if used as
part of proper names, as proper names, or as proper adjectives.
(See Chapter 17, Principal Foreign Countries table.)

United States: the Republic; the Nation; the Union; the Government; also
Federal, Federal Government; *but* republic (when not referring specifically to one such entity); republican (in general sense); a nation devoted
to peace
New York State: the State, a State (a definite political subdivision of first rank);
State of Veracruz; Balkan States; six States of Australia; State rights; *but*
state (referring to a federal government, the body politic); foreign states;
church and state; statehood; state's evidence

> Territory: territory of American Samoa, Guam, Virgin Islands; Yukon, Northwest Territories; the Territory(ies), Territorial
> Dominion of Canada: the Dominion; but dominion (in general sense)
> Ontario Province, Province of Ontario: the Province, Provincial; but province, provincial (in general sense)

3.21. The similar designations *commonwealth, confederation (federal), government, nation (national), powers, republic,* etc., are capitalized only if used as part of proper names, as proper names, or as proper adjectives.

> British Commonwealth, Commonwealth of Virginia: the Commonwealth; *but* a commonwealth government (general sense)
> Swiss Confederation: the Confederation; the Federal Council; the Federal Government; *but* confederation, federal (in general sense)
> French Government: the Government; French and Italian Governments: the Governments; *but* government (in general sense); the Churchill government; European governments
> Cherokee Nation: the Nation; *but* Greek nation; American nations
> National Government (of any specific nation); *but* national customs
> Allied Powers, Allies (in World Wars I and II); *but* our allies, weaker allies; Central Powers (in World War I); *but* the powers; European powers
> Republic of South Africa: the Republic; *but* republic (in general sense)

Names of regions, localities, and geographic features
3.22. A descriptive term used to denote a definite region, locality, or geographic feature is a proper name and is therefore capitalized; also for temporary distinction a coined name of a region is capitalized.

the North Atlantic States	the Continental Divide
the Gulf States	Deep South
the Central States	Midsouth
the Pacific Coast States	the Far East
the Lake States	Far Eastern
East North Central States	the East
Eastern North Central States	Middle East
Far Western States	Middle Eastern
Eastern United States	Mideast
the West	Mideastern (Asia)
the Midwest	Near East (Balkans, etc.)
the Middle West	the Promised Land
the Far West	the Continent (continental Europe)
the Eastern Shore (Chesapeake Bay)	the Western Hemisphere
the Badlands (SD and NE)	the North Pole

the North and South Poles   Western Europe, Central Europe)
the Temperate Zone   (political entities)
the Torrid Zone   *but*
the East Side   lower 48 (States)
Lower East Side (sections of a city) the Northeast corridor

3.23. A descriptive term used to denote direction or position is not a proper name and is therefore not capitalized.

north; south; east; west
northerly; northern; northward
eastern; oriental; occidental
east Pennsylvania
southern California
northern Virginia; *but* Northern Virginia (D.C. suburbs)
west Florida; *but* West Florida (1763–1819)
eastern region; western region
north-central region
east coast; eastern seaboard
northern Italy
southern France
but East Germany; West Germany (former political entities)

Names of calendar divisions

3.24. The names of calendar divisions are capitalized.

January; February; March; etc.
Monday; Tuesday; Wednesday; etc.
but spring; summer; autumn (fall); winter

Names of holidays, etc.

3.25. The names of holidays and ecclesiastic feast and fast days are capitalized.

April Fools' Day   Fourth of July; the Fourth
Arbor Day   Halloween
Armed Forces Day   Hanukkah
Birthday of Martin Luther King, Jr.   Inauguration Day (Federal)
Christmas Day, Eve   Independence Day
Columbus Day   Labor Day
Father's Day   Lincoln's Birthday
Feast of the Passover; the Passover   Memorial Day (also
Flag Day   Decoration Day)

Mother's Day	St. Valentine's Day
New Year's Day, Eve	Thanksgiving Day
Patriot Day	Veterans Day
Presidents Day	Washington's Birthday
Ramadan	Yom Kippur
Rosh Hashanah	*but* election day, primary day

Trade names and trademarks

3.26.   Trade names, variety names, and names of market grades and brands are capitalized. Some trade names have come into usage as generic terms (e.g., cellophane, thermos, and aspirin); when reference is being made to the formal company or specific product name, capitalization should be used. (See Chapter 4 "Capitalization Examples" trade names and trademarks.)

Choice lamb (market grade)	Xerox (the company)
Red Radiance rose (variety)	*but* photocopy (the process)

Scientific names

3.27.   The name of a phylum, class, order, family, or genus is capitalized. The name of a species is not capitalized, even if derived from a proper name. (See rule 11.9.)

> Arthropoda (phylum), Crustacea (class), Hypoparia (order), Agnostidae (family), *Agnostus* (genus)
>
> *Agnostus canadensis; Aconitum wilsonii; Epigaea repens* (genus and species)

3.28.   In scientific descriptions coined terms derived from proper names are not capitalized.

aviculoid	menodontine

3.29.   Any plural formed by adding *s* to a Latin generic name is capitalized.

Rhynchonellas	Spirifers

3.30.   In soil science the 12 soil orders are capitalized.

Alfisols	Gelisols	Oxisols
Andisols	Histosols	Spodosols
Aridisols	Inceptisols	Ultisols
Entisols	Mollisols	Vertisols

3.31.   Capitalize the names of the celestial bodies as well as the planets.

Sun	Mars	Alpha Centauri
Moon	the Big Dipper	Orion
Saturn	Ceres	the Milky Way
Earth	Kepler-1647b	*but* the moons of Jupiter

3.32.   In general, names of diseases, viruses, and syndromes are not capitalized. An exception is when the disease is named for the person who discovered it or the geographic location where the disease occurred.

Alzheimer('s) disease	Hodgkin lymphoma
cancer	Lyme disease
diabetes	measles
Down syndrome	Parkinson('s) disease
Ebola virus	West Nile virus
group A strep infection;	Zika virus
hepatitis C; herpes B virus	

Historical or political events

3.33.   Names of historical or political events used as a proper name are capitalized.

Battle of Bunker Hill	Holocaust, the	Renaissance
Christian Era	Middle Ages	the American
Cold War	New Deal	Revolution; the
D-Day	New Federalism	Revolution
Dust Bowl	New Frontier	V-E Day
Fall of Rome	Prohibition	War of 1812
Great Depression	Restoration	War on Poverty
Great Society	Reformation	

but Korean war; Vietnam war; Gulf war

Personification

3.34.   A vivid personification is capitalized.

The Chair recognizes the gentlewoman from New York;
but I spoke with the chair yesterday.
For Nature wields her scepter mercilessly.
All of a sudden,
   Time stood still.

Religious terms

3.35. Words denoting the Deity except *who, whose,* and *whom;* names for the Bible and other sacred writings and their parts; names of confessions of faith and of religious bodies and their adherents; and words specifically denoting Satan are all capitalized.

> Heavenly Father; the Almighty; Lord; Thee; Thou; He; Him; *but* himself; You, Your; Thy, Thine; [God's] fatherhood
>
> Mass; Communion
>
> Divine Father; *but* divine providence; divine guidance; divine service
>
> Son of Man; Jesus' sonship; the Messiah; *but* a messiah; messiahship; messianic; messianize; christology; christological
>
> Bible, Holy Scriptures, Scriptures, Word; Koran; Talmud; *also* Biblical; Scriptural; Koranic; Talmudic
>
> New Testament; Ten Commandments
>
> Gospel (memoir of Christ); *but* gospel music
>
> Apostles' Creed
>
> Episcopal Church; an Episcopalian; Catholicism; a Protestant
>
> Christian; *also* Christendom; Christianity; Christianize
>
> Black Friars; Brother(s); King's Daughters; Daughter(s); Ursuline Sisters; Sister(s)
>
> Satan; the Devil; *but* a devil; the devils; devil's advocate

Titles of persons

3.36. Civil, religious, military, and professional titles, as well as those of nobility, immediately preceding a name are capitalized.

President Obama	Dr. Bellinger
Queen Elizabeth II	Nurse Joyce Norton
Ambassador Acton	Professor Leverett
Lieutenant Fowler	Examiner Jones (law)
Chairman Williams	Vice-Presidential candidate Smith

> *but* baseball player Harper; maintenance person Flow; foreperson Taylor

3.37. To indicate preeminence or distinction in certain specified instances, a common-noun title immediately following the name of a person or used alone as a substitute for it is capitalized.

> Title of a head or assistant head of state:
>
> Barack Obama, President of the United States: the President; the President-elect; the Executive; the Chief Magistrate; the Commander in Chief; ex-President Bush; former President Reagan; *similarly* the Vice President; the Vice-President-elect; ex-Vice-President Cheney

Terry McAuliffe, Governor of Virginia: the Governor of Virginia; the Governor; *similarly* the Lieutenant Governor; *but* secretary of state of Idaho; attorney general of Maine

Title of a head or assistant head of an existing or a proposed National governmental unit:

John Kerry, Secretary of State: the Secretary; *similarly* the Acting Secretary; the Under Secretary; the Assistant Secretary; the Director; the Chief or Assistant Chief; the Chief Clerk; *but* Secretaries of the military departments; secretaryship

Titles of the military:

General of the Army(ies): United States only; Supreme Allied Commander; General Joseph F. Dunford, Jr., Chairman, Joint Chiefs of Staff; Joint Chiefs of Staff; Chief of Staff, U.S. Air Force; the Chief of Staff; *but* the commanding general; general (military title standing alone not capitalized)

Titles of members of diplomatic corps:

Walter S. Gifford, Ambassador Extraordinary and Plenipotentiary: the American Ambassador; the British Ambassador; the Ambassador; the Senior Ambassador; Her Excellency; *similarly* the Envoy Extraordinary and Minister Plenipotentiary; the Envoy; the Minister; the Chargé d'Affaires; the Chargé; Ambassador at Large; Minister Without Portfolio; *but* the consul general; the consul; the attaché

Title of a ruler or prince:

Elizabeth II, Queen of the United Kingdom of Great Britain and Northern Ireland: the Queen; the Crown; Her Most Gracious Majesty; Her Majesty; *similarly* the Emperor; the Sultan

Charles, Prince of Wales: the Prince; His Royal Highness

Titles not capitalized:

Charles F. Hughes, rear admiral, U.S. Navy: the rear admiral

Steven Knapp, president of The George Washington University: the president

C.H. Eckles, professor of dairy husbandry: the professor

Barbara Prophet, chairwoman of the committee; the chairman; the chairperson; the chair

3.38. In formal lists of delegates and representatives of governments, all titles and descriptive designations immediately following the names should be capitalized if any one is capitalized.

3.39. A title in the second person is capitalized.

Your Excellency	Mr. Chairman	*but* not conversational salutations
Your Highness	Madam Chairman	my dear General
Your Honor	Mr. Secretary	my dear sir

Titles of publications, papers, documents, acts, laws, etc.

3.40.   In the full or short English titles of periodicals, series of publications, annual reports, historic documents, and works of art, the first word and all important words are capitalized.

> Statutes at Large; Revised Statutes; District Code; Bancroft's History; Journal (House or Senate) (short titles); *but* the code; the statutes
>
> Atlantic Charter; Balfour Declaration; *but* British white paper
>
> Chicago's American; *but* Chicago American Publishing Co.
>
> Reader's Digest; *but* New York Times Magazine; Newsweek magazine
>
> Monograph 55; Research Paper 123; Bulletin 420; Circular A; Article 15: Uniform Code of Military Justice; Senate Document 70; House Resolution 45; Presidential Proclamation No. 24; Executive Order No. 24; Royal Decree No. 24; Public Law 89–1; Private and Union Calendars; Calendar No. 80; Calendar Wednesday; Committee Print No. 32, committee print; *but* Senate bill 416; House bill 61; Congressional Record
>
> Annual Report of the Government Publishing Office, 2015; *but* seventh annual report, 19th annual report
>
> Declaration of Independence; the Declaration
>
> Constitution (United States or with name of country); constitutional; *but* New York State constitution: first amendment, 12th amendment
>
> Kellogg-Briand Pact; North Atlantic Pact; Atlantic Pact; Treaty of Versailles; Jay Treaty; *but* treaty of peace, the treaty (descriptive designations); treaty of 1919
>
> *United States* v. *Four Hundred Twenty-two Casks of Wine* (law)
>
> American Gothic, Nighthawks (paintings)

3.41.   All principal words are capitalized in titles of addresses, albums, articles, books, captions, chapter and part headings, editorials, essays, headings, headlines, motion pictures and plays (including television and radio programs), papers, short poems, reports, songs, subheadings, subjects, and themes. The foregoing are also quoted.

3.42.   In the short or popular titles of acts (Federal, State, or foreign) the first word and all important words are capitalized.

> Revenue Act; Walsh-Healey Act; Freedom of Information Act; Classification Act; *but* the act; Harrison narcotic law; Harrison narcotic bill; interstate commerce law; sunset law

3.43.   The capitalization of the titles of books, etc., written in a foreign language is to conform to the national practice in that language.

First words

3.44. The first word following a comma or a colon that introduces a complete sentence or a direct quotation is capitalized. (See also rule 3.45)

> The question is, Shall the bill pass?
> He asked, "And where are you going?"
> The following question came up for discussion: What policy should be adopted?
> His only rule was this: Chickens are not allowed past the front parlor.

3.45. The first word following a colon, an exclamation point, or a question mark is not capitalized if the matter following is merely a supplementary remark making the meaning clearer.

> Revolutions are not made: they come.
> Intelligence is not replaced by mechanism: even the televox must be guided by its master's voice.
> But two months dead! nay, not so much; not two.
> What is this? Your knees to me? to your corrected son?

3.46. The first word of a fragmentary quotation is not capitalized.

> She objected "to the phraseology, not to the ideas."
> "The President," he said, "will veto the bill."

3.47. The first word of a line of poetry is capitalized.

> Lives of great men all remind us
> We can make our lives sublime.

3.48. The first word of a run-in list following a colon is not capitalized. (For lists that are not run in, see rule 8.28.)

> There are three primary pigment colors: magenta, yellow, and cyan.
> The vote was as follows: in the affirmative, 23; in the negative, 11; not voting, 3.
> His goals were these: (1) learn Spanish, (2) see the Grand Canyon, and (3) climb Mt. Everest.

3.49. The first word following *Whereas* in resolutions, contracts, etc., is not capitalized; the first word following an enacting or resolving clause is capitalized.

> Whereas the Constitution provides . . . ; and
> Whereas, moreover, . . . : Therefore be it
> Whereas the Senate provided for the . . . : Now, therefore, be it
> *Resolved,* That . . . ; and be it further
> *Resolved (jointly),* That . . .

Resolved by the House of Representatives (the Senate concurring), That . . . .
(Concurrent resolution, Federal Government.)

*Resolved by the Senate of Oklahoma (the House of Representatives concurring
therein),* That . . . . (Concurrent resolution, using name of State.)

Resolved by the senate (the house of representatives concurring therein), That . . . .
(Concurrent resolution, not using name of State.)

Resolved by the Assembly and Senate of the State of California (jointly), That . . . .
(Joint resolution, using name of State.)

Resolved by the Washington Board of Trade, That . . .

Provided, That . . .

Provided further, That . . .

Provided, however, That . . .

And provided further, That . . .

Ordered, That . . .

Be it enacted, That . . .

Centerheads and sideheads

3.50.   Unless otherwise marked, centerheads are set in capitals, and side-heads are set in sentence case. In centerheads making two lines, wordbreaks should be avoided. The first line should be centered and set as full as possible.

3.51.   In heads set in caps, a small-cap *c* or *ac,* if available, is used in such names as *McLean* or *MacLeod*; otherwise a lowercase *c* or *ac* is used. In heads set in small caps, a thin space is used after the *c* or the *ac.*

3.52.   In such names as *LeRoy, DeHostis, LaFollette,* etc. (one-word forms only), set in caps, the second letter of the particle is made a small cap, if available; otherwise lowercase is used. In heads set in small caps, a thin space is used.

3.53.   In matter set in caps and small caps or caps and lowercase, capital-ize all principal words, including parts of compounds which would be capitalized standing alone. The articles *a, an,* and *the;* the prepo-sitions *at, by, for, in, of, on, per, to,* and *up;* the conjunctions *and, as, but, if, or,* and *nor;* and the second element of a compound numeral are not capitalized. (See also rule 8.133.)

World en Route to All-Out War
Curfew To Be Set for 10 o'Clock (To capitalized in an infinitive verb)
Man Hit With 2-Inch Pipe
No-Par-Value Stock for Sale

Yankees May Be Winners in Zig-Zag Race
Ex-Senator Is To Be Admitted
Notice of Filing and Order on Exemption From Requirements
but Building on Twenty-first Street (if spelled)
One Hundred Twenty-three Years (if spelled)
Only One-tenth of Shipping Was Idle
Many 35-Millimeter Films in Production
Built-Up Stockpiles Are Necessary (*Up* is an adverb here)
The Per Diem Was Increased (*Per Diem* is used as a noun here); Lower Taxes
per Person (*per* is a preposition here)

3.54.   If a normally lowercased short word is used in juxtaposition with a capitalized word of like significance, it should also be capitalized.

Buildings On and Near the National Mall

3.55.   In a heading set in caps and lowercase or in caps and small caps, a normally lowercased last word, if it is the only lowercased word in the heading, should also be capitalized.

All Returns Are In

3.56.   Verbs and the first element of an infinitive are capitalized.

Controls To Be Applied
but Aid Sent to Disaster Area (*to* is a preposition here)

3.57.   In matter set in caps and small caps, such abbreviations as *etc., et al.,* and *p.m.* are set in small caps; in matter set in caps and lowercase, these abbreviations are set in lowercase.

PLANES, GUNS, SHIPS, ETC.   IN RE THE 8 P.M. MEETING
Planes, Guns, Ships, etc.   In re the 8 p.m. Meeting
JAMES BROS. ET AL.
James, Nelson, et al.

3.58.   Paragraph series letters in parentheses appearing in heads set in caps, caps and small caps, small caps, or in caps and lowercase are to be set as in copy.

SECTION 1.580(f)(1)

Addresses, salutations, and signatures

3.59.   The first word and all principal words in addresses, salutations, and signatures are capitalized. See Chapter 16 "Datelines, Addresses, and Signatures."

Interjections

3.60.   The interjection "O" is always capitalized. Other interjections within a sentence are not capitalized.

> Sail on, O Ship of State!
> For lo! the days are hastening on.
> But, oh, how fortunate!

4. Capitalization Examples

A

A-bomb
abstract B, 1, etc.
Academy:
  Air Force; the Academy
  Andover; the academy
  Coast Guard; the Academy
  Merchant Marine; the Academy
  Military; the Academy
  National Academy of Sciences; the
    Academy of Sciences; the academy
  Naval; the Academy
  but service academies
accord, Paris peace (*see* Agreement)
accords, Helsinki
Act (Federal, State, or foreign), short or
    popular title or with number; the act:
  Affordable Care
  Appropriations
  Classification
  Clear Skies
  Economy
  Flood Control
  Military Selective Service
  No Child Left Behind
  Organic Act of Virgin Islands
  Panama Canal
  PATRIOT
  Revenue
  Sarbanes-Oxley
  Stockpiling
  Tariff
  Trademark
  Walsh-Healey Act; *but* Walsh-Healey
    law (or bill)
act, labor-management relations
Acting, if part of capitalized title
Active Duty
Adjutant General, the (*see* The)

Administration, with name; capitalized
    standing alone if Federal unit:
  Farmers Home
  Food and Drug
  Maritime
  Transportation Security
  but Obama administration;
    administration bill, policy, etc.
Administrative Law Judge Davis; Judge
  Davis; an administrative law judge
Admiralty, British, etc.
Admiralty, Lord of the
Adobe Acrobat Reader
Adviser, Legal (Department of State)
Africa:
  east
  East Coast
  north
  South
  South-West (Territory of)
  West Coast
African American (noun)
African-American (adjective)
Agency, if part of name; capitalized
    standing alone if referring to
    Federal unit:
  Central Intelligence; the Agency
Agent Orange
Age(s):
  Age of Discovery
  Dark Ages
  Elizabethan Age
  Golden Age (of Pericles only)
  Middle Ages
  but atomic age; Cambrian age; copper
    age; ice age; missile age; rocket age;
    space age; stone age; etc.
Agreement, with name; the agreement:
  General Agreement on Tariffs and
    Trade (GATT); the general agreement

International Coffee Agreement; the
   coffee agreement
North American Free-Trade
   Agreement (NAFTA)
Status of Forces; *but* status-of-forces
   agreements
United States-Canada Free-Trade
   Agreement; the free-trade agreement
but the Geneva agreement; the Potsdam
   agreement; Paris peace agreement
Air Force:
   Air National Guard (*see* National)
   Base (with name); Air Force base (*see*
      Base; Station)
   Civil Air Patrol; Civil Patrol; the patrol
   Command (*see* Command)
   One (Presidential plane)
   Reserve
   Reserve Officers' Training Corps
Airport: LaGuardia; Reagan National;
   the airport
Alaska Native:
   the Native; *but* Ohio native, a
      native of Alaska, etc.
Al Jazeera
Alliance, Farmers', etc.; the alliance
alliances and coalitions (*see also* powers):
   Allied Powers; the powers (World
      Wars I and II)
   Atlantic alliance
   Axis, the; Axis Powers; the powers
   Benelux (Belgium, Netherlands,
      Luxembourg)
   Big Four (European); of the Pacific
   Big Three
   Central Powers; the powers (World
      War I)
   Coalition of the Willing
   European Economic Community
   Fritalux (France, Italy, Benelux
      countries)
   North Atlantic Treaty Organization
      (*see* Organization)

   Western Powers
Allied (World Wars I and II):
   armies
   Governments
   Nations
   peoples
   Powers; the powers; *but* European
      powers
   Supreme Allied Commander
Allies, the (World Wars I and II); *also*
      members of Western bloc (political
      entity); *but* our allies; weaker allies,
      etc.
al-Qaida
Alzheimer('s) disease
Ambassador:
   British, etc.; the Ambassador; the
      Senior Ambassador; His Excellency
      Extraordinary and Plenipotentiary;
      the Ambassador; Ambassador at
      Large; an ambassador
amendment:
   Baker amendment
   Social Security Amendments of 1983;
      1983 amendments; the Social Security
      amendments; the amendments
   to the Constitution (U.S.); *but* First
      Amendment, 14th Amendment, etc.;
      the Amendment
American:
   Federation of Labor and Congress of
      Industrial Organizations (AFL–CIO);
      the federation
   Gold Star Mothers, Inc.; Gold Star
      Mothers; a Mother
   Legion (*see* Legion)
   National Red Cross; the Red Cross
   War Mothers; a Mother
AmeriCorps Program
Amtrak (National Railroad Passenger
   Corporation)
Ancient Free and Accepted Masons; a
   Mason; a Freemason

Annex, if part of name of building; the
    annex
Antarctic Ocean (*see* Arctic; Ocean)
appendix 1, A, II, etc.; the appendix; *but*
    Appendix II (when part of title);
    Appendix II:[1] Education Directory
appropriation bill (*see also* bill):
    deficiency
    Department of Agriculture
    for any governmental unit
    independent offices
aquaculture; acquiculture
Arab States
Arabic numerals
Arboretum, National; the Arboretum
Archipelago, Philippine, etc.; the
    archipelago
Architect of the Capitol; the Architect
Archivist of the United States; the Archivist
Arctic:
    Circle
    currents
    Ocean
    zone
    but subarctic
arctic (descriptive adjective):
    clothing
    conditions
    fox
    grass
    night
    seas
Area, if part of name; the area:
    Cape Hatteras Recreational
    White Pass Recreation; etc.
    but area 2; free trade area; Metropolitan
        Washington area; bay area;
        nonsmoking area
Arlington:
    Memorial Amphitheater; the Memorial
        Amphitheater; the amphitheater
    Memorial Bridge (*see* Bridge)

National Cemetery (*see* Cemetery)
Arm, Infantry, etc. (military); the arm
Armed Forces (synonym for overall
    Military Establishment):
    British
    Retirement Home (AFRH)
    of the United States
armed services
armistice
Armory, Springfield, etc.; the armory
Army, American or foreign, if part of name;
    capitalized standing alone only if
    referring to U.S. Army:
    Active; Active-Duty
    Adjutant General, the
    All-Volunteer
    Band (*see* Band)
    branches; Gordon Highlanders; Royal
        Guards; etc.
    Brigade, 1st, etc.; the brigade;
        Robinson's brigade
    Command (*see* Command)
    Command and General Staff College
        (*see* College)
    Company A; A Company; the company
    Confederate (referring to Southern
        Confederacy); the Confederates
    Continental; Continentals
    Corps, Reserve (*see* Corps)
    District of Washington (military); the
        district
    Division, 1st, etc.; the division
    Engineers (the Corps of Engineers); the
        Engineers; *but* Army engineer
    Establishment
    Field Establishment
    Field Forces (*see* Forces)
    Finance Department; the Department
    1st, etc.
    General of the Army; *but* the general
    General Staff; the Staff
    Headquarters, 1st Regiment

[1] The colon is preferred; a dash is permissible;
but a comma is too weak.

Headquarters of the; the headquarters
Regiment, 1st, etc.; the regiment
Regular Army officer; a Regular
Revolutionary (American, British,
    French, etc.)
service
Surgeon General, the (*see* Surgeon
    General)
Volunteer; the Volunteers; a Volunteer
army:
    Lee's army; *but* Clark's 5th Army
    mobile
    mule, shoe, etc.
    of occupation; occupation army
    Red
Arsenal, Rock Island, etc.; the arsenal
article 15; *but* Article 15, when part of title:
    Article 15: Uniform Code of
        Military Justice
Articles:
    of Confederation (U.S.)
    of Impeachment; the articles
Asian American (noun)
Asian-American (adjective)
Assembly (*see* United Nations)
Assembly of New York; the assembly (*see*
    also Legislative Assembly)
Assistant, if part of capitalized title; the
    assistant
assistant, Presidential (*see* Presidential)
Assistant Secretary (*see* Secretary)
Associate Justice (*see* Supreme Court)
Association, if part of name; capitalized
    standing alone if referring to
    Federal unit:
    American Association for the
        Advancement of Science; the
        association
    Federal National Mortgage (Fannie
        Mae); the Association
    Young Women's Christian; the
        association

Astrophysical Observatory (*see*
    Observatory)
Atlantic (*see also* Pacific):
    Charter (*see* Charter)
    coast
    Coast States
    community
    Destroyer Flotilla; the destroyer flotilla;
        the flotilla
    Fleet (*see* Fleet)
    mid-Atlantic
    North
    seaboard
    slope
    South
    time, standard time (*see* time)
    but cisatlantic; transatlantic
Attorney General (U.S. or foreign country);
    but attorney general of Maine, etc.
attorney, U.S.
Authority, capitalized standing alone if
    referring to Federal unit:
    National Shipping; the Authority
    Port Authority of New York and New
        Jersey; the port authority; the
        authority
    Tennessee Valley; the Authority
Auto Train (Amtrak)
autumn
Avenue, Constitution, etc.; the avenue
Award:
    Academy
    Distinguished Service
    Merit
    Mother of the Year
    the award (*see also* decorations, etc.)
Axis, the (*see* alliances)
Ayatollah; an ayatollah

B
baby boomer
Badlands (SD and NE)
Balkan States (*see* States)

Baltic States (*see* States)
Band, if part of name; the band:
    Army, Marine, Navy
Bank, if part of name; the bank; capitalized
    standing alone if referring to
    international bank:
    Export-Import Bank of the United States;
        Ex-Im Bank; the Bank
    Farm Loan Bank of Dallas; Dallas Farm
        Loan Bank; farm loan bank; farm loan
        bank at Dallas
    Farmers & Mechanics, etc.
    Federal Land Bank of Louisville;
        Louisville Federal Land Bank; land
        bank at Louisville; Federal land bank
    Federal Reserve Bank of New York;
        Richmond Federal Reserve Bank;
        but Reserve bank at Richmond;
        Federal Reserve bank; Reserve
        bank; Reserve city
    First National, etc.
    German Central; the Bank
    International Bank for Reconstruction
        and Development; the Bank
    but blood bank, central reserve, soil bank
Bar, if part of name; Maryland (State) Bar
    Association; Maryland (State) bar; the
    State bar; the bar association
Barracks, if part of name; the barracks:
    Carlisle
    Disciplinary (Leavenworth)
    Marine (District of Columbia)
    but A barracks; barracks A; etc.
Base, Andrews Air Force; Air Force base;
    the base (*see also* Naval); *but* Sandia
    Base
Basin (*see* geographic terms)
Battery, the (New York City)
Battle, if part of name; the battle:
    of Gettysburg; *but* battle at Gettysburg;
    etc.
    of Fallujah; of the Marne; of the
        Wilderness; of Waterloo; etc.

battlefield, Bull Run, etc.
battleground, Manassas, etc.
Bay, San Francisco Bay area; the bay area
Belt, if part of name; the belt:
    Bible
    Farm
    Rust
    Sun
    but money belt
Beltway, capitalized with name; the beltway
Bench (*see* Supreme Bench)
Benelux (*see* alliances)
Bible; Biblical; Scriptures; Ten
    Commandments; etc. (*see also* book)
bicentennial
bill, Kiess; Senate bill 217; House bill 31 (*see
    also* appropriation bill)
Bill of Rights (historic document); *but* GI
    bill of rights
Bizonia; bizonal; bizone
Black (African American)
Black Caucus (*see* Congressional)
bloc (*see* Western)
block (grants)
Bluegrass region, etc.
Bluetooth
B'nai B'rith
Board, if part of name; capitalized standing
    alone only if referring to Federal or
    international board:
    Employees' Compensation Appeals
    Federal Reserve (*see* Federal)
    Military Production and Supply
        (NATO)
    National Labor Relations
    of Directors (Federal unit); *but* board of
        directors (nongovernmental)
    of Health of Montgomery County;
        Montgomery County Board of Health;
        the board of health; the board
    of Regents (Smithsonian)
    of Visitors (Military and Naval
        Academies)

on Geographic Names
Railroad Retirement
Boko Haram
bond:
  Government
  savings
  series EE
  Treasury
book:
  books of the Bible
  First Book of Samuel; etc.
  Good Book (synonym for Bible)
book 1, I, etc.; *but* Book 1, when part of title:
  Book 1: The Golden Legend
Boolean:
  logic
  operator
  search
border, United States-Mexican
Borough, if part of name: Borough of the
  Bronx; the borough
Botanic Garden (National); the garden (not
  Botanical Gardens)
Bowl, Dust, Rose, Super, etc.; the bowl
Boy Scouts (the organization); a Boy Scout;
  a Scout; Scouting; Eagle Scout;
  Explorer Scout
Branch, if part of name; capitalized
  standing alone only if referring to a
  Federal unit:
  Accounts
  Public Buildings
  but executive, judicial, or legislative
  branch
Bridge, if part of name; the bridge:
  Arlington Memorial; Memorial;
  Francis Scott Key; Key
  but Baltimore & Ohio Railroad bridge
Brother(s) (adherent of religious order)
budget:
  department
  estimate
  Federal

message
performance-type
President's
Budget of the United States Government,
  the Budget (publication)
Building, if part of name; the building:
  Capitol (*see* Capitol Building)
  Colorado
  House (or Senate) Office
  Investment
  Russell Senate Office
  Cannon House Office
  Pentagon
  the National Archives; the Archives
  Treasury; Treasury Annex
Bulletin 420; Farmers' Bulletin No. 420
Bureau, if part of name; capitalized
    standing alone if referring to Federal
  or international unit:
  of Customs (name changed to U.S.
    Customs and Border Protection)
  of Engraving and Printing
  of Indian Affairs

C

C–SPAN
Cabinet, American or foreign, if part of
    name or standing alone (*see also*
    foreign cabinets):
  British Cabinet; the Cabinet
  the President's Cabinet; the Cabinet;
    Cabinet officer, member
Calendar, if part of name; the calendar:
  Consent; etc.
  House
  No. 99; Calendars Nos. 1 and 2
  of Bills and Resolutions
  Private
  Senate
  Unanimous Consent
  Union
  Wednesday (legislative)
Cambrian age (*see* Ages)

Camp Lejeune; David, etc.; the camp
Canal, with name; the canal:
  Cross-Florida Barge
  Isthmian
  Panama
Cape (see geographic terms)
Capital, Capital City, National Capital
    (Washington, DC); but the capital
    (State)
Capitol Building (with State name); the
    capitol
Capitol, the (Washington, DC):
  Architect of
  Building
  caucus room
  Chamber
  Cloakroom
  dome
  Grounds
  Halls (House and Senate)
  Halls of Congress
  Hill; the Hill
  Police (see Police)
  Power Plant
  Prayer Room
  Press Gallery, etc.
  rotunda
  Senate wing
  stationery room
  Statuary Hall
  the well (House or Senate)
  west front
catch-22
Caucasian (see White)
caucus: Republican; but Congressional
    Black Caucus (incorporated name);
    Sun Belt Caucus
CD
Cemetery, if part of name: Arlington
    National; the cemetery
Census:
  Twenty-third Decennial (title);
    Twenty-third (title); the census

2000 census
2000 Census of Agriculture; the census
    of agriculture; the census
the 23d and subsequent decennial
    censuses
Center, if part of name; the Center
    (Federal); the center (non-Federal):
  Agricultural Research, etc.; the Center
    (Federal)
  Kennedy Center for the Performing
    Arts; the Kennedy Center; the
    Center (Federal)
  the Lincoln Center; the center (non-
    Federal)
central Asia, etc.
Central America
Central Europe
Central States
central time (see time)
century, first, 21st, etc.
Chairman, Chairwoman, Chair:
  of the Board of Directors; the
    Chairman (Federal); but chairman of
    the board of directors (non-Federal)
  of the Committee of the Whole House;
    the Chairman
  of the Federal Trade Commission; the
    Chairman
  Vice
chairman, chairwoman, chair
    (congressional):
  of the Appropriations Committee
  of the Subcommittee on Banking
  but Chairman Rogers, Chairwoman
    Capito
Chair, the, if personified
Chamber of Commerce; the chamber:
  of Ada; Ada Chamber of Commerce;
    the chamber of commerce
  of the United States; U.S. Chamber of
    Commerce; the chamber of
    commerce; national chamber
Chamber, the (Senate or House)

channel 3 (TV); the channel
Chaplain (House or Senate); *but* Navy
  chaplain
chapter 5, II, etc.; *but* Chapter 5, when
  part of title: Chapter 5: Research and
  Development; Washington chapter,
  Red Cross
Chargé d'Affaires, British, etc.; the Chargé
  d'Affaires; the Chargé
chart 2, A, II, etc.; *but* Chart 2, when part of
  legend: Chart 2.—Army strength
Charter, capitalized with name; the charter:
  Atlantic
  United Nations
cheese: Camembert, Cheddar, Parmesan,
  Provolone, Roquefort, etc.
Chief, if referring to head of Federal unit;
  the Chief:
  Clerk
  Forester (*see* Forester)
  Intelligence Office
  Judge
  Justice (U.S. Supreme Court); *but* chief
    justice (of a State)
  Magistrate (the President)
  of Division of Publications
  of Engineers (Army)
  of Naval Operations
  of Staff
Christian; Christendom; Christianity;
  Christianize; *but* christen
church and state
church calendar:
  Christmas
  Easter
  Lent
  Pentecost (Whitsuntide)
Church, if part of name of organization or
  building
Circle, if part of name; the circle:
  Arctic
  Logan
  but great circle

Circular 420
cities, sections of, official or popular names:
  East Side
  French Quarter (New Orleans)
  Latin Quarter (Paris)
  North End
  Northwest Washington, etc. (District
    of Columbia); the Northwest; *but*
    northwest (directional)
  the Loop (Chicago)
City, if part of corporate or popular name;
  the city:
  Kansas City; the two Kansas Citys
  Mexico City
  New York City; *but* city of New York
  Twin Cities
  Washington City; *but* city of Washington
  Windy City (Chicago)
  but Reserve city (*see* Bank)
civil action No. 46
civil defense
Civil War (*see* War)
Clan, if part of tribal name; Clan
    MacArthur; the clan
class 2, A, II, etc.; *but* Class 2 when part of
    title: Class 2: Leather Products
Clerk, the, of the House of Representatives;
    of the Supreme Court of the United
    States
clerk, the, of the Senate
client
client-server
cloud computing; the cloud
coal sizes: pea, barley, buckwheat, stove, etc.
coalition; coalition force; coalition
    members, etc.
coast: Atlantic, east, gulf, west, etc.
Coast Guard, U.S.; the Coast Guard;
    Coastguardsman Smith; *but* a
    coastguardsman; a guardsman;
    Reserve
Coastal Plain (Atlantic and Gulf)

Code (in shortened title of a publication);
  the code:
District
Federal Criminal
Internal Revenue (*also* Tax Code)
International (signal)
of Federal Regulations
Penal; Criminal; etc.
Pennsylvania State
Radio
Television
Uniform Code of Military Justice
United States
ZIP Code (copyrighted)
but civil code; flag code; Morse code
codel (congressional delegation)
collection, Brady, etc.; the collection
collector of customs
College, if part of name; the college:
  Armed Forces Staff
  Command and General Staff
  Gettysburg
  National War
  of Bishops
  but electoral college
college degrees: bachelor of arts, master's, etc.
Colonials (American Colonial Army); *but*
  colonial times, etc.
Colonies, the:
  Thirteen
  Thirteen American
  Thirteen Original
  but 13 separate Colonies
colonists, the
Command, capitalize with name; the
  command:
  Air Force Materiel
  Army
  Central (CENCOM)
  Naval Space
  Zone of Interior
Commandant, the (Coast Guard or Marine
  Corps only)

Commandos, the; Commando raid; a
  commando
Commission (if part of name; capitalized
  standing alone if referring to Federal
  or international commission):
International Boundary, United States
  and Canada
of Fine Arts
Public Buildings
Commissioner, if referring to Federal or
  international commission; the
  Commissioner:
Land Bank; *but* land bank
  commissioner loans
of Customs and Border Protection
U.S. (International Boundary
  Commission, etc.)
but a U.S. commissioner
Committee (or Subcommittee) (if part of
  name; the Committee, if referring to
  international or noncongressional
  Federal committee or to the
  Committee of the Whole, the
  Committee of the Whole House, or
  the Committee of the Whole House on
  the state of the Union):
American Medical Association
  Committee on Education; the
  committee on education; the
  committee
Appropriations, etc.; the committee;
  Subcommittee on Appropriations; the
  subcommittee; subcommittee of the
  Appropriations Committee
Democratic National; the national
  committee; the committee;
  Democratic national committeeman
Democratic policy committee; the
  committee
Joint Committee on Printing; the Joint
  Committee; the committee; *but* a joint
  committee

of Defense Ministers (NATO); the
   Committee (*see also* Organization,
   North Atlantic Treaty)
of One Hundred, etc.; the committee
on Finance; the committee
President's Advisory Committee on
   Management; the Committee
Republican National; the national
   committee; the committee;
   Republican national committeeman
Republican policy committee; the
   committee
Senate policy committee
Subcommittee on Immigration; the
   subcommittee
but Baker committee
ad hoc committee
conference committee
Committee Print No. 32; Committee Prints
   Nos. 8 and 9; committee print
Common Cause
Common Core State Standards Initiative;
   Common Core
Commonwealth:
   British Commonwealth; the
      Commonwealth
   of Australia
   of Kentucky
   of Massachusetts
   of Pennsylvania
   of Virginia
Communist Party; a Communist
compact, U.S. marine fisheries, etc.; the
   compact
Company, if part of name; capitalized
   standing alone if referring to unit of
   Federal Government:
   Procter & Gamble Co.; the company
Comptroller of the Currency; the
   Comptroller
Comptroller General (U.S.); the
   Comptroller
Comsat

Concor
Confederacy (of the South)
Confederate:
   Army
   flag
   Government
   soldier
   States
Confederation, Articles of
Conference, if referring to governmental
   (U.S.) or international conference:
   Bretton Woods; the Conference
   Judicial Conference of the United
      States; U.S. Judicial Conference;
      Judicial Conference; the Conference
   Tenth Annual Conference of the
      United Methodist Churches; the
      conference
Congress (convention), if part of name;
   capitalized standing alone if referring
   to international congress:
   of Industrial Organizations
   of Parents and Teachers, National; the
      congress
Congress (legislature), if referring to
   national congress:
   of Bolivia, etc.; the Congress
   of the United States; First, Second,
      10th, 103d, etc.; the Congress;
   Library of
Congressional:
   Black Caucus; the Black Caucus; the
      caucus
   Directory, the directory
   District, First, 10th, etc.; the First
      District; the congressional district; the
      district
   Medal of Honor (*see* decorations)
   but congressional action, committee, etc.
Congressman; Congresswoman;
   Congressman at Large; Member of
   Congress; Member; membership
Conservative Party; a Conservative

Constitution, with name of country; capitalized standing alone when referring to a specific national constitution; *but* New York State Constitution; the constitution

constitutional

consul, British, general, etc.

consulate, British, etc.

Consumer Price Index (official title); the price index; the index; *but* a consumers' price index (descriptive)

Continent, only if following name; North American Continent; the continent; *but* the Continent (continental Europe)

Continental:
    Army; the Army
    Congress; the Congress
    Divide (*see* Divide)
    Outer Continental Shelf
    Shelf; the shelf; a continental shelf

continental Europe, United States, etc.

Continentals (Revolutionary soldiers)

Convention, governmental (U.S.), international, or national political; the convention:
    89th National Convention of the American Legion
    Constitutional (United States, 1787); the Convention
    Democratic National; Democratic
    Genocide (international)
    on International Civil Aviation
    Republican National; Republican
    Universal Postal Union; Postal Union
    also International Postal; Warsaw

copper age (*see* Ages)

Corporation, if part of name; the Corporation, if referring to unit of Federal Government:
    Commodity Credit
    Federal Deposit Insurance
    National Railroad Passenger (Amtrak)

Rand Corp.; the corporation

Saint Lawrence Seaway Development (American)

St. Lawrence Seaway Management (Canadian)

Union Carbide Corp.; the corporation

Virgin Islands

Corps, if part of name; the corps, all other uses:
    Adjutant General's
    Army Reserve
    Chemical
    Finance
    Foreign Service Officer (*see* Foreign Service)
    Job
    Judge Advocate General's
    Marine (*see* Marine Corps)
    Medical
    Military Police
    Nurse
    of Cadets (West Point)
    of Engineers; Army Engineers; the Engineers; *but* Army engineer; the corps
    Ordnance
    Peace; Peace Corpsman; the corpsman
    Quartermaster
    Reserve Officers' Training (ROTC)
    VII Corps, etc.
    Signal
    Transportation
    Youth
    but diplomatic corps

corpsman; hospital corpsman

corridor, Northeast

Council, if part of name; capitalized standing alone if referring to Federal or international unit (*see also* United Nations):
    Boston City; the council
    Her Majesty's Privy Council; the Privy Council; the Council

National Security; the Council
of Foreign Ministers (NATO); the
   Council
of the Organization of American States;
   the Council
Philadelphia City; the council
counsel; general counsel
County, Prince George's; county of Prince
   George's; County Kilkenny, etc.;
   Loudoun and Fairfax Counties; the
   county
country
Court (of law) capitalized if part of name;
   capitalized standing alone if referring
   to the Supreme Court of the United
   States, to the Court of Impeachment
   (U.S. Senate), or to an international
   court:
Circuit Court of the United States for the
   Tenth Circuit; Circuit Court for the
   Tenth Circuit; the circuit court; the
   court; the tenth circuit
Court of Appeals for the State of North
   Carolina, etc.; the Tenth Circuit Court
   of Appeals; the court of appeals; the
   court
Court of Claims; the court
Court of Impeachment, the Senate; the
   Court
District Court of the United States for
   the Eastern District of Missouri; the
   district court; the court
International Court of Justice; the Court
Permanent Court of Arbitration; the
   Court
Superior Court of the District of
   Columbia; the superior court; the
   court
Supreme Court of the United States (*see*
   Supreme Court)
Supreme Court of Virginia, etc.; the
   supreme court; the court

Tax Court; the court
U.S. Court of Appeals for the District
   of Columbia; the court
Covenant, League of Nations; the covenant
Creed, Apostles'; the Creed
Crown, if referring to a ruler; *but* crown
   colony, lands, etc.
Current, if part of name; the current:
   Humboldt
   Japan
   North Equatorial
customhouse; customs official
czar; czarist

D
D-Day
Dalai Lama
Dalles, The; *but* the Dalles region
Dark Ages (*see* Ages)
Daughters of the American Revolution;
   a Daughter
daylight saving time
Declaration, capitalized with name:
   of Independence; the Declaration
   of Panama; the declaration
decorations, medals, etc., awarded by
       United States or any foreign national
       government; the medal, the cross, the
       ribbon (*see also* Award):
Air Medal
Bronze Star Medal
Commendation Ribbon
Congressional Medal of Honor
Croix de Guerre
Distinguished Flying Cross
Distinguished Service Cross
Distinguished Service Medal
Good Conduct Medal
Legion of Merit
Medal for Merit
Medal of Freedom
Medal of Honor

Purple Heart
Silver Star Medal
Soldier's Medal
Victoria Cross
Victory Medal
but oakleaf cluster
also Carnegie Medal; Olympic Gold
    Medal; Mother of the Year ;
    but gold medal
Decree (*see* Executive); Royal Decree
Deep South
Defense Establishment (*see* Establishment)
Deity, words denoting, capitalized
Delegate (U.S. Congress)
Delegates, Virginia House of
delegate (to a conference); the delegate; the
    delegation
Delta, Mississippi River; the delta
Democratic Party; a Democrat
Department, if part of name; capitalized
    standing alone if referring to a Federal
    or international unit:
    of Agriculture
    of the Treasury
    of Veterans Affairs
    Yale University Department of
        Economics; the department of
        economics; the department
Department of New York, American
    Legion
department:
    executive
    judicial
    legislative
Depot, if part of name; the depot (*see also*
    Station)
Depression, Great
Deputy, if part of capitalized title; *but* the
    deputy

derivatives of proper names:

alaska seal (fur)
angora wool
angstrom unit
argyle wool
artesian well
astrakhan fabric
babbitt metal
benday process
bologna
bordeaux
bourbon whiskey
bowie knife
braille
brazil nut
brazilwood
brewer's yeast
bristolboard
brussel sprouts
brussels carpet
bunsen burner
burley tobacco
canada balsam
    (microscopy)
carlsbad twins
    (petrography)
cashmere shawl
castile soap
cesarean section
chantilly lace
chesterfield coat
china clay
chinese blue
collins (drink)
congo red
cordovan leather
coulomb
curie
degaussing apparatus
delftware
derby hat
diesel engine, dieselize
dixie cup
dotted swiss
epsom salt
fedora hat
frankfurter
french chalk
french dressing
french-fried potatoes
fuller's earth
gargantuan
gauss
georgette crepe
german silver
gilbert
glauber salt
gothic type
graham cracker
herculean task
hessian fly

holland cloth
hoolamite detector
hudson seal (fur)
india ink
india rubber
italic type
jamaica ginger
japan varnish
jersey fabric
johnin test
joule
knickerbocker
kraft paper
lambert
leghorn hat
levant leather
levantine silk
lilliputian
logan tent
london purple
lyonnaise potatoes
macadamized road
mach (no period)
    number
madras cloth
maginot line
    (nonliteral)
manila paper
maraschino cherry
mason jar
maxwell
melba toast
mercerized fabric
merino sheep
molotov cocktail
morocco leather
morris chair
murphy bed
navy blue
nelson, half nelson, etc.
neon light
newton
nissen hut
norfolk jacket
oriental rug
oxford shoe
panama hat
parianware
paris green
parkerhouse roll
pasteurized milk
persian lamb
petri dish
pharisaic
philistine
photostat
pitman arm
pitot tube
plaster of paris
prussian blue

quisling	stillson wrench	myasthenia gravis
quixotic idea	surah silk	Parkinson('s) disease
quonset hut	swiss cheese	post-traumatic stress disorder (PTSD)
rembert wheel	timothy grass	spina bifida
roentgen	turkey red	Zika virus
roman candle	turkish towel	
roman cement	utopia, utopian	
roman type	vandyke collar	
russia leather	vaseline	
russian bath	venetian blind	
rutherford	venturi tube	
sanforize	victoria (carriage)	
saratoga chips	vienna bread	
scotch plaid, *but*	virginia reel	
Scotch tape	wedgwoodware	
(trademark)	wheatstone bridge	
shanghai	wilton rug	
siamese twins	zeppelin	
spanish omelet		

dial-up

Diet, Japanese (legislative body)

diplomatic corps (*see also* Corps; service)

Director, if referring to head of Federal or
international unit; the Director:

Director, if referring to head of Federal or
international unit; the Director:

District Director of Internal Revenue

of the Government Publishing Office

of the Fish and Wildlife Service

of National Intelligence

of the Mint

Office of Management and Budget

but director, board of directors
(nongovernmental)

Director General of Foreign Service; the
Director General; the Director

diseases and related terms (see rule 3.32):

AIDS (acquired immunodeficiency
syndrome)

Alzheimer('s) disease

autism, autism spectrum disorder (ASD)

cerebral palsy

Down syndrome

Ebola virus

German measles

HIV (human immunodeficiency virus)

Hodgkin: lymphoma; disease

Lyme disease

Marfan syndrome

Ménierè's disease

Distinguished Service Medal, etc. (*see*
decorations)

District, if part of name; the district:

Alexandria School District No. 4;
school district No. 4

Congressional (with number)

Federal (*see* Federal)

Los Angeles Water; the water district

but customs district No. 2; first assembly
district; public utility district

District of Columbia; the District:

Anacostia Flats; the flats

Arlington Memorial Bridge; the
Memorial Bridge; the bridge

Children's Hospital; the hospital

District jail; the jail; DC jail

Ellipse, the

Mall, The National; The Mall

Mayor (when pertaining to the District
of Columbia only)

Metropolitan Police; Metropolitan
police officer; the police

police court

Public Library; the library

Reflecting Pool; the pool

Tidal Basin; the basin

Washington Channel; the channel

Divide, Continental (Rocky Mountains);
the divide

Divine Father; *but* divine guidance, divine
providence, divine service

Division, Army, if part of name: 1st Cavalry
Division; 1st Air Cavalry Division; the
division

Division, if referring to Federal
governmental unit; the Division:

Buick Motor Division; the division;
a division of General Motors

Passport; the Division
but Trinity River division
   (reclamation); the division
Dixie
docket No. 66; dockets Nos. 76 and 77
Doctrine, Monroe; the doctrine; *but*
   Truman, Eisenhower doctrine
doctrine, fairness
Document, if part of name; the document:
   Document No. 130
   Document Numbered One Hundred
      Thirty
draconian
drawing II, A, 3, etc.; *but* Drawing 2 when
   part of title: Drawing 2.—
   Hydroelectric Power Development
dumpster
Dust Bowl (*see* Bowl)

E

Earth (planet)
East:
   Coast (Africa)
   Middle, Mideast (Asia)
   Near (Balkans)
   Side of New York
   South Central States
   the East (section of United States)
east:
   Africa
   coast (U.S.)
   Pennsylvania
Eastern:
   Gulf States
   Middle, Mideastern (Asia)
   North Central States
   Shore (Chesapeake Bay)
   States
   United States
eastern:
   France
   seaboard
   Wisconsin

easterner
Ebola virus
eBook
EE bond
electoral college; the electors
Elizabethan Age (*see* Ages)
email (lowercase within a sentence)
Email (uppercase "E" to start a sentence)
Emancipation Proclamation (*see*
   Proclamation)
Embassy, British, etc.; the Embassy
Emperor, Japanese, etc.; the Emperor
Empire, Roman; the empire
Engine Company, Bethesda; engine
   company No. 6; No. 6 engine
   company; the company
Engineer officer, etc. (of Engineer Corps);
   the Engineers
Engineers, Chief of (Army)
Engineers, Corps of (*see* Corps)
Envoy Extraordinary and Minister
   Plenipotentiary; the Envoy; the
   Minister
Equator, the; equatorial
Establishment, if part of name; the
   establishment:
   Army
   Army Field
   Defense
   Federal
   Military
   Naval
   Naval Establishments Regs
   Navy
   Postal
   Regular
   Reserve
   Shore
   but civil establishment; legislative
      establishment
Estate, Girard (a foundation); the estate
estate, third (the commons); fourth
   (the press); tax; etc.

Eurodollar, euro
Excellency, His, Her; Their Excellencies
Exchange, New York Stock; the stock
    exchange; the exchange
Executive (President of United States):
    Chief
    Decree No. 100; Decree 100; *but*
        Executive decree; direction
    Mansion; the mansion; the White House
    Office; the Office
    Order No. 34; Order 34; *but* Executive
        order
    power
executive:
    agreement
    branch
    communication
    department
    document
    paper
    privilege
exhibit 2, A, II, etc.; *but* Exhibit 2, when
    part of title: Exhibit 2: Capital
    Expenditures, 1935–49
Expedition, Byrd; Lewis and Clark; the
    expedition
Exposition, California-Pacific
    International, etc.; the exposition

F

Fair Deal
Fair, World's, etc.; the fair; Texas State Fair
fall (season)
Falls, Niagara; the falls
Far East, Far Eastern; Far West (U.S.); *but*
    far western
Farm, if part of name; the farm:
    Johnson Farm; *but* Johnson's farm
    San Diego Farm
    Wild Tiger Farm
Fascist; fascism
Father of our Country (Washington)
FDsys

Fed, the (no period)
Federal (synonym for United States or other
    sovereign power):
    Depository Library Program *but* Federal
        depository library, libraries
    Digital System
    District (Mexico)
    Establishment
    Government (of any national
        government)
    grand jury; the grand jury
    land bank (*see* Bank)
    Register (publication); the Register
    Reserve Board, the Board; *also* Federal
        Reserve System, the System; Federal
        Reserve Board Regulation W, *but*
        Federal regulation W
    but a federal form of government
federally
fellow, fellowship (academic)
Field, Wrigley, Frank Wiley, etc.; the field
figure 2, A, II, etc. (illustration); *but* Figure
    2, when part of legend: Figure 2.—
    Market scenes
firewall
firm names:
    ACDelco
    Amazon
    America Online (AOL)
    Apple
    Bausch & Lomb Inc.
    BP
    Bristol-Myers Squibb
    Carson, Pirie, Scott & Co.
    Coldwell Banker
    Colgate-Palmolive Co.
    Comcast
    DIRECTV
    Dow Jones & Co., Inc.
    Dun & Bradstreet
    eBay
    E.I. du Pont de Nemours & Co.
    Facebook

FedEx
GlaxoSmithKline
Google
Hamilton Beach/Proctor Silex, Inc.
Hartmarx Corp.
Hewlett-Packard
Houghton Mifflin Co.
Ingersoll-Rand Co.
Intel Corp.
J.C. Penney Co., Inc.
Johns-Manville Corp.
Kennecott Exploration Co.
Kmart
Libbey-Owens-Ford Co.
LinkedIn
Macmillan Co.
Merck & Co., Inc.
Merrill Lynch
Microsoft
Pfizer Inc.
Phelps Dodge Corp.
PricewaterhouseCoopers
Procter & Gamble Co.
Rand McNally & Co.
Rolls-Royce
Sun Microsystems
3M
Twitter
Underwriters Laboratories, Inc.
Walmart
Wal-Mart Stores, Inc.
Weyerhaeuser Co.
Xerox Corp.
YouTube
First Family (Presidential)
First Lady (wife of President)
First World War (*see* War)
flag code
flag, U.S.:
    Old Flag, Old Glory
    Stars and Stripes
    Star-Spangled Banner

flags, foreign:
    Tricolor (French)
    Union Jack (British)
    United Nations
Fleet, if part of name; the fleet:
    Atlantic
    Channel
    Grand
    High Seas
    Marine Force
    Naval Reserve
    Pacific
    6th Fleet, etc.
    U.S.
flex fuel
floor (House or Senate)
flyway; Canadian flyway, etc.
Force(s), if part of name; the force(s):
    Active Forces
    Active-Duty
    Air (*see also* Air Force)
    All-Volunteer
    Armed Forces (synonym for overall
        U.S. Military Establishment)
    Army Field Forces; the Field Forces
    Fleet Marine
    Navy Battle (*see* Navy)
    Navy Scouting (*see* Navy)
    Rapid Deployment
    Task Force 70; the task force; *but* task
        force report
    United Nations Emergency; the
        Emergency Force; the Force; *but*
        United Nations police force
foreign cabinets:
    Minister of Foreign Affairs; Foreign
        Minister; the Minister
    Ministry of Foreign Affairs; the Ministry
    Office of Foreign Missions; the Office
    Minister Plenipotentiary
    Premier
    Prime Minister
Foreign Legion (French); the legion

Foreign Service; the Service:
  officer
  Officer Corps; the corps
  Reserve officer; the Reserve officer
  Reserve Officer Corps; the Reserve
    Corps; the corps
  Staff officer; the Staff officer
  Staff Officer Corps; the Staff Corps; the
    corps
Forest, if part of name; the national forest;
    the forest:
  Angeles National
  Black
  Coconino and Prescott National Forests
  but State and National forests (*see*
    System)
Forester (Chief of Forest Service); the Chief;
    also Chief Forester
form 2, A, II, etc.; *but* Form 2, when part of
    title: Form 1040: Individual Income
    Tax Return; *but* withholding tax form
Fort McHenry, etc.; the fort
Foundation, if part of name; capitalized
    standing alone if referring to Federal
    unit:
  Chemical; the foundation
  Ford; the foundation
  National Science; the Foundation
  Russell Sage; the foundation
Founding Fathers; Founders/Founder (of
    this Nation, Country)
four freedoms
Framers (of the U.S. Constitution; of the
    Bill of Rights)
free world
Frisco (for San Francisco; no apostrophe)
Fritalux (*see* alliances)
Fund, if part of name; capitalized standing
    alone if referring to international or
    United Nations fund:
  Democracy (United Nations); the Fund
  International Monetary; the Fund

but civil service retirement fund;
    highway trust fund; mutual security
    fund; national service life insurance
    fund; revolving fund

G

Gadsden Purchase
Gallery of Art, National (*see* National)
Gallup Poll; the poll
Gambia, The
GAO (Government Accountability Office)
Geiger counter
General Order No. 14; General Orders No.
    14; a general order
General Schedule
Generation X
gentile
Geographer, the (State Department)
geographic terms (terms, such as those
    listed below,[2] are capitalized if part of
    name; are lowercased in general sense
    (rivers of Virginia and Maryland)):

Archipelago	Cascade
Area	Cave
Arroyo	Cavern
Atoll	Channel; *but*
Bank	Mississippi River
Bar	channel(s)
Basin, Upper (Lower)	Cirque
Colorado River,	Coulee
etc. (legal entity);	Cove
but Hansen	Crag
flood-control basin;	Crater
Missouri River	Creek
basin (drainage);	Crossroads
upper Colorado	Current (ocean
River storage project	feature)
Bay	Cut
Bayou	Cutoff
Beach	Dam
Bench	Delta
Bend	Desert
Bight	Divide
Bluff	Dome (not geologic)
Bog	Draw (stream)
Borough (boro)	Dune
Bottom	Escarpment
Branch (stream)	Estuary
Brook	Falls
Butte	Fault
Canal; the canal	Flat(s)
(Panama)	Floodway
Canyon	Ford
Cape	Forest

---

[2] List compiled with cooperation of the U.S.
Board on Geographic Names.

Fork (stream)
Gap
Geyser
Glacier
Glen
Gorge
Gulch
Gulf
Gut
Harbor
Head
Hill
Hogback
Hollow
Hook
Horn
Hot Spring
Icefield
Ice Shelf
Inlet
Island
Isle
Islet
Keys (Florida only)
Knob
Lagoon
Lake
Landing
Ledge
Lowland
Marsh
Massif
Mesa
Monument
Moraine
Mound
Mount
Mountain
Narrows
Neck
Needle
Notch
Oasis
Ocean
Oxbow

Palisades
Park
Pass
Passage
Peak
Peninsula
Plain
Plateau
Point
Pond
Pool
Port (water body)
Prairie
Range (mountain)
Rapids
Ravine
Reef
Reservoir
Ridge
River
Roads (anchorage)
Rock
Run (stream)
Sea
Seaway
Shoal
Sink
Slough
Sound
Spit
Spring
Spur
Strait
Stream
Summit
Swamp
Terrace
Thoroughfare
Trench
Trough
Valley
Volcano
Wash
Waterway
Woods

Geological Survey (*see* Survey)

GI bill of rights

Girl Scouts (organization); a Girl Scout; a
    Scout; Scouting

G-man

Gold Star Mothers (*see* American)

Golden Age (*see* Ages)

Golden Rule

Gospel, if referring to the first four books of
    the New Testament; *but* gospel music

Government:
    British, etc.; the Government

department, officials, -owned,
    publications, etc. (U.S. Government)
National and State Governments
Printing Office (historical)
Publishing Office (*see* Office)
U.S.; National; Federal; Tribal
Government information product
government:
    Churchill
    Communist
    District (of Columbia)
    European governments
    Federal, State, and municipal
        governments
    insular; island
    local
    military
    seat of
    State
    State and Provincial governments
    Territorial
governmental
Governor:
    of Louisiana, etc.; the Governor; a
        Governor; State Governor(s);
        Governors' conference
    of Puerto Rico; the Governor
    of the Federal Reserve Board; the
        Governor
Governor General of Canada; the Governor
    General

govinfo (always bold)

grand jury (*see* Federal)

Grange, the (National)

grant, Pell

graph 2, A, II, etc.; *but* Graph 2, when part
    of title: Graph 2.—Production levels

Great:
    Basin
    Depression
    Divide
    Lakes; the lakes; lake(s) traffic
    Plains; *but* southern Great Plains

Seal (any nation)
Society
War (*see* War)
White Way (New York City)
great circle (navigation)
Greater Los Angeles, Greater New York
gross national product (GNP)
Group:
    G8 (Group of 8) (representatives of the
        eight leading industrial nations)
    Helsinki Monitoring; the group
    Military Advisory Group; the group
    Standing (*see* Organization)
    World Bank
group 2, II, A, etc.; *but* Group 2, when part
    of title: Group II: List of Counties by
    States
Guard, National (*see* National)
guardsman (*see* Coast Guard; National
    Guard)
Gulf:
    Coast States; *but* gulf coast
    of Mexico; the gulf
    States
    Stream; the stream

H

Hague, The
Hall (U.S. Senate or House)
Halls of Congress
H-bomb; H-hour
Headquarters:
    Alaskan Command; the command
        headquarters
    4th Regiment Headquarters; regimental
        headquarters
    32d Division Headquarters; the division
        headquarters
hearing examiner
Heaven (religious); heaven (place)
Heimlich maneuver
hell (place)
Hells (no apostrophe) Canyon

Hemisphere, Eastern; Western; etc.; the
    hemisphere
Hezbollah
High Church
High Commissioner
High Court (*see* Supreme Court)
high definition
High School, if part of name: Western; the
    high school
Highway No. 40; Route 40; State Route 9;
    the highway
Hill (the Capitol)
Hispanic
Holocaust, the (World War II); a holocaust
Holy Scriptures; Holy Writ (Bible)
home page
Hoosier
Hospice, if part of name
Hospital, if part of name; the hospital:
    Howard University
    St. Elizabeths (no apostrophe)
    but naval (marine or Army) hospital
hospital corpsman (*see* corpsman)
House, if part of name:
    Blair
    Johnson house (private residence)
    of Representatives; the House (U.S.)
    Office Building (*see* Building)
    Ohio (State); the house
    but both Houses; lower (or upper)
        House (Congress)
House of Representatives (U.S.), titles of
    officers standing alone capitalized:
    Chairman (Committee of the Whole)
    Chaplain
    Clerk; *but* legislative clerk, etc.
    Doorkeeper
    Official Reporter(s) of Debates
    Parliamentarian
    Postmaster
    post office
    Sergeant at Arms

Speaker pro tempore
Speaker; speakership
HUD (Department of Housing and Urban
   Development)
Hudson's Bay Co.
Hurricane Andrew, Katrina, Rita, etc.

I
ice age (*see* Ages)
imam
Independent Party; an Independent
Indians (*see* 3.18):
   Absentee Shawnee
   Alaska (*see* Native)
   Eastern (or Lower) Band of Cherokee;
      the Band
   Five Civilized Tribes; the Tribes
   Native Americans
   Shawnee Tribe; the Tribe
   Six Nations (Iroquois Confederacy)
   Tribe (if federally recognized)
Initiative, Caribbean Basin; *but* strategic
   defense initiative
Inquisition, Spanish; the Inquisition
inspector general
Institute, if part of name; capitalized
      standing alone if referring to Federal
      or international organization:
   National Cancer; the Cancer Institute;
      the Institute
   National Institutes of Health; the
      Institutes
   of International Law; the Institute
   Woman's; the institute
Institution, if part of name; capitalized
      standing alone if referring to
      Federal unit:
   Brookings; the institution
   Carnegie; the institution
   Smithsonian; the Institution
insular government; island government
intercoastal waterway (*see* waterway)
interdepartmental

interface
International Court of Justice; the Court
international:
   banks (*see* Bank)
   boundary
   dateline
   law
   Morse code (*see* Code)
internet (lowercase within a sentence)
Internet (uppercase "I" to start a sentence)
Internet of Things
Interstate 95; I–95; the interstate
Intracoastal Waterway; the waterway (*see
   also* waterway)
intranet
intrastate
Irish potato
Iron Curtain; the curtain
Islam; Islamic
Isthmian Canal (*see* Canal)
Isthmus of Panama; the isthmus

J
Japan Current (*see* Current)
Java (computer language)
Jersey cattle
Job Corps
Joint Chiefs of Staff; Chiefs of Staff
Joint Committee on Printing (*see*
   Committee)
Journal clerk; the clerk
Journal (House or Senate)
Judge Advocate General, the
judge; chief judge; circuit judge; district
      judge; *but* Judge Judy
judiciary, the
Justice; Justice Alito, etc.

K
kaffiyeh (Arabic headdress)
King of Thailand, etc.; the King
Koran, the; Koranic
Krugerrand

L

Laboratory, if part of name; capitalized
    standing alone if referring to Federal
    unit: Forest Products; the Laboratory;
    but laboratory (non-Federal)
Lake: Erie, of the Woods, Great Salt; the lake
Lane, if part of name: Maiden; the lane
Latino, Latina
Latter-day Saints
law, copyright law; Ohm's, etc.
League, Urban; the league
Legion:
    American; the Legion; a Legionnaire
    French Foreign; the legion
Legislative Assembly, if part of name:
        of New York; of Puerto Rico, etc.; the
        legislative assembly; the assembly
legislative branch, clerk, session, etc.
Legislature:
    National Legislature (U.S. Congress);
        the Legislature
    Ohio Legislature; Legislature of Ohio;
        the State legislature; the legislature
Letters Patent No. 378,964; *but* patent No.
        378,964; letters patent
Liberal Party; a Liberal
Libertarian Party; a Libertarian
Liberty Bell
Librarian of Congress; the Librarian
Library:
    Army; the library
    Harry S. Truman; the library
    of Congress; the Library
    Hillsborough Public; the library
Lieutenant Governor of Idaho, etc.; the
        Lieutenant Governor
Light, if part of name; the light:
    Boston
    Buffalo South Pier Light 2; *but* light No.
        2; light 2
    but Massachusetts Bay lights
Lighthouse (*see* Light Station)

Lightship, if part of name; the lightship:
    Grays Reef
    North Manitou Shoal
Light Station, if part of name; the light
        station; the station:
    Minots Ledge
    Watch Hill
Line(s), if part of name; the line(s):
    Greyhound (bus)
    Holland America (cruises)
    Maginot (fortification)
line:
    Mason-Dixon line *or* Mason and
        Dixon's line
    State
listserv
Local:
    Columbia Typographical Union,
        Local 101
    International Brotherhood of Electrical
        Workers Local 180; *but* local No. 180
local time, local standard time (*see* time)
locator service
Loop, the (*see* cities)
Louisiana Purchase
Low Church
Lower, if part of name:
    California (Mexico)
    Colorado River Basin
    Egypt
    Peninsula (of Michigan)
lower:
    48 (States)
    House of Congress
    Mississippi

M

Madam:
    Chair
    Chairman
    Chairwoman
Magna Carta
Majesty, His, Her, Your; Their Majesties

Majority Leader McConnell; Majority
   Leader McCarthy; *but* the majority
   leader (U.S. Congress)
Mall, The National; The Mall (District of
   Columbia)
Mansion, Executive (*see* Executive)
map 3, A, II, etc.; *but* Map 2, when part of
   title: Map 2.—Railroads of Middle
   Atlantic States
mariculture
Marine Corps; the corps:
   Marines (the corps); *but* marines
     (individuals)
   Reserve; the Reserve
   also a marine; a woman marine; the
     women marines (individuals); soldiers,
     sailors, coastguardsmen, and marines
Maritime Provinces (Canada) (*see* Province)
Marshal (*see* Supreme Court)
marshal (U.S.)
medals (*see* decorations)
Medicaid
MediCal
Medicare Act; Medicare plan
Medicare Plus
Medicare Program
Medigap
Member, if referring to Senator,
   Representative, Delegate, or Resident
   Commissioner of U.S. Congress; *also*
   Member at Large; Member of
   Parliament, etc.; *but* membership;
   member of U.S. congressional
   committee
Memorial:
   Jefferson
   Lincoln
   Vietnam
   WWII
   Korean
   Franklin D. Roosevelt etc.; the memorial

Merchant Marine Reserve; the Reserve;
   but U.S. merchant marine; the
   merchant marine
Metroliner
Metropolitan Washington, etc.; *but*
   Washington metropolitan area
midcontinent region
Middle Ages (*see* Ages)
Middle Atlantic States
Middle East; Mideast; Mideastern; Middle
   Eastern (Asia)
Midwest (section of United States);
   Midwestern States; *but* midwestern
   farmers, etc.
Military Academy (*see* Academy)
Military Establishment (*see* Establishment)
milkshed, Ohio, etc. (region)
millennials
millennium
Minister Plenipotentiary; the Minister;
   Minister Without Portfolio (*see also*
   foreign cabinets)
Ministry (*see* foreign cabinets)
Minority Leader Reid; Minority
   Leader Pelosi; *but* the minority
   leader (U.S. Congress)
Mint, Philadelphia, etc.; the mint
minutemen (colonial)
missiles: capitalize such missile names as
   Hellfire, Sparrow, Tomahawk, Scud,
   Trident, etc.; *but* cruise missile, air-to-
   air missile, surface-to-air missile, etc.
Mission, if part of name; the mission:
   Gospel
   but diplomatic mission; military mission;
   Jones mission
Monument:
   Bunker Hill; the monument
   Grounds; the grounds (Washington
     Monument)
   National (*see* National)
   Washington; the monument (District
     of Columbia)

Mountain States
mountain time, mountain standard time
    (*see* time)
Moving Pictures Experts Group (MPEG)
Mr. Chairman; Mr. Secretary; etc.
Mujahedeen
mullah
Museum, capitalize with name; the
    museum:
    Field
    National
    National Air and Space; the Air Museum
    National Museum of African American
        History and Culture
National Museum of the American
    Indian

N

Nation (synonym for United States); *but* a
    nation; nationwide; *also* French
    nation, Balkan nations
nation, in general, standing alone
National, in conjunction with capitalized
    name:
    Academy of Sciences (*see* Academy)
    Archives and Records Administration;
        the National Archives; the Archives
    Capital (Washington); the Capital; *but*
        national capital area
    Endowment for the Arts; the
        Endowment
    Gallery of Art; the National Gallery;
        the gallery
    Grange; the Grange
    Guard, Ohio, etc.; Air National; the
        National Guard; the Guard; a
        guardsman; Reserve; *but* a National
        Guard man; National Guardsman
    Legislature (*see* Legislature)
    Muir Woods National Monument, etc.;
        the national monument; the
        monument
    Museum (*see* Museum)

    Park Service
    Park, Yellowstone, etc.; Yellowstone Park;
        the national park; the park
    Treasury; the Treasury
    War College
    Woman's Party
    Zoological Park (*see* Zoological)
national:
    agency check (NAC)
    anthem, customs, spirit, etc.
    British, Mexican, etc.
    defense agencies
    stockpile
    water policy
Native: Alaska; American; *but* Ohio native,
    etc.
Naval, if part of name:
    Academy (*see* Academy)
    Air Station (NAS) Patuxent River;
        Pensacola; etc.
    Base Guam; the naval base
    Observatory (*see* Observatory)
    Reserve; the Reserve; a reservist
    Reserve Force; the force
    Reserve officer; a Reserve officer
    Shipyard (if preceding or following name):
        Brooklyn Naval Shipyard; Naval
        Shipyard, Brooklyn; *but* the naval
        shipyard
    Volunteer Naval Reserve
    War College; the War College; the college
naval, in general sense:
    command (*see* Command)
    expenditures, maneuvers, officer,
        service, stores, etc.
    petroleum reserves; *but* Naval
        Petroleum Reserve No. 2 (Buena
        Vista Hills Naval Reserve); reserve No. 2
navel orange
Navy, American or foreign, if part of name;
    capitalized standing alone only if
    referring to U.S. Navy:
    Admiral of the; the admiral

Battle Force; the Battle Force; the force
Establishment; the establishment
Hospital Corps; hospital corpsman; the
   corps
Regular
Seabees (construction battalion); a
   Seabee
navy yard
Nazi; Nazism
Near East (Balkans, etc.)
network
New Deal; anti-New Deal
New England States
New Federalism
New Frontier
New World; *but* new world order
North:
   Atlantic
   Atlantic States
   Atlantic Treaty (*see* Treaty)
   Atlantic Treaty Organization (NATO)
     (*see* Organization)
   Equatorial Current (*see* Current)
   Korea
   Pole
   Slope (Alaska)
   Star (Polaris)
   the North (section of United States)
north:
   Africa
   Ohio, Virginia, etc.
north-central region, etc.
Northeast corridor
northern Ohio
Northern States
northerner
Northwest Pacific
Northwest Territory (1799)
Northwest, the (section of the United States)
Northwest Washington (*see* cities)
Northwestern:
   States
   United States

numbers capitalized if spelled out as part of
   a name:
   Air Force One (Presidential plane)
   Charles the First
   Committee of One Hundred
   Twenty-third Census (*see* Census)

O

Observatory, capitalized with name:
   Astrophysical; the Observatory
   Lick; the observatory
     (nongovernmental)
   Naval; the Observatory
Occident, the; occidental
Ocean, if part of name; the ocean:
   Antarctic
   Arctic
   Atlantic
   North Atlantic, etc.
   Pacific
   Southern
   South Pacific, etc.
   Southwest Pacific, etc.
Oceanographer (the Hydrographer), Navy
Office, if referring to unit of Federal
   Government; the Office:
   Executive
   Foreign and Commonwealth (U.K.)
   Government Printing; the Printing
     Office (historical)
   Government Publishing; the Publishing
     Office; the Office
   Naval Oceanographic
   of Chief of Naval Operations
   of General Counsel
   of Management and Budget
   of Personnel Management
   of the Secretary (Defense); Secretary's
     Office
   Patent and Trademark
   but New York regional office (including
     branch, division, or section therein);
     the regional office; the office

officer:
Army
Marine; *but* naval and marine officers
Navy; Navy and Marine officers
Regular Army; Regular; a Regular
Reserve
Old Dominion (Virginia)
Old South
Old World
Olympic Games; Olympiad; XXXI Olympic
Games
ombudsman, Maryland (State)
online
Operation Iraqi Freedom, Desert Storm
Order of Business No. 56 (congressional
calendar)
Ordnance:
Corps (*see* Corps)
Department; the Department
Organization, if part of name; capitalized
standing alone if referring to
international unit:
International Labour (ILO)
North Atlantic Treaty (NATO):
Chiefs of Staff
Committee of Defense Ministers
Council
Council of Foreign Ministers
Defense Committee
Military Committee
Pact
Regional Planning Group; the Group
Standing Group; the Group
of American States (OAS)
United Nations Educational, Scientific,
and Cultural (UNESCO)
but nongovernmental organization (NGO)
Orient, the; oriental (objects)
Osama bin Laden
Outer Continental Shelf (*see* Continental)

P

Pacific (*see also* Atlantic):

Basin
coast
Coast States
Northwest
rim
seaboard
slope
South
States
time, Pacific standard time (*see* time)
but cispacific; transpacific
pan-American games; *but* Pan American
Day
Pan American Union (renamed; *see*
Organization of American States)
Panel, the Federal Service Impasses
(Federal), etc.; the Panel
Panhandle of Texas; Texas Panhandle; the
panhandle; etc.
papers, Woodrow Wilson, etc.; the papers;
but white paper
Parish, Caddo, etc.; *but* parish of Caddo
(Louisiana civil division); the parish
Park, Fairmount, etc.; the park (*see also*
National)
Park Police, U.S.; park policeman
Park Service
Park, Zoological (*see* Zoological)
Parkway, George Washington Memorial;
the memorial parkway; the parkway
Parliament, Houses of; the Parliament
Parliamentarian (U.S. Senate or House)
part 2, A, II, etc.; *but* Part 2, when part of
title: Part 2: Iron and Steel Industry
Party, if part of name; the party
Pass, Brenner, capitalized if part of name;
the pass
patent (*see* Letters Patent)
Peninsula Upper (Lower) (Michigan); the
peninsula
Penitentiary, United States; the penitentiary
petrodollar
phase 2; phase I

Philippines, Republic of the
Pilgrim Fathers (1620); the Pilgrims; a
    Pilgrim
Place, if part of name: Jefferson Place; the
    place
Plains (Great Plains), the
plan:
    controlled materials
    5-year
    Marshall (European Recovery Program)
Planetarium, Fels, Hayden; the planetarium
plant, United States Steel, etc.
plate 2, A, II, etc.; *but* Plate 2, when part of
    title: Plate 2.—Rural Structures
Plaza, Union Station (Washington, DC);
    the plaza
Pledge of Allegiance; the pledge
Pole: North, South; the pole; subpolar
Pole Star (Polaris); polar star
Police, if part of name; the police:
    Capitol
    Park, U.S.
    White House
political action committee (PAC)
political parties and adherents (*see* specific
    political party)
Pool, Northwest Power, etc.; the pool
Pope; *but* papal, patriarch, pontiff, primate
Port, if part of name; Port of Norfolk;
    Norfolk Port; the port (*see* Authority)
Post Office, Chicago, etc.; the post office
P.O. Box (with number); *but* post office box
    (in general sense)
Postmaster General
PostScript; *but* a postscript
Powers, if part of name; the powers (*see*
    also alliances):
    Allied (World Wars I and II)
    Axis (World War II)
    Western
    but European powers
precinct; first, 10th precinct
Premier (*see* foreign cabinets)

Preserve, Sullys Hill, National Game
Presidency (office of the head of Government)
President:
    of the United States; the Executive; the
      Chief Magistrate; the Commander
      in Chief; the President-elect; ex-
      President; former President; *also*
      preceding name
    of any other country; the President of
      Federal or international unit
    but president of the Norfolk Southern
      Railway; president of the Federal
      Reserve Bank of New York
Presidential assistant, authority, order,
    proclamation, candidate, election,
    timber, year, etc.
Prime Minister (*see* foreign cabinets)
Prison, New Jersey State; the prison
Privy Council, Her Majesty's (*see* Council)
Prize, Nobel, Pulitzer, etc.; the prize
Proclamation, Emancipation; Presidential
    Proclamation No. 24; Proclamation
    No. 24; the proclamation; *but*
    Presidential proclamation
Program, if part of name:
    European Recovery
    Fulbright
    Mutual Defense Assistance
    but universal military training;
      government bailout
Progressive Party; a Progressive
Project:
    Gutenberg
    Manhattan
    Vote Smart
Proposition 13
Prosecutor; Special Prosecutor (Federal)
Province, Provincial, if referring to an
    administrative subdivision: Ontario
    Province; Province of Ontario;
    Maritime Provinces (Canada); the
    Province

Proving Ground, Aberdeen, etc.; the
    proving ground
Public Law; Public Law 110–161, etc.
Public Printer; the Government Printer;
    the Printer (historical)
public utility district (*see* District)
Pueblo, Santa Clara; the pueblo (place);
    the Pueblo (Tribe)
Purchase, Gadsden, Louisiana, etc.
Puritan; puritanical
Pyrrhic victory

Q

Quad Cities (Davenport, Rock Island,
    Moline, East Moline, and Bettendorf)
query
queue

R

Radio Free Europe/Radio Liberty
Railroad, Alaska; the railroad
Ranch, King, etc.; the ranch
Range, Cascade, etc. (mountains); the range
Rebellion, if part of name; the rebellion:
    Boxer
    Whisky
Reconstruction period (post-Civil War)
Red army
Red Cross, American, American National
Reds, the; a Red (political)
Reformatory, Michigan; the reformatory
Refuge, Blackwater National Wildlife, etc.;
    Blackwater Refuge; the refuge
region, north-central, etc.; first region,
    10th region; region 7; midcontinent
Regular Army, Navy; a Regular (*see also*
    officer)
regulation:
    greenhouse gas
    W (*see also* Federal Reserve Board)
    but Veterans Entitlements Regulations
religious terms:
    Baha'i
    Baptist

Brahman
Buddhist
Catholic; Catholicism; *but* catholic
    (universal)
Christian
Christian Science
Evangelical United Brethren
Hindu; Hinduism
Islam; Islamic
Jewish
Latter-day Saints
Muslim: Shiite; Sunni
New Thought
Protestant; Protestantism
Scientology
Seventh-day Adventists
Seventh Day Baptists
Sikh
Zoroastrian
Renaissance, the (era)
Report, if part of name (with date or
    number); the annual report;
    the report:
    2015 Report of the Chief of the Forest
        Service
    9/11 Commission Report
    Annual Report of the Secretary of
        Defense for the year ended
        September 30, 2015
    President's Economic Report; the
        Economic Report
    Railroad Retirement Board Annual
        Report, 2015; *but* annual report of
        the Railroad Retirement Board
    Report No. 31
    United States Reports (publication)
Reporter, the (U.S. Supreme Court)
Representative; Representative at Large
    (U.S. Congress); U.N.
Republic, capitalized if part of name;
    capitalized standing alone if referring
    to a specific government:
    Czech

French
Irish
of Bosnia and Herzegovina
of Panama
of the Philippines
Slovak
also the American Republics; South
American Republics; the Latin
American Republics; the Republics
Republican Party; a Republican
Reservation (forest, military, or Indian), if
part of name; the reservation:
Hill Military
Standing Rock
Reserve, if part of name; the Reserve (*see
also* Air Force; Army Corps; Coast
Guard; Foreign Service; Marine
Corps; Merchant Marine; Naval;
National Guard):
Active
Air Force
Army
bank (*see* Bank)
Board, Federal (*see* Federal)
city (*see* Bank)
components
Enlisted
Establishment
Inactive
Naval
officer
Officers' Training Corps
Ready
Retired
Standby
Strategic
Reserves, the; reservist
Resolution, with number; the resolution:
House Joint Resolution 3
Senate Concurrent Resolution 18
War Powers Resolution (short title)
but Tonkin resolution

Revised Statutes (U.S.); Supplement to the
Revised Statutes; the statutes; Statutes
at Large (U.S.)
Revolution, Revolutionary (if referring to
the American, French, or English
Revolution) (*see also* War)
rim; the Pacific rim
Road, if part of name: Benning; the road
Roman numerals, common nouns used
with, not capitalized:
book II; chapter II; part II; etc.
but Book II: Modern Types (complete
heading); Part XI: Early Thought
(complete heading)
Route 66, State Route 9 (highways)
rule 21; rule XXI; *but* Rule 21, when part of
title: Rule 21: Renewal of Motion
Rules:
of the House of Representatives; *but* rules
of the House; House rule X
Standing Rules of the Senate
(publication); *but* rules of the Senate
also Commission rules

S
Sabbath; Sabbath Day
savings bond (*see* bond)
schedule 2, A, II, etc.; *but* Schedule 2, when
part of title; Schedule 2: Open and
Prepay Stations
School, if part of name; the school:
any school of U.S. Armed Forces
Hayes
Pawnee Indian
Public School 13; P.S. 13
school district (*see* District)
Scriptures; Holy Scriptures (the Bible)
Seabees (*see* Navy)
seaboard, Atlantic, eastern, etc.
seasons:
autumn (fall)
spring
summer
winter

seaway (*see* geographic terms; Corporation)
Second World War (*see* War)
Secretariat (*see* United Nations)
Secretaries of the Army and the Navy; *but*
    Secretaries of the military
    departments; secretaryship
Secretary, head of national governmental
    unit:
    of Defense; of State; etc.; the Secretary
    of State for Foreign Affairs (British); for
    the Commonwealth, etc.; the
    Secretary
    of the Smithsonian Institution; the
    Secretary
    also the Assistant Secretary; the
    Executive Secretary
Secretary General; the Secretary General:
    Organization of American States
    United Nations
section 2, A, II, etc.; *but* Section 2, when
    part of title: Section 2: Test
    Construction Theory
Selective Service (*see* Service; System)
Senate (U.S.), titles of officers standing
    alone capitalized:
    Chaplain
    Chief Clerk
    Doorkeeper
    Official Reporter(s)
    Parliamentarian
    Postmaster
    President of the
    President pro tempore
    Presiding Officer
    Secretary
    Sergeant at Arms
Senate, Ohio (State); the senate
Senator (U.S. Congress); *but* lowercased if
    referring to a State senator, unless
    preceding a name
senatorial
Sergeant at Arms (U.S. Senate or House)

Sermon on the Mount
server
Service, if referring to Federal unit; the
    Service:
    Extension
    Federal Mediation and Conciliation
    Fish and Wildlife
    Foreign (*see* Foreign Service)
    Forest
    Internal Revenue
    Marshals
    National Park
    Natural Resources Conservation
    Postal
    Secret (Homeland Security)
    Selective (*see also* System); *but* selective
    service, in general sense; selective
    service classification 1–A, 4–F, etc.
    Senior Executive
service:
    airmail
    Army
    city delivery
    consular
    customs
    diplomatic
    employment (State)
    extension (State)
    general delivery
    naval
    Navy
    parcel post
    postal field
    rural free delivery; rural delivery; free
    delivery
    special delivery
    star route
Shelf, Continental (*see* Continental)
ship of state (unless personified)
Sister(s) (adherent of religious order)
Six Nations (*see* Indians)
Smithsonian Institution (*see* Institution)

Social Security Administration (U.S.),
    application, check, number, pension,
    trust fund, system, etc.
Socialist Party; a Socialist
Society, if part of name; the society:
    American Cancer Society, Inc.
    of the Cincinnati
soil bank
soil orders (see rule 3.30)
Soldiers' Home; the soldiers' home; (*see*
    Armed Forces Retirement Home)
Solicitor for the Department of Labor, etc.;
    the Solicitor
Solicitor General (Department of Justice)
Son of Man (Christ)
Sons of the American Revolution
    (organization); a Son; a Real Son
South:
    American Republics (*see* Republic)
    American States
    Atlantic
    Atlantic States
    Deep South (U.S.)
    Korea
    Midsouth (U.S.)
    Pacific
    Pole
    the South (section of United States);
        Southland
Southeast Asia
southern California, southeastern
    California, etc.
Southern States
Southern United States
southerner
Southwest, the (section of United States)
space shuttle; the shuttle
space station
spam (email)
Spanish-American War (*see* War)
Speaker of the House of Representatives;
    the Speaker

special agent
specialist
Special Order No. 12; Special Orders, No.
    12; a special order
Spirit of '76 (painting); *but* spirit of '76 (in
    general sense)
Sputnik
Square, Lafayette, etc.; the square
Staff, Foreign Service (*see* Foreign Service);
    Air (U.K.)
standard time (*see* time)
Star of Bethlehem
Star-Spangled Banner (*see* flag)
State:
    Champion
    government
    legislature (*see* Legislature)
    line, Iowa; Ohio-Indiana, etc.
    New York
    of Israel
    of Maryland
    of the Union Message/Address
    of Veracruz
    out-of-State (adjective); *but* out-of-stater
    prison
    Vatican City
state:
    church and
    of the art: state-of-the-art technology
    welfare
    also downstate, instate, multistate,
        statehood, statehouse, stateside,
        statewide, substate, tristate, upstate
State's attorney
state's evidence
states' rights (international)
States:
    Arab
    Balkan
    Baltic
    East North Central
    East South Central

Eastern; *but* eastern industrial States
Eastern Gulf
Eastern North Central, etc.
Far Western
Gulf; Gulf Coast
Lake
Latin American
lower 48
Middle
Middle Atlantic
Middle Western
Midwestern
Mountain
New England
North Atlantic
Northwestern, etc.
Organization of American
Pacific
Pacific Coast
rights (U.S.)
South American
South Atlantic
Southern
the six States of Australia; a foreign state
Thirteen Original; original 13 States
Western; *but* western Gulf; western
    farming States
Station, if part of name; the station; not
    capitalized if referring to surveying
    or similar work:
Grand Central
Naval Air Engineering
television station WSYR–TV
Union; Union Depot; the depot
WAMU station; station WMAL; radio
    station WSM; broadcasting station
    WJSV
station 9; substation A
Statue of Liberty; the statue
Statutes at Large (U.S.) (*see also* Revised
    Statutes)
Stealth: bomber, fighter
Stockpile, Strategic National

stone age (*see* Ages)
storage facility
Stream, Gulf (*see* Gulf; geographic terms)
Street, if part of name; the street:
    I Street (not Eye Street)
    110th Street
    U Street (not You Street)
subcommittee (*see* Committee)
subtropical, subtropic(s) (*see* tropical)
summit meeting; Earth summit
Sun; a sun
Super Bowl
Superfund; the fund
Superintendent, if referring to head of
        Federal unit; the Superintendent:
    of Documents (Government
        Publishing Office)
    of the Naval (or Military) Academy
Supplement to the Revised Statutes (*see*
        Revised Statutes)
Supreme Bench; the Bench; *also* High
        Bench; High Tribunal
Supreme Court (U.S.); the Court; *also* High
    Court; titles of officers standing alone
    capitalized:
    Associate Justice
    Chief Justice
    Clerk
    Marshal
    Reporter
    but Ohio Supreme Court; the supreme
    court
Surgeon General, the (Air Force, Army,
    Navy, and Public Health Service)
Survey, if part of name of Federal unit; the
        Survey: Geodetic; Geological
System, if referring to Federal unit; the
        System:
    Federal Home Loan Bank; the System
    Federal Reserve; the System
    National Forest; the System
    National Highway; Interstate Highway;
        the System

National Park; the System
National Trails; the System
National Wild and Scenic Rivers; the
    System
Regional Metro System; Metro system
Selective Service (*see also* Service)
State and National forests
but Amtrak railway system; Amtrak
    system; the system
also Federal land bank system

T

table 2, II, A, etc.; *but* Table 2, when part of
    title: Table 2: Degrees of Land
    Deterioration
task force (*see* Force)
Team, USAREUR Technical Assistance,
    etc.; the team
television station (*see* Station)
Telnet
Ten Commandments
Territorial, if referring to a political
    subdivision
Territory:
    Northwest (1799); the territory
    Trust Territory of the Pacific Islands;
        Pacific Islands Trust Territory; the
        trust territory; the territory
    Yukon, Northwest Territories; the
        Territory(ies), Territorial (Canada)
    but territory of: American Samoa, Guam,
        Virgin Islands
The, part of name, capitalized:
    The Dalles; The Gambia; The Hague;
        The Weirs; *but* the Dalles Dam; the
        Dalles region; the Hague Conference;
        the Weirs streets
    but the Adjutant General; the National
        Archives; the Archives; the Times; the
        Mermaid
Third World
Thirteen American Colonies, etc. (*see*
    Colonies)

Thirteen Original States
Thruway, New York State; the thruway
time:
    Alaska, Alaska standard
    Atlantic, Atlantic standard
    central, central standard
    eastern, eastern daylight, eastern daylight
        saving (no *s*), eastern standard
    Greenwich mean time (GMT)
    Hawaii-Aleutian standard
    local, local standard
    mountain, mountain standard
    Pacific, Pacific standard
    universal
title 2, II, A, etc.; *but* Title 2, when part of
    title: Title 2: General Provisions
Tomb:
    Grant's; the tomb
    of the Unknowns; of the Unknown
        Soldier; Unknown Soldier's Tomb;
        the tomb (*see also* Unknown Soldier)
Tower, Eiffel, etc.; the tower
Township, Union; township of Union
trade names and trademarks:

Blu-Ray	MasterCard
Coca-Cola	TiVo
Dr Pepper	U-Haul
Hersheypark	UNIX
iPhone	VISA
iPod	Yahoo!
iTunes	ZIP Code (Postal)

Trade Representative (U.S.)
transatlantic; transpacific; trans-Siberian,
    etc.; *but* Transjordan; Trans-Alaska
Treasurer, Assistant, of the United States;
    the Assistant Treasurer; *but* assistant
    treasurer at New York, etc.
Treasurer of the United States; the Treasurer
Treasury notes; Treasurys
Treasury, of the United States; General;
    National; Public
Treaty, if part of name; the treaty:
    Jay
    North Atlantic; North Atlantic Defense

of Versailles
   but treaty of 1919
triad
Tribe; Tribal (federally recognized)
   (*see* Indians)
Tribunal, standing alone capitalized only in
   minutes and official reports of a
   specific arbitration; *also* High
   Tribunal; the Tribunal (Supreme
   Court)
Tropic of Cancer, of Capricorn; the Tropics
tropical; neotropic, neotropical, sub-
   tropic(s), subtropical
Trust, Power, etc.
trust territory (*see* Territory)
Tunnel, Lincoln, etc.; the tunnel; *but*
   irrigation, railroad, etc., tunnel
Turnpike, Pennsylvania, etc.; the turnpike
Twin Cities (Minneapolis and St. Paul)

U

U-boat
Under Secretary, if referring to officer of
   Federal Government; the Under
   Secretary:
   of Agriculture
   of State
   of the Treasury
Uniform Code of Military Justice (*see* Code)
Union (if part of proper name; capitalized
   standing alone if synonym for United
   States or if referring to international
   unit):
   Columbia Typographical
   European
   Pan American (former name; *see*
      Organization of American States)
   Station; *but* union passenger station;
      union freight station
   Teamsters; the Teamsters; the
      union; *also* the Auto Workers, etc.
   Universal Postal; the Postal Union
   Woman's Christian Temperance

   but a painters union; printers union
United Nations:
   Charter; the charter
   Educational, Scientific, and Cultural
      Organization (UNESCO) (*see*
      Organization)
   Food and Agriculture Organization
      (FAO)
   General Assembly; the Assembly
   International Children's Emergency
      Fund (UNICEF)
   International Court of Justice; the Court
   Permanent Court of Arbitration (*see*
      Court)
   Secretariat, the
   Secretary General
   Security Council; the Council
   World Employment Conference
   World Health Organization (WHO);
      the Organization
universal:
   military training (*see* Program)
   time (*see* time)
University, if part of name: Stanford; the
   university
Unknown Soldier; Unknown of World War
   II; World War II Unknown;
   Unknown of Korea; Korea
   Unknown; the Unknowns (*see also*
   Tomb)
Upper, if part of name:
   Colorado River Basin
   Egypt
   Peninsula (of Michigan)
   but upper House of Congress
U.S.S.R. (former Union of Soviet Socialist
   Republics)

V

Valley, Shenandoah, etc.; the valley; *but* the
   valleys of Virginia and Maryland
V–E Day; V–J Day; V-chip
veteran, World War II; Vietnam

Veterans Affairs, Department of (*see* Department)
Vice Chairman, etc. (same as Chairman)
vice consul, British, etc.
Vice President (same as President)
Voice of America; the Voice
volume 2, A, II, etc.; *but* Volume 2, when part of title; Volume 2: Five Rivers in America's Future

W
War, if part of formal name:
  Between the States
  Civil
  First World War; World War I; World War; Great War; Second World War; World War II
  for Independence (1776)
  French and Indian (1754–63)
  Mexican
  of 1812
  of the Rebellion; the rebellion
  on Crime
  on Drugs
  on Poverty
  on Terrorism, Global
  Revolutionary; of the Revolution; the Revolution
  Seven Years'
  Six-Day (Arab-Israeli)
  Spanish-American
  the two World Wars
  also post-World War II
war, descriptive or undeclared:
  cold, hot
  European
  French and Indian wars
  Indian
  Korean
  Persian Gulf; Gulf
  third world; world war III
  Vietnam
  with Mexico

War College, National (*see* College)
War Mothers (*see* American)
ward 1, 2, etc.; first, 11th, etc.
Washington's Farewell Address
water district (*see* District)
waterway, inland, intercoastal, etc.; *but* Intracoastal Waterway
web (lowercase within a sentence):
  #address
  #page
  site
Web (upper case "W" to start a sentence)
Week, Fire Prevention; etc.
Weirs, The; *but* the Weirs streets
welfare state
West:
  Bank (Jordan)
  Coast (Africa); *but* west coast (U.S.)
  End, etc. (section of city)
  Europe (political entity)
  Far West; Far Western States
  Florida (1763–1819)
  Middle (United States); Midwest
  South Central States, etc.
  the West (section of United States; *also* world political entity)
west, western Pennsylvania
Western:
  bloc
  civilization
  countries
  Europe(an) (political entity)
  Hemisphere; the hemisphere
  ideas
  Powers
  States
  United States
  World
  but far western; western farming States (U.S.)
westerner
Whip, Majority; Minority
Whisky Rebellion (*see* Rebellion)

White (*see* Caucasian)
White House:
    Blue Room
    East Room
    Oval Office
    Police (*see* Police)
    Red Room
    Rose Garden
    State Dining Room
white paper, British, etc.
Wi-Fi
Wilderness, capitalized with name; San
    Joaquin Wilderness, CA; the
    wilderness; *but* the Wilderness
    (Virginia battlefield)
Wood, if part of name:
    Belleau
    County
    Fort Leonard
World: New, Old, Third; *but* free world
World Bank; the Bank
World Series
World War (*see* War)
World War II veteran
world wide web, the web

X

x ray (note: no hyphen)

Y

year, calendar, fiscal
Your Excellency; Your Honor; Your
    Majesty; etc.
Youth Corps; the Corps

Z

Zika virus
ZIP Code number; ZIP+4
Zone, if part of name; the zone:
    British (in Germany)
    Canal (Panama)
    Eastern, Western (Germany)
    Frigid
    Hot (infectious area)
    of Interior (*see* Command)
    Temperate, Torrid; the zone
    U.S. Foreign Trade; Foreign
        Trade Zone; *but* the foreign trade
        zone, free trade zone
zone:
    Arctic
    eastern standard time
    no-fly
    polar
    tropical
Zoological Park (National); the zoo;
    the park

5. Spelling
(See also Chapter 7 "Compounding Examples" and Chapter 9 "Abbreviations and Letter Symbols")

5.1. GPO uses Webster's Third New International Dictionary as its guide for the spelling of words not appearing in the GPO STYLE MANUAL. Colloquial and dialect spellings are not used unless required by the subject matter or specially requested. The tendency of some producers of computer-assisted publications to rely on the limited capability of some spell-checking programs adds importance to this list.

Preferred and difficult spellings

5.2. In addition to indicating the preferred forms of words with variant spellings, the list also contains other words frequently misspelled or causing uncertainty.

A
abattoir
aberration
abetter
  abettor (law)
abridgment
absorb (take in)
  adsorb (adhesion)
abysmal
a cappella
accede (yield)
  exceed (surpass)
accepter
  acceptor (law)
accessory
accommodate
accordion
accouter
accursed
acetic (acid)
  ascetic (austere)
acknowledgment
acoustic
adapter
adjurer
adjuster
ad nauseam

adviser
  advisor (law)
adz
aegis
aesthetic
affect (influence, v.)
  effect (result, finish, n., v.)
afterward(s)
  afterword
aging
aid (n., v.)
aide
aide-de-camp
albumen (egg)
  albumin (chemistry)
align
allottee
all ready (prepared)
  already (previous)
all right
altogether (completely)
all together (collectively)
aluminum

ambidextrous
amoeba
ampoule
analog
analogous
anemia
anesthetic
aneurysm
anomalous
anonymous
antediluvian
antibiotics (n.)
  antibiotic (adj.)
anyway (adv.)
anywise (adv.)
appall, -ed, -ing
appareled, -ing
aquatic
aqueduct
archaeology
arrester
artifact
artisan
ascendance, -ant
ascent (rise)
  assent (consent)
assassinate

athenaeum
attester
autogiro
awhile (for some time)
a while (a short time)
ax
aye

B
backward
baloney (nonsense)
  bologna (sausage)
bandanna
bargainer
  bargainor (law)
baritone
bark (boat)
barreled, -ing
bastille
bathyscaph
battalion
bazaar (event)
  bizarre (strange or absurd)
behoove
beneficent

benefited, -ing
bettor (wagerer)
beveled, -ing
biased, -ing
blessed
bloc (group)
  block (grants)
blond(e)
bluing
born (birth)
  borne (carried)
bouillon (soup)
  bullion (metal)
boulder
bourgeoisie
breach (gap)
  breech (lower part)
brier
briquet, -ted, -ting
Britannia
broadax
bronco
brunet(te)
buccaneer
buncombe
bunion
bur
burned
bus, bused, buses,
  busing
butadiene

C

caffeine
calcareous
calcimine
caldron
calendar
calender (paper
  finish)
caliber
caliper
calk (spike)
  caulk (seal)

calligraphy
callus (n.)
  callous (adj.)
calorie
canceled, -ing
cancellation
candor
canister
cannot
canoeing
cantaloupe
canvas (cloth)
  canvass (solicit)
capital (city, money)
  capitol (building)
carabao (sing., pl.)
  carat (gem weight)
    caret (omission
      mark)
    karat (gold weight)
carbureted, -ing
carburetor
Caribbean
caroled, -ing
carotene
carrot
cartilage
caster (roller)
  castor (oil)
casual (informal)
  causal (cause)
catalog, -ed, -ing
cataloger
catsup
caviar
caviled, -er, -ing
center
centipede
centrifugal
cesarean
chairmaned
chaise longue;
  lounge
chancellor

channeled, -ing
chaperon(e)
chautauqua
chauvinism
chiffonier
chile con carne
chili (pepper)
chiseled, -ing
chlorophyll
cigarette
citable
cite (quote)
  site (place)
clamor
climactic (climax)
  climatic (climate)
cocaine
coconut
cocoon
coleslaw
colloquy
colossal
combated, -ing
commenter
  commentor (law)
commingle
commiserate
complement
  (complete)
compliment
  (praise)
confectionery
confidant(e)
  confident (sure)
confirmer
  confirmor (law)
conjurer
connecter
  connector (road)
connoisseur
consecrator
consensus
consignor
consulter

consummate
contradicter
control, -lable, -ling
converter
conveyor
cookie
cornetist
corollary
corvette
councilor (of
  council)
  counselor
    (adviser)
counseled, -ing
cozy
crawfish
creneled, -ing
crystaled, -ing
crystalline
crystallize
cudgeled, -ing
cyclopedia
czar

D

darndest
debarkation
decaffeinated
decalogue
defense
deliverer
  deliveror (law)
demagogue
demarcation
de minimis
dependent
descendant (n., adj.)
desecrater
desiccate
desuetude
  (suspended)
  destitute (bereft)
detractor
develop, -ment

device (contrivance)
  devise (convey)
dextrous (syllable
  division)
diaeresis
diaeretic
  diuretic (water pill)
diagramed, -ing
diagrammatic
dialed, -ing
dialogue
dialysis
diaphragm
diarrhea
dickey
dietitian
diffuser
dike
dilettante
dinghy (boat)
diphtheria
discreet (prudent)
  discrete (distinct)
disheveled, -ing
disc (computer)
dispatch
dissension
distention
distill, -ed, -ing,
  -ment
distributor
diverter
divorcee (masc.,
  fem.)
doctoral
doctrinaire
doggerel
dossier
doweled, -ing
downward
dreadnought
dreamed
drought
dueled, -ing

duffelbag
dullness
dumbfound
dwelt
dyeing (coloring)
  dying (death)

E

eastward
ecstasy
edema
edgewise
electronics (n.)
  electronic (adj.)
eleemosynary
elicit (to draw)
  illicit (illegal)
embarrass
embed
embellish
emboweled, -ing
emboweler
emigrant (go from)
  immigrant (go
  into)
emigree
eminent (famous)
  imminent (soon)
emoji
employee
enameled, -ing
encage
encase
encave
enclasp
enclose
enclosure
encumber
encumbrance
encyclopedia
endorse, -ment
endwise
enfeeble
enforce, -ment

engraft
enroll, -ed, -ing,
  -ment
enshade
ensheathe
ensnare
ensure (guarantee)
  insure (protect)
entrench
entrepreneur
entrust
entwine
envelop (v.)
  envelope (n.)
enwrap
eon
epaulet, -ed, -ing
epiglottis
epilogue
equaled, -ing
erysipelas
escallop
escapable
esophagus
etiology
evacuee
evanescent
eviscerate
evocative
exhibitor
exhilarate
exonerate
exorbitant
expellant
exposé (n.,
  exposure)
  expose (v., to lay
  open)
exsiccate
extant (in existence)
  extent (range)
extoll, -ed, -ing
eyeing
eyrie

F

fantasy
farther (distance)
  further (degree)
favor
fecal
feces
fetal
fetish
fetus
fiance(e)
fiber
fiche (microfiche)
filigree
finable
finagle
financier
fjord
flammable (*not*
  inflammable)
flection
fledgling
flextime
flier
flotage
flotation
fluorescent
focused, -ing
folderol
forbade
forbear (endurance)
  forebear (ancestor)
foresee
forgettable
forgo (relinquish)
  forego (precede)
format, formatted,
  formatting
forswear
fortissimo
forward (ahead)
  foreword (preface)
fricassee
fuchsia

fueler
fulfill, -ed, -ing,
　-ment
fulsome
fungus (n., adj.)
funneled, -ing
furor
fuse (all meanings)
fuselage
fusillade

G

gaiety
gaily
galosh
gamboled, -ing
garrote
gauge
gazetteer
gelatin
genealogy
generalissimo
germane
glamorous
glamour
glycerin
gobbledygook
goodbye
govinfo
　(always bold)
graveled, -ing
gray
grievous
groveled, -ing
gruesome
guarantee (n., v.)
　guaranty (n., law)
guerrilla (warfare)
　gorilla (ape)
guesstimate
guttural
gypsy

H

hallelujah
hara-kiri
harass
harebrained
healthful (for
　health)
healthy (with
　health)
heinous
hemoglobin
hemorrhage
hiccup
highfalutin
hijack
homeopath
homogeneity
homogeneous
　(mixed uniformly)
homogenous (of
　similar origin)
homologue
hors d'oeuvre
hypocrisy
hypotenuse

I

idiosyncrasy
idle (inactive)
　idol (statue)
idyll
imminent (soon)
　eminent (famous)
impaneled, -ing
impasse
imperiled, -ing
impostor
impresario
imprimatur
inculcate
indict (to accuse)
　indite (to compose)
inequity (unfairness)
　iniquity (sin)

inferable
infold
ingenious (skillful)
　ingenuous (simple)
innocuous
innuendo
inoculate
inquire, inquiry
install, -ed, -ing,
　-ment
installation
instill, -ed, -ing
insure (protect)
　ensure (guarantee)
intelligentsia
interceptor
interment (burial)
　internment (jail)
intern
intervener
　intervenor (law)
intransigent (n., adj.)
in vitro
in vivo
iridescent
italic

J

jalopy
jalousie
jerry-(built)
　jury-(rigged)
jeweled, -ing, -er
jewelry
judgeship
judgment
jujitsu
juxtaposition

K

karat
kerneled, -ing
kerosene
ketchup

kidnapped, -ing
kidnapper
kilogram
knapsack
kopek
kumquat

L

labeled, -ing
lacquer
landward
lath (wood)
　lathe (machine)
laureled
leukemia
leveled, -ing
leveler
liable (responsible)
　libel (legal)
liaison
libelant
libeled, -ing
libelee
libeler
license
licenser (issuer)
　licensor (grantor)
licorice
likable
lilliputian
linage (lines)
　lineage (descent)
liquefy
liquor
　liqueur
liter
livable
loath (reluctant)
　loathe (detest)
lodestar
lodestone
lodgment
logistics (n.)
　logistic (adj.)

louver
luster
lyonnaise

M
madam
Mafia
maim
maize (corn)
  maze (labyrinth)
maneuver
manifold
manikin (dwarf)
mannequin (model)
mantel (shelf)
  mantle (cloak)
marbleize
marijuana
marshaled, -ing
marshaler
marveled, -ing
marvelous
material (goods)
  materiel (military)
meager
medaled, -ing
medalist
medieval
meme
metaled, -ing
metalize
meteorology
  (weather)
  metrology
  (weights and
  measures)
meter
mil (1/1000 inch)
  mill (1/1000 dollar)
mileage
miliary
  (tuberculosis)
milieu
milk cow

millenary (1,000)
  millinery (hats)
millennium
minable
missilery
misspell
miter
mnemonic
moccasin
modeled, -ing
modeler
mold
mollusk
molt
moneys
monogramed, -ing
monologue
mortise
movable
mucilage
mucus (n.)
  mucous (adj.)
Muslim
mustache

N
naphtha
Navajo
Nazism
neophyte
niacin
nickel
niter
nonplused
northward
Novocain
  (trademark)
novocaine
  (anesthetic)

O
obbligato
obloquy
ocher

octet
offal
offense
omelet
ophthalmology
opossum
orangutan
orbited, -ing
ordinance (law)
  ordnance
  (military)
organdy
overseas or oversea

P
pajamas
palate (mouth)
  palette (colors)
  pallet (bed or
  freight)
paleontology
paneled, -ing
paraffin
paralleled, -ing
parallelepiped
parceled, -ing
partisan
pastime
patrol, -led, -ling
peccadillo
pedant (n.)
  pedantic (adj.)
peddler
penciled, -ing
pendant (n.)
  pendent (u.m.)
percent
peremptory
  (decisive)
  preemptory
  (preference)
perennial
periled, -ing
permittee

perquisite (privilege)
  prerequisite
  (requirement)
personal (individual)
  personnel (staff)
perspective (view)
  prospective
  (expected)
petaled, -ing
pharaoh
pharmacopeia
phoenix
phlegm
phony
phosphorus (n.)
  phosphorous (adj.)
photostated
pickax
picnicking
pipet
plaque
plastics (n.)
  plastic (adj.)
pledger
  pledgor (law)
plenitude
pliers
plow
poleax
pollination
pommeled, -ing
pontoon
porcelaneous
practice (n., v.)
precedence
  (priority)
  precedents (usage)
prerogative
pretense
preventive
principal (chief)
  principle
  (proposition)
privilege

proffer
programmatic
programmed, -mer,
  -ming
prologue
promissory
pronunciation
propel, -led, -ling
propellant (n.)
  propellent (adj.)
prophecy (n.)
  prophesy (v.)
ptomaine
pubic (anatomy)
pulmotor
pusillanimous

Q

quarreled, -ing
quartet
quaternary
questionnaire
queue

R

raccoon
racket (all meanings)
rapprochement
rarefy
rarity
ratable
rational (adj.)
  rationale (n.)
rattan
raveled, -ing
reconnaissance
reconnoiter
recyclable
referable
refuse
registrar
reinforce
relater
  relator (law)
remodeler

renaissance
reparable
repellant (n.)
  repellent (adj.)
requester
  requestor (law)
rescission
responder
  (electronics)
responser
  (electronics)
reveled, -er, -ing
rhyme, rhythmic
RIFing, RIFed, RIFs
rivaled, -ing
roweled, -ing
ruble

S

saccharin (n.)
  saccharine (adj.)
sacrilegious
salable
sandaled, -ing
savable
savanna
savior
  Saviour (Christ)
scalloped, -ing
schizophrenia
scion (horticulture)
scurrilous
seismology
selvage (edging)
  salvage (save)
sentineled, -ing
separate (v., adj.)
sepulcher
seriatim
settler
  settlor (law)
sewage (waste)
  sewerage (drain
    system)

sextet
Shakespearean
shellacking
shoveled, -ing
shriveled, -ing
sideward
signaled, -ing
siphon
site (place)
  cite (quote)
sizable
skeptic
skillful
skulduggery
sleight (deft)
  slight (meager)
smolder
sniveled, -ing
snorkel
soliloquy
sometime
  (formerly)
  some time (some
    time ago)
  some times (at
    times)
southward
spacious (space)
  specious
    (deceptive)
specter
spirituous (liquor)
spirochete
spoliation
stationary (fixed)
  stationery (paper)
statue (sculpture)
  stature (height)
  statute (law)
staunch
stenciled, -ing
stenciler
stifling
stratagem

stubbornness
stultify
stupefy
subpoena, -ed
subtlety
succor
sulfur (also
    derivatives)
sulfanilamide
  sulfureted, -ing
supererogation
surfeit
surreptitious
surveillance
swiveled, -ing
sylvan
synonymous
syrup

T

taboo
tactician
tasseled, -ing
tattoo
taxied, -ing
technique
teetotaler
tercentenary
theater
therefor (for it)
  therefore (for that
    reason)
thiamine
thralldom
thrash (beat)
  thresh (grain)
threshold
tie, tied, tying
timber (wood)
  timbre (tone)
tinseled, -ing
titer
tonsillitis
tormenter

totaled, -ing
toward
toweled, -ing
toxemia
trafficking
trammeled, -ing
tranquilize(r)
tranquillity
transcendent
transferable
transferor
transferred
transonic
transponder
 (electronics)
transshipment
traveled, -ing
traveler
travelogue

triptych
trolley
troop (soldiers)
 troupe (actors)
troweled, -ing
tryptophan
tularemia
tunneled, -ing
tunneler
turquoise
typify
tyrannical
tyro

U
unctuous
unwieldy
upward
uremia
usable

V
vacillate
valance (drape)
 valence
  (chemistry)
veld
veranda
vermilion
vicissitude
victualed, -ing
victualer
vilify
villain
visa, -ed, -ing
vitamin
vitrify
volcanism
voluntarism
votable

vying

W
wainscoting
warranter
 warrantor (law)
warranty
weeviled, -ing
welder
westward
whimsy
whiskey, -s
willful
withe
woeful
woolen
woolly
worshiped, -er, -ing

Anglicized and foreign words

5.3.   Diacritical marks are not used with anglicized words.

A
abaca
aide memoire
a la carte
a la king
a la mode
angstrom
aperitif
applique
apropos
auto(s)-da-fe

B
blase
boutonniere
brassiere

C
cabana
cafe
cafeteria

caique
canape
cause celebre
chateau
cliche
cloisonne
comedienne
comme ci
 comme ca
communique
confrere
consomme
cortege
coulee
coup de grace
coup d'etat
coupe
creme
crepe
crepe de chine

critique
critiquing

D
debacle
debris
debut
debutante
decollete
dejeuner
denouement
depot
dos-a-dos

E
eclair
eclat
ecru
elan
elite
entree

etude

F
facade
faience
faux pas
fete
fiance (masc., fem.)
frappe

G
garcon
glace
grille
gruyere

H
habitue

I
ingenue

J

jardiniere

L

laissez faire

litterateur

M

materiel

matinee

melange

melee

menage

mesalliance

metier

moire

N

naive

naivete

nee

O

opera bouffe

opera comique

P

papier mache

piece de resistance

pleiade

porte cochere

porte lumiere

portiere

pousse cafe

premiere

protege (masc., fem.)

puree

R

rale

recherche

regime

risque

role

rotisserie

roue

S

saute

seance

senor

smorgasbord

soiree

souffle

suede

T

table d'hote

tete-a-tete

tragedienne

V

vicuna

vis-a-vis

5.4. Foreign words carry the diacritical marks as an essential part of their spelling.

à l'américaine	chargé d'affaires	entrepôt	passé (masc., fem.)
attaché	congé	exposé	pâté
béton	crédit foncier	longéron	père
blessé	crédit mobilier	mañana	piña
calèche	curé	maté	précis
cañada	déjà vu	mère	raisonné
cañon	détente	nacré	résumé
chargé	doña	outré	touché

Plural forms

5.5. Nouns ending in *o* immediately preceded by a vowel add *s* to form the plural; nouns ending in *o* preceded by a consonant add *es* to form the plural, except as indicated in the following list.

albinos	falsettos	merinos	sextodecimos
armadillos	gauchos	mestizos	sextos
avocados	ghettos	octavos	siroccos
banjos	halos	octodecimos	solos
cantos	indigos	pianos	tangelos
cascos	infernos	piccolos	tobaccos
centos	juntos	pomelos	twos
didos	kimonos	provisos	tyros
duodecimos	lassos	quartos	virtuosos
dynamos	magnetos	salvos	zeros
escudos	mementos		

5.6. When a noun is hyphenated with an adverb or preposition, the plural is formed on the noun.

comings-in	hangers-on	markers-up
fillers-in	listeners-in	passers-by
goings-on	lookers-on	swearers-in

5.7. When neither word is a noun, the plural is formed on the last word.

also-rans	go-betweens	run-ins
come-ons	higher-ups	tie-ins

5.8. In forming the plurals of compound terms, the significant word takes the plural form.

Significant word first:

adjutants general
aides-de-camp
ambassadors at large
attorneys at law
attorneys general
billets-doux
bills of fare
brothers-in-law
chargés d'affaires
chiefs of staff
commanders in chief
comptrollers general
consuls general
courts-martial
crepes suzette
daughters-in-law
governors general
grants-in-aid
heirs at law
inspectors general
men-of-war
ministers-designate
mothers-in-law
notaries public
pilots-in-command
postmasters general
presidents-elect
prisoners of war
reductions in force

rights-of-way
secretaries general
sergeants at arms
sergeants major
solicitors general
surgeons general

Significant word in middle:

assistant attorneys general
assistant chiefs of staff
assistant comptrollers general
assistant surgeons general

Significant word last:

assistant attorneys
assistant commissioners
assistant corporation counsels
assistant directors
assistant general counsels
brigadier generals
deputy judges
deputy sheriffs
general counsels
judge advocates
judge advocate generals
lieutenant colonels
major generals
provost marshals
provost marshal generals
quartermaster generals

<table>
<tr><td>trade unions</td><td>men employees</td></tr>
<tr><td>under secretaries</td><td>secretaries-treasurers</td></tr>
<tr><td>vice chairmen</td><td>women aviators</td></tr>
</table>

Both words equally significant:	No word significant in itself:
Bulletins Nos. 27 and 28 *not*	forget-me-nots
Bulletin Nos. 27 and 28 *but*	hand-me-downs
Bulletin No. 27 or 28	jack-in-the-pulpits
coats of arms	man-of-the-earths
masters at arms	pick-me-ups
men buyers	will-o'-the-wisps

5.9. Nouns ending with *ful* form the plural by adding *s* at the end; if it is necessary to express the idea that more than one container was filled, the two elements of the solid compound are printed as separate words and the plural is formed by adding *s* to the noun.

five bucketfuls of the mixture (one bucket filled five times)
five buckets full of earth (separate buckets)
three cupfuls of flour (one cup filled three times)
three cups full of coffee (separate cups)

5.10. The following list comprises other words the plurals of which may cause difficulty.

addendum, addenda
adieu, adieus
agendum, agenda
alga, algae
alumnus, alumni (masc.); alumna, alumnae (fem.)
antenna, antennas (antennae, zoology)
appendix, appendixes
aquarium, aquariums
automaton, automatons
axis, axes
bandeau, bandeaux
basis, bases
bateau, bateaux
beau, beaus
cactus, cactuses
calix, calices
cargo, cargoes
chassis (singular and plural)

cherub, cherubs
cicatrix, cicatrices
Co., Cos.
coccus, cocci
consortium, consortia
corrigendum, corrigenda
crisis, crises
criterion, criteria
curriculum, curriculums, curricula
datum (singular), data (plural, but singular in collective sense)
desideratum, desiderata
dilettante, dilettanti
dogma, dogmas
ellipsis, ellipses
equilibrium, equilibriums (equilibria, scientific)
erratum, errata
executrix, executrices
flambeau, flambeaus

focus, focuses
folium, folia
formula, formulas
forum, forums
fungus, fungi
genius, geniuses
genus, genera
gladiolus (singular and plural)
helix, helices
hypothesis, hypotheses
index, indexes (indices, scientific)
insigne, insignia
italic (singular and plural)
Kansas Citys
lacuna, lacunae
larva, larvae
larynx, larynxes
lens, lenses
lira, lire
locus, loci
madam, mesdames
Marys
matrix, matrices
maximum, maximums, maxima
medium, mediums *or* media
memorandum, memorandums,
  memoranda
minimum, minimums, minima
minutia, minutiae
monsieur, messieurs
nucleus, nuclei
oasis, oases
octopus, octopuses
opus, opera

parenthesis, parentheses
phenomenon, phenomena
phylum, phyla
plateau, plateaus
podium, podiums
procès-verbal, procès-verbaux
radius, radii
radix, radixes
referendum, referendums
sanatorium, sanatoriums
sanitarium, sanitariums
septum, septa
sequela, sequelae
seraph, seraphs
seta, setae
ski, skis
stadium, stadiums
stimulus, stimuli
stratum, strata
stylus, styluses
syllabus, syllabuses
symposium, symposia
synopsis, synopses
tableau, tableaus
taxi, taxis
terminus, termini
testatrix, testatrices
thesaurus, thesauri
thesis, theses
thorax, thoraxes
vertebra, vertebras (vertebrae,
  zoology)
virtuoso, virtuosos
vortex, vortexes

Endings "ible" and "able"

5.11. The following words end in *ible*; other words in this class end in *able*.

abhorrible	appetible	coctible	combustible
accendible	apprehensible	coercible	comestible
accessible	audible	cognoscible	commonsensible
addible	avertible	cohesible	compactible
adducible	bipartible	collapsible	compatible
admissible	circumscriptible	collectible(s)	competible

compossible	distractible	impersuasible	inexpressible
comprehensible	divertible	implausible	infallible
compressible	divestible	impossible	infeasible
conducible	divisible	imprescriptible	inflexible
conductible	docible	imputrescible	infractible
confluxible	edible	inaccessible	infrangible
congestible	educible	inadmissible	infusible
contemptible	effectible	inapprehensible	innascible
controvertible	effervescible	inaudible	inscriptible
conversable (oral)	eligible	incircumscriptible	insensible
conversible	eludible	incoercible	instructible
(convertible)	erodible	incognoscrible	insubmergible
convertible	evasible	incombustible	insuppressible
convincible	eversible	incommiscible	insusceptible
corrigible	evincible	incompatible	intactible
corrodible	exemptible	incomprehensible	intangible
corrosible	exhaustible	incompressible	intelligible
corruptible	exigible	inconcussible	interconvertible
credible	expansible	incontrovertible	interruptible
crucible	explosible	inconvertible	intervisible
cullible	expressible	inconvincible	invendible
decoctible	extensible	incorrigible	invertible
deducible	fallible	incorrodible	invincible
deductible	feasible	incorruptible	invisible
defeasible	fencible	incredible	irascible
defectible	flexible	indefeasible	irreducible
defensible	fluxible	indefectible	irrefrangible
delible	forcible	indefensible	irremissible
deprehensible	frangible	indelible	irreprehensible
depressible	fungible	indeprehensible	irrepressible
descendible	fusible	indestructible	irresistible
destructible	gullible	indigestible	irresponsible
diffrangible	horrible	indiscernible	irreversible
diffusible	ignitible	indivertible	legible
digestible	illegible	indivisible	mandible
dimensible	immersible	indocible	marcescible
discernible	immiscible	inducible	miscible
discerpible	impartible	ineffervescible	negligible
discerptible	impatible	ineligible	nexible
discussible	impedible	ineludible	omissible
dispersible	imperceptible	inevasible	ostensible
dissectible	impermissible	inexhaustible	partible
distensible	imperscriptible	inexpansible	passable (open)

passible (feeling)	reflectible	sensible	transmissible
perceptible	reflexible	sponsible	transvertible
perfectible	refrangible	suasible	tripartible
permissible	remissible	subdivisible	unadmissible
persuasible	renascible	submergible	uncorruptible
pervertible	rendible	submersible	unexhaustible
plausible	reprehensible	subvertible	unexpressible
possible	repressible	suggestible	unintelligible
prehensible	reproducible	supersensible	unresponsible
prescriptible	resistible	suppressible	unsusceptible
producible	responsible	susceptible	vendible
productible	reversible	suspensible	vincible
protrusible	revertible	tangible	visible
putrescible	risible	tensible	vitrescible
receptible	runcible	terrible	
redemptible	sconcible	thurible	
reducible	seducible	traducible	

Endings "ise," "ize," and "yze"

5.12. A large number of words have the termination *ise*, *ize*, or *yze*. The letter *l* is followed by *yze* if the word expresses an idea of loosening or separating, as *analyze*; all other words of this class, except those ending with the suffix *wise* and those in the following list, end in *ize*.

advertise	compromise	excise	prise (to force)
advise	demise	exercise	prize (to value)
affranchise	despise	exorcise	reprise
apprise (to inform)	devise	franchise	revise
apprize (to	disenfranchise	improvise	rise
appraise)	disfranchise	incise	supervise
arise	disguise	merchandise	surmise
chastise	emprise	misadvise	surprise
circumcise	enfranchise	mortise	televise
comprise	enterprise	premise	

Endings "cede," "ceed," and "sede"

5.13. Only one word ends in *sede* (supersede); only three end in *ceed* (exceed, proceed, succeed); all other words of this class end in *cede* (precede, secede, etc.).

Doubled consonants

5.14.   A single consonant following a single vowel and ending in a monosyllable or a final accented syllable is doubled before a suffix beginning with a vowel.

		but
bag, bagging	red, reddish	
format, formatting	rob, robbing	total, totaled, totaling
input, inputting	transfer, transferred	travel, traveled, traveling

5.15.   If the accent in a derivative falls upon an earlier syllable than it does in the root word, the consonant is not doubled.

refer, reference	prefer, preference	infer, inference

Indefinite articles

5.16.   The indefinite article *a* is used before a consonant and an aspirated *h*; *an* is used before a silent *h* and all vowels except *u* pronounced as in *visual* and *o* pronounced as in *one*.

		but
a historic occasion	an herbseller	
a hotel	an hour	an H-U-D directive
a human being	an honor	a HUD directive
a humble man	an onion	
a union	an oyster	

5.17.   When a group of initials begins with *b, c, d, g, j, k, p, q, t, u, v, w, y,* or *z,* each having a consonant sound, the indefinite article *a* is used.

a BLS compilation	a GAO limitation	a WWW search
a CIO finding	a UFO sighting	

5.18.   When a group of initials begins with *a, e, f, h, i, l, m, n, o, r, s,* or *x,* each having a vowel sound, the indefinite article *an* is used.

an AEC report	an NSC (en) proclamation
an FCC (ef) ruling	an RFC (ahr) loan

5.19.   Use of the indefinite article *a* or *an* before a numerical expression is determined by the consonant or vowel sound of the beginning syllable.

an 11-year-old	an VIII (eight) classification
a onetime winner	a IV–F (four ef) category (military draft)
a III (three) group	a 4–H Club

Geographic names

5.20.   The spelling of geographic names must conform to the decisions of the U.S. Board on Geographic Names (BGN) (http://geonames. usgs.gov). In the absence of such a decision, the U.S. Directory of Post Offices is to be used.

5.21.   If the decisions or the rules of the BGN permit the use of either the local official form or the conventional English form, it is the prerogative of the originating office to select the form that is most suitable for the matter in hand; therefore, in marking copy or reading proof, it is required only to verify the spelling of the particular form used. GPO's preference is for the conventional English form. Copy will be followed as to accents, but these should be consistent throughout the entire job.

Nationalities, etc.

5.22.   The table on Demonyms in Chapter 17 "Useful Tables" shows forms to be used for nouns and adjectives denoting nationality.

5.23.   In designating the natives of the States, the following forms will be used.

Alabamian	Kentuckian	North Dakotan
Alaskan	Louisianian	Ohioan
Arizonan	Mainer	Oklahoman
Arkansan	Marylander	Oregonian
Californian	Massachusettsan	Pennsylvanian
Coloradan	Michiganian	Rhode Islander
Connecticuter	Minnesotan	South Carolinian
Delawarean	Mississippian	South Dakotan
Floridian	Missourian	Tennessean
Georgian	Montanan	Texan
Hawaii resident	Nebraskan	Utahn
Hoosier	Nevadan	Vermonter
(Indiana)	New Hampshirite	Virginian
Idahoan	New Jerseyan	Washingtonian
Illinoisan	New Mexican	West Virginian
Iowan	New Yorker	Wisconsinite
Kansan	North Carolinian	Wyomingite

5.24.   Observe the following forms:

Alaska Native
Asian American
Black or African American
Hispanic or Latino
Native American or American Indian
Native Hawaiian
Pacific Islander
Puerto Rican
White

Native American words
5.25.   Words, including Tribal and other proper names of Indian, Alaska Native, Hawaiian, and other groups, are to be followed literally as to spelling and the use of spaces, diacriticals, hyphens, etc.

Transliteration
5.26.   In the spelling of nongeographic words transliterated from Chinese, Japanese, or any other language that does not have a Latin alphabet, copy is to be followed literally.

6. Compounding Rules

(See also Chapter 7 "Compounding Examples")

6.1. A compound word is a union of two or more words, either with or without a hyphen. It conveys a unit idea that is not as clearly or quickly conveyed by the component words in unconnected succession. The hyphen is a mark of punctuation that not only unites but also separates the component words; it facilitates understanding, aids readability, and ensures correct pronunciation. When compound words must be divided at the end of a line, such division should be made leaving prefixes and combining forms of more than one syllable intact.

6.2. In applying the rules in this chapter and in using the list of examples in the following chapter, "Compounding Examples," the fluid nature of our language should be kept in mind. Word forms constantly undergo modification. Although it is often the case that hyphenated compound words eventually lose their hyphen, many of them start out unhyphenated.

6.3. The rules, therefore, are somewhat flexible. Exceptions must necessarily be allowed. Current language trends continue to point to closing up certain words which, through either frequent use or widespread dissemination through modern media exposure, have become fixed in the reader's mind as units of thought. The tendency to merge two short words continues to be a natural progression toward better communication.

General rules

6.4. In general, omit the hyphen when words appear in regular order and the omission causes no ambiguity in sense or sound.

banking hours	eye opener	real estate
blood pressure	fellow citizen	rock candy
book value	living costs	training ship
census taker	palm oil	violin teacher
day laborer	patent right	

6.5.   Words are usually combined to express a literal or nonliteral (figurative) unit idea that would not be as clearly expressed in unconnected succession.

afterglow	forget-me-not	right-of-way
bookkeeping	gentleman	whitewash
cupboard	newsprint	

6.6.   A derivative of a compound retains the solid or hyphenated form of the original compound unless otherwise indicated.

coldbloodedness	outlawry	Y-shaped
footnoting	praiseworthiness	
ill-advisedly	railroader	

6.7.   A hyphen is used to avoid doubling a vowel or tripling a consonant, except after the short prefixes *co, de, pre, pro,* and *re,* which are generally printed solid. (See also rules 6.29 and 6.32.)

cooperation	semi-independent	shell-like
deemphasis	brass-smith	hull-less
preexisting	Inverness-shire	*but*
anti-inflation	thimble-eye	co-occupant
micro-organism	ultra-atomic	cross section

Solid compounds

6.8.   Print solid two nouns that form a third when the compound has only one primary accent, especially when the prefixed noun consists of only one syllable or when one of the elements loses its original accent.

airship	cupboard	footnote
bathroom	dressmaker	locksmith
bookseller	fishmonger	workman

6.9.   Print solid a noun consisting of a short verb and an adverb as its second element, except when the use of the solid form would interfere with comprehension.

blowout	builddown	flareback
breakdown	cooldown	giveaway
hangover	runoff	*but*
holdup	setup	cut-in
makeready	showdown	phase-in
markoff	thowaway	run-in
pickup	tradeoff	sit-in

6.10. Compounds beginning with the following nouns are usually printed solid.

book	mill	snow
eye	play	way
horse	school	wood
house	shop	work

6.11. Compounds ending in the following are usually printed solid, especially when the prefixed word consists of one syllable.

berry	keeping	room
bird	land	shop
blossom	light	site
board	like	skin
boat	line	smith
book	load	stone
borne	maid	store
bound	maker	tail
box	making	tight
boy	man	time (not clock)
brained	master	ward
bug	mate	ware
bush	mill	water
cam	mistress	way
craft	monger	wear
field	over	weed
fish	owner	wide
flower	*but* #ownership	wise
fly	person	woman
girl	picker	wood
grower	picking	work
headed	piece	worker
hearted	plane	working
holder	power	worm
hopper	proof	worthy
house	roach	writer
keeper		

6.12.   Print solid *any, every, no,* and *some* when combined with *body, thing,* and *where.* When *one* is the second element, print as two words if meaning a single or particular person or thing. To avoid mispronunciation, print *no one* as two words at all times.

anybody	everywhere	somebody
anything	everyone	something
anywhere	nobody	somewhere
anyone	nothing	someone
everybody	nowhere	
everything	no one	

but any one of us may stay; every one of the pilots is responsible; every body was accounted for

6.13.   Print compound personal pronouns as one word.

herself	oneself	yourself
himself	ourselves	yourselves
itself	themselves	
myself	thyself	

6.14.   Print as one word compass directions consisting of two points, but use a hyphen after the first point when three points are combined.

northeast	north-northeast
southwest	south-southwest

also north-south alignment

Unit modifiers

6.15.   Print a hyphen between words, or abbreviations and words, combined to form a unit modifier immediately preceding the word modified, except as indicated in rule 6.16 and elsewhere throughout this chapter. This applies particularly to combinations in which one element is a present or past participle.

agreed-upon standards	Federal-State-local cooperation
Baltimore-Washington road	German-English descent
collective-bargaining talks	guided-missile program
contested-election case	hearing-impaired class
contract-bar rule	high-speed line
cost-of-living increase	large-scale project
drought-stricken area	law-abiding citizen
English-speaking nation	long-term loan
fire-tested material	line-item veto

long-term-payment loan
low-cost housing
lump-sum payment
most-favored-nation clause
multiple-purpose uses
no-par-value stock
one-on-one situation
part-time personnel
rust-resistant covering
service-connected disability
state-of-the-art technology
supply-side economics
tool-and-die maker
up-or-down vote

U.S.-owned property; U.S.-flagship
1-inch diameter; 2-inch-diameter
  pipe
a 4-percent increase, the 10-percent
  rise

but

4 percent citric acid
4 percent interest. (Note the absence
  of an article: *a, an,* or *the. The*
  word *of* is understood here.)

6.16. Where meaning is clear and readability is not aided, it is not necessary to use a hyphen to form a temporary or made compound. Restraint should be exercised in forming unnecessary combinations of words used in normal sequence.

atomic energy power
bituminous coal industry
child welfare plan
civil rights case
civil service examination
durable goods industry
flood control study
free enterprise system
ground water levels
high school student
elementary school grade
income tax form
interstate commerce law
land bank loan
land use program
life insurance company
mutual security funds

national defense appropriation
natural gas company
per capita expenditure
Portland cement plant
production credit loan
public at large
public utility plant
real estate tax
small businessman
Social Security pension
soil conservation measures
special delivery mail
parcel post delivery
speech correction class

but no-hyphen rule (readability
      aided); *not* no hyphen rule

6.17. Print without a hyphen a compound predicate (either adjective or noun) whose second element is a present participle.

The duties were price fixing.
The effects were far reaching.

The shale was oil bearing.
The area is used for beet raising.

6.18. Print without a hyphen a compound predicate adjective the second element of which is a past participle. Omit the hyphen in a predicate modifier of comparative or superlative degree.

The area is drought stricken.	This material is fire tested.
The paper is fine grained.	The cars are higher priced.
Moderately fine grained wood.	The reporters are better informed.

6.19. Print without a hyphen a two-word modifier the first element of which is a comparative or superlative.

better drained soil	*but*
best liked books	uppercrust society
higher level decision	lowercase, uppercase type
highest priced apartment	upperclassman
larger sized dress	bestseller (noun)
better paying job	lighter-than-air craft
lower income group	higher-than-market price

6.20. Do not use a hyphen in a two-word unit modifier the first element of which is an adverb ending in *ly*, nor use hyphens in a three-word unit modifier the first two elements of which are adverbs.

eagerly awaited moment	*but*
wholly owned subsidiary	ever-normal granary
unusually well preserved specimen	ever-rising flood
very well defined usage	still-new car
longer than usual lunch period	still-lingering doubt
not too distant future	well-known lawyer
most often heard phrase	well-kept secret

6.21. Proper nouns used as unit modifiers, either in their basic or derived form, retain their original form; but the hyphen is printed when combining forms.

Latin American countries	Seventh-day Adventists
North Carolina roads	*but*
a Mexican American	Minneapolis-St. Paul region
South American trade	North American-South American
Spanish-American pride	sphere
Winston-Salem festival	French-English descent
African-American program	Washington–Wilkes-Barre route
Anglo-Saxon period	*or* Washington/Wilkes-Barre
Franco-Prussian War	route

6.22.   Do not confuse a modifier with the word it modifies.

elderly clothesman	well-trained schoolteacher
old-clothes man	elementary school teacher
competent shoemaker	preschool children (kindergarten)
wooden-shoe maker	pre-school children (before school)
field canning factory	rezoned wastesite
tomato-canning factory	hazardous-waste site
brave servicemen	
service men and women	*but*
light blue hat (weight)	common stockholder
light-blue hat (color)	stock ownership
average taxpayer	small businessman
income-tax payer	working men and women
American flagship (military)	steam powerplant site
American-flag ship	meat packinghouse owner

6.23.   Where two or more hyphenated compounds have a common basic element but this element is omitted in all but the last term, the hyphens are retained.

2- to 3- and 4- to 5-ton trucks
2- by 4-inch boards, *but* boards 2 to 6 inches wide
8-, 10-, and 16-foot boards
6.4-, 3.1-, and 2-percent pay raises
moss- and ivy-covered walls, *not* moss and ivy-covered walls
long- and short-term money rates, *not* long and short-term money rates
but twofold or threefold, *not* two or threefold
goat, sheep, and calf skins, *not* goat, sheep, and calfskins
intrastate and intracity, *not* intra-state and -city
American owned and managed companies
preoperative and postoperative examination

6.24.   Do not use a hyphen in a unit modifier consisting of a foreign phrase.

ante bellum days	ex officio member	per diem employee
bona fide transaction	per capita tax	prima facie evidence

6.25.   Do not print a hyphen in a unit modifier containing a letter or a numeral as its second element.

abstract B pages	class II railroad	point 4 program
article 3 provisions	grade A milk	ward D beds

6.26. Do not use a hyphen in a unit modifier enclosed in quotation marks unless it is normally a hyphenated term, but quotation marks are not to be used in lieu of a hyphen.

"blue sky" law   *but*
"good neighbor" policy   right-to-work law
"tie-in" sale   line-item veto

6.27. Print combination color terms as separate words, but use a hyphen when such color terms are unit modifiers.

bluish green   bluish-green feathers
dark green   iron-gray sink
orange red   silver-gray body

6.28. Do not use a hyphen between independent adjectives preceding a noun.

big gray cat   a fine old southern gentleman

Prefixes, suffixes, and combining forms

6.29. Print solid combining forms and prefixes, except as indicated elsewhere.

*after*birth	*infra*red	*peri*patetic
*Anglo*mania	*inter*view	*plano*convex
*ante*date	*intra*spinal	*poly*nodal
*anti*slavery	*intro*vert	*post*script
*bi*weekly	*iso*metric	*pre*exist
*by*law	*macro*analysis	*pro*consul
*circum*navigation	*meso*thorax	*pseudo*scholastic
*cis*alpine	*meta*genesis	*re*enact
*co*operate	*micro*phone	*retro*spect
*contra*position	*mis*state	*semi*official
*counter*case	*mono*gram	*step*father
*de*energize	*multi*color	*sub*secretary
*demi*tasse	*neo*phyte	*super*market
*ex*communicate	*non*neutral	*thermo*couple
*extra*curricular	*off*set	*trans*onic
*fore*tell	*out*bake	*trans*ship
*heroi*comic	*over*active	*tri*color
*hyper*sensitive	*pan*cosmic	*ultra*violet
*hypo*acid	*para*centric	*un*necessary
*in*bound	*parti*coated	*under*flow

6.30. Print solid combining forms and suffixes, except as indicated elsewhere.

port*able*	ge*ography*	inner*most*
cover*age*	man*hood*	partner*ship*
oper*ate*	sel*fish*	lone*some*
plebis*cite*	meat*less*	home*stead*
twenty*fold*	out*let*	north*ward*
spoon*ful*	wave*like*	clock*wise*
kilo*gram*	procure*ment*	

6.31. Print solid words ending in *like*, but use a hyphen to avoid tripling a consonant or when the first element is a proper name.

lifelike	girllike	Scotland-like
lilylike	bell-like	McArtor-like

6.32. Use a hyphen or hyphens to prevent mispronunciation, to ensure a definite accent on each element of the compound, or to avoid ambiguity.

anti-hog-cholera serum	re-creation (create again)
co-occurrence	re-lay (lay again)
co-op	re-sign (sign again)
mid-decade	re-sorting (sort again)
multi-ply (several plies)	re-treat (treat again)
non-civil-service position	un-ionized
non-tumor-bearing tissue	un-uniformity
pre-midcourse review	
pre-position (before)	*but*
pro-choice	rereferred
pro-life	rereviewed
re-cover (cover again)	

6.33. Use a hyphen to join duplicated prefixes.

re-redirect	sub-subcommittee	super-superlative

6.34. Print with a hyphen the prefixes *ex, self,* and *quasi.*

ex-governor	quasi-argument
ex-serviceman	quasi-corporation
ex-son-in-law	quasi-young
ex-vice-president	
self-control	*but*
self-educated	selfhood
quasi-academic	selfsame

6.35. Unless usage demands otherwise, use a hyphen to join a prefix or combining form to a capitalized word. (The hyphen is retained in words of this class set in caps.)

anti-American	non-Federal
pro-British	
un-American	*but*
non-Government	nongovernmental
neo-Nazi	overanglicize
post-World War II	transatlantic
or post-Second World War	

Numerical compounds

6.36. Print a hyphen between the elements of compound numbers from twenty-one to ninety-nine and in adjective compounds with a numerical first element.

twenty-one	three-and-twenty
twenty-first	two-sided question
6-footer	multimillion-dollar fund
6-foot-11-inch man	10-dollar-per-car tax
24-inch ruler	thirty- (30-) day period
3-week vacation	
8-hour day	*but*
10-minute delay	one hundred twenty-one
20th-century progress	100-odd
3-to-1 ratio	foursome
5-to-4 vote	threescore
.22-caliber cartridge	foursquare
2-cent-per-pound tax	$20 million airfield
four-in-hand tie	second grade children

6.37. Print without a hyphen a modifier consisting of a possessive noun preceded by a numeral. (See also rule 8.14.)

1 month's layoff	3 weeks' vacation
1 week's pay	1 minute's delay
2 hours' work	*but* a 1-minute delay

6.38. Print a hyphen between the elements of a fraction, but omit it between the numerator and the denominator when the hyphen appears in either or in both.

one-thousandth	twenty-three thirtieths
two-thirds	twenty-one thirty-seconds
two one-thousandths	three-fourths of an inch

6.39. A unit modifier following and reading back to the word or words modified takes a hyphen and is printed in the singular.

motor, alternating-current, 3-phase, 60-cycle, 115-volt
glass jars: 5-gallon, 2-gallon, 1-quart
belts: 2-inch, 1¼-inch, ½-inch, ¼-inch

Civil and military titles

6.40. Do not hyphenate a civil or military title denoting a single office, but print a double title with a hyphen.

ambassador at large	secretary-treasurer
assistant attorney general	sergeant at arms
commander in chief	treasurer-manager
comptroller general	under secretary
Congressman at Large	*but* under-secretaryship
major general	vice president
notary public	*but* vice-presidency
secretary general	

6.41. The adjectives *elect* and *designate,* as the last element of a title, require a hyphen.

President-elect (Federal)	ambassador-designate
Vice-President-elect (Federal)	minister-designate
Secretary of Housing and Urban Development-designate	

Scientific and technical terms

6.42. Do not print a hyphen in scientific terms (names of chemicals, diseases, animals, insects, plants) used as unit modifiers if no hyphen appears in their original form.

carbon monoxide poisoning	whooping cough remedy
guinea pig raising	*but*
hog cholera serum	Russian-olive plantings
methyl bromide solution	Douglas-fir tree
stem rust control	
equivalent uranium content	

6.43. Chemical elements used in combination with full-size figures use a hyphen; chemical symbols do not.

polonium-210	^{235}U	^{234}U$_{92}$
uranium-235	^{90}Sr	

6.44. Note use of hyphens and closeup punctuation in chemical formulas.

9-nitroanthra(1,9,4,10)bis(1)oxathiazone-2,7-bisdioxide
Cr-Ni-Mo
2,4-D

6.45. Print a hyphen between the elements of technical or contrived compound units of measurement.

candela-hour	light-year	work-year
crop-year	passenger-mile	*but* kilowatthour
horsepower-hour	staff-hour	

Improvised compounds

6.46. Print with a hyphen the elements of an improvised compound.

blue-pencil (v.)	George "Pay-As-You-Go" Miller
18-year-old (n., u.m.)	stick-in-the-mud (n.)
know-it-all (n.)	let-George-do-it attitude
know-how (n.)	how-to-be-beautiful course
lick-the-finger-and-test-the-wind	hard-and-fast rule
economics	penny-wise and pound-foolish policy
make-believe (n., u.m.)	first-come-first-served basis
one-man-one-vote principle	*but* a basis of first come, first served
roll-on/roll-off ship	

6.47. Use hyphens in a prepositional-phrase compound noun consisting of three or more words.

cat-o'-nine-tails	man-of-war	*but*
government-in-exile	mother-in-law	heir at law
grant-in-aid	mother-of-pearl	next of kin
jack-in-the-box	patent-in-fee	officer in charge

6.48. When the corresponding noun form is printed as separate words, the verb form is always hyphenated.

cold-shoulder	blue-pencil	cross-brace

6.49. Print a hyphen in a compound formed of repetitive or conflicting terms and in a compound naming the same thing under two aspects.

boogie-woogie	hanky-panky	young-old
comedy-ballet	murder-suicide	*but*
dead-alive	nitty-gritty	bowwow
devil-devil	pitter-patter	dillydally
even-stephen	razzle-dazzle	hubbub
farce-melodrama	walkie-talkie	nitwit
fiddle-faddle	willy-nilly	riffraff

6.50. Use a hyphen in a nonliteral compound expression containing an apostrophe in its first element.

asses'-eyes	bull's-eye	crow's-nest
ass's-foot	cat's-paw	

6.51. Use a hyphen to join a single capital letter to a noun or a participle.

H-bomb	C-section	*but*
I-beam	V-necked	x ray
T-shaped	S-iron	x raying
U-boat	T-square	S turns
C-chip	X-ed out	

6.52. Print idiomatic phrases without hyphens.

come by	insofar as	nowadays
inasmuch as	Monday week	

7. Compounding Examples

7.1. The following examples are based on the rules for compounding found in chapter 6. Obviously, this list or any other list of compound words could not possibly be a complete reference due to sheer volume. However, an analogy of the words listed with like prefixes and suffixes together with an application of the rules will result in easier handling of those compound words not listed.

7.2. In order to keep the list from becoming cumbersome, certain restrictions had to be adopted.

7.3. The listing of hyphenated compounds ending in *ed* was kept to a minimum. The rationale was to provide one or two examples under a keyword rather than needless repetition.

7.4. Similarly, many two-word forms which create no difficulty were omitted.

7.5. Care was exercised to achieve fuller coverage of solid compounds, particularly when the adopted form is different than that of Webster's Third New International Dictionary. This dictionary is GPO's guide for spelling with the exception of those words listed in rule 5.2. It is not GPO's guide to compounding.

7.6. A distinction exists between words used in a literal sense and a nonliteral sense. With few exceptions, one-word forms usually express a nonliteral interpretation, while two-word forms invariably convey a literal meaning. For example, a person may have an interesting *sideline* or hobby, but be forced to sit on the *side line* during periods of inactivity.

7.7. Distinction should also be made in the compounding of two words to form an adjective modifier and the use of the same words as a predicate adjective; e.g., "crystal-clear water," *but* "the spring water is crystal clear"; "fire-tested material," *but* "the material is fire tested."

7.8.   Caution should be exercised when distinguishing whether a succession of words is being used as a compound or whether they simply appear together. Consider, for example, "We know *someone* should do it and who that *some one* ought to be."

7.9.   Combining forms and prefixes are usually printed solid. For greater readability, the hyphen is sometimes used to avoid doubling a vowel (*anti-inflation, naso-orbital*); to facilitate a normally capitalized word (*mid-April, non-European*); to assure distinct pronunciation of each element of a compound or ready comprehension of intended meaning (*contra-ion, un-ionized*); or to join a combining form or prefix to a hyphenated compound (*equi-gram-molar, pro-mother-in-law*).

7.10.   As nouns and adjectives, *holdup, calldown, layout, makeup,* and similar words should be printed solid. Their *er* derivatives, (*holder-up, caller-down, layer-out,* and *maker-up*) require hyphens. Such compounds as *run-in, run-on,* and *tie-in* resist quick comprehension when solid. They are therefore hyphenated.

7.11.   Words spelled alike but pronounced differently, such as *tear-dimmed* and *tearsheet, wind tunnel* and *windup,* are listed under the same keyword.

7.12.   Words printed flush in the following list combine with the words which follow to indicate solid or hyphenated compounds. A spacemark (#) appearing before an indented entry indicates a two-word form, but two-word forms appearing in the adjective position usually take a hyphen.

7.13.   To indicate word function, several abbreviations have been appended. They are: *adv.,* adverb; *n.,* noun; *v.,* verb; *u.m.,* unit modifier; *pref.,* prefix; *c.f.,* combining form; and *conj.,* conjunction.

A

A
  BC(s) (n.)
  –B–C (u.m.)
  -bomb
  -day
  -flat
  -frame
  -pole
  -sharp
a
  borning, etc.
  foot
  while (adv.)
abdomino (c.f.)
  all one word
able
  -bodied (u.m.)
  -minded (u.m.)
about-face
above
  -cited (u.m.)
  deck
  -found (u.m.)
  -given (u.m.)
  ground (u.m.)
  -mentioned (u.m.)
  -named (u.m.)
  -said (u.m.)
  -water (u.m.)
  -written (u.m.)
absentminded
ace-high (u.m.)
acid
  fast
  -treat (v.)
  works
ack-ack
acre
  -foot
  -inch
actino (c.f.)
  all one word

addle
  brain
  head
  pate
add-on (n., u.m.)
adeno (c.f.)
  all one word
aero (c.f.)
  -otitis
  rest one word
afore
  all one word
after (c.f.)
  all one word
agar-agar
age
  less
  long
  -old (u.m.)
  -stricken (u.m.)
  -weary (u.m.)
agribusiness
ague
  -faced (u.m.)
  -plagued (u.m.)
  -sore (u.m.)
aide-de-camp
air
  bag
  base
  bill
  blast
  -blasted (u.m.)
  blown
  brake
  brush
  burst
  cargo
  -clear (u.m.)
  coach
  -condition (all
    forms)
  -cool (v.)

  -cooled (u.m.)
  course
  crew
  -dried (u.m.)
  -driven (u.m.)
  drome
  drop
  -dry (u.m., v.)
  fare
  -floated (u.m.)
  flow
  foil
  -formed (u.m.)
  frame
  freight
  gap
  glow
  hammer
  head
  hole
  hose
  lane
  lift
  #line (line for air)
  line (aviation)
  liner
  link
  locked
  mail
  mark (v.)
  marker
  mass
  minded
  park
  path
  photo
  port (all
    meanings)
  #raid
  scoop
  ship
  show
  sick

  -slaked (u.m.)
  sleeve
  space
  speed
  stream
  strike
  strip
  #time (radio and
    TV)
  wave
  woman
  worthy
alder-leaved (u.m.)
ale
  cup
  -fed (u.m.)
  glass
alkali#land
all
  -absorbing (u.m.)
  -aged (u.m.)
  -American
  -clear (n., u.m.)
  -fired (u.m.)
  -flotation
    (mining)
  #fours
  #in
  -inclusive (u.m.)
  mark (printing)
  -out (u.m.)
  -possessed (u.m.)
  -round (u.m.)
  spice
  -star (u.m.)
  time (u.m.)
  wise
alleyway
allo (c.f.)
  all one word
almsgiver
along
  ship

shore
side
alpen
glow
stock
alpha
-cellulose
-iron
-naphthol
also-ran (n., u.m.)
alto
cumulus
relievo
stratus
amber
-clear (u.m.)
-colored (u.m.)
-tipped (u.m.)
ambi (c.f.)
all one word
amidships
amino
#acid
as prefix, all one word
ampere
-foot
-hour
meter
-minute
-second
amphi (pref.)
all one word
amylo (c.f.)
all one word
anchor
hold
#light
plate
angel
cake
-eyed (u.m.)
-faced (u.m.)

food
angio (c.f.)
all one word
angle
hook
meter
wing
worm
Anglo (c.f.)
-American, etc.
rest one word
anhydr(o) (c.f.)
all one word
ankle
bone
-deep (u.m.)
jack
ant
eater
hill
ante (pref.)
#bellum, etc.
-Christian, etc.
#mortem
mortem
(nonliteral)
rest one word
antero (c.f.)
all one word
anthra (c.f.)
all one word
anthropo (c.f.)
all one word
anti (pref.)
-American, etc.
-choice
christ
god
-hog-cholera
(u.m.)
-icer
-imperial
-inflation, etc.

-life
-missile-missile
(u.m.)
missile
-New#Deal, etc.
personnel
trust, etc.
rest one word
antro (c.f.)
all one word
anvil
-faced (u.m.)
-headed (u.m.)
any
body
how
one
#one (one thing
or one of
a group)
place (adv.)
aorto (c.f.)
all one word
apo (pref.)
all one word
apple
cart
jack
#juice
sauce
-scented (u.m.)
April-fool (v.)
aqua
culture
lung
marine
meter
puncture
tint
tone
aquo (c.f.)
-ion
rest one word

arc
-over (n., u.m.)
-weld (v.)
arch (pref.)
band
bishop
duke
enemy
-Protestant
archeo (c.f.)
all one word
archi (pref.)
all one word
archo (c.f.)
all one word
areo (c.f.)
all one word
aristo (c.f.)
all one word
arithmo (c.f.)
all one word
arm
band
bone
chair
hole
lift
pit
plate
rack
rest
-shaped (u.m.)
armor
-clad (u.m.)
-piercing (u.m.)
plate
-plated (u.m.)
smith
arm's-length (u.m.)
arrow
head
-leaved (u.m.)
plate

-shaped (u.m.)
shot
-toothed (u.m.)
arseno (c.f.)
all one word
art-colored (u.m.)
arterio (c.f.)
all one word
arthro (c.f.)
all one word
artillery
man
woman
asbestos
-covered (u.m.)
-packed (u.m.)
ash
bin
can
-colored (u.m.)
-free (u.m.)
-gray (u.m.)
#heap
pan
pile
pit
tray
assembly
#line
man
#room
astro (c.f.)
all one word
attorney#at#law
audio
frequency
gram
meter
tape
visual
auri (c.f.)
-iodide
rest one word

authorship
auto (c.f.)
-logon
matic#backup
-objective
-observation
-omnibus
-ophthalmoscope
rest one word
awe
-bound (u.m.)
-filled (u.m.)
-inspired (u.m.)
some
ax
-adz
-grinding (u.m.)
hammer
head
-shaped (u.m.)
axletree
axo (c.f.)
all one word
azo (c.f.)
-orange
-orchil
-orseilline
rest one word

B

B-flat
baby
#boomer
face (n.)
#food
sit (v.)
sitter
back
ache
band
bite (v.)
biter
bone

breaker
cap
chain
charge
-country (u.m.)
cross
date
down (n., u.m.)
drop
face
feed
fill
fire
flap
flash
flow
-focus (v.)
furrow
ground
hand
haul
-in (n., u.m.)
lash
list (v.)
log
lotter
packer (n.)
paddle (v.)
pay
payment
pedal (v.)
plate
rest
road
run
saw
scatter
set
shift
slide
space
spin
spread

staff
stage
stairs
stamp
stay
stitch
stop
strap
-streeter
stretch (n.)
string
strip (book)
stroke
-swath (v.)
swept
swing
tack
talk
tender
tenter
-titrate (v.)
track (v.)
trail
up (n., u.m.)
wall
wash
water
backer
-down
-off
-up
bag
boy
-cheeked (u.m.)
girl
pipe
-shaped (u.m.)
baggage
man
#rack
#room
#train
bailout (n., u.m.)

bake
  oven
  pan
  shop
bald
  faced
  head (n.)
ball
  field
  #game
  -like
  park (nonliteral)
  #park (literal)
  player
  point (n., u.m.)
  stock
ballot#box
band
  aid
  box
  cutter
  saw
  stand
  string
  -tailed (u.m.)
  wagon
  width
bandy
  ball
  -legged (u.m.)
bangup (n., u.m.)
bank
  book
  note
  #paper
  side (stream)
bantamweight
bar
  #bit
  code
  keeper
  maid
  post

  tender
  -wound (u.m.)
bare
  -armed (u.m.)
  back
  bone
  faced
  foot
  handed
  legged
  necked
  worn
barge-laden (u.m.)
bark
  cutter
  peel
  -tanned (u.m.)
barley
  corn
  mow
  #water
barnstormer
barrel
  head
  -roll (v.)
  -shaped (u.m.)
base
  ball
  ball#bat
  line
  #line (surveying)
  -minded (u.m.)
basi (c.f.)
  all one word
basketball
bas-relief
bat
  blind
  -eyed (u.m.)
  fowl
  wing
batch#file

bath
  mat
  robe
  #towel
  tub
batswing (cloth)
battercake
battle
  ax
  -fallen (u.m.)
  front
  ground
  -scarred (u.m.)
  ship
  stead
  wagon
baybolt
beach
  comber
  head
  wagon
bead
  flush
  roll
beak
  head
  iron
  -shaped (u.m.)
beam
  filling
  -making (u.m.)
bean
  bag
  cod
  -fed (u.m.)
  pole
  pot
  setter
  -shaped (u.m.)
  stalk
bear
  baiting
  herd

  hide
  hound
  off (n., u.m.)
  trap
beater
  -out
  -up
beauty
  -blind (u.m.)
  -clad (u.m.)
  #shop
beaverpelt
bed
  board
  bug
  chair
  chamber
  clothes
  cord
  cover
  -fallen (u.m.)
  fast
  fellow
  frame
  lamp
  linen
  pad
  pan
  plate
  post
  quilt
  rail
  #rest
  ridden
  rock
  sheet
  sick
  side
  sore
  space
  spread
  spring
  stand

stead
straw
time
bee
bread
-eater
herd
hive
keeper
line
way
beechnut
beef
eater
#extract
-faced (u.m.)
head
steak
bees
wax
wing
beet
field
#sugar
beetle
-browed (u.m.)
head
stock
before
-cited (u.m.)
hand
-mentioned (u.m.)
-named (u.m.)
behindhand
bell
-bottomed (u.m.)
crank
-crowned (u.m.)
hanger
hop
mouthed
ringer
wether

belly
ache
band
buster
button
fed (u.m.)
pinch
belowstairs
belt
-driven (u.m.)
saw
bench
fellow
-hardened (u.m.)
made (u.m.)
mark (nonliteral)
#mark (surveying)
warmer
#warrant
bentwing (n., u.m.)
benzo (c.f.)
all one word
berry-brown (u.m.)
best
#man
seller (n.)
beta
-glucose
tron
between
decks
whiles
bi (pref.)
-iliac
rest one word
big
-eared (u.m.)
-eyed (u.m.)
head (ego)
horn (sheep)
-horned (u.m.)
-leaguer
mouthed

name (top rank)
(n., u.m.)
bill
back
beetle
broker
fold
head
hook
poster
sticker
billet
-doux
head
billingsgate
bio (c.f.)
-aeration
-osmosis
rest one word
birchbark
bird
bath
bander
cage
call
catcher
#dog (literal)
dog (nonliteral)
-eyed (u.m.)
-faced (u.m.)
life
lime
lore
mouthed
seed
shot
watcher
bird's
-eye
#nest (literal) (n.)
-nest (n., u.m., v.)
birth
bed

#date
day
mark
place
right
#year
biscuit-shaped
(u.m.)
bismuto (c.f.)
all one word
bit
coin
-mapped
stock
bitter
-ender
head
sweet
-tongued (u.m.)
black
ball (nonliteral)
-bordered (u.m.)
-eyed (u.m.)
guard
jack
leg
list
mail
mark
#market (n.)
-market (u.m., v.)
-marketer
out (n., u.m.)
plate (printing)
print
-robed (u.m.)
#sheep (all
meanings)
shirted
snake
strap (n.)
-tie (u.m.)
top

#widow
blast
  hole
  plate
blasto (c.f.)
  all one word
bleach
  ground
  works
blear
  eye
  -eyed (u.m.)
  -witted (u.m.)
blepharo (c.f.)
  all one word
blight-resistant
  (u.m.)
blind
  -bomb (v.)
  -flying (u.m.)
  fold
  -loaded (u.m.)
  #man
  spot
  stitch
  story
blink-eyed (u.m.)
blithe-looking (u.m.)
blitzkrieg
block
  buster
  head
  hole (v.)
  ship
blood
  -alcohol (u.m.)
  bath
  beat
  curdling
  -drenched (u.m.)
  -giving (u.m.)
  guilty
  -hot (u.m.)

hound
letting
mobile
-red (u.m.)
ripe
shed
shot
spiller
spot
stain
stock
stream
sucker
thirsty
-warm (u.m.)
bloody
  -nosed (u.m.)
  -red (u.m.)
blossom
  -bordered (u.m.)
  -laden (u.m.)
blow
  back
  by (n., u.m.)
  cock
  down (n., u.m.)
  gun
  hard (n.)
  hole
  iron
  lamp
  off (n., u.m.)
  out (n., u.m.)
  pipe
  spray
  through (u.m.)
  torch
  tube
  up (n., u.m.)
blue
  -annealed (u.m.)
  beard (n.)
  blood

bonnet
book (nonliteral)
bottle
coat (n.)
-eyed (u.m.)
gill
grass
-gray (u.m.)
-green (u.m.)
-hot (u.m.)
jack
jacket
nose
-pencil (v.)
point (oyster)
print
stocking
streak (nonliteral)
tongue (n.)
blunder
  buss
  head
blunt
  -edged (u.m.)
  -spoken (u.m.)
boar
  spear
  staff
board
  #foot
  rack
  walk
boat
  builder
  crew
  head
  hook
  house
  loader
  owner
  #people
  setter

shop
side
swain
wright
yard
bob
  cat
  sled
  stay
  tail
  white
bobby
  pin
  -soxer
body
  bearer
  bending
  builder
  -centered (u.m.)
  guard
  -mind
  plate
bog
  -eyed (u.m.)
  land
  man
  trot (v.)
boil
  down (n., u.m.)
  off (n., u.m.)
  out (n., u.m.)
  over (n., u.m.)
boiler
  -off
  -out
  plate
  works
boiling#house
bold
  face (printing)
  -spirited (u.m.)

bolt
cutter
head
hole
-shaped (u.m.)
strake
bomb
drop
fall
shell
sight
thrower
-throwing (u.m.)
bone
ache
#ash
black
breaker
-bred (u.m.)
-dry (u.m.)
-eater
-hard (u.m.)
head
lace
meal
set
shaker
-white (u.m.)
boobytrap
boogie-woogie
book
binder
case
dealer
#end
fair
-fed (u.m.)
fold
-learned (u.m.)
-lined (u.m.)
list
lore
lover

mark
mobile
plate
rack
rest
sale
seller
shelf
stack
stall
stamp
stand
stitch
-stitching (u.m.)
-taught (u.m.)
wright
boom
town
truck
boondoggling
boot
black
hose
jack
lace
last
leg
lick
strap
bore
hole
safe
sight
bosom
-deep (u.m.)
-folded (u.m.)
-making (u.m.)
bottle
-fed (u.m.)
neck
-nosed (u.m.)
bottom#land
boughpot

bow
back
bent
grace
head
knot
legged
-necked (u.m.)
pin
shot
sprit
stave
string
wow
box
car
haul
head (printing)
truck
boxer
-off
-up
brachio (c.f.)
all one word
brachy (c.f.)
all one word
brain
cap
child
-cracked (u.m.)
pan
sick
-spun (u.m.)
storm
-tired (u.m.)
wash
brake
drum
head
meter
shoe
brandnew (u.m.)

brandy
-burnt (u.m.)
wine
brass
-armed (u.m.)
-bold (u.m.)
-smith
works
brave
hearted
-looking (u.m.)
-minded (u.m.)
brazen
-browed (u.m.)
face
bread
basket
crumb
earner
fruit
#knife
liner
plate
seller
stuff
#tray
winner
break
away (n., u.m.)
ax
back (n., u.m.)
bone (fever)
#circuit
down (n., u.m.)
-even (u.m.)
fast
fast#room
front
-in (n., u.m.)
neck
off (n., u.m.)
out (n., u.m.)
point

through (n., u.m.)
up (n., u.m.)
wind (n.)
breaker
-down
-off
-up
breast
band
beam
bone
-deep (u.m.)
-fed (u.m.)
feed
-high (u.m.)
hook
mark
piece
pin
plate
plow
rail
rope
work
breath
-blown (u.m.)
-tainted (u.m.)
taking
breech
block
cloth
loader
-loading (u.m.)
lock
pin
plug
sight
breeze
-borne (u.m.)
-lifted (u.m.)
-swept (u.m.)
way

bribe
-free (u.m.)
giver
taker
bric-a-brac
brick
bat
-built (u.m.)
-colored (u.m.)
kiln
layer
liner
mason
-red (u.m.)
setter
work
yard
bride
bed
bowl
cake
chamber
cup
groom
knot
lace
maiden
stake
bridge
builder
head
pot
tree
#wall
work
briefcase
bright
-colored (u.m.)
-eyed (u.m.)
brilliant
-cut (u.m.)
-green (u.m.)
brine-soaked (u.m.)

bringer-up
bristle
cone (u.m.)
-pointed (u.m.)
broad
acre
ax
band (n., u.m.)
-beamed (u.m.)
brim
cast
cloth
head
#jump
leaf (n.)
-leaved (u.m.)
loom
minded
-mouthed (u.m.)
share (n., v.)
sheet (n.)
side
sword
wife
woven
broken
-down (u.m.)
-legged (u.m.)
-mouthed (u.m.)
bromo (c.f.)
all one word
bronchio (c.f.)
all one word
broncho (c.f.)
all one word
broncobuster
bronze
-clad (u.m.)
-covered (u.m.)
-red (u.m.)
broom
#handle
-leaved (u.m.)

-making (u.m.)
stick
brother
hood
-in-law
brow
beat
point
post
brown
back
-eyed (u.m.)
out (n., u.m.)
print
brush
ball
#holder
off (n., u.m.)
-treat (v.)
#up
brusher
-off
-up
buck
eye
-eyed (u.m.)
horn
hound
passer
plate
pot
saw
shot
skinned
stall
stay
stove
tooth
wagon
wash
bucketshaped (u.m.)
buff
-tipped (u.m.)

ware
-yellow (u.m.)
bug
  bear
  bite
  -eyed (u.m.)
build
  down (n., u.m.)
  up (n., u.m.)
built
  -in (u.m.)
  -up (u.m.)
  bulb-tee (u.m.)
bulbo (c.f.)
  all one word
bulk
  head
  -pile (v.)
  weigh (v.)
bull
  baiting
  dog
  doze
  -faced (u.m.)
  fight
  frog
  head
  -mouthed (u.m.)
  neck
  nose
  pen
  ring
  #terrier
  toad
  -voiced (u.m.)
  whack
  whip
bullet
  head
  maker
  proof
bull's
  -eye (nonliteral)

-foot
bumble
  bee
  foot
  kite
bung
  hole
  start
burn
  -in (n., u.m.)
  out (n., u.m.)
  up (n., u.m.)
  burned-over (u.m.)
  burner-off
burnt
  -out (u.m.)
  -up (u.m.)
bus
  boy
  #conductor
  driver
  fare
  girl
  line
  load
bush
  beater
  buck
  fighter
  -grown (u.m.)
  hammer
  -leaguer
  ranger
  whacker
  bustup (n., u.m.)
busy
  body
  -fingered (u.m.)
  head
butt
  -joint (v.)

saw
stock
strap
-weld (v.)
butter
  ball
  -colored (u.m.)
  fat
  fingers
  head
  milk
  mouth
  nut
  print
  -rigged (u.m.)
  scotch
  -smooth (u.m.)
  -yellow (u.m.)
button
  -eared (u.m.)
  -headed (u.m.)
  hold
  hole
  hook
  mold
by
  -and-by
  -the-way (n., u.m.)
  -your-leave (n., u.m.)
  rest one word

C

C
  -sharp
  -star
  -tube
cab
  driver
  fare
  #owner
  stand

cabbagehead
cabinet
  maker
  making
  cable-laid (u.m.)
caco (c.f.)
  all one word
  cage#bird
cake
  baker
  bread
  -eater
  mixer
  -mixing (u.m.)
  pan
  walk
calci (c.f.)
  all one word
  calk-weld (v.)
call
  back (n., u.m.)
  box
  down (n., u.m.)
  -in (n., u.m.)
  note
  -off (n., u.m.)
  out (n., u.m.)
  -over (n., u.m.)
  up (n., u.m.)
  camshaft
camel
  back (rubber)
  -backed (u.m.)
  case
  driver
  -faced (u.m.)
  camel's-hair (u.m.)
camp
  fire
  ground
  stool
can
  capper

not
#opener
canalside
candle
  bomb
  -foot
  holder
  -hour
  lighter
  lit
  -meter
  power
  -shaped (u.m.)
  stand
  stick
  wick
  wright
candystick
cane
  -backed (u.m.)
  brake
  crusher
  cutter
  #sugar
canker
  -eaten (u.m.)
  -mouthed (u.m.)
cannonball
canvas-covered
  (u.m.)
cap
  -flash (v.)
  nut
  screw
  sheaf
  shore
car
  barn
  break
  builder
  fare
  goose
  hop

jacker
lot
-mile
owner
pool
port
sick
wash
carbo (c.f.)
  all one word
carbol (c.f.)
  all one word
carcino (c.f.)
  all one word
card
  case
  -index (u.m., v.)
  player
  sharp
  stock
cardio (c.f.)
  -aortic
  rest one word
care
  free
  giver
  -laden (u.m.)
  taker
  -tired (u.m.)
  worn
carpet
  bagger
  beater
  #cleaner
  -cleaning (u.m.)
  -covered (u.m.)
  fitter
  layer
  -smooth (u.m.)
  -sweeping (u.m.)
  weaver
  -weaving (u.m.)
  web

woven
carpo (c.f.)
  -olecranal
  rest one word
carriage-making
  (u.m.)
carrot
  -colored (u.m.)
  head (nonliteral)
  juice
  top (nonliteral)
carry
  all (n., u.m.)
  around (n., u.m.)
  back (n., u.m.)
  forward (n.)
  -in (n., u.m.)
  out (n., u.m.)
  over (n., u.m.)
cart
  load
  wheel (coin)
  whip
  wright
case
  bearer
  finding
  hammer
  harden
  load
  mated
  worker
caser-in
cashflow
cast
  away (n., u.m.)
  back (n., u.m.)
  -by (u.m.)
  off (n., u.m.)
  out (n., u.m.)
  -ridden (u.m.)
  -weld (v.)

caster
  -off
  -out
castlebuilder
  (nonliteral)
cat
  back
  beam
  bird
  call
  -eyed (u.m.)
  face (n.)
  fall
  gut
  head
  hole
  hook
  -ion
  like
  nap
  nip
  -o'-nine-tails
  stitch
  walk
CAT scan
catch
  all (n., u.m.)
  -as-catch-can
    (u.m.)
  cry
  penny
  plate
  up (n., u.m.)
  weight
  word
cater
  corner
  wauling
cat's
  -eye (nonliteral)
  -paw (nonliteral)
cattle
  #boat

feed
-raising (u.m.)
yak
cauliflower
-eared (u.m.)
#ware
causeway
cave
dweller
-dwelling (u.m.)
#fish
-in (n., u.m.)
cease-fire (n., u.m.)
cedar-colored (u.m.)
celi (c.f.)
all one word
celio (c.f.)
all one word
cell
cement
-covered (u.m.)
mason
-temper (v.)
census
#taker
-taking
center
#field (sports)
head (printing)
line
most
piece
-second
centi (c.f.)
all one word
centimeter-gram-
second
centri (c.f.)
all one word
centro (c.f.)
all one word
cephalo (c.f.)
all one word

cerato (c.f.)
all one word
cerebro (c.f.)
-ocular
rest one word
certificate holder
cervico (c.f.)
-occipital
-orbicular
rest one word
cess
pipe
pit
pool
chaffcutter
chain
#belt
-driven (u.m.)
#gang
stitch
chair
fast
mender
person
-shaped (u.m.)
warmer
chalk
cutter
line
-white (u.m.)
chamber
maid
woman
changeover
chapfallen
chapelgoing
char
broiler
coal
pit
woman
charge
#book

off (n., u.m.)
out (n., u.m.)
chartbook
chattermark
cheapskate
check
bite
forger
hook
-in (n., u.m.)
list
mark
nut
off (n., u.m.)
out (n., u.m.)
passer (n.)
point
rack
rail
rein
ring
roll
rope
row
sheet
strap
string
up (n., u.m.)
washer
weigher
writer
checker
-in
-off
-out
-up
cheek
bone
strap
cheerleader
cheese
burger
cake

cloth
curd
cutter
head
lip
parer
plate
chemico (c.f.)
all one word
chemo (c.f.)
all one word
cherry
-colored (u.m.)
stone (nonliteral)
#stone (literal)
chestnut
-colored (u.m.)
-red (u.m.)
chicken
bill
-billed (u.m.)
#breast
breasted
#coop
#farm
feed
heart
pox
#yard
chief
#justice
-justiceship
#mate
child
bearing
bed
birth
care
crowing
hood
kind
life
-minded (u.m.)

ridden
#support
wife
chill-cast (u.m., v.)
chin
band
-bearded (u.m.)
-chin
cloth
cough
-high (u.m.)
rest
strap
china
-blue (u.m.)
#shop
ware
Chinatown
chipmunk
chiro (c.f.)
all one word
chisel
-cut (u.m.)
-edged (u.m.)
#maker
chitchat
chitter-chatter
chloro (c.f.)
all one word
chock
ablock
-full (u.m.)
chocolate
-brown (u.m.)
-coated (u.m.)
#maker
choir
boy
#master
choke
bore
chain
damp

out (n., u.m.)
point
strap
chole (c.f.)
all one word
chondro (c.f.)
-osseous
rest one word
chop
-chop
stick
chowchow
Christ
-given (u.m.)
-inspired (u.m.)
like
chromo (c.f.)
all one word
chrono (c.f.)
all one word
chuck
hole
plate
wagon
church
#choir
goer
like
work
yard
churn
-butted (u.m.)
milk
cigar
case
cutter
-shaped (u.m.)
cigarette
#holder
#maker
-making (u.m.)
cine (c.f.)
all one word

circuitbreaker
circum (pref.)
arctic, pacific,
etc.
-Saturnal, etc.
rest one word
cirro (c.f.)
all one word
cis (pref.)
alpine
atlantic
-trans (u.m.)
rest one word
city
-born (u.m.)
-bred (u.m.)
folk
#man
scape
clam
bake
shell
clampdown (n.,
u.m.)
clap
net
trap
clasphook
class
book
-conscious (u.m.)
#consciousness
#day
work
claw
bar
-footed (u.m.)
hammer
hatchet
-tailed (u.m.)
clay
bank
-colored (u.m.)

pan
pit
works
clean
-cut (u.m.)
handed
out (n., u.m.)
-shaved (u.m.)
-smelling (u.m.)
up (n., u.m.)
clear
cole
-cut (u.m.)
cut (forestry) (n.,
v.)
-eyed (u.m.)
headed
-sighted (u.m.)
up (n., u.m.)
wing
clearinghouse
cleft
-footed (u.m.)
-graft (v.)
client/server
cliff
dweller
-dwelling (u.m.)
hanger
side
top
-worn (u.m.)
clinch-built (u.m.)
clink-clank
clinker-built (u.m.)
clip
-clop
-edged (u.m.)
sheet
clipper-built (u.m.)
cloak
-and-dagger (n.,
u.m.)

room

clock
  case
  face
  -minded (u.m.)
  setter
  #speed
  watcher

close
  bred
  -connected (u.m.)
  cross
  -cut (u.m.)
  down (n.)
  -fertilize (v.)
  fisted
  handed
  -knit
  minded
  mouthed
  out (n., u.m.)
  up (n., u.m.)

closed
  -circuit (u.m.)
  #end
  #shop
cloth-backed (u.m.)

clothes
  bag
  basket
  brush
  #closet
  horse
  pin
  line
  press
  rack
  #tree

cloud
  base
  burst
  cap
  -hidden (u.m.)

clover
  bloom
  leaf
  seed
  sick

club
  #car
  foot
  hand
  haul
  mobile
  ridden
  room
  root
  -shaped (u.m.)

co (pref.)
  -op
  exist, operate, etc.
  processor
  rest one word

coach
  -and-four
  builder
  whip

coal
  bag
  bed
  bin
  -black (u.m.)
  breaker
  #car
  dealer
  digger
  -faced (u.m.)
  hole
  -laden (u.m.)
  #loader
  #mine
  #oil
  pit
  rake
  sack (astron. only)
  shed

ship
  #tar
  #truck
  yard
coastside

coat
  hanger
  rack
  tailed

cob
  head
  meal
  shed
  web

cock
  bill
  brain
  crow
  eye
  fight
  head
  pit
  #robin
  spur
  sure
  -tailed (u.m.)
  up (n., u.m.)
cockleshell
cockscomb

cod
  bank
  fishing
  head
  #liver
  piece
  pitchings
  smack

code
  #name
  -named (u.m.)

coffee
  break
  cake

  -colored (u.m.)
  -growing (u.m.)
  pot
  room
cofferdam
cogwheel
coin-operated
  (u.m.)

cold
  blooded
  -chisel (v.)
  cuts
  -draw (v.)
  finch
  -flow (v.)
  -forge (v.)
  frame
  -hammer (v.)
  -hammered (u.m.)
  pack
  -press (v.)
  -roll (v.)
  -rolled (u.m.)
  -short (u.m.)
  -shortness
  -shoulder (v.)
  type (printing)
  #war
  #wave
  -work (v.)

cole
  seed
  slaw

coli (c.f.)
  all one word

collar
  bag
  band
  bone

colo (c.f.)
  all one word

color
  bearer

blind
#blindness
fast
-free (u.m.)
#line
  type (printing)
  (n.)
-washed (u.m.)
comb-toothed
  (u.m.)
come
-along (tool)
  back (n., u.m.)
-between (n.)
  down (n.)
-off (n., u.m.)
-on (n., u.m.)
-out (n.)
-outer
  uppance
comic#book
command
-line
#prompt
commander#in
  #chief
common
-carrier
#law
  place
#sense (n.)
  sense (u.m.)
  weal
  wealth
companionship
compressed#file
comptime
cone
-shaped (u.m.)
  speaker
conference#room
Congressman#at
  #Large

contra (pref.)
-acting
-approach
-ion
  rest one word
cook
  book
  off (n., u.m.)
  out (n., u.m.)
  shack
  stove
coolheaded
cooped
-in (u.m.)
-up (u.m.)
cop
#out (v.)
  out (n.)
copper
-bottomed (u.m.)
-colored (u.m.)
  head
-headed (u.m.)
#mine
  nose
  plate
-plated (u.m.)
  smith
  works
copy
  cat
  cutter
  desk
#editor
  fitter
  holding
  reader
  right
  writer
coral
-beaded (u.m.)
-red (u.m.)

cork
-lined (u.m.)
  screw
corn
  bin
  bread
  cake
  cob
  cracker
  crib
  crusher
  cutter
  dodger
-fed (u.m.)
  husk
  loft
  meal
#pone
  stalk
  starch
corner
  bind
  post
corpsmember
cost
#effective (n.)
-effectiveness
  wise
costo (c.f.)
  all one word
cotton
-clad (u.m.)
-covered (u.m.)
-growing (u.m.)
#mill
  mouth (snake)
  packer
  picker, ing
  seed
  sick
countdown (n., u.m.)
counter
#check (banking)

#septum
-off
  act, propaganda,
  top, etc.
  *as combining
  form, one
  word*
country
-born (u.m.)
-bred (u.m.)
  folk
  people
  side
  wide
county
#seat
  wide
court
  bred
-martial
  ship
cousin
  hood
-in-law
cover
  alls
  let
  side
  up (n., u.m.)
cow
  barn
  bell
  catcher
-eyed (u.m.)
  gate
  hand
  herd
  hide
  hitch
  lick
  path
  pen
#pony

pox
puncher
shed
sucker
crab
  cake
  catcher
  eater
  faced
  hole
  meat
  stick
crack
  down (n., u.m.)
  #house
  jaw
  pot
  -the-whip (n., u.m.)
  up (n., u.m.)
cradle
  side
  #snatcher
  song
cranio (c.f.)
  all one word
crank
  case
  -driven (u.m.)
  pin
  pit
  shaft
crapehanger
crashdive (v.)
crazy
  bone
  cat
cream
  cake
  -colored (u.m.)
creditworthiness
creek
  bed
  side

creep
  hole
  mouse
  crepe#de#chine
  crestfallen
crew
  cut
  member
  cribstrap
crime
  fighter
  solver
  wave
crisscross
crook
  all one word
crooked
  -foot (n.)
  -legged (u.m.)
  -nosed (u.m.)
crop
  -bound (u.m.)
  -haired (u.m.)
  head
  mark
  -year
cross
  -appeal
  arm
  band
  bar
  beam
  bearer
  bedded
  belt
  bench
  -bidding
  bill (bird)
  #bill (legal)
  bind
  bolt
  bond
  bones

bred
breed
-bridge (v.)
-brush (v.)
-carve (v.)
-channel (u.m.)
-check
-claim
-compound (v.)
-connect (v.)
-country (u.m.)
-cultivate (v.)
current
-curve (math.) (n.)
cut
-date (v.)
-drain (v.)
-dye (v.)
-dyeing (n.)
-examine (v.)
-eye (n., u.m.)
-eyed (u.m.)
fall
feed
-fertile (u.m.)
-fertilize (v.)
-fiber (u.m.)
file
fire
flow
foot
-grained (u.m.)
hair
hand
hatch
haul
head
-immunity
-index (u.m.)
-interrogate (v.)
-interrogatory
-invite (v.)
legged

legs
-level (v.)
-license (v.)
lift (v.)
lock
lots
mark
member
patch
path
plow (v.)
-pollinate (v.)
-purpose (n.)
-question
rail
-reaction
-refer (v.)
-reference
road
row
-service
-shaft
-slide
-staff
-sterile
-stitch
-stone
-stratification
-sue (v.)
-surge (v.)
talk
tie
town
track
trail
tree
under (n., u.m.)
-vote
walk
web
wind
word

crow
  bait
  bar
  foot
crowd
  funding
  sourcing
crownbar
crow's
  -foot (nonliteral)
  -nest (nonliteral)
crybaby
crypto (c.f.)
  -Christian, etc.
  rest one word
crystal
  -clear (u.m.)
  -girded (u.m.)
  -smooth (u.m.)
cubbyhole
cumulo (c.f.)
  all one word
cup
  bearer
  cake
  ful
  head
curb
  side
  stoner
cure-all (n., u.m.)
curly
  head
  locks (n.)
currycomb
cussword
custom
  -built (u.m.)
  -made (u.m.)
  -tailored (u.m.)
cut
  away (n., u.m.)
  back (n., u.m.)

glass
  -in (n., u.m.)
  off (n., u.m.)
  out (n., u.m.)
  rate (u.m.)
  throat
  -toothed (u.m.)
  -under (u.m.)
  -up (n., u.m.)
cutter
  -built (u.m.)
  -down
  head
  -off
  -out
  -rigged (u.m.)
  -up
cuttlebone
cyano (c.f.)
  all one word
cyber
  bullying
  security
  cyclecar
cyclo (c.f.)
  -olefin
  rest one word
cysto (c.f.)
  all one word
cyto (c.f.)
  all one word

D

D
  -Day
  -major
  -plus-4-day
dairy
  -fed (u.m.)
  -made (u.m.)
daisy#chain
damp
  proofing

  -stained (u.m.)
damping-off (n.,
  u.m.)
dancehall
danger#line
dare
  -all (n., u.m.)
  devil
  say
dark
  -eyed (u.m.)
  horse (nonliteral)
  room (n.)
  -skinned (u.m.)
dash
  plate
  wheel
data
  bank
  base
  set
date
  lined
  mark
daughter-in-law
dawn
  -gray (u.m.)
  streak
day
  beam
  bed
  break
  -bright (u.m.)
  care
  dream
  -fly (aviation) (v.)
  -flying (u.m.)
  going
  lighted
  lit
  long (u.m.)
  mark
  side

  star
  -to-day (u.m.)
  worker
de (pref.)
  -air
  icer
  -ink
  -ion
  centralize,
    energize, etc.
  rest one word
dead
  -alive
  beat (n.)
  born
  -burn (v.)
  #center
  -cold (u.m.)
  -dip (v.)
  -drunk (u.m.)
  -ender
  eye (n.)
  -eyed (u.m.)
  fall
  head
  -heated (u.m.)
  -heater
  -heavy (u.m.)
  latch
  #load
  lock
  pan
  -roast (v.)
  weight (n., u.m.)
  wood
death
  bed
  blow
  day
  -divided (u.m.)
  -doom (v.)
  #house
  -struck (u.m.)

trap
watch
-weary (u.m.)
decision
#making (n.)
-making (u.m., v.)
deckhand
deep
-affected (u.m.)
-cut (u.m.)
-felt (u.m.)
-freeze (u.m., v.)
-frying (u.m.)
going
-grown (u.m.)
-laid (u.m.)
most
mouthed
-rooted (u.m.)
#sea
-seated (u.m.)
-set (u.m.)
-sunk (u.m.)
-voiced (u.m.)
water (u.m.)
deer
drive (n.)
-eyed (u.m.)
food
herd
horn
hound
meat
stalker
stand
tick
dehydr(o) (c.f.)
all one word
demi (pref.)
-Christian, etc.
-incognito
rest one word
dermato (c.f.)
all one word

desk
#room
top (n., u.m.)
dessert
#fork
#knife
spoon
deutero (c.f.)
all one word
devil
-devil
dog (a marine)
-inspired (u.m.)
-ridden (u.m.)
dew
beam
cap
-clad (u.m.)
claw
damp
-drenched (u.m.)
drop
fall
-fed (u.m.)
-laden (u.m.)
lap
point
dextro (c.f.)
all one word
di (pref.)
all one word
dia (pref.)
all one word
dialog#box
dial-up
diamond
back
-backed (u.m.)
-shaped (u.m.)
diazo (c.f.)
-oxide
rest one word

dice
cup
play
die
-away (u.m.)
back
case
-cast (u.m., v.)
caster
-cut (u.m., v.)
cutter
hard (n., u.m.)
head
#proof (philately)
(n.)
setter
sinker
-square (u.m.)
stock
diesel
-driven (u.m.)
-electric (u.m.)
dillydally
dim
-lighted (u.m.)
lit
out (n., u.m.)
diner-out
ding
bat
dong
dining#room
dinitro (c.f.)
#spray
rest one word
dip
-dye (v.)
-grained (u.m.)
head
stick
dipper-in
direct
-connected (u.m.)

-indirect
direction-finding
(u.m.)
dirt
-cheap (u.m.)
fast
-incrusted (u.m.)
plate
dirty
-faced (u.m.)
-minded (u.m.)
#work
dis (pref.)
all one word
disc drive
dish
cloth
#cover
pan
rack
rag
#towel
washer
disk
jockey
pack
plow
-shaped (u.m.)
ditch
bank
digger
rider
side
dive
-bomb (v.)
#bomber
do
-all (n., u.m.)
-gooder
-little (n., u.m.)
-nothing (n.,
u.m.)

dock
- hand
- head
- side
- worker

dog
- bite
- -bitten (u.m.)
- breeder
- cart
- catcher
- #days
- -drawn (u.m.)
- -ear (v.)
- -eared (u.m.)
- face (soldier)
- -faced (u.m.)
- fall
- fight
- #food
- -headed (u.m.)
- hole
- leg
- #owner
- race
- shore
- sled
- -tired (u.m.)
- tooth
- -toothed (u.m.)
- trick
- trot
- watch
- -weary (u.m.)

doll
- face
- -faced (u.m.)
- dollyhead

donkey
- back
- -drawn (u.m.)
- -eared (u.m.)
- doomsday

door
- bed
- bell
- case
- check
- frame
- head
- jamb
- keeper
- knob
- knocker
- mat
- nail
- #opener
- plate
- post
- -shaped (u.m.)
- sill
- step
- stop

dope
- fiend
- passer
- pusher
- sheet

dorsi (c.f.)
- *all one word*

dorso (c.f.)
- -occipital
- *rest one word*

dot
- -matrix
- #pitch

double
- -barrel (n., u.m.)
- -barreled (u.m.)
- -bitt (v.)
- -breasted (u.m.)
- -charge (v.)
- check (n., v.)
- checked (u.m., v.)
- -chinned (u.m.)
- -click

- cross (nonliteral)
- deal (v.)
- -decker
- dipper (nonliteral)
- -duty (u.m.)
- -dye (v.)
- -edged (u.m.)
- -ender
- -entendre
- handed
- -headed (u.m.)
- header
- -jointed
- -leaded (u.m.)
- -quick (u.m.)
- -sided
- #space (v.)
- #take
- talk
- tone (printing)
- tree
- -trouble
- -up (u.m., v.)
- #work

dough
- boy
- -colored (u.m.)
- mixer
- nut

down
- beat
- by
- cast
- check
- coast
- come
- -covered (u.m.)
- crier
- cry
- curved
- cut
- dale

- draft
- drag
- face
- fall
- feed
- filled
- flow
- fold
- grade
- gradient
- growth
- hanging
- haul
- hearted
- hill
- lead
- load
- lock (n.)
- look
- most
- payment
- pour
- rate
- right
- river
- rush
- shore
- side
- sitting
- slip
- slope
- -soft (u.m.)
- spout
- stage
- stairs
- state
- stream
- street
- stroke
- sun (adv., u.m.)
- swing
- take
- throw

thrust
time
town
trampling
trend
trodden
turn
valley
weigh
weight
wind

draft
  age (allowance)
  #age
  -exempt (u.m.)

drag
  bar
  bolt
  net
  pipe
  rope
  saw
  staff
  wire

dragger
  -down
  -in
  -out
  -up

dragon
  -eyed (u.m.)
  fly
  #piece

drain
  cleaner
  pipe
  plug
  tile

drainage
  #area
  #basin
  way

draw
  -arch (n.)
  arm
  back
  bar
  beam
  bench
  bolt
  bore
  bridge
  cut
  down (n., u.m.)
  file
  gate
  gear
  glove
  head
  horse
  knife
  knot
  link
  loom
  net
  off (n., u.m.)
  out (n., u.m.)
  pin
  plate
  point
  sheet
  span
  stop
  string
  tongs
  tube

drawer
  -down
  -in
  -off
  -out

drawing
  #board
  #room

dream
  -haunted (u.m.)
  land
  lore
  world

dredge#net
dressup (n., u.m.)
dressing#room

drift
  #boat
  bolt
  meter
  -mining (u.m.)
  #net
  pin
  wind

drill
  case
  -like
  stock

drip
  cock
  -drip
  -dry (u.m., v.)
  sheet
  stick

drive
  away (n., u.m.)
  belt
  bolt
  by (n., u.m.)
  cap
  head
  -in (n., u.m.)
  pipe
  screw
  #shaft
  way

drop
  away (n., u.m.)
  bolt
  cloth
  -down

-forge (v.)
front
hammer
head
kick
leaf (n., u.m.)
leg
off (n., u.m.)
out (n., u.m.)
sonde
stitch

drug
  -addicted (u.m.)
  mixer
  passer
  pusher
  seller
  #user

drum
  beat
  fire
  head
  stick
  -up (n., u.m.)

dry
  -burnt (u.m.)
  #cell
  clean
  -cure (v.)
  dock
  -dye (v.)
  -farm (v.)
  farming (n., u.m.)
  gulch (nonliteral)
  lot
  -pack (u.m., v.)
  -rotted (u.m.)
  -salt (v.)
  wash

duck
  bill

-billed (u.m.)
bore
#breast
foot (tool)
-footed (u.m.)
pin
pond
walk
due
-in (n., u.m.)
out (n., u.m.)
duffelbag
dug
out (n.)
-up (u.m.)
dull
-edged (u.m.)
head
-looking (u.m.)
-witted (u.m.)
dumdum
dumb
bell
waiter
dump
car
cart
site
duo (c.f.)
all one word
dust
bag
bin
brush
cloth
-covered (u.m.)
fall
-gray (u.m.)
-laden (u.m.)
pan
storm
duty
bound

-free (u.m.)
dwelling#house
dye
mixer
stuff
works
dys (pref.)
all one word
E
E-minor
e
Book
-commerce
file
Government
Library
mail
eagle
#eye
-eyed (u.m.)
ear
ache
cap
drop
drum
flap
guard
hole
lap
lobe
mark
#muff
phone
-piercing (u.m.)
plug
ring
screw
shot
sore
splitting
tab
wax
wig

witness
earth
bank
born
-bred (u.m.)
fall
fast
-fed (u.m.)
fill
grubber
#house
kin
lit
mover
nut
quake
-shaking (u.m.)
slide
-stained (u.m.)
wall
east
bound
-central (u.m.)
going
-northeast
#side
-sider
-southeast
Eastertime
easy
going
mark (n.)
-rising (u.m.)
-spoken (u.m.)
eavesdrop
ebbtide
edge
#plane
shot
ways
wise
eel
cake

catcher
fare
pot
pout
skin
spear
egg
beater (all
    meanings)
cup
eater
fruit
head (nonliteral)
hot (n.)
nog
plant
-shaped (u.m.)
shell
-white (u.m.)
eight
-angled (u.m.)
#ball
fold
penny (nail)
-ply (u.m.)
score
-wheeler
elbowchair
elder
#brother
-leaved (u.m.)
electro (c.f.)
-optics
-osmosis
-ultrafiltration
rest one word
embryo (c.f.)
all one word
empty
handed
-looking (u.m.)
en
#banc

#gros
#route
encephalo (c.f.)
all one word
end
-all (n., u.m.)
bell
game
-measure (v.)
ender
-on
-up
endo (c.f.)
all one word
engine
#shop
-sized (u.m.)
work
#worker
#yard
entero (c.f.)
all one word
entry
#book
way
envelope
#holder
#maker
epi (pref.)
all one word
equi (c.f.)
-gram-molar
rest one word
ere
long
now
errorproof
erythro (c.f.)
all one word
even
glow
handed
minded

-numbered (u.m.)
song
-tempered (u.m.)
ever
-abiding (u.m.)
bearing
blooming
-constant (u.m.)
-fertile (u.m.)
glade
going
green
lasting
more
-normal (u.m.)
-present (u.m.)
-ready (u.m.)
sporting (biol.)
which
every
day (n., u.m.)
#day (each day)
one (all)
#one (distributive)
#time
evil
doer
#eye
-eyed (u.m.)
-faced (u.m.)
-looking (u.m.)
minded (u.m.)
sayer
speaker
wishing
ex
#cathedra
cathedral
communicate
-Governor
#libris
#officio
#post#facto

#rights
-serviceman
-trader
-vice-president
extra
-alimentary
-American
bold
-Britannic
-condensed (u.m.)
curricular
-fine (u.m.)
hazardous
judicial
-large (u.m.)
-long (u.m.)
marginal
mural
ordinary
polar
-strong (u.m.)
territorial
vascular
eye
#appeal
ball
bank
bar
blink
-blurred (u.m.)
bolt
brow
-conscious (u.m.)
cup
flap
glance
glass
hole
lash
lens
lid
mark
-minded (u.m.)

#opener
peep
pit
point
service
shade
shield
shot
sick
sight
sore
spot
-spotted (u.m.)
stalk
strain
string
tooth
wash
#weariness
wink
witness

F

F
-flat
-horn
-sharp
fable
#book
teller
face
-arbor (v.)
cloth
-harden (v.)
-hardened (u.m.)
lifting
mark
-off (n.)
-on (n., u.m.)
plate
up (n., u.m.)
fact
book

finding
sheet
fade
  away (n., u.m.)
  -in (n., u.m.)
  out (n., u.m.)
fail-safe
faint
  hearted
  -voiced (u.m.)
fair
  ground
  -lead (n., u.m.)
  minded
  play
  -skinned (u.m.)
  #trade
fairy
  folk
  hood
  tale
faithbreaker
fall
  away (n., u.m.)
  back (n., u.m.)
  #guy
  -in (n., u.m.)
  out (n., u.m.)
  -plow (v.)
  -sow (v.)
  trap
fallow#land
false
  -bottomed (u.m.)
  #face
  -faced (u.m.)
  hood
  -tongued (u.m.)
fame
  -crowned (u.m.)
  -thirsty (u.m.)
fan
  back

bearer
#belt
fare
fold
foot
-jet
-leaved (u.m.)
marker
-shaped (u.m.)
-tailed (u.m.)
fancy
  -free (u.m.)
  -loose (u.m.)
  -woven (u.m.)
  -wrought (u.m.)
far
  -aloft (u.m.)
  away (n., u.m.)
  -borne (u.m.)
  -distant (u.m.)
  -eastern (u.m.)
  -famed (u.m.)
  fetched
  flung (u.m.)
  gone
  -off (u.m.)
  #out
  -reaching (u.m.)
  seeing
  -seen (u.m.)
  -set (u.m.)
  sight
farm
  -bred (u.m.)
  hand
  hold
  owner
  people
  place
  stead
  worker
fashion
  -led (u.m.)

#piece (naut.)
#plate
-setting (u.m.)
fast
  -anchored (u.m.)
  back
  -dyed (u.m.)
  going
  hold
  -moving (u.m.)
  -read (v.)
  -reading (u.m.)
fat
  back
  -bellied (u.m.)
  -free (u.m.)
  -soluble (u.m.)
father
  -confessor
  -in-law
  land
fault
  finder
  line
  slip
faux#pas
fax
  -and-voice#
    mailbox
  #modem
  -on-demand
fear
  -free (u.m.)
  nought
  -pursued (u.m.)
  -shaken (u.m.)
feather
  bed (v.)
  bedding
  bone
  brain
  edge
  -footed (u.m.)

head
-leaved (u.m.)
stitch
-stitched (u.m.)
-stitching
-tongue (v.)
weight
wing (moth)
fed-up (u.m.)
feeble
  -bodied (u.m.)
  minded
feed
  back (n., u.m.)
  bag
  bin
  box
  crusher
  cutter
  head
  lot
  mixer
  pipe
  rack
  store
  stuff
feeder
  -in
  -up
fellow
  craft
  ship
  rest two words
felt
  cutter
  -lined (u.m.)
  packer
fence
  post
  #row
fern
  -clad (u.m.)
  leaf

-leaved (u.m.)
ferro (c.f.)
  -carbon-titanium
  -uranium
  rest one word
ferry
  boat
  #car
  #slip
fever
  less
  -stricken (u.m.)
  trap
  -warm (u.m.)
fiber
  -faced (u.m.)
  glass
  #optics
  stitch
  Fiberglas
  (copyright)
fibro (c.f.)
  -osteoma
  rest one word
  fickleminded
fiddle
  back
  -faddle
  head
  -shaped (u.m.)
  stick
  string
field
  ball
  glass
  goal
  -strip
fierce
  -eyed (u.m.)
  -looking (u.m.)
fiery
  -flaming (u.m.)
  -hot (u.m.)

-red (u.m.)
-tempered (u.m.)
fig
  bar
  eater
  leaf
  shell
figure
  head
  -of-eight (u.m.)
  #work (printing)
file
  card
  -hard (u.m.)
  name
  setter
  -soft (u.m.)
fill
  -in (n., u.m.)
  out (n., u.m.)
  -up (n., u.m.)
filler
  cap
  -in
  -out
  -up
film
  cutter
  goer
  going
  #paper
  slide
  strip
  -struck (u.m.)
fin
  back
  -shaped (u.m.)
fine
  -cut (u.m., v.)
  -draw (v.)
  -drawn (u.m.)
  -featured (u.m.)
  -looking (u.m.)

-set (u.m.)
finger
  breadth
  -cut (u.m.)
  hold
  hole
  hook
  mark
  nail
  parted
  post
  print
  shell
  space
  spin
  stall
  tip
fire
  arm
  back (n.)
  ball
  bell
  bolt
  bomb
  brand
  brat
  break
  brick
  -burnt (u.m.)
  -clad (u.m.)
  coat
  cracker
  crest
  -cure (v.)
  damp
  #drill
  -eater
  fall
  fang
  fighter
  guard
  -hardened (u.m.)
  horse

hose
lit
pit
place
plow
plug
-polish (v.)
power
proof
-red (u.m.)
-resistant (u.m.)
safe
side
spout
trap
truck
wall
warden
firm
  -footed (u.m.)
  -set (u.m.)
  -up (n., u.m.)
first
  #aid
  -aider
  -born (u.m.)
  -class (u.m.)
  comer
  hand (u.m.)
  -made (u.m.)
  -named (u.m.)
  -nighter
  -rate (u.m.)
fish
  back
  bed
  -bellied (u.m.)
  bolt
  bone
  bowl
  cake
  eater
  eye

-eyed (u.m.)
fall
#farm
-fed (u.m.)
food
garth
hook
-joint (v.)
kill
#ladder
meal
mouth
plate
pond
pool
pot
pound
trap
weir
works
fisher
folk
man
people
fishyback (n., u.m.)
fit
out (n.)
strip
five
bar
fold
-ply (u.m.)
-pointed (u.m.)
-reeler
score
flag
bearer
pole
post
-raising (u.m.)
ship
-signal (v.)
staff

stick
flame
-colored (u.m.)
-cut (v.)
out (n.)
proof
-retardant
thrower
flannelmouth
flap
cake
doodle
-eared (u.m.)
jack
flare
back (n., u.m.)
out (n., u.m.)
path
up (n., u.m.)
flash
back (n., u.m.)
bulb
card
gun
lamp
pan
point
flat
back
    (bookbinding)
bed (printing)
-bottomed (u.m.)
car
-compound (v.)
fold
foot (n.)
hat
head
iron
nose
out (n., u.m.)
-rolled (u.m.)
sawn

top
-topped (u.m.)
woods
flax
drop
-leaved (u.m.)
-polled (u.m.)
seed
flea
bite
-bitten (u.m.)
trap
fleet
foot
-footed (u.m.)
wing
flesh
brush
hook
-pink (u.m.)
pot
#wound
fleur-de-lis
flextime
flight
crew
-hour
path
-test (v.)
flimflam
flip
-flap
-flop
-up (n., u.m.)
flood
cock
flow
gate
lamp
lighting
mark
#plain
tide

wall
water
floor
beam
cloth
head
lamp
mat
mop
#show
space
stain
walker
#wax
-waxing (u.m.)
flophouse
floppy#disc
flour
bag
bin
#mill
sack
#sifter
flow
chart
meter
off (n., u.m.)
sheet
through (n.,
    u.m.)
flower
bed
bud
-crowned (u.m.)
#grower
-hung (u.m.)
#piece
pot
-scented (u.m.)
#shop
flue-cure (v.)
fluid
-compressed (u.m.)

extract (pharm.)
(n.)
glycerate
fluo (c.f.)
all one word
fluoro (c.f.)
all one word
flush
-cut (u.m.)
-decked (u.m.)
-decker
gate
fluvio (c.f.)
all one word
fly
away
back
ball
-bitten (u.m.)
blow
blown
-by-night (n.,
u.m.)
catcher
eater
-fish (v.)
-fisher
-fisherman
#fishing
flap
-free (u.m.)
leaf
paper
sheet
speck
-specked (u.m.)
tier
trap
weight
wheel
winch
flying
#boat

#fish
foam
bow
-crested (u.m.)
-white (u.m.)
fog
bound
bow
dog
eater
-hidden (u.m.)
horn
#light
-ridden (u.m.)
fold
-in
up (n., u.m.)
folk
#dance
lore
song
follow
-on
through (n.,
u.m.)
up (n., u.m.)
follower-up
food
-fasted (u.m.)
-fasting (v.)
packer
store
stuff
foolhardy
foolscap
foot
-and-mouth
(u.m.)
ball
band
bath
blower
board

brake
breadth
bridge
candle
fall
-free (u.m.)
gear
-grain
hill
hold
lambert
licker
light(s)
lining
locker
loose
mark
note
pad
path
pick
plate
-pound
-pound-second
print
race
rail
rest
rope
scald
-second
slogger
sore
stalk
stall
step
stick
stock
stool
-ton
walk
wall
-weary (u.m.)

worn
for (pref.)
all one word
fore
-age
-and-aft (n., u.m.)
-and-after (n.)
-edge
-end
-exercise
word
rest one word
forest
-clad (u.m.)
-covered (u.m.)
#land
side
fork
head
lift
-pronged (u.m.)
tail
-tailed (u.m.)
form
fitting
#work (printing)
forth
coming
right
with
fortune
#hunter
teller
forty-niner
foul
#line
-looking (u.m.)
mouthed
-spoken (u.m.)
-tongued (u.m.)
up (n., u.m.)
fountainhead

four
 -bagger
 -eyed (u.m.)
 flusher
 fold
 -footed (u.m.)
 -in-hand (n., u.m.)
 -masted (u.m.)
 -master
 penny (nail)
 -ply (u.m.)
 score
 some
 square
 -wheeler
fox
 -faced (u.m.)
 hole
 hound
 #hunting
 skinned
 tailed
 trot
fracto (c.f.)
 all one word
frame-up
free
 booter
 born
 drop
 -for-all (n., u.m.)
 -grown (u.m.)
 hand (drawing)
 handed
 hold
 lance
 loader
 -minded
 masonry
 #post
 -spoken (u.m.)
 standing (u.m.)

 thinker
 trader
 wheel (u.m., v.)
 wheeler (n.)
 #will (n.)
 will (u.m.)
 freedom#fighter
freeze
 down (n., u.m.)
 out (n., u.m.)
 up (n., u.m.)
freight
 #house
 -mile
 #room
 #train
fresh
 -looking (u.m.)
 -painted (u.m.)
 water
frog
 belly
 -eyed (u.m.)
 face
 man
 mouth
 nose
 pond
 tongue
  (medicine)
front
 -end (u.m.)
 -focused (u.m.)
 runner
 stall
 -wheel (u.m.)
fronto (c.f.)
 -occipital
 -orbital
 rest one word
frost
 bite
 bow

 -free (u.m.)
 -hardy (u.m.)
 -heaving (u.m.)
 -killed (u.m.)
 lamp
 line
fruit
 cake
 #fly
 growing
 #shop
 stalk
 frying#pan
fuel
 #line
 #oil
full
 back
 -bellied (u.m.)
 blood
 -bound (u.m.)
 -duplex
 face
 -fashioned (u.m.)
 -flowering (u.m.)
 -grown (u.m.)
 -handed (u.m.)
 -headed (u.m.)
 -lined (u.m.)
 #load
 mouth
 -strength (u.m.)
 -text
 -time (u.m.)
 fundraising
 funlover
funnel
 form
 -shaped (u.m.)
fur
 -clad (u.m.)
 coat
 -lined (u.m.)

 skin
 -trimmed (u.m.)
fuse
 box
 #gauge
 plug

G

G
 -major
 -man
 -minor
 -sharp
 gabfest
gad
 about (n., u.m.)
 fly
 gaff-topsail
gag
 -check (v.)
 #order
 root
 #rule
gain
 say
 -sharing (u.m.)
galact(o) (c.f.)
 all one word
 gallbladder
 galley#proof
  (printing)
galvano (c.f.)
 all one word
game
 bag
 cock
gang
 boss
 plank
 saw
 garnet-brown
  (u.m.)

gas
bag
bomb
-driven (u.m.)
field
-fired (u.m.)
firing
fitter
-heated (u.m.)
-laden (u.m.)
lamp
lighted
line (auto)
#line (queue)
lock
#main
#mask
meter
works
gastro (c.f.)
-omental
rest one word
gate
house
keeper
leg (u.m.)
pin
post
tender
works
gauge pin
gear
box
case
-driven (u.m.)
fitter
-operated (u.m.)
set
shift
wheel
gelatin
-coated (u.m.)
-making (u.m.)

gelatino (c.f.)
bromide
chloride
gem
cutter
-set (u.m.)
#stone
genito (c.f.)
all one word
gentle
folk
-looking (u.m.)
man
-mannered (u.m.)
mouthed
-spoken (u.m.)
woman
geo (c.f.)
all one word
germ-free (u.m.)
gerrymander
get
away (n., u.m.)
#off
-together (n., u.m.)
up (n., u.m.)
ghost
-haunted (u.m.)
write (v.)
gilt-edge (u.m.)
ginger
#ale
bread
-colored (u.m.)
snap
spice
give
-and-take (n., u.m.)
away (n., u.m.)
glacio (c.f.)
all one word

glass
blower
#ceiling
cutter
-eater
-eyed (u.m.)
-hard (u.m.)
house
works
glauco (c.f.)
all one word
glidepath
globetrotter
glosso (c.f.)
all one word
glow
lamp
meter
gluc(o) (c.f.)
all one word
glue
pot
stock
glycero (c.f.)
all one word
glyco (c.f.)
all one word
go
-ahead (n., u.m.)
-around (n., u.m.)
-as-you-please (u.m.)
-back (n., u.m.)
-between (n.)
by (n.)
cart
-devil (n.)
-getter
-getting (n., u.m.)
-off (n., u.m.)
goal
post
#setter

goat
-bearded (u.m.)
-eyed (u.m.)
herd
goat's
-hair
-horn
God
-conscious (u.m.)
-fearing (u.m.)
-forsaken (u.m.)
-given (u.m.)
head
-man
-ordained (u.m.)
-sent (u.m.)
-sped (u.m.)
speed
-taught (u.m.)
god
child
daughter
father
head
hood
less
mother
parent
send
ship
son
sonship
goggle-eyed (u.m.)
goings-on
gold
beater
brick (shirker)
#brick (of real gold)
-bright (u.m.)
-brown (u.m.)
digger
#dust
-filled (u.m.)

foil
-inlaid (u.m.)
leaf
plate (v.)
-plated (u.m.)
-plating (u.m.)
smithing
-wrought (u.m.)
golden
-fingered (u.m.)
-headed (u.m.)
good
-bye
-for-nothing (n., u.m.)
-looker
-looking (u.m.)
-natured (u.m.)
#will (kindness)
will (salable asset)
goose
bone
bumps
-cackle
#egg
-eyed (u.m.)
flesh
-footed (u.m.)
herd
mouth
neck
pimples
rump
step
wing
gospel
like
-true (u.m.)
Government (U.S. or foreign)
-in-exile

-owned (u.m.)
wide
governmentwide (State, city, etc.)
grab
-all (n., u.m.)
#bag
hook
rope
grade
finder
mark
grain
-cut (u.m.)
field
-laden (u.m.)
mark
sick
gram
-fast (u.m.)
-meter
-molecular
-negative (u.m.)
-positive (u.m.)
grand
aunt
child, etc.
stand
grant-in-aid
grape
fruit
#juice
-leaved (u.m.)
seed
stalk
vine
graph
alloy
#paper
grapho (c.f.)
all one word
grass
-clad (u.m.)

-covered (u.m.)
cutter
flat
-green (u.m.)
hop
nut
plot
roots (nonliteral)
#roots (literal)
widow
grave
clothes
digger
side
stead
gravel
-blind (u.m.)
stone
gray
back (n., u.m.)
beard (n.)
-clad (u.m.)
coat (n.)
-eyed (u.m.)
-haired (u.m.)
head
-headed (u.m.)
out (n., u.m.)
grease
#gun
#pit
proof
great
-aunt
coat
-eared (u.m.)
-grandchild, etc.
-headed (u.m.)
heart
mouthed
green
back (n., u.m.)
belt

(community)
-clad (u.m.)
-eyed (u.m.)
gage (plum)
gill
grocer
horn
keeper
-leaved (u.m.)
sand (geology)
sick
stuff
sward
town (community)
#wood (literal)
wood (forest)
greyhound
grid
iron
lock
griddlecake
grillroom
grip
sack
wheel
gross
-minded (u.m.)
#weight
ground
breaking
hog
mass
nut
path
plot
speed
#water
wave
work
group-connect (v.)
grownup (n., u.m.)
grubstake

guard
 house
 plate
 rail
guest
 chamber
 house
 room
guided-missile
 (u.m.)
guidepost
guider-in
gum
 boil
 chewer
 digger
 drop
 -gum
 lac
 -saline (n.)
 shoe
gun
 #barrel
 bearer
 blast
 builder
 cotton
 crew
 deck
 fight
 fire
 flint
 lock
 paper
 pit
 play
 point
 powder
 rack
 -rivet (v.)
 runner
 shop
 shot

 -shy (u.m.)
 sight
 stock
 wale
gut
 less
 string
gutter
 blood
 -bred (u.m.)
 snipe
 spout
gymno (c.f.)
 all one word
gyneco (c.f.)
 all one word
gyro
 #horizon
 #mechanism
 #pelorus
 plane, compass,
 etc.

H

H
 -bar
 -beam
 -bomb
 -hour
hack
 barrow
 hammer
 log
 saw
hailstorm
hair
 band
 breadth
 brush
 -check (n.)
 cloth
 cut (n.)
 do

 dresser
 -fibered (u.m.)
 lock
 pin
 #ribbon
 space (printing)
 splitting
 spring
 streak
 stroke (printing)
 #trigger
half
 -and-half (n.,
 u.m.)
 -afraid
 -alive
 -angry
 back (football)
 -backed (u.m.)
 -baked (u.m.)
 -bound (u.m.)
 caste
 -clear
 cock (v.)
 cocked
 (nonliteral)
 -dark
 #day
 deck
 -decked (u.m.)
 -decker
 -feed (v.)
 hearted
 -hourly (u.m.)
 -life
 #load
 -loaded (u.m.)
 -mast
 -miler
 -monthly (u.m.)
 -on (n., u.m.)
 pace
 penny

 -ripe
 -shy
 -sole (v.)
 staff
 stitch
 -strength (u.m.)
 title
 tone (printing)
 track
 -true
 -truth
 -weekly (u.m.)
 -yearly (u.m.)
hallmark
ham
 shackle
 string
hammer
 cloth
 dress (v.)
 -hard (u.m.)
 -harden (v.)
 -hardened (u.m.)
 head
 lock
 #thrower
 toe
 -weld (v.)
 -wrought (u.m.)
hand
 bag
 ball
 bank (v.)
 barrow
 bill
 book
 -bound (u.m.)
 bow
 brake
 breadth
 brush
 -built (u.m.)
 car

-carry (v.)
cart
-carve (v.)
clap
clasp
-clean (v.)
crank
cuff
-cut (v.)
-embroidered
  (u.m.)
-fed (v.)
fold
grasp
grenade
grip
guard
gun
-held (u.m.)
-high (u.m.)
hold
hole
-in-hand (u.m.)
kerchief
-knit (v.)
-knitter
laid
-letter (v.)
lift (truck)
liner
made
-me-down (n.,
  u.m.)
mix (v.)
mold (v.)
mower
off (n., u.m.)
out (n., u.m.)
pick (v.)
post
press
print
rail

reading
saw
scrape (v.)
set
shake
spade
spike
splice
split
spring
spun
-stamp (v.)
stand
stitch
stroke
stuff
-tailored (u.m.)
tap
tool
-tooled (u.m.)
-tooling (u.m.)
truck
weave
wheel
worked
woven
write (v.)
written
wrought
hands#free
handlebar
hang
  dog
  nail
  net
  out (n., u.m.)
  up (n.)
hanger
  -back
  -on
  -up
happy-go-lucky
hara-kiri

harbor
  master
  side
hard
  -and-fast (u.m.)
  back (beetle)
  -baked (u.m.)
  -bitten (u.m)
  -boiled (u.m.)
  case
  copy (n.)
  core
  #disc
  #drive
  fist (n.)
  handed
  hat (n.)
  -hit (u.m.)
  -looking (u.m.)
  mouthed
  nose
  pan
  -pressed (u.m.)
  -set (u.m.)
  #shell (n.)
  ship
  spun
  stand
  tack
  top (auto)
  ware
  -won (u.m.)
  #work
  -working (u.m.)
  wrought
hare
  brain
  foot
  hound
  -mad (u.m.)
harness-making
  (u.m.)
harum-scarum

harvesttime
has-been (n.)
hashmark
hat
  band
  box
  brim
  brush
  cleaner
  pin
  rack
  rail
  stand
  #tree
hatchback
hatchet-faced (u.m.)
haul
  about (n., u.m.)
  away (n., u.m.)
  back (n.)
have-not (n., u.m.)
haversack
hawk
  bill
  -billed (u.m.)
  head
  -nosed (u.m.)
hawse
  hole
  pipe
hay
  band
  cap
  cart
  cock
  #fever
  field
  fork
  lift
  loft
  market
  mow
  rack

rake
rick
-scented (u.m.)
seed
stack
wire
hazardous
    #waste#site
hazel
-eyed (u.m.)
nut
he-man
head
ache
achy
band
bander
block
cap
chair
cheese
chute
cloth
count
dress
-ender
first
frame
gate
gear
hunter
lamp
ledge
lighting
liner
lock
long
master
mistress
mold
most
note
-on (u.m.)

phone
plate
post
quarters
rail
reach
rest
ring
rope
set
shake
sill
space
spin
spring
stall
stand
start
stick
stock
stream
strong
waiter
wall
wind
header-up
heal-all (n., u.m.)
healthcare
heart
ache
aching
beat
block
blood
break
burn
deep
felt
free (u.m.)
grief
heavy
leaf
-leaved (u.m.)

nut
quake
seed
sick
sore
string
struck
throb
-throbbing (u.m.)
-weary (u.m.)
hearth
rug
warming
heat
drops
#pump
#rash
-resistant (u.m.)
stroke
treat (v.)
-treating (u.m.)
#wave
heaven
bound
-inspired (u.m.)
-sent (u.m.)
heaver
-off
-out
-over
heavy
back
-duty (u.m.)
-eyed (u.m.)
-footed (u.m.)
handed
-looking (u.m.)
-set (u.m.)
#water
weight (n., u.m.)
hecto (c.f.)
    all one word

hedge
born
breaker
#fund
hog
hop
pig
row
#trimmer
heel
ball
band
block
cap
fast
grip
pad
path
plate
post
print
ring
stay
strap
tap
helio (c.f.)
    all one word
helpmeet
helter-skelter
hema (c.f.)
    all one word
hemato (c.f.)
    all one word
hemi (pref.)
    all one word
hemo (c.f.)
    all one word
hemp
seed
string
hemstitch
hen
bill

coop
-feathered (u.m.)
house
pecked
roost
hence
forth
forward
hepato (c.f.)
all one word
hepta (c.f.)
all one word
here
about
after
at
by
from
in
inabove
inafter
inbefore
into
of
on
to
tofore
under
unto
upon
with
herringbone
hetero (c.f.)
-ousia, etc.
rest one word
hexa (c.f.)
all one word
hi-fi
hide
-and-seek (n., u.m.)
away (n., u.m.)
out (n., u.m.)

high
ball
binder
born
bred
brow (nonliteral)
-caliber (u.m.)
-class (u.m.)
-density
flier (n.)
flying (u.m.)
-foreheaded (u.m.)
#frequency
handed
-hat (v.)
jinks
lander
#light (literal)
light (nonlit.)
-minded (u.m.)
-power (u.m.)
-pressure (u.m., v.)
-priced (u.m.)
#proof
-reaching (u.m.)
-rigger (n.)
rise (building)
road
#seas
-speed (u.m.)
stepper
-tension (u.m.)
#tide
-up (u.m.)
#water
higher-up (n.)
hill
culture (farming)
side
top

hind
brain
cast
gut (n.)
head
leg
most
quarter
saddle
sight
wing
hip
bone
mold
shot
hippo (c.f.)
all one word
histo (c.f.)
all one word
hit
-and-miss (u.m.)
-and-run (u.m.)
-or-miss (u.m.)
hitchhiker
hoarfrost
hoary-haired (u.m.)
hob
goblin
nail
nob
hobbyhorse
hockshop
hocus-pocus
hod#carrier
hodgepodge
hog
back
-backed (u.m.)
-faced (u.m.)
fat
frame
hide
nose (machine)

-nosed (u.m.)
pen
sty
-tie (v.)
wash
-wild (u.m.)
hog's-back (geol.)
hogshead
hoistaway (n.)
hold
all (n., u.m.)
back (n., u.m.)
-clear (n., u.m.)
down (n., u.m.)
fast (n., u.m.)
off (n., u.m.)
out (n., u.m.)
up (n., u.m.)
holder
-forth
-on
-up
hole
#in#one
-high (u.m.)
-in-the-wall (n.)
through
hollow
back (bookbinding)
-backed (u.m.)
-eyed (u.m.)
faced
-ground (u.m.)
holo (c.f.)
all one word
holy
#day
stone
home
-baked (u.m.)
body
born

bred
brew
builder
#buyer
comer
coming
-fed (u.m.)
felt
folk
freeze (u.m., v.)
front
furnishings (n.)
going
grown
lander
life
made
maker
owner
#ownership
#page
plate
#rule
seeker
sick
spun
stead
stretch
town
woven
homeo (c.f.)
   all one word
homo
   #legalis
   #sapiens
homo (c.f.)
   -ousia, etc.
   rest one word
honey
   -colored (u.m.)
   comb
   -cured (u.m.)
   dew

drop
eater
-laden (u.m.)
lipped
moon
mouthed
pot
sucker
sweet
honor
   bound
   #guard
   #man
hood
   cap
   mold
   wink
hoof
   beat
   mark
   print
   -printed (u.m.)
hook
   ladder
   nose
   -nosed (u.m.)
   pin
   up (n., u.m.)
hooker
   -off
   -on
   -out
   -over
   -up
hoopstick
hop
   about (n., u.m.)
   off (n., u.m.)
   scotch
   toad
hope#chest
hopper
   burn

dozer
horehound
hormono (c.f.)
   all one word
horn
   bill
   blende
   blower
   -eyed (u.m.)
   pipe
   stay
   tip
hornyhanded
horse
   back
   breaker
   car
   cloth
   dealer
   fair
   fight
   flesh
   hair
   head
   herd
   hide
   hoof
   -hour
   jockey
   laugh
   meat
   mint
   play
   pond
   power-hour
   power-year
   pox
   race
   #sense (n.)
   shoe
   thief
   #trade
   whip

hot
   bed
   blood
   -blooded (u.m.)
   brain
   cake
   -cold
   dog
   foot
   head (n.)
   -mix (u.m.)
   pack
   patch
   plate
   -press (v.)
   rod (nonliteral)
   -roll (v.)
   -rolled (u.m.)
   spot
   -work (v).
hotelkeeper
houndshark
hourglass
house
   breaking
   broken
   builder
   #call
   cleaner
   -cleaning (u.m.)
   coat
   dress
   father
   furnishing(s) (n.)
   guest
   hold
   husband
   mother
   owner
   parent
   pest
   plant
   -raising (u.m.)

ridden
top
trailer
wares
warming
wife
how
  -do-you-do (n.)
  ever
  soever
hub
  cap
  -deep (u.m.)
humankind
humble
  bee
  -looking (u.m.)
  mouthed
  -spirited (u.m.)
humdrum
hump
  back
  -shouldered
    (u.m.)
humpty-dumpty
hunchback
hundred
  fold
  -legged (u.m.)
  -percenter
  -pounder
  weight
hung-up (u.m.)
hunger
  -mad (u.m.)
  -worn (u.m.)
hurly-burly
hush
  -hush
  #money
  up (n., u.m.)
hydro (c.f.)
  all one word

hydro#station
hygro (c.f.)
  all one word
hyper (pref.)
  -Dorian, etc.
  linked
  text
  rest one word
hypo (c.f.)
  all one word
hystero (c.f.)
  -oophorectomy
  -salpingo-oopho-
    rectomy
  rest one word

I

I
  -bar
  -beam
  -iron
  -rail
ice
  berg
  blind
  #blindness
  blink
  block
  bone
  breaker
  cap
  -clad (u.m.)
  -cold (u.m.)
  -cooled (u.m.)
  -covered (u.m.)
  #cream
  fall
  #fishing
  floe (island)
  flow (current)
  -free (u.m.)
  maker
  melt

pack
plant
plow
quake
#storm
#water
ideo (c.f.)
  -unit
  rest one word
idle
  headed
  -looking (u.m.)
  -minded (u.m.)
ileo (c.f.)
  all one word
ilio (c.f.)
  all one word
ill
  -advised (u.m.)
  -being (n.)
  -born (u.m.)
  -bred (u.m.)
  #breeding (n.)
  -doing (n., u.m.)
  -fated (u.m.)
  -humored (u.m.)
  -looking (u.m.)
  -treat (v.)
  -use (v.)
  #will
  -wisher
  -wishing (u.m.)
in
  -and-in (u.m.)
  -and-out (u.m.)
  -and-outer
  -being (u.m.)
  -flight (u.m.)
  -house
  -law (n.)
  asmuch, sofar
  #re, #rem, #situ,
    etc.

in (pref.)
  active (u.m.)
  breeding
  depth (u.m.)
  hospital (u.m.)
  migration (u.m.)
  service
    (u.m.), etc.
inch
  -deep (u.m.)
  -long (u.m.)
  meal
  -pound
  -ton
  worm
index-digest
indigo
  -blue (u.m.)
  -carmine (u.m.)
Indo (c.f.)
  china
  chinese
  -European, etc.
infra (pref.)
  -anal
  -auricular
  -axillary
  -esophageal
  -umbilical
  rest one word
ink
  -black (u.m.)
  mixer
  pot
  slinger
  spot
  -spotted (u.m)
  stain
  stand
  well
inner
  -city (u.m.)
  #man

spring
ino (c.f.)
  all one word
insect-borne (u.m.)
inter (pref.)
  -American, etc.
  rest one word
intra (pref.)
  -atomic, etc.
  rest one word
intro (pref.)
  all one word
Irish
  -American (u.m.)
  -born (u.m.)
iron
  #age
  back
  -braced (u.m.)
  clad
  fisted
  -free (u.m.)
  handed
  hard
  -lined (u.m.)
  mold
  -red (u.m.)
  shod
  shot (mineral)
    (u.m.)
  #shot (golf)
  side
  -willed (u.m.)
  works
ironer-up
island
  -born (u.m.)
  -dotted (u.m.)
iso (c.f.)
  -octane
  -oleic
  -osmosis
  rest one word

ivory
  -tinted (u.m.)
  type (photog.)
  -white (u.m.)
ivy
  -clad (u.m.)
  -covered (u.m.)

J

J-bolt
jack
  ass
  hammer
  head
  -in-the-box
  knife
  -of-all-trades
  -o'-lantern
  -plane (v.)
  pot
  rabbit
  screw
jail
  bird
  house
jam
  nut
  packed
Java
  #applets
  Beans
  Script
jaw
  bone
  breaker
  -locked (u.m.)
  twister
jay
  hawk
  walk
jelly
  bean
  roll

jerry
  -build (v.)
  builder
  -built (u.m.)
jet
  #airliner
  #airplane
  -black (u.m.)
  lag
  liner
  port
  -powered (u.m.)
  prop
  -propelled (u.m.)
  #propulsion
  stream
  wash
jewel
  -bright (u.m.)
  -studded (u.m.)
jib
  head
  -o-jib
  stay
jig
  -a-jig
  back
  -drill (v.)
  saw
job
  #lot
  seeker
  #shop
  site
joggle#piece
joint#owner
joulemeter
joy
  hop
  ride
  stick
jump
  master

off (n., u.m.)
  rock
jungle
  -clad (u.m.)
  -covered (u.m.)
  #gym
  side
junkpile
jury
  #box
  -fixing (u.m.)
  -rigged (u.m.)
just#in#time
juxta (c.f.)
  -ampullar
  -articular
  rest one word

K

K
  -ration
  -term
keel
  block
  fat
  haul
  -laying (u.m.)
  #line
keepsake
kerato (c.f.)
  all one word
kettle
  drum
  stitch
key
  board
  bolt
  hole
  lock
  note
  punch
  ring
  seat

stone
stop
word
worker
kick
  about (n., u.m.)
  back (n., u.m.)
  -in (n., u.m.)
  off (n., u.m.)
  out (n., u.m.)
  up (n., u.m.)
killjoy
kiln
  -dry (u.m., v.)
  eye
  hole
  rib
  stick
  tree
kilo (pref.)
  gram-meter
  voltampere
  watthour
  rest one word
kindheart
king
  bolt
  #crab
  head
  hood
  hunter
  maker
  piece
  pin
kins
  folk
  people
kiss-off (n., u.m.)
kite
  flier
  flying
knapsack

knee
  -braced (u.m.)
  brush
  cap
  -deep (u.m.)
  -high (u.m.)
  hole
  -jerk (u.m.)
  pad
  pan
  strap
knick
  knack
  point
knight
  -errant
  head
  hood
knitback
knock
  about (n., u.m.)
  away (n., u.m.)
  down (n., u.m.)
  -knee (n.)
  -kneed (u.m.)
  off (n., u.m.)
  -on (n., u.m.)
  out (n., u.m.)
  up (n., u.m.)
knocker
  -off
  -up
knot
  hole
  horn
know
  -all (n., u.m.)
  -how (n., u.m.)
  -it-all (n., u.m.)
  -little (n., u.m.)
  -nothing (n.,
    u.m.)

knuckle
  bone
  buster
  -deep (u.m.)
  -kneed (u.m.)

L

L
  -bar
  -beam
  -block
  -shaped
  -square
labio (c.f.)
  all one word
laborsaving
lace
  -edged (u.m.)
  #edging
  wing (insect)
  -winged (u.m.)
  worked
lackluster
ladder-backed
  (u.m.)
lady
  beetle
  finger
  killer
  ship
lake
  bed
  front
  lander
  shore
  side
lameduck
  (nonliteral)
  (n., u.m.)
lamp
  black
  -blown (u.m.)
  -foot

hole
-hour
house
lighter
lit
post
shade
stand
wick
land
  #base
  -based (u.m.)
  #bird
  borne
  fall
  fast
  fill
  flood
  form
  grabber
  -grant (u.m.)
  holding
  lady
  locked
  look
  lord
  lubber
  mark
  mass
  mine
  #office
  owner
  -poor (u.m.)
  right
  scape
  sick
  side
  slide
  slip
  spout
  storm
  wash
  wire

wrack
lantern-jawed
  (u.m.)
lap
  belt
  -lap
  robe
  streak
  top
  weld (v.)
  -welded (u.m.)
  -welding (u.m.)
large
  -eyed
  -handed (u.m.)
  -minded (u.m.)
  mouthed
  -scale (u.m.)
lark
  -colored (u.m.)
  spur
laryngo (c.f.)
  all one word
last
  -born (u.m.)
  -cited (u.m.)
  -ditcher
  -named (u.m.)
latch
  bolt
  key
  string
late
  -born (u.m.)
  comer
  -lamented (u.m.)
  -maturing (u.m.)
latero (c.f.)
  all one word
lath-backed (u.m.)
lathe-bore (v.)
latter
  -day (u.m.)

most
lattice
  #stitch
  work
laughing
  #gas
  stock
launch
  #pad
  site
laundry#room
law
  -abiding (u.m.)
  book
  breaker
  -fettered (u.m.)
  giver
  #office
  suit
lawnmower
lay
  away (n., u.m.)
  back (n., u.m.)
  -by (n.)
  down (n., u.m.)
  -minded (u.m.)
  off (n., u.m.)
  on (n., u.m.)
  out (n., u.m.)
  up (n., u.m.)
layer
  -on
  -out
  -over
  -up
lazy
  bones
  boots
  #guy
  legs
lead
  -alpha
  -burn (v.)

  -filled (u.m.)
  -gray (u.m.)
  -in (n., u.m.)
  line
  #line (medical,
    naut. only)
  off (n., u.m.)
  out (n., u.m.)
  #pencil
  time
leaden
  -eyed (u.m.)
  pated
  -souled (u.m.)
leader#line
leaf
  bud
  -clad (u.m.)
  -eating (u.m.)
  -shaped (u.m.)
  stalk
lean
  -faced (u.m.)
  -looking (u.m.)
  -to (n., u.m.)
leap
  frog
  #year
lease
  back (n., u.m.)
  hold
leased-line
leather
  back
  -backed (u.m.)
  -bound (u.m.)
  -brown (u.m.)
  -covered (u.m.)
  head
  neck
  side
  ware
leavetaking

lee-bow (v.)
leech
  eater
  #rope
left
  -bank (v.)
  #field (sports)
  -hand (u.m.)
  -handed (u.m.)
  -hander
  most
  -sided (u.m.)
  wing (political)
leg
  band
  puller
  rope (v.)
  work
lend-lease (n., u.m.)
length
  ways
  wise
lepto (c.f.)
  all one word
let
  down (n., u.m.)
  off (n., u.m.)
  up (n., u.m.)
letter
  bomb
  #carrier
  drop
  gram
  head
  -perfect (u.m.)
  press
  space
  writer
leuc(o) (c.f.)
  all one word
liberal-minded
  (u.m.)

lieutenant
#colonel
-colonelcy
#governor
-governorship
life
belt
blood
boat
#buoy
#cycle
-cycle (u.m.)
drop
float
giver
giving
guard
hold
jacket
long
#net
raft
ring
saver
-size (u.m.)
-sized (u.m.)
span
spring
stream
style
tide
time
vest
weary (u.m.)
lift-off (n., u.m.)
light
-armed (u.m.)
-clad (u.m.)
-colored (u.m.)
-drab (u.m.)
-draft (u.m.)
face (printing)
-footed (u.m.)

handed
house#keeping
(nautical)
#housekeeping
(domestic)
mouthed
-producing (u.m.)
ship
-struck (u.m.)
weight (n., u.m.)
-year
lighter-than-air
(u.m.)
like
-looking (u.m.)
-minded (u.m.)
lily
handed
-shaped (u.m.)
-white (u.m.)
lime
#juice
kiln
lighter
pit
quat
stone
wash
water
linch
bolt
pin
line
-bred (u.m.)
-breed (v.)
casting
crew
cut (printing)
finder
-item (u.m.)
up (n., u.m.)
walker

link
up (n., u.m.)
#up (v.)
lion
-bold (u.m.)
-headed (u.m.)
hearted
-maned (u.m.)
lip
read
service
stick
listener-in
litho (c.f.)
-offset
rest one word
little
-known (u.m.)
neck (clam)
-used (u.m.)
live
#load
long
stock
#stream
#wire
wire (nonliteral)
liver
-brown (u.m.)
-colored (u.m.)
wurst
living#room
loadmeter
loanword
lob
fig
lolly
lobster-tailed (u.m.)
lock
box
fast
hole
jaw

nut
out (n., u.m.)
pin
ring
step
stitch
up (n., u.m.)
washer
locker#room
lode
star
stone
log
book
in
jam
on
off
roll
sheet
loggerhead
logo (c.f.)
all one word
long
-awaited (u.m.)
beard (n.)
-bearded (u.m.)
-billed (u.m.)
bow
cloth
-distance (u.m.)
-drawn (u.m.)
felt
hair (n.)
-haired (u.m.)
hand (nonliteral)
-handed (u.m.)
-handled (u.m.)
head (n.)
horn (cattle)
-horned (u.m.)
johns
#jump

leaf
-leaved (u.m.)
-legged (u.m.)
legs (n.)
-lived (u.m.)
mouthed
-necked (u.m.)
nose (n.)
-nosed (u.m.)
-past (u.m.)
play (records)
playing (u.m.)
run (u.m.)
shoreman
spun
standing (u.m.)
stitch
#term (n.)
-term (u.m.)
wave (radio)
ways
wool (sheep)
look
down (n., u.m.)
-in (n., u.m.)
out (n., u.m.)
over (n., u.m.)
#over (v.)
through (n., u.m.)
looker-on
loop
hole
#knot
stitch
loose
leaf (u.m.)
mouthed
-tongued (u.m.)
lop
-eared (u.m.)
sided

loud
mouthed
#speaker (orator)
speaker (radio)
-voiced (u.m.)
love
bird
born
-inspired (u.m.)
#knot
lorn
seat
sick
low
born
boy
bred
brow (nonliteral)
browed
(nonliteral)
-built (u.m.)
down (n., u.m.)
-downer
-lander
-lived (u.m.)
-lying (u.m.)
-power (u.m.)
-pressure (u.m.)
rise
#water
lower
case (printing)
#deck
most
lug
bolt
mark
sail
lukewarm
lumber
jack
#room

lumbo (c.f.)
-ovarian
rest one word
lumen-hour
lunch
box
#hour
room
time
lying-in (n., u.m.)

M

M-day
macebearer
machine
-finished (u.m.)
gun
-hour
-made (u.m.)
#shop
#work
macro (c.f.)
all one word
mad
brain
cap
man (n.)
#money
made
-over (u.m.)
-up (u.m.)
magnetite
-basalt
-olivinite
-spinellite
magneto (c.f.)
-optics
rest one word
mahjong
maid
#of#honor
servant

maiden
hair
head
hood
#name
mail
bag
clad
clerk
guard
-order (u.m.)
pouch
room
slot
truck
main
frame
mast
pin
sail
sheet
spring
stay
stream
(nonliteral)
top
topmast
#yard
major
-domo
#league
-leaguer
-minor
make
-believe (n., u.m.)
fast (n.)
over
ready (printing)
shift
up (n., u.m.)
weight
maker
-off

-up
space
making#up
mal (c.f.)
  all one word
man
  back
  -child
  -created (u.m.)
  -day
  eater
  -fashion (u.m.)
  -grown (u.m.)
  handle
  hater
  -high (u.m.)
  hole
  -hour
  killer
  kind
  -made (u.m.)
  -minute
  -of-war (ship)
  power
  servant
  -size (u.m.)
  slaughter
  slayer
  stealer
  stopper
  trap
  -woman
  -year
manic-depressive
manifold
mantel
  piece
  shelf
  tree
many
  -colored (u.m.)
  -folded (u.m.)
  -layered (u.m.)

plies
-sided (u.m.)
mapreader
marble
  head
  -looking (u.m.)
  -topped (u.m.)
  -white (u.m.)
mare's
  -nest
  -tail
mark
  down (n., u.m.)
  off (n., u.m.)
  shot
  up (n., u.m.)
marker
  -down
  -off
  -up
marketplace
marrowbone
marsh
  buck
  mallow
    (confection)
  #mallow (plant)
mass
  -minded (u.m.)
  -produce (v.)
mast
  -brown (u.m.)
  head
master
  #at#arms
  mind
  #of#ceremonies
  piece
  ship
  #stroke
  #workman
mat-covered (u.m.)

match
  book
  head
  -lined (u.m.)
  mark
  safe
  stick
maxi (n.)
maxi (pref.)
  all one word
May
  #Day
  -day (u.m.)
  pole
  tide
may
  be (adv.)
  beetle
  day (distress call)
  hap
mealymouth
mean
  -acting (u.m.)
  -spirited (u.m.)
  time
    (meanwhile)
  #time
    (astronomical)
  tone (u.m.)
  while
meat
  ball
  cutter
  -eater
  -fed (u.m.)
  hook
  -hungry (u.m.)
  packer
  works
  wrapper
mechanico (c.f.)
  all one word

medico (c.f.)
  all one word
medio (c.f.)
  all one word
medium
  -brown (u.m.)
  -size(d) (u.m.)
  weight (n., u.m.)
meek
  -eyed (u.m.)
  hearted
  -spirited (u.m.)
meetingplace
megalo (c.f.)
  all one word
melon
  grower
  -laden (u.m.)
  -shaped (u.m.)
melt
  down (n., u.m.)
  water
men
  folk
  kind
meningo (c.f.)
  all one word
menu-driven
merry
  -go-round
  -meeting
  -minded (u.m.)
meshbag
meso (c.f.)
  all one word
mess
  hall
  kit
  room
  tin
  -up (n., u.m.)
meta (pref.)
  all one word

metal
 ammonium
 -clad (u.m.)
 -coated (u.m.)
 -lined (u.m.)
 works
meter
 -amperes
 -kilogram
 -kilogram-second
metro (c.f.)
 all one word
mezzo
 graph
 relievo
 soprano
 tint
micro (c.f.)
 -organism
 rest one word
mid (c.f.)
 -American, etc.
 -April
 day
 -decade
 -dish
 -ice
 -level
 -1958
 -Pacific, etc.
 -Victorian, etc.
 rest one word
middle
 -aged (u.m.)
 breaker
 brow (nonliteral)
 -burst (v.)
 buster
 #ear
 #ground
 man (nonliteral)
 most
 -of-the-roader

-sized (u.m.)
 splitter
 weight
midi (n.)
midi (pref.)
 all one word
mighty-handed
 (u.m.)
mil-foot
mild
 -cured (u.m.)
 -mannered (u.m.)
 -spoken (u.m.)
mile
 -long (u.m.)
 -ohm
 post
 -pound
 -ton
 -wide (u.m.)
milk
 -fed (u.m.)
 head
 #run
 shake
 shed
 sick
 sop
 -white (u.m.)
mill
 cake
 course
 dam
 feed
 hand
 -headed (u.m.)
 pond
 post
 race
 ring
 stock
 stream
 wright

milli (c.f.)
 gram-hour
 rest one word
mincemeat
mind
 #healer
 -healing (u.m.)
 reader
 set (n.)
 sight
mine
 field
 layer
 ship
 sweeper
 thrower
 works
mini (n.)
mini (pref.)
 all one word
minor
 #league
 -leaguer
minute#book
mirror
 -faced (u.m.)
 scope
mis (pref.)
 all one word
mischiefmaking
mist
 bow
 -clad (u.m.)
 -covered (u.m.)
 fall
miter
 #box
 -lock (v.)
mix
 blood
 up (n.)
mixing#room
mizzenmast

mock
 -heroic (u.m.)
 #turtle
 up (n., u.m.)
mocker-up
mocking
 stock
 -up (u.m.)
mold
 made (u.m.)
 #shop
mole
 catcher
 -eyed (u.m.)
 head
 hill
money
 bag
 changer
 getter
 grubber
 lender
 -mad (u.m.)
 maker
 saver
monkey
 -faced (u.m.)
 nut
 pod
 pot
 shine
 #wrench
mono (c.f.)
 -ideistic
 -iodo
 -iodohydrin
 -ion
 -ousian
 rest one word
month
 end
 long (u.m.)

moon
  beam
  blind
  #blindness
  blink
  born
  -bright (u.m.)
  eye
  face
  gazing
  glow
  head
  lighter
  lit
  -mad (u.m.)
  path
  rise
  sail
  set
  shade
  shine
  shot
  sick
  struck
  tide
  walker
  -white (u.m.)
moosecall
mop
  head
  stick
  up (n., u.m.)
mopper-up
mopping-up (u.m.)
morning
  #sickness
  #star
  tide
mosquito
  -free (u.m.)
  #net
moss
  back

  -clad (u.m.)
  -green (u.m.)
  -grown (u.m.)
  head
  -lined (u.m.)
  most-favored-nation
    (u.m.)
moth
  ball
  -eaten (u.m.)
  hole
  proof
mother
  board
  hood
  -in-law
  -of-pearl
moto (c.f.)
  all one word
motor
  bike
  bus
  cab
  cade
  car
  coach
  cycle
  -driven (u.m.)
  jet
  -minded (u.m.)
  #scooter
  ship
  truck
  van
moundbuilder
mountain
  -high (u.m.)
  side
  top
  -walled (u.m.)
mouse
  -brown (u.m.)
  -eared (u.m.)

  -eaten (u.m.)
  hole
  trap
mouth
  -filling (u.m.)
  -made (u.m.)
  piece
  wash
muck
  rake (v.)
  raker
  sweat
muco (c.f.)
  all one word
mud
  bank
  bath
  -colored (u.m.)
  flat
  flow
  guard
  head
  hole
  lark
  sill
  slinger
  -splashed (u.m.)
  stain
  sucker
  track
  #turtle
mule
  back
  #deer
  skinner
multi (c.f.)
  all one word
multiple-purpose
    (u.m.)
muscle
  bound
  power

music
  lover
  -mad (u.m.)
  maker
  room
musico (c.f.)
  all one word
musk
  #deer
  melon
  #ox
  rat
mutton
  #chop (meat)
  chop (shape)
  fist
  head
myria (c.f.)
  all one word
mytho (c.f.)
  all one word
myxo (c.f.)
  all one word

N
nail
  bin
  brush
  head
  -headed (u.m.)
  #hole
  print
  puller
  rod
  -shaped (u.m.)
  -studded (u.m.)
name
  -calling (u.m.)
  -dropping (u.m.)
  plate
  sake
nano (c.f.)
  all one word

naptime
narco (c.f.)
all one word
narrow
-mouthed (u.m.)
minded
naso (c.f.)
-occipital
-orbital
rest one word
nationwide
native-born (u.m.)
navy-blue (u.m.)
naysayer
near
by
-miss
sighted
neat's-foot (u.m.)
neck
band
bone
-breaking (u.m.)
cloth
-deep (u.m.)
fast
guard
-high (u.m.)
hole
lace
line
mold
tie
necro (c.f.)
all one word
needle
bill
case
-made (u.m.)
nose (pliers)
point
-shaped (u.m.)
-sharp (u.m.)

worked
ne'er-do-well
neo (c.f.)
-Greek, etc.
rest one word
nephro (c.f.)
all one word
nerve
ache
-celled (u.m.)
-racked (u.m.)
net
ball
braider
-veined (u.m.)
work
#worth
nettle
fire
foot
some
neuro (c.f.)
all one word
never
-ending (u.m.)
more
theless
new
born
-car (u.m.)
comer
-created (u.m.)
fangled
-fashioned (u.m.)
-front (v.)
-made (u.m.)
-mown (u.m.)
-rich (u.m.)
newlywed
news
boy
case
cast

clip
dealer
#editor
letter
#media
paper
paper#work
photo
print
reader
reel
sheet
stand
story
teller
nick
-eared (u.m.)
name
nickel
plate (v.)
-plated (u.m.)
-plating (u.m.)
type
night
-black (u.m.)
#blindness
cap
-clad (u.m.)
clothes
club
dress
fall
-fly (aviation) (v.)
-flying (u.m.)
gown
-grown (u.m.)
hawk
long (u.m.)
mare
#school
shade
#shift
shirt

side
tide
walker
nimble
-fingered (u.m.)
footed
nimbostratus
(clouds)
nine
fold
#holes
-lived (u.m.)
pin
score
nitpicker
nitro (c.f.)
-hydro-carbon
rest one word
no
-account (n., u.m.)
-fault
-fee
-good (n., u.m.)
-hitter (n.)
how
#man's land
#one
-par (u.m.)
-par-value (u.m.)
-show (n., u.m.)
-thoroughfare (n.)
whit
-year (funds)
noble
-born (u.m.)
-featured (u.m.)
heartedness
-looking (u.m.)
-minded (u.m.)
nol-pros (v.)
non
-civil-service (u.m.)

-European, etc.
interactive
-pros (v.)
#sequitur, etc.
-tumor-bearing
(u.m.)
*as prefix, one
word*
none
such
theless
noon
day
tide
time
north
-central (u.m.)
east
going
most
-northeast
-sider
nose
bag
bleed
bone
dive
down (n., u.m.)
gay
guard
-high (u.m.)
hole
-led (u.m.)
over (n., u.m.)
pipe
ring
-thumbing (u.m.)
up (n., u.m.)
wheel
note
book
#paper
worthy

notwithstanding
novel
-reading (u.m.)
#writer
-writing (u.m.)
nucleo (c.f.)
all one word
nut
breaker
-brown (u.m.)
cake
cracker
hatch
hook
pecker
pick
-shaped (u.m.)
shell
sweet

O

oak
-beamed (u.m.)
-clad (u.m.)
-green (u.m.)
#leaf
-leaved (u.m.)
oar
-footed (u.m.)
lock
oarsman
oat
bin
cake
-fed (u.m.)
meal
seed
oathbreaker
object-oriented
oblong
-elliptic (u.m.)
-leaved (u.m.)
-linear (u.m.)

-ovate (u.m.)
-shaped (u.m.)
-triangular (u.m.)
occipito (c.f.)
-otic
rest one word
ocean
-born (u.m.)
borne
-girdled (u.m.)
going
side
-spanning (u.m.)
octo (c.f.)
all one word
odd
-jobber
-job man
-looking (u.m.)
man (arbiter)
-numbered (u.m.)
off
-and-on (u.m.)
beat
cast
center (u.m.)
color (u.m.)
-colored (u.m.)
cut (printing)
day
-fall (v.)
-flavor (n., u.m.)
-flow
-go (n.)
going
grade
hand
-hours
line
loading
look
-lying (u.m.)
peak

print
put
-reckoning (n.)
saddle
scape
scour
scum
-season
set
shoot
shore
side
site
-sorts (n.)
spring
stage
street
take
-the-record (u.m.)
type
-wheel (n.)
-wheeler (n.)
-white (u.m.)
#year
office
#boy
holder
seeker
-seeking (u.m.)
oftentimes
ofttimes
ohm
-ammeter
meter
-mile
oil
#burner
cake
can
cloth
coat
cup
-driven (u.m.)

-fed (u.m.)
field
-forming (u.m.)
-harden (v.)
hole
meal
paper
proofing
seed
#shale
skinned
-soaked (u.m.)
spill (n.)
stove
-temper (v.)
tightness
#well

old
-fashioned (u.m.)
-fogy (u.m.)
-growing (u.m.)
-looking (u.m.)
#maid
-maidish (u.m.)
#man
-new
style (printing)
timer
#woman
-young

oleo
#gear
margarine
#oil
#strut
as combining
form, one word

olive
-brown (u.m.)
-clad (u.m.)
-drab (u.m.)
-growing (u.m.)
#oil

-skinned (u.m.)
wood
#wood (color)

omni (c.f.)
all one word

on
-and-off (n., u.m.)
board (u.m.)
-go (n.)
going
line#service
site
noun, adjective,
one word

once
-over (n.)
-run (u.m.)

one
-armed (u.m.)
-decker
-eyed (u.m.)
fold
-half
-handed (u.m.)
ness
-piece (u.m.)
self
-sided (u.m.)
-sidedness
signed (u.m.)
-step (dance)
-striper
time (formerly)
(u.m.)
-time (one action)
(u.m.)
-two-three
-way (u.m.)

onion
peel
skin
op-ed
(newspaper)

open
-air (u.m.)
-armed (u.m.)
-back (u.m.)
-backed (u.m.)
band (yarn)
cast
cut (mining)
-end (u.m.)
-ended
-faced (u.m.)
handed
#house
minded
mouthed
#shop
side (u.m.)
-sided (u.m.)
worked

opera
goer
going
#house
operating#system

ophthalmo (c.f.)
all one word

orange
ade
colored (u.m.)
peel
-red (u.m.)
stick
orchard#house
orderly#room

organo (c.f.)
all one word

ornitho (c.f.)
all one word
orrisroot

ortho (c.f.)
all one word

osteo (c.f.)
all one word

other
wise
#world
worldly

oto (c.f.)
all one word

out
-and-out (u.m.)
-and-outer (n.)
-loud (u.m.)
-Machiavelli, etc.
migration
-of-date (u.m.)
-of-door(s) (u.m.)
-of-State (u.m.)
-of-the-way (u.m.)
placement
-to-out (u.m.)
as prefix, one
word

outer
-city (u.m.)
#man
most
wear

outward
-bound (u.m.)
-bounder

ovate
-acuminate (u.m.)
-oblong (u.m.)

ovato (c.f.)
-oblong
-orbicular
rest one word

oven
baked
dried
peel
ware

over
age (surplus)

age (older) (n.,
  u.m.)
all (n., u.m.)
-the-counter
  (u.m.)
  as combining
  form, one word
owl-eyed (u.m.)
ox
  biter
  blood (color)
  bow
  brake
  cart
  cheek
  eye
  -eyed (u.m.)
  gall
  harrow
  hide
  horn
  shoe
  tail
  #team
oxy (c.f.)
  all one word
oyster
  bed
  #crab
  house
  root
  seed
  shell
  -white (u.m.)

P
pace
  maker
  #setter
  -setting (u.m.)
pachy (c.f.)
  all one word
pack
  builder

cloth
horse
-laden (u.m.)
sack
saddle
staff
thread
up (n., u.m.)
packing#box
padlock
paddlefoot
page
  -for-page (u.m.)
  #proof (printing)
painkiller
painstaking
paint
  box
  brush
  mixer
  pot
  spray
  stained (u.m.)
pale
  belly
  -blue (u.m.)
  buck
  -cheeked (u.m.)
  -faced (u.m.)
  -looking (u.m.)
  -reddish (u.m.)
paleo (c.f.)
  -Christian, etc.
  rest one word
pallbearer
palm
  -green (u.m.)
  #leaf
  #oil
  -shaded (u.m.)
palmi (c.f.)
  all one word

pan
  -American, etc.
  -broil (v.)
  #ice
  rest one word
Pan
  #American Union
  hellenic
panel-lined (u.m.)
panic-stricken
  (u.m.)
panto (c.f.)
  all one word
panty hose
paper
  back (n.)
  #box
  #carrier
  cutter
  hanger
  shell (n., u.m.)
  -shelled (u.m.)
  -thin (u.m.)
  weight
  -white (u.m.)
papier#mache
para (c.f. or pref.)
  -analgesia
  -anesthesia
  legal
  medic
  rest one word
parcel
  #carrier
  -plate (v.)
  #post
parchment
  -covered (u.m.)
  #maker
  -making (u.m.)
parieto (c.f.)
  -occipital
  rest one word

parimutuel
park
  #forest
  land
  way
part
  -finished (u.m.)
  #owner
  -time (u.m.)
  -timer (n.)
  #way
parti (c.f.)
  all one word
party#line
parvi (c.f.)
  all one word
pass
  back (n.)
  book
  key
  out (n., u.m.)
  port
  through (n.,
    u.m.)
  way
  word
passenger-mile
passer(s)-by
passion
  -driven (u.m.)
  -feeding (u.m.)
  -filled (u.m.)
  #play
paste
  down (n., u.m.)
  pot
  up (n., u.m.)
pastureland
patent-in-fee
path
  breaker
  finder
  way

patho (c.f.)
all one word
patri (c.f.)
all one word
patrol
man
#wagon
pattycake
pawn
broker
shop
pay
back (n., u.m.)
check
#cut
day
dirt
load
off (n., u.m.)
out (n., u.m.)
#raise
roll
sheet
-TV
pea
#coal
coat
cod
-green (u.m.)
hen
jacket
nut
pod
shooter
-sized (u.m.)
stick
peace
-blessed (u.m.)
breaker
-loving (u.m.)
maker
#pipe
time

peach
bloom
blow (color)
-colored (u.m.)
pear-shaped (u.m.)
pearl
-eyed (u.m.)
fishing
-pure (u.m.)
-set (u.m.)
-studded (u.m.)
-white (u.m.)
peat
-roofed (u.m.)
moss
stack
pebble
-paved (u.m.)
-strewn (u.m.)
peeloff (n., u.m.)
peep
eye
hole
show
sight
peer-to-peer
pegleg
pellmell
pen
-cancel (v.)
head
knife
manship
#name
point
pusher
rack
script
-shaped (u.m.)
stock
trough
pencil
#box

holder
-mark (v.)
penny
-a-liner
pincher
weight
winkle
worth
pent-up (u.m.)
penta (c.f.)
-acetate
rest one word
pepper
corn
#jelly
mint
pot
-red (u.m.)
peptalk
per
#annum
cent
#centum
compound
(chemical)
current
(botanical)
#diem
salt (chemical)
#se
sulfide
peri (pref.)
-insular
rest one word
permafrost
pest
hole
-ridden (u.m.)
petcock
petit
grain
#jury
#larceny

#point
petro (c.f.)
-occipital
rest one word
pharmaco (c.f.)
-oryctology
rest one word
pharyngo (c.f.)
-esophageal
-oral
rest one word
phase
-in (n., u.m.)
meter
out (n., u.m.)
-wound (u.m.)
pheno (c.f.)
all one word
philo (c.f.)
-French, etc.
rest one word
phlebo (c.f.)
all one word
phonebook
phono (c.f.)
all one word
phospho (c.f.)
all one word
photo (c.f.)
-offset
-oxidation
-oxidative
rest one word
phrasemark (music)
phreno (c.f.)
all one word .
phyllo (c.f.)
all one word
phylo (c.f.)
all one word
physico (c.f.)
all one word

physio (c.f.)
  all one word
phyto (c.f.)
  all one word
piano
  forte
  graph
  #player
pick
  aback
  ax
  lock
  -me-up (n., u.m.)
  off (n., u.m.)
  over (n., u.m.)
  #over (v.)
  pocket
  pole
  shaft
  up (n., u.m.)
picker-up
picket#line
pickle-cured (u.m.)
picture
  #book
  #writing
pie
  bald
  crust
  -eater
  -eyed
  marker
  pan
  plant
  #plate
  -stuffed (u.m.)
  #tin
piece
  -dye (v.)
  #goods
  meal
  mold

piezo (c.f.)
  -oscillator
  rest one word
pig
  -back (v.)
  -backed (u.m.)
  -bellied (u.m.)
  belly
  -eyed (u.m.)
  face
  -faced (u.m.)
  foot
  -footed (u.m.)
  headed
  herd
  #iron
  out
  pen
  root
  stick
  sty
  tailed
  wash
pigeon
  gram
  hole
  -toed (u.m.)
  wing
piggyback
pike
  -eyed (u.m.)
  staff
pile
  driver
  -driving (u.m.)
  hammer
  up (n., u.m.)
  #weave
  woven
pill
  pusher
  rolling
  taker

pillow
  case
  made
  slip
  top
pilot
  #boat
  house
  #light
pin
  ball
  block
  bone
  case
  cushion
  -eyed (u.m.)
  fall
  feather
  fire
  fold
  head
  hold
  hole
  hook
  lock
  paper
  point
  prick
  rail
  setter
  spot
  stripe
  -tailed (u.m.)
  up (n., u.m.)
  wheel
pinch
  back
  bar
  beck
  cock
  fist
  -hit (v.)
  -hitter

  penny
pine
  apple
  -bearing (u.m.)
  -clad (u.m.)
  #cone
  -fringed (u.m.)
  #needle
  #oil
  -shaded (u.m.)
  #tar
pink
  -blossomed (u.m.)
  eye (n.)
  -eyed (u.m.)
pipe
  -drawn (u.m.)
  dream
  fitter
  layer
  line
  -shaped (u.m.)
  stem
  walker
  welder
pisci (c.f.)
  all one word
pistol-whipped (v.)
piston
  head
  #pin
  #rod
  #valve
pit
  #boss
  #bull
  -eyed (u.m.)
  fall
  head
  -headed (u.m.)
  hole
  mark
  -marked (u.m.)

-rotted (u.m.)
saw
side
pitch
-black (u.m.)
blende
#box
-colored (u.m.)
-dark (u.m.)
#darkness
fork
hole
-lined (u.m.)
man
-marked (u.m.)
out (n., u.m.)
#pipe
up (n., u.m.)
place
card
kick
plague-infested
(u.m.)
plain
back (fabric)
-bodied (u.m.)
clothes (u.m.)
clothesman
-headed (u.m.)
-looking (u.m.)
-spoken (u.m.)
woven (u.m.)
plane
#curve
load
-mile
-parallel (u.m.)
table (surveying)
plani (c.f.)
all one word
plano (c.f.)
all one word

plant
#food
life
site
plasterboard
plate
cutter
#glass
-incased (u.m.)
layer
mark
#proof (printing)
-roll (v.)
-rolled (u.m.)
platy (c.f.)
all one word
play
-act (v.)
back (n., u.m.)
bill
book
boy
broker
day
down (n., u.m.)
fellow
goer
going
ground
mate
off (n., u.m.)
pen
reader
room
script
suit
thing
time
wright
#yard
pleasure
-bent (u.m.)
#boat

-seeking (u.m.)
-tired (u.m.)
-weary (u.m.)
pleo (c.f.)
all one word
pleuro (c.f.)
all one word
plow
back (n., u.m.)
-bred (u.m.)
hand
horse
pan
point
-shaped (u.m.)
share
shoe
sole
staff
#tail
wright
plug
-and-play
hole
-in (n., u.m.)
tray
plumbline
plume-crowned
(u.m.)
pluri (c.f.)
all one word
pluto (c.f.)
all one word
pneumato (c.f.)
-hydato-genetic
(u.m.)
rest one word
pneumo (c.f.)
all one word
pock
mark
-marked (u.m.)
-pit (v.)

pocket
book (purse)
#book (book)
-eyed (u.m.)
knife
-sized (u.m.)
-veto (v.)
poet
-artist
#laureate
-painter
pointblank
Point-to-Point
poison-dipped
(u.m.)
pole
arm
-armed (u.m.)
ax
burn
cat
-dried (u.m.)
horse
-pile (v.)
setter
-shaped (u.m.)
sitter
-stack (v.)
star
timber
trap
-vault (v.)
#vaulter
policy
maker
making
politico (c.f.)
-orthodox
rest one word
poll
book
#parrot
#tax

poly (c.f.)
  all one word
poor
  -blooded (u.m.)
  farm
  -spirited (u.m.)
pop
  corn
  eye
  gun
  up (n., u.m.)
poppy
  -bordered (u.m.)
  cock
  -red (u.m.)
  seed
pork
  barrel (n., u.m.)
  #chop
  fish
  #pie
port
  cullis
  fire
  folio
  hole
  hook
  manteau
  -mouthed (u.m.)
  side
  #wine
post
  #bellum
  #boat
  card
  -Christian, etc.
  -cold-war (u.m.)
  #diem
  -free (u.m.)
  haste
  #hospital
    (military)
  #meridiem

#mortem (literal)
  mortem
    (nonliteral)
#partum
#school (military)
  traumatic
  -traumatic
    (PTSD)
  audit, graduate,
    etc.
  as prefix, one
    word
postal#card
pot
  ash
  bellied
  boil
  eye
  hanger
  herb
  hole
  hook
  hunter
  latch
  lid
  luck
  pie
  pourri
  rack
  #roast
  shot
potato#field
poultry
  #keeper
  -keeping (u.m.)
  #raiser
  -raising (u.m.)
  #yard
pound
  cake
  -foolish (u.m.)
  -foot
  worth

powder
  -blue (u.m.)
  box
  #house
  #keg
  #mill
  #room
  -scorched (u.m.)
power
  boat
  #mower
  -operated (u.m.)
  pack
  plant
praise
  -deserving (u.m.)
  -spoiled (u.m.)
  worthiness
pre (pref.)
  -Incan, etc.
  audit, existing,
    etc.
  rest one word
president
  -elect
  #pro#tempore
press
  #agent
  -agentry
  board
  feeder
  -forge (v.)
  -made (u.m.)
  mark
  pack (v.)
  plate
  #proof (printing)
preter (pref.)
  all one word
price
  #cutter
  -cutting (u.m.)
  #fixer

  -fixing (u.m.)
  #index
  list
  -support (u.m.)
  tag
prick
  -eared (u.m.)
  mark
  seam
priesthood
prime
  #minister
  -ministerial
    (u.m.)
  -ministership
  -ministry
prince
  hood
  -priest
print
  cloth
  out
  script
printing
  -in (n., u.m.)
  #ink
  #office
  -out (n., u.m.)
prison
  bound
  -free (u.m.)
  -made (u.m.)
prisoner-of-war
  (u.m.)
prize
  fighter
  #ring
  taker
  winner
  -winning (u.m.)
pro
  -Ally, etc.
  -choice

#football, etc.
#forma
-life
#rata
#tem
#tempore
as prefix, one word
problem-solver
procto (c.f.)
all one word
profit
-and-loss (u.m.)
-sharing (u.m.)
prong
buck
-hoe (v.)
horn
-horned (u.m.)
proof
#press
read
reader
room
sheet
prop
jet
wash
proso (c.f.)
all one word
proto (c.f.)
-Egyptian, etc.
rest one word
proud
hearted
-looking (u.m.)
-minded (u.m.)
psalmbook
pseudo (c.f.)
-Messiah, etc.
-occidental
-official
-orthorhombic

-osteomalacia
-owner
rest one word
psycho (c.f.)
-organic
rest one word
ptero (c.f.)
all one word
public
hearted
-minded (u.m.)
-spirited (u.m.)
#works
pug
nose
-pile (v.)
pull
back (n., u.m.)
#box
down (n., u.m.)
-in (n., u.m.)
off (n., u.m.)
-on (n., u.m.)
out (n., u.m.)
-push (u.m.)
through (n., u.m.)
up (n., u.m.)
puller
-in
-out
pulp
board
wood
punch
board
bowl
card
-drunk (u.m.)
mark
-marked (u.m.)
out (n.)

punctureproof
pup#tent
pure
blood
bred
#line (biological)
purple
-blue (u.m.)
-clad (u.m.)
-colored (u.m.)
heart (wood)
purse
making
-proud (u.m.)
#strings
push
button
card
cart
off (n., u.m.)
-pull (u.m.)
up (n., u.m.)
pussy
cat
foot
#willow
put
back (n., u.m.)
off (n., u.m.)
-on (n., u.m.)
out (n., u.m.)
-put (n.)
-up (n., u.m.)
putter
-forth
-in
-off
-on
-out
-through
-up

pyo (c.f.)
all one word
pyro (c.f.)
all one word
Q
Q
-boat
-fever
quadri (c.f.)
-invariant
rest one word
quarrystone
quarter
-angled (u.m.)
back
-bloom (u.m.)
#boards
-bound (u.m.)
-breed (u.m.)
-cast (u.m.)
-cut (u.m.)
deck
-miler
#note
pace
-phase (u.m.)
saw (v.)
staff
stretch
-yearly (u.m.)
quartermaster
#general
-generalship
quasi
all hyphened
queen#bee
quick
-change (u.m., v.)
-drawn (u.m., v.)
freeze (u.m., v.)
lime
sand

set
silver
step
#time
-witted (u.m.)
quin (c.f.)
   all one word
quit
   claim
   rent

R

rabbit
   -backed (u.m.)
   -eared (u.m.)
   #fever
   #foot
   skin
race
   about (n., u.m.)
   course
   goer
   horse
   track
   way
radarscope
radio
   generally two
   words except
   the following
   forms
   frequency
   isotope
   telegraph
   telephone
rag
   bolt
   #doll
   -made (u.m.)
   sorter
   tag
   time

rail
   bird
   car
   guard
   head
   -ridden (u.m.)
   road
   setter
   splitter
   #train
   way#maker
   wayman
rain
   band
   -beaten (u.m.)
   bow
   check
   coat
   drop
   fall
   #forest
   -soft (u.m.)
   spout
   storm
   wash
   water
rakeoff (n., u.m.)
ram
   jet
   rod
   shackle
ranch
   #hand
   house
random-access
   (u.m.)
range
   finder
   #light
   rider
rapid
   #fire
   #transit

rat
   bite
   catcher
   hole
   -infested (u.m.)
   #race
   -tailed (u.m.)
   -tight (u.m.)
   trap
rate
   #cutter
   -cutting (u.m.)
   -fixing (u.m.)
   payer
   -raising (u.m.)
   setting
rattle
   brain
   snake
   trap
raw
   boned
   -edged (u.m.)
   hide
   -looking (u.m.)
razor
   back
   -billed (u.m.)
   #blade
   edge
   -keen (u.m.)
   -sharp (u.m.)
   strop
razzle-dazzle
re (pref.)
   -cover (cover
      again)
   -create (create
      again), etc.
   -cross-
      examination
   -ice
   -ink

   -redirect
   evaluate, process,
      etc.
   rest one word
reading#room
read
   out (n.)
   through (n., u.m.)
real
   time (n.)
   -time (u.m.)
ready
   -built (u.m.)
   -handed (u.m.)
   made (u.m.)
   -mix (u.m.)
   #reference
   room
   -witted (u.m.)
rear
   #end
   guard
   most
   view (u.m.)
   ward
reception#room
recordbreaker
recti (c.f.)
   all one word
recto (c.f.)
   all one word
red
   bait (v.)
   -billed (u.m.)
   -blooded (u.m.)
   buck
   cap (porter)
   coat (n.)
   eye (n.)
   -eyed (u.m.)
   -faced (u.m.)
   -haired (u.m.)
   handed

head (n.)
-hot (u.m.)
-legged (u.m.)
#line (literal)
out (n., u.m.)
-skinned (u.m.)
tape (nonliteral)
#tape (literal)
-throated (u.m.)
-yellow (u.m.)
reformat
regionwide
religio (c.f.)
   all one word
remote-access
repair#shop
representative
   #at#large
   -elect
research#worker
resino (c.f.)
   all one word
retro (c.f.)
   -ocular
   -omental
   -operative
   -oral
   rest one word
rheo (c.f.)
   all one word
rhino (c.f.)
   all one word
rhizo (c.f.)
   all one word
rhod(o) (c.f.)
   all one word
rhomb(o) (c.f.)
   all one word
rice
   growing
   #water
rich
   -bound (u.m.)

-clad (u.m.)
-looking (u.m.)
rickrack
ridge
   band
   pole
   top
riffraff
rifleshot
rig
   out (n., u.m.)
   -up (n., u.m.)
right
   about
   about-face
   -angle (u.m., v.)
   -angled (u.m.)
   #away
   #field (sports)
   -handed (u.m.)
   -hander
   -headed (u.m.)
   most
   -of-way
   wing (political)
rim
   -deep (u.m.)
   fire
   lock
   rock
ring
   -adorned (u.m.)
   -banded (u.m.)
   -billed (u.m.)
   bolt
   giver
   head
   -in (n., u.m.)
   lead (v.)
   leader
   -necked (u.m.)
   -off (n., u.m.)
   pin

-porous (u.m.)
-shaped (u.m.)
side
sight
stand
stick
-tailed (u.m.)
-up (n., u.m.)
worm
rip
   cord
   -off (n., u.m.)
   rap
   roaring
   sack
   saw
   snorter
   tide
   -up (n., u.m.)
river
   bank
   bed
   #bottom
   flow
   -formed (u.m.)
   front
   head
   scape
   side
   wash
   -worn (u.m.)
road
   bank
   bed
   block
   builder
   head
   hog
   kill
   map
   #runner (bird)
   #show
   side

-test (v.)
way
-weary (u.m.)
rock
   abye
   bottom
    (nonliteral)
   #climber
   -climbing (u.m.)
   fall (n.)
   -fallen (u.m.)
   fill
   firm
   pile
   -ribbed (u.m.)
   #salt
   shaft
   slide
rod-shaped (u.m.)
roe
   buck
   #deer
roentgeno (c.f.)
   all one word
roll
   about (n., u.m.)
   back (n., u.m.)
   call
   -fed (v.)
   film
   off (n., u.m.)
   -on (n., u.m.)
   out (n., u.m.)
   over (n., u.m.)
   top
   up (n., u.m.)
roller
   #blade
   #coaster
   -made (u.m.)
   -milled (u.m.)
   #skate

Romano (c.f.)
  -canonical, etc.
  -Gallic, etc.
roof
  garden
  line
  top
  tree
room
  #clerk
  keeper
  mate
  roominghouse
root
  bound
  cap
  -cutting (u.m.)
  fast
  hold
  #mean#square
  #rot
  stalk
  stock
rope
  dance
  layer
  stitch
  walk
rose
  -bright (u.m.)
  bud
  bush
  head
  -headed (u.m.)
  -scented (u.m.)
  -sweet (u.m.)
  tan
  #water
rotor
  craft
  ship
rotten
  -dry (u.m.)

-minded (u.m.)
rough
  -and-ready (u.m.)
  -and-tumble (n., u.m.)
  cast (u.m., v.)
  -coat (v.)
  -cut (u.m.)
  draw (v.)
  dress (v.)
  dry (u.m., v.)
  -face (v.)
  -faced (u.m.)
  hew
  house
  -legged (u.m.)
  -looking (u.m.)
  neck
  rider
  setter
  shod
  -sketch (v.)
  stuff
  tailed
  #work (n.)
  work (v.)
  wrought
rougher
  -down
  -out
  -up
  roughing-in (u.m.)
round
  about (n., u.m.)
  about-face
  -faced (u.m.)
  head
  -made (u.m.)
  mouthed
  nose (tool)
  out (n., u.m.)
  robin (petition)
  seam

table (panel)
  -tailed (u.m.)
  -topped (u.m.)
  #trip
  -tripper
  up (n., u.m.)
rub
  -a-dub
  down (n., u.m.)
rubber
  band
  -down
  -lined (u.m.)
  neck
  -off
  -set (u.m.)
  stamp (nonliteral) (n., u.m., v.)
  #stamp (n.)
  -stamped (u.m.)
ruby
  -hued (u.m.)
  -red (u.m.)
  -set (u.m.)
  -throated (u.m.)
rudder
  head
  hole
  post
  stock
  rule#of#thumb
rum
  -crazed (u.m.)
  runner
  seller
  rumpus#room
run
  about (n., u.m.)
  around (n., u.m.)
  away (n., u.m.)
  back (n., u.m.)
  by (n.)

down (n., u.m.)
  -in (n., u.m.)
  off (n., u.m.)
  -on (n., u.m.)
  out (n., u.m.)
  over (n., u.m.)
  through (n., u.m.)
  up (n., u.m.)
  runner-up
Russo (c.f.)
  -Chinese, etc.
  rest one word
rust
  -brown (u.m.)
  -eaten (u.m.)
  proofing
  -resistant (u.m.)
  -stained (u.m.)
  rye#field

S

S
  -bend
  -brake
  -iron
  -ray
  -shaped
  -trap
  -wrench
saber
  -legged (u.m.)
  tooth
  -toothed (u.m.)
  sable-cloaked (u.m.)
  Sabrejet
saccharo (c.f.)
  all one word
sack
  bearer
  cloth
  #coat
  -coated (u.m.)
  -making (u.m.)

-shaped (u.m.)
sacro (c.f.)
all one word
sad
-eyed (u.m.)
iron
#sack
-voiced (u.m.)
saddle
back
-backed (u.m.)
bag
bow
cloth
-graft (v.)
#horse
-making (u.m.)
nose
-nosed (u.m.)
sore
-stitched (u.m.)
tree
-wire (u.m.)
safe
blower
cracker
-deposit (u.m.)
guard
hold
#house
#site
sage
brush
leaf
-leaved (u.m.)
sail
cloth
-dotted (u.m.)
flying
saintlike
sales
book
clerk

manship
people
person
salmon
-colored (u.m.)
-red (u.m.)
salpingo (c.f.)
-oophorectomy
-oophoritis
-ovariotomy
-ovaritis
rest one word
salt
box
cellar
-cured (u.m.)
#lick
mouth
pack
pan
peter
pit
pond
shaker
spoon
sprinkler
water
works
salver
form
-shaped (u.m.)
same-sex (u.m.)
sample
#book
#box
maker
-making (u.m.)
sand
bag
bank
bar
bath
bin

blast
blown
box
-built (u.m.)
-buried (u.m.)
-cast (u.m., v.)
culture
#dune
fill
flea
glass
heat
hill
-hiller
hog
hole
lapper
lot
paper
pile
pipe
pit
-pump (u.m., v.)
shoe
spit
storm
table
weld (v.)
-welded (u.m.)
-welding (u.m.)
sandy-bottomed
(u.m.)
sangfroid
sans
#serif
#souci
sapphire
-blue (u.m.)
-colored (u.m.)
sarco (c.f.)
all one word
sashcord

satin
#cloth
-lined (u.m.)
-smooth (u.m.)
sauce
dish
pan
sauer
braten
kraut
save-all (n., u.m.)
saw
back
belly
bill (bird)
-billed (u.m.)
bones (n.)
buck
dust
-edged (u.m.)
horse
setter
timber
tooth
-toothed (u.m.)
sax
cornet
horn
tuba
say
-nothing (n., u.m.)
-so (n.)
scale
bark
down (n., u.m.)
pan
-reading (u.m.)
scapegoat
scapulo (c.f.)
all one word
scar
-clad (u.m.)
face

-faced (u.m.)
#tissue
scare
  crow
  head
scarfpin
scarlet
  -breasted (u.m.)
  #fever
  -red (u.m.)
scatter
  brain
  good
  #rug
scene
  shifter
  wright
schisto (c.f.)
  all one word
schizo (c.f.)
  all one word
school
  bag
  #board
  book
  bus
  children
  day
  -made (u.m.)
  mate
  ship
  teacher
  -trained (u.m.)
  #year
scientifico (c.f.)
  all one word
scissor
  bill
  -tailed (u.m.)
  -winged (u.m.)
scissors
  hold
  -shaped (u.m.)

#smith
sclero (c.f.)
  -oophoritis
  -optic
  rest one word
score
  board
  book
  card
  sheet
scot-free
Scoto (c.f.)
  -Britannic, etc.
Scotsman
scout
  #badge
  #car
  hood
  master
scrap
  basket
  book
  #paper
  works
scratch
  brush
  -brusher
  -coated (u.m.)
  #pad
  #test
screen
  out (n., u.m.)
  play
screw
  ball
  bolt
  cap
  down (u.m.)
  drive (v.)
  -driven (u.m.)
  driver
  head
  hook

jack
-lifted (u.m.)
nut
ship
#thread
-threaded (u.m.)
-turned (u.m.)
scroll
  -back
  head
  work
scuttlebutt
scythe-shaped
  (u.m.)
sea
  #base
  -based (u.m.)
  -bathed (u.m.)
  beach
  -beaten (u.m.)
  bed
  #bird
  -blue (u.m.)
  board
  #boat
  -born (u.m.)
  borne
  bound
  -bred (u.m.)
  coast
  -deep (u.m.)
  dog
  -driven (u.m.)
  drome
  -encircled (u.m.)
  fare (food)
  fighter
  #floor
  folk
  food
  front
  girt
  goer

going
hound
lane
#level
lift
#lion
mark
port
quake
#room
scape
#scout
scouting
shell
shine
shore
sick
side
stroke
#time (clock)
wall
weed
wing
worn
worthiness
-wrecked (u.m.)
seam
  blasting
  rend (v.)
  stitch
  weld (v.)
  -welded (u.m.)
search
  #engine
  light
  plane
seat
  belt
  #cover
  -mile
second
  -class (u.m.)
  -degree (u.m.)

-foot
-guess (v.)
hand (adv., u.m.)
#hand (n.)
#in#command
-rate (u.m.)
#sight
-sighted (u.m.)
Secret Service
secretary
#general
-generalcy
-generalship
section#man
seed
bed
cake
case
coat
kin
stalk
seer
band
hand
sucker
seesaw
seismo (c.f.)
all one word
self
dom
-extracting
hood
less
ness
same
reflexive prefix,
use hyphen
sell
off (n., u.m.)
out (n., u.m.)
semi (pref.)
-armor-piercing
(u.m.)

-Christian, etc.
-idleness
-indirect, etc.
annual, arid, etc.
rest one word
send
off (n., u.m.)
out (n., u.m.)
senso (c.f.)
all one word
septi (c.f.)
all one word
septo (c.f.)
all one word
sergeant#at#arms
serio (c.f.)
all one word
sero (c.f.)
all one word
serrate
-ciliate (u.m.)
-dentate (u.m.)
server-based
service
-connected (u.m.)
man
#man#and
#woman
member
person
wide
woman
servo
accelerometer
amplifier
control
mechanism
motor
system
sesqui (c.f.)
all one word
set
-aside (n., u.m.)

back (n., u.m.)
bolt
down (n., u.m.)
-fair (n.)
head
-in (n., u.m.)
off (n., u.m.)
-on (n., u.m.)
out (n., u.m.)
over (n., u.m.)
pin
screw
-stitched (u.m.)
-to (n., u.m.)
up (n., u.m.)
setter
-forth
-in
-on
-out
-to
-up
seven
-branched (u.m.)
fold
penny (nail)
score
-shooter
-up (n.)
severalfold
shade
-giving (u.m.)
-grown (u.m.)
shadow
boxing
gram
graph
#line
shag
bark
-haired (u.m.)
#rug

shake
down (n., u.m.)
out (n., u.m.)
up (n., u.m.)
shallow
-draft (u.m.)
-headed (u.m.)
shame
-crushed (u.m.)
faced
shank
bone
#mill
shapeup (n., u.m.)
share
bone
broker
cropper
holder
out (n., u.m.)
ware
sharp
-angled (u.m.)
-cut (u.m.)
-edged (u.m.)
-freeze (u.m., v.)
-freezer
-looking (u.m.)
naysayer
-set (u.m.)
shod
shooter
-tailed (u.m.)
-witted (u.m.)
shavetail
shear
pin
waters
shedhand
sheep
biter
crook
dip

#dog
faced
#farm
fold
gate
herder
hook
kill
-kneed (u.m.)
nose (apple)
pen
shank
shear (v.)
shearer (n.)
shed
stealer
walk
-white (u.m.)
sheer
off (n., u.m.)
up (n., u.m.)
sheet
block
flood
#glass
rock
ways
shell
back
burst
fire
fishery
#game
hole
-like
shocked
shelterbelt
shield-shaped
(u.m.)
shilly-shally
shin
bone
guard

plaster
shiner-up
ship
breaker
broken
broker
builder
lap
mast
owning
-rigged (u.m.)
shape
side
wreck
shipping
#master
#room
shirt
band
#sleeve
tail
waist
shock
#therapy
#troops
#wave
shoe
black
brush
horn
lace
pack
scraper
shine
store
string
tree
shootoff (n., u.m.)
shop
folk
lifter
-made (u.m.)
mark

owner
-soiled (u.m.)
talk
walker
window
shore
#bird
#boat
fast
going
#leave
side
short
-armed (u.m.)
bread
cake
change (v.)
changer
#circuit
-circuited (u.m.)
coming
cut (n., u.m., v.)
fall (n.)
-fed (u.m.)
hand (writing)
-handed (u.m.)
head (whale)
horn (n., u.m.)
-horned (u.m.)
-lasting (u.m.)
leaf (u.m.)
-lived (u.m.)
rib
run (u.m.)
sighted
staff
stop
#term
-term (u.m.)
wave (radio)
shot
gun
hole

put
star
shoulder
#belt
#blade
-high (u.m.)
#strap
show
boat
card
case
down (n., u.m.)
off (n., u.m.)
piece
place
room
through
(printing) (n.,
u.m.)
up (n., u.m.)
shredout (n., u.m.)
shroud
-laid (u.m.)
plate
shut
away (n., u.m.)
down (n., u.m.)
eye (n., u.m.)
-in (n., u.m.)
-mouthed (u.m.)
off (n., u.m.)
out (n., u.m.)
up (u.m.)
shuttlecock
sick
bay
bed
#call
#leave
list
room
sickle cell (n.)
sickle-cell (u.m.)

side
arms
band
board
bone
burns
car
check
-cut (u.m.)
dress (v.)
flash
head (printing)
hill
hook
kick
lap
#light (literal)
light (nonliteral)
#line (literal)
line (nonliteral)
long
note
plate
play
saddle
show
slip
splitting
step
stitch
-stitched (u.m.)
sway
swipe
track
walk
wall
-wheeler
winder
sight
hole
read
saver
seeing

setter
sign
off (n., u.m.)
-on (n., u.m.)
post
up (n., u.m.)
silico (c.f.)
all one word
silk
#screen
-stockinged (u.m.)
works
siltpan
silver
-backed (u.m.)
beater
-bright (u.m.)
fish
-gray (u.m.)
-haired (u.m.)
-lead (u.m.)
-leaved (u.m.)
plate (v.)
-plated (u.m.)
point (drawing)
print
tip
-tongued (u.m.)
top
simon-pure (u.m.)
simple
-headed (u.m.)
-minded (u.m.)
-rooted (u.m.)
-witted (u.m.)
simulcast
sin
-born (u.m.)
-bred (u.m.)
sine#die
single
bar
-breasted (u.m.)

-decker
-edged (u.m.)
handed
hood
-loader
-minded (u.m.)
-phase (u.m.)
-seater
stick
#stitch
tree
singsong
sink
head
hole
Sino (c.f.)
-Japanese, etc.
sister
hood
-in-law
sit
down (n., u.m.)
-downer
fast (n., u.m.)
-in
up (n., u.m.)
sitter
-by
-in
-out
sitting#room
sitz
#bath
mark
six
-cylinder (u.m.)
fold
penny (nail)
-ply (u.m.)
-shooter
-wheeler
sizeup (n., u.m.)

ski
#jump
#lift
plane
#suit
skid
lift (truck)
road
#row
skin
-clad (u.m.)
deep
diver
flint
-graft (v.)
skipjack
skirtmarker
skullcap
sky
-blue (u.m.)
gazer
-high (u.m.)
jacker
lift
look (v.)
rocket
sail
scape
scraper
shine
writer
slab-sided (u.m.)
slack
-bake (v.)
-filled (u.m.)
#water
slambang
slap
bang
dab
dash
down (n., u.m.)
happy

jack
stick
-up (n., u.m.)
slate
-blue (u.m.)
-colored (u.m.)
works
slaughter
house
pen
slave
holding
#market
owner
pen
Slavo (c.f.)
-Hungarian, etc.
sledge
#hammer
-hammered (u.m.)
meter
sleep
-filled (u.m.)
talker
walker
sleepy
-eyed (u.m.)
head
-looking (u.m.)
sleetstorm
sleeveband
sleuthhound
slide
film
knot
#rule
sling
ball
shot
slip
along (u.m.)
band
case

cover
knot
#law
-on (n., u.m.)
#proof (printing)
proof
ring
sheet
shod
sole
step
stitch
stream
-up (n., u.m.)
washer
slit
shell
#skirt
slop
-molded (u.m.)
seller
slopeways
slow
belly
down (n., u.m.)
-footed (u.m.)
going
-motion (u.m.)
mouthed
poke
#time
up (n., u.m.)
-witted (u.m.)
sluice
box
#gate
slum
dweller
gullion
gum
lord
slumber-bound
(u.m.)

small
#arms
#businessman
pox
-scale (u.m.)
sword
talk
-time (u.m.)
town (u.m.)
smart
#aleck
-alecky (u.m.)
-looking (u.m.)
#set
-tongued (u.m.)
smashup (n., u.m.)
smearcase
smoke
-blinded (u.m.)
bomb
chaser
-dried (u.m.)
-dry (v.)
-dyed (u.m.)
-filled (u.m.)
house
jack
jumper
-laden (u.m.)
pot
screen
stack
smoking#room
smooth
bore
-browed (u.m.)
-cast (u.m.)
-mouthed (u.m.)
-tongued (u.m.)
-working (u.m.)
snackbar
snail
-paced (u.m.)

-slow (u.m.)
snail's#pace
snake
bite
-bitten (u.m.)
-eater
-eyed (u.m.)
head
hole
pit
snap
dragon
head
hook
-on (n., u.m.)
out (n.)
ring
roll
shooter
shot
-up (u.m.)
snapper
-back
-up
snipe
bill
#eel
-nosed (u.m.)
sniperscope
snooperscope
snow
ball
bank
berg
blind
#blindness
blink
block
-blocked (u.m.)
blower
break
capped
-choked (u.m.)

clad (u.m.)
#cover
-covered (u.m.)
drift
fall
field
flake
line
melt
-melting (u.m.)
mobile
pack
pit
plow
scape
shade
shed
shine
shoe
sled
slide
slip
storm
suit
-topped (u.m.)
#water
-white (u.m.)
snuffbox
so
-and-so
beit (n., conj.)
-called (u.m.)
-seeming (u.m.)
-so
soap
box
bubble
dish
flakes
#opera
rock
stock
suds

sob
#sister
#story
sober
-minded (u.m.)
sides
social
#work
#worker
socio (c.f.)
-official
economic, etc.
sod
buster
culture
#house
soda
jerk
#pop
#water
sofa
#bed
#maker
-making (u.m.)
-ridden (u.m.)
soft
ball
-boiled (u.m.)
#coal
#copy
#drink
#goods
head
-pedal (v.)
-shelled (u.m.)
-soap (nonliteral) (v.)
-soaper (nonliteral) (n.)
-spoken (u.m.)
tack
ware
wood

sole
cutter
plate
somato (c.f.)
all one word
some
day
how
one (anyone)
#one (distributive)
place (adv.)
time (adv., u.m.)
#time (some time ago)
what
son-in-law
song
bird
fest
writer
sonobuoy
sooth
fast
sayer
sore
-eyed (u.m.)
foot (n.)
footed (u.m.)
head (n., u.m.)
sorry-looking (u.m.)
soul
-deep (u.m.)
mate
-searching (u.m.)
sick
sound
-absorbing (u.m.)
#field
film
-minded (u.m.)
off (n., u.m.)
track
#wave

soup
bone
#bowl
#kitchen
#plate
spoon
sour
belly
bread
dough (n.)
faced
-natured (u.m.)
-sweet
source
book
#code
#file
south
-born (u.m.)
bound
-central (u.m.)
east
going
lander
paw
#side
-sider
-southeast
west
soybean
sow
back
belly
space
bar
craft
-cramped (u.m.)
#key
mark
ship
#time
spade
-dug (u.m.)

foot
-footed (u.m.)
-shaped (u.m.)
Spanish
-American (u.m.)
-born (u.m.)
-speaking (u.m.)
spare
-bodied (u.m.)
rib
#room
spark
#plug (literal)
plug (nonliteral)
speakeasy (n.)
spear
cast
head
-high (u.m.)
-shaped (u.m.)
spectro (c.f.)
all one word
speech
-bereft (u.m.)
-read (v.)
speed
boating
trap
up (n., u.m.)
spell
binding
check
down (n., u.m.)
-free (u.m.)
spend
-all (n.)
thrift
spermato (c.f.)
all one word
spermo (c.f.)
all one word
spheno (c.f.)
-occipital

rest one word
sphygmo (c.f.)
all one word
spice
-burnt (u.m.)
cake
-laden (u.m.)
spider
#crab
-legged
-spun (u.m.)
#web (n.)
web (u.m., v.)
spike
horn
-kill (v.)
-pitch (v.)
spill
over (n., u.m.)
way
spin
back
#doctor (slang)
off
spindle
-formed (u.m.)
head
-legged (u.m.)
legs
shanks
spine
bone
-broken (u.m.)
-pointed (u.m.)
spino (c.f.)
-olivary
rest one word
spirit
-born (u.m.)
-broken (u.m.)
#writing
spit
ball

fire
splanchno (c.f.)
all one word
splay
footed
mouthed
spleen
-born (u.m.)
sick
-swollen (u.m.)
spleno (c.f.)
all one word
split
finger
(crustacean)
fruit
mouth
saw
#second
-tongued (u.m.)
up (n., u.m.)
spoilsport
spondylo (c.f.)
all one word
sponge
#bath
cake
diver
-diving (u.m.)
-shaped (u.m.)
spongio (c.f.)
all one word
spool#winder
spoon
-beaked (u.m.)
-billed (u.m.)
bread
-fed (u.m.)
-shaped (u.m.)
ways
sporeformer
sporo (c.f.)
all one word

sports
#editor
person
wear
writer
spot
#check
-checked (u.m.)
-face (v.)
light
weld (v.)
welded (u.m.)
-welding (u.m.)
spray-washed (u.m.)
spread
-eagle (u.m., v.)
head
out (n., u.m.)
over (n., u.m.)
-set (v.)
spring
back
(bookbinding)
bok
-born (u.m.)
buck
-clean (v.)
#fever
finger
-grown (u.m.)
halt
head
-plow (v.)
-plowed (u.m.)
tide (season)
time
trap
spritsail
spur
-clad (u.m.)
-driven (u.m.)
gall
-galled (u.m.)

-heeled (u.m.)
spy
  glass
  hole
  tower
square
  -bottomed (u.m.)
  -built (u.m.)
  -faced (u.m.)
  flipper
  head
  -headed
  #mile
  -rigged (u.m.)
  #root
  -set (u.m.)
  shooter
squeeze
  -in (n., u.m.)
  out (n., u.m.)
  up (n., u.m.)
squirrel-headed
  (u.m.)
stackup (n., u.m.)
staff
  -herd (v.)
  -hour
  time
stag
  -handled (u.m.)
  head
  -headed (u.m.)
  horn
  -horned (u.m.)
  hound
  hunter
stage
  coach
  hand
  #set
  -struck (u.m.)
stair
  case

head
step
well
stake
  head
  holder
  out (n.)
stale-worn (u.m.)
stall
  -fed (u.m.)
  -feed (v.)
stand
  by (n., u.m.)
  down (n., u.m.)
  fast (n., u.m.)
  -in (n., u.m.)
  off (n., u.m.)
  offish
  out (n., u.m.)
  pat
  pipe
  point
  post
  still (n., u.m.)
  up (n., u.m.)
standard
  #bearer
  bred
  #gauge
  #time
staphylo (c.f.)
  all one word
star
  blind
  bright
  dust
  gazer
  -led (u.m.)
  light
  lit
  lite (gem)
  nose (mole)
  shake

shine
shoot
-spangled (u.m.)
stroke
-studded (u.m.)
#time
stark
  -blind (u.m.)
  -mad (u.m.)
  -naked (u.m.)
  -raving (u.m.)
starter-off
start-stop
startup (n., u.m.)
stat (pref.)
  all one word
State
  -aided (u.m.)
  #line
  -owned (u.m.)
state
  hood
  -of-the-art (u.m.)
  quake
  room
  side
station#house
stato (c.f.)
  all one word
statute
  -barred (u.m.)
  #book
stay
  -at-home (n., u.m.)
  #bar
  bolt
  boom
  lace
  log
  pin
  plow
  sail
  wire

steam
  boating
  car
  -cooked (u.m.)
  -driven (u.m.)
  fitter
  pipe
  plant
  -pocket (v.)
  power (n.)
  #powerplant
  -propelled (u.m.)
  roll (v.)
  roller (u.m., v.)
  ship
  table
  tightness
steamer#line
steel
  -blue (u.m.)
  -bright (u.m.)
  -cased (u.m.)
  clad
  -framed (u.m.)
  -hard (u.m.)
  head
  plate
  works
steep
  -rising (u.m.)
  -to (u.m.)
  -up (u.m.)
  -walled (u.m.)
steeple
  chase
  -high (u.m.)
  jack
  top
stem
  head
  post
  winder
stencil-cutting (u.m.)

steno (c.f.)
  all one word
step
  aunt
  child, etc.
  dance
  down (n., u.m.)
  -in (n., u.m.)
  ladder
  off (n., u.m.)
  -on (n., u.m.)
  over (n., u.m.)
  -up (n., u.m.)
stepping
  -off (u.m.)
  -out (u.m.)
  stone
stereo (c.f.)
  all one word
stern
  castle
  -faced (u.m.)
  -heavy (u.m.)
  -looking (u.m.)
  most
  post
  #wheel
  -wheeler
sterno (c.f.)
  all one word
stetho (c.f.)
  all one word
stew
  pan
  pot
stick
  -at-it (n., u.m.)
  fast (n.)
  -in-the-mud (n., u.m.)
  out (n., u.m.)
  pin
  -to-it-iveness (n.)

up (n., u.m.)
sticker
  -in
  -on
  -up
stiff
  -backed (u.m.)
  neck
  -necked (u.m.)
still
  -admired (u.m.)
  birth
  born
  -burn (v.)
  -fish (v.)
  -hunt (v.)
  #life
  -recurring (u.m.)
  stand
stink
  ball
  bomb
  bug
  damp
  pot
stir
  about (n., u.m.)
  fry
  -up (n., u.m.)
stitch
  down (n., u.m.)
  up (n., u.m.)
stock
  breeder
  broker
  #car
  feeder
  holding
  jobber
  judging
  list
  pile
  pot

rack
raiser
-still (u.m.)
taker
truck
stoke
  hold
  hole
stomach
  #ache
  -filling (u.m.)
  #pump
  -shaped (u.m.)
  -sick (u.m.)
  -weary (u.m.)
stomato (c.f.)
  all one word
stone
  biter
  blind
  brash
  breaker
  broke
  brood
  cast
  -cold (u.m.)
  #crab
  crusher
  cutter
  -dead (u.m.)
  -deaf (u.m.)
  -eyed (u.m.)
  head
  layer
  lifter
  mason
  shot
  #wall (n.)
  wall (u.m., v.)
  #writing
stony
  -eyed (u.m.)
  #land

stop
  back (n.)
  block
  clock
  cock
  gap
  hound
  list
  log
  -loss (u.m.)
  off (n., u.m.)
  watch
storage#room
store
  front
  house
storm
  -beaten (u.m.)
  cock
  flow
  -laden (u.m.)
  -swept (u.m.)
  -tossed (u.m.)
  #trooper
  wind
  #window
storyteller
stout
  -armed (u.m.)
  heartedness
  -minded (u.m.)
stove
  brush
  -heated (u.m.)
  pipe
stow
  away (n., u.m.)
  down (n., u.m.)
straddle
  back
  -face (v.)
  -legged (u.m.)

straight
  away
  -backed (u.m.)
  -cut (u.m.)
  edge
  -edged (u.m.)
  #face
  -faced (u.m.)
  forward
  head
  -legged (u.m.)
  #line
  -lined (u.m.)
  -out (n., u.m.)
  -spoken (u.m.)
  #time
  -up (u.m.)
  -up-and-down
    (u.m.)
strainslip
strait
  -chested (u.m.)
  jacket
  laced
stranglehold
strap
  -bolt (v.)
  hanger
  head
  -shaped (u.m.)
  watch
strato (c.f.)
  all one word
straw
  berry#field
  boss
  -built (u.m.)
  hat
  #poll
  -roofed (u.m.)
  splitting
  stack
  -stuffed (u.m.)

#vote
walker
-yellow (u.m.)
stray
  away (n., u.m.)
  #line
  mark
stream
  bank
  bed
  flow
  head
  lined
  side
street
  -bred (u.m.)
  car
  cleaner
  -cleaning (u.m.)
  sweeper
  walker
strepto (c.f.)
  all one word
stretchout (n., u.m.)
strike
  breaker
  -in (n., u.m.)
  out (n., u.m.)
  -over (n., u.m.)
striker
  -in
  -out
  -over
string
  course
  halt
  #proof (density)
  ways
strip
  cropping
  #mine
  tease

strong
  -arm (u.m., v.)
  back (nautical)
  -backed (u.m.)
  box
  hold
  #man (literal)
  man (nonliteral)
  -minded (u.m.)
  point (n.)
stub
  runner
  -toed (u.m.)
  wing
stubble
  #field
  -mulch (u.m.)
stubbornminded
stucco-fronted
  (u.m.)
stuck
  up (n., u.m.)
  -uppish (u.m.)
stud
  bolt
  horse
  mare
stuntman
sturdy-limbed (u.m.)
stylebook
stylo (c.f.)
  all one word
sub (pref.)
  -Himalayan, etc.
  machinegun
  #rosa, #specie, etc.
  -subcommittee
  polar, standard,
    etc.
  rest one word
subject
  -object
  -objectivity

subter (pref.)
  all one word
such-and-such
suck
  -egg (n., u.m.)
  hole
  -in (n., u.m.)
sugar
  #beet
  #bowl
  cake
  cane
  -coat (v.)
  -coated (u.m.)
  -cured (u.m.)
  loaf
  plum
  spoon
  sweet
  #water
  works
sulfa (c.f.)
  all one word
sulfo (c.f.)
  all one word
sulfon (c.f.)
  all one word
sullen
  hearted
  -natured (u.m.)
summer
  -clad (u.m.)
  -dried (u.m.)
  -fallow (v.)
  -made (u.m.)
  tide
  time (season)
  #time (daylight
    saving)
sun
  -baked (u.m.)
  bath
  -bathed (u.m.)

beam
blind
#blindness
bonnet
bow
break
burn
burst
-cured (u.m.)
dial
dog
down
dress
-dried (u.m.)
-dry (v.)
fall
fast
glade
glare
glow
#hat
lamp
lit
quake
ray
rise
scald
set
shade
shine
-shot (u.m.)
shower
spot
stricken
stroke
struck
tan
#time (measure)
time (dawn)
up
sunny
-looking (u.m.)
-natured (u.m.)

super (pref.)
-Christian, etc.
#high frequency
-superlative
highway, market,
etc.
rest one word
Super Bowl
supra (pref.)
-abdominal
-acromial
-aerial
anal
-angular
-arytenoid
-auditory
-auricular
-axillary
-Christian, etc.
rest one word
sur (pref.)
all one word
sure
-fire (u.m.)
-footed (u.m.)
-slow
surf
-battered (u.m.)
board
#fish
-swept (u.m.)
swallow
pipe
-tailed (u.m.)
swampside
swan
-bosomed (u.m.)
dive
herd
mark
neck
song
swansdown

swash
buckler
plate
sway
back (n., u.m.)
-backed (u.m.)
bar
-brace (v.)
swearer-in
sweat
band
#gland
shirt
shop
sweep
back (aviation)
(n., u.m.)
forward
(aviation) (n.,
u.m.)
stake
through (n., u.m.)
washer
sweet
bread
-breathed (u.m.)
brier
faced
heart
meat
mouthed
-pickle (v.)
-sour
swell
-butted (u.m.)
head
toad
swelled-headed
(u.m.)
swept
back (n., u.m.)
forward (n., u.m.)
wing (n., u.m.)

swift
foot
-footed (u.m.)
-handed (u.m.)
-running (u.m.)
swill
bowl
tub
swimsuit
swine
-backed (u.m.)
bread
head
herd
pox
sty
swing
back (n., u.m.)
bar
dingle
#gate
#shift
stock
tree
swingle
bar
tree
switch
back
blade
box
gear
plate
plug
rail
tender
swivel
#chair
eye
-eyed (u.m.)
-hooked (u.m.)
sword
-armed (u.m.)

bearer
#belt
bill
fishing
play
-shaped (u.m.)
stick
syn (pref.)
all one word
synchro
cyclotron
flash
mesh
tron
Syro (c.f.)
-Arabian, etc.
phenician

T

T
-ball
-bandage
-beam
-boat
-bone
-cloth
-iron
-man
-rail
-scale (score)
-shape
-shaped
-shirt
-square
table
cloth
-cut (u.m.)
cutter
-cutting (u.m.)
-formed (u.m.)
#linen
-shaped (u.m.)
spoon

talk
top
ware
tachy (c.f.)
all one word
tag
-affixing (u.m.)
lock
rag
sore
tail
band
#coat
-cropped (u.m.)
#end
-ender
first
foremost
gate
head
-heavy (u.m.)
hook
lamp
pin
pipe
race
spin
stock
-tied (u.m.)
twister
-up (n., u.m.)
wheel
wind
tailor
-cut (u.m.)
made (u.m.)
-suited (u.m.)
take
-all (n.)
down (n., u.m.)
-home (n., u.m.)
-in (n., u.m.)
off (n., u.m.)

out (n., u.m.)
over (n., u.m.)
up (n., u.m.)
taker
-down
-in
-off
-over
-up
tale
bearer
carrier
teller
talkfest
talking-to (n.)
tall
boy (n.)
-built (u.m.)
-looking (u.m.)
tallow
-faced (u.m.)
-pale (u.m.)
tally
#board
#clerk
ho
#room
#sheet
tame
-grown (u.m.)
-looking (u.m.)
tan
bark
works
tangent
-cut (v.)
-saw (v.)
tangle
foot
-haired (u.m.)
tank
#car
farm

ship
town
tap
bolt
dance
hole
net
off (n., u.m.)
-riveted (u.m.)
room
root
-tap
water
tape
#deck
#drive
#measure
string
-tied (u.m.)
taper
bearer
-fashion (u.m.)
-headed (u.m.)
tapestry
-covered (u.m.)
#maker
-making (u.m.)
#work
tar
-brand (v.)
brush
-coal (u.m.)
-dipped (u.m.)
#paper
-paved (u.m.)
pot
-roofed (u.m.)
works
tariff-protected
(u.m.)
tarpaulin
-covered (u.m.)
#maker

-making (u.m.)
tarso (c.f.)
  all one word
task
  #force
  setter
  tattletale
tauro (c.f.)
  all one word
tax
  -burdened (u.m.)
  #collector
  eater
  -exempt (u.m.)
  -free (u.m.)
  gatherer
  -laden (u.m.)
  paid
  payer
  #roll
  -supported (u.m.)
taxi
  auto
  bus
  cab
  meter
  stand
tea
  ball
  cake
  cart
  -colored (u.m.)
  cup
  dish
  kettle
  #party
  pot
  room
  -scented (u.m.)
  spoon
  taster
teamplay

tear
  bomb
  -dimmed (u.m.)
  down (n., u.m.)
  drop
  #gas
  -off (n., u.m.)
  -out (n., u.m.)
  pit
  sheet
  stain
  -stained (u.m.)
teen
  age (u.m.)
  ager
  teeter-totter
tele (c.f.)
  all one word
teleo (c.f.)
  all one word
tell
  tale
  truth
telo (c.f.)
  all one word
  tempest-rocked
  (u.m.)
temporo (c.f.)
  -occipital
  rest one word
ten
  fold
  penny (nail)
  pins
tender
  #boat
  -faced (u.m.)
  foot
  -footed (u.m.)
  footish
  -handed (u.m.)
  heart
  loin

-looking (u.m.)
tenement#house
tent
  -dotted (u.m.)
  pole
  -sheltered (u.m.)
  #show
terra
  #cotta
  #firma
  mara
terrace-fashion
  (u.m.)
test-fly (v.)
tetra (c.f.)
  all one word
thanksgiving
thatch-roofed
  (u.m.)
text
  -based
  #file
  #mode
theater
  goer
  going
thenceforth
theo (c.f.)
  all one word
theologico (c.f.)
  all one word
there
  about(s)
  above
  across
  after
  against
  among
  around
  at
  away
  before
  between

  by
  for
  fore
  from
  in
  inafter
  inbefore
  into
  on
  over
  through
  tofore
  under
  until
  unto
  upon
  with
thermo (c.f.)
  all one word
thick
  -blooded (u.m.)
  head
  -looking (u.m.)
  pated
  set (n., u.m.)
  skinned
  skull (n.)
  skulled
  -tongued (u.m.)
  wit
  -witted (u.m.)
  -wooded (u.m.)
  -woven (u.m.)
thin
  -clad (u.m.)
  down (n., u.m.)
  set (u.m.)
  -voiced (u.m.)
thio (c.f.)
  all one word
third
  -class (u.m.)
  -degree (u.m.)

hand (adv., u.m.)
#house
-rate (u.m.)
-rater
thistledown
thoraco (c.f.)
all one word
thorn
  back
  bill
  -covered (u.m.)
  -set (u.m.)
  -strewn (u.m.)
  tail
thorough
  -bind (v.)
  bred
  -dried (u.m.)
  fare
  going
  -made (u.m.)
  paced
  pin
thought
  -free (u.m.)
  -out (u.m.)
  -provoking (u.m.)
thousand
  fold
  -headed (u.m.)
  -legged (u.m.)
  legs (worm)
thrall
  born
  dom
  -less
thread
  bare
  -leaved (u.m.)
  worn
three
  -bagger
  -cornered (u.m.)

-dimensional
  (u.m.)
fold
-in-hand
-master
penny (nail)
-piece (u.m.)
-ply (u.m.)
score
some
-spot
-square
-striper
throat
  band
  cutter
  latch
  strap
thrombo (c.f.)
all one word
through
  out
  put
  #road
  way
throw
  away (n., u.m.)
  back (n., u.m.)
  -in (n., u.m.)
  #line
  off (n., u.m.)
  -on (n., u.m.)
  out (n., u.m.)
  over (n., u.m.)
  -weight
thrust-pound
thumb
  #hole
  -made (u.m.)
  mark
  -marked (u.m.)
  nail
  print

screw
stall
string
sucker
tack
worn
thunder
  bearer
  blast
  bolt
  clap
  cloud
  head
  peal
  shower
  storm
  struck
thymo (c.f.)
all one word
thyro (c.f.)
all one word
tibio (c.f.)
all one word
tick
  #feed
  seed
  tacktoe
  tick
  tock
ticket
  #seller
  -selling (u.m.)
  #writer
tidal#wave
tiddlywink
tide
  flat
  head
  mark
  -marked (u.m.)
  race
  table
  -tossed (u.m.)

waiter
-worn (u.m.)
tie
  back (n.)
  #bar
  #beam
  down (n., u.m.)
  -in (n., u.m.)
  -on (n., u.m.)
  -out (n., u.m.)
  pin
  -plater
  #rod
  #tack
  up (n., u.m.)
tierlift (truck)
tiger
  eye
  #lily
  #shark
  -striped (u.m.)
tight
  -belted (u.m.)
  fisted
  -fitting (u.m.)
  lipped
  rope
  -set (u.m.)
  -tie (v.)
  wad
  wire
tile
  -clad (u.m.)
  #drain
  -red (u.m.)
  setter
  works
  wright
tilt
  hammer
  rotor
  up (n.)

timber
  -built (u.m.)
  head
  -headed (u.m.)
  jack
  line
  -propped (u.m.)
  #wolf
  wright
time
  bomb
  born
  card
  clerk
  clock
  -consuming (u.m.)
  frame
  -honored (u.m.)
  keeper
  killer
  lag
  lock
  outs (n., u.m.)
  piece
  pleaser
  saver
  server
  sheet
  slip
  slot
  span
  -stamp (v.)
  study
  table
  taker
  waster
  worn
tin
  -bearing (u.m.)
  #can
  -capped (u.m.)
  -clad (u.m.)
  #cup

  #fish (torpedo)
  foil
  horn
  kettle
  -lined (u.m.)
  man
  pan
  plate
  -plated (u.m.)
  pot
  -roofed (u.m.)
  type
  -white (u.m.)
tinsel
  -bright (u.m.)
  -clad (u.m.)
  -covered (u.m.)
  #town
  tintblock (printing)
tip
  burn
  cart
  -curled (u.m.)
  head
  -in (n., u.m.)
  most
  off (n., u.m.)
  over (n., u.m.)
  staff
  stock
  tank
  -tap
  toe
  top
  -up (u.m.)
tire
  changer
  dresser
  fitter
  #gauge
  #iron
  -mile
  #rack

  shaper
  some
tit
  bit
  #for#tat
  mouse
titano (c.f.)
  all one word
tithe
  book
  -free (u.m.)
  payer
  right
title
  holder
  -holding (u.m.)
  #page
  winner
  -winning (u.m.)
to
  -and-fro
  -do (n.)
  #wit
toad
  back
  -bellied (u.m.)
  blind
  fish
  -green (u.m.)
  stool
tobacco
  #grower
  -growing (u.m.)
  #shop
toe
  cap
  #dance
  hold
  -in (n., u.m.)
  -mark (v.)
  nail
  plate
  print

toil
  -beaten (u.m.)
  some
  -stained (u.m.)
  -weary (u.m.)
  worn
  toilet#room
toll
  bar
  #bridge
  #call
  gate
  gatherer
  house
  #line
  payer
  road
  taker
tom
  boy
  cat
  foolery
  -tom
tommy
  gun
  rot
ton
  -hour
  -kilometer
  -mile
  -mileage
  -mile-day
tone
  -deaf (u.m.)
  down (n., u.m.)
  -producing (u.m.)
  up (n., u.m.)
tongue
  -baited (u.m.)
  -bound (u.m.)
  -free (u.m.)
  -lash (v.)
  #lashing

play
-shaped (u.m.)
shot
sore
tack
-tied
tip
#twister
-twisting (u.m.)
tool
 bag
 #belt
 box
 builder
 #chest
 crib
 dresser
 fitter
 #grinder
 -grinding (u.m.)
 head
 holding
 kit
 mark
 plate
 post
 rack
 setter
 shed
 slide
 stock
tooth
 ache
 #and#nail
 -billed (u.m.)
 brush
 drawer
 mark
 -marked (u.m.)
 paste
 pick
 plate
 powder

puller
-pulling (u.m.)
-set (u.m.)
-shaped (u.m.)
some
wash
top
 #brass
 cap (n.)
 coat
 cutter
 #dog
 -drain (v.)
 #drawer
 dress (v.)
 flight (u.m.)
 full
 gallant (n., u.m.)
 -graft (v.)
 hat
 -hatted (u.m.)
 heavy
 kick
 knot
 liner
 mark
 mast
 milk
 most
 notch (nonliteral)
 rail
 rope
 sail
 -secret (u.m.)
 side (naut.)
 soil
topo (c.f.)
 all one word
topsy-turvy
torch
 bearer
 #holder

lighted
lit
torpedo
 #boat
 #room
torquemeter
toss
 pot
 up (n., u.m.)
touch
 #and#go
 back (n., u.m.)
 down (n., u.m.)
 hole
 -me-not (n., u.m.)
 pan
 reader
 stone
 up (n., u.m.)
tough
 -headed (u.m.)
 -looking (u.m.)
 -skinned (u.m.)
tow
 away
 boat
 head
 line
 mast
 #net
 -netter
 path
 rope
 #truck
tower
 -high (u.m.)
 -shaped (u.m.)
town
 -bred (u.m.)
 #clerk
 #crier
 -dotted (u.m.)
 folk

gate
going
hall
lot
ship
side
site
talk
-weary (u.m.)
towns
 fellow
 people
toy
 #dog
 -sized (u.m.)
 town
tracheo (c.f.)
 all one word
trachy (c.f.)
 all one word
track
 barrow
 hound
 layer
 mark
 -mile
 side
 walker
tractor-trailer
trade
 #board
 -in (n., u.m.)
 -laden (u.m.)
 -made (u.m.)
 mark
 #name
 off
 #union
 #wind
tradespeople
traffic-mile
tragico (c.f.)
 all one word

trail
  blazer
  breaker
  -marked (u.m.)
  side
  sight
  -weary (u.m.)
train
  bearer
  bolt
  crew
  line
  -mile
  shed
  sick
  stop
tram
  -borne (u.m.)
  car
  rail
  road
  way
trans (pref.)
  alpine
  atlantic
  -Canadian, etc.
  gender
  pacific
  uranic
  rest one word
transit#time
trap
  door
  fall
  shoot
trashrack
travel
  -bent (u.m.)
  time
  -tired (u.m.)
  -worn (u.m.)
trawlnet

tread
  mill
  wheel
treasure
  -filled (u.m.)
  #house
  -laden (u.m.)
treaty
  breaker
  -sealed (u.m.)
tree
  #belt
  -clad (u.m.)
  #line
  -lined (u.m.)
  nail
  -ripe (u.m.)
  scape
  top
  #trunk
  trellis-covered
    (u.m.)
trench
  back
  coat
  foot
  #knife
  mouth
  #plow
  -plowed (u.m.)
tri (c.f.)
  -iodide
  -ply (u.m.)
  state, etc.
  rest one word
tribespeople
tribo (c.f.)
  all one word
tricho (c.f.)
  all one word
trim
  -cut (u.m.)
  -dressed (u.m.)

  -looking (u.m.)
trinitro (c.f.)
  all one word
trip
  -free (u.m.)
  hammer
  wire
triple
  -acting (u.m.)
  back (sofa)
  branched (u.m.)
  -edged (u.m.)
  fold
  #play
  -tailed (u.m.)
  tree (n.)
trolley#line
troop
  ship
  #train
tropho (c.f.)
  all one word
tropo (c.f.)
  all one word
trouble
  -free (u.m.)
  -haunted (u.m.)
  maker
  shooter
  some
truce
  breaker
  -seeking (u.m.)
truck
  driver
  #farm
  -mile
  stop
true
  -aimed (u.m.)
  -blue (u.m.)
  born
  bred

  -eyed (u.m.)
  -false
  love (n., u.m.)
  penny (n.)
  #time
trunk
  back
  nose
trust
  breaking
  buster
  -controlled (u.m.)
  -ridden (u.m.)
  worthy
truth
  -filled (u.m.)
  lover
  seeker
  -seeking (u.m.)
  teller
try
  -on (n., u.m.)
  out (n., u.m.)
  square
  works
tube
  -eyed (u.m.)
  -fed (u.m.)
  head
  -nosed (u.m.)
  works
tuberculo (c.f.)
  all one word
tubo (c.f.)
  -ovarian
  rest one word
tug
  boat
  #of#war
tumbledown (n.,
  u.m.)
tune
  out (n., u.m.)

up (n., u.m.)
tunnel
  -boring (u.m.)
  -shaped (u.m.)
  #vision
turbo (c.f.)
  -ramjet (u.m.)
  rest one word
turf
  -built (u.m.)
  -clad (u.m.)
  -covered (u.m.)
  #war
turkey
  back
  #buzzard
  #gobbler
  #trot
Turko (c.f.)
  -Greek, etc.
  rest one word
turn
  about (n., u.m.)
  about-face
  again (n., u.m.)
  around (n., u.m.)
  back (n., u.m.)
  buckle
  cap
  coat
  cock
  down (n., u.m.)
  gate
  -in (n., u.m.)
  key
  off (n., u.m.)
  out (n., u.m.)
  over (n., u.m.)
  pike
  pin
  plate
  round (n., u.m.)
  screw

sheet
sole
stile
stitch
table
tail
-to (n.)
under (n., u.m.)
up (n., u.m.)
turned
  -back (u.m.)
  -down (u.m.)
  -in (u.m.)
  -on (u.m.)
  -out (u.m.)
  -over (u.m.)
turner-off
turtle
  back
  dove
  -footed (u.m.)
  neck (u.m.)
  #shell
twelve
  fold
  penny (nail)
  score
twenty
  -first
  fold
  -one
twice
  -born (u.m.)
  -reviewed (u.m.)
  -told (u.m.)
twin
  #boat
  born
  -engined (u.m.)
  fold
  -jet (u.m.)
  -motor (u.m.)
  -screw (u.m.)

two
  -a-day (u.m.)
  -along (n.)
    (bookbinding)
  -decker
  -faced (u.m.)
  fold
  -handed (u.m.)
  penny (nail)
  -piece (u.m.)
  -ply (u.m.)
  score
  -seater
  some
  -spot
  -step (dance)
  -striper
  -suiter
  -up (n., u.m.)
  -way (u.m.)
  -wheeler
tympano (c.f.)
  all one word
type
  case
  cast
  cutter
  face
  foundry
  script
  set
  write (v.)
typho (c.f.)
  all one word
typo (c.f.)
  all one word
tyro (c.f.)
  all one word

U

U
  -boat
  -cut

-magnet
-rail
-shaped
-tube
ultra (pref.)
  -ambitious,
    -atomic, etc.
  -English, etc.
  high#frequency
  -high-speed (u.m.)
  #valorem, etc.
  rest one word
un (pref.)
  -American, etc.
  called-for (u.m.)
  heard-of (u.m.)
  -ionized (u.m.)
  self-conscious
  sent-for (u.m.)
  thought-of (u.m.)
  rest one word
under
  age (deficit)
  age (younger)
    (n., u.m.)
  #cultivation
    (tillage)
  cultivation
    (insufficient)
  #secretary
  -secretaryship
  way
  as prefix, one
  word
uni (c.f.)
  -univalent
  rest one word
union
  -made (u.m.)
  #shop
  unit-set (u.m.)
up
  -anchor (u.m., v.)

-and-coming
(u.m.)
#and#up
beat
coast
country
dip
end (v.)
front (n., u.m.)
grade
gradient
keep
lift
load
-over (u.m.)
rate
river
stairs
state
stream
swing
take
tight (n., u.m.)
#tight (v.)
-to-date (u.m.)
#to#date
town
trend
turn
wind
upper
case (printing)
#class
classman
crust (n., u.m.)
cut
#deck
most
urano (c.f.)
all one word
uretero (c.f.)
all one word

urethro (c.f.)
all one word
uro (c.f.)
all one word
used-car (u.m.)
user
#default
-defined
-friendly
#group
#interface
utero (c.f.)
all one word

V

V
-connection
-curve
-engine
-neck
-shaped
-type
vacant
-eyed (u.m.)
-looking (u.m.)
-minded (u.m.)
vagino (c.f.)
all one word
vainglorious
valve
-grinding (u.m.)
-in-head (u.m.)
van
driver
guard
pool
vapor
-filled (u.m.)
-heating (u.m.)
#lock
vase-shaped (u.m.)
vaso (c.f.)
all one word

vegeto (c.f.)
all one word
vein
-mining (u.m.)
-streaked (u.m.)
vellum
-bound (u.m.)
-covered (u.m.)
velvet
-crimson (u.m.)
-draped (u.m.)
-green (u.m.)
-pile (u.m.)
venthole
ventri (c.f.)
all one word
ventro (c.f.)
all one word
vertebro (c.f.)
all one word
vesico (c.f.)
all one word
vibro (c.f.)
all one word
vice
#admiral
-admiralty
#consul
-consulate
#governor
-governorship
#minister
-ministry
-presidency
#president
-president-elect
-presidential
#rector
-rectorship
regal
-regency
#regent
royal

#squad
#versa
#warden
videotape
Vietcong
view
finder
point
vile-natured (u.m.)
vine
-clad (u.m.)
-covered (u.m.)
dresser
growing
stalk
vinegar
-flavored (u.m.)
-hearted (u.m.)
-making (u.m.)
-tart (u.m.)
violet
-blue (u.m.)`
-colored (u.m.)
-eared (u.m.)
#ray
-rayed (u.m.)
#water
violin-shaped (u.m.)
vis-a-vis
viscero (c.f.)
all one word
vitreo (c.f.)
all one word
vitro (c.f.)
-clarain
-di-trina
rest one word
vivi (c.f.)
all one word
voice
-capable
#mail
over (n.)

volleyball
volt
  ammeter
  -ampere
  -coulomb
  meter
  ohmmeter
  -second
volta (c.f.)
  all one word
vote
  -casting (u.m.)
  getter
  -getting (u.m.)
vow
  -bound (u.m.)
  breaker
  -pledged (u.m.)
vulvo (c.f.)
  all one word

W

W
  -engine
  -shaped
  -surface
  -type
wage
  #earner
  -earning (u.m.)
  #scale
  worker
waist
  band
  belt
  cloth
  coat
  -deep (u.m.)
  -high (u.m.)
  line
waiting
  #list
  #man

#room
#woman
walk
  around (n., u.m.)
  away (n., u.m.)
  -on (n., u.m.)
  out (n., u.m.)
  over (n., u.m.)
  up (n., u.m.)
  way
walkie-talkie
wall
  board
  eyed
  flower
  -like
  -painting (u.m.)
  paper
  plate
  -sided (u.m.)
walled
  -in (u.m.)
  -up (u.m.)
war
  #dance
  -disabled (u.m.)
  -famed (u.m.)
  fare
  head
  horse (nonliteral)
  like
  monger
  -made (u.m.)
  path
  plane
  ship
  -swept (u.m.)
  #time (clock)
  time (duration)
ward
  #heeler
  robe
  ship

warm
  blooded
  -clad (u.m.)
  up (n., u.m.)
warmed-over (u.m.)
warpsetter
wash
  basin
  basket
  board
  bowl
  cloth
  -colored (u.m.)
  day
  down (n., u.m.)
  -in (n., u.m.)
  off (n., u.m.)
  out (n., u.m.)
  pot
  rag
  #sale
  stand
  tray
  trough
  tub
  up (n., u.m.)
washed
  -out (u.m.)
  -up (u.m.)
waste
  basket
  land
  leaf
    (bookbinding)
  paper
  site
  word
watch
  band
  case
  #chain
  cry
  dog

-free (u.m.)
glass
tower
water
bag
bank
bearer
-bearing (u.m.)
-beaten (u.m.)
-bind (v.)
#blister
bloom
buck
color
-colored (u.m.)
-cool (v.)
-cooled (u.m.)
#cooler
course
craft
dog
-drinking (u.m.)
drop
fall
-filled (u.m.)
finder
flood
flow
fog
-free (u.m.)
front
gate
head
hole
horse
-inch
-laden (u.m.)
lane
leaf
#line
-lined (u.m.)
locked
log

#main
mark
melon
meter
plant
pot
power
proofing
quake
-rot (v.)
scape
shed
shoot
side
-soak (v.)
-soaked (u.m.)
-soluble (u.m.)
spout
stain
#table
tight
wall
works
worn

watt
-hour
meter
-second

wave
-cut (u.m.)
form
guide
-lashed (u.m.)
length
mark
meter
-moist (u.m.)
-on (n., u.m.)
off (n., u.m.)
-swept (u.m.)
-worn (u.m.)

wax
bill

-billed (u.m.)
chandler
cloth
-coated (u.m.)
-headed (u.m.)
#paper
#stone
-yellow (u.m.)

way
back (n., u.m.)
beam
bill
down (n., u.m.)
farer
fellow
going
laid
lay
mark
post
side
-sore (u.m.)
-up (n., u.m.)
worn

weak
-backed (u.m.)
-eyed (u.m.)
handed
-kneed (u.m.)
minded
mouthed

weather
beaten
blown
-borne (u.m.)
break
cock
glass
going
-hardened (u.m.)
#house
-marked (u.m.)
most

proofing
-stain (v.)
strip
-stripped (u.m.)
worn

web
-fingered (u.m.)
foot
-footed (u.m.)
master
#page
#press
site

wedge
-billed (u.m.)
-shaped (u.m.)

weed
-choked (u.m.)
-hidden (u.m.)
hook
killer

week
day
end
-ender
-ending (u.m.)
long (u.m.)
-old (u.m.)

weigh
bridge
-in (n., u.m.)
lock
out (n., u.m.)
shaft

well
-being (n.)
-beloved (u.m.)
-born (u.m.)
-bound (u.m.)
-bred (u.m.)
-clad (u.m.)
-deserving (u.m.)
-doer

-doing (n., u.m.)
-drained (u.m.)
-drilling (u.m.)
#field
-grown (u.m.)
head
-headed (u.m.)
hole
-informed (u.m.)
-known (u.m.)
-looking (u.m.)
-meaner
-nigh (u.m.)
-off (u.m.)
-read (u.m.)
-set-up (u.m.)
-settled (u.m.)
side
-spoken (u.m.)
spring
stead
-thought-of (u.m.)
-thought-out
   (u.m.)
-to-do (u.m.)
-wisher
-wishing (u.m.)
-worn (u.m.)
welterweight
werewolf

west
bound
-central (u.m.)
#end
-faced (u.m.)
going
most
-northwest
#side
-sider

wet
#bar
-cheeked (u.m.)

-clean (v.)
land
-nurse (v.)
pack
wash
whale
back
-backed (u.m.)
bone
-built (u.m.)
-headed (u.m.)
-mouthed (u.m.)
ship
wharf
#boat
hand
head
side
what
abouts (n.)
ever
-is-it (n.)
not (n.)
soever
-you-may-call-it
(n.)
wheat
cake
-colored (u.m.)
ear
-fed (u.m.)
field
grower
-rich (u.m.)
stalk
wheel
band
barrow
base
chair
-cut (u.m.)
going
horse (nonliteral)

#load
-made (u.m.)
plate
race
spin
stitch
-worn (u.m.)
wright
when
ever
-issued (u.m.)
soever
where
abouts
after
as
at
by
for
fore
from
in
insoever
into
of
on
over
soever
through
to
under
upon
with
withal
wherever
which
ever
soever
whiffletree
whip
cord
crack
-graft (v.)

#hand
lash
-marked (u.m.)
post
saw
-shaped (u.m.)
socket
staff
stalk
stall
stick
stitch
stock
-tailed (u.m.)
whipper
-in
snapper
whirl
about (n., u.m.)
blast
pool
-shaped (u.m.)
wind
whirlybird
whisk
broom
#tail
whistle
blower
(nonliteral)
#blower (literal)
stop
white
back
beard (n.)
#book
(diplomatic)
cap (n.)
coat (n.)
-collar (u.m.)
comb (n.)
corn
-eared (u.m.)

-eyed (u.m.)
face
-faced (u.m.)
foot (n.)
-footed (u.m.)
handed
-hard (u.m.)
head
-headed (u.m.)
-hot (u.m.)
#line
out (u.m., v.)
pot
tail
-tailed (u.m.)
-throated (u.m.)
top (n.)
vein
wash
who
ever
soever
whole
-headed (u.m.)
#hog
-hogger
sale
some
whomsoever
whooping#cough
wicker-woven (u.m.)
wicket
keeper
keeping
wide
-angle (u.m.)
-awake (u.m.)
-handed (u.m.)
mouthed
-open (u.m.)
spread
-spreading (u.m.)

widow
  #bird
  hood
wigwag
wild
  cat (n.)
  -eyed (u.m.)
  fire
  #land
  life
  #man
  wind
will
  -less
  -o'-the-wisp
  power
wilt-resistant (u.m.)
wind (v.)
  down (n., u.m.)
  up (n., u.m.)
  bag
  ball
  blown
  brace
  breaker
  burn
  catcher
  -chapped (u.m.)
  chill
  fall
  #farm
  fast
  -fertilized (u.m.)
  firm
  flow
  #force
  gall
  -galled (u.m.)
  #gauge
  hole
  -hungry (u.m.)
  jammer
  lass

mill
pipe
-pollinated (u.m.)
#power
-rode (u.m.)
row
screen
-shaken (u.m.)
-shear (u.m.)
shield
shock
side
sleeve
sock
speed
stop
storm
stream
swept
#tunnel
worn
window
  breaker
  -breaking (u.m.)
  #cleaner
  -cleaning (u.m.)
  #dresser
  -dressing (u.m.)
  pane
  #shade
  -shop (v.)
  -shopping (u.m.)
  sill
  #work
wine
  bag
  -black (u.m.)
  -drinking (u.m.)
  glass
  growing
  -hardy (u.m.)
  pot
  #press

-red (u.m.)
seller
taster
tester
vat
wing
  band
  bar
  beat
  bolt
  bone
  borne
  bow
  cut
  #flap
  -footed (u.m.)
  handed
  -heavy (u.m.)
  -loading (u.m.)
  -loose (u.m.)
  nut
  over (n., u.m.)
  -shaped (u.m.)
  -shot (u.m.)
  span
  -swift (u.m.)
  tip
  top
  wall
  -weary (u.m.)
winter
  -beaten (u.m.)
  -clad (u.m.)
  -fallow (v.)
  -fed (u.m.)
  feed
  #green (color)
  green (plant, etc.)
  -hardy (u.m.)
  kill
  -made (u.m.)
  -sown (u.m.)
  tide

time
-worn (u.m.)
wire
  bar
  -caged (u.m.)
  -cut (u.m.)
  cutter
  dancer
  draw (v.)
  -edged (u.m.)
  #gauge
  hair (dog)
  -haired (u.m.)
  less
  #line
  photo
  puller
  #rope
  spun
  stitch
  -stitched (u.m.)
  -tailed (u.m.)
  tap
  walker
  works
  -wound (u.m.)
wise
  acre
  crack
  guy
  head (n.)
  -headed (u.m.)
  -spoken (u.m.)
wishbone
witch
  craft
  #hazel
  #hunt
  -hunting (u.m.)
with
  draw
  hold
  in

out
stand
within
-bound (u.m.)
-named (u.m.)
woe
begone
worn
wolf
-eyed (u.m.)
#fish
hound
pack
woman
folk
hood
kind
womenfolk
wonder
land
strong
-struck (u.m.)
wood
bark (color)
bin
bined
block
-built (u.m.)
-cased (u.m.)
chipper
chopper
chuck
craft
cut
grub
hole
horse
hung (u.m.)
land
-lined (u.m.)
lot
-paneled (u.m.)
pecker

pile
-planing (u.m.)
print
pulp
ranger
rock
#rot
shed
side
stock
turner
-turning (u.m.)
-walled (u.m.)
wind (music)
working (u.m.)
wooden
head (n.)
-hulled (u.m.)
wool
fell
gatherer
grader
growing
head
-laden (u.m.)
-lined (u.m.)
pack
press
shearer
shed
sorter
stock
washer
wheel
-white (u.m.)
winder
woolly
-coated (u.m.)
-headed (u.m.)
-looking (u.m.)
-white (u.m.)
word
-blind (u.m.)

book
builder
catcher
-clad (u.m.)
-deaf (u.m.)
flow
list
-perfect (u.m.)
play
seller
smith
work
aday (n., u.m.)
-and-turn (u.m.)
away (n., u.m.)
bag
basket
bench
book
card
day
-driven (u.m.)
fare
flow
folk
force
group
hand
-hardened (u.m.)
horse
-hour (u.m.)
housed
life
load
manship
out (n., u.m.)
pace
pan
paper
people
place
room
saving

sheet
shoe
shop
-shy (n., u.m.)
-shyness
site
slip
space
-stained (u.m.)
stand
station
stream
study
table
time
up (n., u.m.)
ways
-weary (u.m.)
week
worn
working
#capital
#load
#room
world
beater
-conscious (u.m.)
#consciousness
#line
#power
-shaking (u.m.)
-weary (u.m.)
worm
-eaten (u.m.)
-eating (u.m.)
hole
-riddled (u.m.)
-ripe (u.m.)
seed
shaft
wood
worn
#away

down (u.m.)
out (u.m.)
outness
worrywart
worth
less
while (n., u.m.)
whileness (n.)
wrap
around (n., u.m.)
-up (n., u.m.)
wreath-crowned
(u.m.)
wreck-free (u.m.)
wring
bolt
staff
wrist
band
bone
drop
fall
lock
#pin
plate
watch
write
back (n., u.m.)
-in (n., u.m.)
off (n., u.m.)
-protect
up (n., u.m.)
writing#room
wrong
doer
-ended (u.m.)
-minded (u.m.)
-thinking (u.m.)
wrought
#iron

-up (u.m.)
wry
bill
-billed (u.m.)
-faced (u.m.)
-looking (u.m.)
-mouthed (u.m.)
neck
-set (u.m.)

X

X
-body
-chromosome
-disease
#rated
-shaped
-virus
x
-axis
#ray (n.)
-ray (u.m.)
xantho (c.f.)
all one word
xeno (c.f.)
all one word
xero (c.f.)
all one word
xylo (c.f.)
all one word

Y

Y
-chromosome
-joint
-level
-potential
-shaped
-track
-tube

Yankee-Doodle
yard
arm
-deep (u.m.)
-long (u.m.)
stick
-wide (u.m.)
yaw
meter
-sighted (u.m.)
year
book
day
end
-hour (u.m.)
long (u.m.)
-old (u.m.)
-round (u.m.)
yellow
back
-backed (u.m.)
-bellied (u.m.)
belly
-billed (u.m.)
brush
#fever
-headed (u.m.)
-tailed (u.m.)
-throated (u.m.)
top
yes
-man
-no
yester
day
year
yoke
fellow
mating
-toed (u.m.)

young
eyed (u.m.)
-headed (u.m.)
-ladylike
-looking (u.m.)
-manlike
-old
-womanhood
youthtide
yuletide

Z

Z
-bar
zero
axial
-dimensional
(u.m.)
#gravity
#hour
zigzag
zinc
-coated (u.m.)
-white (u.m.)
zip
#gun
line
-lipped (u.m.)
lock
zoo (c.f.)
all one word
zoologico (c.f.)
all one word
zygo (c.f.)
all one word
zygomatico (c.f.)
-orbital
rest one word
zymo (c.f.)
all one word

8. Punctuation

8.1.   Punctuation is used to clarify the meaning of written or printed language. Well-planned word order requires a minimum of punctuation. The trend toward less punctuation calls for skillful phrasing to avoid ambiguity and to ensure exact interpretation. The GPO STYLE MANUAL can offer only general rules of text treatment. A rigid design or pattern of punctuation cannot be laid down, except in broad terms. The adopted style, however, must be consistent and based on sentence structure.

8.2.   The general principles governing the use of punctuation are: If it does not clarify the text it should be omitted; and, in the choice and placing of punctuation marks, the sole aim should be to bring out more clearly the author's thought. Punctuation should aid reading and prevent misreading.

Apostrophes and possessives

8.3.   The possessive case of a singular or plural noun not ending in *s* is formed by adding an apostrophe and *s*. The possessive case of a singular or plural noun ending in *s* or with an *s* sound is formed by adding an apostrophe only. Some irregular plurals require both an apostrophe and an *s*. (For possessives of italicized nouns, see rule 11.6.)

boss', bosses'	man's, men's
child's, children's	medium's, media's
citizen's, citizens'	people's, peoples'
Congress', Congresses'	Essex's, Essexes'
criterion's, criteria's	Jones', Joneses'
Co.'s, Cos.'	Jesus'
erratum's, errata's	Mars'
hostess', hostesses'	Dumas'
lady's, ladies'	Schmitz'

8.4.   In compound nouns, the *'s* is added to the element nearest the object possessed.

comptroller general's decision	attorney at law's fee
attorneys general's appointments	John White, Jr.'s (no comma) account
Mr. Brown of New York's motion	

8.5.   Joint possession is indicated by placing an apostrophe on the last element of a series, while individual or alternative possession requires the use of an apostrophe on each element of a series.

soldiers and sailors' home	editor's or proofreader's opinion
Brown & Nelson's store	Bush's or Obama's administration
men's, women's, and children's clothing	Mrs. Smith's and Mrs. Allen's children
St. Michael's Men's Club	the Army's and the Navy's work
	master's and doctor's degrees

8.6.   In the use of an apostrophe in firm names, the names of organizations and institutions, the titles of books, and geographic names, the authentic form is to be followed. (Note use of "St.")

Masters, Mates & Pilots' Association	Johns Hopkins University
Dentists' Supply Co. of New York	Hinds' Precedents
International Ladies' Garment Workers' Union	Hells Canyon
Court of St. James's	Reader's Digest
St. Peter's Church	Actor's Equity Association
St. Elizabeths Hospital	Harpers Ferry
	but Martha's Vineyard

8.7.   Generally, the apostrophe should not be used after names of countries and other organized bodies ending in *s*, or after words more descriptive than possessive (not indicating personal possession), except when plural does not end in *s*.

United States control	teachers college
United Nations meeting	merchants exchange
Southern States industries	children's hospital
Massachusetts laws	Young Men's Christian Association
Bureau of Ships report	
House of Representatives session	*but*
Teamsters Union	Veterans' Administration
editors handbook	(now Department of Veterans Affairs)
syrup producers manual	Congress' attitude
technicians guide	

8.8.   Possessive pronouns do not take an apostrophe.

its	yours
ours	hers
theirs	whose

8.9.   Possessive indefinite or impersonal pronouns require an apostrophe.

each other's books   another's idea
some others' plans   someone's guesstimate
one's home is his castle

8.10.   The singular possessive case is used in such general terms as the
following:

arm's length   fuller's earth
attorney's fees   miner's inch
author's alterations   printer's ink
confectioner's sugar   traveler's checks
cow's milk   writer's cramp
distiller's grain

8.11.   While an apostrophe is used to indicate possession and contractions, it is not generally necessary to use an apostrophe simply to
show the plural form of most acronyms, initialisms, or abbreviations, except where clarity and sense demand such inclusion.

49ers   e'er (ever)
TVers   class of '08 (2008)
OKs   spirit of '76 (1776)
MCing
RIFing   *not* in her '70s (age)
RIFs   better: in her seventies
RIFed
YWCAs   *not* during the '90s
ABCs   better: during the 1990s or
1920s   during the nineties
IOUs
10s (thread)   *but*
4½s (bonds)   he never crosses his t's
3s (golf)   she fails to dot her i's
2 by 4s   a's, &'s, 7's
IQs   watch your p's and q's
don't (do not)   are they l's or 1's
I've (I have)   the Oakland A's
it's (it is/it has)   a number of s's
ne'er (never)   his résumé had too many I's

When the plural form of an acronym appears in parentheses, a lowercase *s* is included within the parentheses.

(MPDs)	(IPOs)
(MP3s)	(SUVs)
(JPEGs)	(EVs)

8.12. The apostrophe is omitted in abbreviations, and also in shortened forms of certain other words.

Danl., *not* Dan'l	Halloween, *not* Hallowe'en
phone, *not* 'phone	copter, *not* 'copter
coon, *not* 'coon	
possum, *not* 'possum	*but* ma'am

8.13. The plural of spelled-out numbers, of words referred to as words, and of words containing an apostrophe is formed by adding *s* or *es*; but *'s* is added to indicate the plural of words used as words if omission of the apostrophe would cause difficulty in reading.

twos, threes, sevens	yeses and noes
ands, ifs, and buts	yeas and nays
ins and outs	
the haves and have-nots	*but*
ups and downs	do's and don'ts
whereases and wherefores	which's and that's
pros and cons	

8.14. The possessive case is often used in lieu of an objective phrase even though ownership is not involved.

1 day's labor (labor for 1 day)	for charity's sake
12 days' labor	for pity's sake
2 hours' traveltime	several billion dollars' worth
a stone's throw	
2 weeks' pay	*but* $10 billion worth

8.15. The possessive case is not used in such expressions as the following, in which one noun modifies another.

day labor (labor by the day)	State prison
quartermaster stores	States rights

8.16. For euphony, nouns ending in *s* or *ce* and followed by a word beginning with *s* form the possessive by adding an apostrophe only.

for goodness' sake   for acquaintance' sake
Mr. Hughes' service   for conscience' sake
for old times' sake

8.17. A possessive noun used in an adjective sense requires the addition of *'s*.

He is a friend of John's.   Stern's is running a sale.

8.18. A noun preceding a gerund should be in the possessive case.

in the event of Mary's leaving   the ship's hovering nearby

Brackets

Brackets, in pairs, are used—

8.19. In transcripts, congressional hearings, the Congressional Record, testimony in courtwork, etc., to enclose interpolations that are not specifically a part of the original quotation, such as a correction, explanation, omission, editorial comment, or a caution that an error is reproduced literally.

We found this to be true at the Government Publishing Office [GPO].
He came on the 3d [2d] of July.
Our conference [lasted] 2 hours.
The general [Washington] ordered him to leave.
The paper was as follows [reads]:
I do not know. [Continues reading:]
[Chorus of "Mr. Chairman."]
They fooled only themselves. [Laughter.]
Our party will always serve the people [applause] in spite of the opposition [loud applause]. (If more than one bracketed interpolation, both are included within the sentence.)
The WITNESS. He did it that way [indicating].
Q. Do you know these men [handing witness a list]?
The bill had *not* been paid. [Italic added.] *or* [Emphasis added.]
The statue [sic] was on the statute books.
The WITNESS. This matter is classified. [Deleted.]
[Deleted.]
Mr. JONES. Hold up your hands. [Show of hands.]
Answer [after examining list]. Yes; I do.
Q. [Continuing.]
A. [Reads:]

A. [Interrupting.]

[Discussion off the record.]

[Pause.]

The WITNESS [interrupting]. It is known——

Mr. JONES [continuing]. Now let us take the next item.

Mr. SMITH [presiding]. Do you mean that literally?

Mr. JONES [interposing]. Absolutely.

[The matter referred to is as follows:]

The CHAIRMAN [to Mr. Smith].

The CHAIRMAN [reading]:

Mr. KELLEY [to the chairman]. From 15 to 25 percent.

[Objected to.]

[Mr. Smith nods.]

[Mr. Smith aside.]

[Mr. Smith makes further statement off the record.]

Mr. JONES [for Mr. Smith].

A VOICE FROM AUDIENCE. Speak up.

SEVERAL VOICES. Quiet!

8.20. In bills, contracts, laws, etc., to indicate matter that is to be omitted.

8.21. In mathematics, to denote that enclosed matter is to be treated as a unit.

8.22. When matter in brackets makes more than one paragraph, start each paragraph with a bracket and place the closing bracket at end of last paragraph.

Colon

The colon is used—

8.23. To introduce any matter that forms a question or a quotation.

> The following question came up for discussion: What policy should be adopted?
> She said: "We believe the time is now or never."

8.24. After an introductory independent clause that describes or defines what follows. If a complete sentence follows the colon, capitalize its first word.

> And then came the surprise: cake all around!
> His only rule was this: Chickens are not allowed past the front parlor.

8.25.   Before a final clause that extends or amplifies the preceding in-dependent clause. Even if a complete sentence follows the colon, lowercase its first word.

> Give up conveniences; do not demand special privileges; do not stop work: these are necessary while we are at war.
>
> Railroading is not a variety of outdoor sport: it is service.

8.26.   Following a sentence introducing an extract.

> The Clerk will read as follows:
>> Amendment by Mr. STEARNS: In line 4, after the word "pay", add a comma and the following words: "out of any money in the Treasury not otherwise appropriated".

8.27.   To introduce a run-in list.

> There are three primary pigment colors: magenta, yellow, and cyan.
>
> The vote was as follows: in the affirmative, 23; in the negative, 11; not voting, 3.
>
> These are what he missed most: walking along the river at dawn, napping under the old maple tree, chasing birds in the park.
>
> His goals were these: (1) learn Spanish, (2) see the Grand Canyon, and (3) climb Mt. Everest.

8.28.   To introduce a bulleted or enumerated list that is not run in. There are many ways to construct such a list—far too many to detail here—depending on the contents of the list and the intent of the author; however, a few guidelines concerning consistency should be kept in mind.

Punctuation at the end of each list item may be commas, semi-colons, periods, or even none at all, as long as its use is consistent within a list. The exception to this is that if commas or semicolons are used, the last item should end with a period, unless the list is part of a sentence that continues on after the list.

List items should be lowercased in a list using commas or semico-lons after each list item. For lists using periods or no punctuation, capitalization should be determined by context—lists of single words are usually lowercased, whereas lists of independent clauses are more appropriately capitalized. Whatever choice is made con-cerning capitalization, it should be applied to all the list items; the first item is not handled differently.

49-

A conjunction (and, or, nor) should follow the penultimate item in a list using commas or semicolons after each list item, but not otherwise.

His goals were these:
- Learn Spanish.
- See the Grand Canyon.
- Climb Mt. Everest.

His goals were these:
(1) learn Spanish,
(2) see the Grand Canyon, and
(3) climb Mt. Everest.

His goals were these:
(a) learn Spanish,
(b) see the Grand Canyon, and
(c) climb Mt. Everest;
but he knew it was unlikely he would meet them.

8.29. To introduce subentries in tables and leaderwork. Single subentries are run in following the colon and are initial cap.

Seward Peninsula: Council district: (single subentry runs in).
    Mining and manufacturing.
    Shipping and trade.

Seward Peninsula:
    Council district:
        Mining and manufacturing.
        Shipping and trade.
    Fairhaven district: Tourism (single subentry runs in).

8.30. After a salutation.

MY DEAR SIR:
Ladies and Gentlemen:
To Whom It May Concern:

8.31. In expressing clock time.

2:40 p.m.

8.32. In Biblical and other citations.

Luke 4:3.
I Corinthians 13:13.
Journal of Education 3:342–358.

8.33. In bibliographic references, between place of publication and name of publisher.

> Congressional Directory. Washington: U.S. Government Publishing Office.

8.34. To separate book titles and subtitles.

> Financial Aid for College Students: Graduate
> Germany Revisited: Education in the Federal Republic

8.35. In imprints before the year (en space each side of colon).

> U.S. Government Publishing Office
> Washington : 2016

8.36. In proportions.

> Concrete mixed 5:3:1
> *but* 5–2–1 *or* 5-2-1 (when so in copy)

8.37. In double colon as ratio sign.

> 1:2::3:6

Comma

The comma is used—

8.38. To separate two words or figures that might otherwise be misunderstood.

> Instead of hundreds, thousands came.
> Instead of 20, 50 came.
> December 7, 1941.
> In 2003, 400 men were dismissed.
> To John, Smith was very kind.
> What the difficulty is, is not known.
> *but* He suggested that that committee be appointed.

8.39. Before a direct quotation of only a few words following an introductory phrase.

> He said, "Now or never."

8.40. To indicate the omission of a word or words.

> Then we had much; now, nothing.

8.41. After each of a series of coordinate qualifying words.

> short, swift streams; *but* short tributary streams

8.42. Between an introductory modifying phrase and the subject modified.

> Beset by the enemy, they retreated.

8.43. Before and after *Jr., Sr., Esq., Ph.D., F.R.S., Inc.,* etc., within a sentence except where possession is indicated.

Henry Smith, Jr., chairman	*but*
Peter Johns, F.R.S., London	John Smith 2d (*or* II); Smith, John, II
Washington, DC, schools	Mr. Smith, Junior, also spoke
Google, Inc., technology	(where only last name is used)
Brown, A.H., Jr. (*not* Brown, Jr., A.H.)	Alexandria, VA's waterfront
Milan, Italy, vacation	
University of California, Santa Cruz, mascot	

8.44. To set off parenthetic words, phrases, or clauses.

> Mr. Jefferson, who was then Secretary of State, favored the location of the National Capital at Washington.
> It must be remembered, however, that the Government had no guarantee.
> It is obvious, therefore, that this office cannot function.
> The atom bomb, which was developed at the Manhattan project, was first used in World War II.
> Their high morale might, he suggested, have caused them to put success of the team above the reputation of the college.
> The restriction is laid down in title IX, chapter 8, section 15, of the code.
> *but* The man who fell [restrictive clause] broke his back.
> The dam that gave way [restrictive clause] was poorly constructed.
> He therefore gave up the search.

8.45. To set off words or phrases in apposition or in contrast.

> Mr. Green, the lawyer, spoke for the defense.
> Mr. Jones, attorney for the plaintiff, signed the petition.
> Mr. Smith, not Mr. Black, was elected.
> James Roosevelt, Democrat, of California.
> Jean's sister, Joyce, was the eldest. (Jean had one sister.)
> *but* Jonathan's brother Moses Taylor was appointed. (Jonathan had more than one brother.)

8.46. After each member within a series of three or more words, phrases, letters, or figures used with *and, or,* or *nor.*

> red, white, and blue
> horses, mules, and cattle; *but* horses and mules and cattle
> by the bolt, by the yard, or in remnants

a, b, and c
neither snow, rain, nor heat
2 days, 3 hours, and 4 minutes (series); *but* 70 years 11 months 6 days (age)

8.47. Before the conjunction in a compound sentence containing two or more independent clauses, each of which could have been written as a simple sentence.

> Fish, mollusks, and crustaceans were plentiful in the lakes, and turtles frequented the shores.
> The boy went home alone, and his sister remained with the crowd.

8.48. After a noun or phrase in direct address.

> Senator, will the measure be defeated?
> Mr. Chairman, I will reply to the gentleman later.
> *but* Yes, sir; he did see it.
> No, ma'am; I do not recall.

8.49. After an interrogative clause, followed by a direct question.

> You are sure, are you not?   You will go, will you not?

8.50. Between the title of a person and the name of an organization in the absence of the words *of* or *of the*.

> Chief, Division of Finance   colonel, 12th Cavalry Regiment
> chairman, Committee on   president, University of Virginia
> Appropriations

8.51. Inside closing quotation mark.

> He said "four," not "five."
> "Freedom is an inherent right," he insisted.
> Items marked "A," "B," and "C," inclusive, were listed.

8.52. To separate thousands and millions in numerical figures.

> 4,230   *but* 1,000,000,000 is more clearly
> 50,491   illustrated as 1 billion
> 1,250,000

8.53. After the year in complete dates (month, day, year) within a sentence.

> The dates of September 11, 1993, to June 12, 1994, were erroneous.
> This was reflected in the June 13, 2007, report.
> *but* Production for June 2008 was normal.
> The 10 February 2008 deadline passed.

The comma is omitted—

8.54. Between superior figures or letters in footnote references.

Numerous instances may be cited.[1][2]
Data are based on October production.[a][b]

8.55. Before ZIP (Zone Improvement Plan) Code postal-delivery number.

Washington, DC 20401–0003, for the GPO
East Rochester, OH 44625–9701 USA, was his hometown

8.56. Between month, holiday, or season and year in dates.

June 2016	150 B.C.
22d of May 2016	Labor Day 2016
February and March 2016	Easter Sunday 2016
January, February, and March 2016	5 January 2016 (military usage)
January 24 A.D. 2016; 15th of June	spring 2016
A.D. 2016	autumn 2016

8.57. Between the name and number of an organization.

Columbia Typographical Union No. 101–12
American Legion Post No. 33

8.58. In fractions, in decimals, and in serial numbers, except patent numbers.

$\frac{1}{2500}$
1.0947
page 2632
202–512–1800 (telephone number)
1721–1727 St. Clair Avenue
Executive Order 11242
motor No. 189463
1450 kilocycles; 1100 meters

8.59. Between two nouns one of which identifies the other.

The Children's Bureau's booklet "Infant Care" continues to be a bestseller.

8.60. Before an ampersand (&).

Brown, Wilson & Co.
Mine, Mill & Smelter Workers

8.61. Before abbreviations of compass directions.

6430 Princeton Dr. SW

8.62. In bibliographies, between name of the publication and volume or similar number.

> American Library Association Bulletin 34:238, April 1940.

8.63. Wherever possible without danger of ambiguity.

> $2 gold
> Executive Order No. 21
> General Order No. 12; *but* General Orders, No. 12
> Public Law 85–1
> He graduates in the year 2010 (not the year 2,010)
> My age is 30 years 6 months 12 days.
> John Lewis 2d (*or* II)
> Murphy of Illinois; Murphy of New York (where only last name is used)
> Carroll of Carrollton; Henry of Navarre (person closely identified with place);
>   *but* Clyde Leo Downs, of Maryland; President Levin, of Yale University
> James Bros. et al.; but James Bros., Nelson Co., et al. (last element of series)

Dash

A 1-em dash is used—

8.64. To mark a sudden break or abrupt change in thought.

> He said—and no one contradicted him—"The battle is lost."
> If the bill should pass—which God forbid!—the service will be wrecked.
> The auditor—shall we call him a knave or a fool?—approved an inaccurate statement.

8.65. To indicate an interruption or an unfinished word or sentence. A 2-em dash is used when the interruption is by a person other than the speaker, and a 1-em dash will show self-interruption. Note that extracts must begin with a true paragraph. Following extracts, colloquy must start as a paragraph.

> "Such an idea can scarcely be——"
> "The word 'donation'——"
> "The word 'dona'——"
> He said: "Give me lib——"
> The bill reads "repeal," not "am——"
> Q. Did you see——
> A. No, sir.

> Mr. BROWN [reading]: "The report goes on to say that"—Observe this closely—"during the fiscal year . . . ."

8.66. Instead of commas or parentheses if the meaning may thus be clarified.

> These are shore deposits—gravel, sand, and clay—but marine sediments underlie them.

8.67. Before a final clause that summarizes a series of ideas.

> Freedom of speech, freedom of worship, freedom from want, freedom from fear—these are the fundamentals of moral world order.

8.68. After an introductory phrase reading into the following lines and indicating repetition of such phrase.

> I recommend—
>> that we submit them for review and corrections;
>> that we then accept them as corrected; and
>> that we also publish them.

8.69. With a preceding question mark, in lieu of a colon.

> How can you explain this?—"Fee paid, $5."

8.70. To precede a credit line or a run-in credit or signature.

>> Lay the proud usurpers low!
>> Tyrants fall in every foe!
>> Liberty's in every blow!
>> Let us do or die!
>>> —Robert Burns.

> Every man's work shall be made manifest.—I Corinthians 3:13.
> This statement is open to question.—GERALD H. FORSYTHE.

8.71. After a run-in sidehead.

8.72. To separate run-in questions and answers in testimony.

> Q. Did he go?—A. No.

A 1-em dash is not used—

8.73. At the beginning of any line of type, except as shown in rule 8.70.

8.74. Immediately after a comma, colon, or semicolon.

A 3-em dash is used—

8.75. In bibliographies to indicate repetition.

> Powell, James W., Jr., Hunting in Virginia's lowlands. 1972. 200 pp.
> ———Fishing off Delmarva. 1972. 28 pp.

An en dash is used—

8.76. In a combination of figures and/or letters, including acronyms (even if the acronym spells out a word (e.g. PATRIOT)). But use a hyphen to combine such letters and/or figures with a word or abbreviation, or in chemical nomenclature.

figures:
5–20 (bonds)
85–1—85–20 (Public laws; use em dash between two elements with en dashes)
1–703–555–6593 (telephone number)
123–45–6789 (Social Security number)
$15–$20 (range)

letters:
WTOP–AM–FM–TV (radio and television stations)
CBS–TV
AFL–CIO
C–SPAN
s–NOM (scientific term)

figures and letters:
6–A (exhibit identification)
DC–14 (airplane)
MiG–25 (airplane, mixed letters with figure)
I–95 (interstate roadway)
4–H (Club)
LK–66–A(2)–74, 15A–x–3 (serial numbers)
SE–BatsCZX–2015–65 (SEC file number)
rule 13e–4
Section 12(a)–(d) (range)

but a hyphen is used with:
ACF-Brill Motors Co. (hyphen with capital letters and a word)
loran-C (coined word plus letter)
ALL-AMERICAN ESSAY CONTEST (hyphen in capitalized heading)
Four Corners Monument, AZ-NM-UT-CO (hyphen with two-letter state abbreviations)
U-235, Cr-Ni-Mo (chemical symbols)
δ-HCH (chemical nomenclature)

8.77. In the absence of the word *to* when denoting a span of time.

2005–2008   January–June   Monday–Friday

An en dash is not used—

8.78. For *to* when the word *from* precedes the first of two related figures or expressions.

> From June 1 to July 30, 2016; *not* from June 1–July 30, 2016

8.79. For *and* when the word *between* precedes the first of two related figures or expressions.

> Between 2000 and 2016; *not* between 2000–16

Ellipses

8.80. Three periods or three asterisks, separated by en spaces, are used to denote an ellipsis within a sentence, at the beginning or end of a sentence, or in two or more consecutive sentences. To achieve faithful reproduction of excerpt material, editors using period ellipses should indicate placement of the terminal period in relation to an ellipsis at the end of a sentence. Note, in the following examples, the additional spacing necessary to clearly define commas and the terminal period when period ellipses are employed.

> The Senate having tried Andrew Johnson, President of the United States, upon articles of impeachment exhibited against him by the House of Representatives, and two-thirds of the Senators present not having found him guilty of the charges contained in the second, third, and eleventh articles of impeachment, it is therefore
>
> *Ordered and adjudged.* That the said Andrew Johnson, President of the United States be, and he is, acquitted of the charges in said articles made and set forth.

> The Senate having tried Andrew Johnson . . . upon articles of impeachment . . . , and two-thirds of the Senators present not having found him guilty of the charges . . . , it is therefore
>
> *Ordered and adjudged.* That the said Andrew Johnson, President of the United States be . . . acquitted of the charge . . . .

> The Senate having tried Andrew Johnson * * * upon articles of impeachment * * *, and two-thirds of the Senators present not having found him guilty of the charges * * *, it is therefore
>
> *Ordered and adjudged.* That the said Andrew Johnson, President of the United States be * * * acquitted of the charges * * *.

8.81. Ellipses are not overrun alone at the end of a paragraph.

8.82. Copy will be followed for period or asterisk ellipses, even if inconsistent.

8.83. A line of asterisks indicates an omission of one or more entire paragraphs. In 26½-pica or wider measure, a line of "stars" means seven asterisks indented 2 ems at each end of the line, with the remaining space divided evenly between the asterisks. In measures less than 26½ picas, five asterisks are used. Quotation marks are not used on a line of asterisks in quoted matter. Where an ellipsis line ends a complete quotation, no closing quote is used.

*   *   *   *   *   *   *

8.84. Indented matter in 26½-pica or wider measure also requires a seven-asterisk line to indicate the omission of one or more entire paragraphs.

8.85. If an omission occurs in the last part of a paragraph immediately before a line of asterisks, three periods or asterisks are used, in addition to the line of asterisks, to indicate such an omission.

8.86. Equalize spacing above and below an ellipsis line.

Exclamation point

8.87. The exclamation point is used to mark surprise, incredulity, admiration, appeal, or other strong emotion which may be expressed even in a declarative or interrogative sentence.

> Who shouted, "All aboard!" [Note omission of question mark.]
> "Great!" he shouted. [Note omission of comma.]
> He acknowledged the fatal error!
> How breathtakingly beautiful!
> Timber!
> Mayday! Mayday!

8.88. In direct address, either to a person or a personified object, O is used without an exclamation point, or other punctuation; but if strong feeling is expressed, an exclamation point is placed at the end of the statement.

> O my friend, let us consider this subject impartially.
> O Lord, save Thy people!

8.89. In exclamations without direct address or appeal, *oh* is used instead
of *O*, and the exclamation point is omitted.

> Oh, but the gentleman is mistaken.
> Oh dear; the time is so short.

Hyphen

The hyphen (a punctuation mark, not an element in the spelling of words)
is used—

8.90. To connect the elements of certain compound words. (See Chapter 6 "Compounding Rules.")

8.91. To indicate continuation of a word divided at the end of a line.

8.92. Between the letters of a spelled word.

> The Style Board changed New Jerseyite to New J-e-r-s-e-y-a-n.
> A native of Halifax is a H-a-l-i-g-o-n-i-a-n.
> The Chinese repressive action took place in T-i-a-n-a-n-m-e-n Square.

8.93. To separate elements of chemical formulas.

The hyphen, as an element, may be used—

8.94. To represent letters deleted or illegible words in copy.

> Oakland's - - bonic plague   Richard Emory H - - - -

Parentheses

Parentheses are used—

8.95. To set off important matter not intended to be part of the main
statement that is not a grammatical element of the sentence. In
colloquy, brackets must be substituted.

> This case (124 U.S. 329) is not relevant.
> The result (see fig. 2) is most surprising.
> The United States is the principal purchaser (by value) of these exports (23 percent in 1995 and 19 percent in 1996).

8.96. To enclose a parenthetic clause where the interruption is too great to
be indicated by commas.

> You can find it neither in French dictionaries (at any rate, not in Littré) nor in
> English dictionaries.

8.97. To enclose an explanatory word not part of a written or printed statement.

> the Winchester (VA) Star; *but* the Star of Winchester, VA
> Portland (OR) Chamber of Commerce; *but* Athens, GA, schools

8.98. To enclose letters or numbers designating items in a series, either at the beginning of paragraphs or within a paragraph.

> The order of delivery will be: (a) food, (b) clothing, and (c) tents and other housing equipment.
> You will observe that the sword is (1) old fashioned, (2) still sharp, and (3) unusually light for its size.
> Paragraph 7(B)(1)(*a*) will be found on page 6. (Note parentheses closed up.)

8.99. To enclose a figure inserted to confirm a written or printed statement given in words if double form is specifically requested.

> This contract shall be completed in sixty (60) days.

8.100. A reference in parentheses at the end of a sentence is placed before the period, unless it is a complete sentence in itself.

> The specimen exhibits both phases (pl. 14, *A, B*).
> The individual cavities show great variation. (See pl. 4.)

8.101. If a sentence contains more than one parenthetic reference, the one at the end is placed before the period.

> This sandstone (see pl. 6) is in every county of the State (see pl. 1).

8.102. When a figure is followed by a letter in parentheses, no space is used between the figure and the opening parenthesis; but, if the letter is not in parentheses and the figure is repeated with each letter, the letter is closed up with the figure.

> 15(*a*). Classes, grades, and sizes.
> 15*a*. Classes, grades, and sizes.

8.103. If both a figure and a letter in parentheses are used before each paragraph, a period and an en space are used after the closing parenthesis. If the figure is not repeated before each letter in parentheses but is used only before the first letter, the period is placed after the figure. However, if the figure is not repeated before each letter in parentheses and no period is used, space is inserted after the number if at least one other lettered subsection appears.

> 15(*a*). When the figure is used before the letter in each paragraph—
> 15(*b*). The period is placed after the closing parenthesis.
> 15. (*a*) When the figure is used before the letter in the first paragraph but not repeated with subsequent letters—
> (*b*) The period is used after the figure only.
> Sec. 12 (a) When no period is used and a letter in parentheses appears after a numbered item—
> (b) Space must be used after the number if at least one other lettered subsection is shown.

8.104. Note position of the period relative to closing parenthesis:

> The vending stand sells a variety of items (sandwiches, beverages, cakes, etc.).
> The vending stand sells a variety of items (sandwiches, beverages, cakes, etc. (sometimes ice cream)).
> The vending stand sells a variety of items. (These include sandwiches, beverages, cakes, etc. (sometimes ice cream).)

8.105. To enclose bylines in congressional work.

> (By Harvey Hagman, archeological correspondent)

8.106. When matter in parentheses makes more than one paragraph, start each paragraph with a parenthesis and place the closing parenthesis at the end of the last paragraph.

Period

The period is used—

8.107. After a declarative sentence that is not exclamatory or after an imperative sentence.

> Stars are suns.
> He was employed by Sampson & Company.
> Do not be late.
> On with the dance.

8.108. After an indirect question or after a question intended as a suggestion and not requiring an answer.

> Tell me how he did it.
> May we hear from you.
> May we ask prompt payment.

8.109.   In place of a closing parenthesis after a letter or number denoting a series.

a. Bread well baked	1. Punctuate freely
b. Meat cooked rare	2. Compound sparingly
c. Cubed apples stewed	3. Index thoroughly

8.110.   To indicate an ellipsis. (See rules 8.80 and 8.82.)

8.111.   After a run-in sidehead.

> *Conditional subjunctive.*—The conditional subjunctive is required for all unreal and doubtful conditions.
>
> **2. Peacetime preparation.**—*a.* The Chairman of the National Security Resources Board, etc.
>
> *2. Peacetime preparation.*—*Industrial mobilization plans.*—The Chairman of the National Security Resources Board, etc.
>
> **2. Peacetime preparation.**—*Industrial mobilization.*—The Chairman of the National Security Resources Board, etc.
>
> *62. Determination of types.*—*a. Statement of characteristics.*—Before types of equipment, etc.
>
> **Steps in planning for procurement.**—(1) *Determination of needs.*—To plan for the procurement of such arms, etc.
>
> *62. Determination of types.*—*(a) Statement of characteristics.*—Before, etc.
>
> **DETERMINATION OF TYPES.**—**Statement of characteristics.**—Before types of, etc.
>
> *but* NOTE.—The source material was furnished.
>
> Source: U.S. Department of Commerce, Bureau of the Census.

8.112.   Paragraphs and subparagraphs may be arranged according to the following scheme. The sequence is not fixed, and variations, in addition to the use of center and side heads or indented paragraphs, may be adopted, depending on the number of parts.

> I. Outlines can begin with a capital Roman numeral.
>> A. The number of levels and the width of the column determine alignment and indention.
>>> 1. A set space (en space) following the identifier aids alignment.
>>>> *a.* Usually, typefaces and sizes are chosen to agree with the hierarchy of the head breakdowns.
>>>>> (1) Aligning runover lines with the first word which follows the number or letter aids readability.

(*a*) It is important to vary (alternate) the use of letters and numbers in any outline.

    (i) The lowercase Roman numerals (i), (ii), etc. may be used as parts of the outline or to identify subparts of any previous parts.

      (*aa*) When absolutely necessary, double (or triple) lowercase letters may be used.

II. Where not needed, the capital Roman numerals may be discarded and the outline can begin with the letter A. As in any composition, consistency in indentions and order is essential.

8.113. To separate integers from decimals in a single expression.

13.75 percent	1.25 meters
$3.50	0.08 mile

8.114. In continental European languages, to indicate thousands.

1.317	72.190.175

8.115. After abbreviations, unless otherwise specified. (See Chapter 9, "Abbreviations and Letter Symbols.")

Apr.	*but*
Co.	m (meter)
fig.	kc (kilocycle)
Ry.	NY (New York)
Ph.D.	RR
p.m.	SSE (south-southeast)

8.116. After legends and explanatory matter beneath illustrations. Legends without descriptive language do not receive periods.

Figure 1.—Schematic drawing.
Figure 1.—Continued.
but Figure 1 (without legend, no period)

8.117. After *Article 1, Section 1,* etc., at the beginning of paragraphs.

A center period is sometimes used—

8.118. To indicate multiplication. (Use of a multiplication sign is preferable.)

$a \cdot b$ $a \times b$

The period is omitted—
8.119.   After—

> Lines in title pages
> Center, side, and running heads; *but* is not omitted after run-in
>> sideheads
> Continued lines
> Boxheads of tables
> Scientific, chemical, or other symbols
>
> This rule does not apply to abbreviation periods.

8.120.   After a quotation mark that is preceded by a period.

> She said: "I believe the time is now or never."

8.121.   After letters used as names without specific designation.

> Officer B, Subject A, Brand X, etc.
> A said to B that all is well.
> Mr. A told Mr. B that the case was closed.
> Mr. X (for unknown or censored name).
> *but* Mr. A. [for Mr. Andrews]. I do not want to go.
> Mr. K. [for Mr. King]. The meeting is adjourned.

8.122.   After a middle initial which is merely a letter and not an abbreviation of a name.

> Daniel D Tompkins
> Ross T McIntire
> *but* Harry S. Truman (President Truman's preference)

8.123.   After a short name which is not an abbreviation of the longer form.

> Alex   Mac
> Ed   Sam

8.124.   After Roman numerals used as ordinals.

> King George V   Super Bowl XLIX, LI
> Apollo XII insigne   *but* Super Bowl 50

8.125.   After words and incomplete statements listed in columns. Full-measure matter is not to be regarded as a column.

8.126.   After explanatory matter under leaders or rules.

> ....
> (Name)   (Address)   (Position)

8.127. Immediately before leaders, even if an abbreviation precedes the leaders.

Question mark

The question mark is used—

8.128. To indicate a direct query, even if not in the form of a question.

> Did he do it?
> He did what?
> Can the money be raised? is the question.
> Who asked, "Why?" [Note single question mark.]
> "Did you hurt yourself, my son?" she asked.

8.129. To express more than one query in the same sentence.

> Can he do it? or you? or anyone?

8.130. To express doubt.

> He said the boy was 8(?) feet tall. (No space before question mark.)
> The statue(?) was on the statute books.
> The scientific identification *Dorothia?* was noted. (Roman "?".)

Quotation marks

Quotation marks are used—

8.131. To enclose direct quotations. (Each part of an interrupted quotation begins and ends with quotation marks.)

> The answer is "No."
> He said, "John said, 'No.' " (Note thin space between single and double closing quotes.)
> "John," asked Henry, "why do you go?"

8.132. To enclose any matter following such terms as *entitled, the word, the term, marked, designated, classified, named, endorsed, cited as, referred to as,* or *signed;* however, quotation marks are not used to enclose expressions following the terms *known as, called, so-called,* etc., unless such expressions are misnomers or slang.

> Congress passed the act entitled "An act . . . ."
> After the word "treaty," insert a comma.
> Of what does the item "Miscellaneous debts" consist?
> The column "Imports from foreign countries" was not well written.
> The document will be marked "Exhibit No. 21;" *but* The document may be made exhibit No. 21.
> The check was endorsed "John Adamson."

It was signed "John."
but Beryllium is known as glucinium in some European countries.
It was called profit and loss.
The so-called investigating body.

8.133. To enclose titles of addresses, albums, articles, awards, books, captions, editorials, essays, headings, headlines, hearings, motion pictures and plays (including television and radio programs), operas, papers, short poems, reports, songs, studies, subheadings, subjects, and themes. All principal words are to be capitalized.

An address on "Uranium-235 in the Atomic Age"
The article "Germany Revisited" appeared in the last issue.
He received the "Man of the Year" award.
"The Conquest of Mexico," a published work (book)
Under the caption "Long-Term Treasurys Rise"
The subject was discussed in "Punctuation." (chapter heading)
It will be found in "Part XI: Early Thought."
The editorial "Haphazard Budgeting"
"Compensation," by Emerson (essay)
"United States To Appoint Representative to U.N." (heading or headline)
In "Search for Paradise" (motion picture)
"South Pacific" (play)
A paper on "Constant-Pressure Combustion" was read.
"O Captain! My Captain!" (short poem)
The report "Atomic Energy: What It Means to the Nation"; *but* annual report
    of the Director of the Government Publishing Office
This was followed by the singing of "The Star-Spangled Banner."
The information is located under the subhead "Sixty Days of Turmoil."
The subject (or theme) of the conference is "Peaceful Uses of Atomic Energy."
also Account 5, "Management fees."
Under the heading "Management and Operation."
Under the appropriation "Building of ships, Navy."

8.134. At the beginning of each paragraph of a quotation, but at the end of the last paragraph only.

8.135. To enclose a letter or communication that bears both date and signature.

8.136. To enclose misnomers, slang expressions, sobriquets, coined words, or ordinary words used in an arbitrary way.

His report was "bunk."
It was a "gentlemen's agreement."

> The "invisible government" is responsible.
> George Herman "Babe" Ruth.
> *but* He voted for the lameduck amendment.

8.137.   To close up characters except when they precede a fraction or an apostrophe or precede or follow a superior figure or letter, in which case a thin space is used. A thin space is used to separate double and single quotation marks.

8.138.   The comma and the final period will be placed inside the quotation marks. Other punctuation marks should be placed inside the quotation marks only if they are a part of the matter quoted.

> Ruth said, "I think so."
> "The President," he said, "will veto the bill."
> The conductor shouted, "All aboard!"
> Who asked, "Why?"
> The President suggests that "an early occasion be sought."
> Why call it a "gentlemen's agreement"?

8.139.   In congressional and certain other classes of work showing amendments, and in courtwork with quoted language, punctuation marks are printed after the quotation marks when not a part of the quoted matter.

> Insert the words "growth", "production", and "manufacture".
> To be inserted after the words "cadets, U.S. Coast Guard;".
> Change "February 1, 1983", to "June 30, 2016".
> "Insert in lieu thereof 'July 1, 1983,'."

8.140.   When occurring together, quotation marks should precede footnote reference numbers.

> The commissioner claimed that the award was "unjustified."[1]
> Kelly's exact words were: "The facts in the case prove otherwise."[2]

8.141.   Quotation marks should be limited, if possible, to three sets (double, single, double).

> "The question in the report is, 'Can a person who obtains his certificate of naturalization by fraud be considered a "bona fide" citizen of the United States?' "

Quotation marks are not used—

8.142.   To enclose titles of works of art: paintings, statuary, etc.

8.143. To enclose names of newspapers or magazines.

8.144. To enclose complete letters having date and signature.

8.145. To enclose extracts that are indented or set in smaller type, or solid extracts in leaded matter; but indented matter in text that is already quoted carries quotation marks.

8.146. In indirect quotations.

> Tell her yes.   He could not say no.

8.147. Before a display initial which begins a quoted paragraph.

Semicolon

The semicolon is used—

8.148. To separate clauses containing commas.

> Donald A. Peters, Jr., president of the First National Bank, was also a director of New York Central; Harvey D. Jones was a director of Oregon Steel Co. and New York Central; Thomas W. Harrison, chairman of the board of McBride & Co., was also on the board of Oregon Steel Co.
>
> Reptiles, amphibians, and predatory mammals swallow their prey whole or in large pieces, bones included; waterfowl habitually take shellfish entire; and gallinaceous birds are provided with gizzards that grind up the hardest seeds.
>
> Yes, sir; he did see it.
>
> No, sir; I do not recall.

8.149. To separate statements that are too closely related in meaning to be written as separate sentences, and also statements of contrast.

> Yes; that is right.
>
> No; we received one-third.
>
> It is true in peace; it is true in war.
>
> War is destructive; peace, constructive.

8.150. To set off explanatory abbreviations or words that summarize or explain preceding matter.

> The industry is related to groups that produce finished goods; i.e., electrical machinery and transportation equipment.
>
> There were three metal producers involved; namely, Jones & Laughlin, Armco, and Kennecott.

The semicolon is not used—

8.151.   Where a comma will suffice.

> Offices are located in New York, NY, Chicago, IL, and Dallas, TX.

Single punctuation

8.152.   Single punctuation should be used wherever possible without ambiguity.

> 124 U.S. 321 (no comma)
> Sir: (no dash)
> Joseph replied, "It is a worthwhile effort." (no outside period)

Type

8.153.   All punctuation marks, including parentheses, brackets, and superior reference figures, are set to match the type of the words which they adjoin. A lightface dash is used after a run-in boldface sidehead followed by lightface matter. Lightface brackets, parentheses, or quotation marks shall be used when both boldface and lightface matter are enclosed.

> Charts: C&GS 5101 (N.O. **18320**), page **282 (see above)**; N.O. **93491 (Plan)**; page **271**.

9. Abbreviations and Letter Symbols

9.1. Abbreviations and letter symbols are used to save space and to avoid distracting the reader by use of repetitious words or phrases.

9.2. The nature of the publication governs the extent to which abbreviations are used. In the text of technical and legal publications, and in parentheses, brackets, footnotes, sidenotes, tables, leaderwork, and bibliographies, many words are frequently abbreviated. Heads, legends, tables of contents, and indexes follow the style of the text.

9.3. Internal and terminal punctuation in symbols representing units of measure are to be omitted to conform with practice adopted by scientific, technical, and industrial groups. Where the omission of terminal punctuation causes confusion; e.g., the symbol *in* (inch) mistaken for the preposition *in*, the symbol should be spelled out.

9.4. Standard and easily understood forms are preferable, and they should be uniform throughout a job. Abbreviations not generally known should be followed in the text by the spelled-out forms in parentheses the first time they occur; in tables and leaderwork such explanatory matter should be supplied in a footnote. As the printer cannot rewrite the copy, the author should supply these explanatory forms.

9.5. In technical matter, symbols for units of measure should be used only with figures; similarly, many other abbreviations and symbols should not appear in isolation. For example, *energy is measured in foot-pounds*, NOT *energy is measured in ft•lbs*. See ASME Y14.38 ("Abbreviations and Acronyms for use on Drawings and Related Documents") for an extended list of technical abbreviations.

Capitals, hyphens, periods (points), and spacing

9.6. In general, an abbreviation follows the capitalization and hyphenation of the word or words abbreviated. It is followed by a period unless otherwise indicated.

c.o.d.	St.	*but* ft•lb

9.7.   Abbreviations and initials of a personal name with points are set without spaces. Abbreviations composed of contractions and initials or numbers, will retain space.

F.D.R.	i.e., e.g. (*but* op. cit.)
J.F.K.	B.S., LL.D., Ph.D., B.Sc.
L.B.J.	H.R. 116 (*but* S. 116, S. Con.
B.C. Forrest, D.D.S.	Res. 116)
U.S.	C.A.D.C. (*but* App. D.C.)
U.N.	*but*
U.S.C. (*but* Rev. Stat.)	AT&T
A.F. of L.-CIO (AFL–CIO	Texas A&M
preferred)	R&D
A.D., B.C.	

9.8.   Except as otherwise designated, points and spaces are omitted after initials used as shortened names of governmental agencies and of other organized bodies. "Other organized bodies" will be interpreted to mean organized bodies that have become popularly identified with a symbol, such as MIT (Massachusetts Institute of Technology), GM (General Motors), AFLAC (American Family Life Assurance Company), etc. (See also rule 9.61.) Symbols, when they appear in copy, may be used for acts of Congress. Example: ARA (Area Redevelopment Act).

VFW	TVA	ARC
NLRB	AFL–CIO	ASTM

Geographic terms

9.9.   *United States* must be spelled out when appearing in a sentence containing the name of another country. The abbreviation *U.S.* will be used when preceding the word *Government* or the name of a Government organization, except in formal writing (treaties, Executive orders, proclamations, etc.); congressional bills; legal citations and courtwork; and covers and title pages.

> U.S. Government
> U.S. Congress
> U.S. Department of Health and Human Services
> U.S. district court
> U.S. Supreme Court (*but* Supreme Court of the United States)
> U.S. Army (*but* Army of the United States)
> U.S. monitor *Nantucket*

U.S.-NATO assistance
U.S. Government efforts to control inflation must be successful if the
     United States is to have a stable economy.
but British, French, and United States Governments; United States-British
     talks

9.10. With the exceptions in the preceding rule, the abbreviation *U.S.*
is used in the adjective position, but is spelled out when used as a
noun.

U.S. foreign policy	United States Steel Corp.
U.S. farm-support program	(legal title)
U.S. attorney	Foreign policy of the
U.S. citizen	United States
United States Code (official title)	*not* Temperatures vary in the U.S.

9.11. The names of foreign countries are not abbreviated, with the exception of the former U.S.S.R., which is abbreviated due to its
length.

9.12. In other than formal usage as defined in rule 9.9, all States of the
United States, Puerto Rico, the Virgin Islands, and freely associated
states are abbreviated immediately following any capitalized geographic term, including armory, arsenal, airbase, airport, barracks,
depot, fort, Indian agency, military camp, national cemetery (also
forest, historic site, memorial, seashore, monument, park), naval
shipyard, proving ground, reservation (forest, Indian, or military),
and reserve or station (military or naval).

Prince George's County, MD	Arlington National Cemetery, VA
Mount Rainier National Forest, WA	Aberdeen Proving Ground, MD
	Washington Dulles
Stone Mountain, GA	International Airport, VA
National Naval Medical Center, Bethesda, MD	Redstone Arsenal, AL
Mark Twain National Wildlife Refuge, IL-IA-MO (note use of hyphens here)	*but*
	Leavenworth freight yards, Kansas
Richmond, VA	Altoona sidetrack, Wisconsin

9.13. The Postal Service style of two-letter State, Province, and freely
associated State abbreviations is to be used.

United States
[Including freely associated States]

Alabama..........................AL	Kentucky........................KY	Ohio...............................OH
Alaska............................AK	Louisiana.......................LA	Oklahoma......................OK
American Samoa...........AS	Maine.............................ME	Oregon...........................OR
Arizona.........................AZ	Marshall Islands............MH	Palau.............................PW
Arkansas.......................AR	Maryland........................MD	Pennsylvania.................PA
California......................CA	Massachusetts...............MA	Puerto Rico...................PR
Colorado.......................CO	Michigan........................MI	Rhode Island.................RI
Connecticut..................CT	Minnesota......................MN	South Carolina..............SC
Delaware.......................DE	Mississippi.....................MS	South Dakota................SD
District of Columbia.....DC	Missouri.........................MO	Tennessee......................TN
Federated States of	Montana.........................MT	Texas.............................TX
Micronesia..............FM	Nebraska........................NE	Utah..............................UT
Florida..........................FL	Nevada...........................NV	Vermont........................VT
Georgia.........................GA	New Hampshire..............NH	Virgin Islands................VI
Guam.............................GU	New Jersey.....................NJ	Virginia.........................VA
Hawaii...........................HI	New Mexico....................NM	Washington....................WA
Idaho.............................ID	New York........................NY	West Virginia.................WV
Illinois..........................IL	North Carolina...............NC	Wisconsin......................WI
Indiana..........................IN	North Dakota.................ND	Wyoming.......................WY
Iowa..............................IA	Northern Mariana	
Kansas...........................KS	Islands.....................MP	

Canada

Alberta..........................AB	Northwest Territories.....NT	Prince Edward Island.....PE
British Columbia...........BC	Nova Scotia....................NS	Quebec..........................QC
Manitoba.......................MB	Nunavut.........................NU	Saskatchewan................SK
New Brunswick..............NB	Ontario..........................ON	Yukon............................YT
Newfoundland and Labrador...NL		

9.14. The names of other insular possessions, trust territories, and *Long Island, Staten Island,* etc., are not abbreviated.

9.15. The names of Canadian Provinces and other foreign political subdivisions are not abbreviated except as noted in rule 9.13.

Addresses

9.16. Words such as *Street, Avenue, Place, Road, Square, Boulevard, Terrace, Drive, Court,* and *Building,* following a name or number, are abbreviated in footnotes, sidenotes, tables, leaderwork, and lists.

9.17. In addresses, no period is used with the abbreviations *NW, SW, NE, SE* (indicating sectional divisions of cities) following name or number. *North, South, East,* and *West* are spelled out at all times.

9.18. The word *Street* or *Avenue* as part of a name is not abbreviated even in parentheses, footnotes, sidenotes, tables, lists, or leaderwork.

    14th Street Bridge   Ninth Avenue Bldg.

9.19. The words *County, Fort, Mount, Point,* and *Port* are not abbreviated. *Saint* (*St.*) and *Sainte* (*Ste.*) should be abbreviated.

Descriptions of tracts of land

9.20. In the description of tracts of public land the following abbreviations are used (periods are only used after compass directional abbreviations that describe township(s) (T./Tps.) and range(s) (R./Rs.)):

SE¼NW¼ sec. 4, T. 12 S., R. 15 E., of the Boise Meridian
lot 6, NE¼ sec. 4, T. 6 N., R. 1 W.
N½ sec. 20, T. 7 N., R. 2 W., sixth principal meridian
Tps. 9, 10, 11, and 12 S., Rs. 12 and 13 W.
T. 2 S., Rs. 8, 9, and 10 E., sec. 26
T. 3 S., R. 1 E., sec. 34, W½E½, W½, and W½SE¼SE¼
sec. 32 (with or without a township number)

9.21. If fractions are spelled out in land descriptions, *half* and *quarter* are used (not *one-half* or *one-quarter*).

south half of T. 47 N., R. 64 E.

9.22. In case of an unavoidable break in a land-description symbol group at end of a line, use no hyphen and break after fraction.

Names and titles

9.23. The following forms are not always abbreviations, and copy should be followed as to periods:

Al	Ben	Fred	Walt
Alex	Ed	Sam	Will

9.24. In signatures, an effort should be made to retain the exact form used by the signer.

George Wythe   Geo. Taylor

9.25. In company and other formal names, if it is not necessary to preserve the full legal title, such forms as *Bro., Bros., Co., Corp., Inc., Ltd.,* and *&* are used. *Association* and *Manufacturing* are not abbreviated.

Radio Corp. of America   Electronics Manufacturing Co.
Aluminum Co. of America   Texas College of Arts & Industries
Standard Oil Co. of New Jersey   Robert Wilson & Associates, Inc.
H.J. Baker & Bro.   U.S. News & World Report
Jones Bros. & Co.   Baltimore & Ohio Railroad
American Telephone &   Mine, Mill & Smelter Workers
    Telegraph Co.
Norton Enterprises, Inc.
Maryland Steamship Co., Ltd.   *but*
Chesapeake & Delaware Canal   Little Theater Company
Fairmount Building & Loan   Senate Banking, Housing and
    Association   Urban Affairs Committee

9.26. *Company* and *Corporation* are not abbreviated in names of Federal Government units.

Commodity Credit Corporation
Federal Savings and Loan Insurance Corporation
Pension Benefit Guaranty Corporation

9.27. In parentheses, footnotes, sidenotes, tables, and leaderwork, abbreviate the words *railroad* and *railway* (*RR* and *Ry.*), except in such names as "Washington Railway & Electric Co." and "Florida Railroad & Navigation Corp." *SS* for *steamship, MS* for *motorship*, etc., preceding name are used at all times.

9.28. In the names of informal companionships the word *and* is spelled out.

Lennon and McCartney   Currier and Ives

9.29. In other than formal usage, a civil, military, or naval title preceding a name is abbreviated if followed by first or given name or initial; but *Mr., Mrs., Miss, Ms., M., MM., Messrs., Mlle., Mme.*, and *Dr.* are abbreviated with or without first or given name or initial.

United States military titles and abbreviations

Officer rank

Officer ranks in the United States military consist of commissioned officers and warrant officers. The commissioned ranks are the highest in the military. These officers hold presidential commissions and are confirmed at their ranks by the Senate. Army, Air Force, and Marine Corps officers are called company grade officers in the pay grades of O–1 to O–3, field grade officers in pay grades O–4 to O–6, and general officers in pay grades O–7 and higher. The equivalent officer groupings in the Navy are called junior grade, mid-grade, and flag.

Warrant officers hold warrants from their service secretary and are specialists and experts in certain military technologies or capabilities. The lowest ranking warrant officers serve under a warrant, but they receive commissions from the President upon promotion to chief warrant officer 2. These commissioned warrant officers are direct representatives of the President of the United States. They derive their authority from the same source as commissioned officers but remain specialists, in contrast to commissioned officers, who are generalists. There are no warrant officers in the Air Force.

	Army	Navy Coast Guard	Marines	Air Force
	General of the Army (Reserved for wartime only)	Fleet Admiral (Reserved for wartime only)		General of the Air Force (Reserved for wartime only)
O10	General GEN Army Chief of Staff	Admiral ADM Chief of Naval Operations and Commandant of the Coast Guard	General Gen. Commandant of the Marine Corps	General Gen. Air Force Chief of Staff
O9	Lieutenant General LTG	Vice Admiral VADM	Lieutenant General Lt. Gen.	Lieutenant General Lt. Gen.
O8	Major General MG	Rear Admiral Upper Half RADM	Major General Maj. Gen.	Major General Maj. Gen.
O7	Brigadier General BG	Rear Admiral Lower Half RDML	Brigadier General Brig. Gen.	Brigadier General Brig. Gen.
O6	Colonel COL	Captain CAPT	Colonel Col.	Colonel Col.
O5	Lieutenant Colonel LTC	Commander CDR	Lieutenant Colonel Lt. Col.	Lieutenant Colonel Lt. Col.
O4	Major MAJ	Lieutenant Commander LCDR	Major Maj.	Major Maj.
O3	Captain CPT	Lieutenant LT	Captain Capt.	Captain Capt.

	Army	Navy Coast Guard	Marines	Air Force
O2	First Lieutenant 1LT	Lieutenant Junior Grade LTJG	First Lieutenant 1st Lt.	First Lieutenant 1st Lt.
O1	Second Lieutenant 2LT	Ensign ENS	Second Lieutenant 2nd Lt.	Second Lieutenant 2nd Lt.
W5	Chief Warrant Officer CW5	Chief Warrant Officer CWO5	Chief Warrant Officer 5 CWO5	NO WARRANT
W4	Chief Warrant Officer 4 CW4	Chief Warrant Officer 4 CWO4	Chief Warrant Officer 4 CWO4	NO WARRANT
W3	Chief Warrant Officer 3 CW3	Chief Warrant Officer 3 CWO3	Chief Warrant Officer 3 CWO3	NO WARRANT
W2	Chief Warrant Officer 2 CW2	Chief Warrant Officer 2 CWO2	Chief Warrant Officer 2 CWO2	NO WARRANT
W1	Warrant Officer 1 WO1	Warrant Officer 1 WO1	Warrant Officer 1 WO	NO WARRANT

Source: http://www.defense.gov/About-DoD/Insignias/Officers.

Enlisted rank

Service members in pay grades E–1 through E–3 are usually either in some kind of training status or on their initial assignment. The training includes the basic training phase where recruits are immersed in military culture and values and are taught the core skills required by their service component.

Basic training is followed by a specialized or advanced training phase that provides recruits with a specific area of expertise or concentration. In the Army and Marines, this area is called a military occupational specialty; in the Navy it is known as a rate; and in the Air Force it is simply called an Air Force specialty.

Leadership responsibility significantly increases in the mid-level enlisted ranks. This responsibility is given formal recognition by use of the terms noncommissioned officer and petty officer. An Army sergeant, an Air Force staff sergeant, and a Marine corporal are considered NCO ranks. The Navy NCO equivalent, petty officer, is achieved at the rank of petty officer third class.

At the E–8 level, the Army, Marines, and Air Force have two positions at the same pay grade. Whether one is, for example, a senior master sergeant or a first sergeant in the Air Force depends on the person's job. The same is true for the positions at the E–9 level. Marine Corps master gunnery sergeants and sergeants major receive the same pay but have different responsibilities. E–8s and E–9s have 15 to 30 years on the job, and are commanders' senior advisers for enlisted matters.

A third E–9 element is the senior enlisted person of each service. The sergeant major of the Army, the sergeant major of the Marine Corps, the master chief petty officer of the Navy, and the chief master sergeant of the Air Force are the spokespersons of the enlisted force at the highest levels of their services.

	Army		Navy / Coast Guard		Marines		Air Force		
E9	Sergeant Major of the Army (SMA)		Master Chief Petty Officer of the Navy (MCPON) and Coast Guard (MCPOCG)		Sergeant Major of the Marine Corps (SgtMajMC)		Chief Master Sergeant of the Air Force (CMSAF)		
E9	Sergeant Major (SGM)	Command Sergeant Major (CSM)	Master Chief Petty Officer (MCPO)	Fleet/ Command Master Chief Petty Officer	Sergeant Major (SgtMaj)	Master Gunnery Sergeant (MGySgt)	Chief Master Sergeant (CMSgt)	First Sergeant	Command Chief Master Sergeant (CCM)
E8	Master Sergeant (MSG)	First Sergeant (1SG)	Senior Chief Petty Officer (SCPO)		Master Sergeant (MSgt)	First Sergeant	Senior Master Sergeant (SMSgt)	First Sergeant	
E7	Sergeant First Class (SFC)		Chief Petty Officer (CPO)		Gunnery Sergeant (GySgt)		Master Sergeant (MSgt)	First Sergeant	
E6	Staff Sergeant (SSG)		Petty Officer First Class (PO1)		Staff Sergeant (SSgt)		Technical Sergeant (TSgt)		
E5	Sergeant (SGT)		Petty Officer Second Class (PO2)		Sergeant (Sgt)		Staff Sergeant (SSgt)		
E4	Corporal (CPL)	Specialist (SPC)	Petty Officer Third Class (PO3)		Corporal (Cpl)		Senior Airman (SrA)		

	Army	Navy Coast Guard	Marines	Air Force
E3	Private First Class (PFC)	Seaman (SN)	Lance Corporal (LCpl)	Airman First Class (A1C)
E2	Private E–2 (PV2)	Seaman Apprentice (SA)	Private First Class (PFC)	Airman (Amn)
E1	Private	Seaman Recruit (SR)	Private	Airman Basic

Source: http://www.defense.gov/About-DoD/Insignias/Enlisted.

9.30.   Spell out *Senator, Representative,* and *commandant.*

9.31.   Unless preceded by *the,* abbreviate *Honorable, Reverend,* and *Monsignor* when followed by the first name, initials, or title.

> Hon. John Kerry; the Honorable John Kerry; the Honorable Mr. Kerry
>
> the Honorables John Roberts, Elena Kagan, and Ruth Bader Ginsberg
>
> Rev. Martin Luther King, Jr.; the Reverend Dr. King; Rev. Dr. King; Reverend King (*not* Rev. King, *nor* the Reverend King)
>
> Rt. Rev. James E. Freeman; the Right Reverend James E. Freeman; Very Rev. Henry Boyd; the Very Reverend Henry Boyd
>
> Rt. Rev. Msgr. John Bird; the Right Reverend Monsignor John Bird

9.32.   The following and similar forms are used after a name:

> Esq., Jr., Sr.
>
> 2d, 3d (*or* II, III) (not preceded by comma)
>
> Degrees: LL.D., M.A., Ph.D., etc.
>
> Fellowships, orders, etc.: FSA Scot, F.R.S., K.C.B., C.P.A., etc.

9.33.   The abbreviation *Esq.* and other titles such as *Mr., Mrs.,* and *Dr.,* should not appear with any other title or with abbreviations indicating scholastic degrees.

> John L. Smith, Esq., *not* Mr. John L. Smith, Esq., *nor* John L. Smith, Esq., A.M.; *but* James A. Jones, Jr., Esq.
>
> Ford Maddox, A.B., Ph.D., *not* Mr. Ford Maddox, A.B., Ph.D.
>
> George Gray, M.D., *not* Mr. George Gray, M.D., *nor* Dr. George Gray, M.D.
>
> Dwight A. Bellinger, D.V.M., *but* Major John P. Pryor, M.D.

9.34.   *Sr.* and *Jr.* should not be used without first or given name or initials, but may be used in combination with any title.

> A.K. Jones, Jr., or Mr. Jones, Junior, *not* Jones, Jr., *nor* Jones, Junior
>
> President J.B. Nelson, Jr.

9.35.   When name is followed by abbreviations designating religious and fraternal orders and scholastic and honorary degrees, their sequence is as follows: Orders, religious first; theological degrees; academic degrees earned in course; and honorary degrees in order of bestowal.

>   Henry L. Brown, D.D., A.M., D.Lit.
>   T.E. Holt, C.S.C., S.T.Lr., LL.D., Ph.D.
>   Samuel J. Deckelbaum, P.M.

9.36.   Academic degrees standing alone may be abbreviated.

>   John was graduated with a B.A. degree; *but* bachelor of arts degree (lowercase
>   when spelled out).
>   She earned her Ph.D. by hard work.

9.37.   In addresses, signatures, lists of names, and leaderwork but not in tables nor in centerheads, *Mr., Mrs.,* and other titles preceding a name, and *Esq., Ph.D., Jr.,* and *Sr.* following a name, are set in roman caps and lowercase if the name is in caps and small caps. If the name is in caps, they are set in caps and small caps, if small caps are available—otherwise in caps and lowercase.

Parts of publications

9.38.   The following abbreviations are used for parts of publications mentioned in parentheses, brackets, footnotes, sidenotes, list of references, tables, and leaderwork, when followed by figures, letters, or Roman numerals.

app., apps. (appendix, appendixes)	pl., pls. (plate, plates)
art., arts. (article, articles)	pt., pts. (part, parts)
bull., bulls. (bulletin, bulletins)	sec., secs. (section, sections)
ch., chs. (chapter, chapters)	subch., subchs. (subchapter, subchapters)
col., cols. (column, columns)	subpar., subpars. (subparagraph, subparagraphs)
ed., eds. (edition, editions)	subpt., subpts. (subpart, subparts)
fig., figs. (figure, figures)	subsec., subsecs. (subsection, subsections)
fn., fns. (footnote, footnotes)	supp., supps. (supplement, supplements)
No., Nos. (number, numbers)	vol., vols. (volume, volumes)
p., pp. (page, pages)	
par., pars. (paragraph, paragraphs)	

9.39.   The word *article* and the word *section* are abbreviated when appearing at the beginning of a paragraph and set in caps and small caps followed by a period and an en space, except that the first of a series is spelled out.

> ART. 2; SEC. 2; etc.; *but* ARTICLE 1; SECTION 1
> ART. II; SEC. II; etc.; *but* ARTICLE I; SECTION I

9.40.   At the beginning of a legend, the word *figure* preceding the legend number is not abbreviated.

FIGURE 4.—Landscape.

Terms relating to Congress

9.41.   The words *Congress* and *session*, when accompanied by a numerical reference, are abbreviated in parentheses, brackets, and text footnotes. In sidenotes, lists of references, tables, leaderwork, and footnotes to tables and leaderwork, the following abbreviations are used:

> 106th Cong., 1st sess.   Public Law 84, 102d Cong.
> 1st sess., 106th Cong.   Private Law 68, 102d Cong.

9.42.   In references to bills, resolutions, documents and reports in parentheses, brackets, footnotes, sidenotes, tables, and leaderwork, the following abbreviations are used:

> H.R. 416 (House bill)   H. Conf. Rept. 10 (House
> S. 116 (Senate bill)   conference report)
> The examples above may be   H. Doc. 35 (House document)
>   abbreviated or spelled   S. Doc. 62 (Senate document)
>   out in text.   H. Rept. 214 (House report)
> H. Res. 5 (House resolution)   S. Rept. 410 (Senate report)
> H. Con. Res. 10 (House concurrent   Ex. Doc. B (Executive document)
>   resolution)   Ex. F (92d Cong., 2d sess.)
> H.J. Res. 21 (House joint resolution) Ex. Rept. 9 (92d Cong., 1st sess.)
> S. Res. 50 (Senate resolution)   Misc. Doc. 16 (miscellaneous
> S. Con. Res. 17 (Senate concurrent   document)
>   resolution)   Public Res. 47
> S.J. Res. 45 (Senate joint resolution)

9.43.   References to statutes in parentheses, footnotes, sidenotes, tables, leaderwork, and congressional work are abbreviated.

> Rev. Stat. (Revised Statutes); 43 Rev. Stat. 801; 18 U.S.C. 38
> Supp. Rev. Stat. (Supplement to the Revised Statutes)
> Stat. L. (Statutes at Large)
> *but* Public Law 85–1; Private Law 68

Calendar divisions

9.44.   Names of months followed by the day, or day and year, are abbreviated in footnotes, tables, leaderwork, sidenotes, and in bibliographies. (See examples, rule 9.45.) *May, June,* and *July* are always spelled out. In narrow columns in tables, however, the names of months may be abbreviated even if standing alone. Preferred forms follow:

Jan.	Apr.	Oct.
Feb.	Aug.	Nov.
Mar.	Sept.	Dec.

9.45.   In text only, dates as part of a citation or reference within parentheses or brackets are also abbreviated.

> (Op. Atty. Gen., Dec. 4, 2005)
> (Congressional Record, Sept. 25, 2007)
> [From the New York Times, Mar. 4, 2008]
> [From the Mar. 4 issue]
> On Jan. 25 (we had commenced on Dec. 26, 2005) the work was finished. (In footnotes, tables, leaderwork, and sidenotes)
> On January 25, a decision was reached (Op. Atty. Gen., Dec. 4, 2006). (Text, but with citation in parentheses)
>
> *but* On January 25 (we had commenced on December 26, 2008) the work was finished. (Not a citation or reference in text)

9.46.   Weekdays are not abbreviated, but the following forms are used, if necessary, in lists or in narrow columns in tables:

Sun.	Wed.	Fri.
Mon.	Thurs.	Sat.
Tues.		

Time zones

9.47.   The following forms are to be used when abbreviating names of time zones:

AKDT—Alaska daylight time

AKST—Alaska standard time

AKT—Alaska time (implies
   standard or daylight time)

AST—Atlantic standard time

AT—Atlantic time

CDT—central daylight time

CST—central standard time

CT—central time

ChST—Chamorro standard time
   (DST not observed)

DST—daylight saving (no "s") time

EDT—eastern daylight time

EST—eastern standard time

ET—eastern time

GCT—Greenwich civil time

GMAT—Greenwich mean
   astronomical time

GMT—Greenwich mean time

HDT—Hawaii-Aleutian daylight time
   (not observed in HI)

HST—Hawaii-Aleutian standard time

LST—local standard time

MDT—mountain daylight time

MST—mountain standard time

MT— mountain time

PDT—Pacific daylight time

PST—Pacific standard time

PT—Pacific time

SST—Samoan standard time
   (DST not observed)

UTC—coordinated universal time

Acronyms and coined words

9.48.   To obtain uniform treatment in the formation of acronyms and coined words, apply the formulas that follow:

Use all capital letters when only the first letter of each word or selected words is used to make up the symbol:

   APPR (Army package power reactor)

   EPCOT (Experimental Prototype Community of Tomorrow)

   MAG (Military Advisory Group)

   MIRV (multiple independently targetable reentry vehicle)

   SALT (strategic arms limitation talks); (*avoid* SALT talks)

Use all capital letters where first letters of prefixes and/or suffixes are utilized as part of established expressions:

   CPR (*c*ardio*p*ulmonary *r*esuscitation)

   ESP (*e*xtra*s*ensory *p*erception)

   FLIR (*f*orward-*l*ooking *i*nfra*r*ed)

Copy must be followed where an acronym or abbreviated form is copyrighted or established by law:

   ACTION (agency of Government; not an acronym)

   MARAD (*Mar*itime *Ad*ministration)

   NACo (*N*ational *A*ssociation of *Co*unties)

   MEDLARS (*Med*ical *L*iterature *A*nalysis and *R*etrieval *S*ystem)

Use caps and lowercase when proper names are used in shortened form, any word of which uses more than the first letter of each word:

Conrail (Consolidated Rail Corporation)
Pepco (Potomac Electric Power Co.)
Inco (International Nickel Co.)
Aramco (Arabian-American Oil Co.)
Unprofor (United Nations Protection Force)
but USAJOBS

Use lowercase in common-noun combinations made up of more than the first letter of lowercased words:

loran (*long-ra*nge *n*avigation)
sonar (*sound n*avigation *r*anging)
secant (*se*paration *c*ontrol of *a*ircraft by *n*onsynchronous *t*echniques)

9.49. The words *infra* and *supra* are not abbreviated.

Terms of measure

9.50. The only instance where a period is used with a compass directonal abbreviation is in a land tract description with township(s) (T./Tps.) and range(s) (R./Rs.). (See rule 9.20.) Compass directionals are abbreviated as follows:

N	S	ESE
NE	NNW	10° N 25° W
E	W	*but*
NW by N ¼ W	SW	T. 2 S., R. 1 E.

9.51. The words *latitude* and *longitude,* followed by figures, are abbreviated in parentheses, brackets, footnotes, sidenotes, tables, and leaderwork, and the figures are always closed up.

lat. 52°33'05" N   long. 13°21'10" E

9.52. Avoid breaking latitude and longitude figures at end of line; space out line instead. In case of an unavoidable break at end of line, use hyphen.

9.53. Temperature and gravity are expressed in figures. When the degree mark is used, it must appear closed up to the capital letter, not against the figures. Note the following related abbreviations and letter symbols and their usages:

abs, absolute	API, American Petroleum
Bé, Baumé	Institute
°C,[1] degree Celsius[2]	Twad, Twaddell
°F, degree Fahrenheit	100 °C
°R, degree Rankine	212 °F[1]
K, kelvin; *but* Kelvin scale	671.67 °R
273.15 K	18 °API
°API	

9.54. References to meridian in statements of time are abbreviated as follows:

10 a.m. (*not* 10:00 a.m.)	12 p.m. (12 noon)
2:30 p.m.	12 a.m. (12 midnight)

9.55. The word *o'clock* is not used with abbreviations of time.

not 10 o'clock p.m.

9.56. Metric unit letter symbols are set lowercase roman unless the unit name has been derived from a proper name, in which case the first letter of the symbol is capitalized (for example Pa for pascal and W for watt). The exception is the letter L for liter. The same form is used for singular and plural. The preferred symbol for *cubic centimeter* is *cm³*; use *cc* only when requested.

A space is used between a figure and a unit symbol except in the case of the symbols for degree, minute, and second of plane angle.

3 m	45 mm	25 °C	*but* 33°15'21"

Prefixes for multiples and submultiples				Metric units	
Y	yotta (10^{24})	d	deci (10^{-1})	m	meter (for length)
Z	zetta (10^{21})	c	centi (10^{-2})	g	gram (for weight or mass)
E	exa (10^{18})	m	milli (10^{-3})	L	liter (for capacity)
P	peta (10^{15})	μ	micro (10^{-6})		
T	tera (10^{12})	n	nano (10^{-9})		
G	giga (10^{9})	p	pico (10^{-12})		
M	mega (10^{6})	f	femto (10^{-15})		
k	kilo (10^{3})	a	atto (10^{-18})		
h	hecto (10^{2})	z	zepto (10^{-21})		
da	deka (10)	y	yocto (10^{-24})		

---

[1] Without figures preceding it, ˚C or ˚F should be used only in boxhead and over figure columns in tables.
[2] Preferred form (superseding Centigrade).

	Length		*Area*		*Volume*
km	kilometer	km²	square kilometer	km³	cubic kilometer
hm	hectometer	hm²	square hectometer	hm³	cubic hectometer
dam	decameter	dam²	square decameter	dam³	cubic dekameter
m	meter	m²	square meter	m³	cubic meter
dm	decimeter	dm²	square decimeter	dm³	cubic decimeter
cm	centimeter	cm²	square centimeter	cm³	cubic centimeter
mm	millimeter	mm²	square millimeter	mm³	cubic millimeter

	Weight		*Land area*		*Capacity of containers*
kg	kilogram	ha	hectare	kL	kiloliter
hg	hectogram	a	acre	hL	hectoliter
dag	dekagram			daL	dekaliter
g	gram			L	liter
dg	decigram			dL	deciliter
cg	centigram			cL	centiliter
mg	milligram			mL	milliliter
μg	microgram				

9.57. A similar form of abbreviation applies to any unit of the metric system.

A	ampere	V	volt	mF	millifarad
VA	voltampere	W	watt	mH	millihenry
F	farad	kc	kilocycle	μF	microfarad (one-
H	henry	kV	kilovolt		millionth of a farad)
Hz	hertz	kVA	kilovoltampere		
J	joule	kW	kilowatt		

9.58. The following forms are used when units of English weight and measure and units of time are abbreviated, the same form of abreviation being used for both singular and plural:

	Length		*Area and volume*
in	inch	in²	square inch
ft	foot	in³	cubic inch
yd	yard	mi²	square mile
mi	mile (statute)	ft³	cubic foot

Time		Weight		Capacity	
yr	year	gr	grain	gill	(not abbreviated)
mo	month	dr	dram	pt	pint
d	day	oz	ounce	qt	quart
h	hour	lb	pound	gal	gallon
min	minute	cwt	hundredweight	pk	peck
s	second	dwt	pennyweight	bu	bushel
		ton(s)	(not abbreviated)	bbl	barrel
		but t	metric ton (tonne)		

9.59. In astrophysical and similar scientific matter, magnitudes and units of time may be expressed as follows:

$$5^h3^m9^s \qquad\qquad 4.5^h$$

Money

9.60. The following are some of the abbreviations and symbols used for indicating money:

(For the abbreviations of other terms indicating currency, see the table "Currency" in Chapter 17 "Useful Tables.")

$, dol (dollar)   Mex $2,650

c, ct, ¢ (cent, cents)   ₱ (peso)

TRL175 (Turkish)   £ (pound)

USD15,000   d (pence)

€ (euro)

Use "USD" if omission would result in confusion.

Standard word abbreviations

9.61. For a more complete list of Government acronyms visit the U.S. Government Manual: https//www.govinfo.gov/content/pkg/GOVMAN-2015-07-01/pdf/GOVMAN-2015-07-01-Commonly-Used-Agency-Acronyms-105.pdf. Use these forms if abbreviations are required:

2,4D (insecticide)   A1 (rating)

2d—second   A.A.—Alcoholics Anonymous

3d—third   AARP—American Association of

3D—three dimensional   Retired Persons

4°—quarto   abbr.—abbreviation

8°—octavo   abs.—abstract

acct.—account

ACTH—adrenocorticotropic hormone

A.D.—(anno Domini) in the year of our Lord (A.D. 937)

ADDH—attention deficit disorder with hyperactivity

ADHD—attention deficit hyperactivity disorder

AF—audiofrequency

AFB—Air Force Base

AFL-CIO—American Federation of Labor and Congress of Industrial Organizations

AIDS—acquired immunodeficiency syndrome

a.k.a.—also known as

A.L.R.—American Law Reports

ALS—amyotrophic lateral sclerosis

AM—amplitude modulation (no periods)

A.M.—(anno mundi) in the year of the world

A.M. or M.A.—master of arts

a.m.—(ante meridiem) before noon

Am. Repts.—American Reports

Amtrak—National Railroad Passenger Corporation

AMVETS—American Veterans; Amvet(s) (individual)

ANSI—American National Standards Institute

antilog—antilogarithm (no period)

AOA—Administration on Aging

APEC—Asia-Pacific Economic Cooperation

API—American Petroleum Institute

APO—Army post office (no periods)

App. D.C.—District of Columbia Appeal Cases

App. Div.—Appellate Division

approx.—approximately

ARC—American Red Cross

ARS—Agricultural Research Service

ASD—autism spectrum disorder

ASME—American Society of Mechanical Engineers

ASTM—American Society for Testing and Materials

ATM—automatic teller machine

Atl.—Atlantic Reporter; A.2d, Atlantic Reporter, second series

AUS—Army of the United States

Ave.—avenue

AWACS—airborne warning and control system

AWOL—absent without leave

B.A. or A.B.—bachelor of arts

BAC—billing address code

BBB—Better Business Bureau

B.C.—before Christ (1200 B.C.)

B.C.E.—Before Common Era

BCG—(bacillus Calmette-Guerin) antituberculosis vaccine

bf.—boldface

BGN—Board on (*not* of) Geographic Names

BIA—Bureau of Indian Affairs

BIS—Bank for International Settlements

Blatch. Pr. Cas.—Blatchford's Prize Cases

Bldg.—building

B.Lit(t). or Lit(t).B.—bachelor of literature

BLM—Bureau of Land Management

BLS—Bureau of Labor Statistics

Blvd.—boulevard

b.o.—buyer's option

B.S. or B.Sc.—bachelor of science

c. and s.c.—caps and small caps

ca.—(circa) about

ca—centiare

CACM—Central American
    Common Market
CAD—computer-aided design
CAP—Civil Air Patrol
CAT scan—computerized axial
    tomography
C.C.A.—Circuit Court of Appeals
CCC—Commodity Credit
    Corporation
C.Cls.—Court of Claims
C.Cls.R.—Court of Claims Reports
C.C.P.A.—Court of Customs and
    Patents Appeals
CCSDS—Consultative Committee
    for Space Data Systems
CDC—Centers for Disease Control
    and Prevention
C.E.—Common Era
CEA—Council of Economic
    Advisers
cf.—(confer) compare or see
CFR—Code of Federal Regulations
CFR Supp.—Code of Federal
    Regulations Supplement
CHAMPUS—Civilian Health
    and Medical Program of the
    Uniformed Services
CIA—Central Intelligence Agency
C.J.—(corpus juris) body of law;
    Chief Justice
CMYK—cyan, magenta, yellow,
    black
CNN—Cable News Network
CO—commanding officer
Co.—company (commercial)
c.o.d.—cash on delivery
COLA—cost-of-living adjustment
Comp. Dec.—Comptroller's
    Decisions (Treasury)
Comp. Gen.—Comptroller
    General Decisions
con.—continued
Conus—continental United States

Corp.—corporation (commercial)
cos—cosine (no period)
cosh—hyperbolic cosine (no
    period)
cot—cotangent (no period)
coth—hyperbolic cotangent (no
    period)
c.p.—chemically pure
C.P.A.—certified public
    accountant
CPI—Consumer Price Index
CPR—cardiopulmonary
    resuscitation
cr.—credit; creditor
C-SPAN—Cable Satellite Public
    Affairs Network
csc—cosecant (no period)
csch—hyperbolic cosecant (no
    period)
Ct.—court
Dall.—Dallas (U.S. Supreme
    Court Reports)
DAR—Daughters of the American
    Revolution
d.b.a.—doing business as
d.b.h.—diameter at breast height
D.D.—doctor of divinity
D.D.S.—doctor of dental surgery
DDT—dichlorodiphenyl-
    trichloroethane
DHS—Department of Homeland
    Security
Dist. Ct.—District Court
D.Lit(t). or Lit(t).D.—doctor of
    literature
DNC—Domestic Names
    Committee (BGN)
do.—(ditto) the same
DOC—Department of Commerce
DoD—Department of Defense
DOE—Department of Energy
DOI—Department of the Interior
DOJ—Department of Justice

DOL—Department of Labor
DoS—Department of State
DOT—Department of Transportation
DP—displaced person (no period)
D.P.H.—doctor of public health
D.P.Hy.—doctor of public hygiene
DPT—diphtheria, pertussis, tetanus innoculation
dr.—debit; debtor
Dr.—doctor; drive
DST—daylight saving (no "s") time
D.V.M.—doctor of veterinary medicine
E—east
e–CFR—electronic Code of Federal Regulations
EDGAR—Electronic Data Gathering, Analysis and Retrieval (SEC)
EEOC—Equal Employment Opportunity Commission
EFTA—European Free Trade Association
EFTS—electronic funds transfer system
e.g.—(exempli gratia) for example
EHF—extremely high frequency
emcee—master of ceremony
e.o.m.—end of month
EOP—Executive Office of the President
EPA—Environmental Protection Agency
ESE—east-southeast
et al.—(et alii) and others
et seq.—(et sequentia) and the following
etc.—(et cetera) and so forth
EU—European Union
Euratom—European Atomic Energy Community
Euro—currency (common)

Eurodollars—U.S. dollars used to finance foreign trade
Ex. Doc. (with letter)—executive document
EXIM Bank—Export-Import Bank of the United States
f., ff.—and following page (pages)
FAA—Federal Aviation Administration
FACS—Faculty of the American College of Surgeons
Fannie Mae—Federal National Mortgage Association
FAO—Food and Agriculture Organization
FAQ—frequently asked question
FAR—Federal Acquisition Regulation
f.a.s.—free alongside ship
FAS—Foreign Agricultural Service
FBI—Federal Bureau of Investigation
FCA—Farm Credit Administration
FCC—Federal Communications Commission
FCIC—Federal Crop Insurance Corporation
FCSC—Foreign Claims Settlement Commission
FDA—Food and Drug Administration
FDIC—Federal Deposit Insurance Corporation
FDLP—Federal Depository Library Program
Fed.—Federal Reporter; F.3d, Federal Reporter, third series
FEOF—Foreign Exchange Operations Fund
FERC—Federal Energy Regulatory Commission

FHA—Federal Housing
Administration
FHFA—Federal Housing
Finance Agency
FmHA—Farmers Home
Administration
FHWA—Federal Highway
Administration
FICA—Federal Insurance
Contributions Act
FLSA—Fair Labor Standards Act
FM—frequency modulation
FMC—Federal Maritime
Commission
FMCS—Federal Mediation and
Conciliation Service
FNS—Food and Nutrition Service
f°—folio
FOB—free on board
FPO—fleet post office (no periods)
FR—Federal Register
(publication)
FRG—Federal Republic of
Germany
FRS—Federal Reserve System
FS—Forest Service
FSLIC—Federal Savings and Loan
Insurance Corporation
F. Supp.—Federal Supplement
FTC—Federal Trade Commission
FWS—Fish and Wildlife Service
GAO—Government
Accountability Office
GATT—General Agreement on
Tariffs and Trade
GDP—Gross Domestic Product
GFE—government furnished
equipment
GFI—government furnished
information
GI—general issue; Government
issue
GIS—geographic information
system

G.M.&S.—general, medical, and
surgical
GNMA—Government National
Mortgage Association
(Ginnie Mae)
Gov.—Governor
GPO—Government Publishing
Office
GPS—Global Positioning System
gr. wt.—gross weight
GSA—General Services
Administration
GSE—Government-Sponsored
Enterprise
G7—Group of Seven
H.C.—House of Commons
H. Con. Res. (with number)—
House concurrent resolution
H. Doc. (with number)—House
document
hazmat—hazardous material
HDTV—high definition television
HE—high explosive (no periods)
HF—high frequency (no periods)
HHS—Health and Human
Services (Department of)
HIV—human immunodeficiency
virus
H.J. Res. (with number)—House
joint resolution
HMO—health-maintenance
organization
HOV—high-occupancy vehicle
How.—Howard (U.S. Supreme
Court Reports)
H.R. (with number)—House bill
H. Rept. (with number)—House
report
H. Res. (with number)—House
resolution
HUD—Housing and Urban
Development (Department of)
IADB—Inter-American Defense
Board

IAEA—International Atomic
   Energy Agency
ibid.—(ibidem) in the same place
ICBM—intercontinental ballistic
   missile
id.—(idem) the same
ID—Information Dissemination
IDA—International Development
   Association
IDE—integrated drive electronics
i.e.—(id est) that is
IEEE—Institute of Electrical and
   Electronic Engineers
IF—intermediate frequency (no
   periods)
IFC—International Finance
   Corporation
IMF—International Monetary
   Fund
Insp. Gen. (also IG)—inspector
   general
Interpol—International Criminal
   Police Organization
IOU—I owe you
IQ—intelligence quotient
IRA—individual retirement
   account
IRBM—intermediate range
   ballistic missile
IRE—Institute of Radio Engineers
IRS—Internal Revenue Service
ISIL—Islamic State of Iraq and
   the Levant (Intelligence
   Community standard)
ISIS—Islamic State of Iraq and Syria
ISO—International Organization
   for Standardization
ISS—International Space Station
ISSN—International Standard
   Serial Number
JAG—Judge Advocate General
jato—jet-assisted takeoff
J.D.—(jurum or juris doctor)
   doctor of laws

JOBS—Job Opportunities in the
   Business Sector
JIT—just in time
Jpn.—Japan or Japanese where
   necessary to abbreviate
Jr.—junior
Judge Adv. Gen.—Judge Advocate
   General
lat.—latitude
LC—Library of Congress
LCD—liquid crystal display
lc.—lowercase
L.Ed.—Lawyer's edition (U.S.
   Supreme Court Reports)
LGBTQ—Lesbian, Gay, Bisexual,
   Transgender, and Questioning
liq.—liquid
lf.—lightface
LF—low frequency
LL.B.—bachelor of laws
LL.D.—doctor of laws
loc. cit.—(loco citato) in the place
   cited
log (no period)—logarithm
long.—longitude
loran (no periods)—long-range
   navigation
lox (no periods)—liquid oxygen
LPG—liquefied petroleum gas
Ltd.—limited
Lt. Gov.—lieutenant governor
M—money supply: M1, M2, etc.
M.—monsieur; MM., messieurs
m.—(meridies) noon
M—more
MAC—Military Airlift Command
MARAD—Maritime
   Administration
MC—Member of Congress
   (emcee, master of ceremonies)
M.D.—doctor of medicine
MDAP—Mutual Defense
   Assistance Program
Medi-Cal—Medicaid California

memo—memorandum
MF—medium frequency;
    microfiche
MFN—most favored nation
MIA—missing in action (plural
    MIAs)
MIRV—multiple independently
    targetable reentry vehicle
Misc. Doc. (with number)—
    miscellaneous document
Mlle.—mademoiselle
MMAR—Materials Management
    Acquisition Regulation
Mme.—madam
Mmes.—mesdames
mo.—month
MOS—military occupational
    specialty
M.P.—Member of Parliament
MP—military police
Mr.—mister (plural Messrs.)
MRI—magnetic resonance
    imaging
Mrs.—mistress
Ms.—feminine title (plural Mses.)
M.S.—master of science
MS.—MSS., manuscript,
    manuscripts
MSC—Military Sealift Command
Msgr.—monsignor
m.s.l.—mean sea level
MTN—multilateral trade
    negotiations
N—north
NA—not available; not applicable
NACo.—National Association of
    Counties
NAFTA—North American Free
    Trade Agreement
NAS—National Academy of
    Sciences
NASA—National Aeronautics and
    Space Administration

NATO—North Atlantic Treaty
    Organization
NCUA—National Credit Union
    Administration
NE—northeast
n.e.c.—not elsewhere classified
n.e.s.—not elsewhere specified
net wt.—net weight
N.F.—National Formulary
NFC—National Finance Center
NIH—National Institutes of
    Health
NIST—National Institute of
    Standards and Technology
NGA—National Geospatial-
    Intelligence Agency
n.l.—natural log or logarithm
NLRB—National Labor Relations
    Board
NNTP—Network News Transfer
    Protocol
NNW—north-northwest
No.—Nos., number, numbers
NOAA—National Oceanic and
    Atmospheric Administration
n.o.i.b.n.—not otherwise indexed
    by name
n.o.p.—not otherwise provided
    (for)
n.o.s.—not otherwise specified
NPR—National Public Radio
NPS—National Park Service
NRC—Nuclear Regulatory
    Commission
NS—nuclear ship
NSA—National Security Agency
NSC—National Security Council
NSF—National Science
    Foundation
n.s.k.—not specified by kind
n.s.p.f.—not specifically provided
    for
NW—northwest

OAPEC—Organization of Arab
    Petroleum Exporting
    Countries
OAS—Organization of American
    States
OASDHI—Old-Age, Survivors,
    Disability, and Health
    Insurance Program
OASI—Old-Age and Survivors
    Insurance
OD—officer of the day
OD—overdose; Odd, overdosed
O.D.—doctor of optometry
OK—Oked, Oking, Oks
OMB—Office of Management and
    Budget
Op. Atty. Gen.—Opinions of the
    Attorney General
op. cit.—(opere citato) in the work
    cited
OPEC—Organization of
    Petroleum Exporting
    Countries
OSD—Office of the Secretary of
    Defense
PA—public address system;
    physician assistant
Pac.—Pacific Reporter; P.2d,
    Pacific Reporter, second
    series
PAC—political action committee
    (plural PACs)
PBS—Public Broadcasting Service;
    Public Buildings Service
PCV—Peace Corps Volunteer
Pet.—Peters (U.S. Supreme Court
    Reports)
Ph—phenyl
Phar.D.—doctor of pharmacy
Ph.B. or B.Ph.—bachelor of
    philosophy
Ph.D. or D.Ph.—doctor of
    philosophy

Ph.G.—graduate in pharmacy
PHS—Public Health Service
PIN—personal identification
    number
Pl.—place
p.m.—(post meridiem) after noon
P.O. Box (with number)—*but* post
    office box (in general sense)
POP—Point of Presence; Post
    Office Protocol
POW—prisoner of war (plural
    POWs)
Private Res. (with number)—
    private resolution
Prof.—professor
pro tem—(pro tempore)
    temporarily
P.S.—(post scriptum) postscript;
    public school (with number)
PTA—parent-teachers' association
PTSD—post-traumatic stress
    disorder
Public Res. (with number)—public
    resolution
PX—post exchange
QT—on the quiet
R.—Rs., range, ranges
racon—radar beacon
radar—radio detection and
    ranging
R&D—research and development
rato—rocket-assisted takeoff
Rd.—road
RDT&E—research, development,
    testing, and evaluation
Rev.—reverend
Rev. Stat.—Revised Statutes
RF—radio frequency
R.F.D.—rural free delivery
RGB—red, green, blue
Rh—Rhesus (blood factor)
RIF—reduction(s) in force; RIFed,
    RIFing, RIFs

R.N.—registered nurse
ROTC—Reserve Officers'
     Training Corps
RR—railroad
RRB—Railroad Retirement Board
RSS—Really Simple Syndication
Rt. Rev.—right reverend
Ry.—railway
S—south
S.—Senate bill (with number)
SAE—Society of Automotive
     Engineers
S&L(s)—savings and loan(s)
SALT—strategic arms limitation
     talks
SAR—Sons of the American
     Revolution
SBA—Small Business
     Administration
sc.—(scilicet) namely (see also ss)
s.c.—small caps
S. Con. Res. (with number)—
     Senate concurrent resolution
s.d.—(sine die) without date
S. Doc. (with number)—Senate
     document
SE—southeast
SEATO—Southeast Asia Treaty
     Organization
SEC—Securities and Exchange
     Commission
sec—secant
sech—hyperbolic secant
2d—second
SEO—Search Engine Optimization
SHF—superhigh frequency
shoran—short range (radio)
SI—Systeme International d'Unités
sic—thus
sin—sine
sinh—hyperbolic sine
S.J. Res. (with number)—Senate
     joint resolution

sonar—sound, navigation, and
     ranging (no period)
SOP—standard operating
     procedure
SOS—wireless distress signal
SP—shore patrol
SPA—simplified purchase
     agreement
SPAR—Coast Guard Women's
     Reserve (*semper paratus*—
     always ready)
sp. gr.—specific gravity
Sq.—square (street)
Sr.—senior
S. Rept. (with number)—Senate
     report
S. Res. (with number)—Senate
     resolution
SS—steamship
ss—(scilicet) namely (in law) (see
     also sc.)
SSA—Social Security
     Administration
SSE—south-southeast
SSS—Selective Service System
St.—Ste., SS., Saint, Sainte, Saints
St.—street
Stat.—Statutes at Large
STEAM—Science, Technology,
     Engineering, Art and
     Mathematics
STEM—Science, Technology,
     Engineering and Mathematics
STP—standard temperature and
     pressure
Sup. Ct.—Supreme Court
     Reporter
Supp. Rev. Stat.—Supplement to
     the Revised Statutes
Supt.—superintendent
Surg.—surgeon
Surg. Gen.—Surgeon General
SW—southwest

S.W.2d—Southwestern Reporter, second series
SWAT—special weapons and tactics (team)
T.—Tps., township, townships
tan—tangent
tanh—hyperbolic tangent
TB—tuberculosis
T.D.—Treasury Decisions
TDY—temporary duty
Ter.—terrace
3d—third
t.m.—true mean
TNT—trinitrotoluol
TPP—Trans-Pacific Partnership
TV—television
TVA—Tennessee Valley Authority
uc.—uppercase
UHF—ultrahigh frequency
U.N.—United Nations
UNESCO—United Nations Educational, Scientific, and Cultural Organization
UNCHR—United Nations High Commissioner for Refugees
UNICEF—United Nations Children's Fund
U.S.—U.S. Supreme Court Reports
U.S.A.—United States of America
USA—U.S. Army
USAF—U.S. Air Force
USAID—U.S. Agency for International Development
U.S.C.—United States Code
U.S.C.A.—United States Code Annotated
USCCR—U.S. Commission on Civil Rights
U.S.C. Supp.—United States Code Supplement
USCG—U.S. Coast Guard

USDA—U.S. Department of Agriculture
USES—U.S. Employment Service
U.S. 61—U.S. No. 61, U.S. Highway No. 61
USGS—U.S. Geological Survey
USMC—U.S. Marine Corps
USN—U.S. Navy
USNR—U.S. Navy Reserve
U.S.P.—United States Pharmacopeia
USPS—U.S. Postal Service
U.S.S.—U.S. Senate
v. or vs.—(versus) against
VA—Department of Veterans Affairs
VAT—value added tax
VCR—video cassette recorder
VHF—very high frequency
VIP—very important person
viz—(videlicet) namely
VLF—very low frequency
VTR—video tape recording
W—west
w.a.e.—when actually employed
Wall.—Wallace (U.S. Supreme Court Reports)
wf—wrong font
Wheat.—Wheaton (U.S. Supreme Court Reports)
WHO—World Health Organization
WIPO—World Intellectual Property Organization
WNW—west-northwest
w.o.p.—without pay
Yale L.J.—Yale Law Journal
ZIP Code—Zone Improvement Plan Code (Postal Service)
ZIP+4—9-digit ZIP Code

Standard letter symbols for units of measure

9.62. The same form is used for singular and plural senses.

A—ampere
Å—angstrom
a—are
a—atto (prefix, one-quintillionth)
aA—attoampere
abs—absolute (temperature and
      gravity)
ac—alternating current
AF—audiofrequency
Ah—ampere-hour
A/m—ampere per meter
AM—amplitude modulation
asb—apostilb
At—ampere-turn
at—atmosphere, technical
atm—atmosphere
at wt—atomic weight
au—astronomical units
avdp—avoirdupois
b—barn
B—bel
b—bit
bbl—barrel
bbl/d—barrel per day
Bd—baud
bd. ft.—board foot (obsolete); use fbm
Bé—Baumé
Bev (obsolete); see GeV
Bhn—Brinell hardness number
bhp—brake horsepower
bm—board measure
bp—boiling point
Btu—British thermal unit
bu—bushel
c—¢, ct; cent(s)
c—centi (prefix, one-hundredth)
C—coulomb
°C—degree Celsius
cal—calorie (also: cal_{IT}, International
      Table; cal_{th}—thermochemical)
cd/in²—candela per square inch

cd/m²—candela per square meter
cg—centigram
cd•h—candela-hour
Ci—curie
cL—centiliter
cm—centimeter
c/m—cycles per minute
cm²—square centimeter
cm³—cubic centimeter
cmil—circular mil
cp—candlepower
cP—centipoise
cSt—centistokes
cwt—hundredweight
D—darcy
d—day
d—deci (prefix, one-tenth)
d—pence
da—deka (prefix, 10)
dag—dekagram
daL—dekaliter
dam—dekameter
dam²—square dekameter
dam³—cubic dekameter
dB—decibel
dBu—decibel unit
dc—direct current
dg—decigram
dL—deciliter
dm—decimeter
dm²—square decimeter
dm³—cubic decimeter
dol—dollar
doz—dozen
dr—dram
dwt—deadweight tons
dwt—pennyweight
dyn—dyne
EHF—extremely high frequency
emf—electromotive force
emu—electromagnetic unit

erg—erg
esu—electrostatic unit
eV—electronvolt
°F—degree Fahrenheit
F—farad
f—femto (prefix, one-quadrillionth)
fbm—board foot; board foot measure
fc—footcandle
fL—footlambert
fm—fentometer
FM—frequency modulation
ft—foot
ft²—square foot
ft³—cubic foot
ftH$_2$O—conventional foot of water
ft•lb—foot-pound
ft•lbf—foot-pound force
ft/min—foot per minute
ft²/min—square foot per minute
ft³/min—cubic foot per minute
ft-pdl—foot poundal
ft/s—foot per second
ft²/s—square foot per second
ft³/s—cubic foot per second
ft/s²—foot per second squared
ft/s³—foot per second cubed
G—gauss
G—giga (prefix, 1 billion)
g—gram; acceleration of gravity
Gal—gal cm/s²
gal—gallon
gal/min—gallons per minute
gal/s—gallons per second
GB—gigabyte
Gb—gilbert
g/cm³—gram per cubic centimeter
GeV—gigaelectronvolt
GHz—gigahertz (gigacycle per second)
gr—grain; gross
h—hecto (prefix, 100)
H—henry
h—hour
ha—hectare
HF—high frequency

hg—hectogram
hL—hectoliter
hm—hectometer
hm²—square hectometer
hm³—cubic hectometer
hp—horsepower
hph—horsepower-hour
Hz—hertz (cycles per second)
id—inside diameter
ihp—indicated horsepower
in—inch
in²—square inch
in³—cubic inch
in/h—inch per hour
inH$_2$O—conventional inch of water
inHg—conventional inch of mercury
in-lb—inch-pound
in/s—inch per second
J—joule
J/K—joule per kelvin
K—kayser
K—kelvin (use without degree symbol)
k—kilo (prefix, 1,000)
k—thousand (7k=7,000)
kc—kilocycle; see also kHz (kilohertz),
    kilocycles per second
kcal—kilocalorie
keV—kiloelectronvolt
kG—kilogauss
kg—kilogram
kgf—kilogram-force
kHz—kilohertz (kilocycles per second)
kL—kiloliter
klbf—kilopound-force
km—kilometer
km²—square kilometer
km³—cubic kilometer
km/h—kilometer per hour
kn—knot (speed)
kΩ—kilohm
kt—kiloton; carat
kV—kilovolt
kVA—kilovoltampere
kvar—kilovar

kW—kilowatt
kWh—kilowatthour
L—lambert
L—liter
lb—pound
lb ap—apothecary pound
lb—avdp, avoirdupois pound
lbf—pound-force
lbf/ft—pound-force foot
lbf/ft²—pound-force per square foot
lbf/ft³—pound-force per cubic foot
lbf/in²—pound-force per square inch
  (see psi)
lb/ft—pound per foot
lb/ft²—pound per square foot
lb/ft³—pound per cubic foot
lct—long calcined ton
ldt—long dry ton
LF—low frequency
lin ft—linear foot
l/m—lines per minute
lm—lumen
lm/ft²—lumen per square foot
lm/m²—lumen per square meter
lm•s—lumen second
lm/W—lumen per watt
l/s—lines per second
L/s—liter per second
lx—lux
M—mega (prefix, 1 million)
M—million (3 M=3 million)
m—meter
m—milli (prefix, one-thousandth)
M1—monetary aggregate
m²—square meter
m³—cubic meter
µ—micro (prefix, one-millionth)
µm—micrometer
mA—milliampere
µA—microampere
MB—megabyte
mbar—millibar
µbar—microbar

Mc—megacycle; see also MHz
  (megahertz), megacycles per
  second
mc—millicycle; see also mHz
  (millihertz), millicycles per
  second
mD—millidarcy
meq—milliquivalent
MeV—megaelectronvolts
mF—millifarad
µF—microfarad
mG—milligauss
mg—milligram
µg—microgram
Mgal/d—million gallons per day
mH—millihenry
µH—microhenry
MHz—megahertz
mHz—millihertz
mi—mile (statute)
mi²—square mile
mi/gal—mile(s) per gallon
mi/h—mile(s) per hour
mil—mil
min—minute (time)
µin—microinch
mL—milliliter
mm—millimeter
mm²—square millimeter
mm³—cubic millimeter
µm²—square micrometer
µm³—cubic micrometer
µµ—micromicron (use of compound
  prefixes obsolete; use pm,
  picometer)
µµf—micromicrofarad (use of
  compound prefixes obsolete; use
  pF)
mmHg—conventional millimeter of
  mercury
mΩ—megohm
mo—month
mol—mole (unit of substance)

mol wt—molecular weight
mp—melting point
ms—millisecond
μs—microsecond
Mt—megaton
mV—millivolt
μV—microvolt
MW—megawatt
mW—milliwatt
μW—microwatt
MWd/t—megawatt-days per ton
Mx—maxwell
n—nano (prefix, one-billionth)
N—newton
nA—nanoampere
nF—nanofarad
N•m—newton meter
N/m²—newton per square meter
nmi—nautical mile
Np—neper
ns—nanosecond
N•s/m²—newton second per square
    meter
nt—nit
od—outside diameter
Oe—oersted (use of A/m, amperes per
    meter, preferred)
oz—ounce (avoirdupois)
p—pico (prefix, one-trillionth)
P—poise
Pa—pascal
pA—picoampere
pct—percent
pdl—poundal
pF—picofarad
pF—water-holding energy
pH—hydrogen-ion concentration
ph—phot; phase
pk—peck
pm—picometer
p/m—parts per million
ps—picosecond
psi—pounds per square inch
pt—pint

pW—picowatt
qt—quart
quad—quadrillion (10^{15})
R—rankine
R—roentgen (measurement of
    radiation)
°R—degree Rankine
rad—radian
rd—rad (radiation-absorbed dose)
rem—roentgen equivalent man
r/min—revolutions per minute
rms—root mean square
r/s—revolutions per second
s—second (time)
s—shilling
S—siemens
sb—stilb
scp—spherical candlepower
s•ft—second-foot
shp—shaft horsepower
slug—slug
sr—steradian
sSf—standard saybolt fural
sSu—standard saybolt universal
stdft³—standard cubic foot (feet)
Sus—saybolt universal second(s)
T—tera (prefix, 1 trillion)
Tft³—trillion cubic feet
T—tesla
t—tonne (metric ton)
tbsp—tablespoonful
thm—therm
ton—ton
tsp—teaspoonful
Twad—twaddell
u—(unified) atomic mass unit
UHF—ultrahigh frequency
V—volt
VA—voltampere
var—var
VHF—very high frequency
V/m—volt per meter
W—watt
Wb—weber

Wh—watthour
W/(m•K)—watt per meter kelvin
W/sr—watt per steradian
W/(sr•m²)—watt per steradian square
    meter

x—unknown quantity (italic)
yd—yard
yd²—square yard
yd³—cubic yard
yr—year

Standard Latin abbreviations

9.63.   When Latin abbreviations are used, follow this list.

a.—annus, year; ante, before

A.A.C.—anno ante, Christum in the year before Christ

A.A.S.—Academiae Americanae Socius, Fellow of the American Academy [Academy of Arts and Sciences]

A.B.—artium baccalaureus, bachelor of arts

ab init.—ab initio, from the beginning

abs. re.—absente reo, the defendant being absent

A.C.—ante Christum, before Christ

A.D.—anno Domini, in the year of our Lord

a.d.—ante diem, before the day

ad fin.—ad finem, at the end, to one end

ad h.l.—ad hunc locum, to this place, on this passage

ad inf.—ad infinitum, to infinity

ad init.—ad initium, at the beginning

ad int.—ad interim, in the meantime

ad lib.—ad libitum, at pleasure

ad loc.—ad locum, at the place

ad val.—ad valorem, according to

A.I.—anno inventionis, in the year of the discovery

al.—alia, alii, other things, other persons

A.M.—anno mundi, in the year of the world; Annus mirabilis, the wonderful year [1666]

a.m.—ante meridiem, before noon

an.—anno, in the year; ante, before

ann.—annales, annals; anni, years

A.R.S.S.—Antiquariorum Regiae Societatis Socius, Fellow of the Royal Society of Antiquaries

A.U.C.—anno urbis conditae, ab urbe conolita, in [the year from] the building of the City [Rome], 753 B.C.

B.A.—baccalaureus artium, bachelor of arts

B.S. or B. Sc.—baccalaureus scientiae, bachelor of science

C.—centum, a hundred; condemno, I condemn, find guilty

c.—circa, about

cent.—centum, a hundred

cf.—confer, compare

C.M.—chirurgiae magister, master of surgery

coch.—cochlear, a spoon, spoonful

coch. amp.—cochlear amplum, a tablespoonful

coch. mag.—cochlear magnum, a large spoonful

coch. med.—cochlear medium, a dessert spoonful

coch. parv.—cochlear parvum, a teaspoonful

con.—contra, against; conjunx, wife

C.P.S.—custos privati sigilli, keeper of the privy seal

C.S.—custos sigilli, keeper of the seal

cwt.—c. for centum, wt. for weight, hundredweight

D.—Deus, God; Dominus, Lord; d.,
decretum, a decree; denarius, a
penny; da, give

D.D.—divinitatis doctor, doctor of
divinity

D.G.—Dei gratia, by the grace of God;
Deo gratias, thanks to God

D.N.—Dominus noster, our Lord

D.S. or D. Sc.—doctor scientiae,
doctor of science

d.s.p.—decessit sine prole, died
without issue

D.V.—Deo volente, God willing

dwt.—d. for denarius, wt. for weight
pennyweight

e.g.—exempli gratia, for example

et al.—et alibi, and elsewhere; et alii, or
aliae, and others

etc.—et cetera, and others, and so forth

et seq.—et sequentes, and those that
follow

et ux.—et uxor, and wife

F.—filius, son

f.—fiat, let it be made; forte, strong

fac.—factum similis, facsimile, an
exact copy

fasc.—fasciculus, a bundle

fl.—flores, flowers; floruit, flourished;
fluidus, fluid

f.r.—folio recto, right-hand page

F.R.S.—Fraternitatis Regiae Socius,
Fellow of the Royal Society

f.v.—folio verso, on the back of the leaf

guttat.—guttatim, by drops

H.—hora, hour

h.a.—hoc anno, in this year; hujus
anni, this year's

hab. corp.—habeas corpus, have the
body—a writ

h.e.—hic est, this is; hoc est, that is

h.m.—hoc mense, in this month; huius
mensis, this month's

h.q.—hoc quaere, look for this

H.R.I.P.—hic requiescat in pace, here
rests in peace

H.S.—hic sepultus, here is buried; hic
situs, here lies; h.s., hoc sensu, in
this sense

H.S.S.—Historiae Societatis Socius,
Fellow of the Historical Society

h.t.—hoc tempore, at this time; hoc
titulo, in or under this title

I—Idus, the Ides; i., id, that;
immortalis, immortal

ib. or ibid.—ibidem, in the same place

id.—idem, the same

i.e.—id est, that is

imp.—imprimatur, sanction, let it be
printed

I.N.D.—in nomine Dei, in the name of
God

in f.—in fine, at the end

inf.—infra, below

init.—initio, in the beginning

in lim.—in limine, on the threshold, at
the outset

in loc.—in loco, in its place

in loc. cit.—in loco citato, in the place
cited

in pr.—in principio, in the beginning

in trans.—in transitu, on the way

i.q.—idem quod, the same as

i.q.e.d.—id quod erat demonstrandum,
what was to be proved

J.—judex, judge

J.C.D.—juris civilis doctor, doctor of
civil law

J.D.—jurum or juris doctor, doctor of
laws

J.U.D.—juris utriusque doctor, doctor
of both civil and canon law

L.—liber, a book; locus, a place

£—libra, pound; placed before figures
thus £10; if l, to be placed after, as
40l.

L.A.M.—liberalium artium magister, master of the liberal arts

L.B.—baccalaureus literarum, bachelor of letters

lb.—libra, pound (singular and plural)

L.H.D.—literarum humaniorum doctor, doctor of the more humane letters

Litt. D.—literarum doctor, doctor of letters

LL.B.—legum baccalaureus, bachelor of laws

LL.D.—legum doctor, doctor of laws

LL.M.—legum magister, master of laws

loc. cit.—loco citato, in the place cited

loq.—loquitur, he, or she, speaks

L.S.—locus sigilli, the place of the seal

l.s.c.—loco supra citato, in the place above cited

£ s. d.—librae, solidi, denarii, pounds, shillings, pence

M.—magister, master; manipulus, handful; medicinae, of medicine; m., meridies, noon

M.A.—magister artium, master of arts

M.B.—medicinae baccalaureus, bachelor of medicine

M. Ch.—magister chirurgiae, master of surgery

M.D.—medicinae doctor, doctor of medicine

m.m.—mutatis mutandis, with the necessary changes

m.n.—mutato nomine, the name being changed

MS.—manuscriptum, manuscript; MSS., manuscripta, manuscripts

Mus. B.—musicae baccalaureus, bachelor of music

Mus. D.—musicae doctor, doctor of music

Mus. M.—musicae magister, master of music

N.—Nepos, grandson; nomen, name; nomina, names; noster, our; n., natus, born; nocte, at night

N.B.—nota bene, mark well

ni. pri.—nisi prius, unless before

nob.—nobis, for (or on) our part

nol. pros.—nolle prosequi, will not prosecute

non cul.—non culpabilis, not guilty

n.l.—non licet, it is not permitted; non liquet, it is not clear; non longe, not far

non obs.—non obstante, notwithstanding

non pros.—non prosequitur, he does not prosecute

non seq.—non sequitur, it does not follow logically

O.—octarius, a pint

ob.—obiit, he, or she, died; obiter, incidentally

ob. s.p.—obiit sine prole, died without issue

o.c.—opere citato, in the work cited

op.—opus, work; opera, works

op. cit.—opere citato, in the work cited

P.—papa, pope; pater, father; pontifex, bishop; populus, people; p., partim, in part; per, by, for; pius, holy; pondere, by weight; post, after; primus, first; pro, for

p.a.—or per ann., per annum, yearly; pro anno, for the year

p. ae.—partes aequales, equal parts

pass.—passim, everywhere

percent.—per centum, by the hundred

pil.—pilula, pill

Ph. B.—philosophiae baccalaureus, bachelor of philosophy

P.M.—post mortem, after death

p.m.—post meridiem, afternoon

pro tem.—pro tempore, for the time being

prox.—proximo, in or of the next [month]

P.S.—postscriptum, postscript; P.SS.,
    postscripta, postscripts
q.d.—quasi dicat, as if one should say;
    quasi dictum, as if said; quasi
    dixisset, as if he had said
q.e.—quod est, which is
Q.E.D.—quod erat demonstrandum,
    which was to be demonstrated
Q.E.F.—quod erat faciendum, which
    was to be done
Q.E.I.—quod erat inveniendum, which
    was to be found out
q.l.—quantum libet, as much as you
    please
q. pl.—quantum placet, as much as
    seems good
q.s.—quantum sufficit, sufficient
    quantity
q.v.—quantum vis, as much as you
    will; quem, quam, quod vide,
    which see; qq. v., quos, quas, or
    quae vide, which see (plural)
R.—regina, queen; recto, right-hand
    page; respublica, commonwealth
℞—recipe, take
R.I.P.—requiescat, or requiescant, in
    pace, may he, she, or they, rest in
    peace
R.P.D.—rerum politicarum doctor,
    doctor of political science
R.S.S.—Regiae Societatis Sodalis,
    Fellow of the Royal Society
S.—sepultus, buried; situs, lies;
    societas, society; socius or
    sodalis, fellow; s., semi, half;
    solidus, shilling
s.a.—sine anno, without date;
    secundum artem, according to
    art
S.A.S.—Societatis Antiquariorum
    Socius, Fellow of the Society of
    Antiquaries
sc.—scilicet, namely; sculpsit, he, or
    she, carved or engraved it

S.B. or Sc. B.—scientiae baccalaureus,
    bachelor of science
S.D. or Sc. D.—scientiae doctor,
    doctor of science
S.D.—salutem dicit, sends greetings
s.d.—sine die, indefinitely
sec.—secundum, according to
sec. leg.—secundum legem, according
    to law
sec. nat.—secundum naturam,
    according to nature, or naturally
sec. reg.—secundum regulam,
    according to rule
seq.—sequens, sequentes, sequentia,
    the following
S.H.S.—Societatis Historiae Socius,
    Fellow of the Historical Society
s.h.v.—sub hac voce or sub hoc verbo,
    under this word
s.l.a.n.—sine loco, anno, vel nomine,
    without place, date, or name
s.l.p.—sine legitima prole, without
    lawful issue
s.m.p.—sine mascula prole, without
    male issue
s.n.—sine nomine, without name
s.p.—sine prole, without issue
S.P.A.S.—Societatis Philosophiae
    Americanae Socius, Fellow of the
    American Philosophical Society
s.p.s.—sine prole superstite, without
    surviving issue
S.R.S.—Societatis Regiae Socius or
    Sodalis, Fellow of the Royal
    Society
ss—scilicet, namely (in law)
S.S.C.—Societas Sanctae Crucis,
    Society of the Holy Cross
stat.—statim, immediately
S.T.B.—sacrae theologiae
    baccalaureus, bachelor of sacred
    theology
S.T.D.—sacrae theologiae doctor,
    doctor of sacred theology

S.T.P.—sacrae theologiae professor, professor of sacred theology
sub.—subaudi, understand, supply
sup.—supra, above
t. or temp.—tempore, in the time of
tal. qual.—talis qualis, just as they come; average quality
U.J.D.—utriusque juris doctor, doctor of both civil and canon law
ult.—ultimo, last month (may be abbreviated in writing but should be spelled out in printing)
ung.—unguentum, ointment
u.s.—ubi supra, in the place above mentioned

ut dict.—ut dictum, as directed
ut sup.—ut supra, as above
ux.—uxor, wife
v.—versus, against; vide, see; voce, voice, word
v. —— a., vixit —— annos—lived [so many] years
verb. sap.—verbum [satis] sapienti, a word to the wise suffices
v.g.—verbi gratia, for example
viz—videlicet, namely
v.s.—vide supra, see above

Information technology acronyms and initialisms

9.64. Use these forms, if abbreviations are required:

3DES—Triple DES encryption
3DM—Data Driven Decision Making
ABLS—Automated Bid List System
ACES—access certificates for electronic services
ACID—Atomicity, Consistency, Isolation and Durability
ACL—Access Control List
ACP—Access Content Package
AES—advanced Encryption Standard
AI—Artificial Intelligence
AIDC—Automatic identification and capture
AIFF—audio interchange file format
AIO—Asynchronous I/O
AIP—Archival Information Package
AJAX—Asynchronous JavaScript and XML
ALPN—Application-Layer Protocol Negotiation
API—Application Programming Interface
ARK—archival resource key
ARP—address resolution protocol
ASCII—American Standard Code for Information Interchange

ASP—application service provider
ATO—Authority to Operate
AWS—Amazon Web Services
BASE—Basically Available, Soft-State, Eventually Consistent
BDA—Big Data Analytics
BI—Business Intelligence
BLOB —Binary Large OBject
BPEL—business process execution language
BPI—business process information
C&I—Cataloging and Indexing
CA—certificate authority
CAP—Consistency, Availability, Partition tolerance
CBC—Cipher Block Chaining
CD—compact disc
CDM—Copy Data Management
CDN—content delivery network
CDR—critical design review
CD-ROM—compact disc read only memory
CE—content evaluator
CentOS—Community Enterprise Operating System

CERN—(European) Centre for Nuclear Research
CGP—Catalog of U.S. Government Publications
CI—Clustered Index
CIM—Common Interface Model
CISCAT—Center for Internet Security -Configuration Assessment Tool
CISSP—Certified Information Systems Security Professional
CK—Candidate Key
CLOB—Character Large Object
CMS—content management system
CN—Canonical Name
CO—content originator
COG—Continuity of Government
COOP—continuity of operations plan
CP—content processor
CPS—Certificate Practice Statement
CRC—cyclic redundancy checks
CRL—Certificate Revocation List
CRM—Customer Relationship Management
CRUD—Create, Read, Update, and Delete
CSS—Cascading Style Sheets
CSV—comma separated variable
CTE—Common Table Expression
CVS—Concurrent Versioning Services
DaaS—Database as a Service
DBA—Database Administrator
DB—Database
DBMS—database management system
DCL—Data Control Language
DDL—Data Definition Language
DDoS—Distributed Denial of Service
DES—data encryption standard
DHCP—Dynamic Host Control Protocol
DH—Diffie-Hellman (Exchange)
DHE—Diffie-Hellman Ephemeral
DHSL—Distributed Hadoop Storage Layer

DIP—Dissemination Information Package
DMD—Data Management Definition
DMI—desktop management interface
DML—Data Manipulation Language
DMV—Dynamic Management Views
DN—Distinguished Name
DNS—domain name system
DO—digital objects
DOI—Digital Object Identifier
DoS—denial of service
DPI—dots per inch
DR—Disaster Recovery
DSL—digital subscriber line
DSR—deployment system review
DSSL—document style and semantics language
DVD—digital versatile disc
DW—Database Warehouse
E_Port—Expansion port, also known as ISL
EAC—estimate at completion
EAD—encoded archival description
EA—enterprise architecture
EAP—enterprise application platform
EBCDIC—Extended Binary Coded Decimal Interchange Code
ECC—Elliptic Curve Cryptography
ECDHE—Elliptic Curve Diffie-Hellman Key Exchange
EPS—Encapsulated PostScript
ERD—Entity Relationship Diagram
ESXi—Elastic Sky X Integrated
ETL—Extract, Transform, Load
EV—Extended Validation
FBCA—Federal Bridge Certificate Authority
FC–AL—Fibre Channel Arbitrated Loop
FCIA—Fibre Channel Industry Association
FC–IP—Fibre Channel Over IP
FCP—Fibre Channel Protocol
FC–SW—Fibre Channel Switched

FDDI—fiber distributed data interface
FDsys—Federal Digital System
FICC—Federal Identity Credentialing
    Committee
FIFO—first in first out
FIPNet—Federal Information
    Preservation Network
FIPS—Federal Information Processing
    Standard
FISMA—Federal Information Security
    Management Act of 2002
FK—Foreign Key
FOSI—format output specifi cation
    instance
FTP—file transfer protocol
GBIC—Gigabit Interface Converter
Gbps—Gigabits per second
GDI—graphical device interface
GGP—gateway-to-gateway protocol
GIF—graphics interchange format
GILS—Government Information
    Locator Service
GUI—graphical user interface
HBA—Host Bus Adapter
HDFS—Hadoop Distributed File
    System
HDTV—high definition television
HMAC—key hashed message
    authentication code
HPC—High-Performance Computing
HSM—hardware security module
HSM—Hierarchical Storage
    Management
HSTS—HTTP Strict Transport
    Security
HTML—hypertext markup language
HTTP—hypertext transfer protocol
HTTPS—HyperText Transfer Protocol
    Secure
Hz—Hertz
Iaas—Infrastructure as a Service
IAM—Identity and Access
    Management

ICMP—internet control message
    protocol
IDD—interface design description
IDE—Integrated Development
    Environment
IDE—Integrated Drive Electronics
IEEE—Institute of Electrical and
    Electronics Engineers
IETF—Internet Engineering Task
    Force
iFCP—Internet Fibre Channel
    Protocol
ILS—Integrated Library System
IOPS—I/O operations per second
IOS—Apple Operating System
IOT—Index Organized Table
IoT—Internet of Things
IP—internet protocol
IPR—internal progress review
IPSEC—internet protocol security
IPS—Intrusion Prevention System
ISAM—Indexed Sequential Access
    Method
ISL—Inter switch link
ISP—internet service provider
IT—information technology
ITU—International
    Telecommunications Union
JBOD—Just a bunch of disks
JDBC—Java Database Connectivity
JDF—Job Definition Format
JITS—Just-in-time storage
JPEG—Joint Photographic Experts
    Group
JS—JavaScript
JSON—JavaScript Object Notation
L_Port—Loop port
LAMP—Linux, Apache, MySQL and
    PHP
LAN—local area network
LDAP—lightweight directory access
    protocol
LHC—Large Hadron Collider

LOB—Large Object
LPAR—Logical Partition
LPI—lines per inch
LRU—Last Recently Used (algorithm)
LUN—Logical Unit Number
MAC—message authentication code
MAN—Metropolitan area network
MARC—Machine Readable
    Cataloging
MDC—Multidimensional Clustering
    Table
METS—Metadata Encoding and
    Transmission Standard
MIME—multipurpose internet mail
    extensions
MIPS—millions of instructions per
    second
MODS—Metadata Object Descriptive
    Schema
MOOC—massive online open courses
MP3—MPEG-2 Audio Layer III
MPCF—marginally punched
    continuous forms
MVC—Model View Controller
MV—Materialized View
NAS—Network Attached Storage
NAT—network address translation
NDIIPP—National Digital
    Information Infrastructure and
    Preservation Program
NDLP—National Digital Library
    Program
NF—Normal Form
NNTP—network news transfer protocol
NOSQL—Not Only Structured Query
    Language
OAI—Open Archives Initiative
OAI-PMH—Open Archives Initiative
    Protocol for Metadata Harvesting
OAIS—open archival information
    system
OCLC—Online Computer Library
    Center

OCR—optical character recognition
OCSP—Online Certificate Status
Protocol
ODBC—Open Database Connectivity
OLAP—Online Analytical Processing
OLTP—online transaction processing
OODBMS—Object-Oriented Database
    Management System
ORM—Object-Relational Mapping
PAAS—Platform as a service
PDF—Portable Document Format
PGP—Pretty Good Privacy
PHP—PHP Hypertext Preprocessor
PKI—Public Key Cryptography
PK—Primary Key
PL/pgSQL—Procedural Language/
    SQL
PL/SQL—Procedural Language/SQL
PNG—portable network graphics
PREMIS—Preservation Metadata:
    Implementation Strategies
PRONOM—Practical Online
    Compendium of File Formats
PTR—program tracking report
PURL—persistent uniform resource
    locator
QoS—Quality of service
QPS—Queries Per Second
RAC—Real Application Clusters
    (Oracle)
RAID—redundant array of
    inexpensive disks
RAM—random access memory
RC4—Rivest Cipher 4
RDA—Resource Description and
    Access
REGEX—Regular Expression
REST—Representational State
    Transfer
RFC—Request for Comments or
    Request for Change
RHEL—Red Hat Enterprise Linux
RI—representation information

RMA—reliability, maintainability, availability

RPC—remote procedure call

RPM—RPM Package Manager

RSA—Rivest, Shamir, and Adelman (public key cryptosystem)

RTF—rich text format

RVTM—requirements verification traceability matrix

S4—Simple Scalable Streaming System

SAAS—Software as a Service

SAML—security assertion markup language

SAN—Storage-area network

SASL—Simple Authentication and Security Layer

SASS—Syntactically Awesome Stylesheets

SDD—System Design Diagram

SDD—System Design Document

SDK—Software Development Kit

SDLC—software/system development lifecycle

SDR—system design review

Section 508—Section 508 of the Rehabilitation Act

SFTP—Secure File Transfer Protocol

SGML—standard generalized markup language

SHA—Secure Hash Algorithm

SIP—Submission Information Package

SMTP—simple mail transfer protocol

SNMP—simple network management protocol

SOAP—Simple Object Access Protocol

SOA—Service Oriented Architecture

SQL—Structured Query Language

SQL PL—SQL Procedure Language used for writing stored procedures. Also see PL/SQL

SQL/XML—an extension of the SQL language used for querying XML

SSD—Solid State Drive

SSD—System Security Diagram

SSH—Secure Shell

SSL —Secure Sockets Layer

SSP—system security plan

SSR—software specification review

SUSE—Software und System Entwicklung (Software and Systems Development)

SVN—Subversion

TDES—Triple Data Encryption Standard

TFS—Team Foundation Server

TIFF—tagged image file format

TLS—transport layer security

TPS—Transactions Per Second, a measurement of database performance

UAT—User Acceptance Testing

UDF—User Defined Function

UDP—user datagram protocol

UDT—User Defined Type

UID—Unique Identifier

URL—uniform resource locator

URN—uniform resource name/number

UUID—Universal Unique Identifer

VC—Virtual Center

VDC—Virtual Data Center

VIP—Virtual Internet Protocol

VI—Virtual Interface

VLAN—virtual local area network

VM—Virtual Machine

VMW—Vmware

VPN—virtual private network

VSAN—Virtual Storage Area Network

W3C—World Wide Web Consortium

WAI–ARIA—Worldwide Accessibility Initiative - Accessible Rich Internet Applications

WAIS—wide area information service

WAN—Wide Area Network

WAP—wireless application protocol
WAV—waveform audio format
WCAG—Web Content Accessibility
    Guidelines
Wi-Fi—wireless fidelity
WIP—work in process
WML—wireless markup language
www—world wide web
WYSIWYG—what you see is what
    you get
XAML—Extensible Application
    Markup Language
XDW—Extended Data Warehouse
XMLDsig—xml signature

XMLENC—xml encryption
XML—Extensible Markup Language
XPATH—XML Path Language
XQUERY—XML Query
XSD—XML Schema Definition
XSL—Extensible Stylesheet Language
XSL-FO—XSL Formatting Objects
XSLT—Extensible Stylesheet Language
    Transformations
YAML—Yet Another Markup
    Language
YARN—Yet Another Resource
    Negotiator

10. Signs and Symbols

10.1. The increased use of signs and symbols and their importance in technical and scientific work have emphasized the necessity of standardization on a national basis and of the consistent use of the standard forms.

10.2. Certain symbols are standardized—number symbols (the digits, 0, 1, 2, 3, 4, 5, 6, 7, 8, 9); letter symbols (the letters of the alphabet, a, b, c, d, etc.); and graphic symbols (the mathematical signs +, −, ±, ×, ÷).

10.3. The signs +, −, ±, ×, and ÷, etc., are closed against accompanying figures and symbols. When the × is used to indicate "crossed with" (in plant or animal breeding) or magnification, it will be separated from the accompanying words by a space.

i–vii+1–288 pages	Early June × Bright (crossed with)
The equation A+B	× 4 (magnification)
The result is 4×4	miles ÷ gallons
20,000±5,000	

Symbols with figures

10.4. In technical publications the degree mark is used in lieu of the word *degree* following a figure denoting measurement.

10.5. Following a figure, the spelled form is preferred. The percent symbol is used in areas where space will not allow the word *percent* to be used.

> In that period the price rose 12, 15, and 19 percent.
> *not* In that period the price rose 12 percent, 15 percent, and 19 percent.

10.6. Any symbol set close up to figures, such as the degree mark, number mark, dollar mark, or cent mark, is used before or after each figure in a group or series.

$5 to $8 price range	*but*
5'–7' long, *not* 5–7' long	§ 12 (thin space)
3¢ to 5¢ (no spaces)	¶ 1951 (thin space)
±2 to ±7; 2°±1°	from 15 to 25 percent
#61 to #64	45 to 65 °F *not* 45° to 65° F

Letter symbols

10.7.   Letter symbols are set in italic (see rule 10.8) or in roman (see rule 9.56) without periods and are capitalized only if so shown in copy, since the capitalized form may have an entirely different meaning.

Equations

10.8.   In mathematical equations, use italic for all letter symbols—capitals, lowercase, small capitals, and superiors and inferiors (exponents and subscripts); use roman for figures, including superiors and inferiors.

10.9.   If an equation or a mathematical expression needs to be divided, break before +, −, =, etc. However, the equal sign is to clear on the left of other beginning mathematical signs.

10.10.   A short equation in text should not be broken at the end of a line. Space out the line so that the equation will begin on the next line; or better, center the equation on a line by itself.

10.11.   An equation too long for one line is set flush left, the second half of the equation is set flush right, and the two parts are balanced as nearly as possible.

10.12.   Two or more equations in a series are aligned on the equal signs and centered on the longest equation in the group.

10.13.   Connecting words of explanation, such as *hence, therefore,* and *similarly,* are set flush left either on the same line with the equation or on a separate line.

10.14.   Parentheses, braces, brackets, integral signs, and summation signs should be of the same height as the mathematical expressions they include.

10.15.   Inferiors precede superiors if they appear together; but if either inferior or superior is too long, the two are aligned on the left.

Chemical symbols

10.16.   The names and symbols listed below are approved by the International Union of Pure and Applied Chemistry. They are set in roman without periods.

Element	Symbol	Atomic No.	Element	Symbol	Atomic No.
Actinium	Ac	89	Mendelevium	Md	101
Aluminum	Al	13	Mercury	Hg	80
Americium	Am	95	Molybdenum	Mo	42
Antimony	Sb	51	Moscovium	Mc	115
Argon	Ar	18	Neodymium	Nd	60
Arsenic	As	33	Neon	Ne	10
Astatine	At	85	Neptunium	Np	93
Barium	Ba	56	Nickel	Ni	28
Berkelium	Bk	97	Nihonium	Nh	113
Beryllium	Be	4	Niobium	Nb	41
Bismuth	Bi	83	Nitrogen	N	7
Bohrium	Bh	107	Nobelium	No	102
Boron	B	5	Oganesson	Og	118
Bromine	Br	35	Osmium	Os	76
Cadmium	Cd	48	Oxygen	O	8
Calcium	Ca	20	Palladium	Pd	46
Californium	Cf	98	Phosphorus	P	15
Carbon	C	6	Platinum	Pt	78
Cerium	Ce	58	Plutonium	Pu	94
Cesium	Cs	55	Polonium	Po	84
Chlorine	Cl	17	Potassium	K	19
Chromium	Cr	24	Praseodymium	Pr	59
Cobalt	Co	27	Promethium	Pm	61
Copernicium	Cn	112	Protactinium	Pa	91
Copper	Cu	29	Radium	Ra	88
Curium	Cm	96	Radon	Rn	86
Darmstadtium	Ds	110	Rhenium	Re	75
Dubnium	Db	105	Rhodium	Rh	45
Dysprosium	Dy	66	Roentgenium	Rg	111
Einsteinium	Es	99	Rubidium	Rb	37
Erbium	Er	68	Ruthenium	Ru	44
Europium	Eu	63	Rutherfordium	Rf	104
Fermium	Fm	100	Samarium	Sm	62
Flerovium	Fl	114	Scandium	Sc	21
Fluorine	F	9	Seaborgium	Sg	106
Francium	Fr	87	Selenium	Se	34
Gadolinium	Gd	64	Silicon	Si	14
Gallium	Ga	31	Silver	Ag	47
Germanium	Ge	32	Sodium	Na	11
Gold	Au	79	Strontium	Sr	38
Hafnium	Hf	72	Sulfur	S	16
Hassium	Hs	108	Tantalum	Ta	73
Helium	He	2	Technetium	Tc	43
Holmium	Ho	67	Tellurium	Te	52
Hydrogen	H	1	Tennessine	Ts	117
Indium	In	49	Terbium	Tb	65
Iodine	I	53	Thallium	Tl	81
Iridium	Ir	77	Thorium	Th	90
Iron	Fe	26	Thulium	Tm	69
Krypton	Kr	36	Tin	Sn	50
Lanthanum	La	57	Titanium	Ti	22
Lawrencium	Lr	103	Tungsten	W	74
Lead	Pb	82	Uranium	U	92
Lithium	Li	3	Vanadium	V	23
Livermorium	Lv	116	Xenon	Xe	54
Lutetium	Lu	71	Ytterbium	Yb	70
Magnesium	Mg	12	Yttrium	Y	39
Manganese	Mn	25	Zinc	Zn	30
Meitnerium	Mt	109	Zirconium	Zr	40

Standardized symbols

10.17.   Symbols duly standardized by any national scientific, professional, or technical group are accepted as preferred forms within the field of the group. The issuing office desiring or requiring the use of such standardized symbols should see that copy is prepared accordingly.

Signs and symbols

10.18.   The following list contains some signs and symbols frequently used in printing. The forms and style of many symbols vary with the method of reproduction employed. It is important that editors and writers clearly identify signs and symbols when they appear within a manuscript.

ACCENTS

⁄ acute
˘ breve
¸ cedilla
ʌ circumflex
·· dieresis
ˋ grave
¯ macron
~ tilde

ARROWS

→ direction
↖ direction
↪ direction
↷ direction
↶ direction
← bold arrow
◊ open arrow
⇌ reversible reaction

BULLETS

● solid circle; bullet
• bold center dot
• movable accent

CHEMICAL

°⁄₀₀ salinity
m minim
ↄ exchange
↑ gas

CIRCLED SYMBOLS

Ⓐ angle in circle
Ⓞ circle with parallel rule
Ⓐ triangle in circle
Ⓞ dot in circle
Ⓐ dot in triangle in circle
⊕ cross in circle
© copyright
① Ceres
② Pallas
③ Juno
④ Vesta

CODE

· No. 1 6 pt. code dot
· No. 2 8 pt. code dot
· No. 3 10 pt. code dot
● No. 4 8 pt. code dot
● No. 4 10 pt. code dot
— No. 1 6 pt. code dash
— No. 2 8 pt. code dash
— No. 3 10 pt. code dash
▬ No. 4 8 pt. code dash
▬ No. 4 10 pt. code dash

COMPASS

° degree
°. degree with period
′ minute
′. minute with period
″ second
″. second with period
″ canceled second

DECORATIVE

✚ bold cross
✛ cross patte
■ cross patte
✠ cross patte

● (184 N)
⚷ key
⚣ (206 N)
¶ paragraph

ELECTRICAL

ℛ reluctance
↔ reaction goes both right and left
↕ reaction goes both up and down
↕ reversible
→ direction of flow; yields
→ direct current
⇄ electrical current
⇄ reversible reaction
⇌ reversible reaction
⇄ alternating current
⇌ alternating current
⇌ reversible reaction beginning at left
⇋ reversible reaction beginning at right
Ω ohm; omega
MΩ megohm; omega
μΩ microohm; mu omega
ω angular frequency, solid angle; omega
Φ magnetic flux; phi
Ψ dielectric flux; electrostatic flux; psi
γ conductivity; gamma

ELECTRICAL—Con.

ρ resistivity; rho
Λ equivalent conductivity
HP horsepower

MATHEMATICAL

— vinculum (above letters)
$\div$ geometrical proportion
—: difference, excess
‖ parallel
‖s parallels
$\neq$ not parallels
| | absolute value
· multiplied by
: is to; ratio
÷ divided by
∴ therefore; hence
∵ because
:: proportion; as
≪ is dominated by
> greater than
⊏ greater than
≥ greater than or equal to
≧ greater than or equal to
≷ greater than or less than
≯ is not greater than
< less than
⊐ less than
≶ less than or greater than
≮ is not less than
< smaller than
≤ less than or equal to
≦ less than or equal to
≧ or ≥ greater than or equal to
≲ equal to or less than
≣ equal to or less than
≩ is not greater than equal to or less than
≳ equal to or greater than
≩ is not less than equal to or greater than
⊥ equilateral
⊥ perpendicular to
⊢ assertion sign
≑ approaches

MATHEMATICAL—Con.

≐ approaches a limit
⊻ equal angles
≠ not equal to
≡ identical with
≢ not identical with
𝍦 score
≈ or ≒ nearly equal to
= equal to
∼ difference
≃ perspective to
≅ congruent to approximately equal
≏ difference between
⬦ geometrically equivalent to
(included in
) excluded from
⊂ is contained in
∪ logical sum or union
∩ logical product or intersection
√ radical
√ root
∛ square root
∛ cube root
∜ fourth root
∜ fifth root
∜ sixth root
π pi
ε base (2.718) of natural system of logarithms; epsilon
ε is a member of; dielectric constant; mean error; epsilon
+ plus
+ bold plus
− minus
− bold minus
/ shill(ing); slash; virgule
± plus or minus
∓ minus or plus
× multiplied by
= bold equal
number
℔ per
% percent
∫ integral
| single bond
\ single bond
/ single bond

MATHEMATICAL—Con.

‖ double bond
⦦ double bond
∥ double bond
◯ benzene ring
∂ or δ differential; variation
∂ Italian differential
→ approaches limit of
∼ cycle sine
⌡ horizontal integral
∮ contour integral
∝ variation; varies as
Π product
Σ summation of; sum; sigma
! or ⌐ factorial product

MEASURE

℔ pound
ʒ dram
ƒʒ fluid dram
℥ ounce
ƒ℥ fluid ounce
O pint

MISCELLANEOUS

§ section
† dagger
‡ double dagger
⅊ account of
℅ care of
𝍦 score
¶ paragraph
þ Anglo-Saxon
₵ center line
♂ conjunction
⊥ perpendicular to
″ or " ditto
∝ variation
℞ recipe
⌐ move right
⌐ move left
◯ or ⊙ or ① annual
⊙⊙ or ② biennial
∈ element of
℈ scruple
ƒ function
! exclamation mark
⊞ plus in square
♃ perennial

MISCELLANEOUS—Con.

- φ   diameter
- c̄   mean value of c
- U   mathmodifier
- ⊂   mathmodifier
- ⊡   dot in square
- △   dot in triangle
- ⊠   station mark
- @   at

MONEY

- ¢   cent
- ¥   yen
- £   pound sterling
- ₥   mills

MUSIC

- ♮   natural
- ♭   flat
- ♯   sharp

PLANETS

- ☿   Mercury
- ♀   Venus
- ⊕   Earth
- ♂   Mars
- ♃   Jupiter
- ♄   Saturn
- ♅   Uranus
- ♆   Neptune
- ☊   dragon's head, ascending node
- ☋   dragon's tail, descending node
- ☌   conjunction
- ☍   opposition
- ☉ or ⊙ Sun
- ♁   Sun's lower limb
- ☉   Sun's upper limb
- ☼   solar corona
- ⊕   solar halo
- ☽   Moon
- ●   new Moon
- ☽   first quarter
- ◑   first quarter
- ◕   third quarter
- ◐   last quarter
- ☾   last quarter
- ◑   last quarter
- ○   full Moon
- ⊕   full Moon
- ⊖   eclipse of Moon

PLANETS—Con.

- ☋   lunar halo
- ☋   lunar corona
- ⚳   Ceres
- ⚵   Juno

PUNCTUATION

- { }   braces
- [ ]   brackets
- ( )   parentheses
- ⟨ ⟩   square parentheses; angle brackets
- ¡   inverted exclamation mark
- ¿   inverted question mark

SEX

- ♂ or ⚦ male
- ☐   male, in charts
- ♀   female
- ○   female, in charts
- ⚥   hermaphrodite

SHAPES

- ◆   solid diamond
- ◇   open diamond
- ○   circle
- ▲   solid triangle
- △   triangle
- ☐   square
- ■   solid square
- ▱   parallelogram
- ▭   rectangle
- ▭   double rectangle
- ★   solid star
- ☆   open star
- ∟   right angle
- ∠   angle
- √   check
- ✔   check
- ß   German ss
- ß   italic German ss
- ☛   solid index
- ☚   solid index
- ☜   index
- ☞   index

GEOLOGIC SYSTEMS [1]

- Q   Quaternary
- T   Tertiary
- K   Cretaceous

- J   Jurassic
- Ŧ   Triassic
- P   Permian
- **P**   Pennsylvanian
- M   Mississippian
- D   Devonian
- S   Silurian
- O   Ordovician
- €   Cambrian
- p€ Precambrian
- C   Carboniferous

VERTICAL

- | 5 unit vertical
- | 8 point vertical
- | 9 unit vertical

WEATHER

- T   thunder
- ⚡   thunderstorm; sheet lightning
- <   sheet lightning
- ↓   precipitate
- ◍   rain
- ←   floating ice crystals
- ↔   ice needles
- ▲   hail
- ⊗   sleet
- ∞   glazed frost
- ⊔   hoarfrost
- V   frostwork
- *   snow or sextile
- ⊠   snow on ground
- +   drifting snow (low)
- ≡   fog
- ∞   haze
- △   Aurora

ZODIAC

- ♈   Aries; Ram
- ♉   Taurus; Bull
- ♊   Gemini; Twins
- ♋   Cancer; Crab
- ♌   Leo; Lion
- ♍   Virgo; Virgin
- ♎   Libra; Balance
- ♏   Scorpio; Scorpion
- ♐   Sagittarius; Archer
- ♑   Capricornus; Goat
- ♒   Aquarius; Water bearer
- ♓   Pisces; Fishes

[1] Standard letter symbols used by the Geological Survey on geologic maps. Capital letter indicates the system and one or more lowercased letters designate the formation and member where used.

11. Italic
(See also Chapter 9 "Abbreviations and Letter Symbols"
and Chapter 16 "Datelines, Addresses, and Signatures")

11.1.   Italic is sometimes used to differentiate or to give greater prominence
          to words, phrases, etc. However, an excessive amount of italic defeats
          this purpose and should be restricted.

Emphasis, foreign words, and titles of publications

11.2.   Italic is not used for mere emphasis, foreign words, or the titles of
          publications.

11.3.   In nonlegal work, *ante, post, infra,* and *supra* are italicized only when
          part of a legal citation. Otherwise these terms, as well as the abbrevia-
          tions *id., ibid., op. cit., et seq.,* and other foreign words, phrases, and
          their abbreviations, are printed in roman.

11.4.   When [emphasis in original], [emphasis supplied], [emphasis added],
          or [emphasis ours] appears in copy, it should not be changed; but
          "underscore supplied" should be changed to "italic supplied."
          Therefore, when emphasis in quoted or extracted text is referred to
          by the foregoing terms, such emphasized text must be reflected and
          set in italic.

11.5.   When copy is submitted with instructions to set "all roman (no
          italic)," these instructions will not apply to *Ordered, Resolved, Be it
          enacted,* etc.; titles following signatures or addresses; or the parts of
          datelines that are always set in italic.

Names of aircraft, vessels, and spacecraft

11.6.   The names of aircraft, vessels, and manned spacecraft are italicized
          unless otherwise indicated. In lists set in columns and in stubs and
          reading columns of tables consisting entirely of such names, they will
          be set in roman. Missiles and rockets will be set in caps and lowercase
          and will not be italicized.

SS *America*; the liner *America*
USS *Los Angeles* (submarine)
USS *Wisconsin*
ex-USS *Savannah*
USCGS (U.S. Coast and Geodetic
   Survey) ship *Pathfinder*
CSS *Virginia*
CG cutter *Thetus*
the *U–7*
destroyer *31*
HMS *Hornet*
HS (hydrofoil ship) *Denison*
MS (motorship) *Richard*
GTS (gas turbine ship) *Alexander*
NS (nuclear ship) *Savannah*
MV (motor vessel) *Havtroll*

Apollo 13, Atlantis (U.S. spaceships)
West Virginia class or type
the *Missouri*'s (roman "s") turret
the *U–7*'s (roman "s") deck
Enola Gay
but
Air Force One (President's plane)
B–50 (type of plane)
DD–882
LST–1155
MiG; MiG–35
PT–109
F–22 Raptor
F–117 Nighthawk (Stealth fighter)
A–10 Thunderbolt

11.7. Names of vessels are quoted in matter printed in other than capitals and lowercase roman, even if there is italic type available in the series.

Sinking of the "Lusitania"
Sinking of the "Lusitania"

Sinking of the "Lusitania"
SINKING OF THE "LUSITANIA"

Names of legal cases

11.8. The names of legal cases are italicized, except for the *v.*, which is always set in lowercase. When requested, the names of such cases may be set in roman with an italic *v.* In matter set in italic, legal cases are set in roman with the *v.* being set roman.

"The Hornet" and "The Hood,"
  124 F.2d 45
Smith v. *Brown et al.*
Smith Bros. case (172 App.
  Div. 149)
Smith Bros. case, *supra*
Smith Bros. case
As cited in *Smith Bros.*

Smith v. Brown et al. (heading)
SMITH v. BROWN ET AL.
  (heading)
Durham rule
Brown decision
John Doe v. Richard Roe
but John Doe against Richard Roe,
  the *Cement* case.

Scientific names

11.9. The scientific names of genera, subgenera, species, and subspecies (varieties) are italicized but are set in roman in italic matter; the names of groups of higher rank than genera (phyla, classes, orders, families, tribes, etc.) are printed in roman.

> *A.s. perpallidus*
> *Dorothia?* sp. (roman "?")
> *Tsuga canadensis*
> *Cypripedium parviflorum* var. *pubescens*
> the genera *Quercus* and *Liriodendron*
> the family Leguminosae; the family Nessiteras rhombopteryx
> *Measurements of specimens of* Cyanoderma erythroptera neocara

11.10. Quotation marks should be used in place of italic for scientific names appearing in lines set in caps, caps and small caps, or boldface, even if there is italic type available in the series.

Words and letters

11.11. The words *Resolved, Resolved further, Provided, Provided, however, Provided further, And provided further,* and *ordered,* in bills, acts, resolutions, and formal contracts and agreements are italicized; also the words *To be continued, Continued on p. —, Continued from p. —,* and *See* and *see also* (in indexes and tables of contents only).

> *Resolved,* That (resolution)
> *Resolved by the Senate and House of Representatives of the United States of America in Congress assembled,* That
> [*To be continued*] (centered; no period)
> [*Continued from p. 3*] (centered; no period)
> *see also* Mechanical data (index entry)

11.12. All letters (caps, small caps, lowercase, superiors, and inferiors) used as symbols are italicized. In italic matter, roman letters are used. Chemical symbols (even in italic matter) and certain other standardized symbols are set in roman.

> nth degree; x dollars
> $D \div 0.025V_m^{2.7} = 0.042/G - 1V_m^{2.7}$
> $5Cu_2S \cdot 2(Cu,Fe,Zn)S \cdot 2Sb_2S_3O_4$

11.13.   Letter designations in mathematical and scientific matter, except chemical symbols, are italicized.

11.14.   Letter symbols used in legends to illustrations, drawings, etc., or in text as references to such material, are set in italic without periods and are capitalized if so shown in copy.

11.15.   Letters (*a*), (*b*), (*c*), etc., and *a, b, c,* etc., used to indicate sections or paragraphs, are italicized in general work but not in laws or other legal documents.

11.16.   Internet websites and email addresses should be set in roman.

12. Numerals
(See also Chapter 13 "Tabular Work" and Chapter 14 "Leaderwork")

12.1. Most rules for the use of numerals are based on the general principle that the reader comprehends numerals more readily than numerical word expressions, particularly in technical, scientific, or statistical matter. However, for special reasons, numbers are spelled out in certain instances, except in FIC & punc. and Fol. Lit. matter.

12.2. The following rules cover the most common conditions that require a choice between the use of numerals and words. Some of them, however, are based on typographic appearance rather than on the general principle stated above.

12.3. Arabic numerals are preferable to Roman numerals.

Numbers expressed in figures

12.4. A figure is used for a single number of *10* or more with the exception of the first word of the sentence. (See also rules 12.9 and 12.23.)

50 ballots	24 horses	nearly 13 buckets
10 guns	about 40 men	10 times as large

Numbers and numbers in series

12.5. When 2 or more numbers appear in a sentence and 1 of them is *10* or larger, figures are used for each number. (See supporting rule 12.6.)

Each of 15 major commodities (9 metal and 6 nonmetal) was in supply.

but Each of nine major commodities (five metal and four nonmetal) was in supply.

Petroleum came from 16 fields, of which 8 were discovered in 1956.

but Petroleum came from nine fields, of which eight were discovered in 1956.

That man has 3 suits, 2 pairs of shoes, and 12 pairs of socks.

but That man has three suits, two pairs of shoes, and four hats.

Of the 13 engine producers, 6 were farm equipment manufacturers, 6 were principally engaged in the production of other types of machinery, and 1 was not classified in the machinery industry.

but Only nine of these were among the large manufacturing companies, and only three were among the largest concerns.

There were three 6-room houses, five 4-room houses, and three 2-room cottages, and they were built by 20 carpenters. (See rule 12.21.)

There were three six-room houses, five four-room houses, and three two-room cottages, and they were built by nine carpenters.

but If two columns of sums of money add or subtract one into the other and one carries points and ciphers, the other should also carry points and ciphers.

At the hearing, only one Senator and one Congressman testified.

There are four or five things that can be done.

12.6.   A unit of measurement, time, or money (as defined in rule 12.9), which is always expressed in figures, does not affect the use of figures for other numerical expressions within a sentence.

Each of the five girls earned 75 cents an hour.

Each of the 15 girls earned 75 cents an hour.

A team of four men ran the 1-mile relay in 3 minutes 20 seconds.

This usually requires from two to five washes and a total time of 2 to 4 hours.

This usually requires 9 to 12 washes and a total time of 2 to 4 hours.

The contractor, one engineer, and one surveyor inspected the 1-mile road.

but There were two six-room houses, three four-room houses, and four two-room cottages, and they were built by nine workers in thirty 5-day weeks. (See rule 12.21.)

12.7.   Figures are used for serial numbers.

Bulletin 725	290 U.S. 325
Document 71	Genesis 39:20
pages 352–357	202–512–0724 (telephone number)
lines 5 and 6	the year 2001
paragraph 1	1721–1727 St. Clair Avenue
chapter 2	*but* Letters Patent No. 2,189,463

12.8.   A colon preceding figures does not affect their use.

The result was as follows: 12 voted yea, 4 dissented.

The result was as follows: nine voted yea, seven dissented.

Measurement and time

12.9.   Units of measurement and time, actual or implied, are expressed in figures.

a. Age:

6 years old	a 3-year-old
52 years 10 months 6 days	at the age of 3 (years implied)

b. Clock time (see also Time):

4:30 p.m.; half past 4
10 o'clock *or* 10 p.m. (*not* 10 o'clock p.m.; 2 p.m. in the afternoon; 10:00 p.m.)
12 p.m. (12 noon)
12 a.m. (12 midnight)
$4^h 30^m$ *or* 4.5^h, in scientific work, if so written in copy
0025, 2359 (astronomical and military time)
08:31:04 (stopwatch reading)

c. Dates:

9/11 (referring to the attack on the United States that occurred on September 11, 2001)
June 1985 (*not* June, 1985); June 29, 1985 (*not* June 29th, 1985)
March 6 to April 15, 1990 (*not* March 6, 1990, to April 15, 1990)
May, June, and July 1965 (*but* June and July 1965)
15 April 1951; 15–17 April 1951 (military)
4th of July (*but* Fourth of July, meaning the holiday)
the 1st [day] of the month (*but* the last of April or the first [part] of May, not referring to specific days)
in the year 2000 (*not* 2,000)

In referring to a fiscal year, consecutive years, or a continuous period of 2 years or more, when contracted, the forms 1900–11, 1906–38, 1931–32, 1801–2, 1875–79 are used (*but* upon change of century, 1895–1914 and to avoid multiple ciphers together, 2000–2001). For two or more separate years not representing a continuous period, a comma is used instead of a dash (1875, 1879); if the word *from* precedes the year or the word *inclusive* follows it, the second year is not shortened and the word *to* is used in lieu of the dash (from 1933 to 1936; 1935 to 1936, inclusive).

In dates, *A.D.* precedes the year (A.D. 937); *B.C.* follows the year (254 B.C.); C.E. and B.C.E. follow the year.

d. Decimals: In text a cipher should be supplied before a decimal point if there is no whole unit, and ciphers should be omitted after a decimal point unless they indicate exact measurement.

0.25 inch; 1.25 inches	*but* .30 caliber (meaning 0.30 inch,
silver 0.900 fine	bore of small arms); 30 calibers
specific gravity 0.9547	(length)
gauge height 10.0 feet	

e. Use spaces to separate groups of three digits in a decimal fraction. (See rule 12.27.)

0.123 456 789; *but* 0.1234

f. Degrees, etc. (spaces omitted):

longitude 77°04'06" E	*but*
35°30'; 35°30' N	two degrees of justice; 12
a polariscopic test of 85°	degrees of freedom
an angle of 57°	32d degree Mason
strike N 16° E	150 million degrees Fahrenheit
dip 47° W *or* 47° N 31° W	30 Fahrenheit degrees
25.5' (preferred) *also* 25'.5	

g. Game scores:

1 up (golf)	7 to 6 (football), etc.
3 to 2 (baseball)	2 all (tie)

h. Market quotations:

4½ percent bonds	gold is 109
Treasury bonds sell at 95	wheat at 2.30
Metropolitan Railroad, 109	sugar, .03; *not* 0.03
Dow Jones average of 18500.76	

i. Mathematical expressions:

multiplied by 3	a factor of 2
divided by 6	square root of 4

j. Measurements:

7 meters	3 ems
about 10 yards	20/20 (vision)
8 by 12 or 8 x 12 inches	30/30 (rifle)
8- by 12-inch page	12-gauge shotgun
2 feet by 1 foot 8 inches by 1 foot 3	2,500 horsepower
inches	15 cubic yards
2 by 4 or 2 x 4 (lumber) (*not* 2×4)	6-pounder
1½ miles	80 foot-pounds
6 acres	10s (for yarns and threads)
9 bushels	*f*/2.5 (lens aperture)
1 gallon	4 by 4 or 4 x 4 truck

but	six bales
tenpenny nail	two dozen
fourfold	one gross
three-ply	zero miles
five votes	seven-story building

k. Money:

$3.65; $0.75; 75 cents; 0.5 cent	*but*
$3 (*not* $3.00) per 200 pounds	two pennies
75 cents apiece	three quarters
Rs32,25,644 (Indian rupees)	one half
CHF 2.5 (Swiss francs)	six bits, etc.
9 euros or 9€	
65 yen	
₱265	

l. Percentage:

12 percent; 25.5 percent; 0.5 percent (*or* one-half of 1 percent)	50–50 (colloquial expression)
thirty-four one hundredths of 1 percent	5 percentage points
	a 1,100-percent increase, *or* an 1100-percent increase
3.65 bonds; 3.65s; 5–20 bonds; 5–20s; 4½s; 3s	

m. Proportion:

1 to 4	1:62,500
1–3–5	

n. Time (see also Clock time):

6 hours 8 minutes 20 seconds	*but*
10 years 3 months 29 days	four centuries
7 minutes	three decades
8 days	three quarters (9 months)
4 weeks	statistics of any one year
1 month	in a year or two
3 fiscal years; third fiscal year	four afternoons
1 calendar year	one-half hour
millennium	the eleventh hour
FY 2010	FY10

o. Unit modifiers:

5-day week	a 5-percent increase
8-year-old wine	20th-century progress
8-hour day	
10-foot pole	*but*
½-inch pipe	two-story house
5-foot-wide entrance	five-member board
10-million-peso loan	$20 million airfield

p. Vitamins:

B_{12}, B_T, A_1, etc.

Ordinal numbers

12.10. Except as indicated in rules 12.11 and 12.19, and also for day preceding month, figures are used in text and footnotes to text for serial ordinal numbers beginning with *10th*. In tables, leaderwork, footnotes to tables and leaderwork, and in sidenotes, figures are used at all times. Military units are expressed in figures at all times when not the beginning of a sentence, except *Corps*. (For ordinals in addresses, see rule 12.13.)

29th of May, *but* May 29	eighth parallel; 38th parallel
First Congress; 102d Congress	fifth ward; 12th ward
ninth century; 21st century	ninth birthday; 66th birthday
Second Congressional District; 20th Congressional District	first grade; 11th grade
	1st Army
seventh region; 17th region	1st Cavalry Division
323d Fighter Wing	
12th Regiment	*but*
9th Naval District	XII Corps (Army usage)
7th Fleet	Court of Appeals for the Tenth Circuit
7th Air Force	
7th Task Force	Seventeenth Decennial Census (title)

12.11. When ordinals appear in juxtaposition and one of them is *10th* or more, figures are used for such ordinal numbers.

This legislation was passed in the 1st session of the 102d Congress.
He served in the 9th and 10th Congresses.

From the 1st to the 92d Congress.

Their children were in 1st, 2d, 3d, and 10th grades.

We read the 8th and 12th chapters.

but The district comprised the first and second precincts.

He represented the first, third, and fourth regions.

The report was the sixth in a series of 14.

12.12. Ordinals and numerals appearing in a sentence are treated according to the separate rules dealing with ordinals and numerals standing alone or in a group. (See rules 12.4, 12.5, and 12.24.)

The fourth group contained three items.

The fourth group contained 12 items.

The 8th and 10th groups contained three and four items, respectively.

The eighth and ninth groups contained 9 and 12 items, respectively.

12.13. Beginning with *10th*, figures are used in text matter for numbered streets, avenues, etc. However, figures are used at all times and *street, avenue,* etc. are abbreviated in sidenotes, tables, leaderwork, and footnotes to tables and leaderwork.

First Street NW.; *also* in parentheses: (Fifth Street) (13th Street); 810 West 12th Street; North First Street; 1021 121st Street; 2031 18th Street North; 711 Fifth Avenue; 518 10th Avenue; 51–35 61st Avenue

Punctuation

12.14. The comma is used in a number containing four or more digits, except in serial numbers, common and decimal fractions, astronomical and military time, and kilocycles and meters of not more than four figures pertaining to radio.

Chemical formulas

12.15. In chemical formulas full-sized figures are used before the symbol or group of symbols to which they relate, and inferior figures are used after the symbol.

$$6PbS \cdot (Ag,Cu)_2 S \cdot 2As_2 S_3 O_4$$

Numbers spelled out

12.16. Spell out numbers at the beginning of a sentence or head. Rephrase a sentence or head to avoid beginning with figures. (See rule 12.25 for related numbers.)

> Five years ago . . . ; *not* 5 years ago . . .
> Five hundred fifty men hired . . . ; *not* 550 men hired . . .
> "Five-Year Plan Announced"; *not* "5-Year Plan Announced" (head)
> The year 2065 seems far off . . . ; *not* 2065 seems far off . . .
> Workers numbering 207,843 . . . ; *not* 207,843 workers . . .
> Benefits of $69,603,566 . . . ; *not* $69,603,566 worth of benefits . . .
>
> 1958 REPORT *change to* THE 1958 REPORT
> $3,000 BUDGETED *change to* THE SUM OF $3,000 BUDGETED
> 4 MILLION JOBLESS *change to* JOBLESS NUMBER 4 MILLION

12.17. In verbatim testimony, hearings, transcripts, and question-and-answer matter, figures are used immediately following Q. and A. or name of interrogator or witness for years (e.g., 2015), sums of money, decimals, street numbers, and for numerical expressions beginning with *101*.

> Mr. BIRCH, Junior. 2015 was a good year.
> Mr. BELL. $1 per share was the return. Two dollars in 1956 was the alltime high. Two thousand twenty-nine may be another story.
> Colonel DAVIS. 92 cents.
> Mr. SMITH. 12.8 people.
> Mr. JONES. 1240 Pennsylvania Avenue NW, Washington, DC 20004.
> Mr. SMITH. Ninety-eight persons.
> Q. 101 years? *But* Q. One hundred years?
> A. 200 years.
> Mr. SMITH. Ten-year average would be how much?

12.18. A spelled-out number should not be repeated in figures, except in legal documents. In such instances use these forms:

> five (5) dollars, *not* five dollars (5)
> ten dollars ($10), *not* ten ($10) dollars

12.19. Numbers appearing as part of proper names, used in a hypothetical or inexact sense, or mentioned in connection with serious and dignified subjects such as Executive orders, legal proclamations, and in formal writing are spelled out.

Three Rivers, PA, Fifteenmile Creek, etc.	three score years and ten
the Thirteen Original States	Ten Commandments
in the year two thousand eight	Air Force One (Presidential plane)
the One Hundred Tenth Congress	back to square one
millions for defense but not one cent for tribute	behind the eight ball
	our policy since day one

12.20. If spelled out, whole numbers should be set in the following form:

two thousand twenty
one thousand eight hundred fifty
one hundred fifty-two thousand three hundred five
eighteen hundred fifty (serial number)

When spelled out, any number containing a fraction or piece of a whole should use the word "and" when stating the fraction or piece:

sixty-two dollars and four cents
ninety-nine and three-tenths degrees
thirty-three and seventy-five one-hundredths shares

12.21. Numbers below *100* preceding a compound modifier containing a figure are spelled out.

two ¾-inch boards	*but*
twelve 6-inch guns	120 8-inch boards
two 5-percent discounts	three four-room houses

12.22. Indefinite expressions are spelled out.

the seventies; the early seventies; *but* the early 1870s *or* 1970s	midthirties (age, years, money)
in his eighties, *not* his '80's *nor* 80's	a thousand and one reasons
between two and three hundred horses (*better* between 200 and 300 horses)	*but*
	1 to 3 million
	mid-1971; mid-1970s
twelvefold; thirteenfold; fortyfold; hundredfold; twentyfold to thirtyfold	40-odd people; nine-odd people
	40-plus people
	100-odd people
	3½-fold; 250-fold; 2.5-fold; 41-fold

Words such as *nearly, about, around, approximately,* etc., do not reflect indefinite expressions.

> The bass weighed about 6 pounds.
> She was nearly 8 years old.

12.23. Except as indicated in rules 12.5 and 12.9, a number less than *10* is spelled out within a sentence.

six horses	*but*
five wells	3½ cans
eight times as large	2½ times or 2.5 times

12.24. For typographic appearance and easy grasp of large numbers beginning with *million,* the word *million, billion,* or *trillion* is used.

The following are guides to treatment of figures as submitted in copy. If copy reads—

> $12,000,000, *change to* $12 million
> 2,750,000,000 dollars, *change to* $2,750 million
> 2.7 million dollars, *change to* $2.7 million
> 2⅜ million dollars, *change to* $2⅜ million
> two and one-half million dollars, *change to* $2½ million
> a hundred cows, *change to* 100 cows
> a thousand dollars, *change to* $1,000
> a million and a half, *change to* 1½ million
> two thousand million dollars, *change to* $2,000 million
> less than a million dollars, *change to* less than $1 million
> *but* $2,700,000, *do not convert* to $2.7 million
> *also* $10 to $20 million; 10 or 20 million; between 10 and 20 million
> 4 million of assets
> amounting to 4 trillion
> $1,270,000
> $1,270,200,000
> $2¾ billion; $2.75 billion; $2,750 million
> $500,000 to $1 million

300,000; *not* 300 thousand

$½ billion to $1¼ billion (note full figure with second fraction); $1¼ to $1½ billion

three-quarters of a billion dollars

5 or 10 billion dollars' worth

12.25. Related numbers appearing at the beginning of a sentence, separated by no more than three words, are treated alike.

Fifty or sixty more miles away is snowclad Mount Everest.

Sixty and, quite often, seventy listeners responded.

but Fifty or, in some instances, almost 60 applications were filed.

Fractions

12.26. Mixed fractions are always expressed in figures. Fractions standing alone, however, or if followed by *of a* or *of an*, are generally spelled out. (See also rule 12.28.)

three-fourths of an inch; *not* ¾ inch *nor* ¾ of an inch	two one-hundredths
	one-thousandth
one-half inch	five one-thousandths
one-half of a farm; *not* ½ of a farm	thirty-five one-thousandths
one-fourth inch	*but*
seven-tenths of 1 percent	½ to 1¾ pages
three-quarters of an inch	½-inch pipe
half an inch	½-inch-diameter pipe
a quarter of an inch	3½ cans
one-tenth portion	2½ times
one-hundredth	

12.27. Fractions (¼, ½, ¾, ⅜, ⅝, ⅞, ¹⁄₂₉₅₄) or full-sized figures with the shilling mark (1/4, 1/2954) may be used only when either is specifically requested. Mixed fractions in full-sized figures are joined with a hyphen (2-2/3). A comma should not be used in any part of a built-up fraction of four or more digits or in decimals. (See rule 12.9e.)

12.28. Fractions are used in a unit modifier.

½-inch pipe; *not* one-half-inch pipe	¼-mile run	⅞-point rise

Roman numerals

12.29.   A repeated letter repeats its value; a letter placed after one of greater value adds to it; a letter placed before one of greater value subtracts from it; a dashline over a letter denotes multiplied by 1,000.

Numerals

I	1	XXV	25	LXX	70	D	500
II	2	XXIX	29	LXXV	75	DC	600
III	3	XXX	30	LXXIX	79	DCC	700
IV	4	XXXV	35	LXXX	80	DCCC	800
V	5	XXXIX	39	LXXXV	85	CM	900
VI	6	XL	40	LXXXIX	89	M	1,000
VII	7	XLV	45	XC	90	MD	1,500
VIII	8	XLIX	49	XCV	95	MM	2,000
IX	9	L	50	IC	99	MMM	3,000
X	10	LV	55	C	100	MMMM	
XV	15	LIX	59	CL	150	or $\overline{\text{MV}}$	4,000
XIX	19	LX	60	CC	200	$\overline{\text{V}}$	5,000
XX	20	LXV	65	CCC	300	$\overline{\overline{\text{M}}}$	1,000,000
		LXIX	69	CD	400		

Dates

MDC	1600	MCMXX	1920	MCMLXX	1970
MDCC	1700	MCMXXX	1930	MCMLXXX	1980
MDCCC	1800	MCMXL	1940	MCMXC	1990
MCM or MDCCCC	1900	MCML	1950	MM	2000
MCMX	1910	MCMLX	1960	MMX	2010

13. Tabular Work
(See also Chapter 9 "Abbreviations and Letter Symbols" and Chapter 14 "Leaderwork")

13.1. The object of a table is to present in a concise and orderly manner information that cannot be presented as clearly in any other way.

13.2. Tabular material should be kept as simple as possible, so that the meaning of the data can be easily grasped by the user.

13.3. Tables shall be set without down (vertical) rules when there is at least an em space between columns, except where: (1) in GPO's judgment down rules are required for clarity; or (2) the agency has indicated on the copy they are to be used. The mere presence of down rules in copy or enclosed sample is not considered a request that down rules be used. The publication dictates the type size used in setting tables. Tabular work in the Congressional Record is set 6 on 7. The balance of congressional tabular work sets 7 on 8. If down rules are used they will be set as hairlines, unless a specific weight is requested.

Abbreviations

13.4. To avoid burdening tabular text, commonly known abbreviations are used in tables. Metric and unit-of-measurement abbreviations are used with figures.

13.5. The names of months (except May, June, and July) when followed by the day are abbreviated.

13.6. The words *street, avenue, place, road, square, boulevard, terrace, drive, court,* and *building,* following name or number, are abbreviated. For numbered streets, avenues, etc., figures are used.

13.7. Abbreviate the words *United States* if preceding the word *Government,* the name of any Government organization, or as an adjective generally.

13.8. Use the abbreviations *RR* and *Ry.* following a name, and *SS, MS,* etc., preceding a name.

13.9. Use *lat.* and *long.* with figures.

13.10.   Abbreviate, when followed by figures, the various parts of publications, as *article, part, section,* etc.

13.11.   Use, generally, such abbreviations and contractions as *98th Cong., 1st sess., H. Res. 5, H.J. Res. 21, S. Doc. 62, S. Rept. 410, Rev. Stat.,* etc.

13.12.   In columns containing names of persons, copy is followed as to abbreviations of given names.

13.13.   Periods are not used after abbreviations followed by leaders.

Bearoff or inset

13.14.   An en space is used for all bearoffs or insets.

13.15.   In a crowded table, when down rules are necessary, the bearoff or inset may be reduced in figure columns.

13.16.   Fractions are set flush right to the bearoff or inset of the allotted column width, and not aligned.

13.17.   Mathematical signs, parentheses, fractions, and brackets are set with a normal bearoff or inset.

Boxheads

13.18.   Periods are omitted after all boxheads, but a dash is used after any boxhead which reads into the matter following.

13.19.   Boxheads run crosswise.

13.20.   Boxheads are set solid, even in leaded tables.

13.21.   Boxheads are centered horizontally and vertically.

Down-rule style (see rule 13.3)

Sex and age	Employed students whose work records were obtained						
	Total		Time of year at beginning work [depth of this box does not influence the depth of box on left]				
			June to August		September to May		Not reported
	Number	Distribution (percent)	Number	Distribution (percent)	Number	Distribution (percent)	
Female (16 to 18)	3,869	45.5	1,415	9.6	2,405	15.8	49

No-down-rule style (preferred)

TABLE 9.—*Mine production of gold, silver, copper, lead, and zinc in 2008*

Class of material	Short tons	Gold (fine ounces)	Silver (fine ounces)	Copper (pounds)	Lead (pounds)	Zinc (pounds)
	Concentrate shipped to smelters and recoverable metals					
Copper	220,346	763	70,357	14,242,346	9,950	6,260
Lead	3,931	392	48,326	72,500	5,044,750	290,980
Zinc	25,159	269	41,078	263,400	581,590	26,441,270
Total:						
2008	249,436	1,424	159,756	14,578,246	5,636,290	26,738,510
2007	367,430	1,789	432,122	10,622,155	13,544,875	11,923,060
	Crude material shipped to smelters					
Dry gold, dry gold-silver ore	134	52	2,839	2,200	....	....
Copper:						
Crude ore	107,270	844	39,861	2,442,882	124,100	2,200
Slag	421	10	165	285,421	....	....
Lead	528	12	1,693	5,950	110,870	300
Mill cleanings (lead-zinc)	31	....	254	1,450	8,100	4,300
Total:						
2008	125,749	919	45,444	30,375,754	249,710	6,890
2007	166,184	1,042	47,176	41,601,845	497,125	26,940

13.22. In referring to quantity of things, the word *Number* in boxheads is spelled if possible.

13.23. Column numbers or letters in parentheses may be set under boxheads and are separated by one line space below the deepest head. (If alignment of parentheses is required within the table, use brackets in boxhead.) These column references align across the table. Units of quantity are set in parentheses within boxheads.

States	Department of Agriculture				Department of Commerce		
	Commodity Credit Corporation, value of commodities donated	Special school milk program[1]	Value of commodities distributed within States	Disaster loans, etc. (payments to assist States in furnishing hay in droughtstriken areas)	Civil Aeronautics Administration— Federal airport program— regular grants	Bureau of Public Roads: Highway construction	
						Regular grants[2]	Emergency grants[3]
	(1)	(2)	(3)	(4)	(5)	(6)	(7)
Alabama	$4,730,154	$1,520,362	$7,970,875	....	$79,284	$1,176,401	$247,515
Alaska	393,484	269,274	591,487	....	297,266	12,366,106	472,749
Arizona	4,545,983	823,136	6,512,639	....	127,749	9,317,853	....

13.24. Leaders may be supplied in a column consisting entirely of symbols or years or dates or any combination of these.

Centerheads, flush entries, and subentries

13.25. Heads follow the style of the tables as to the use of figures and abbreviations.

13.26. Punctuation is omitted after centerheads. Flush entries and subentries over subordinate items are followed by a colon (single subentry to run in, preserving the colon), but a dash is used instead of a colon when the entry reads into the matter below.

25	Miscellaneous: Powerplant equipment	$245,040.37
26	Roads, railroads, and bridges	275,900.34
	Total	520,940.71

TRANSMISSION PLANT

42	Structures and improvements	26,253.53
43	Station equipment	966,164.41
	Total	992,417.94

GENERAL PLANT

General plant:

Norris	753,248.97
Other	15,335.81
Total	768,584.78
Grand total	2,281,943.43

13.27. In reading columns if the centerhead clears the reading matter below by at least an em, the space is omitted; if it clears by less than an em, a space is used. If an overrun, rule, etc., in another column, or in the same column, creates a blank space above the head, the extra space is not added.

13.28. Units of quantity and years used as heads in reading and figure columns are set in italic with space above but no space below.

No-down-rule style (preferred)

The rules are used here to aid readability.

2015								
Oct. 1	35.6	15	Jan. 16	45.2	15	May 8	46.5	15
Oct. 31	45.0	15	Feb. 4	50.2	15	May 22	45.1	18
Nov. 14	40.9	18	Feb. 17	43.4	15	June 9	47.1	14
Dec. 24	41.7	15	Mar. 4	45.6	15	June 24	48.2	16
			Mar. 19	42.7	15	July 9	46.6	17
2016			Apr. 2	40.9	15	July 24	45.9	16
Jan. 3	43.9	15	Apr. 28	47.7	13	Aug. 6	46.5	16

Down-rule style (see rule 13.3)

2015								
Oct. 1	35.6	15	Jan. 16..................	45.2	15	May 8	46.5	15
Oct. 31	45.0	15	Feb. 4	50.2	15	May 22	45.1	18
Nov. 14	40.9	18	Feb. 17	43.4	15	June 9	47.1	14
Dec. 24	41.7	15	Mar. 4	45.6	15	June 24	48.2	16
			Mar. 19	42.7	15	July 9	46.6	17
2016			Apr. 2....................	40.9	15	July 24	45.9	16
Jan. 3.................	43.9	15	Apr. 28	47.7	13	Aug. 6...................	46.5	16

Ciphers

13.29. Where the first number in a column or under a cross rule is wholly a decimal, a cipher is added at the left of its decimal point. A cipher used alone in a money or other decimal column is placed in the unit row and is not followed by a period. The cipher repeats in mixed units before decimals unless the group totals.

January..............	+26.4	0	0	0	0	0	[1] +$0.7	27.1+	+40.4
February............	+66.7	0	0	0	0	0	−.9	65.8+	+98.1
March................	+143.1	+2.6	−7.5	0	0	0	+12.4	150.6	+224.1

13.30. In columns containing both dollars and cents, ciphers will be supplied on right of decimal point in the absence of figures.

13.31. Where column consists of single decimal, supply a cipher on the right unless the decimal is a cipher.

$$0.6$$
$$0$$
$$3.0$$
$$4.2$$
$$5.0$$

13.32. Where column has mixed decimals of two or more places, do not supply ciphers but follow copy.

$$0.22453$$
$$1.263$$
$$4$$
$$2.60$$
$$3.4567$$
$$78$$
$$12.6$$

$$\overline{102.14423}$$

13.33. Copy is followed in the use of the word *None* or a cipher to indicate *None* in figure columns. If neither one appears in the copy, leaders are inserted, unless a clear (no leaders) is specifically requested.

13.34. In columns of figures under the heading £ *s d,* if a whole number of pounds is given, one cipher is supplied under *s* and one under *d;* if only shillings are given, one cipher is supplied under *d.*

13.35. In columns of figures under *Ft In,* if only feet are given, supply cipher under *In;* if only inches are given, clear under *Ft;* if ciphers are used for *None,* place one cipher under both *Ft* and *In.*

13.36. In any column containing sums of money, the period and ciphers are omitted if the column consists entirely of whole dollars.

Continued heads

13.37. In continued lines an em dash is used between the head and the word (*Continued*) (in italic). No period is carried after a continued line.

13.38. Continued heads over tables will be worded exactly like the table heading. Notes above tables are repeated; footnote references are repeated in boxheads and in continued lines.

Dashes or rules

13.39. Rules are not carried in reading columns or columns consisting of serial or tracing numbers, but are carried through all figure columns.

13.40. Parallel rules are used to cut off figures from other figures below that are added or subtracted; also, generally, above a grand total.

Ditto (do.)

13.41. The abbreviation *do.* is used to indicate that the previous line is being repeated instead of repeating the line, verbatim, over and over. It is used in reading columns only, lowercased and preceded by leaders (6 periods) when there is matter in preceding column. If ditto marks are requested, closing quotes will be used.

13.42. Capitalize *Do.* in the first and last columns. These are indented 1 or 2 ems, depending on the length of the word being repeated, or the width of the column; the situation will determine as it is encountered.

13.43. In mixed columns made up of figure and reading-matter items, *do.* is used only under the latter items.

13.44. *Do.* is not used—

(1) In a figure or symbol column (tracing columns are figure columns);

(2) In the first line under a centerhead in the column in which the centerhead occurs;

(3) Under a line of leaders or a rule;

(4) Under an item italicized or set in boldface type for a specific reason (italic or boldface *do.* is never used; item is repeated);

(5) Under an abbreviated unit of quantity or other abbreviations; or

(6) Under words of three letters or less.

13.45. *Do.* is used, however, under a clear space and under the word *None* in a reading column.

13.46. *Do.* does not apply to a reference mark on the preceding item. The reference mark, if needed, is added to *do.*

13.47. Leaders are not used before *Do.* in the first column or before or after *Do.* in the last column.

13.48. In a first and/or last column 6 ems or less in width, a 1-em space is used before *Do.* In all other columns 6 ems or less in width, six periods are used. Bearoff is not included.

13.49. In a first and/or last column more than 6 ems in width, 2 ems of space are used before *Do.* In all other columns more than 6 ems in width, six periods are used. Bearoff space is not included. If the preceding line is indented, the indention of *Do.* is increased accordingly.

13.50. *Do.* under an indented item in an inside reading column, with or without matter in preceding column, is preceded by six periods which are indented to align with item above.

Dollar mark

13.51. The dollar mark or any other money symbol is placed close to the figure; it is used only at the head of the table and under cross rules when the same unit of value applies to the entire column.

13.52. In columns containing mixed amounts (as money, tons, gallons, etc.), the dollar mark, pound mark, peso mark, or other symbol, as required, is repeated before each sum of money.

13.53. If several sums of money are grouped together, they are separated from the nonmoney group by a parallel rule, and the symbol is placed on the first figure of the separated group only.

	1958	1967
Water supply available (gallons)	4,000,000	3,000,000
Wheat production (bushels)	9,000,000	8,000,000
Operations:		
Water-dispatching operations	$442,496	$396,800
Malaria control	571,040	426,600
Plant protection	134,971	58,320
Total	1,148,507	881,720
Number of plants	642	525
Percent of budget	96.8	78.8

NOTE.—Preliminary figures.
Source: U.S. Department of Commerce, Bureau of the Census.

13.54. In a double money column, dollar marks are used in the first group of figures only; en dashes are aligned.

$7–$9
10–12
314–316
1,014–1,016

13.55. The dollar mark is omitted from a first item consisting of a cipher.

0	*but* $0.12
$300	13.43
500	15.07
700	23.18

13.56. The dollar mark should be repeated in stub or reading columns.

0 to $0.99 ....
$1 to $24 ....
$25 to $49 ....
$50 to $74 ....

Figure columns

13.57. Figures align on the right, with an en space bearoff. There is no bearoff on leaders.

13.58. In a crowded table the bearoff may be reduced in figure columns only. It is preferable to retain the bearoff.

13.59. Figures in parentheses align.

13.60. In double rows of figures in a single column, connected by a dash, a plus, or minus sign, and in dates appearing in the form 9–4–08, the dashes or signs can be aligned.

13.61. Plus or minus signs at the left of figures are placed against the figures regardless of alignment; plus and minus signs at the right of figures are cleared.

13.62. Words and Roman numerals in figure columns are aligned on the right with the figures, without periods.

Median value of livestock	$224	$62	
Median value of machinery	$54	Small	
Median value of furniture	$211	$100	
Possessing automobiles (percent)	25	17	
Median age (years)			5.5
Median value			$144
Fraternal membership:			
Men		IV	486
Women			None

13.63. Figures (including decimal and common fractions) expressing mixed units of quantity (feet, dollars, etc.) and figures in parentheses are aligned on the right.

13.64. Decimal points are aligned except in columns containing numbers that refer to mixed units (such as pounds, dollars, and percentage) and have irregular decimals.

Footnotes and references

13.65. Footnotes to tables are numbered independently from footnotes to text unless requested by committee or department.

13.66. Superior figures are used for footnote references, beginning with 1 in each table.

13.67. If figures might lead to ambiguity (for example, in connection with a chemical formula), asterisks, daggers, or italic superior letters, etc., may be used.

13.68. When items carry several reference marks, the superior-figure reference precedes an asterisk, dagger, or similar character used for reference. These, in the same sequence, precede mathematical signs. A thin space is used to bear off an asterisk, dagger, or similar character.

13.69. Footnote references are repeated in boxheads or in continued lines over tables.

13.70. References to footnotes are numbered consecutively across the page from left to right.

13.71. Footnote references are placed at the right in reading columns and symbol columns, and at the left in figure columns (also at the left of such words as *None* in figure columns), and are separated by a thin space.

13.72. Two or more footnote references occurring together are separated by spaces, not commas.

13.73. In a figure column, a footnote reference standing alone is set in parentheses and flushed right. In a reading column, it is set at the left in parentheses and is followed by leaders, but in the last column it is followed by a period, as if it were a word. In a symbol column it is set at the left and cleared.

13.74. Numbered footnotes are placed immediately beneath the table. If a sign or letter reference in the heading of a table is to be followed, it is not changed to become the first numbered reference mark. The footnote to it precedes all other footnotes. The remaining footnotes in a table will follow this sequence: footnotes (numbers, letters, or symbols); NOTE.—; then Source:.

13.75. For better makeup or appearance, footnotes may be placed at the end of a lengthy table. A line reading "Footnotes at end of table." is supplied.

13.76. If the footnotes to both table and text fall together at the bottom of a page, the footnotes to the table are placed above the footnotes to the text, and the two groups are separated by a 50-point rule flush left; but if there are footnotes to the text and none to the table, the 50-point rule is retained.

13.77. Footnotes to cut-in and indented tables and tables in rules are set full measure, except when footnotes are short, they can be set in 1 em under indented table.

13.78. Footnotes are set as paragraphs, but two or more short footnotes should be combined into one line, separated by not less than 2 ems.

13.79. The footnotes and notes to tables are set solid.

13.80. Footnotes and notes to tables and boxheads are set the same size, but not smaller than 6 point, unless specified otherwise.

13.81. Footnotes to tables follow tabular style in the use of abbreviations, figures, etc.

13.82. In footnotes, numbers are expressed in figures, even at the beginning of a note or sentence.

13.83. If a footnote consists entirely or partly of a table or leaderwork, it should always be preceded by introductory matter carrying the reference number; if necessary, the copy preparer should add an introductory line, such as "[1] See the following table:".

13.84. An explanatory paragraph without specific reference but belonging to the table rather than to the text follows the footnotes, if any, and is separated from them or from the table by space.

Fractions

13.85. All fractions are set flush right to the bearoff.

Total length	$40\frac{3}{4}$	41	0.42	43	44	0.455	46	47	48	½ in.
Sleeve length	$10\frac{5}{8}$	10	10	10	11	11	11	11	11	1 in.
Armhole length	$8\frac{5}{8}$	8½	9	9½	9½	10	10½	10½	11	1 in.
Sleeve cuff length (if cuff is used).	5½	5½	5½	$5\frac{7}{12}$	5½	$5\frac{7}{12}$	5½	5½	5½	Maximum.
Neck opening	26½	26	$27\frac{17}{32}$	$28\frac{15}{32}$	28	$29\frac{17}{32}$	30	30	31	2 in.
Waist:										
7, 8, 9, 10 cut	23½	24	25½	$27\frac{15}{32}$	28	29½	31	32	33½	6 pct.
11, 12, 14 cut	22½	23½	25	26½	27½	29	30½	31½	33	6 pct.

13.86. Fractions standing alone are expressed in figures, even at the beginning of a line, but should be spelled out at the beginning of a footnote.

Headnotes

13.87. Headnotes should be set lowercase, but not smaller than 6 point, bracketed, and period omitted at end, even if the statement is a complete sentence; but periods should not be omitted internally if required by sentence structure.

13.88. Headnotes are repeated under continued heads but the word *Continued* is not added to the headnote.

Indentions and overruns

Subentries

13.89. The indention of subentries is determined by the width of the stub or reading column. Subentries in columns more than 15 ems wide are indented in 2-em units; in columns 15 ems or less, with short entry lines and few overruns, 2-em indentions are also used. All overruns are indented 1 em more.

13.90. Subentries in columns of 15 ems or less are indented in 1-em units. Overruns are indented 1 additional em space.

Total, mean, and average lines

13.91. All total (also mean and average) lines are indented 3 ems. In very narrow stub columns, total lines may be reduced to 1- or 2-em indentions, depending on length of line.

13.92. Where overrun of item above conflicts, the total line is indented 1 em more. Runovers of total lines are also indented 1 additional em space.

13.93. It is not necessary to maintain uniform indention of the word *Total* throughout the same table. The word *Total* is supplied when not in copy.

Wide stub column—subentries 2 ems	Total, all banks	National banks	Non-national banks	Building associations
ASSETS				
Loans and discounts:				
Loans to banks...	$74,518	$1,267,493	$947,289	$135,619
Commercial and industrial loans..................................	2,753,456	450,916	211,597	18,949
Total (total lines generally indent 3 ems)................	2,827,974	718,409	1,158,886	154,568
Real estate loans:				
Secured by farmland..	12,532	29,854	186,228	19,044
Secured by residential property other than rural and farm	1,011,856	167,765	1,554,084	3,172,837
Total (indent 1 em more to avoid conflict with line above)...	1,024,388	194,619	1,740,312	3,191,881
Securities:				
U.S. Government obligations:				
Direct obligations:				
U.S. savings bonds..	1,149,764	3,285,721	2,361,796	23,506
Nonmarketable bonds (including investment series A–1965)...................................	242,500	490,677	732,689	167,735
Total (indent 1 em more than runover above)..	1,392,264	3,776,398	3,094,485	191,241

Italic

13.94.   Names of vessels and aircraft (except in columns consisting entirely of such names), titles of legal cases (except *v.* for *versus*), and certain scientific terms are set in italic. The word "Total" and headings in the column do not affect the application of this rule. In gothic typefaces without italic, quotes are allowed.

13.95.   Set "See" and "See also" in roman.

Leaders

13.96.   Leaders run across the entire table except that they are omitted from a last reading column.

13.97.   The style of leadering is guided by two rules: (1) tables with a single reading column leader from the bottom line, or (2) tables with any combination of more than one reading or symbol column leader from the top line.

13.98.   If leadering from the top line, overruns end with a period.

13.99.   A column of dates is regarded as a reading column only if leaders are added; in all other cases it is treated as a figure column.

13.100.   In tables with tracing figures on left and right of page, leader from top line.

Numerals in tables

13.101.   Figures, ordinals, and fractions are used in all parts of a table, except fractions that will be spelled out at the beginning of a footnote.

Parallel and divide tables

13.102.   Parallel tables are set in pairs of pages; beginning on a left-hand page and running across to facing right-hand page, leader from the top line.

13.103.   Heads and headnotes center across the pair of pages, with 2-em hanging indention for three or more lines when combined measure exceeds 30 picas in width. Two-line heads are set across the pair of pages. A single-line head or headnote is divided evenly, each part set flush right and left, respectively. Words are not divided between pages.

13.104.   Boxheads and horizontal rules align across both pages.

13.105.   Boxheads are not divided but are repeated, with *Continued* added.

13.106.   Tracing figures are carried through from the outside columns of both pages and are set to "leader from the top line."

13.107.   In divide tables that are made up parallel, with stub column repeated, the head and headnote repeat on each succeeding page, with *Continued* added to the head only.

13.108.   Tables with tracing figures or stub, or both, repeating on the left of odd pages, are divide tables and not parallel tables. Over such tables the heads are repeated, with *Continued* added.

Reading columns

13.109. Figures or combinations of figures and letters used to form a reading column align on left and are followed by leaders. *Do.* is not used under such items.

13.110. The en dash is not to be used for *to* in a reading column; if both occur, change to *to* throughout.

13.111. Cut-in items following a colon are indented 2 ems.

13.112. A single entry under a colon line should be run in; retain the colon.

13.113. Numerical terms, including numbered streets, avenues, etc., are expressed in figures, even at the beginning of an item.

Symbol columns

13.114. A column consisting entirely of letters, letters and figures, symbols, or signs, or any combination of these, is called a symbol column. It should be set flush left and cleared, except when it takes the place of the stub, it should then be leadered. No closing period is used when such column is the last column. Blank lines in a last column are cleared. *Do.* is not used in a symbol column.

Symbol	Typical commercial designation	Army product symbol	Filing order symbol	General description	Specification symbol
GM(2)	Gasoline and diesel engine oil, SAE10 and SAE10W grades.	OR10	A	Fuel, grease, chassis, or soap base.	G.&D.
CG	Ball and roller bearing grease.	4l–X–59	N	Extreme pressure	BR
CW[1]	Wheel-bearing grease	OE20[2]	X	......do	WBG[3]
	Grease not typified			Further tests being conducted.	
G090	Universal gear lubricant	S.&T.	B	Water-pump grease	80D

13.115. Columns composed of both symbols and figures are treated as figure columns and are set flush right. In case of blank lines in a last column, leaders will be used as in figure columns.

Symbol or catalog number	Typical commercial designation	Symbol or product number	Symbol or filing order symbol	General description	Symbol or specification number
WBD	Chassis grease, cup grease, under pressure.	961	A	Especially adapted to very cold climates.	1359
14L88	Water-pump bearing grease	SWA	352	Under moderate pressure	
5190	Exposed gear chain lubricant	12L	N	High-speed use	AE10
	E.P. hypoid lubricant	863	X	For experimental use only..	NXL
376	Special grade for marine use		468	Free flowing in any weather	749

Tables without rules

13.116. It is preferable to set all tables alike; that is, without either down rules or cross rules and with roman boxheads. When so indicated on copy, by ordering agency, tabular matter may be set without rules, with italic boxheads.

13.117. Column heads over figure columns in 6- or 8-point leaderwork are set in 6-point italic.

13.118. Horizontal rules (spanner) used between a spread or upper level column heading carried over two or more lower level column headings are set continuous and without break, from left to right, between the two levels of such headings.

TABLE 9.—*Changes in fixed assets and related allowances*

| | *Balance June 30, 2008 (table 9–a)* | *Fixed assets* | | | | |
| | | *Investment* | | *Operations* | | |
		Current additions	*Adjustments*	*Transfers*	*Retirements*	*Balance June 30, 2008*
Supporting and general facilities:						
Transportation and utilities:						
Panama Railroad......	$12,123,197	$306	....	($539)	($284,358)	$11,838,606
Motor Transportation Division	2,242,999	122,597	....	2,143	(147,561)	2,220,178
Steamship line...........	13,653,989	10,247	....	....	....	13,664,236
Power system..............	19,364,373	366,311	....	(342)	(290,174)	19,440,168
Communication system..................	2,739,012	151,819	($113,261)	....	(26,100)	2,751,470
Water system and hydroelectric facilities.................	10,590,820	104,039	....	1,661	(48,920)	10,647,600
Total, transportation and utilities ..	60,714,390	755,319	(113,261)	2,923	(797,113)	60,562,258
Employee service and facilities:						
Commissary Division	7,012,701	105,952	(130,891)	21,777	(36,418)	6,973,121
Service centers..................	3,684,670	29,086	....	530	(230,276)	3,484,010
Housing Division..............	35,729,465	(10,336)	....	(485,548)	(937,916)	34,295,665
Total employee service and facilities..............	46,426,836	124,702	(130,891)	(463,241)	(1,204,610)	44,752,796
Grand total	107,141,236	880,021	(244,152)	(466,164)	(2,001,723)	105,315,054

13.119. More than one figure column, also illustrating use of dollar mark, rule, bearoff, etc.

For property purchased from—
  Central Pipeline Distributing Co.:
    Capital stock issued recorded amount.................................... $75,000
    Undetermined consideration recorded.................................... 341
  Pan American Bonded Pipeline Co.: Recorded money outlay .. 3,476
  M.J. Mitchell: Recorded money outlay.. 730
  R. Lacy, Inc., and Lynch Refining Co.:
    Recorded money outlay... $157,000
    Note issued... 100,000
                                                                                    _____
    Subtotal... 257,000
  Less value of oil in lines and salvaged construction
    material.. 26,555   230,445 $309,992

For construction, improvements, and replacements, recorded money outlay...... 522
For construction work in progress, recorded money outlay................................... 933,605
  Total 1,244,119

	Quantity (million cubic feet)	Value at point of consumption
Use:		
Residential	34,842	$21,218,778
Commercial...	14,404	5,257,468
Industrial:		
Field (drilling, pumping, etc.)	144,052	10,419,000
All other industrial:		
Fuel for petroleum refineries...	96,702	....
Other, including electric utility plants	346,704	61,440,000
Total	636,704	98,335,246

	Estimated		
	2004	2008	Change
General account:			
Receipts	$64,800	$69,800	+$5,000
Expenditures..	(70,300)	(67,100)	(-3,200)
Net improvement, 2008 over 2004			1,800
Deduct 2004 deficit			1,500
Net surplus, estimated for 2008...			300

[In U.S.-dollar equivalent]

Balance with the Treasury Department July 1, 2008..	$165,367,704.85
Receipts:	
Collections $564,944,502.99	
Return from agency accounts of currencies advanced for liquidation of obligations incurred prior to July 1, 2007...................... 4,450,577.07	
Total receipts..	569,395,080.06
Total available...	734,762,784.91

Units of quantity

13.120. Units of quantity in stub columns are set in lowercase in plural form and placed in parentheses.

Coke (short tons)	4,468,437	[1] 25,526,646	5,080,403	[2] 29,519,871
Diatomite...	([123])	([1])	([1])	([123])
Emery (pounds)	765	6,828	1,046	9,349
Feldspar (crude) (long tons)	([1])	([1])	([1])	([1])
Ferroalloys (short tons)	183,465	[2] 18,388,766	259,303	[2] 30,719,756

13.121. Units of quantity and other words as headings over figure columns are used at the beginning of a table or at the head of a continued page or continued column in a double-up table.

13.122. Over figure columns, units of quantity and other words used as headings, and the abbreviations *a.m.* and *p.m.*, if not included in the boxheads, are set in italic and are placed immediately above the figures, without periods other than abbreviating periods. In congressional work (gothic), or at any time when italic is not available, these units should be placed in the boxheads in parentheses. Any well-known abbreviation will be used to save an overrun, but if one unit of quantity is abbreviated, all in the same table will be abbreviated. If units change in a column, the new units are set in italic with space above and no space below. The space is placed both above and below only when there is no italic available.

Quoted tabular work

13.123. When a table is part of quoted matter, quotation marks will open on each centerhead and each footnote paragraph, and, if table is end of quoted matter, quotation marks close at end of footnotes. If there are no footnotes and the table is the end of the quotation, quotation marks close at end of last item.

14. Leaderwork

(See also Chapter 9 "Abbreviations and Letter Symbols" and Chapter 13 "Tabular Work")

14.1. Leaderwork is a simple form of tabular work without boxheads or rules and is separated from text by 4 points of space above and below in solid matter or 6 points of space in leaded matter. It consists of a reading (stub) column and a figure column, leadered from the bottom line. It may also consist of two reading columns, aligning on the top line. In general, leaderwork (except indexes and tables of contents, which are set the same style as text) is governed by the same rules of style as tabular work. Unless otherwise indicated, leaderwork is set in 8 point. The period is omitted immediately before leaders.

Bearoff or inset

14.2. No bearoff or inset is required at the right in a single reading column.

Columns

14.3. A figure column is at least an en quad wider than the largest group of figures but not less than 3 ems in single columns or 2 ems in double-up columns. Total rules are to be the full width of all figure columns.

	Pounds
Year: 2000	655,939
Fiscal year:	
2009	368,233
2010	100,000
Total	1,124,172

14.4. Where both columns are reading columns, they are separated by an em space.

Particulars	*Artist*
To the French Government:	
The entire collection of French paintings on loan, with the exception of Mlle. DuBourg (Mme. Fantin-Latour).	Degas.
Avant la Course	Do.
To Col. Axel H. Oxholm, Washington, DC:	
Martha Washington, George Washington, and Thomas Jefferson.	Attributed to Jonathan E. Earl, Los Angeles, CA.
Roses	Renoir.
Do	Forain.
Roses in a Chinese Vase and Sculpture by Maillol	Vuillard.
Maternity	Gauguin.

Continued heads

14.5.   The use of continued heads in leaderwork is not necessary.

Ditto (do.)

14.6.   The abbreviation *do.* is indented and capitalized in the stub. It is capitalized and cleared (no leaders) in the last reading column (see above).

Dollar mark and ciphers

14.7.   In a column containing mixed amounts (as money, tons, gallons, etc.) the figures are aligned on the right, and the dollar mark or other symbol is repeated before each sum of money. If several sums of money are grouped and added or subtracted to make a total, they are separated from the nonmoney group by a parallel rule, and the symbol is placed on the first figure of the separated group only.

14.8.   If two columns of sums of money add or subtract one into the other and one carries points and ciphers, the other should also carry points and ciphers.

Flush items and subheads

14.9.   Flush items clear the figure column.

14.10.   Subheads are centered in full measure.

Footnotes

14.11. Footnotes to leaderwork follow the style of footnotes to tables.

14.12. Footnote references begin with 1 in each leadered grouping, and footnotes are placed at the end, separated from it by 4 points of space. Separate notes from matter following by not less than 6 points of space.

14.13. If the leaderwork runs over from one page to another, the footnotes will be placed at the bottom of the leadered material.[1]

Units of quantity

14.14. Units of quantity or other words over a stub or figure column are set italic.

14.15. The following example shows the style to be observed where there is a short colon line at left. In case of only one subentry, run in with colon line and preserve the colon.

	Tons
Baltimore & Ohio RR:	
Freight carried:	
May	50,000
June	52,000
Coal carried	90,000
Dixie RR: Freight carried Jan. 1, 1999, including freight carried by all its subsidiaries	[1] 2,000

    [1] Livestock not included.

14.16. If there is no colon line, the style is as follows:

	Tons
Freight carried by the Dixie RR and the Baltimore & Ohio RR in May	71,500

14.17. Explanatory matter is set in 6 point under leaders (note omission of period):

(Name)	(Address)	(Position)

---

[1] If footnotes to leaderwork and text fall at bottom of page, leaderwork footnotes are placed above text footnotes. The two groups are separated by a 50-point rule.

14.18. In blank forms, leaders used in place of complete words to be supplied are preceded and followed by a space.

On this .... day of .... 20 ....

14.19. In half measure doubled up, units of quantity are aligned across the page.

	Inches		*Inches*
Seedlings:			
Black locust	27	Osage-orange	20
Honey locust	16	Catalpa	16
Green ash	7	Black walnut	10

14.20. Mixed units of quantity and amounts and words in a figure column are set as follows:

Capital invested	$8,000
Value of implements and stock	$3,000
Land under cultivation (acres)	128.6
Orchard (acres)	21.4
Forest land (square miles)	50
Livestock:	
Horses:	
Number	8
Value	$1,500
Cows:	
Number	18
Estimated weekly production of butter per milk cow (pounds)	7½
Hogs:	
Number	46
Loss from cholera	None

15. Footnotes, Indexes, Contents, and Outlines

Footnotes and reference marks

15.1. Text footnotes follow the style of the text with the exception of those things noted in Chapter 9 "Abbreviations and Letter Symbols." Footnotes appearing in tabular material follow the guidelines set forth in Chapter 13 "Tabular Work."

15.2. In a publication divided into chapters, sections, or articles, each beginning a new page, text footnotes begin with 1 in each such division. In a publication without such divisional grouping, footnotes are numbered consecutively from 1 to 99, and then begin with 1 again. However, in supplemental sections, such as appendixes and bibliographies, which are not parts of the publication proper, footnotes begin with 1.

15.3. Copy preparers must see that references and footnotes are plainly marked.

15.4. If a reference is repeated on another page, it should carry the original footnote; but to avoid repetition of a long note, the copy preparer may use the words "See footnote 3 (6, 10, etc.) on p.—." instead of repeating the entire footnote.

15.5. Unless the copy is otherwise marked: (1) footnotes to 12-point text are set in 8 point; (2) footnotes to 11-point text are set in 8 point, except in Supreme Court reports, in which they are set in 9 point; (3) footnotes to 10- and 8-point text are set in 7 point.

15.6. Footnotes are set as paragraphs at the bottom of the page and are separated from the text by a 50-point rule, set flush left, with no less than 2 points of space above and below the rule.

15.7. Footnotes to indented matter (other than excerpt footnotes) are set full measure.

15.8. To achieve faithful reproduction of indented excerpt material (particularly legal work) containing original footnotes, these footnotes are also indented and placed at the bottom of the excerpt, separated by 6 points of space. No side dash is used. Reference numbers are not changed to fit the numbering sequence of text footnotes.

15.9. Footnotes must always begin on the page where they are referenced. If the entire footnote will not fit on the page where it is cited, it will be continued at the bottom of the next page.[1]

15.10. Footnotes to charts, graphs, and other illustrations should be placed immediately beneath such illustrative material.

15.11. A cutoff rule is not required between a chart or graph and its footnotes.

15.12. For reference marks use: (1) roman superior figures, (2) italic superior letters, and (3) symbols. Superior figures (preferred), letters, and symbols are separated from the words to which they apply by thin spaces, unless immediately preceded by periods or commas.

15.13. Where reference figures might lead to ambiguity (for example, in matter containing exponents), asterisks, daggers, etc., or italic superior letters may be used.

15.14. When symbols or signs are used for footnote reference marks, their sequence should be (*) asterisk, (†) dagger, (‡) double dagger, and (§) section mark. Should more symbols be needed, these may be doubled or tripled, but for simplicity and greater readability, it is preferable to extend the assortment by adding other single-character symbols.

15.15. Symbols with established meanings, such as the percent sign (%) and the number mark (#), are likely to cause confusion and should not be used for reference marks.

15.16. To avoid possible confusion with numerals and letters frequently occurring in charts and graphs, it is preferable in such instances to use symbols as reference marks.

---

[1] When a footnote breaks from an odd (right-hand) page to an even (left-hand) page, the word (*Continued*) is set inside parentheses in italic below the last line of the footnote where the break occurs.

A 50-point rule is used above each part of the footnote.

When a footnote break occurs on facing pages, i.e., from an even page to an odd page, the (*Continued*) line is not set, but the 50-point rule is duplicated.

15.17. When items carry several reference marks, the superior-figure reference precedes an asterisk, dagger, or similar character used for reference.

15.18. A superior reference mark follows all punctuation marks except a dash, but it falls inside a closing parenthesis or bracket if applying only to matter within the parentheses or brackets.

15.19. Two or more superior footnote references occurring together are separated by thin spaces.

Indexes and tables of contents

15.20. Indexes and tables of contents are set in the same style as the text, except that *See* and *see also* are set in italic.

15.21. Where a word occurs in an index page column, either alone or with a figure, it is set flush on the right. If the word extends back into the leaders, it is preceded by an en space.

Page

Explanatory diagram.. Frontispiece
General instructions.. VIII
Capitalization (*see also* Abbreviations).. 16
Correct imposition (diagram).. Facing 34
Legends. (*See* Miscellaneous rules.)
Appendixes A, B, C, and D, maps, illustrations,
   and excerpts.. In supplemental volume

15.22. For better appearance, Roman numerals should be set in small caps in the figure columns of tables of contents and indexes.

15.23. In indexes set with leaders, if the page numbers will not fit in the leader line, the first number only is set in that line and the other numbers are overrun. If the entry makes three or more lines and the last line of figures is not full, do not use a period at the end.

If page folios overrun due to an excessive amount of figures
   use this form 220,
                                       224, 227, 230, 240

And this way when overrun folios make two or more lines 220,
        224–225, 230–240, 245, 246, 250–255, 258, 300, 320, 330, 350,
        360, 370, 380, 390, 400, 410–500, 510, 520, 530, 540, 550, 560,
        570, 580, 590, 600–620, 630, 640, 650

(For examples of item indentions in a reading column of indexes, see the index in this MANUAL.)

15.24.   Overrun page numbers are indented 3½ ems in measures not over 20 picas and 7 ems in wider measures, more than one line being used if necessary. These indentions are increased as necessary to not less than 2 ems more than the line immediately above or below.

15.25.   When copy specifies that all overs are to be a certain number of ems, the runovers of the figure column shall be held in 2 ems more than the specified indention.

15.26.   Examples of block-type indexes:

Example 1	*Example 2*
Medical officer, radiological defense, 3	Brazil—Continued
Medicolegal dosage, 44	Exchange restrictions—Continued
Military Liaison Committee, 4	Williams mission (*see also*
Monitoring, 58	Williams, John H., special
Air, 62	mission), exchange control
Personnel, 59	situation, 586–588
Civilian, 60	Trade agreement with United
Military, 59	States, proposed:
Sea, 61	Draft text, 558–567
Ship, 61	Proposals for:
Monitors, radiological defense, 3	Inclusion of all clauses, 531

15.27.   In index entries the following forms are used:

Brown, A.H., Jr. (*not* Brown, Jr., A.H.)
Brown, A.H., & Sons (*not* Brown & Sons, A.H.)
Brown, A.H., Co. (*not* Brown Co., A.H.)
Brown, A.H., & Sons Co. (*not* Brown & Sons Co., A.H.)

15.28.   In a table of contents, where *chapter, plate,* or *figure* is followed by a number and period, an en space is used after the period. The periods are aligned on the right.

Chapter   Page

    I. Introduction.. I
   II. Summary.. 1
  VI. Conclusions.. 7

15.29.   Subheads in indexes and tables of contents are centered in the full measure.

15.30. In contents using two sizes of lightface type, or a combination of boldface and lightface type, all leaders and page numbers will be set in lightface roman type. Contents set entirely in boldface will use boldface page numbers. All page numbers will be set in the predominant size.

                                                                                       Page

PART I. MAINTENANCE OF PEACE AND SECURITY   5
    Disarmament   6
    Peaceful Uses of Atomic Energy   7

                                                                                       Page

Part I. Maintenance of Peace and Security   5
    Disarmament   6
    Peaceful Uses of Atomic Energy   7

                                                                                       Page

Part I. Maintenance of Peace and Security **5**
    Disarmament **6**
    Peaceful Uses of Atomic Energy **7**

Outlines

15.31. Outlines vary in appearance because there is no one set style to follow in designing them. The width of the measure, the number of levels required for the indentions, and the labeling concept selected to identify each new level all contribute to its individuality.

The following sample outline demonstrates a very basic and structured arrangement. It uses the enumerators listed in rule 8.112 to identify each new indented level.

The enumerators for the first four levels are followed by a period and a fixed amount of space. The enumerators for the second four levels are set in parentheses and followed by the same amount of fixed space.

Each new level indents 2 ems more than the preceding level, and data that runs over to the next line aligns with the first word following the enumerator.

Outline example:
I. Balancing a checkbook
   A. Open your check register
      1. Verify all check numbers
         a. Verify no check numbers were duplicated
         b. Verify no check numbers were skipped
   B. Open your bank statement
      1. Put canceled checks in sequence
      2. Compare amounts on checks to those in register
         a. Correct any mistakes in register
         b. Indicate those check numbers cashed
            (1) Mark off check number on the statement
               (a) Verify amount of check
                  (i) Highlight discrepancies on statement
                     (aa) Enter figures on back
                  (ii) Enter missing check numbers on back with amounts
                     (aa) Identify missing check numbers in register
                     (bb) Verify those check numbers were not cashed previously

16. Datelines, Addresses, and Signatures

16.1. The general principle involved in the typography of datelines, addresses, and signatures is that they should be set to stand out clearly from the body of the letter or paper that they accompany. This is accomplished by using caps and small caps and italic, as set forth below. Other typographic details are designed to ensure uniformity and good appearance. Street addresses and ZIP Code numbers are not to be used. In certain lists that carry ZIP Code numbers, regular spacing will be used preceding the ZIP Code. Certain general instructions apply alike to datelines, addresses, and signatures.

General instructions

16.2. Principal words in datelines, addresses, and titles accompanying signatures are capitalized.

16.3. *Mr., Mrs., Miss, Ms.,* and all other titles preceding a name, and *Esq., Jr., Sr.,* and *2d* following a name in address and signature lines, are set in roman caps and lowercase if the name is in caps and small caps or caps and lowercase; if the name is in caps, they are set in caps and small caps, if small caps are available—otherwise in caps and lowercase.

Spacing

16.4. At least 2 points of space should appear between dateline and text or address, address and text, text and signature, or signature and address.

Datelines

16.5. Datelines at the beginning of a letter or paper are set at the right side of the page, the originating office in caps and small caps, the address and date in italic; if the originating office is not given, the address is set in caps and small caps and the date in italic; if only the date is given, it is set in caps and small caps. Such datelines are indented from the right 1 em for a single line; 3 ems and 1 em, successively, for two lines; or 5 ems, 3 ems, and 1 em, successively, for three lines. In measures 30 picas or wider, these indentions are increased by 1 em.

THE WHITE HOUSE,☐☐☐
Washington, DC, January 1, 2016.☐
THE WHITE HOUSE, *July 30, 2016.*☐

TREASURY DEPARTMENT,☐☐☐☐☐
OFFICE OF THE TREASURER,☐☐☐
Washington, DC, January 1, 2016.☐

TREASURY DEPARTMENT, *July 30, 2016.*☐

DEPARTMENT OF COMMERCE,☐☐☐
July 30, 2016.☐

FAIRFAX COUNTY, VA.☐

OFFICE OF JOHN SMITH & CO.,☐☐☐
New York, NY, June 6, 2016.☐

WASHINGTON, *May 20, 2016—10 a.m.*☐

THURSDAY, MAY 5, 2016—2 P.M.☐

JANUARY 24, 2016.☐

WASHINGTON, *November 28, 2016.*☐☐☐
[Received December 5, 2016].☐

ON BOARD USS "CONNECTICUT,"☐☐☐
January 22, 2016.☐

16.6. Congressional hearings:

THURSDAY, NOVEMBER 19, 2015 [1]

HOUSE OF REPRESENTATIVES,☐☐☐☐☐☐☐
COMMITTEE ON THE JUDICIARY,☐☐☐☐☐
SUBCOMMITTEE ON IMMIGRATION☐☐☐
AND BORDER SECURITY,☐☐☐
Washington, DC.☐

U.S. SENATE,☐☐☐☐☐
COMMITTEE ON ARMED SERVICES,☐☐☐
Washington, DC.☐

CONGRESS OF THE UNITED STATES,☐☐☐☐☐
JOINT COMMITTEE ON PRINTING,☐☐☐
Washington, DC.☐

---

[1] Normally, dates in House hearings on appropriation bills are set on the right in 10-point caps and small caps.

16.7. Datelines at the end of a letter or paper, either above or below signatures, are set on left in caps and small caps for the address and italic for the date. When the word *dated* is used, dateline is set in roman caps and lowercase.

☐MAY 7, 2016.
☐ROANOKE, VA.
☐ROANOKE, VA, *July 1, 2016.*
☐Dated July 1, 2016.
☐Dated Albany, March 13, 2016.

16.8. Datelines in newspaper extracts are set at the beginning of the paragraph, the address in caps and small caps and the date in roman caps and lowercase, followed by a period and a 1-em dash.

☐ABOARD USS *Ronald Reagan* April 3, 2016.—
☐NEW YORK, NY, August 21, 2016.—A message received here from . . . .

Addresses

16.9. Addresses are set flush left at the beginning of a letter or paper in congressional work (or at end in formal usage).

16.10. At beginning or at end:

To SMITH & JONES and
☐BROWN & GREEN, Esqs.,
Attorneys for Claimant.
(Attention of Mr. Green.)

Hon. PATTY MURRAY,
U.S. Senate.

Hon. NANCY PELOSI,
U.S. House of Representatives. (Collective address.)

The PRESIDENT,
The White House.

16.11. A long title following an address is set in italic caps and lowercase, the first line flush left and right, overruns indented 2 ems to clear a following 1-em paragraph indention.

Hon. MIKE ROUNDS,
Chairman, Subcommittee on Superfund, Waste Management,
☐☐*and Regulatory Oversight, U.S. Senate, Washington, DC.*

16.12. The name or title forming the first line of the address is set in caps and small caps, but *Mr., Mrs.,* or other title preceding a name, and *Esq., Jr., Sr.,* or *2d* following a name, are set in roman caps and lowercase; the matter following is set in italic. The words *U.S. Army* or *U.S. Navy* immediately following a name are set in roman caps and lowercase in the same line as the name.

> Lt. Gen. Todd T. Semonite, U.S. Army,
> *Chief of Engineers.*

> Chief of Engineers, U.S. Army. (Full title, all caps and small caps.)

> Lt. Gen. Todd T. Semonite,
> *Chief of Engineers, U.S. Army,*
> *Washington, DC.*

> Hon. Karen L. Haas,
> *Clerk of the House of Representatives.*

> Hon. Richard J. Durbin,
> *U.S. Senator, Washington, DC.*

> Hon. Cory Gardner,
> *Russell Senate Office Building, Washington, DC.*

> The Committee on Appropriations,
> *House of Representatives.*

16.13. General (or collective) addresses are set in italic caps and lowercase, flush left, with overruns indented 2 ems and ending with a colon, except when followed by a salutation, in which case a period is used.

16.14. Examples of general addresses when not followed by salutation (note the use of colon at end of italic line):

> *To the Officers and Members of the Daughters of the American*
> *☐☐Revolution, Washington, DC:*

> *To the American Diplomatic and Consular Officers:*

> *To Whom It May Concern:*

> *Collectors of Customs:*

> *To the Congress of the United States:*

16.15. Example of general address when followed by salutation (note the use of period at end of italic line):

> *Senate and House of Representatives.*
> ☐Gentlemen: You are hereby * * *.

16.16. Examples illustrating other types of addresses:

To the EDITOR:

To JOHN L. NELSON, *Greeting:*

To JOHN L. NELSON, *Birmingham, AL, Greeting:*

To the CLERK OF THE HOUSE OF REPRESENTATIVES:

CHIEF OF ENGINEERS
(Through the Division Engineer).
☐MY DEAR SIR: I have the honor . . . .
☐MR. REED: I have the honor . . . .
☐DEAR MR. REED: I have the honor . . . .

Lt. (jg.) JOHN SMITH,
Navy Department:
☐The care shown by you . . . .

STATE OF NEW YORK,
County of New York, ss:
☐Before me this day appeared . . . .

DISTRICT OF COLUMBIA, *ss:*
☐Before me this day appeared . . . .

Envelope addresses

U.S. House of Representatives
Committee on Education and the Workforce
2176 Rayburn House Office Building
Washington, DC 20515

Signatures

16.17. Signatures, preceded by an em dash, are sometimes run in with the last line of text.

16.18. Signatures are set at the right side of the page. They are indented 1 em for a single line; 3 ems and 1 em, successively, for two lines; and 5 ems, 3 ems, and 1 em, successively, for three lines. In measures 30 picas or wider, these indentions are increased by 1 em.

16.19. The name or names are set in caps and small caps; *Mr., Mrs.,* and all other titles preceding a name, and *Esq., Jr., Sr.,* and *2d* following a name, are set in roman caps and lowercase; the title following name is set in italic. Signatures as they appear in copy must be followed in regard to abbreviations.

16.20. If name and title make more than half a line, they are set as two lines.

16.21. Two to eight independent signatures, with or without titles, are aligned on the left, at approximately the center of the measure.

> ROBERT E. SCHWENK.
> QUEEN E. HUGHES.
> ERICA N. PROPHET.
> ANDRE RODGERS,
> _Commander, U.S. Navy (Retired)._ ☐
> WILLIAM H. COUGHLIN, _Chairman._

16.22. More than eight signatures, with or without titles, are set full measure, roman caps and lowercase, run in, indented 5 and 7 ems in measures of 26½ picas or wider; in measures less than 26½ picas, indent 2 and 3 ems.

> ☐☐☐☐☐Brown, Shipley & Co.; Denniston, Cross & Co.; Fruhling &
> ☐☐☐☐☐☐Groschen, Attorneys; C.J. Hambro & Sons; Hardy,
> ☐☐☐☐☐☐Nathan & Co.; Heilbut, Symons & Co.; Harrison Bros. &
> ☐☐☐☐☐☐Co., by George Harrison; Hoare, Miller & Co.; Thomas
> ☐☐☐☐☐☐Eaton Co.

16.23. The punctuation of closing phrases is governed by the sense. A detached complimentary close is made a new paragraph.

16.24. Examples of various kinds of signatures:

> UNITED STATES IMPROVEMENT CO.,
> (By) JOHN SMITH, _Secretary._
>
> TEXARKANA TEXTILE MERCHANTS &
>   MANUFACTURERS' ASSOCIATION,
> JOHN L. JONES, _Secretary._
>
> TEXARKANA TEXTILE MERCHANTS &
>   MANUFACTURERS' ASSOCIATION,
> JOANNE WILDER,
>   _Board Member and Secretary._ ☐
>
> JOHN W. SMITH ☐☐☐
> (And 25 others). ☐
>
> JOHN SMITH, ☐☐☐☐☐
> _Lieutenant Governor_ ☐☐☐
> (For the Governor of Maine). ☐

NORTH AMERICAN ICE CO.,
SYLVIA ROONEY, *Secretary.*
JOHN [his thumbmark] SMITH.☐

NITA M. LOWEY,
BARBARA COMSTOCK,
Managers on the Part of the House.☐

CHRIS COONS,
AMY KLOBUCHAR,
Managers on the Part of the Senate.☐

☐I am, very respectfully, yours,
(Signed)☐FRED C. KLEINSCHMIDT,☐☐☐
Assistant Clerk, Court of Claims.☐

☐On behalf of the Philadelphia Chamber of Commerce:
GEO. W. PHILIPS.
SAML. CAMPBELL.

☐I have the honor to be,
☐☐☐Very respectfully, your obedient servant,
(Signed)☐ John R. King
(Typed)☐ JOHN R. KING,
Secretary.☐

or

(S)☐ John R. King
JOHN R. KING,
Secretary.☐

☐Attest:
RICHARD ROE, *Notary Public.*☐

☐By the Governor:
NATHANIEL COX, *Secretary of State.*☐

☐Approved.
JOHN SMITH, *Governor.*☐

☐By the President:
JOHN KERRY, *Secretary of State.*☐

☐Respectfully submitted.
MARY FARRELL, *U.S. Indian Agent.*☐

☐☐☐Yours truly,
Capt. JAMES STALEY, Jr.,☐☐☐
Superintendent.☐

☐☐☐Respectfully yours,
Mrs. BETTY SHEFFIELD.☐

☐☐☐Very respectfully,
RON GOLDEN, *U.S. Indian Agent.*☐

16.25.   In quoted matter:

□□□"Very respectfully,

> "Todd S. Gilbert.
> "Paul Hartman.
> "Dolores Hicks.
> "Albert H. Jones.
> "Joan C. Nugent.
> "Brandon Proctor."

16.26.   Examples of various kinds of datelines, addresses, and signatures:

Re weather reports submitted by the International Advisory Committee of □□the Weather Council.

Mr. Fred Upton,
Chairman, House Committee on Energy and Commerce,
Washington, DC.

□Dear Mr. Upton: We have been in contact with your office, etc.

Dr. Louis W. Uccellini,□□□□□
Executive Director,□□□
National Weather Service.□

———

Lincoln Park, MI, *February 15, 2016.*□

Re Romeo O. Umanos, Susanna M. Umanos, case No. S–254, U.S. □□Citizenship and Immigration Services, application pending.

Hon. John Cornyn,
Chairman, Subcommittee on the Constitution,
Committee on the Judiciary, Washington, DC.

□Dear Mr. Cornyn: You have for some time . . . .
□□□Sincerely yours,

Edward Pultorak,□□□
Architectural Designer.□

Hon. TREY GOWDY,
Chairman, Subcommittee on Immigration and Border Security
□□*of the Committee on the Judiciary, House of Representatives,*
□□*Washington, DC.*

□DEAR MR. GOWDY: You have for some time . . . .

———

　　　U.S. DEPARTMENT OF □□□□□
　　　　　　COMMERCE,□□□□□
　　NATIONAL WEATHER SERVICE,□□□
　　　Washington, March 3, 2016.□

Hon. GENE GREEN,
House of Representatives,
Washington, DC.
□DEAR MR. GREEN: We will be glad to
give you any further information.
□□□Sincerely yours,
　　　　F.W. REICHELDERFER,□□□
　　　　　　Chief of Service.□

———

　　　　　　　　　　NEW YORK, NY, *February 8, 2016.*□

To: All supervisory employees of production plants, northern and
□□eastern divisions, New York State.
From: Production manager.
Subject: Regulations concerning vacations, health and welfare plans,
□□and wage contract negotiations.
□It has come to our attention that the time . . . .

———

　　　　　　　　　　WASHINGTON, DC, *May 16, 2016.*□

The Honorable the SECRETARY OF THE NAVY.
□DEAR MR. SECRETARY: This is in response to your letter . . . .
□□□Very sincerely yours,
　　　　　　　[SEAL]□BARACK OBAMA.□

EAST LANSING, MI, *June 10, 2016.*□
To Whom It May Concern:
□I have known Kyu Yawp Lee for 7 years and am glad to testify as to his fine character. He has been employed . . . .
□Wishing you success in your difficult and highly important job, we are,
□□□Sincerely yours,
AGOSTINO J. GONINO.
LOUISE M. GONINO.

———

U.S. DEPARTMENT OF VETERANS AFFAIRS,□□□□□□□
OFFICE OF THE SECRETARY OF□□□□□
VETERANS AFFAIRS,□□□
Washington, DC.□
Hon. CHARLES E. GRASSLEY,
Chairman, Committee on the Judiciary,
U.S. Senate, Washington, DC.
□DEAR SENATOR GRASSLEY: Further reference is made to your reply . . . .
□□□Sincerely yours,
GORDON M. MANSFIELD,□□□□□□□
Deputy Secretary□□□□□
(For and in the absence of□□□
James B. Peake, Secretary).□

———

WASHINGTON, DC, *September 16, 2016.*□
Mr. WILLIAM E. JONES, Jr.,
Special Assistant to the Attorney General, Attorney for Howard
□□*Sutherland, Director, Office of Alien Property.*
□DEAR MR. JONES: In reply to your letter . . . .
□□□Yours truly,
(Signed)□THOMAS E. RHODES,□□□
Special Assistant to the Attorney General.□
□P.S.—A special word of thanks to you from J.R. Brown for your fine
□□help.
T.E.R.□

Tokyo, Japan, *November 13, 2016.*□
U.S. Department of Homeland Security,
U.S. Citizenship and Naturalization Services,
Detroit, MI.
□Gentlemen: This letter will testify to the personal character . . . .
□□□Very truly yours,

Mrs. Grace C. Lohr,□□□□□
Inspector General Section, HQ, AFFE,□□□
APO 343, San Francisco, CA.□

16.27. The word *seal* appearing with the signature of a notary or of an organized body, such as a company, is spaced 1 em from the signature. The word *seal* is to be set in small caps and bracketed.

[seal]□Richard Roe,□□□
Notary Public.□

[seal]□J.M. Wilber.□

[seal]□Bartlett, Robins & Co.□

16.28. Presidential proclamations after May 23, 1967, do not utilize the seal except when they pertain to treaties, conventions, protocols, or other international agreements. Copy will be followed literally with respect to the inclusion of and between elements of numerical expressions.

In 1872, the Congress established Yellowstone National Park—the first park of its kind anywhere in the world. Decades later, the passage of the Antiquities Act in 1906 created our first national historic preservation policy. Under this new authority, and heavily inspired by his time in nature with conservationist John Muir, President Theodore Roosevelt set aside 18 new monuments and landmarks, adding to the scattered collection of existing parks throughout our country. One decade later, in order to provide the leadership necessary for maintaining our growing system of parks, the Congress passed monumental legislation—which President Woodrow Wilson signed on August 25, 1916—to create the National Park Service (NPS). . . .

*   *   *   *   *   *   *

Now, Therefore, I, Barack Obama, President of the United States of America, by virtue of the authority vested in me by the Constitution and the laws of the United States, do hereby proclaim August 25, 2016, as the 100th Anniversary of the National Park Service. I invite all Americans to observe this day with appropriate programs, ceremonies, and activities that recognize the National Park Service for maintaining and protecting our public lands for the continued benefit and enjoyment of all Americans.

IN WITNESS WHEREOF, I have hereunto set my hand this twenty-second day of August, in the year of our Lord two thousand sixteen, and of the Independence of the United States of America the two hundred and forty-first.

BARACK OBAMA.☐

17. Useful Tables

This chapter contains useful tables presented in GPO style. The tables display various design features most frequently used in Government publications and can be considered examples of GPO style.

U.S. Presidents and Vice Presidents

President	Years	Vice President	Years
George Washington	(1789–1797)	John Adams	(1789–1797)
John Adams	(1797–1801)	Thomas Jefferson	(1797–1801)
Thomas Jefferson	(1801–1809)	Aaron Burr	(1801–1805)
		George Clinton	(1805–1809)
James Madison	(1809–1817)	George Clinton	(1809–1812)
		Vacant	(1812–1813)
		Elbridge Gerry	(1813–1814)
		Vacant	(1814–1817)
James Monroe	(1817–1825)	Daniel D. Tompkins	(1817–1825)
John Quincy Adams	(1825–1829)	John C. Calhoun	(1825–1829)
Andrew Jackson	(1829–1837)	John C. Calhoun	(1829–1832)
		Vacant	(1832–1833)
		Martin Van Buren	(1833–1837)
Martin Van Buren	(1837–1841)	Richard M. Johnson	(1837–1841)
William Henry Harrison	(1841)	John Tyler	(1841)
John Tyler	(1841–1845)	Vacant	(1841–1845)
James K. Polk	(1845–1849)	George M. Dallas	(1845–1849)
Zachary Taylor	(1849–1850)	Millard Fillmore	(1849–1850)
Millard Fillmore	(1850–1853)	Vacant	(1850–1853)
Franklin Pierce	(1853–1857)	William R. King	(1853)
		Vacant	(1853–1857)
James Buchanan	(1857–1861)	John C. Breckinridge	(1857–1861)
Abraham Lincoln	(1861–1865)	Hannibal Hamlin	(1861–1865)
		Andrew Johnson	(1865)
Andrew Johnson	(1865–1869)	Vacant	(1865–1869)
Ulysses S. Grant	(1869–1877)	Schuyler Colfax	(1869–1873)
		Henry Wilson	(1873–1875)
		Vacant	(1875–1877)
Rutherford B. Hayes	(1877–1881)	William A. Wheeler	(1877–1881)
James A. Garfield	(1881)	Chester A. Arthur	(1881)
Chester A. Arthur	(1881–1885)	Vacant	(1881–1885)
Grover Cleveland	(1885–1889)	Thomas A. Hendricks	(1885)
		Vacant	(1885–1889)
Benjamin Harrison	(1889–1893)	Levi P. Morton	(1889–1893)
Grover Cleveland	(1893–1897)	Adlai E. Stevenson	(1893–1897)
William McKinley	(1897–1901)	Garret A. Hobart	(1897–1901)
		Theodore Roosevelt	(1901)
Theodore Roosevelt	(1901–1909)	Vacant	(1901–1905)
		Charles W. Fairbanks	(1905–1909)
William H. Taft	(1909–1913)	James S. Sherman	(1909–1912)
		Vacant	(1912–1913)
Woodrow Wilson	(1913–1921)	Thomas R. Marshall	(1913–1921)
Warren G. Harding	(1921–1923)	Calvin Coolidge	(1921–1923)
Calvin Coolidge	(1923–1929)	Vacant	(1923–1925)
		Charles G. Dawes	(1925–1929)
Herbert Hoover	(1929–1933)	Charles Curtis	(1929–1933)
Franklin D. Roosevelt	(1933–1945)	John Nance Garner	(1933–1941)
		Henry A. Wallace	(1941–1945)
		Harry S. Truman	(1945)
Harry S. Truman	(1945–1953)	Vacant	(1945–1949)
		Alben W. Barkley	(1949–1953)
Dwight D. Eisenhower	(1953–1961)	Richard M. Nixon	(1953–1961)

U.S. Presidents and Vice Presidents—Continued

President	Years	Vice President	Years
John F. Kennedy	(1961–1963)	Lyndon B. Johnson	(1961–1963)
Lyndon B. Johnson	(1963–1969)	Vacant	(1963–1965)
		Hubert H. Humphrey	(1965–1969)
Richard M. Nixon	(1969–1974)	Spiro T. Agnew	(1969–1973)
		Gerald R. Ford	(1973–1974)
Gerald R. Ford	(1974–1977)	Nelson A. Rockefeller	(1974–1977)
James Earl "Jimmy" Carter	(1977–1981)	Walter F. Mondale	(1977–1981)
Ronald Reagan	(1981–1989)	George H.W. Bush	(1981–1989)
George H.W. Bush	(1989–1993)	J. Danforth Quayle	(1989–1993)
William J. Clinton	(1993–2001)	Albert Gore, Jr.	(1993–2001)
George W. Bush	(2001–2009)	Richard B. Cheney	(2001–2009)
Barack Obama	(2009–)	Joseph R. Biden, Jr.	(2009–)

State Populations and Their Capitals
[As of July 1, 2015 Census estimates]

State, capital	State population	State, capital	State population
Alabama, Montgomery	4,858,979	Montana, Helena	1,032,949
Alaska, Juneau	738,432	Nebraska, Lincoln	1,896,190
Arizona, Phoenix	6,828,065	Nevada, Carson City	2,890,845
Arkansas, Little Rock	2,978,204	New Hampshire, Concord	1,330,608
California, Sacramento	39,144,818	New Jersey, Trenton	8,958,013
Colorado, Denver	5,456,574	New Mexico, Santa Fe	2,085,109
Connecticut, Hartford	3,590,886	New York, Albany	19,795,791
Delaware, Dover	945,934	North Carolina, Raleigh	10,042,802
District of Columbia, Washington	672,228	North Dakota, Bismarck	756,927
Florida, Tallahassee	20,271,272	Ohio, Columbus	11,613,423
Georgia, Atlanta	10,214,860	Oklahoma, Oklahoma City	3,911,338
Hawaii, Honolulu	1,431,603	Oregon, Salem	4,028,977
Idaho, Boise	1,654,930	Pennsylvania, Harrisburg	12,802,503
Illinois, Springfield	12,859,995	Rhode Island, Providence	1,056,298
Indiana, Indianapolis	6,619,680	South Carolina, Columbia	4,896,146
Iowa, Des Moines	3,123,899	South Dakota, Pierre	858,469
Kansas, Topeka	2,911,641	Tennessee, Nashville	6,600,299
Kentucky, Frankfort	4,425,092	Texas, Austin	27,469,114
Louisiana, Baton Rouge	4,670,724	Utah, Salt Lake City	2,995,919
Maine, Augusta	1,329,328	Vermont, Montpelier	626,042
Maryland, Annapolis	6,006,401	Virginia, Richmond	8,382,993
Massachusetts, Boston	6,794,422	Washington, Olympia	7,170,351
Michigan, Lansing	9,922,576	West Virginia, Charleston	1,844,128
Minnesota, St. Paul	5,489,594	Wisconsin, Madison	5,771,337
Mississippi, Jackson	2,992,333	Wyoming, Cheyenne	586,107
Missouri, Jefferson City	6,083,672		

Principal Foreign Countries as of October 2016

Country	UN member	Capital	Chief of state	Legislative body	Government type
Afghanistan	Yes	Kabul	President	National Assembly of House of People, House of Elders	Islamic Republic.
Albania	do	Tirana (Tirane)	do	Assembly (unicameral)	Emerging Democracy.
Algeria	do	Algiers	do	National People's Assembly, Council of Nations.	Republic.
Andorra	do	Andorra la Vella	Executive Council President	General Council of the Valleys (unicameral)	Parliamentary Democracy.
Angola	do	Luanda	President	National Assembly (unicameral)	Republic: multiparty presidential regime.
Antigua and Barbuda	do	Saint John's	Queen (represented by Governor General)	Parliament (bicameral)	Constitutional Monarchy with a parliamentary system of government.
Argentina	do	Buenos Aires	President	National Congress (bicameral)	Republic.
Armenia	do	Yerevan	do	National Assembly (Parliament)	Do.
Australia	do	Canberra	Queen (represented by Governor General)	Federal Parliament (bicameral)	Federal Parliamentary Democracy.
Austria	do	Vienna	President	Federal Assembly (bicameral)	Federal Republic.
Azerbaijan	do	Baku (Baki, Baky)	do	National Assembly (unicameral)	Republic.
Bahamas, The	do	Nassau	Queen (represented by Governor General)	Parliament (bicameral)	Constitutional Parliamentary Democracy.
Bahrain	do	Manama	King	Legislature (bicameral)	Constitutional Monarchy.
Bangladesh	do	Dhaka	President	National Parliament (unicameral)	Parliamentary Democracy.
Barbados	do	Bridgetown	Queen (represented by Governor General)	Parliament (bicameral)	Do.
Belarus	do	Minsk	President	National Assembly (bicameral)	Republic in name, although in fact a dictatorship.
Belgium	do	Brussels	King	Parliament (bicameral)	Federal Parliamentary Democracy under a Constitutional Monarchy.
Belize	do	Belmopan	Queen (represented by Governor General)	National Assembly (bicameral)	Parliamentary Democracy.

Principal Foreign Countries as of October 2016—Continued

Country	UN member	Capital	Chief of state	Legislative body	Government type
Benin	Yes	Porto-Novo	President	National Assembly (unicameral)	Republic.
Bhutan	do	Thimphu	King	Parliament (bicameral)	In transition to Constitutional Monarchy; special treaty relationship with India.
Bolivia	do	La Paz (administrative) Sucre (legislative/judiciary)	President	National Congress (bicameral)	Republic.
Bosnia and Herzegovina	do	Sarajevo	Chairman of the Presidency	Parliamentary Assembly (bicameral)	Emerging Federal Democratic Republic.
Botswana	do	Gaborone	President	Parliament (bicameral)	Parliamentary Republic.
Brazil	do	Brasilia	do	National Congress (bicameral)	Federal Republic.
Brunei	do	Bandar Seri	Sultan and Prime Minister	Legislative Council	Constitutional Sultanate.
Bulgaria	do	Sofia	President	National Assembly (unicameral)	Parliamentary Democracy.
Burkina Faso	do	Ouagadougou	do	do	Parliamentary Republic.
Burma (Myanmar)[1]	do	Rangoon. Nay Pyi Taw (administrative)	Chairman of the State Peace and Development Council SPDC)	People's Assembly (unicameral)	Military Junta.
Burundi	do	Bujumbura	President	Parliament (bicameral)	Republic.
Cabo Verde[2]	do	Praia	President	National Assembly (unicameral)	Republic.
Cambodia	do	Phnom Penh	King	National Assembly (bicameral)	Multiparty Democracy under a Constitutional Monarchy.
Cameroon	do	Yaounde	President	National Assembly (unicameral)	Republic; Multiparty Presidential Regime.
Canada	do	Ottawa	Queen (represented by Governor General)	Parliament (bicameral)	Constitutional Monarchy that is also a Parliamentary Democracy and a Federation
Central African Republic	do	Bangui	do	do	Do.
Chad	do	N'Djamena	do	do	Do.

Country		Capital	Chief of State	Legislature	Government type
Chile	...do...	Santiago	President	National Congress (bicameral)	Do.
China[3]	...do...	Beijing	...do...	National People's Congress (unicameral)	Communist State.
Colombia	...do...	Bogotá	...do...	Congress (bicameral)	Republic, Executive Branch dominates government structure.
Comoros	...do...	Moroni	...do...	Assembly of the Union (unicameral)	Republic.
Congo, Democratic Republic of the [4]	...do...	Kinshasa	...do...	Legislature (bicameral)	Do.
Congo, Republic of the [4]	...do...	Brazzaville	...do...	Parliament (bicameral)	Do.
Costa Rica	...do...	San José	...do...	Legislative Assembly (unicameral)	Democratic Republic.
Côte d'Ivoire, Republic of	...do...	Yamoussoukro	...do...	National Assembly (bicameral)	Republic; multiparty presidency
Croatia	...do...	Zagreb	...do...	Assembly (unicameral)	Presidential/Parliamentary Democracy.
Cuba	...do...	Havana	...do...	National Assembly of People's Power (unicameral)	Communist State.
Cyprus	...do...	Nicosia	...do...	House of Representatives (unicameral)	Republic.
Czechia[5]	...do...	Prague	...do...	Parliament (bicameral)	Parliamentary Democracy.
Denmark	...do...	Copenhagen	Queen	People's Assembly (unicameral)	Constitutional Monarchy.
Djibouti	...do...	Djibouti	President	Chamber of Deputies (unicameral)	Republic.
Dominica	...do...	Roseau	...do...	House of Assembly (unicameral)	Parliamentary Democracy.
Dominican Republic	...do...	Santo Domingo	...do...	National Congress (bicameral)	Democratic Republic.
Ecuador	...do...	Quito	President	National Congress (unicameral)	Republic.
Egypt	...do...	Cairo	...do...	People's Assembly (bicameral)	Do.
El Salvador	...do...	San Salvador	...do...	Legislative Assembly (unicameral)	Do.
Equatorial Guinea	...do...	Malabo	...do...	House of People's Representatives (unicameral)	Do.
Eritrea	...do...	Asmara	...do...	National Assembly (unicameral)	Transitional Government.
Estonia	...do...	Tallinn	...do...	Parliament (unicameral)	Parliamentary Republic.
Ethiopia	...do...	Addis Ababa	...do...	Parliament (bicameral)	Federal Republic.

Principal Foreign Countries as of October 2016—Continued

Country	UN member	Capital	Chief of state	Legislative body	Government type
Fiji	Yes	Suva	President	do	Republic.
Finland	do	Helsinki	do	Parliament (unicameral)	Do.
France	do	Paris	do	Parliament (bicameral)	Do.
Gabon	do	Libreville	do	Legislature (bicameral)	Republic; Multiparty Presidential Regime.
Gambia, The	do	Banjul	do	National Assembly (unicameral)	Republic.
Georgia	do	Tbilisi	do	Parliament (unicameral, also known as Supreme Council)	Do.
Germany	do	Berlin	do	Parliament (bicameral)	Federal Republic.
Ghana	do	Accra	do	Parliament (unicameral)	Constitutional Democracy.
Greece	do	Athens	do	do	Parliamentary Republic.
Grenada	do	Saint George's	Queen (represented by Governor General)	Parliament (bicameral)	Parliamentary Democracy.
Guatemala	do	Guatemala City	President	Congress of the Republic (unicameral).	Constitutional Democratic Republic.
Guinea	do	Conakry	do	People's National Assembly (unicameral)	Republic.
Guinea-Bissau	do	Bissau	do	National People's Asssembly (unicameral)	Do.
Guyana	do	Georgetown	do	National Assembly (unicameral)	Do.
Haiti	do	Port-au-Prince	do	National Assembly (bicameral)	Do.
Holy See (Vatican City)	No	Vatican City	Pope	Pontifical Commission for the State of Vatican City (unicameral)	Ecclesiastical.
Honduras	Yes	Tegucigalpa	President	National Congress (unicameral)	Democratic Constitutional Republic.
Hungary	do	Budapest	do	National Assembly (unicameral)	Parliamentary Democracy.
Iceland	do	Reykjavik	do	Parliament (unicameral)	Constitutional Republic.
India	do	New Delhi	do	Parliament (bicameral)	Federal Republic.
Indonesia	do	Jakarta	do	House of Representatives	Republic.

Country		Capital	Chief of State	Legislature	Type of Government
Iran	...do...	Tehran	Supreme Leader	Islamic Consultative Assembly (unicameral)	Theocratic Republic.
Iraq	...do...	Baghdad	President	Council of Representatives	Parliamentary Democracy.
Ireland	...do...	Dublin	...do...	Parliament (bicameral)	Republic, Parliamentary Democracy.
Israel	...do...	Jerusalem [6]	...do...	Knesset (unicameral)	Parliamentary Democracy.
Italy	...do...	Rome	...do...	Parliament (bicameral)	Republic.
Jamaica	...do...	Kingston	Queen (represented by Governor General)	Parliament (bicameral)	Constitutional Parliamentary Democracy.
Japan	...do...	Tokyo	Emperor	Diet (bicameral)	Constitutional Monarchy with a Parliamentary Government.
Jordan	...do...	Amman	King	National Assembly (bicameral)	Constitutional Monarchy.
Kazakhstan	...do...	Astana	President	Parliament (bicameral)	Republic, Authoritarian Presidential rule, with little power outside the Executive Branch.
Kenya	...do...	Nairobi	...do...	National Assembly (unicameral)	Republic.
Kiribati	...do...	Tarawa	...do...	House of Parliament (unicameral)	Do.
Korea, North	...do...	Pyongyang	Premier	Supreme People's Assembly (unicameral)	Communist State one-man dictatorship.
Korea, South	...do...	Seoul	President	National Assembly (unicameral)	Republic.
Kosovo	No	Pristina (Pristine)	...do...	Kosovo Assembly of the Provisional Government (unicameral)	Do.
Kuwait	Yes	Kuwait City	Amir	National Assembly (unicameral)	Constitutional Emirate.
Kyrgyzstan	...do...	Bishkek	President	Supreme Council (unicameral)	Republic.
Laos	...do...	Vientiane	...do...	National Assembly (unicameral)	Communist State.
Latvia	...do...	Riga	...do...	Parliament (unicameral)	Parliamentary Democracy.
Lebanon	...do...	Beirut	...do...	National Assembly (unicameral)	Republic.
Lesotho	...do...	Maseru	King	Parliament (bicameral)	Parliamentary Constitutional Monarchy.
Liberia	...do...	Monrovia	President	National Assembly (bicameral)	Republic.
Libya	...do...	Tripoli	Chairman, Presidential Council	Council of Deputies (unicameral)	In transition.
Liechtenstein	...do...	Vaduz	Prince	Parliament or Landtag (unicameral)	Constitutional Monarchy.

Principal Foreign Countries as of October 2016—Continued

Country	UN member	Capital	Chief of state	Legislative body	Government type
Lithuania	Yes	Vilnius	President	Parliament or Seimas (unicameral)	Parliamentary Democracy.
Luxembourg	do	Luxembourg	Grand Duke	Chamber of Deputies (unicameral)	Constitutional Monarchy.
Macedonia, Republic of[7]	do	Skopje	President	Assembly or Sobranie (unicameral)	Parliamentary Republic.
Madagascar	do	Antananarivo	do	Legislature (bicameral)	Republic.
Malawi	do	Lilongwe	do	National Assembly (unicameral)	Multiparty Democracy.
Malaysia	do	Kuala Lumpur	Paramount Ruler	Parliament (bicameral)	Constitutional Monarchy.
Maldives	do	Male	President	People's Council (unicameral)	Republic.
Mali	do	Bamako	do	National Assembly (unicameral)	Do.
Malta	do	Valletta	do	House of Representatives (unicameral)	Do.
Marshall Islands	do	Majuro	do	Legislature (unicameral)	Constitutional Government in free association with the U.S.
Mauritania	do	Nouakchott	President	Legislature (bicameral)	Democratic Republic.
Mauritius	do	Port Louis	do	National Assembly (unicameral)	Parliamentary Democracy.
Mexico	do	Mexico City	do	National Congress (bicameral)	Federal Republic.
Micronesia, Federated States of	do	Palikir	do	Congress (unicameral)	Constitutional Government in free association with the U.S.
Moldova, Republic of	do	Chisinau	do	Parliament (unicameral)	Republic.
Monaco	do	Monaco	Prince	National Council (unicameral)	Constitutional Monarchy.
Mongolia	do	Ulaanbaatar	President	State Great Hural (unicameral)	Mixed Parliamentary/Presidential.
Montenegro	do	Podgorica	do	Assembly (unicameral)	Republic.
Morocco	do	Rabat	King	Parliament (bicameral)	Constitutional Monarchy.
Mozambique	do	Maputo	President	Assembly of the Republic (unicameral)	Republic.
Namibia	do	Windhoek	do	Legislature (bicameral)	Do.
Nauru	do	No official capital; government offices in Yaren District	do	Parliament (unicameral)	Do.

Country	Capital		Legislature	Government type
Nepal	Kathmandu	...do...	330 seat Interim Parliament	Constitutional Monarchy.
Netherlands	Amsterdam; The Hague (seat of government)	...do...	States General (bicameral)	Do.
New Zealand	Wellington	...do...	House of Representatives (unicameral)	Parliamentary Democracy.
Nicaragua	Managua	...do...	National Assembly (unicameral)	Republic.
Niger	Niamey	...do...	...do...	Do.
Nigeria	Abuja	...do...	National Assembly (bicameral)	Federal Republic.
Norway	Oslo	...do...	Parliament (Storting), (modified unicameral)[8]	Constitutional Monarchy.
Oman	Muscat	...do...	Majlis Oman (bicameral)	Monarchy.
Pakistan	Islamabad	...do...	Parliament (bicameral)	Federal Republic.
Palau	Ngerulmud	...do...	National Congress (bicameral)	Constitutional Government in free association with the U.S.
Panama	Panama City	...do...	National Assembly (unicameral)	Constitutional Democracy.
Papua New Guinea	Port Moresby	...do...	National Parliament (unicameral)	Constitutional Parliamentary Democracy.
Paraguay	Asunción	...do...	Congress (bicameral)	Constitutional Republic.
Peru	Lima	...do...	Congress of the Republic of Peru (unicameral)	Do.
Philippines	Manila	...do...	Congress (bicameral)	Republic.
Poland	Warsaw	...do...	National Assembly (bicameral)	Do.
Portugal	Lisbon	...do...	Assembly of the Republic (unicameral)	Parliamentary Democracy.
Qatar	Doha	...do...	Advisory Council (unicameral)	Emirate.
Romania	Bucharest	...do...	Parliament (bicameral)	Republic.
Russia	Moscow	...do...	Federal Assembly (bicameral)	Federation.
Rwanda	Kigali	...do...	Parliament (bicameral)	Republic; presidential, multiparty system.
Saint Kitts and Nevis	Basseterre	...do...	National Assembly (unicameral)	Parliamentary Democracy.
Saint Lucia	Castries	...do...	Parliament (bicameral)	Parliamentary Democracy.

Principal Foreign Countries as of October 2016—Continued

Country	UN member	Capital	Chief of state	Legislative body	Government type
Saint Vincent and the Grenadines	Yes	Kingstown	do.	House of Assembly (unicameral)	Do.
Samoa	do	Apia	Chief of State	Legislative Assembly (unicameral)	Do.
San Marino	do	San Marino	Co-Chiefs of State (Captains Regent)	Grand and General Council (unicameral)	Republic.
Sao Tome and Principe	do	São Tomé	President	National Assembly (unicameral)	Do.
Saudi Arabia	do	Riyadh	King and Prime Minister	Consultative Council	Monarchy.
Senegal	do	Dakar	President	Parliament (bicameral)	Republic.
Serbia	do	Belgrade	do	National Assembly (unicameral)	Do.
Seychelles	do	Victoria	do	do	Do.
Sierra Leone	do	Freetown	do	Parliament (unicameral)	Constitutional Democracy.
Singapore	do	Singapore	do	do	Parliamentary Republic.
Slovakia	do	Bratislava	do	National Council (unicameral)	Parliamentary Democracy.
Slovenia	do	Ljubljana	do	Parliament (bicameral)	Parliamentary Republic.
Solomon Islands	do	Honiara	Queen	National Parliament (unicameral)	Parliamentary Democracy.
Somalia	do	Mogadishu	Transitional Federal President	National Assembly (unicameral)	No permanent National Government; transitional Parliamentary Federal Government.
South Africa	do	Pretoria (administrative) Cape Town (legislative) Bloemfontein (judiciary)	President	Parliament (bicameral)	Republic.
South Sudan, Republic of[9]	do	Juba	President	National Legislature (bicameral)	Presidential Republic.
Spain	do	Madrid	King	General Courts or National Assembly (bicameral)	Parliamentary Monarchy.

Country		Capital		Legislature	
Sri Lanka	...do...	Colombo; Sri Jayewardenepura Kotte (legislative)	President	Parliament (unicameral)	Republic.
Sudan	...do...	Khartoum	...do...	National Legislature (bicameral)	Government of National Unity (GNU).
Suriname	...do...	Paramaribo	...do...	National Assembly (unicameral)	Constitutional Democracy.
Swaziland	...do...	Mbabane (administrative), Lobamba (legislative)	King	Parliament (bicameral)	Monarchy.
Sweden	...do...	Stockholm	King	Parliament (unicameral)	Constitutional Monarchy.
Switzerland	...do...	Bern	President	Federal Assembly (bicameral)	Formally a Confederation but similar in structure to a Federal Republic.
Syria	...do...	Damascus	...do...	People's Council (unicameral)	Republic under an authoritarian military-dominated regime.
Tajikistan	...do...	Dushanbe	...do...	Supreme Assembly (bicameral)	Republic.
Tanzania	...do...	Dar es Salaam, Dodoma (legislative)	...do...	National Assembly (unicameral)	Republic.
Thailand	...do...	Bangkok	King	National Assembly (bicameral)	Constitutional Monarchy.
Timor-Leste	...do...	Dili	President	National Parliament (unicameral)	Republic.
Togo	...do...	Lomé	President	National Assembly (unicameral)	Republic under transition to multiparty democratic rule.
Tonga	...do...	Nuku'alofa	King	Legislative Assembly (unicameral)	Constitutional Monarchy.
Trinidad and Tobago	...do...	Port-of-Spain	President	Parliament (bicameral)	Parliamentary Democracy.
Tunisia	...do...	Tunis	...do...	Chamber of Deputies and the Chamber of Advisors (bicameral)	Republic.
Turkey	...do...	Ankara	...do...	Grand National Assembly of Turkey (unicameral)	Republican Parliamentary Democracy
Turkmenistan	...do...	Ashgabat (Ashkhabad)	...do...	Two Parliamentary Bodies: People's Council and a National Assembly	Republic; Authoritarian Presidential rule, with little power outside the executive branch.
Tuvalu	...do...	Funafuti	Queen	Parliament (also called House of Assembly; unicameral)	Constitutional Monarchy with a Parliamentary Democracy.
Uganda	...do...	Kampala	President	National Assembly (unicameral)	Republic.

Principal Foreign Countries as of October 2016—Continued

Country	UN member	Capital	Chief of state	Legislative body	Government type
Ukraine	Yes	Kyiv (Kiev)	do	Supreme Council (unicameral)	Do.
United Arab Emirates	do	Abu Dhabi	do	Federal National Council (FNC) (unicameral)	Federation with specified powers delegated to the UAE federal government and other powers reserved to member emirates
United Kingdom	do	London	Queen	Parliament (bicameral)	Constitutional Monarchy.
Uruguay	do	Montevideo	President	General Assembly (bicameral)	Constitutional Republic.
Uzbekistan	do	Tashkent	do	Supreme Assembly (bicameral)	Republic; authoritarian presidential rule, with little power outside the executive branch.
Vanuatu	do	Port-Vila (on Efate)	do	Parliament (unicameral)	Parliamentary Republic.
Venezuela	do	Caracas	do	National Assembly (unicameral)	Federal Republic.
Vietnam	do	Hanoi	do	do	Communist State.
Yemen	do	Sanaa	do	Legislature (bicameral)	Republic.
Zambia	do	Lusaka	do	National Assembly (unicameral)	Do.
Zimbabwe	do	Harare	Executive President	Parliament (bicameral)	Parliamentary Democracy.

[1] Since 1989, the military authorities in Burma have promoted the name Myanmar as a conventional name for their state; this decision was not approved by any sitting legislature in Burma, and the U.S. Government did not adopt the name, which is a derivative of the Burmese short-form name Myanma Naingngandaw.

[2] In a diplomatic note sent on November 27, 2013, the Embassy of Cape Verde requested that the U.S. Government change the name of the country from "Cape Verde" to "Cabo Verde". The U.S. Board on Geographic Names approved the change on December 9, 2013.

[3] With the establishment of diplomatic relations with China on January 1, 1979, the U.S. Government recognized the People's Republic of China as the sole legal government of China and acknowledged the Chinese position that there is only one China and that Taiwan is part of China.

[4] "Congo" is the official short-form name for both the Democratic Republic of the Congo and the Republic of the Congo. To distinguish one from the other, see capital names.

[5] Following U.N. and U.S. State Department notification, the Czech Republic officially changed its English short-form name to Czechia as of July 1, 2016.

[6] In 1950, the Israel Parliament proclaimed Jerusalem as the capital. The United States does not recognize Jerusalem as the capital and the U.S. Embassy continues to be located in Tel Aviv.

[7] In November 2004, the United States recognized the country under its constitutional name: the Republic of Macedonia.

[8] No accurate English equivalents.

[9] The United States recognized South Sudan as a sovereign, independent state on July 9, 2011 following its secession from Sudan.

Source: World Factbook, Central Intelligence Agency, https://www.cia.gov/library/publications/resources/the-world-factbook/index.html and the U.S. Department of State.

Demonyms: Names of Nationalities

[Demonym is a name given to a people or inhabitants of a place.]

Country	Demonym*	Country	Demonym*
Afghanistan	Afghan.	Croatia	Croat or Croatian.
Albania	Albanian.	Cuba	Cuban.
Algeria	Algerian.	Curacao	Curacaoan.
American Samoa	American Samoan.	Cyprus	Cypriot.
Andorra	Andorran.	Czechia	Czech.
Angola	Angolan.	Denmark	Dane.
Anguilla	Anguillan.	Djibouti	Djiboutian.
Antigua and Barbuda	Antiguan, Barbudan.	Dominica	Dominican.
Argentina	Argentine.	Dominican Republic	Dominican.
Armenia	Armenian.	Ecuador	Ecuadorian.
Aruba	Aruban.	Egypt	Egyptian.
Australia	Australian.	El Salvador	Salvadoran.
Austria	Austrian.	Equatorial Guinea	Equatorial Guinean or Equatoguinean.
Azerbaijan	Azerbaijani.		
The Bahamas	Bahamian.	Eritrea	Eritrean.
Bahrain	Bahraini.	Estonia	Estonian.
Bangladesh	Bangladeshi.	Ethiopia	Ethiopian.
Barbados	Barbadian or Bajan.	Falkland Islands	Falkland Islander.
Belarus	Belarusian.	Faroe Islands	Faroese (singular and plural).
Belgium	Belgian.		
Belize	Belizean.	Fiji	Fijian.
Benin	Beninese (singular and plural).	Finland	Finn.
		France	French, Frenchman (men), or Frenchwoman (women).
Bermuda	Bermudian.		
Bhutan	Bhutanese (singular and plural).		
Bolivia	Bolivian.	French Polynesia	French Polynesian.
Bosnia and Herzegovina	Bosnian, Herzegovinian.	Gabon	Gabonese (singular and plural).
Botswana	Motswana (singular), Batswana (plural).		
		The Gambia	Gambian.
Brazil	Brazilian.	Georgia	Georgian.
British Virgin Islands	British Virgin Islander.	Germany	German.
Brunei	Bruneian.	Ghana	Ghanaian.
Bulgaria	Bulgarian.	Gibraltar	Gibraltarian.
Burkina Faso	Burkinabe (singular and plural).	Greece	Greek.
		Greenland	Greenlander.
Burma (Myanmar[1])	Burmese (singular and plural).	Grenada	Grenadian.
		Guam	Guamanian.
Burundi	Burundian.	Guatemala	Guatemalan.
Cabo Verde	Cabo Verdean.	Guernsey	Channel Islander.
Cambodia	Cambodian.	Guinea	Guinean.
Cameroon	Cameroonian.	Guinea-Bissau	Bissau-Guinean.
Canada	Canadian.	Guyana	Guyanese (singular and plural).
Cayman Islands	Caymanian.		
Central African Republic	Central African.	Haiti	Haitian.
Chad	Chadian.	Honduras	Honduran.
Chile	Chilean.	Hong Kong	Chinese/Hong Konger.
China	Chinese (singular and plural).	Hungary	Hungarian.
		Iceland	Icelander.
Christmas Island	Christmas Islander.	India	Indian.
Cocos (Keeling) Islands	Cocos Islander.	Indonesia	Indonesian.
Colombia	Colombian.	Iran	Iranian.
Comoros	Comoran.	Iraq	Iraqi.
Congo, Democratic Republic of the.	Congolese (singular and plural).	Ireland	Irishman (men), Irishwoman (women), Irish (collective plural).
Congo, Republic of the	Congolese (singular and plural).		
		Israel	Israeli.
Cook Islands	Cook Islander.	Italy	Italian.
Costa Rica	Costa Rican.	Jamaica	Jamaican.
Côte d'Ivoire	Ivorian.		

Demonyms: Names of Nationalities—Continued

[Demonym is a name given to a people or inhabitants of a place.]

Country	Demonym*	Country	Demonym*
Japan	Japanese (singular and plural).	New Caledonia	New Caledonian.
Jersey	Channel Islander.	New Zealand	New Zealander.
Jordan	Jordanian.	Nicaragua	Nicaraguan.
Kazakhstan	Kazakhstani.	Niger	Nigerien.
Kenya	Kenyan.	Nigeria	Nigerian.
Kiribati	I-Kiribati (singular and plural).	Niue	Niuean.
Korea, North	Korean.	Norfolk Island	Norfolk Islander.
Korea, South	Korean.	Norway	Norwegian.
Kosovo	Kosovar (Albanian), Kosovski (Serbian).	Oman	Omani.
		Pakistan	Pakistani.
Kuwait	Kuwaiti.	Palau	Palauan.
Kyrgyzstan	Kyrgyzstani.	Panama	Panamanian.
Laos	Lao or Laotian.	Papua New Guinea	Papua New Guinean.
Latvia	Latvian.	Paraguay	Paraguayan.
Lebanon	Lebanese (singular and plural).	Peru	Peruvian.
		Philippines	Filipino.
Lesotho	Mosotho (singular), Basotho (plural).	Pitcairn Islands	Pitcairn Islander.
		Poland	Pole.
Liberia	Liberian.	Portugal	Portuguese (singular and plural).
Libya	Libyan.		
Liechtenstein	Liechtensteiner.	Qatar	Qatari.
Lithuania	Lithuanian.	Romania	Romanian.
Luxembourg	Luxembourger.	Russia	Russian.
Macau	Chinese (singular and plural).	Rwanda	Rwandan.
		Saint Helena	Saint Helenian.
Macedonia	Macedonian.	Saint Kitts and Nevis	Kittian, Nevisian.
Madagascar	Malagasy (singular and plural).	Saint Lucia	Saint Lucian.
		Saint Pierre and Miquelon	French, Frenchman (men), or Frenchwoman (women).
Malawi	Malawian.		
Malaysia	Malaysian.		
Maldives	Maldivian.	Saint Vincent and the Grenadines.	Saint Vincentian or Vincentian.
Mali	Malian.	Samoa	Samoan.
Malta	Maltese (singular and plural).	San Marino	Sammarinese (singular and plural).
Marshall Islands	Marshallese (singular and plural).	Sao Tome and Principe	Sao Tomean.
Mauritania	Mauritanian.	Saudi Arabia	Saudi, Saudi Arabian.
Mauritius	Mauritian.	Senegal	Senegalese (singular and plural).
Mexico	Mexican.		
Micronesia, Federated States of.	Micronesian.	Serbia	Serb.
		Seychelles	Seychellois (singular and plural).
Moldova	Moldovan.	Sierra Leone	Sierra Leonean.
Monaco	Monegasque or Monacan.	Singapore	Singaporean.
		Slovakia	Slovak.
Mongolia	Mongolian.	Slovenia	Slovene.
Montenegro	Montenegrin.	Solomon Islands	Solomon Islander.
Montserrat	Montserratian.	Somalia	Somali.
Morocco	Moroccan.	South Africa	South African.
Mozambique	Mozambican.	South Sudan	South Sudanese.
Namibia	Namibian.	Spain	Spaniard.
Nauru	Nauruan.	Sri Lanka	Sri Lankan.
Nepal	Nepali (singular and plural).	Sudan	Sudanese (singular and plural).
Netherlands	Dutchman (men), Dutchwoman (women), Dutch (collective).	Suriname	Surinamer.
		Swaziland	Swazi.
		Sweden	Swede.
Netherlands Antilles	Dutch Antillean.	Switzerland	Swiss (singular and plural).

Demonyms: Names of Nationalities—Continued

[Demonym is a name given to a people or inhabitants of a place.]

Country	Demonym*	Country	Demonym*
Syria	Syrian.	United Arab Emirates	Emirati.
Taiwan	Taiwan (singular and plural).	United Kingdom	Briton, British (collective plural).
Tajikistan	Tajikistani.	United States	American.
Tanzania	Tanzanian.	Uruguay	Uruguayan.
Thailand	Thai (singular and plural).	Uzbekistan	Uzbekistani.
Timor-Leste	Timorese (singular and plural).	Vanuatu	Ni-Vanuatu (singular and plural).
Togo	Togolese (singular and plural).	Venezuela	Venezuelan.
		Vietnam	Vietnamese (singular and plural).
Tokelau	Tokelauan.	Virgin Islands	Virgin Islander.
Tonga	Tongan.	Wallis and Futuna	Wallisian, Futunan, or Wallis and Futuna Islander.
Trinidad and Tobago	Trinidadian, Tobagonian.		
Tunisia	Tunisian.	Western Sahara	Sahrawi, Sahraoui.
Turkey	Turk.	Yemen	Yemeni.
Turkmenistan	Turkmen.	Zambia	Zambian.
Tuvalu	Tuvaluan.	Zimbabwe	Zimbabwean.
Uganda	Ugandan.		
Ukraine	Ukrainian.		

[1] Since 1989 the military authorities in Burma have promoted the name Myanmar as a conventional name for their state; this decision was not approved by any sitting legislature in Burma, and the U.S. Government did not adopt the name, which is a derivative of the Burmese short-form name Myanma Naingngandaw.

*NOTE.—Plural references add *s* unless otherwise indicated.

Source: Information courtesy of World Factbook as of September 2016; for more information see https://www.cia.gov/library/publications/resources/the-world-factbook/fields/2110.html.

Currency

[As of July 2016]

Country	Currency	Alphabetic code
Afghanistan	Afghani	AFN
Åland Islands	Euro	EUR
Albania	Lek	ALL
Algeria	Algerian dinar	DZD
American Samoa	U.S. dollar	USD
Andorra	Euro	EUR
Angola	Kwanza	AOA
Anguilla	East Caribbean dollar	XCD
Antarctica	No universal currency	
Antigua and Barbuda	East Caribbean dollar	XCD
Argentina	Argentine peso	ARS
Armenia	Armenian dram	AMD
Aruba	Aruban florin	AWG
Australia	Australian dollar	AUD
Austria	Euro	EUR
Azerbaijan	Azerbaijanian manat	AZN
Bahamas (The)	Bahamian dollar	BSD
Bahrain	Bahraini dinar	BHD
Bangladesh	Taka	BDT
Barbados	Barbados dollar	BBD
Belarus	Belarusian ruble	BYN
Belarus	Belarusian ruble	BYR
Belgium	Euro	EUR
Belize	Belize dollar	BZD

Currency—Continued
[As of July 2016]

Country	Currency	Alphabetic code
Benin	CFA franc BCEAO	XOF
Bermuda	Bermudian dollar	BMD
Bhutan	Indian rupee	INR
Bhutan	Ngultrum	BTN
Bolivia (Plurinational State of)	Boliviano	BOB
Bolivia (Plurinational State of)	Mvdol	BOV
Bonaire, Sint Eustatius and Saba	U.S. dollar	USD
Bosnia and Herzegovina	Convertible mark	BAM
Botswana	Pula	BWP
Bouvet Island	Norwegian krone	NOK
Brazil	Brazilian real	BRL
British Indian Ocean Territory (The)	U.S. dollar	USD
Brunei Darussalam	Brunei dollar	BND
Bulgaria	Bulgarian lev	BGN
Burkina Faso	CFA franc BCEAO	XOF
Burundi	Burundi franc	BIF
Cabo Verde	Cabo Verde escudo	CVE
Cambodia	Riel	KHR
Cameroon	CFA franc BEAC	XAF
Canada	Canadian dollar	CAD
Cayman Islands (The)	Cayman Islands dollar	KYD
Central African Republic (The)	CFA franc BEAC	XAF
Chad	CFA franc BEAC	XAF
Chile	Chilean peso	CLP
Chile	Unidad de Fomento	CLF
China	Yuan renminbi	CNY
Christmas Island	Australian dollar	AUD
Cocos (Keeling) Islands (The)	Australian dollar	AUD
Colombia	Colombian peso	COP
Colombia	Unidad de Valor real	COU
Comoros (The)	Comoro franc	KMF
Congo (The Democratic Republic of the)	Congolese franc	CDF
Congo (The)	CFA franc BEAC	XAF
Cook Islands (The)	New Zealand dollar	NZD
Costa Rica	Costa Rican colon	CRC
Côte d'Ivoire	CFA franc BCEAO	XOF
Croatia	Kuna	HRK
Cuba	Cuban peso	CUP
Cuba	Peso convertible	CUC
Curaçao	Netherlands Antillean guilder	ANG
Cyprus	Euro	EUR
Czech Republic (The)	Czech koruna	CZK
Denmark	Danish krone	DKK
Djibouti	Djibouti franc	DJF
Dominica	East Caribbean dollar	XCD
Dominican Republic (The)	Dominican peso	DOP
Ecuador	U.S. dollar	USD
Egypt	Egyptian pound	EGP
El Salvador	El Salvador colon	SVC
El Salvador	U.S. dollar	USD
Equatorial Guinea	CFA franc BEAC	XAF
Eritrea	Nakfa	ERN
Estonia	Euro	EUR
Ethiopia	Ethiopian birr	ETB
European Union	Euro	EUR
Falkland Islands (The) [Malvinas]	Falkland Islands pound	FKP
Faroe Islands (The)	Danish krone	DKK
Fiji	Fiji dollar	FJD
Finland	Euro	EUR

Currency—Continued

[As of July 2016]

Country	Currency	Alphabetic code
France	Euro	EUR
French Guiana	Euro	EUR
French Polynesia	CFP franc	XPF
French Southern Territories (The)	Euro	EUR
Gabon	CFA franc BEAC	XAF
Gambia (The)	Dalasi	GMD
Georgia	Lari	GEL
Germany	Euro	EUR
Ghana	Ghana cedi	GHS
Gibraltar	Gibraltar pound	GIP
Greece	Euro	EUR
Greenland	Danish krone	DKK
Grenada	East Caribbean dollar	XCD
Guadeloupe	Euro	EUR
Guam	U.S. dollar	USD
Guatemala	Quetzal	GTQ
Guernsey	Pound sterling	GBP
Guinea	Guinea franc	GNF
Guinea-Bissau	CFA franc BCEAO	XOF
Guyana	Guyana dollar	GYD
Haiti	Gourde	HTG
Haiti	U.S. dollar	USD
Heard Island and McDonald Islands	Australian dollar	AUD
Holy See (The)	Euro	EUR
Honduras	Lempira	HNL
Hong Kong	Hong Kong dollar	HKD
Hungary	Forint	HUF
Iceland	Iceland krona	ISK
India	Indian rupee	INR
Indonesia	Rupiah	IDR
International Monetary Fund (IMF)	SDR (Special Drawing Right)	XDR
Iran (Islamic Republic of)	Iranian rial	IRR
Iraq	Iraqi dinar	IQD
Ireland	Euro	EUR
Isle of Man	Pound sterling	GBP
Israel	New Israeli sheqel	ILS
Italy	Euro	EUR
Jamaica	Jamaican dollar	JMD
Japan	Yen	JPY
Jersey	Pound sterling	GBP
Jordan	Jordanian dinar	JOD
Kazakhstan	Tenge	KZT
Kenya	Kenyan shilling	KES
Kiribati	Australian dollar	AUD
Korea (The Democratic People's Republic of)	North Korean won	KPW
Korea (The Republic of)	Won	KRW
Kuwait	Kuwaiti dinar	KWD
Kyrgyzstan	Som	KGS
Lao People's Democratic Republic (The)	Kip	LAK
Latvia	Euro	EUR
Lebanon	Lebanese pound	LBP
Lesotho	Loti	LSL
Lesotho	Rand	ZAR
Liberia	Liberian dollar	LRD
Libya	Libyan dinar	LYD
Liechtenstein	Swiss franc	CHF
Lithuania	Euro	EUR
Luxembourg	Euro	EUR
Macao	Pataca	MOP

Currency—Continued

[As of July 2016]

Country	Currency	Alphabetic code
Macedonia (The Former Yugoslav Republic of)..	Denar	MKD
Madagascar	Malagasy ariary	MGA
Malawi	Malawi kwacha	MWK
Malaysia	Malaysian ringgit	MYR
Maldives	Rufiyaa	MVR
Mali	CFA franc BCEAO	XOF
Malta	Euro	EUR
Marshall Islands (The)	U.S. dollar	USD
Martinique	Euro	EUR
Mauritania	Ouguiya	MRO
Mauritius	Mauritius rupee	MUR
Mayotte	Euro	EUR
Member Countries of the African Development Bank Group	ADB Unit of Account	XUA
Mexico	Mexican peso	MXN
Mexico	Mexican Unidad de Inversion (UDI)	MXV
Micronesia (Federated States of)	U.S. dollar	USD
Moldova (The Republic of)	Moldovan leu	MDL
Monaco	Euro	EUR
Mongolia	Tugrik	MNT
Montenegro	Euro	EUR
Montserrat	East Caribbean dollar	XCD
Morocco	Moroccan dirham	MAD
Mozambique	Mozambique metical	MZN
Myanmar	Kyat	MMK
Namibia	Namibia dollar	NAD
Namibia	Rand	ZAR
Nauru	Australian dollar	AUD
Nepal	Nepalese rupee	NPR
Netherlands (The)	Euro	EUR
New Caledonia	CFP franc	XPF
New Zealand	New Zealand dollar	NZD
Nicaragua	Cordoba oro	NIO
Niger (The)	CFA franc BCEAO	XOF
Nigeria	Naira	NGN
Niue	New Zealand dollar	NZD
Norfolk Island	Australian dollar	AUD
Northern Mariana Islands (The)	U.S. dollar	USD
Norway	Norwegian krone	NOK
Oman	Rial omani	OMR
Pakistan	Pakistan rupee	PKR
Palau	U.S. dollar	USD
Palestine, State of	No universal currency	
Panama	Balboa	PAB
Panama	U.S. dollar	USD
Papua New Guinea	Kina	PGK
Paraguay	Guarani	PYG
Peru	Sol	PEN
Philippines (The)	Philippine peso	PHP
Pitcairn	New Zealand dollar	NZD
Poland	Zloty	PLN
Portugal	Euro	EUR
Puerto Rico	U.S. dollar	USD
Qatar	Qatari rial	QAR
Réunion	Euro	EUR
Romania	Romanian leu	RON
Russian Federation (The)	Russian ruble	RUB
Rwanda	Rwanda franc	RWF
Saint Barthélemy	Euro	EUR

Currency—Continued

[As of July 2016]

Country	Currency	Alphabetic code
Saint Helena, Ascension and Tristan Da Cunha	Saint Helena pound	SHP
Saint Kitts and Nevis	East Caribbean dollar	XCD
Saint Lucia	East Caribbean dollar	XCD
Saint Martin (French Part)	Euro	EUR
Saint Pierre and Miquelon	Euro	EUR
Saint Vincent and the Grenadines	East Caribbean dollar	XCD
Samoa	Tala	WST
San Marino	Euro	EUR
Sao Tome and Principe	Dobra	STD
Saudi Arabia	Saudi riyal	SAR
Senegal	CFA franc BCEAO	XOF
Serbia	Serbian dinar	RSD
Seychelles	Seychelles rupee	SCR
Sierra Leone	Leone	SLL
Singapore	Singapore dollar	SGD
Sint Maarten (Dutch Part)	Netherlands Antillean guilder	ANG
Sistema Unitario De Compensacion Regional De Pagos "Sucre"	Sucre	XSU
Slovakia	Euro	EUR
Slovenia	Euro	EUR
Solomon Islands	Solomon Islands dollar	SBD
Somalia	Somali shilling	SOS
South Africa	Rand	ZAR
South Georgia and the South Sandwich Islands	No universal currency	
South Sudan	South Sudanese pound	SSP
Spain	Euro	EUR
Sri Lanka	Sri Lanka rupee	LKR
Sudan (The)	Sudanese pound	SDG
Suriname	Surinam dollar	SRD
Svalbard and Jan Mayen	Norwegian krone	NOK
Swaziland	Lilangeni	SZL
Sweden	Swedish krona	SEK
Switzerland	Swiss franc	CHF
Switzerland	WIR Euro	CHE
Switzerland	WIR franc	CHW
Syrian Arab Republic	Syrian pound	SYP
Taiwan (Province of China)	New Taiwan dollar	TWD
Tajikistan	Somoni	TJS
Tanzania, United Republic of	Tanzanian shilling	TZS
Thailand	Baht	THB
Timor-Leste	U.S. dollar	USD
Togo	CFA franc BCEAO	XOF
Tokelau	New Zealand dollar	NZD
Tonga	Pa'anga	TOP
Trinidad and Tobago	Trinidad and Tobago dollar	TTD
Tunisia	Tunisian dinar	TND
Turkey	Turkish lira	TRY
Turkmenistan	Turkmenistan new manat	TMT
Turks and Caicos Islands (The)	U.S. dollar	USD
Tuvalu	Australian dollar	AUD
Uganda	Uganda shilling	UGX
Ukraine	Hryvnia	UAH
United Arab Emirates (The)	UAE dirham	AED
United Kingdom of Great Britain and Northern Ireland (The)	Pound sterling	GBP
United States Minor Outlying Islands (The)	U.S. dollar	USD
United States of America (The)	U.S. dollar	USD

Currency—Continued
[As of July 2016]

Country	Currency	Alphabetic code
United States of America (The)	U.S. dollar (Next day)	USN
Uruguay	Peso Uruguayo	UYU
Uruguay	Uruguay peso en Unidades Indexadas (URUIURUI)	UYI
Uzbekistan	Uzbekistan sum	UZS
Vanuatu	Vatu	VUV
Venezuela (Bolivarian Republic of)	Bolívar	VEF
Viet Nam	Dong	VND
Virgin Islands (British)	U.S. dollar	USD
Virgin Islands (U.S.)	U.S. dollar	USD
Wallis and Futuna	CFP franc	XPF
Western Sahara	Moroccan dirham	MAD
Yemen	Yemeni rial	YER
Zambia	Zambian kwacha	ZMW
Zimbabwe	Zimbabwe dollar	ZWL

Source: http://www.currency-iso.org/en/home/tables/table-a.1.html.

Metric and U.S. Measures [1]

Length

Metric unit	U.S. unit
10 millimeters....................................1 centimeter.	12 inches..1 foot (ft).
10 centimeters...................................1 decimeter.	3 feet...1 yard.
10 decimeters...................................1 meter.	22 yards...1 chain.
10 meters...1 dekameter.	10 chains...1 furlong (660 ft).
10 dekameters...................................1 hectometer.	8 furlongs..1 mile (5,280 ft).
10 hectometers.................................1 kilometer.	1 nautical mile..................................1.1508 mile.
1 kilometer...1,000 meters.	1 league..3 nautical miles.

Mass Weight

Metric unit	U.S. unit
10 milligrams (mg).........................1 centigram.	16 ounces...1 pound.
10 centigrams..................................1 decigram (100 mg).	100 pounds (lbs)..............................1 hundredweight.
10 decigrams...................................1 gram (1,000 mg).	2,000 lbs..1 ton.
10 grams (g).....................................1 dekagram.	
10 dekagrams...................................1 hectogram (100 g).	
10 hectograms.................................1 kilogram (1,000 g).	
1,000 kilograms...............................1 metric ton.	

Volume

Metric unit	U.S. liquid capacity
10 milliliters......................................1 centiliter.	3 teaspoons......................................1 tablespoon.
10 centiliters.....................................1 deciliter.	2 tablespoons...................................1 fluid ounce (fl oz).
10 deciliters......................................1 liter.	1 cup..8 fl oz.
1,000 liters..1 cubic meter.	2 cups..1 pint.
	2 pints...1 quart.
	4 quarts...1 gallon.
	42 gallons...1 petroleum barrel.
	U.S. dry measure [2]
	2 pints...1 quart.
	4 quarts...1 gallon.
	2 gallons...1 peck.
	4 pecks..1 bushel.
	8 bushels...1 quarter.

Temperature Conversion [3]

Celsius	Fahrenheit	Kelvin	Celsius	Fahrenheit	Kelvin
100....................................	212	373.1	0...	32	273.1
50......................................	122	323.1	−10......................................	14	263.1
40......................................	104	313.1	−20......................................	−4	253.1
30......................................	86	303.1	−30......................................	−22	243.1
20......................................	68	293.1	−40......................................	−40	233.1
10......................................	50	283.1	−50......................................	−58	223.1
			−273.1.................................	−459.7	0

[1] At this time, only three countries—Burma, Liberia, and the United States—have not significantly transitioned to the International System of Units (SI, or metric system) as their official system of weights and measures.

[2] Dry measurements are mainly used for measuring grain or fresh produce. Do not confuse dry measure for liquid measure, as they are not the same.

[3] The equation for converting temperatures is as follows: °C to °F: multiply by 9, then divide by 5, then add 32; °F to °C: subtract 32, then multiply by 5, then divide by 9.

Common Measures and Their Metric Equivalents

U.S. to metric	Metric to U.S.
Inch....................2.54 centimeters.	Centimeter...............0.3937 inch.
Foot....................0.3048 meter.	Meter...............3.2808 feet.
Yard....................0.9144 meter.	Do...............1.0936 yards.
Mile....................1.6093 kilometers.	Kilometer...............0.6214 mile.
Nautical mile....................1.852 kilometers.	Do...............0.5399 nautical mile.
League....................5.556 kilometers.	Do...............0.1799 league.
Square inch....................6.452 square centimeters.	Square centimeter...............0.155 square inch.
Square foot....................0.0929 square meter.	Square meter...............10.7639 square feet.
Square yard....................0.836 square meter.	Do...............1.196 square yards.
Acre....................0.4047 hectare.	Hectare...............2.471 acres.
Square mile....................259 hectares.	Do...............0.0039 square mile.
Cubic inch....................16.39 cubic centimeters.	Cubic centimeter...............0.06 cubic inch.
Cubic foot....................0.0283 cubic meter.	Cubic meter...............35.3146 cubic feet.
Cubic yard....................0.7646 cubic meter.	Do...............1.3079 cubic yards.
Cord....................128 cubic feet.	
Ounce (liquid)....................29.574 milliliters.	Milliliter...............0.0338 ounce (liquid).
Pint (liquid)....................473.176 milliliters.	
Quart (liquid)....................946.35 milliliters.	Liter...............1.06 quarts (liquid).
Gallon (liquid)....................3.79 liters.	Do...............0.26 gallon (liquid).
Pint (dry)....................550.61 milliliters.	
Quart (dry)....................1101 milliliters.	Do...............0.91 quart (dry).
Quart, imperial....................1137 milliliters.	
Gallon (dry)....................4.40 liters.	Do...............0.23 gallon (dry).
Gallon, imperial....................4.55 liters.	
Peck....................8.810 liters.	Do...............0.1135 peck.
Peck, imperial....................9.092 liters.	
Bushel....................35.24 liters.	Do...............0.028 bushel.
Bushel, imperial....................36.37 liters.	
Grain[1]....................64.799 milligrams.	
Ounce[2]....................28.35 grams.	Gram...............0.04 ounce.
Ounce, troy[3]....................31.103 grams.	Do...............0.032 troy ounce.
Pound[2]....................0.4536 kilogram.	Kilogram...............2.20 pounds.
Pound, troy....................12 troy ounces.	
Ton, short....................907.185 kilograms.	
Do....................2,000 pounds.	
Ton, metric....................1,000 kilograms.	
Do....................2,204.6 pounds.	
Ton, long....................1,016.047 kilograms.	
Do....................2,240 pounds.	

[1] The grain is used to measure in ballistics and archery; grains were originally used in medicine but have been replaced by milligrams.

[2] Avoirdupois; avoirdupois is the measure of mass of everyday items.

[3] The troy ounce is used in pricing silver, gold, platinum, and other precious metals and gemstones.

Measurement Conversion

Fractional inch	Decimal inches	Milli-meters	Picas	Points	Fractional inch	Decimal inches	Milli-meters	Picas	Points
1/16	.0625	1.587	0p4.5	4.5	7/8	.875	22.225	5p3	63
1/8	.125	3.175	0p9	9	15/16	.9375	23.812	5p7.5	67.5
3/16	.1875	4.762	1p1.5	13.5	1	1	25.4	6	72
1/4	.25	6.35	1p6	18	1¼	1.25	31.75	7p6	90
5/16	.3125	7.937	1p10.5	22.5	1½	1.5	38.1	9	108
3/8	.375	9.525	2p3	27	1¾	1.75	44.5	10p6	126
7/16	.4375	11.112	2p7.5	31.5	2	2	50.8	12	144
1/2	.5	12.7	3	36	2½	2.5	63.5	15	180
9/16	.5625	14.287	3p4.5	40.5	3	3	76.2	18	216
5/8	.625	15.875	3p9	45	3½	3.5	88.9	21	252
11/16	.6875	17.462	4p1.5	49.5	4	4	100.6	24	288
3/4	.75	19.05	4p6	54	5	5	127	30	360
13/16	.8125	20.637	4p10.5	58.5	6	6	152.4	36	432

18. Geologic Terms and Geographic Divisions

Geologic terms

For capitalization, compounding, and use of quotations in geologic terms, copy is to be followed. Geologic terms quoted verbatim from published material should be left as the original author used them; however, it should be made clear that the usage is that of the original author.

Formal geologic terms are capitalized: Proterozoic Eon, Cambrian Period. Structural terms such as arch, anticline, or uplift are capitalized when preceded by a name: Cincinnati Arch, Cedar Creek Anticline, Ozark Uplift. See Chapter 4 geographic terms for more information.

Divisions of Geologic Time
[Most recent to oldest]

Eon	Era	Period
Phanerozoic..............	Cenozoic...........................	Quaternary.
		Tertiary (Neogene, Paleogene).
	Mesozoic..........................	Cretaceous.
		Jurassic.
		Triassic.
	Paleozoic	Permian.
		Carboniferous (Pennsylvanian, Mississippian).
		Devonian.
		Silurian.
		Ordovician.
		Cambrian.
Proterozoic..............	Neoproterozoic	Ediacaran.
		Cryogenian.
		Tonian.
	Mesoproterozoic............	Stenian.
		Ectasian.
		Calymmian.
	Paleoproterozoic............	Statherian.
		Orosirian.
		Rhyacian.
		Siderian.
Archean......................	Neoarchean.	
	Mesoarchean.	
	Paleoarchean.	
	Eoarchean.	
Hadean.		

Source: Information courtesy of the U.S. Geological Survey; for graphic see http://pubs.usgs.gov/fs/2007/3015/fs2007-3015.pdf.

Physiographic regions

Physiographic regions are based on terrain texture, rock type, and geologic structure and history. The classification system has three tiers: divisions, which are broken into provinces, and some provinces break further into sections. All names are capitalized, not the class; for graphic see http://tapestry.usgs.gov/physiogr/physio.html.

Physiographic Regions of the Lower 48 United States

Division	Province	Section
Laurentian Upland	Superior Upland.	
Atlantic Plain	Continental Shelf.	
	Coastal Plain	Embayed.
		Sea Island.
		Floridian.
		East Gulf Coastal Plain.
		Mississippi Alluvial Plain.
		West Gulf Coastal Plain.
Appalachian Highlands	Piedmont	Piedmont Upland.
		Piedmont Lowlands.
	Blue Ridge	Northern.
		Southern.
	Valley and Ridge	Tennessee.
		Middle.
		Hudson Valley.
	St. Lawrence Valley	Champlain.
		Northern.
	Appalachian Plateaus	Mohawk.
		Catskill.
		Southern New York.
		Allegheny Mountain.
		Kanawha.
		Cumberland Plateau.
		Cumberland Mountain.
	New England	Seaboard Lowland.
		New England Upland.
		White Mountain.
		Green Mountain.
		Taconic.
	Adirondack.	
Interior Plains	Interior Low Plateaus	Highland Rim.
		Lexington Plain.
		Nashville Basin.
	Central Lowland	Eastern Lake.
		Western Lake.
		Wisconsin Driftless.
		Till Plains.
		Dissected Till Plains.
		Osage Plains.

Division	Province	Section
	Great Plains..............................	Missouri Plateau, glaciated.
		Missouri Plateau, unglaciated.
		Black Hills.
		High Plains.
		Plains Border.
		Colorado Piedmont.
		Raton.
		Pecos Valley.
		Edwards Plateau.
		Central Texas.
Interior Highlands......................	Ozark Plateaus............................	Springfield-Salem Plateaus.
		Boston "Mountains."
	Ouachita......................................	Arkansas Valley.
		Ouachita Mountains.
Rocky Mountain System............	Southern Rocky Mountains.	
	Wyoming Basin.	
	Middle Rocky Mountains.	
	Northern Rocky Mountains.	
Intermontane Plateaus	Columbia Plateau	Walla Walla Plateau.
		Blue Mountain.
		Payette.
		Snake River Plain.
		Harney.
	Colorado Plateaus	High Plateaus of Utah.
		Uinta Basin.
		Canyon Lands.
		Navajo.
		Grand Canyon.
		Datil.
	Basin and Range	Great Basin.
		Sonoran Desert.
		Salton Trough.
		Mexican Highland.
		Sacramento.
Pacific Mountain System............	Cascade-Sierra Mountains........	Northern Cascade Mountains.
		Middle Cascade Mountains.
		Southern Cascade Mountains.
		Sierra Nevada.
	Pacific Border	Puget Trough.
		Olympic Mountains.
		Oregon Coast Range.
		Klamath Mountains.
		California Trough.
		California Coast Ranges.
		Los Angeles Ranges.
	Lower California.	

Source: Information courtesy of the U.S. Geological Survey.

Geographic divisions

The Public Land Survey System has a hierarchy of lines. Principal meridians and base lines and their related townships, sections, and subdivisions of sections are incorporated in the description of land conveyed by the Federal Government and others.

The Principal Meridians and Base Lines of the United States [1]

Black Hills Meridian and Base Line.
  (South Dakota)

Boise Meridian and Base Line. (Idaho)

Chickasaw Meridian and Base Line.
  (Mississippi-Tennessee)

Choctaw Meridian and Base Line. (Mississippi)

Cimarron Meridian and Base Line.
  (Oklahoma)

Copper River Meridian and Base Line. (Alaska)

Fairbanks Meridian and Base Line. (Alaska)

Fifth Principal Meridian and Base Line.
  (Arkansas-Iowa-Minnesota-Missouri-
  North Dakota-South Dakota)

First Principal Meridian and Base Line.
  (Ohio-Indiana)

Fourth Principal Meridian and Base Line.
  (Illinois)

Fourth Principal Meridian and Base Line
  Wisconsin. (Minnesota-Wisconsin)

Gila and Salt River Meridian and Base Line.
  (Arizona)

Humboldt Meridian and Base Line.
  (California)

Huntsville Meridian and Base Line.
  (Alabama-Mississippi)

Indian Meridian and Base Line. (Oklahoma)

Kateel River Principal Meridian and Base
  Line. (Alaska)

Louisiana Meridian and Base Line.
  (Louisiana-Texas)

Michigan Meridian and Base Line.
  (Michigan-Ohio)

Mount Diablo Meridian and Base Line.
  (California-Nevada)

Navajo Meridian and Base Line. (Arizona-
  New Mexico)

New Mexico Principal Meridian and Base
  Line. (New Mexico-Colorado)

Point of Beginning and Geographer's
  Line. (Ohio)

Principal Meridian and Base Line.
  (Montana)

Salt Lake Meridian and Base Line. (Utah)

San Bernardino Meridian and Base Line.
  (California-Nevada)

Second Principal Meridian and Base Line.
  (Illinois-Indiana)

Seward Principal Meridian and Base Line.
  (Alaska)

Sixth Principal Meridian and Base Line.
  (Colorado-Kansas-Nebraska-South
  Dakota-Wyoming)

St. Helena Meridian and Base Line.
  (Louisiana)

St. Stephens Meridian and Base Line.
  (Alabama-Mississippi)

Tallahassee Meridian and Base Line.
  (Florida)

Third Principal Meridian and Base Line.
  (Illinois)

Uintah Special Meridian and Base Line.
  (Utah)

Umiat Principal Meridian and Base Line.
  (Alaska)

Ute Principal Meridian and Base Line.
  (Colorado)

Washington Meridian and Base Line.
  (Mississippi)

Willamette Meridian and Base Line.
  (Oregon-Washington)

Wind River Meridian and Base Line.
  (Wyoming)

[1] Information courtesy of the U.S. Department of the Interior, Bureau of Land Management.

Public Land Surveys Having No Initial Point as an Origin for Both Township and Range Numbers[1]

Between the Miamis, north of Symmes Purchase. (Ohio)	Scioto River Base. (Ohio)
	Twelve-Mile-Square Reserve. (Ohio)
Muskingum River Survey. (Ohio)	United States Military Survey. (Ohio)
Ohio River Base. (Indiana)	West of the Great Miami. (Ohio)
Ohio River Survey. (Ohio)	

[1] Information courtesy of the U.S. Department of the Interior, Bureau of Land Management.

Sources: Manual of Surveying Instructions: For the Survey of the Public Lands of the United States, Bureau of Land Management, 2009, GPO; Initial Points of the Rectangular Survey System, C. Albert White, 1996.

See http://www.blm.gov/wo/st/en/prog/more/cadastralsurvey.html for more information on prinicipal meridians and base lines.

Major Rivers of the World

River	Length (in miles)	River	Length (in miles)
Nile (Africa)	4,160	MacKenzie (Canada)	2,635
Amazon (S. America)	4,000	Mekong (Vietnam)	2,600
Yangtze (China)	3,964	Niger (Africa)	2,590
Yellow (China)	3,395	Yenisey (Russia)	2,543
Ob-Irtysh (Russia)	3,362	Missouri (U.S.)	2,540
Amur (Asia)	2,744	Parana (S. America)	2,485
Lena (Russia)	2,734	Mississippi (U.S.)	2,340
Congo (Africa)	2,718	Murray-Darling (Australia)	2,310

NOTE.—Information compiled from numerous public domain websites; references cite different lengths for the same river depending on origin.

Major Rivers of the United States

River	Length (in miles)	River	Length (in miles)
Missouri	2,540	Ohio	1,310
Mississippi	2,340	Red	1,290
Yukon	1,980	Brazos	1,280
Rio Grande	1,900	Columbia	1,249
St. Lawrence	1,900	Snake	1,040
Arkansas	1,469	Platte	990
Colorado	1,450	Pecos	926
Atchafalaya	1,420	Canadian	906

Source: Information courtesy of the U.S. Geological Survey; see http://water.usgs.gov/edu/riversofworld.html.

States, capitals, and counties

The following includes parishes, boroughs, census divisions, districts, islands, municipalities, and "municipios" of the 50 States, U.S. possessions, and territories. County totals include city counties as defined by the National Association of Counties. See www.naco.org for more information.

ALABAMA (AL) (67 counties)
Capital: Montgomery

Autauga	Cleburne	Fayette	Lowndes	Russell
Baldwin	Coffee	Franklin	Macon	St. Clair
Barbour	Colbert	Geneva	Madison	Shelby
Bibb	Conecuh	Greene	Marengo	Sumter
Blount	Coosa	Hale	Marion	Talladega
Bullock	Covington	Henry	Marshall	Tallapoosa
Butler	Crenshaw	Houston	Mobile	Tuscaloosa
Calhoun	Cullman	Jackson	Monroe	Walker
Chambers	Dale	Jefferson	Montgomery	Washington
Cherokee	Dallas	Lamar	Morgan	Wilcox
Chilton	DeKalb	Lauderdale	Perry	Winston
Choctaw	Elmore	Lawrence	Pickens	
Clarke	Escambia	Lee	Pike	
Clay	Etowah	Limestone	Randolph	

ALASKA (AK) (29 entities: 19 boroughs,* 10 census areas)
Capital: Juneau

Aleutians East*	Haines*	Kusilvak	Petersburg*	Wrangell*
Aleutians West	Hoonah-	Lake and	Prince of	Yakutat*
Anchorage*	Angoon	Peninsula*	Wales-Hyder	Yukon-
Bethel	Juneau*	Matanuska-	Sitka*	Koyukuk
Bristol Bay*	Kenai	Susitna*	Skagway*	
Denali*	Peninsula*	Nome	Southeast	
Dillingham	Ketchikan	North Slope*	Fairbanks	
Fairbanks	Gateway*	Northwest	Valdez-	
North Star*	Kodiak Island*	Arctic*	Cordova	

AMERICAN SAMOA (AS) (5 entities: 2 islands,* 3 districts)
Capital: Pago Pago

Eastern	Manu'a	Rose*	Swains*	Western

ARIZONA (AZ) (15 counties)
Capital: Phoenix

Apache	Gila	La Paz	Navajo	Santa Cruz
Cochise	Graham	Maricopa	Pima	Yavapai
Coconino	Greenlee	Mohave	Pinal	Yum

ARKANSAS (AR) (75 counties)
Capital: Little Rock

Arkansas	Craighead	Howard	Miller	Randolph
Ashley	Crawford	Independence	Mississippi	St. Francis
Baxter	Crittenden	Izard	Monroe	Saline
Benton	Cross	Jackson	Montgomery	Scott
Boone	Dallas	Jefferson	Nevada	Searcy
Bradley	Desha	Johnson	Newton	Sebastian
Calhoun	Drew	Lafayette	Ouachita	Sevier
Carroll	Faulkner	Lawrence	Perry	Sharp
Chicot	Franklin	Lee	Phillips	Stone
Clark	Fulton	Lincoln	Pike	Union
Clay	Garland	Little River	Poinsett	Van Buren
Cleburne	Grant	Logan	Polk	Washington
Cleveland	Greene	Lonoke	Pope	White
Columbia	Hempstead	Madison	Prairie	Woodruff
Conway	Hot Spring	Marion	Pulaski	Yell

CALIFORNIA (CA) (58 counties)
Capital: Sacramento

Alameda	Imperial	Modoc	San Diego	Solano
Alpine	Inyo	Mono	San Francisco	Sonoma
Amador	Kern	Monterey	San Joaquin	Stanislaus
Butte	Kings	Napa	San Luis	Sutter
Calaveras	Lake	Nevada	Obispo	Tehama
Colusa	Lassen	Orange	San Mateo	Trinity
Contra Costa	Los Angeles	Placer	Santa Barbara	Tulare
Del Norte	Madera	Plumas	Santa Clara	Tuolumne
El Dorado	Marin	Riverside	Santa Cruz	Ventura
Fresno	Mariposa	Sacramento	Shasta	Yolo
Glenn	Mendocino	San Benito	Sierra	Yuba
Humboldt	Merced	San Bernardino	Siskiyou	

COLORADO (CO) (64 counties)
Capital: Denver

Adams	Crowley	Gunnison	Mesa	Rio Blanco
Alamosa	Custer	Hinsdale	Mineral	Rio Grande
Arapahoe	Delta	Huerfano	Moffat	Routt
Archuleta	Denver	Jackson	Montezuma	Saguache
Baca	Dolores	Jefferson	Montrose	San Juan
Bent	Douglas	Kiowa	Morgan	San Miguel
Boulder	Eagle	Kit Carson	Otero	Sedgwick
Broomfield	Elbert	Lake	Ouray	Summit
Chaffee	El Paso	La Plata	Park	Teller
Cheyenne	Fremont	Larimer	Phillips	Washington
Clear Creek	Garfield	Las Animas	Pitkin	Weld
Conejos	Gilpin	Lincoln	Prowers	Yuma
Costilla	Grand	Logan	Pueblo	

CONNECTICUT (CT) (8 counties)
Capital: Hartford

Fairfield	Litchfield	New Haven	Tolland
Hartford	Middlesex	New London	Windham

DELAWARE (DE) (3 counties)
Capital: Dover

Kent	New Castle	Sussex

DISTRICT OF COLUMBIA (DC) (single entity)

FEDERATED STATES OF MICRONESIA (FM) (4 States)
Capital: Palikir

Chuuk	Kosrae	Pohnpei	Yap

FLORIDA (FL) (67 counties)
Capital: Tallahassee

Alachua	Charlotte	Duval	Gulf	Holmes
Baker	Citrus	Escambia	Hamilton	Indian River
Bay	Clay	Flagler	Hardee	Jackson
Bradford	Collier	Franklin	Hendry	Jefferson
Brevard	Columbia	Gadsden	Hernando	Lafayette
Broward	DeSoto	Gilchrist	Highlands	Lake
Calhoun	Dixie	Glades	Hillsborough	Lee

Leon	Miami-Dade	Palm Beach	Santa Rosa	Volusia
Levy	Monroe	Pasco	Sarasota	Wakulla
Liberty	Nassau	Pinellas	Seminole	Walton
Madison	Okaloosa	Polk	Sumter	Washington
Manatee	Okeechobee	Putnam	Suwannee	
Marion	Orange	St. Johns	Taylor	
Martin	Osceola	St. Lucie	Union	

GEORGIA (GA) (159 counties)
Capital: Atlanta

Appling	Cobb	Grady	Madison	Sumter
Atkinson	Coffee	Greene	Marion	Talbot
Bacon	Colquitt	Gwinnett	Meriwether	Taliaferro
Baker	Columbia	Habersham	Miller	Tattnall
Baldwin	Cook	Hall	Mitchell	Taylor
Banks	Coweta	Hancock	Monroe	Telfair
Barrow	Crawford	Haralson	Montgomery	Terrell
Bartow	Crisp	Harris	Morgan	Thomas
Ben Hill	Dade	Hart	Murray	Tift
Berrien	Dawson	Heard	Muscogee	Toombs
Bibb	Decatur	Henry	Newton	Towns
Bleckley	DeKalb	Houston	Oconee	Treutlen
Brantley	Dodge	Irwin	Oglethorpe	Troup
Brooks	Dooly	Jackson	Paulding	Turner
Bryan	Dougherty	Jasper	Peach	Twiggs
Bulloch	Douglas	Jeff Davis	Pickens	Union
Burke	Early	Jefferson	Pierce	Upson
Butts	Echols	Jenkins	Pike	Walker
Calhoun	Effingham	Johnson	Polk	Walton
Camden	Elbert	Jones	Pulaski	Ware
Candler	Emanuel	Lamar	Putnam	Warren
Carroll	Evans	Lanier	Quitman	Washington
Catoosa	Fannin	Laurens	Rabun	Wayne
Charlton	Fayette	Lee	Randolph	Webster
Chatham	Floyd	Liberty	Richmond	Wheeler
Chattahoochee	Forsyth	Lincoln	Rockdale	White
Chattooga	Franklin	Long	Schley	Whitfield
Cherokee	Fulton	Lowndes	Screven	Wilcox
Clarke	Gilmer	Lumpkin	Seminole	Wilkes
Clay	Glascock	McDuffie	Spalding	Wilkinson
Clayton	Glynn	McIntosh	Stephens	Worth
Clinch	Gordon	Macon	Stewart	

GUAM (GU) (single entity)
Capital: Agana

HAWAII (HI) (4 counties)
Capital: Honolulu

Hawaii	Honolulu	Kalawao	Kauai	Maui

IDAHO (ID) (44 counties)
Capital: Boise

Ada	Bonneville	Custer	Kootenai	Owyhee
Adams	Boundary	Elmore	Latah	Payette
Bannock	Butte	Franklin	Lemhi	Power
Bear Lake	Camas	Fremont	Lewis	Shoshone
Benewah	Canyon	Gem	Lincoln	Teton
Bingham	Caribou	Gooding	Madison	Twin Falls
Blaine	Cassia	Idaho	Minidoka	Valley
Boise	Clark	Jefferson	Nez Perce	Washington
Bonner	Clearwater	Jerome	Oneida	

ILLINOIS (IL) (102 counties)
Capital: Springfield

Adams	DuPage	Jo Daviess	Massac	Schuyler
Alexander	Edgar	Johnson	Menard	Scott
Bond	Edwards	Kane	Mercer	Shelby
Boone	Effingham	Kankakee	Monroe	Stark
Brown	Fayette	Kendall	Montgomery	Stephenson
Bureau	Ford	Knox	Morgan	Tazewell
Calhoun	Franklin	Lake	Moultrie	Union
Carroll	Fulton	LaSalle	Ogle	Vermilion
Cass	Gallatin	Lawrence	Peoria	Wabash
Champaign	Greene	Lee	Perry	Warren
Christian	Grundy	Livingston	Piatt	Washington
Clark	Hamilton	Logan	Pike	Wayne
Clay	Hancock	McDonough	Pope	White
Clinton	Hardin	McHenry	Pulaski	Whiteside
Coles	Henderson	McLean	Putnam	Will
Cook	Henry	Macon	Randolph	Williamson
Crawford	Iroquois	Macoupin	Richland	Winnebago
Cumberland	Jackson	Madison	Rock Island	Woodford
DeKalb	Jasper	Marion	St. Clair	
De Witt	Jefferson	Marshall	Saline	
Douglas	Jersey	Mason	Sangamon	

INDIANA (IN) (92 counties)
Capital: Indianapolis

Adams	Elkhart	Jefferson	Ohio	Sullivan
Allen	Fayette	Jennings	Orange	Switzerland
Bartholomew	Floyd	Johnson	Owen	Tippecanoe
Benton	Fountain	Knox	Parke	Tipton
Blackford	Franklin	Kosciusko	Perry	Union
Boone	Fulton	LaGrange	Pike	Vanderburgh
Brown	Gibson	Lake	Porter	Vermillion
Carroll	Grant	LaPorte	Posey	Vigo
Cass	Greene	Lawrence	Pulaski	Wabash
Clark	Hamilton	Madison	Putnam	Warren
Clay	Hancock	Marion	Randolph	Warrick
Clinton	Harrison	Marshall	Ripley	Washington
Crawford	Hendricks	Martin	Rush	Wayne
Daviess	Henry	Miami	St. Joseph	Wells
Dearborn	Howard	Monroe	Scott	White
Decatur	Huntington	Montgomery	Shelby	Whitley
DeKalb	Jackson	Morgan	Spencer	
Delaware	Jasper	Newton	Starke	
Dubois	Jay	Noble	Steuben	

IOWA (IA) (99 counties)
Capital: Des Moines

Adair	Clay	Hancock	Madison	Sac
Adams	Clayton	Hardin	Mahaska	Scott
Allamakee	Clinton	Harrison	Marion	Shelby
Appanoose	Crawford	Henry	Marshall	Sioux
Audubon	Dallas	Howard	Mills	Story
Benton	Davis	Humboldt	Mitchell	Tama
Black Hawk	Decatur	Ida	Monona	Taylor
Boone	Delaware	Iowa	Monroe	Union
Bremer	Des Moines	Jackson	Montgomery	Van Buren
Buchanan	Dickinson	Jasper	Muscatine	Wapello
Buena Vista	Dubuque	Jefferson	O'Brien	Warren
Butler	Emmet	Johnson	Osceola	Washington
Calhoun	Fayette	Jones	Page	Wayne
Carroll	Floyd	Keokuk	Palo Alto	Webster
Cass	Franklin	Kossuth	Plymouth	Winnebago
Cedar	Fremont	Lee	Pocahontas	Winneshiek
Cerro Gordo	Greene	Linn	Polk	Woodbury
Cherokee	Grundy	Louisa	Pottawattamie	Worth
Chickasaw	Guthrie	Lucas	Poweshiek	Wright
Clarke	Hamilton	Lyon	Ringgold	

KANSAS (KS) (105 counties)
Capital: Topeka

Allen	Doniphan	Jackson	Morris	Saline
Anderson	Douglas	Jefferson	Morton	Scott
Atchison	Edwards	Jewell	Nemaha	Sedgwick
Barber	Elk	Johnson	Neosho	Seward
Barton	Ellis	Kearny	Ness	Shawnee
Bourbon	Ellsworth	Kingman	Norton	Sheridan
Brown	Finney	Kiowa	Osage	Sherman
Butler	Ford	Labette	Osborne	Smith
Chase	Franklin	Lane	Ottawa	Stafford
Chautauqua	Geary	Leavenworth	Pawnee	Stanton
Cherokee	Gove	Lincoln	Phillips	Stevens
Cheyenne	Graham	Linn	Pottawatomie	Sumner
Clark	Grant	Logan	Pratt	Thomas
Clay	Gray	Lyon	Rawlins	Trego
Cloud	Greeley	McPherson	Reno	Wabaunsee
Coffey	Greenwood	Marion	Republic	Wallace
Comanche	Hamilton	Marshall	Rice	Washington
Cowley	Harper	Meade	Riley	Wichita
Crawford	Harvey	Miami	Rooks	Wilson
Decatur	Haskell	Mitchell	Rush	Woodson
Dickinson	Hodgeman	Montgomery	Russell	Wyandotte

KENTUCKY (KY) (120 counties)
Capital: Frankfort

Adair	Caldwell	Estill	Harrison	Lee
Allen	Calloway	Fayette	Hart	Leslie
Anderson	Campbell	Fleming	Henderson	Letcher
Ballard	Carlisle	Floyd	Henry	Lewis
Barren	Carroll	Franklin	Hickman	Lincoln
Bath	Carter	Fulton	Hopkins	Livingston
Bell	Casey	Gallatin	Jackson	Logan
Boone	Christian	Garrard	Jefferson	Lyon
Bourbon	Clark	Grant	Jessamine	McCracken
Boyd	Clay	Graves	Johnson	McCreary
Boyle	Clinton	Grayson	Kenton	McLean
Bracken	Crittenden	Green	Knott	Madison
Breathitt	Cumberland	Greenup	Knox	Magoffin
Breckinridge	Daviess	Hancock	Larue	Marion
Bullitt	Edmonson	Hardin	Laurel	Marshall
Butler	Elliott	Harlan	Lawrence	Martin

Mason	Muhlenberg	Perry	Scott	Union
Meade	Nelson	Pike	Shelby	Warren
Menifee	Nicholas	Powell	Simpson	Washington
Mercer	Ohio	Pulaski	Spencer	Wayne
Metcalfe	Oldham	Robertson	Taylor	Webster
Monroe	Owen	Rockcastle	Todd	Whitley
Montgomery	Owsley	Rowan	Trigg	Wolfe
Morgan	Pendleton	Russell	Trimble	Woodford

LOUISIANA (LA) (64 parishes)
Capital: Baton Rouge

Acadia	Concordia	Lafayette	Richland	Terrebonne
Allen	De Soto	Lafourche	Sabine	Union
Ascension	East Baton	La Salle	St. Bernard	Vermilion
Assumption	Rouge	Lincoln	St. Charles	Vernon
Avoyelles	East Carroll	Livingston	St. Helena	Washington
Beauregard	East Feliciana	Madison	St. James	Webster
Bienville	Evangeline	Morehouse	St. John the	West Baton
Bossier	Franklin	Natchitoches	Baptist	Rouge
Caddo	Grant	Orleans	St. Landry	West Carroll
Calcasieu	Iberia	Ouachita	St. Martin	West Feliciana
Caldwell	Iberville	Plaquemines	St. Mary	Winn
Cameron	Jackson	Pointe Coupee	St. Tammany	
Catahoula	Jefferson	Rapides	Tangipahoa	
Claiborne	Jefferson Davis	Red River	Tensas	

MAINE (ME) (16 counties)
Capital: Augusta

Androscoggin	Hancock	Oxford	Somerset
Aroostook	Kennebec	Penobscot	Waldo
Cumberland	Knox	Piscataquis	Washington
Franklin	Lincoln	Sagadahoc	York

MARSHALL ISLANDS (MH) (33 municipalities)
Capital: Majuro

Ailinginae	Bokak	Kili	Mejit	Ujae
Ailinglaplap	Ebon	Kwajalein	Mili	Ujelang
Ailuk	Enewetak	Lae	Namorik	Utirik
Arno	Erikub	Lib	Namu	Wotho
Aur	Jabat	Likiep	Rongelap	Wotje
Bikar	Jaluit	Majuro	Rongrik	
Bikini	Jemo	Maloelap	Toke	

MARYLAND (MD) (24 counties)
Capital: Annapolis

Allegany	Carroll	Garrett	Prince	Talbot
Anne Arundel	Cecil	Harford	George's	Washington
Baltimore	Charles	Howard	Queen Anne's	Wicomico
Calvert	Dorchester	Kent	St. Mary's	Worcester
Caroline	Frederick	Montgomery	Somerset	Baltimore city

MASSACHUSETTS (MA) (14 counties)
Capital: Boston

Barnstable	Dukes	Hampden	Nantucket	Suffolk
Berkshire	Essex	Hampshire	Norfolk	Worcester
Bristol	Franklin	Middlesex	Plymouth	

MICHIGAN (MI) (83 counties)
Capital: Lansing

Alcona	Clare	Iosco	Marquette	Otsego
Alger	Clinton	Iron	Mason	Ottawa
Allegan	Crawford	Isabella	Mecosta	Presque Isle
Alpena	Delta	Jackson	Menominee	Roscommon
Antrim	Dickinson	Kalamazoo	Midland	Saginaw
Arenac	Eaton	Kalkaska	Missaukee	St. Clair
Baraga	Emmet	Kent	Monroe	St. Joseph
Barry	Genesee	Keweenaw	Montcalm	Sanilac
Bay	Gladwin	Lake	Montmorency	Schoolcraft
Benzie	Gogebic	Lapeer	Muskegon	Shiawassee
Berrien	Grand Traverse	Leelanau	Newaygo	Tuscola
Branch	Gratiot	Lenawee	Oakland	Van Buren
Calhoun	Hillsdale	Livingston	Oceana	Washtenaw
Cass	Houghton	Luce	Ogemaw	Wayne
Charlevoix	Huron	Mackinac	Ontonagon	Wexford
Cheboygan	Ingham	Macomb	Osceola	
Chippewa	Ionia	Manistee	Oscoda	

MINNESOTA (MN) (87 counties)
Capital: St. Paul

Aitkin	Brown	Clearwater	Faribault	Hubbard
Anoka	Carlton	Cook	Fillmore	Isanti
Becker	Carver	Cottonwood	Freeborn	Itasca
Beltrami	Cass	Crow Wing	Goodhue	Jackson
Benton	Chippewa	Dakota	Grant	Kanabec
Big Stone	Chisago	Dodge	Hennepin	Kandiyohi
Blue Earth	Clay	Douglas	Houston	Kittson

Koochiching	Martin	Pennington	Roseau	Wabasha
Lac qui Parle	Meeker	Pine	St. Louis	Wadena
Lake	Mille Lacs	Pipestone	Scott	Waseca
Lake of the	Morrison	Polk	Sherburne	Washington
Woods	Mower	Pope	Sibley	Watonwan
Le Sueur	Murray	Ramsey	Stearns	Wilkin
Lincoln	Nicollet	Red Lake	Steele	Winona
Lyon	Nobles	Redwood	Stevens	Wright
McLeod	Norman	Renville	Swift	Yellow
Mahnomen	Olmsted	Rice	Todd	Medicine
Marshall	Otter Tail	Rock	Traverse	

MISSISSIPPI (MS) (82 counties)
Capital: Jackson

Adams	Forrest	Kemper	Noxubee	Tate
Alcorn	Franklin	Lafayette	Oktibbeha	Tippah
Amite	George	Lamar	Panola	Tishomingo
Attala	Greene	Lauderdale	Pearl River	Tunica
Benton	Grenada	Lawrence	Perry	Union
Bolivar	Hancock	Leake	Pike	Walthall
Calhoun	Harrison	Lee	Pontotoc	Warren
Carroll	Hinds	Leflore	Prentiss	Washington
Chickasaw	Holmes	Lincoln	Quitman	Wayne
Choctaw	Humphreys	Lowndes	Rankin	Webster
Claiborne	Issaquena	Madison	Scott	Wilkinson
Clarke	Itawamba	Marion	Sharkey	Winston
Clay	Jackson	Marshall	Simpson	Yalobusha
Coahoma	Jasper	Monroe	Smith	Yazoo
Copiah	Jefferson	Montgomery	Stone	
Covington	Jefferson Davis	Neshoba	Sunflower	
DeSoto	Jones	Newton	Tallahatchie	

MISSOURI (MO) (115 counties)
Capital: Jefferson City

Adair	Boone	Cass	Crawford	Gasconade
Andrew	Buchanan	Cedar	Dade	Gentry
Atchison	Butler	Chariton	Dallas	Greene
Audrain	Caldwell	Christian	Daviess	Grundy
Barry	Callaway	Clark	DeKalb	Harrison
Barton	Camden	Clay	Dent	Henry
Bates	Cape Girardeau	Clinton	Douglas	Hickory
Benton	Carroll	Cole	Dunklin	Holt
Bollinger	Carter	Cooper	Franklin	Howard

Howell	McDonald	Nodaway	Randolph	Shelby
Iron	Macon	Oregon	Ray	Stoddard
Jackson	Madison	Osage	Reynolds	Stone
Jasper	Maries	Ozark	Ripley	Sullivan
Jefferson	Marion	Pemiscot	St. Charles	Taney
Johnson	Mercer	Perry	St. Clair	Texas
Knox	Miller	Pettis	Ste. Genevieve	Vernon
Laclede	Mississippi	Phelps	St. Francois	Warren
Lafayette	Moniteau	Pike	St. Louis	Washington
Lawrence	Monroe	Platte	Saline	Wayne
Lewis	Montgomery	Polk	Schuyler	Webster
Lincoln	Morgan	Pulaski	Scotland	Worth
Linn	New Madrid	Putnam	Scott	Wright
Livingston	Newton	Ralls	Shannon	St. Louis City

MONTANA (MT) (56 counties)
Capital: Helena

Beaverhead	Fallon	Lewis and Clark	Phillips	Stillwater
Big Horn	Fergus		Pondera	Sweet Grass
Blaine	Flathead	Liberty	Powder River	Teton
Broadwater	Gallatin	Lincoln	Powell	Toole
Carbon	Garfield	McCone	Prairie	Treasure
Carter	Glacier	Madison	Ravalli	Valley
Cascade	Golden Valley	Meagher	Richland	Wheatland
Chouteau	Granite	Mineral	Roosevelt	Wibaux
Custer	Hill	Missoula	Rosebud	Yellowstone
Daniels	Jefferson	Musselshell	Sanders	Yellowstone National Park
Dawson	Judith Basin	Park	Sheridan	
Deer Lodge	Lake	Petroleum	Silver Bow	

NEBRASKA (NE) (93 counties)
Capital: Lincoln

Adams	Butler	Dawes	Gage	Holt
Antelope	Cass	Dawson	Garden	Hooker
Arthur	Cedar	Deuel	Garfield	Howard
Banner	Chase	Dixon	Gosper	Jefferson
Blaine	Cherry	Dodge	Grant	Johnson
Boone	Cheyenne	Douglas	Greeley	Kearney
Box Butte	Clay	Dundy	Hall	Keith
Boyd	Colfax	Fillmore	Hamilton	Keya Paha
Brown	Cuming	Franklin	Harlan	Kimball
Buffalo	Custer	Frontier	Hayes	Knox
Burt	Dakota	Furnas	Hitchcock	Lancaster

Lincoln	Nemaha	Polk	Seward	Valley
Logan	Nuckolls	Red Willow	Sheridan	Washington
Loup	Otoe	Richardson	Sherman	Wayne
McPherson	Pawnee	Rock	Sioux	Webster
Madison	Perkins	Saline	Stanton	Wheeler
Merrick	Phelps	Sarpy	Thayer	York
Morrill	Pierce	Saunders	Thomas	
Nance	Platte	Scotts Bluff	Thurston	

NEVADA (NV) (17 counties)
Capital: Carson City

Churchill	Esmeralda	Lincoln	Pershing	Carson City
Clark	Eureka	Lyon	Storey	City
Douglas	Humboldt	Mineral	Washoe	
Elko	Lander	Nye	White Pine	

NEW HAMPSHIRE (NH) (10 counties)
Capital: Concord

| Belknap | Cheshire | Grafton | Merrimack | Strafford |
| Carroll | Coos | Hillsborough | Rockingham | Sullivan |

NEW JERSEY (NJ) (21 counties)
Capital: Trenton

Atlantic	Cumberland	Mercer	Passaic	Warren
Bergen	Essex	Middlesex	Salem	
Burlington	Gloucester	Monmouth	Somerset	
Camden	Hudson	Morris	Sussex	
Cape May	Hunterdon	Ocean	Union	

NEW MEXICO (NM) (33 counties)
Capital: Santa Fe

Bernalillo	Dona Ana	Lincoln	Rio Arriba	Socorro
Catron	Eddy	Los Alamos	Roosevelt	Taos
Chaves	Grant	Luna	Sandoval	Torrance
Cibola	Guadalupe	McKinley	San Juan	Union
Colfax	Harding	Mora	San Miguel	Valencia
Curry	Hidalgo	Otero	Santa Fe	
De Baca	Lea	Quay	Sierra	

NEW YORK (NY) (62 counties)
Capital: Albany

Albany	Dutchess	Madison	Putnam	Sullivan
Allegany	Erie	Monroe	Queens	Tioga
Bronx	Essex	Montgomery	Rensselaer	Tompkins
Broome	Franklin	Nassau	Richmond	Ulster
Cattaraugus	Fulton	New York	Rockland	Warren
Cayuga	Genesee	Niagara	St. Lawrence	Washington
Chautauqua	Greene	Oneida	Saratoga	Wayne
Chemung	Hamilton	Onondaga	Schenectady	Westchester
Chenango	Herkimer	Ontario	Schoharie	Wyoming
Clinton	Jefferson	Orange	Schuyler	Yates
Columbia	Kings	Orleans	Seneca	
Cortland	Lewis	Oswego	Steuben	
Delaware	Livingston	Otsego	Suffolk	

NORTH CAROLINA (NC) (100 counties)
Capital: Raleigh

Alamance	Chowan	Guilford	Mitchell	Rutherford
Alexander	Clay	Halifax	Montgomery	Sampson
Alleghany	Cleveland	Harnett	Moore	Scotland
Anson	Columbus	Haywood	Nash	Stanly
Ashe	Craven	Henderson	New Hanover	Stokes
Avery	Cumberland	Hertford	Northampton	Surry
Beaufort	Currituck	Hoke	Onslow	Swain
Bertie	Dare	Hyde	Orange	Transylvania
Bladen	Davidson	Iredell	Pamlico	Tyrrell
Brunswick	Davie	Jackson	Pasquotank	Union
Buncombe	Duplin	Johnston	Pender	Vance
Burke	Durham	Jones	Perquimans	Wake
Cabarrus	Edgecombe	Lee	Person	Warren
Caldwell	Forsyth	Lenoir	Pitt	Washington
Camden	Franklin	Lincoln	Polk	Watauga
Carteret	Gaston	McDowell	Randolph	Wayne
Caswell	Gates	Macon	Richmond	Wilkes
Catawba	Graham	Madison	Robeson	Wilson
Chatham	Granville	Martin	Rockingham	Yadkin
Cherokee	Greene	Mecklenburg	Rowan	Yancey

NORTH DAKOTA (ND) (53 counties)
Capital: Bismarck

Adams	Divide	LaMoure	Pembina	Stark
Barnes	Dunn	Logan	Pierce	Steele
Benson	Eddy	McHenry	Ramsey	Stutsman
Billings	Emmons	McIntosh	Ransom	Towner
Bottineau	Foster	McKenzie	Renville	Traill
Bowman	Golden Valley	McLean	Richland	Walsh
Burke	Grand Forks	Mercer	Rolette	Ward
Burleigh	Grant	Morton	Sargent	Wells
Cass	Griggs	Mountrail	Sheridan	Williams
Cavalier	Hettinger	Nelson	Sioux	
Dickey	Kidder	Oliver	Slope	

NORTHERN MARIANA ISLANDS (MP) (4 municipalities)
Capital: Saipan

Northern Islands	Rota	Saipan	Tinian

OHIO (OH) (88 counties)
Capital: Columbus

Adams	Darke	Hocking	Miami	Scioto
Allen	Defiance	Holmes	Monroe	Seneca
Ashland	Delaware	Huron	Montgomery	Shelby
Ashtabula	Erie	Jackson	Morgan	Stark
Athens	Fairfield	Jefferson	Morrow	Summit
Auglaize	Fayette	Knox	Muskingum	Trumbull
Belmont	Franklin	Lake	Noble	Tuscarawas
Brown	Fulton	Lawrence	Ottawa	Union
Butler	Gallia	Licking	Paulding	Van Wert
Carroll	Geauga	Logan	Perry	Vinton
Champaign	Greene	Lorain	Pickaway	Warren
Clark	Guernsey	Lucas	Pike	Washington
Clermont	Hamilton	Madison	Portage	Wayne
Clinton	Hancock	Mahoning	Preble	Williams
Columbiana	Hardin	Marion	Putnam	Wood
Coshocton	Harrison	Medina	Richland	Wyandot
Crawford	Henry	Meigs	Ross	
Cuyahoga	Highland	Mercer	Sandusky	

OKLAHOMA (OK) (77 counties)
Capital: Oklahoma City

Adair	Cotton	Jackson	Mayes	Roger Mills
Alfalfa	Craig	Jefferson	Murray	Rogers
Atoka	Creek	Johnston	Muskogee	Seminole
Beaver	Custer	Kay	Noble	Sequoyah
Beckham	Delaware	Kingfisher	Nowata	Stephens
Blaine	Dewey	Kiowa	Okfuskee	Texas
Bryan	Ellis	Latimer	Oklahoma	Tillman
Caddo	Garfield	Le Flore	Okmulgee	Tulsa
Canadian	Garvin	Lincoln	Osage	Wagoner
Carter	Grady	Logan	Ottawa	Washington
Cherokee	Grant	Love	Pawnee	Washita
Choctaw	Greer	McClain	Payne	Woods
Cimarron	Harmon	McCurtain	Pittsburg	Woodward
Cleveland	Harper	McIntosh	Pontotoc	
Coal	Haskell	Major	Pottawatomie	
Comanche	Hughes	Marshall	Pushmataha	

OREGON (OR) (36 counties)
Capital: Salem

Baker	Deschutes	Josephine	Morrow	Wasco
Benton	Douglas	Klamath	Multnomah	Washington
Clackamas	Gilliam	Lake	Polk	Wheeler
Clatsop	Grant	Lane	Sherman	Yamhill
Columbia	Harney	Lincoln	Tillamook	
Coos	Hood River	Linn	Umatilla	
Crook	Jackson	Malheur	Union	
Curry	Jefferson	Marion	Wallowa	

PALAU (PW) (16 States)
Capital: Melekeok

Aimeliik	Kayangel	Ngarchelong	Ngeremlengui
Airai	Koror	Ngardmau	Ngiwal
Angaur	Melekeok	Ngatpang	Peleliu
Hatohobei	Ngaraard	Ngchesar	Sonsorol

PENNSYLVANIA (PA) (67 counties)
Capital: Harrisburg

Adams	Beaver	Blair	Butler	Carbon
Allegheny	Bedford	Bradford	Cambria	Centre
Armstrong	Berks	Bucks	Cameron	Chester

Clarion	Forest	Lebanon	Northumber-land	Tioga
Clearfield	Franklin	Lehigh	Perry	Union
Clinton	Fulton	Luzerne	Philadelphia	Venango
Columbia	Greene	Lycoming	Pike	Warren
Crawford	Huntingdon	McKean	Potter	Washington
Cumberland	Indiana	Mercer	Schuylkill	Wayne
Dauphin	Jefferson	Mifflin	Snyder	Westmoreland
Delaware	Juniata	Monroe	Somerset	Wyoming
Elk	Lackawanna	Montgomery	Sullivan	York
Erie	Lancaster	Montour	Susquehanna	
Fayette	Lawrence	Northampton		

PUERTO RICO (PR) (78 municipios)
Capital: San Juan

Adjuntas	Cataño	Gurabo	Maunabo	San Juan
Aguada	Cayey	Hatillo	Mayagüez	San Lorenzo
Aguadilla	Ceiba	Hormigueros	Moca	San Sebastián
Aguas Buenas	Ciales	Humacao	Morovis	Santa Isabel
Aibonito	Cidra	Isabela	Naguabo	Toa Alta
Añasco	Coamo	Jayuya	Naranjito	Toa Baja
Arecibo	Comerío	Juana Díaz	Orocovis	Trujillo Alto
Arroyo	Corozal	Juncos	Patillas	Utuado
Barceloneta	Culebra	Lajas	Peñuelas	Vega Alta
Barranquitas	Dorado	Lares	Ponce	Vega Baja
Bayamón	Fajardo	Las Marías	Quebradillas	Vieques
Cabo Rojo	Florida	Las Piedras	Rincón	Villalba
Caguas	Guánica	Loíza	Río Grande	Yabucoa
Camuy	Guayama	Luquillo	Sabana Grande	Yauco
Canóvanas	Guayanilla	Manatí	Salinas	
Carolina	Guaynabo	Maricao	San Germán	

RHODE ISLAND (RI) (5 counties)
Capital: Providence

Bristol	Kent	Newport	Providence	Washington

SOUTH CAROLINA (SC) (46 counties)
Capital: Columbia

Abbeville	Beaufort	Chesterfield	Edgefield	Hampton
Aiken	Berkeley	Clarendon	Fairfield	Horry
Allendale	Calhoun	Colleton	Florence	Jasper
Anderson	Charleston	Darlington	Georgetown	Kershaw
Bamberg	Cherokee	Dillon	Greenville	Lancaster
Barnwell	Chester	Dorchester	Greenwood	Laurens

Lee	Marlboro	Pickens	Sumter
Lexington	Newberry	Richland	Union
McCormick	Oconee	Saluda	Williamsburg
Marion	Orangeburg	Spartanburg	York

SOUTH DAKOTA (SD) (66 counties)
Capital: Pierre

Aurora	Corson	Hand	McCook	Spink
Beadle	Custer	Hanson	McPherson	Stanley
Bennett	Davison	Harding	Marshall	Sully
Bon Homme	Day	Hughes	Meade	Todd
Brookings	Deuel	Hutchinson	Mellette	Tripp
Brown	Dewey	Hyde	Miner	Turner
Brule	Douglas	Jackson	Minnehaha	Union
Buffalo	Edmunds	Jerauld	Moody	Walworth
Butte	Fall River	Jones	Pennington	Yankton
Campbell	Faulk	Kingsbury	Perkins	Ziebach
Charles Mix	Grant	Lake	Potter	
Clark	Gregory	Lawrence	Roberts	
Clay	Haakon	Lincoln	Sanborn	
Codington	Hamlin	Lyman	Shannon	

TENNESSEE (TN) (95 counties)
Capital: Nashville

Anderson	Decatur	Henderson	Marion	Sequatchie
Bedford	DeKalb	Henry	Marshall	Sevier
Benton	Dickson	Hickman	Maury	Shelby
Bledsoe	Dyer	Houston	Meigs	Smith
Blount	Fayette	Humphreys	Monroe	Stewart
Bradley	Fentress	Jackson	Montgomery	Sullivan
Campbell	Franklin	Jefferson	Moore	Sumner
Cannon	Gibson	Johnson	Morgan	Tipton
Carroll	Giles	Knox	Obion	Trousdale
Carter	Grainger	Lake	Overton	Unicoi
Cheatham	Greene	Lauderdale	Perry	Union
Chester	Grundy	Lawrence	Pickett	Van Buren
Claiborne	Hamblen	Lewis	Polk	Warren
Clay	Hamilton	Lincoln	Putnam	Washington
Cocke	Hancock	Loudon	Rhea	Wayne
Coffee	Hardeman	McMinn	Roane	Weakley
Crockett	Hardin	McNairy	Robertson	White
Cumberland	Hawkins	Macon	Rutherford	Williamson
Davidson	Haywood	Madison	Scott	Wilson

TEXAS (TX) (254 counties)
Capital: Austin

Anderson	Coke	Freestone	Jasper	Matagorda
Andrews	Coleman	Frio	Jeff Davis	Maverick
Angelina	Collin	Gaines	Jefferson	Medina
Aransas	Collingsworth	Galveston	Jim Hogg	Menard
Archer	Colorado	Garza	Jim Wells	Midland
Armstrong	Comal	Gillespie	Johnson	Milam
Atascosa	Comanche	Glasscock	Jones	Mills
Austin	Concho	Goliad	Karnes	Mitchell
Bailey	Cooke	Gonzales	Kaufman	Montague
Bandera	Coryell	Gray	Kendall	Montgomery
Bastrop	Cottle	Grayson	Kenedy	Moore
Baylor	Crane	Gregg	Kent	Morris
Bee	Crockett	Grimes	Kerr	Motley
Bell	Crosby	Guadalupe	Kimble	Nacogdoches
Bexar	Culberson	Hale	King	Navarro
Blanco	Dallam	Hall	Kinney	Newton
Borden	Dallas	Hamilton	Kleberg	Nolan
Bosque	Dawson	Hansford	Knox	Nueces
Bowie	Deaf Smith	Hardeman	Lamar	Ochiltree
Brazoria	Delta	Hardin	Lamb	Oldham
Brazos	Denton	Harris	Lampasas	Orange
Brewster	DeWitt	Harrison	La Salle	Palo Pinto
Briscoe	Dickens	Hartley	Lavaca	Panola
Brooks	Dimmit	Haskell	Lee	Parker
Brown	Donley	Hays	Leon	Parmer
Burleson	Duval	Hemphill	Liberty	Pecos
Burnet	Eastland	Henderson	Limestone	Polk
Caldwell	Ector	Hidalgo	Lipscomb	Potter
Calhoun	Edwards	Hill	Live Oak	Presidio
Callahan	Ellis	Hockley	Llano	Rains
Cameron	El Paso	Hood	Loving	Randall
Camp	Erath	Hopkins	Lubbock	Reagan
Carson	Falls	Houston	Lynn	Real
Cass	Fannin	Howard	McCulloch	Red River
Castro	Fayette	Hudspeth	McLennan	Reeves
Chambers	Fisher	Hunt	McMullen	Refugio
Cherokee	Floyd	Hutchinson	Madison	Roberts
Childress	Foard	Irion	Marion	Robertson
Clay	Fort Bend	Jack	Martin	Rockwall
Cochran	Franklin	Jackson	Mason	Runnels

Rusk	Smith	Terry	Van Zandt	Willacy
Sabine	Somervell	Throckmorton	Victoria	Williamson
San Augustine	Starr	Titus	Walker	Wilson
San Jacinto	Stephens	Tom Green	Waller	Winkler
San Patricio	Sterling	Travis	Ward	Wise
San Saba	Stonewall	Trinity	Washington	Wood
Schleicher	Sutton	Tyler	Webb	Yoakum
Scurry	Swisher	Upshur	Wharton	Young
Shackelford	Tarrant	Upton	Wheeler	Zapata
Shelby	Taylor	Uvalde	Wichita	Zavala
Sherman	Terrell	Val Verde	Wilbarger	

UTAH (UT) (29 counties)
Capital: Salt Lake City

Beaver	Duchesne	Kane	San Juan	Utah
Box Elder	Emery	Millard	Sanpete	Wasatch
Cache	Garfield	Morgan	Sevier	Washington
Carbon	Grand	Piute	Summit	Wayne
Daggett	Iron	Rich	Tooele	Weber
Davis	Juab	Salt Lake	Uintah	

VERMONT (VT) (14 counties)
Capital: Montpelier

Addison	Chittenden	Grand Isle	Orleans	Windham
Bennington	Essex	Lamoille	Rutland	Windsor
Caledonia	Franklin	Orange	Washington	

VIRGIN ISLANDS (VI) (3 islands)
Capital: Charlotte Amalie

| St. Croix | St. John | St. Thomas |

VIRGINIA (VA) (95 counties)
Capital: Richmond

Accomack	Bedford	Charles City	Essex	Goochland
Albemarle	Bland	Charlotte	Fairfax	Grayson
Alleghany	Botetourt	Chesterfield	Fauquier	Greene
Amelia	Brunswick	Clarke	Floyd	Greensville
Amherst	Buchanan	Craig	Fluvanna	Halifax
Appomattox	Buckingham	Culpeper	Franklin	Hanover
Arlington	Campbell	Cumberland	Frederick	Henrico
Augusta	Caroline	Dickenson	Giles	Henry
Bath	Carroll	Dinwiddie	Gloucester	Highland

Isle of Wight	Madison	Orange	Richmond	Stafford
James City	Mathews	Page	Roanoke	Surry
King and	Mecklenburg	Patrick	Rockbridge	Sussex
Queen	Middlesex	Pittsylvania	Rockingham	Tazewell
King George	Montgomery	Powhatan	Russell	Warren
King William	Nelson	Prince Edward	Scott	Washington
Lancaster	New Kent	Prince George	Shenandoah	Westmoreland
Lee	Northampton	Prince William	Smyth	Wise
Loudoun	Northumber-	Pulaski	Southampton	Wythe
Louisa	land	Rappahannock	Spotsylvania	York
Lunenburg	Nottoway			

WASHINGTON (WA) (39 counties)
Capital: Olympia

Adams	Douglas	King	Pacific	Stevens
Asotin	Ferry	Kitsap	Pend Oreille	Thurston
Benton	Franklin	Kittitas	Pierce	Wahkiakum
Chelan	Garfield	Klickitat	San Juan	Walla Walla
Clallam	Grant	Lewis	Skagit	Whatcom
Clark	Grays Harbor	Lincoln	Skamania	Whitman
Columbia	Island	Mason	Snohomish	Yakima
Cowlitz	Jefferson	Okanogan	Spokane	

WEST VIRGINIA (WV) (55 counties)
Capital: Charleston

Barbour	Grant	Logan	Nicholas	Summers
Berkeley	Greenbrier	McDowell	Ohio	Taylor
Boone	Hampshire	Marion	Pendleton	Tucker
Braxton	Hancock	Marshall	Pleasants	Tyler
Brooke	Hardy	Mason	Pocahontas	Upshur
Cabell	Harrison	Mercer	Preston	Wayne
Calhoun	Jackson	Mineral	Putnam	Webster
Clay	Jefferson	Mingo	Raleigh	Wetzel
Doddridge	Kanawha	Monongalia	Randolph	Wirt
Fayette	Lewis	Monroe	Ritchie	Wood
Gilmer	Lincoln	Morgan	Roane	Wyoming

WISCONSIN (WI) (72 counties)
Capital: Madison

Adams	Douglas	Kewaunee	Ozaukee	Taylor
Ashland	Dunn	La Crosse	Pepin	Trempealeau
Barron	Eau Claire	Lafayette	Pierce	Vernon
Bayfield	Florence	Langlade	Polk	Vilas
Brown	Fond du Lac	Lincoln	Portage	Walworth
Buffalo	Forest	Manitowoc	Price	Washburn
Burnett	Grant	Marathon	Racine	Washington
Calumet	Green	Marinette	Richland	Waukesha
Chippewa	Green Lake	Marquette	Rock	Waupaca
Clark	Iowa	Menominee	Rusk	Waushara
Columbia	Iron	Milwaukee	St. Croix	Winnebago
Crawford	Jackson	Monroe	Sauk	Wood
Dane	Jefferson	Oconto	Sawyer	
Dodge	Juneau	Oneida	Shawano	
Door	Kenosha	Outagamie	Sheboygan	

WYOMING (WY) (23 counties)
Capital: Cheyenne

Albany	Crook	Laramie	Platte	Uinta
Big Horn	Fremont	Lincoln	Sheridan	Washakie
Campbell	Goshen	Natrona	Sublette	Weston
Carbon	Hot Springs	Niobrara	Sweetwater	
Converse	Johnson	Park	Teton	

Common misspellings

Geographers and cartographers omit the possessive apostrophe in placenames; however, apostrophes appearing in legally constituted names of counties should not be changed.

The names of the following counties are often misspelled and/or confused:

Allegany in Maryland and New York
Alleghany in North Carolina and Virginia
Allegheny in Pennsylvania
Andrew in Missouri
Andrews in Texas
Aransas in Texas
Arkansas in Arkansas
Barber in Kansas
Barbour in Alabama and West Virginia
Brevard in Florida
Broward in Florida

Brooke in West Virginia
Brooks in Georgia and Texas
Bulloch in Georgia
Bullock in Alabama
Burnet in Texas
Burnett in Wisconsin
Cheboygan in Michigan
Sheboygan in Wisconsin
Clarke in Alabama, Georgia, Iowa, Mississippi, and Virginia
Clark in all other States

Coffee in Alabama, Georgia, and
   Tennessee
Coffey in Kansas
Coal in Oklahoma
Cole in Missouri
Coles in Illinois
Cook in Illinois and Minnesota
Cooke in Texas
Davidson in North Carolina and
   Tennessee
Davie in North Carolina
Daviess in Indiana, Kentucky,
   and Missouri
Davis in Iowa and Utah
Davison in South Dakota
DeKalb all one word
Dickenson in Virginia
Dickinson in Iowa, Kansas, and
   Michigan
Dickson in Tennessee
Forrest in Mississippi
Forest in all other States
Glascock in Georgia
Glasscock in Texas
Green in Kentucky and Wisconsin
Greene in all other States
Harford in Maryland
Hartford in Connecticut
Huntingdon in Pennsylvania
Huntington in Indiana
Johnston in North Carolina and
   Oklahoma
Johnson in all other States
Kanabec in Minnesota
Kennebec in Maine
Kearney in Nebraska
Kearny in Kansas
Kenedy in Texas
Linn in Iowa, Kansas, Missouri,
   and Oregon
Lynn in Texas
Loudon in Tennessee
Loudoun in Virginia

Manatee in Florida
Manistee in Michigan
Merced in California
Mercer in all other States
Morton in Kansas
Norton in Kansas
Muscogee in Georgia
Muskogee in Oklahoma
Park in Colorado and Montana
Parke in Indiana
Pottawatomie in Kansas and
   Oklahoma
Pottawattamie in Iowa
Prince George in Virginia
Prince George's in Maryland
Sanders in Montana
Saunders in Nebraska
Smyth in Virginia
Smith in all other States
Stafford in Virginia
Strafford in New Hampshire
Stanley in South Dakota
Stanly in North Carolina
Stark in Illinois, North Dakota,
   and Ohio
Starke in Indiana
Stephens in Georgia, Oklahoma,
   and Texas
Stevens in Kansas, Minnesota,
   and Washington
Storey in Nevada
Story in Iowa
Terrell in Georgia and Texas
Tyrrell in North Carolina
Tooele in Utah
Toole in Montana
Vermillion in Indiana
Vermilion in all other States
Woods in Oklahoma
Wood in all other States
Wyandot in Ohio
Wyandotte in Kansas

19. Congressional Record

Code of laws of the United States and rules for publication of the Congressional Record

TITLE 44, SECTION 901. CONGRESSIONAL RECORD: ARRANGEMENT, STYLE, CONTENTS, AND INDEXES.—The Joint Committee on Printing shall control the arrangement and style of the Congressional Record, and while providing that it shall be substantially a verbatim report of proceedings, shall take all needed action for the reduction of unnecessary bulk. It shall provide for the publication of an index of the Congressional Record semimonthly during and at the close of sessions of Congress.

TITLE 44, SECTION 904. CONGRESSIONAL RECORD: MAPS, DIAGRAMS, ILLUSTRATIONS.—Maps, diagrams, or illustrations may not be inserted in the Record without the approval of the Joint Committee on Printing.

General rules

The rules governing document work (FIC & punc.) apply to the Congressional Record, except as may be noted herein. The same general style should be followed in the permanent (bound) Record as is used in the daily Record. It is important to be familiar with the exceptions and the forms peculiar to the Record.

Much of the data printed in the Congressional Record is forwarded to GPO using the captured keystrokes of the floor reporters. Element identifier codes are programmatically inserted, and galley output is accomplished without manual intervention. It is not cost-effective to prepare the accompanying manuscript as per the GPO STYLE MANUAL, and it is too time-consuming to update and change the data once it is already in type form. Therefore, the Record is to be FIC & punc. Because of its volume, it is not necessary to stamp the manuscript FIC & punc. However, Record style will be followed, as stated in the following rules:

Daily and permanent Record texts are set in 8-point type on a 9-point body. Extracts are set in 7-point type on an 8-point body.

An F-dash will be used preceding 8-point cap lines in the proceedings of the Senate and House.

All 7-point extracts and poetry will carry 2 points of space above and below unless heads appear, which generate their own space.

All extracts are set 7 point unless otherwise ordered by the Joint Committee on Printing.

Except as noted below, all communications from the President must be set in 8 point, but if such communications contain extracts, etc., the extracts are set in 7 point.

An address of the President delivered outside of Congress or referred to as an extract is set in 7 point.

A letter from the President to the Senate is set in 7 point when any form of treaty is enclosed that is to be printed in the Record in connection therewith. The letter is set in 7 point whether the treaty follows or precedes it or is separated from it by intervening matter.

In all quoted amendments and excerpts of bills and in reprinting bills, the style and manuscript as printed in the bill will be followed.

Except where otherwise directed, profanity, obscene wording, or extreme vulgarisms are to be deleted and a 3-em dash substituted.

Floor-approved statements in a foreign language, will be printed following their English translation.

Extreme caution must be used in making corrections in manuscript, and no important change will be made without proper authorization.

Observe the lists of names of Senators, Representatives, and Delegates, committees of both Houses, and duplicate names. Changes caused by death, resignation, or otherwise must be noted. There is no excuse for error in the spelling of names of Senators, Representatives, or department officials. In case of doubt, the Congressional Directory will be the authority.

Datelines should be followed on Extensions of Remarks. If any question arises as to the proper date to be used, a supervisor must be consulted.

Indented matter in leaderwork will be 1 em only.

Do not write queries on proofs.

Capitalization
(See also Chapter 3 "Capitalization Rules")

If the name of the Congressional Record is mentioned, it must be set in caps and small caps and never abbreviated, even when appearing in citations, except in extract matter, then cap/lowercase.

The name of a Senator or a Representative preceding his or her direct remarks is set in caps and is followed by a period with equal spacing to be used.

The name of a Senator or a Representative used in connection with a bill or other paper—that is, in an adjectival sense—is lowercased, as the Engel bill, the Fish amendment, etc.; but UDALL's amendment, etc.

The names of Members and Members-elect of both Houses of the Congress, including those of the Vice President and Speaker, will be printed in caps and small caps if mention is made of them, except in extract matter.

Deceased Members' names will be set in caps and small caps in eulogies only on the first day the House or Senate is in session following the death of a Member, in a speech carrying date when the Member was eulogized, or on memorial day in the Senate and House. Eulogy day in one House will be treated the same in the other.

Certificates of Senators-elect of a succeeding Congress are usually presented to the current Congress, and in such cases the names of the Senators-elect must be in caps and small caps.

Names of Members of Congress must be set in caps and lowercase in votes, in lists set in columns, in the list of standing and select committees, in contested-election cases, in lists of pairs, and in all parts of tabular matter (head, body, and footnotes).

Observe that the names of all persons not certified Members of Congress are to be set in caps and lowercase; that is, names of secretaries, clerks, messengers, and others.

Names of proposed Federal boards, commissions, services, etc., are capitalized.

Capitalize principal words and quote after each of the following terms: *address, album, article, book, caption, chapter heading, editorial, essay, heading, headline, motion picture* or *play* (including TV or radio program), *paper, poem, report, song, subheading, subject, theme,* etc. Also, following the word *entitled*, except with reference to bill titles which are treated as follows: "A bill (or an act) transferring certain functions of the Price Administrator to the Petroleum Administrator for War," etc.

Figures

Follow the manuscript as to the use of numerals. Dollar amounts in Record manuscript are to be followed.

Figures appearing in manuscript as "20 billion 428 million 125 thousand dollars" should be followed.

Tabular matter and leaderwork

Record tables may be set either one or three columns in width, as follows:

One-column table: 14 picas (168 points).

Three-column table: 43½ picas (522 points). Footnote(s) will be set 43½ picas.

All short footnotes should be run in with 2 ems between each.

Italic

Italic, boldface, caps, or small caps shall not be used for emphasis; nor shall unusual indentions be used. This does not apply to literally reproduced quotations from historical, legal, or official documents. If italic other than restricted herein is desired, the words should be underscored and "Fol. ital." written on each folio. Do not construe this to apply to *"Provided," "Provided further," "Ordered," "Resolved," "Be it enacted,"* etc.

Names of vessels must be set in italic, except in headings, where they will be quoted.

The prayer delivered in either House must be set in 8-point roman. If prefaced or followed by a quotation from the Bible, such quotation must be set in 8-point italic. Extracts from the Bible or other literature contained in the body of the prayer will be set in 8-point roman and quoted.

When general or passing mention is made of a case in 8 point, the title is set in roman, as Smith Bros. case. When a specific citation is indicated and reference follows, use italic for title, as *Smith Bros.* case (172 App. Div. 149).

In 8-point manuscript, titles of cases are always set in italic if followed by references. In 7 point, manuscript is followed.

In 8-point matter, when only the title of a case is given, set in roman, as United States versus 12 Diamond Rings.

When *versus* is used in other than legal phrases and for the purposes of showing contrast, it is not abbreviated or set in italic, as "airplanes versus battleships."

Miscellaneous

Do not quote any communication carrying date and signature. However, a letter (or other communication) bearing both date and signature that appears within a letter shall be quoted.

Do not put quotation marks on centerheads in 7-point extracts unless centerheads belong to original matter.

In newspaper extracts, insert place and date at beginning of paragraph. Use caps and small caps for name of place and roman lowercase for spelled-out date. Connect date and extract by a period and an em dash. If date and place are credited in a bracket line above extract, they need not be used again at the beginning of the paragraph.

Each *Whereas* in a preamble must begin a new paragraph. The *Therefore be it* must be preceded by a colon and be run in with the last *Whereas*. *Be it* will run in with the word *Therefore, but* it must not be supplied when not in manuscript. Note the following:

Whereas it has been deemed advisable   *Resolved,* That the committee, etc.
to, etc.: Therefore be it

In the titles of legal cases, manuscript is followed as to spelling, abbreviations, and use of figures.

Use single punctuation in citations of cases and statutes:

United States v. *12 Diamond Rings* (124 U.S. 329; R.S. p. 310, sec. 1748).

Indent asterisk lines 2 ems on each side. Use five asterisks.

If a title is used as part of the name of an organization, vessel, etc., spell; thus, General Ulysses S. Grant Post No. 76, Grand Army of the Republic.

The order of subdivision of the Constitution of the United States is as follows: article I, section 2, clause 3.

If an exhibit appears at the end of a speech, the head *Exhibit* is set in 7-point caps and small caps.

In extracts containing votes the names must be run in, as Mr. Smith of Texas, AuCoin, and Clay, etc.

In a Senator's or a Representative's remarks, when amendments, sections, etc., are referred to by number, follow the manuscript.

In text references to Senate and House reports and in executive and miscellaneous documents, follow the manuscript.

In headings and text references to resolutions and memorials, follow the manuscript.

In gross or en gros

When a bill comes to final action, in the presentment of amendments collectively for a vote, either the term "*in gross*" or the French equivalent "*en gros*" may be used.

Examples of Congressional Record

USE OF CAPS AND SMALL CAPS

[Note the use of parentheses and brackets in the following examples. Each will be used as submitted, as long as they are consistent throughout.]

Mr. THUNE. (Name all caps when a Member or visitor addresses Senate or House.)

On motion by [or of] Mr. FRANKEN, it was, etc.

The VICE PRESIDENT resumed the chair.

The PRESIDING OFFICER (Mr. BLUNT). Is there objection?

The SPEAKER called the House to order.

Mr. HUDSON's amendment was adopted.

Mr. FARR. Madam Speaker, I yield to Mr. HOYER.

Mr. HOYER said: If not paired, I would vote "no" on this bill.

A MEMBER. And debate it afterward.

SEVERAL SENATORS. I object.

But: Several Senators addressed the Chair.

Mr. COATS, Mr. DONNELLY (and others). Let it be read.

The ACTING SECRETARY. In line 11, after the word "*Provided*", it is proposed, etc.

Mrs. CAPPS was recognized, and yielded her time to Mr. CÁRDENAS.

[When two Members from the same State have the same surname, full name is used.]

On motion of Ms. LINDA T. SÁNCHEZ of California . . .

On motion of Ms. LORETTA SANCHEZ of California . . .

Mr. DeSANTIS and Mr. MARIO DIAZ-BALART of Florida rose to a point of order.

The CHAIRMAN appointed Mr. POE and Mr. ISRAEL as conferees.

[Extracts that consist of colloquies will use caps and small caps for names of persons speaking, as shown below:]

Mr. DeFAZIO. I think this bill is so well understood that no time will be required for its discussion.

Ms. NORTON. Does this bill come from the Committee on Armed Services?

The SPEAKER. It does.

SPECIAL ORDERS GRANTED

By unanimous consent, permission to address the House, following the legislative and any special orders heretofore entered, was granted to:

Mr. HOYER, for 1 hour, on Wednesday, February 2.

Mr. ENGEL (at the request of Mr. HOYER), for 1 hour, on February 2.

(The following Members (at the request of Mr. KING of New York) and to revise and extend their remarks and include therein extraneous matter:)

Mrs. COMSTOCK, for 5 minutes, today.

Mr. HOLDING, for 5 minutes, today.

Mr. COFFMAN, for 60 minutes, today.

[Note the following double action:]

(Mr. HOYER asked and was given permission to extend his remarks at this point in the RECORD and to include extraneous matter.)

(Mr. HOYER addressed the House. His remarks will appear hereafter in the Extensions of Remarks.)

The SPEAKER pro tempore. Under a previous order of the House, the gentleman from Nebraska (Mr. FORTENBERRY) is recognized for 5 minutes.

(Mr. FORTENBERRY addressed the House. His remarks will appear hereafter in the Extensions of Remarks.)

PUNCTUATION

Mr. REID. Mr. President, I call up my amendment which is identified as "unprinted amendment No. 1296," and ask that it be stated.

The bill was reported to the Senate as amended, and the amendment was concurred in.

The bill was reported to the Senate without amendment, ordered to be engrossed for a third reading, read the third time, and passed.

The bill was ordered to be engrossed for a third reading, read the third time, and passed.

[Use this form when title of bill is given:]

The bill was ordered to be engrossed and read the third time, was read the third time, and passed.

The title was amended so as to read: "A bill for the relief of Maude S. Burman."

A motion to reconsider was laid on the table. [House.]

[Use this form when title of bill is not given:]

The bill was ordered to be engrossed and read a third time, was read the third time, and passed, and a motion to reconsider was laid on the table. [House.]

The bill was ordered to be engrossed and read a third time, and passed.

The amendments were ordered to be engrossed and the bill to be read a third time.

The amendment was agreed to, and the bill as amended was ordered to be engrossed and read a third time; and being engrossed, it was accordingly read the third time and passed.

There was no objection, and, by unanimous consent, the Senate proceeded . . .

The question was taken, and the motion was agreed to.

The question being taken, the motion was agreed to.

Ordered to lie on the table and to be printed.

Ms. EDWARDS. Mr. Chairman, I move to strike the requisite number of words.

(Ms. EDWARDS asked and was given permission to revise and extend her remarks.)

[Note use of interrogation mark in the following:]

Mr. NELSON. Mr. President, what does this mean?—

We have never received a dollar of this amount.

POM–376. A resolution adopted by the House of Representatives of the State of Rhode Island expressing its opposition to federal proposals to authorize increases in the size or weight of commercial motor vehicles; to the Committee on Commerce, Science, and Transportation.

HOUSE RESOLUTION NO. 8296

Whereas, The State of Rhode Island is committed to protecting the safety of motorists on its highways and to protecting taxpayers' investment in our highway infrastructure; and

Whereas, The General Assembly of the State of Rhode Island and Providence Plantations resolved jointly to urge the Congress of the United States to . . .

Resolved, That this House of Representatives of the State of Rhode Island and Providence Plantations hereby reaffirms its opposition to proposals, at all levels of government, that would authorize increases in the size and weight of commercial motor vehicles because of the impact that these increases would have on highway infrastructure, especially bridges; and be it further

Resolved, That the Secretary of State be and he hereby is authorized and directed to transmit duly certified copies of this resolution to the President and Vice President of the United States, the Speaker of the United States House of Representatives, the Majority Leader of the United States Senate and the Rhode Island Delegation to the Congress of the United States.

[Note use of italic in title of cases:]

. . . This is the occasion America did not have to consider what other options might guarantee maternal safety while protecting the unborn. This is our national opportunity to reconsider *Roe* v. *Wade*, 410 U.S. 113 (1973).

Roe against Wade and its companion case, *Doe* v. *Bolton*, 410 U.S. 179 (1973), granted abortion the elevated status of a fundamental constitutional right and invalidated almost all effective restrictions on abortion throughout the 9 months of pregnancy . . . .

PARENTHESES AND BRACKETS

[The use of parentheses and brackets will be followed as submitted for acronyms, symbols, or abbreviations.]

This legislation would exempt certain defined Central Intelligence Agency [CIA] operational files from the search and review process of the Freedom of Information Act [FOIA], thus permitting the Agency to respond much more quickly to those FOIA requests which are at all likely to result in the release of information.

Mr. HUFFMAN. Madam Speaker, I now yield 5 minutes to the gentleman from Indiana (Mr. HIGGINS).

(Mr. BUTTERFIELD asked and was given permission to revise and extend his remarks in the Record.)

Ms. MOORE. There is no "may not" about it. Here is the form in which they are printed.

Mr. DOYLE. I am in hopes we shall be able to secure a vote on the bill tonight.

["Vote! Vote!"]

Mr. HICE. The Chair rather gets me on that question. [Laughter.] I did not rise. [Cries of "Vote! Vote!"]

Mrs. CAPPS [one of the tellers]. I do not desire to press the point that no quorum has voted.

The CHAIRMAN [after a pause]. If no gentleman claims the floor, the Clerk will proceed with the reading of the bill.

Mr. HURD of Texas. Then he is endeavoring to restrict the liberty of the individual in the disbursement of his own money. [Applause on the Republican side.]

Mr. ELLISON. Mr. Speaker, I desire to ask unanimous consent that the time of the gentleman——[Cries of "Regular Order!"]

[Laughter.]

The SPEAKER. Is there objection to the consideration of this bill at this time? [After a pause.] There is no objection.

The CHAIRMAN [rapping with his gavel]. Debate is exhausted.

Mr. HURT of Virginia. Patrick Henry said:

Ceasar had his Brutus, Charles I his Cromwell, and George III——
[here he was interrupted by cries of "Treason, Treason"]
and George III may profit by their example. If this be treason, let us make the most of it!

(Mr. MILLER of Florida addressed the Committee [or House]. His remarks will appear hereafter in the Extensions of Remarks.)

[Names of Senators or Representatives appearing in remarks of other Members of Congress should be enclosed in brackets, except in listing of tellers or when some title other than "Mr." is used, as in the following examples:]

Mr. SCHUMER. Mr. President, I thank my friend from Rhode Island [Senator WHITEHOUSE] for that magnificent exchange of correspondence between the Hebrew congregation of Newport, RI, and President Washington.

May I say that Senator WHITEHOUSE, in his own bearing and substance, lives out the promise of religious freedom that our first President gave to all Americans.

Perhaps I should say I say that as one of the descendants of the Stock of Abraham who is privileged to be a Member of the Senate today. I thank Senator WHITEHOUSE. I thank Senator MORAN.

I am going to take the liberty, if I may, to speak for a few minutes while we are waiting for either Senator MURKOWSKI, Senators WARNER or MENENDEZ, who are going to read documents before I conclude.

[In Senate manuscript a Senator is referred to as "the Senator from —— [Mr. ——]." Do not supply name and brackets if name does not appear in manuscript.]

[Note that brackets are used only when *Mr.*, etc., appears in manuscript.]

[See also use of *Mr.*, *Mrs.*, *Miss*, *Ms.* in explanation of votes under "Pairs."]

VOTING IN THE HOUSE AND IN COMMITTEE OF THE WHOLE

[Note that a dash is used only when a comma is necessary to separate the ayes and noes. If only the ayes or the noes are given, no punctuation is to be used. If the word *and* is used to connect the ayes and noes, as *ayes 52 and noes 65*, or *52 ayes and 65 noes*, the dash is omitted after the word *were* or *being*.]

On the question of ordering the yeas and nays there were 18 ayes and 88 noes.

The House divided; and there were—ayes 52, noes 65.

So (no further count being called for) the amendment of Mr. SCOTT of Virginia was not agreed to.

So (two-thirds having voted in favor thereof) the rules were suspended, and the bill was passed.

So (two-thirds not having voted in favor thereof) the motion was rejected.

The CHAIRMAN. The gentleman raises the point of no quorum. The Chair will count. [After counting.]

Two hundred and seventeen present, a quorum. The noes have it, and the amendment is rejected.

The question being taken on the motion of Mr. HOYER to suspend the rules and pass the bill, it was agreed to (two-thirds voting in favor thereof).

So (the affirmative not being one-fifth of the whole vote) the yeas and nays were not ordered.

The question was taken by a viva voce vote, and the Speaker announced that two-thirds appeared to have voted in the affirmative and [after a pause] that the bill was passed.

The yeas and nays were ordered, there being 43 in the affirmative, more than one-fifth of the last vote.

The question being taken on Mr. SHELBY's motion, there were—ayes 18, noes 35.

The question being taken on concurring in the amendments of the Senate, there were—ayes 101, noes 5.

The question was taken; and on a division [demanded by Mr. HOYER] there were—ayes 17, noes 29.

Mr. HOYER. Mr. Chairman, I demand a recorded vote, and pending that, I make the point of order that a quorum is not present.

The CHAIRMAN. Evidently a quorum is not present.

The Chair announces that pursuant to clause 2, rule XXIII, he will vacate proceedings under the call when a quorum of the Committee appears.

Members will record their presence by electronic device.

The call was taken by electronic device.

□ 1715

[The above box followed by a four-digit number indicates floor time in the House (5:15 p.m.)]

QUORUM CALL VACATED

The CHAIRMAN. One hundred Members have appeared. A quorum of the Committee of the Whole is present. Pursuant to rule XXIII, clause 2, fur-

ther proceedings under the call shall be considered as vacated.

The Committee will resume its business.

The pending business is the demand of the gentleman from Minnesota [Mr. PAULSEN] for a recorded vote.

A recorded vote was refused.

So the amendment to the amendment offered as a substitute for the amendment was rejected.

The CHAIRMAN. The question is on the amendment offered by the gentleman from Pennsylvania [Mr. MEEHAN] as a substitute for the amendment offered by the gentlewoman from South Dakota [Mrs. NOEM].

The question was taken; and the Chairman announced that the noes appeared to have it.

RECORDED VOTE

Mr. MEEHAN. Mr. Chairman, I demand a recorded vote.

A recorded vote was ordered.

The vote was taken by electronic device, and there were—ayes 228, noes 188, answered "present" 1, not voting 47, as follows

[Roll No. 509]

AYES—228

Abraham	Ellmers (NC)	Huelskamp
Babin	Farenthold	Sensenbrenner
Brooks (AL)	Fincher	Walker
Brooks (IN)	Garrett	Westerman
Chabot	Goodlatte	Yoho
Curbelo (FL)	Hartzler	Zeldin

NOES—188

Adams	Matsui	Takano
Bonamici	McCollum	Van Hollen
DeGette	O'Rourke	Vargas
Deutch	Ryan (OH)	Veasey
Hastings	Sarbanes	Wilson (FL)
Langevin	Schakowsky	Yarmuth

ANSWERED "PRESENT"—1

Fleming

NOT VOTING—17

Bishop (UT)	Lipinski	Price (NC)
Duckworth	McKinley	Reichert
Gohmert	Nugent	Ross
Graves (LA)	Palazzo	Valadao

□ 1311

Mr. RYAN of Wisconsin changed his vote from "aye" to "no."

Ms. WASSERMAN SCHULTZ, Ms. ESHOO, and Ms. ROS-LEHTINEN changed their vote from "no" to "aye."

[The Speaker's vote is recorded only in the "Ayes" or "Noes." It is never recorded as "not voting."]

[If the Speaker votes, his name is not used, but at the end of the "yeas" or "nays," according to his vote, insert: "The Speaker."]

So the amendment offered as a substitute for the amendment was agreed to.

The result of the vote was announced as above recorded.

VOTING BY YEAS AND NAYS

Senate

QUORUM CALL

The clerk will call the roll.

The assistant legislative clerk proceeded to call the roll, and the following Senators entered the Chamber and answered to their names:

[Quorum No. 42]

Alexander	Murkowski	Tillis
Feinstein	Nelson	Udall
Grassley	Paul	Vitter
Hatch	Sullivan	Warner
Heinrich	Tester	Whitehouse
Kaine	Thune	Wicker

The PRESIDING OFFICER [Mr. SASSE]. A quorum is not present.

Mr. REID. Mr. President, I move that the Sergeant at Arms be instructed to require the attendance of absent Senators, and I ask for the yeas and nays on the motion.

THE PRESIDING OFFICER. Is there a sufficient second? There is a sufficient second.

The yeas and nays were ordered.

The PRESIDING OFFICER. The question is on agreeing to the motion of the Senator from Nevada. On this question the yeas and nays have been ordered, and the clerk will call the roll.

The Assistant legislative clerk called the roll.

Mr. DURBIN. I announce that the Senator from Ohio (Mr. BROWN), the Senator from Massachusetts (Mr. MARKEY), the Senator from Illinois (Mr. KIRK), the Senator from Arkansas (Mr. BOOZMAN), and the Senator from

Montana (Mr. TESTER) are necessarily absent.

Mr. CORNYN. The following Senators are necessarily absent: the Senator from Minnesota (Mr. FRANKLIN), the Senator from Nevada (Mr. HELLER), the Senator from South Carolina (Mr. GRAHAM), the Senator from New Hampshire (Mrs. SHAHEEN), the Senator from Arizona (Mr. MCCAIN), the Senator from Alaska (Ms. MURKOWSKI), the Senator from South Dakota (Mr. THUNE), the Senator from Louisiana (Mr. VITTER), and the Senator from Mississippi (Mr. WICKER).

Further, if present and voting, the Senator from Minnesota (Ms. KLOBUCHAR) would have voted "yea."

The result was announced—yeas 52, nays 40, as follows:

[Rollcall Vote No. 163 Leg.]

YEAS—76

Baldwin	Heitkamp	Pryor
Begich	Hirono	Reed
Bennet	Johnson (SD)	Reid
Blumenthal	Kaine	Rockefeller
Booker	Klobuchar	Sanders
Boxer	Landrieu	Schatz
Brown	Leahy	Schumer
Cantwell	Levin	Shaheen
Cardin	Manchin	Stabenow
Carper	Markey	Tester
Casey	McCaskill	Udall (CO)
Coons	Menendez	Udall (NM)
Durbin	Merkley	Walsh
Feinstein	Mikulski	Warner
Franken	Murphy	Warren
Gillibrand	Murray	Whitehouse
Hagan	Nelson	Wyden
Heinrich		

NAYS—10

Alexander	Flake	Murkowski
Ayotte	Graham	Paul
Boozman	Grassley	Portman
Burr	Heller	Risch
Coats	Hoeven	Rubio
Coburn	Inhofe	Scott
Cochran	Isakson	Sessions
Collins	Johanns	Shelby
Corker	Johnson (WI)	Thune
Cornyn	King	Toomey
Crapo	Kirk	Vitter
Cruz	Lee	Wicker
Enzi	McCain	
Fischer	McConnell	

NOT VOTING—14

Barrasso	Donnelly	Moran
Blunt	Harkin	Roberts
Chambliss	Hatch	

So the motion was agreed to.

PAIRS

[The word *with* must always be used in pairs in the House, not *and*; and manuscript must be altered to conform thereto, as Mr. Smith with Mr. Jones—*not* Mr. Smith and Mr. Jones. Note use of lowercase for names in list of pairs in House.]

The Clerk announced the following pairs:

On this vote:

Mr. Abraham for, with Mr. Aderholt against.

Until further notice:

Mr. Barr with Mrs. Beatty.

Mrs. Capps with Mr. Calvert.

Ms. Maxine Waters of California with Mr. Sean Patrick Maloney of New York.

Mr. Ackerman with Mr. Young of Alaska.

Mr. HANNA of New York, Mrs. BUSTOS, Messrs. FOSTER, HILL, and ISRAEL changed their votes from "nay" to "yea."

So the bill was passed.

The result of the vote was announced as above recorded.

A motion to reconsider was laid on the table.

Mr. BARR. Mr. Speaker, I voted, but, being paired with the gentlelady from Minnesota, Mrs. BEATTY, I withdraw my vote.

Ms. MAXINE WATERS of California. Mr. Speaker, I have a pair with the gentleman from New York, Mr. SEAN PATRICK MALONEY of New York, who, if present, would have voted "yea." I voted "nay." I withdraw my vote and vote "present."

[In House pairs do not use brackets when members are referred to by name. In Senate pairs observe the following use of brackets:]

Mr. DAWES (when his name was called). I am paired on this question with the senior Senator from Massachusetts [Mr. MARKEY]. If he were here, I should vote "yea."

CALL OF THE HOUSE

Mr. PALLONE. Ms. Speaker, I move a call of the House.

A call of the House was ordered.

The call was taken by electronic device and the following Members responded to their names:

[Roll No. 41]

Abraham	Garamendi	Tiberi
Aguilar	Hurd (TX)	Tipton
Brady (PA)	Hurd (VA)	Tonko
Brady (TX)	Neugebauer	Torres
Davis, Rodney	Perlmutter	Yoho
DeFazio	Ros-Lehtinen	Young (AK)

[No reference will be made of the names of those not voting.]

FORMS OF TITLES

[Always in roman lowercase, flush and hang 1 em, if more than two lines.]

H.J. RES. 2

Joint resolution authorizing the Secretary of the Treasury to issue to the public 2 per centum bonds or certificates, etc.

Resolved by the Senate and House of Representatives of the United States of America in Congress assembled, That the . . .

H.R. 4487

A bill to authorize the Rock Island and Southwestern Railway Company to construct a bridge, etc.

Be it enacted by the Senate and House of Representatives of the United States of

America in Congress assembled, That it shall be lawful for the Rock Island and Southwestern Railway Company, a corporation organized under the general incorporation, etc.

ADDRESSES AND SIGNATURES

[No line spacing, street addresses, or ZIP Code numbers are to be used in communications in the Record.]

The Honorable the SECRETARY OF THE ☐☐NAVY.

☐DEAR MR. SECRETARY: This is in response to your letter, etc.

☐☐☐Very sincerely yours,

GEORGE W. BUSH.☐

COLUMBIA, MO,☐☐☐
January 17, 2016.☐

Hon. CLAIRE MCCASKILL,
Cannon House Office Building,
Washington, DC.

☐The President's farm message of today . . . farmers and prevent the spread of this depression to every part of our country.

MISSOURI FARMERS
ASSOCIATION,
F.V. HEINKEL, *President.*

JANUARY 20, 2016.☐

Hon. JACOB J. LEW,
The Secretary of the Treasury, Department ☐☐of the Treasury, Washington, DC.

☐DEAR MR. SECRETARY: Mindful of the tremendous workload, etc.

I would appreciate your comment on the foregoing proposal.

Your proposal seems to be in the best interest of all concerned.

☐☐☐Sincerely yours,

JOHN P. SARBANES,☐☐☐
Member of Congress.☐☐

ALEXANDRIA, MN,☐☐☐
November 10, 2016.☐

Hon. AMY KLOBUCHAR,
Senate Office Building,
Washington, DC.

☐We oppose the nomination of John Smith for Secretary of Agriculture because he resists family farms.

RAYMOND WAGNER.☐

☐BRANDON, MN.

JANUARY 17, 1972.☐

Re resignation from committee.

Hon. CARL ALBERT,
The Speaker, U.S. House of Representa-☐☐tives, U.S. Capitol, Washington, DC.

☐DEAR MR. SPEAKER: Having changed my politics from Republican to Democrat, etc.

☐With my best wishes.

☐☐☐Sincerely,

VINCENT J. DELLAY.☐

U.S. SENATE,☐☐☐☐☐
PRESIDENT PRO TEMPORE,☐☐☐
Washington, DC, March 17, 2016.☐

To the Senate:

☐Being temporarily absent from the Senate, I appoint Hon. ROB PORTMAN, a Senator from the State of Montana, to perform the duties of the Chair during my absence.

ORRIN G. HATCH,☐☐☐
President pro tempore.☐

DESIGNATION OF SPEAKER PRO TEMPORE

☐The SPEAKER pro tempore laid before the House the following communication from the Speaker:

WASHINGTON, DC,☐☐☐
June 17, 2016.☐

☐I hereby appoint the Honorable KEN BUCK to act as Speaker pro tempore on this day.

PAUL D. RYAN,☐☐☐
Speaker of the House of Representatives.☐

☐☐THE INTERNATIONAL UNION, UNITED☐☐☐
☐☐☐AUTOMOBILE, AEROSPACE AND AGRI-☐☐☐
☐☐☐CULTURAL IMPLEMENT WORKERS OF☐☐☐
☐☐☐AMERICA,

Detroit, MI, March 25, 2016.☐

To the Senate of the United States.

To the United States House of Representa-☐☐tives.

☐HONORABLE SIRS: April 7, 2016, being the 60th anniversary of the modification, etc.

[Two to eight independent signatures, with or without titles, are aligned on the left.]

To the Honorable Senate and House of ☐☐Representatives of the United States of ☐☐America Now Assembled at Washington, ☐☐DC:

☐The undersigned, officers of the Navy of the United States, respectfully show unto your honorable bodies the following information, etc.

JAMES G. GREEN.
W.H. SOUTHERLAND.
THOMAS HARRISON.
F.F. FLETCHER.
ROBERT WHELAN.
C.C. WILSON.

———

☐Respectfully submitted,
KARL F. FELLER,
International President.☐
THOMAS RUSCH,
Director of Organization.☐
ARTHUR GILDEA,
Secretary-Treasurer.☐
JOSEPH E. BRADY,
Director of Legislation.☐

[More than eight signatures, with or without titles, are set full measure, caps and lowercase, run in, indented 2 and 3 ems, as follows:]

Gene H. Rosenblum, Cochairman; Paul H. Ray, Cochairman; Cynthia Asplund, James Pedersen, George Doty, Thomas St. Martin; Joan O'Neill; Lloyd Moosebrugger; Sam Kaplan; Ronald Nemer; Dean Potter; Philip Archer; Thomas McDonough; Mrs. Lloyd Moosebrugger; Minnesota Young Democratic Civil Rights Committee.

———

JOHN SMITH,☐☐☐☐☐
Lieutenant Governor☐☐☐
(For the Governor of Maine).☐

———

TEXARKANA TEXTILE
MERCHANTS &
MANUFACTURERS'
ASSOCIATION,
JOHN L. JONES,
Secretary.

CREDITS

[From the Wall Street Journal, Oct. 31, 2007]

SURVEILLANCE SANITY

(By Benjamin Civiletti, Dick Thornburgh and William Webster)

Following the terrorist attacks of Sept. 11, 2001, President Bush authorized the National Security Agency to target al Qaeda communications into and out of the country. Mr. Bush concluded that this was essential for protecting the country, that using the Foreign Intelligence Surveillance Act would not permit the necessary speed and agility, and that he had the constitutional power to authorize such surveillance without court orders to defend the country.

Since the program became public in 2006, Congress has been asserting appropriate oversight. Few of those who learned the details of the program have criticized its necessity. Instead, critics argued that if the president found FISA inadequate, he should have gone to Congress and gotten the changes necessary to allow the program to proceed under court orders. That process is now underway. The administration has brought the program under FISA, and the Senate Intelligence Committee recently reported out a bill with a strong bipartisan majority of 13–2, that would make the changes to FISA needed for the program to continue. This bill is now being considered by the Senate Judiciary Committee.

POETRY

[If poetry is quoted, each stanza should start with quotation marks, but only the last stanza should end with them. The lines of the poem should align on the left, those that rhyme taking the same indention. Poems are flush left; overs 3 ems; 2 points of space between stanzas, and 2 points of space above and below.]

CASEY AT THE BAT

The outlook wasn't brilliant for the Mudville nine that day:
The score stood four to two, with but one inning more to play.

And then when Cooney died at first, and Barrows did the same,
A pall-like silence fell upon the patrons of the game.

A straggling few got up to go in deep despair.
The rest clung to that hope which springs eternal in the human breast;
They thought, if only Casey could get but a whack at that—
We'd put up even money now, with Casey at the bat.

But Flynn preceded Casey, as did also Jimmy Blake,
And the former was a hoodoo and the latter was a cake;
So upon that stricken multitude grim melancholy sat,
For there seemed but little chance of Casey's getting to the bat.

But Flynn let drive a single, to the wonderment of all,
And Blake, the much despised, tore the cover off the ball;
And when the dust had lifted, and the men saw what had occurred,
There was Jimmy safe at second and Flynn a-hugging third.

Then from five thousand throats and more there rose a lusty yell;
It rumbled through the valley, it rattled in the dell;
It pounded on the mountain and recoiled upon the flat,
For Casey, mighty Casey, was advancing to the bat.

There was ease in Casey's manner as he stepped into his place;
There was pride in Casey's bearing and a smile lit Casey's face.
And when, responding to the cheers, he lightly doffed his hat,
No stranger in the crowd could doubt 'twas Casey at the bat.

Ten thousand eyes were on him as he rubbed his hands with dirt;
Five thousand tongues applauded when he wiped them on his shirt.
Then while the writhing pitcher ground the ball into his hip,
Defiance gleamed in Casey's eye, a sneer curled Casey's lip.

And now the leather-covered sphere came hurtling through the air,
And Casey stood a-watching it in haughty grandeur there.

Close by the sturdy batsman the ball unheeded sped—
"That ain't my style," said Casey. "Strike one," the umpire said.

From the benches, black with people, there went up a muffled roar,
Like the beating of the storm-waves on a stern and distant shore.
"Kill him! Kill the umpire!" shouted someone on the stand;
And it's likely they'd a-killed him had not Casey raised his hand.

With a smile of Christian charity great Casey's visage shone;
He stilled the rising tumult; he bade the game go on;
He signaled to the pitcher, and once more the dun sphere flew;
But Casey still ignored it, and the umpire said, "Strike two."

"Fraud!" cried the maddened thousands, and echo answered fraud;
But one scornful look from Casey and the audience was awed.
They saw his face grow stern and cold, they saw his muscles strain,
And they knew that Casey wouldn't let that ball go by again.

The sneer is gone from Casey's lip, his teeth are clenched in hate;
He pounds with cruel violence his bat upon the plate.
And now the pitcher holds the ball, and now he lets it go,
And now the air is shattered by the force of Casey's blow.

Oh, somewhere in this favored land the sun is shining bright;
The band is playing somewhere, and somewhere hearts are light,
And somewhere men are laughing, and somewhere children shout;
But there is no joy in Mudville—mighty Casey has struck out.

—Ernest Lawrence Thayer.

EXTRACTS

[Extracts must be set in 7 point unless ordered otherwise by the Joint Committee on Printing. This does not refer to a casual quotation of a few words or a quotation that would not make more than 3 lines of 7-point type. The beginning of the 7-point extract must start with a true paragraph; 8-point type following is always a paragraph.]

On February 29, Sue Payton, who is the Air Force's Assistant Secretary for Acquisition, said at a DOD news briefing:

We have been extremely open and

transparent. We have had a very thorough review of what we're doing. We've got it nailed.

A week later, she told the House Appropriations Subcommittee on Defense:

The Air Force followed a carefully structured source selection process,—

They what?

designed to provide transparency, maintain integrity, and ensure a fair competition.

And throughout the last 4 months, Air Force officials have insisted that they selected the cheapest plane that best met their criteria and that they made no mistakes.

[Note, as above, that following an excerpt, the 8 point must begin with a paragraph.]

[An address of the President delivered outside of Congress or referred to as an extract will be set in 7 point.]

SCHEME OF TEXT HEADINGS

[In 8-point, heads are 8-point caps. After the cap head, all sub heads are 7-point small caps, regardless of any perceived hierarchy.

[In 7-point, the progression is as follows (in descending order):

7-point caps and small caps.

7-point small caps.

7-point italic lowercase.

7-point roman caps and lowercase.

7-point roman lowercase.]

USE OF DOUBLE HEADS

This is something which has been entirely overlooked by the . . .

ANALYSIS OF SPECIFIC PROVISIONS OF THE COMMITTEE BILL

AMENDMENTS CHANGING THE INTERSTATE COMMERCE PROVISIONS OF THE ACE

As the law stands today, it applies only to an employee who . . .

EXECUTIVE PROGRAM

———

ESTATE TAX CONVENTION WITH CANADA

AMENDMENTS SUBMITTED

———

RECIPROCAL TRADE AGREEMENTS

———

WARREN AMENDMENT NO. 1194

HEADS USED IN EXTENSIONS OF REMARKS

VA ACCOUNTABILITY FIRST AND APPEALS MODERNIZATION ACT OF 2016

———

SPEECH OF

HON. CHRIS VAN HOLLEN

OF MARYLAND

IN THE HOUSE OF REPRESENTATIVES

Tuesday, September 13, 2016

The House in Committee of the Whole House on the state of the Union had under consideration the bill (H.R. 5620) to amend title 38, United States Code, to provide for the removal or demotion of employees of the Department of Veterans Affairs based on performance or misconduct, and for other purposes:

[The words "Speech of" are to be used only when on manuscript and is an indication that that particular Extension of Remarks is to be inserted in the proceedings of the bound Record of the date used in the heading.]

———

MISSING CHILDREN

———

HON. ORRIN G. HATCH

OF UTAH

IN THE SENATE OF THE UNITED STATES

Wednesday, February 3, 1999

Mr. HATCH. Mr. President, I rise before this distinguished assembly to focus additional attention on the tragedy of missing children. The Department of Health and Human Services has estimated that approximately 1.3 million children disappear each year. A significant number do not leave of their own accord. . . .

CONGRESSIONAL PROCEEDINGS

SENATE

TUESDAY, JULY 12, 2016

(Legislative day of Monday, July 11, 2016)[1]

The Senate met at 9:30 a.m., on the expiration of the recess, and was called to order by the Honorable LISA MERKOWSKI, a Senator from the State of Alaska.

[Above line to be used only when Senate had been in recess.]

The Senate met at 9:30 a.m., and was called to order by the Honorable JAMES LANKFORD, a Senator from the State of Oklahoma.

[Note.—Entire prayer set in 8 point.]

PRAYER

The Chaplain, Dr. Barry C. Black, offered the following prayer:

Let us pray.

Our Father in heaven, we thank You for the beautiful differences in the human family, for its varied shapes and sizes, its features and colors, its abilities and talents. Deliver us from the forces that would destroy our unity by eliminating our diversity.

Bless the Members of this body. Help them in their debates to distinguish between substance and semantics, between rhetoric and reality. Free them from personal and partisan preoccupations that would defeat their aspirations and deprive Americans of just and equitable solutions. May our lawmakers avoid the works of darkness and put on Your armor of light.

We pray in Your holy Name. Amen.

PLEDGE OF ALLEGIANCE

The Presiding Officer led the Pledge of Allegiance, as follows:

[1] To be used only when the Senate had been in recess.

I pledge allegiance to the Flag of the United States of America, and to the Republic for which it stands, one nation under God, indivisible, with liberty and justice for all.

APPOINTMENT OF ACTING PRESIDENT PRO TEMPORE

The PRESIDING OFFICER. The clerk will please read a communication to the Senate from the President pro tempore (Mr. HATCH).

The legislative clerk read the following letter:

U.S. SENATE,
PRESIDENT PRO TEMPORE,
Washington, DC, September 26, 2016.

To the Senate:

Under the provisions of rule I, section 3, of the Standing Rules of the Senate, I hereby appoint the Honorable JONI ERNST, a Senator from the State of Iowa, to perform the duties of the Chair.

ORRIN G. HATCH,
President pro tempore.

Mrs. ERNST thereupon assumed the chair as Acting President pro tempore.

RECOGNITION OF THE MAJORITY LEADER

The ACTING PRESIDENT pro tempore. The majority leader is recognized.

SCHEDULE

Mr. McCONNELL. Mr. President, following my remarks and those of Senator REID, there will be a period of morning business for 1 hour, with Senators permitted to speak therein for up to 10 minutes each. The majority will control the first 30 minutes;

the Republicans will control the second 30 minutes.

Following morning business, the Senate will resume consideration of the motion to proceed to S. 3044, the Consumer-First Energy Act. The first 4 hours of debate will be equally divided and controlled in 30-minute alternating blocks of time, with the majority controlling the first 30 minutes and Republicans controlling the next 30 minutes.

Upon conclusion of the controlled time, Senators will be permitted to speak for up to 10 minutes each.

As a reminder, yesterday, I filed cloture on the motion to proceed to S. 3101, the Medicare Improvements for Patients and Providers Act. That cloture vote will occur tomorrow morning.

RESERVATION OF LEADER TIME

The ACTING PRESIDENT pro tempore. Under the previous order, the leadership time is reserved.

MORNING BUSINESS

The ACTING PRESIDENT pro tempore. Under the previous order, the Senate will proceed to a period of morning business for up to 1 hour, with Senators permitted to speak therein for up to 10 minutes each, with the time equally divided and controlled between the two leaders or their designees, with the majority controlling the first half and the Republicans controlling the final half.

Ms. BALDWIN. Mr. President, I ask unanimous consent that the order for the quorum call be rescinded.

The PRESIDING OFFICER. Without objection, it is so ordered.

CONCLUSION OF MORNING BUSINESS

The PRESIDING OFFICER. Morning business is now closed.

LEGISLATIVE BRANCH APPROPRIATIONS ACT, 2017—MOTION TO PROCEED

The PRESIDING OFFICER. Under the previous order, the Senate will resume consideration of the motion to proceed to H.R. 5325, which the clerk will report.

The senior assistant legislative clerk read as follows:

Motion to proceed to Calendar No. 516, H.R. 5325, a bill making appropriations for the Legislative Branch for the fiscal year ending September 30, 2017, and for other purposes.

The PRESIDING OFFICER. The assistant Democratic leader.

ZIKA VIRUS FUNDING

Mr. DURBIN. Mr. President, I can still recall the first briefing I had as a Member of Congress on something called HIV/AIDS. . . .

LEGISLATIVE BRANCH APPROPRIATIONS ACT, 2017—MOTION TO PROCEED—Continued

[Note the use of bullets signifying that which was not spoken on the floor.]

ADDITIONAL STATEMENTS

TRIBUTE TO GEORGE TAKEI

● Ms. HIRONO. Mr. President, "Oh Myyy!" My friend George Takei is being honored with the National Asian Pacific American Bar Association's NAPABA, Inspire Award. In addition to his many contributions to the arts, George has been on the forefront for decades, fighting for those who don't have a voice. . . . ●

MESSAGES FROM THE PRESIDENT

Messages from the President of the United States were communicated to the Senate by Mr. Pate, one of his secretaries.

EXECUTIVE MESSAGES REFERRED

As in executive session the Presiding Officer laid before the Senate messages from the President of the United States submitting sundry nominations which were referred to the appropriate committees.

(The nominations received today are printed at the end of the Senate proceedings.)

REPORT OF THE VETO OF S. 2040, THE JUSTICE AGAINST SPONSORS OF TERRORISM ACT, RECEIVED DURING ADJOURNMENT OF THE SENATE ON SEPTEMBER 23, 2016—PM 56

The PRESIDING OFFICER laid before the Senate the following message from the President of the United States which was ordered to be printed in the RECORD, spread in full upon the Journal and held at the desk:

To the Senate of the United States:

I am returning herewith without my approval S. 2040, the "Justice Against Sponsors of Terrorism Act" (JASTA) . . . .

The JASTA, however, does not contribute to these goals, does not enhance the safety of Americans from terrorist attacks, and undermines core U.S. interests. For these reasons, I must veto the bill.

BARACK OBAMA.

THE WHITE HOUSE, *September 23, 2016.*

[The above to be 8 point.]
[When communications from the President contain extracts, etc., such extracts must be in 7 point.]

MESSAGES FROM THE HOUSE

At 12:21 p.m., a message from the House of Representatives, delivered by Mr. Novotny, one of its reading clerks, announced that the House has passed the following bill, with an amendment and an amendment to

the title, in which it requests the concurrence of the Senate:

S. 253. An act to amend the Communications Act of 1934 to consolidate the reporting obligations of the Federal Communications Commission in order to improve congressional oversight and reduce reporting burdens.

ENROLLED BILLS SIGNED

At 10:05 a.m., a message from the House of Representatives, delivered by Mr. Novotny, one of its reading clerks, announced that the Speaker has signed the following enrolled bill:

H.R. 5325. An act making continuing appropriations for fiscal year 2017, and for other purposes. The enrolled bill was subsequently signed by the President pro tempore (Mr. HATCH).

The President pro tempore (Mr. HATCH) announced that on today, September 29, 2016, he signed the following enrolled bills, which were previously signed by the Speaker of the House:

S. 1878. An act to extend the pediatric priority review voucher program.

S. 2683. An act to include disabled veteran leave in the personnel management system of the Federal Aviation Administration.

At 12:56 p.m., a message from the House of Representatives, delivered by Mr. Novotny, one of its reading clerks, announced that the House has passed the following bill, in which it requests the concurrence of the Senate:

H.R. 5303. An act to provide for improvements to the rivers and harbors of the United States, to provide for the conservation and development of water and related resources, and for other purposes.

MEASURES REFERRED

The following bills were read the first and the second times by unanimous consent, and referred as indicated:

H.R. 5065. An act to direct the Administrator of the Transportation Security Administration to notify air carriers and security screening personnel of the Transportation Security Administration of such Administration's guidelines regarding permitting baby formula, breast milk, purified deionized water, and juice on airplanes, and for other purposes, to the Committee on Commerce, Science, and Transportation.

MEASURES PLACED ON THE CALENDAR

The following bill was read the second time, and placed on the calendar:

S. 3326. A bill to give States the authority to provide temporary access to affordable private health insurance options outside of Obamacare exchanges.

MEASURES READ THE FIRST TIME

The following bill was read the first time:

H.R. 954. An act to amend the Internal Revenue Code of 1986 to exempt from the individual mandate certain individuals who had coverage under a terminated qualified health plan funded through the Consumer Operated and Oriented Plan (CO-OP) program.

ENROLLED BILL PRESENTED

The Secretary of the Senate reported that on September 12, 2016, she had presented to the President of the United States the following enrolled bill:

S. 2040. An act to deter terrorism, provide justice for victims, and for other purposes.

EXECUTIVE AND OTHER COMMUNICATIONS

The following communications were laid before the Senate, together with accompanying papers, reports, and documents, and were referred as indicated:

EC–7000. A communication from the Secretary of the Commodity Futures Trading Commission, transmitting, pursuant to law, the report of a rule entitled "System Safeguards Testing

Requirements for Derivatives Clearing Organizations" (RIN3038–AE29) received in the Office of the President of the Senate on September 21, 2016; to the Committee on. . . .

REPORT ON CLASSIFIED INFORMATION (S. DOC. NO. 107)

Mr. WARNER. Mr. President, the Committee on Armed Services of the Senate has recently requested the Office of Public Relations of the Department of the Navy to submit to it a report on classified information. The Department of the Navy has complied with the request, and I now present the report and ask that it be published as a Senate document.

The VICE PRESIDENT. Without objection, the report will be printed as a document as requested by the Senator from Virginia.

[Note the insertion of S. Doc. No. — in cases where papers are ordered to be printed as a document. To be inserted only when ordered to be printed or its equivalent is in manuscript.]

Third reading and passage of a bill.

MISSOURI RIVER BRIDGE NEAR ST. CHARLES, MO

The bill (S. 4174) to extend the times for commencing and completing the construction of a bridge across the Missouri River at or near St. Charles, MO, was considered, ordered to be engrossed for a third reading, read the third time, and passed, as follows:

S. 4174

Be it enacted by the Senate and House of Representatives of the United States of America in Congress assembled, That the times for commencing and completing the construction of the bridge across the Missouri River, etc.

GOVERNMENT OF THE TERRITORY OF HAWAII

The Senate proceeded to consider the bill (S. 1881) to amend an act entitled "An act to provide a government for the Territory of Hawaii," approved April 30, 1900, as amended, to establish a Hawaiian Homes Commission, and for other purposes, which had been reported from the Committee on Interior and Insular Affairs with amendments.

The first amendment was, on page 4 line 22, to strike out "Keaaupaha" and insert "Keaaukaha".

The amendment was agreed to.

The next amendment was, on page 6, line 19, after the figure "(1)", to insert "by further authorization of Congress and", so as to make the paragraph read:

(1) by further authorization of Congress and for a period of five years after the first meeting of the Hawaiian Homes Commission only those lands situated on the island of Molokaki, etc.

The Amendment was agreed to.

The bill was ordered to be engrossed for a third reading, read the third time, and passed.

Forms of amendments

The joint resolution (S.J. Res. 4) requesting the President to negotiate a treaty or treaties for the protection of salmon in retrain parts of the Pacific Ocean was announced as next in order.

Mr. INHOFE. Mr. President, I have just had an opportunity to examine this joint resolution. I offer this amendment.

The PRESIDING OFFICER. The Secretary will state the amendment offered by the Senator from Arizona.

The READING CLERK. On page 1, line 11, it is proposed to strike out the words "both within and", so as to make the joint resolution read:

Resolved by the Senate and House of Representatives of the United States of America in Congress assembled, That the President of the United States be, and he is hereby, requested to negotiate on behalf of the United States, as promptly as is practicable, etc.

Mr. McCONNELL. Mr. President, I observe in the report of the bill by the chairman of the Foreign Relations Committee that it is reported as a Senate joint resolution. I ask for a modification of it so that it will be a Senate resolution instead of a Senate joint resolution.

The LEGISLATIVE CLERK. It is proposed to strike out "S.J. Res. 4" and insert "S. Res. 85".

The PRESIDING OFFICER. Is there objection to the modification? The Chair hears one and it will be so modified.

Mr. INHOFE. Would it not be necessary to change the resolving clause also? The resolving clause reads:

Resolved by the Senate and House of Representatives of the United States of America in Congress assembled,

The amendment was agreed to.

[Note use of words, figures, and punctuation in the following example. Follow manuscript.]

The next amendment was, on page 34, in line 9, under the heading "Employees' Compensation Commission", before the word "assistants", to strike out "five" and insert "three"; in line 10, after the word "clerks" and before the words "of class 3", to strike out "seven" and insert "five"; in line 11, before the words "of class 2", to strike out "twelve" and insert "nine"; in the same line, before the words "of class 1", to strike out "twenty-seven" and insert "twenty"; in line 12, before the words "at $1.000 each", to strike out "three" and insert "two"; and in line 18, to strike out "$124,940" and insert "$102,590", so as to read:

EMPLOYEE'S COMPENSATION COMMISSION

Salaries: Three Commissioners at $4,000 each; secretary, $2,750; attorney, $4,000; chief statistician, $3,000; chief of accounts, $2,500; accountant, $2,250; claim examiners—chief $2,250, assistant $2,000, assistant $1,800, three assistants at $1,600 each; special agents—two at $1,800 each, two at $1,600 each; clerks—five of class 3, nine of class 2, twenty of class 1, two at $1,000 each; in all $102,590.

Mr. UDALL submitted an amendment intended to be proposed by him to the sundry civil appropriation bill, which was ordered to lie on the table and to be printed, as follows:

Add a new section, as follows: *"That the President of the Senate appoint three Members of the Senate; and the Speaker of the House three Members of the House."*

The Senate resumed the consideration of the bill (H.R. 4075) to limit the immigration of aliens into the United States.

[An executive session usually being open, the following precedes the recess or adjournment heading:]

REPORT ON THE STATE OF THE UNION DELIVERED TO A JOINT SESSION OF CONGRESS ON JANUARY 12, 2016—PM 36

The PRESIDING OFFICER laid before the Senate the following message from the President of the United States which was ordered to lie on the table.

To the Congress of the United States:

Mr. Speaker, Mr. Vice President, Members of Congress, my fellow Americans:

Tonight marks the eighth year I've come here to report on the State of the Union. And for this final one, I'm going to try to make it shorter. I know some of you are antsy to get back to Iowa. I also understand that because it's an election season, expectations for what we'll achieve this year are low. Still, Mr. Speaker, I appreciate the constructive approach you and the other leaders took at the end of last year to pass a budget and make tax cuts permanent for working families. So I hope we can work together this year on bipartisan priorities like criminal justice reform, and helping people who are battling prescription drug abuse. We just might surprise the cynics agains.

But tonight, I want to go easy on the traditional list of proposals for the year ahead. Don't worry, I've got plenty, from helping students learn to write computer code to personalizing medical treatments for patients. And I'll keep pushing for progress on the work that still needs doing. Fixing a broken immigration system. Protecting our kids from gun violence. Equal pay for equal work, paid leave, raising the minimum wage. All these things still matter to hardworking families; they are still the right thing to do; and I will not let up until they get done. . . .

That's the America I know. That's the country we love. Clear-eyed. Bighearted. Optimistic that unarmed truth and unconditional love will have the final word. That's what makes me so hopeful about our future. Because of you. I believe in you. That's why I stand here confident that the State of our Union is strong.

Thank you, God bless you, and God bless the United States of America.

BARACK OBAMA. ☐
THE WHITE HOUSE, *January 12, 2016.*

To the Senate of the United States:

To the end that I may receive the advice and consent of the Senate to ratification, I transmit herewith a treaty of arbitration and conciliation between the United States and Switzerland, signed at Washington on March 17, 1952.

HARRY S. TRUMAN. ☐
THE WHITE HOUSE, *March 17, 1952.*

[A letter from the President to the Senate is set in 7-point type when any form of treaty is encloses that is to be printed in the Record in connection therewith. The letter is set in 7-point type whether the treaty follows or precedes it or separated from it by intervening matter.]

RECESS UNTIL TOMORROW AT 10:30 A.M.

Mr. McCONNELL. Mr. President, I know of no further business to come before the Senate. I move, in accordance with the order previously entered, that the Senate stand in recess until the hour of 10:30 a.m. tomorrow.

The motion was agreed to and, at 7:34 p.m., the Senate recessed until Wednesday, June 5, 2016, at 10:30 a.m.

[After the recess or adjournment the following may appear:]

NOMINATIONS

Executive Nominations received by the Senate.

[Under the heads *Nominations, Confirmations, Withdrawal,* and *Rejection,* the following scheme for subheads is to be followed:

[Heads indicating service, or branch or department of Government and subheads

indicating subdivision or type of service—
7-point small caps.]

[Subheads indicating new rank of appointee—7-point italic initial cap.

[Text is set in 5-point caps.

[Note: Nominations will be set first name, middle name (or first middle initial), and last name throughout followed by period. Asterisks, if any, precede names as in executive nominations.]

Executive nominations received by the Senate:

NATIONAL FOUNDATION ON
THE ARTS AND THE HUMANITIES

JANE MARIE DOGGETT, OF MONTANA, TO BE A MEMBER OF THE NATIONAL COUNCIL ON THE HUMANITIES FOR A TERM EXPIRING JANUARY 26, 2022, VICE CATHY M. DAVIDSON, TERM EXPIRED.

STATE JUSTICE INSTITUTE

WILFREDO MARTINEZ, OF FLORIDA, TO BE A MEMBER OF THE BOARD OF DIRECTORS OF THE STATE JUSTICE INSTITUTE FOR A TERM EXPIRING SEPTEMBER 17, 2019. (REAPPOINTMENT)

IN THE NAVY

THE FOLLOWING NAMED OFFICER FOR APPOINTMENT IN THE UNITED STATES NAVY TO THE GRADE INDICATED WHILE ASSIGNED TO A POSITION OF IMPORTANCE AND RESPONSIBILITY UNDER TITLE 10, U.S.C., SECTION 601:

To be vice admiral

VICE ADMIN. DIXON R. SMITH

CONFIRMATIONS

Executive nominations confirmed by the Senate September 28, 2016:

IN THE AIR FORCE

THE FOLLOWING NAMED OFFICER FOR APPOINTMENT IN THE UNITED STATES AIR FORCE TO THE GRADE INDICATED UNDER TITLE 10, U.S.C., SECTION 624:

To be brigadier general

COL. KENNETH P. EKMAN

To be brigadier general

COL. ALFRED F. ABRAMSON III
COL. PETER B. ANDRYSIAK, JR.
COL. ROBERT W. BENNETT, JR.

HOUSE OF REPRESENTATIVES

FRIDAY, SEPTEMBER 9, 2016

[When the Speaker is in the Chair, follow this style.]

The House met at noon.

The Chaplain, the Reverend Patrick J. Conroy, offered the following prayer:

Merciful God, we give You thanks for giving us another day.

In this year of post-9/11, we pray that the children of this generation and their children's children may never have to experience another day like the one that flooded our TV screens so many years ago.

Protect and guide this Nation to a new security, built upon human integrity and communal solidarity with all who love freedom and human dignity, while respecting the lives and beliefs of others.

Empower the Members of Congress and governments around the world to establish just laws and seek the common good that will lead to ways of equity and peace.

May all that is done this day be for Your greater honor and glory.

Amen.

[When the Speaker is not in the Chair, follow this style.]

The House met at 12:30 and was called to order by the Speaker pro tempore (Mr. BOST).

DESIGNATION OF SPEAKER PRO TEMPORE

The SPEAKER pro tempore laid before the House the following communication from the Speaker:

WASHINGTON, DC,
June 17, 2016.

I hereby appoint the Honorable MIKE BOST to act as Speaker pro tempore on this day.

PAUL D. RYAN,
Speaker of the House of Representatives.

PRAYER[1]

The Chaplain, the Reverend Patrick J. Conroy, offered the following prayer:

We give You thanks, O God, for giving us another day. In the wake of a great American holiday, we ask Your special blessing on American workers, those fortunate to have jobs during these difficult economic times and those desiring work. May they know and be confident of the nobility and sacredness of their labor.

As the Members of the people's House return to the Capitol, call them, as well, with Your gentling voice of collegiality.

When a sense of alienation shadows all of our souls, we find our differences difficult to bear; we move away from each other. Insofar as this spirit of alienation has descended upon this House, help each Member to overcome unnecessary divisions that hamper productive work on behalf of our Nation.

Bring them to a deeper level of awareness of Your spirit, and make us one Nation. Give the Members listening hearts, ready and willing to respond to Your spirit living in each one.

And may all that is done be for Your greater honor and glory.

Amen.

THE JOURNAL

The SPEAKER pro tempore. The Chair has examined the Journal of the last day's proceedings and announces to the House his approval thereof.

Pursuant to clause 1, rule I, the Journal stands approved.

---

[1] Head is not used when the Speaker is in the chair. See preceding example.

PLEDGE OF ALLEGIANCE

The SPEAKER pro tempore. Will the gentleman from Iowa (Mr. BLUM) come forward and lead the House in the Pledge of Allegiance.

Mr. BLUM led the Pledge of Allegiance as follows:

I pledge allegiance to the Flag of the United States of America, and to the Republic for which it stands, one nation under God, indivisible, with liberty and justice for all.

SWEARING IN OF THE HONORABLE WARREN DAVIDSON, OF OHIO, AS A MEMBER OF THE HOUSE

Ms. KAPTUR. Mr. Speaker, I ask unanimous consent that the gentleman from Ohio, the Honorable WARREN DAVIDSON, be permitted to take the oath of office today.

His certificate of election has not arrived, but there is no contest and no question has been raised with regard to his election.

The SPEAKER. Is there objection to the request of the gentlewoman from Ohio?

There was no objection.

The SPEAKER. Will Representative-elect DAVIDSON and the members of the Ohio delegation present themselves in the well.

All Members will rise and the Representative-elect will please raise his right hand.

Mr. DAVIDSON appeared at the bar of the House and took the oath of office, as follows:

Do you solemnly swear that you will support and defend the Constitution of the United States against all enemies, foreign and domestic; that you will bear true faith and allegiance to the same; that you take this obligation freely, without any mental reservation or purpose of evasion; and that you will well and faithfully discharge the duties of the office on which you are about to enter, so help you God

The SPEAKER. Congratulations. You are now a Member of the 114th Congress.

WELCOMING THE HONORABLE WARREN DAVIDSON TO THE HOUSE OF REPRESENTATIVES

[Welcoming speeches follow.]
[Initial speech of new Representative follows.]

ANNOUNCEMENT BY THE SPEAKER

The SPEAKER. Under clause 5(d) of rule XX, the Chair announces to the House that, in light of the administration of the oath of office to the gentleman from Ohio (Mr. DAVIDSON), the whole number of the House is 435.

OATH OF OFFICE OF MEMBERS

The oath of office required by the sixth article of the Constitution of the United States, and as provided by section 2 of the act of May 13, 1884 (23 Stat. 22), to be administered to Members, Resident Commissioner, and Delegates or the House of Representatives, the text of which is carried in 5 U.S.C. 3331:

"I, AB, do solemnly swear (or affirm) that I will support and defend the Constitution of the united States against all enemies, foreign and domestic; that you will bear true faith and allegiance to the same; that you take this obligation freely, without and mental reservation or purpose of evasion; and that you will well and faithfully discharge the duties of the office on which you are about to enter, so help you God.

has been subscribed to in person and filed in duplicate with the Clerk of the House of Representatives by the following Member of the 110th Congress, pursuant to Public Law 412 of the 80th Congress entitled "An act to amend section 30 of the Revised Statues of the United States" (2 U.S.C. 25, approved February 18, 1948:

WARREN DAVIDSON, 8th District of Ohio.

MESSAGE FROM THE SENATE

A message from the Senate by Ms. Curtis, one of its clerks, announced that the Senate concurs in the amendment of the House to the bill (S. 2146) "An Act to authorize the Administrator of the Environmental Protection Agency to accept, as part of a settlement, diesel emission reduction Supplemental Environmental Projects, and for other purposes."

[Above usage occurs when there is only one bill referenced. For more than one bill, use the following style.]

MESSAGE FROM THE SENATE

A message from the Senate by Ms. Curtis, one of its clerks, announced that the Senate has passed without amendment a bill of the House of the following titles:

H.R. 3969. An act to designate the Department of Veterans Affairs community-based Outpatient clinic in Laughlin, Nevada, as the "Master Chief Petty Officer Jesse Dean VA Clinic".

[Observe that bills from the Senate to the House read *An act*. If the manuscript should read *A bill*, change to *An act* in conformity with this rule, and place number first. Note also the following forms:]

PRESIDENTIAL ALLOWANCE MODERNIZATION ACT OF 2016—VETO MESSAGE FROM THE PRESIDENT OF THE UNITED STATES (H. DOC. NO. 114–155)

The SPEAKER pro tempore laid before the House the following veto message from the President of the United States:

To the House of Representatives:

II am returning herewith without my approval H.R. 1777, the "Presidential Allowance Modernization Act of 2016," which would amend the Former Presidents Act of 1958.

I agree with H.R. 1777's goal of reforming the pensions and allowances provided to former Presidents so as to reduce unnecessary costs to taxpayers. But if implemented as drafted, the bill would have unintended consequences. It would impose onerous and unreasonable burdens on the offices of former Presidents, including by requiring the General Services Administration to immediately terminate salaries and benefits of office employees and to remove furnishings and equipment from offices. It would withdraw the General Services Administration's ability to administer leases and negatively impact operations, with unanticipated implications for the protection and security of former Presidents.

My Administration will work with the authors of the bill and other leaders in the Congress, in consultation with the offices of former Presidents, to explore the best ways to achieve these goals going forward. If the Congress returns the bill having appropriately addressed these concerns, I will sign it. For now, I must veto the bill.

BARACK OBAMA.

THE WHITE HOUSE, *July 22, 2016.*

The SPEAKER pro tempore. The objections of the President will be spread at large upon the Journal, and the veto message and the bill will be printed as a House document.

Without objection, further consideration of the veto message and the bill, H.R. 1777, is postponed until the legislative day of September 23, 2016.

There was no objection.

[Debate and vote follow.]

MESSAGE FROM THE PRESIDENT

A message in writing from the President of the United States was communicated to the House by Mr. Sherman Williams, one of his secretaries, who also informed the House that on the following dates the

President approved and signed bills of the House and Senate of the following titles:

On July 1, 1996:

H.R. 3029. An act to designate the United States courthouse in Washington, District of Columbia, as the "E. Barrett Prettyman United States Courthouse."

On July 2, 1996:

H.R. 2803. An act to amend the anti-car theft provisions of title 49, United States Code, to increase the utility of motor vehicle title information to the State and Federal law enforcement officials, and for other purposes.

On July 3, 1996:

H.R. 3525, An act amend title 18, United States Code, to clarify the Federal jurisdiction over offenses relating to damage to religious property. . . .

[Observe that bills coming from the President take the form of *An act*. This rule must be followed invariably, even if the manuscript reads *A bill*.]

MOURNING THE LOSS OF SHIMON PERES

(Mr. CICILLINE asked and was given permission to address the House for 1 minute.)

Mr. CICILLINE. Mr. Speaker, I rise to express my deep sadness on the passing of former Israeli President and Prime Minister Shimon Peres. Shimon Peres was devoted to the cause of the Jewish state and worked tirelessly to achieve a lasting peace in the Middle East.

He was the founding father of the State of Israel and remained, throughout his life, one of its greatest champions. He was the central architect of the Oslo Accords and was respected around the world for his strong leadership as Prime Minister and President of Israel. His example should be an inspiration to us all, as he fought so long for peace.

My thoughts are with his family and friends as well as the people of Israel, who have lost a beloved leader.

MRS. VIRGINIA THRIFT

Mr. GOSAR. Ms. Speaker, by direction of the Committee on House Administration, I offer a privileged resolution (H. Res. 321) and ask for its immediate consideration.

The Clerk read as follows:

H. Res. 321

Resolved, That there shall be paid out of the contingent fund of the House to Mrs. Virginia Thrift, late an employee of the House, an amount equal to six months' salary compensation at the rate he was receiving at the time of his death, and an additional amount not to exceed $250 to defray funeral expenses of the said Chester R. Thrift.

The Resolution was agreed to.

A motion to reconsider was laid on the table.

BILLS PRESENTED TO THE PRESIDENT

Karen L. Haas, Clerk of the House, reported that on February 23, 2016, she presented to the President of the United States, for his approval, the following bill:

H.R. 644. To reauthorize trade facilitation and trade enforcement functions and activities, and for other purposes.

ENROLLED BILLS SIGNED

Ms. Lorraine C. Miller, Clerk of the House, reported and found truly enrolled bills of the House of the following titles, which were thereupon signed by the Speaker:

H.R. 430. An act to designate the United States bankruptcy courthouse located at 271 Cadman Plaza East in Brooklyn, New York, as the "Conrad B. Duberstein United States Bankruptcy Courthouse".

H.R. 781. An act to redesignate Lock and Dam No. 5 of the McClellan-Kerr Arkansas River Navigation System near Redfield, Arkansas, authorized by the Rivers and Harbors Act approved July 24, 1946, as the "Colonel Charles D. Maynard Lock and Dam".

H.R. 1019. An act to designate the United States customhouse building located at 31 Gonzalez Clemente Avenue in Mayagüez, Puerto Rico, as the "Rafael Martinez Nadal United States Customhouse Building".

PRIVATE CALENDAR

The SPEAKER pro tempore (Mrs. BLACK). This is the day for the call of the Private Calendar.

The Clerk will call the bill on the calendar.

CORINA DE CHALUP TURCINOVIC

The Clerk called called the bill (H.R. 306) for the relief of Corina de Chalup Turcinovic.

There being no objection, the Clerk read the bill as follows:

H.R. 306

Be it enacted by the Senate and House of Representatives of the United States of America in Congress assembled,

SECTION 1. PERMANENT RESIDENT STATUS FOR CORINA DE CHALUP TURCINOVIC.

(a) IN GENERAL.—Notwithstanding subsections (a) and (b) of section 201 of the Immigration and Nationality Act, Corina de Chalup Turcinovic shall be eligible for issuance of an immigrant visa or for adjustment of status to that of an alien lawfully admitted for permanent residence upon filing an application for issuance of an immigrant visa under section 204 of such Act or for adjustment of status to lawful permanent resident. . . .

(e) DENIAL OF PREFERENTIAL IMMIGRATION TREATMENT FOR CERTAIN RELATIVES.—The natural parents, brothers, and sisters of Corina de Chalup Turcinovic shall not, by virtue of such relationship, be accorded any right, privilege, or status under the Immigration and Nationality Act.

The bill was ordered to be engrossed and read a third time, was read the third time,
and passed, and a motion to reconsider was laid on the table.

The SPEAKER pro tempore. This concludes the call of the Private Calendar.

SENATE BILLS REFERRED

Bills of the Senate of the following titles were taken from the Speaker's table and, under the rule, referred as follows:

S. 1479. An act to amend the Comprehensive Environmental Response, Compensation, and Liability Act of 1980 to modify provisions relating to grants, and for other purposes; to the Committee on Energy and Commerce; in addition, to the Committee on Transportation and Infrastructure for a period to be subsequently determined by the Speaker, in each case for consideration of such provisions as fall with the jurisdiction of the committee concerned.

S. 2829. An act to amend and enhance certain maritime programs of the Department of Transportation, and for other purposes; to the Committee on Armed Services; in addition, to the Committee on Transportation and Infrastructure; to the Committee on Natural Resources; to the Committee on Veterans' Affairs; to the Committee on the Judiciary; and to the Committee on Oversight and Government Reform for a period to be subsequently determined by the Speaker, in each case for consideration of such provisions as fall within the jurisdiction of the committee concerned.

[In the reference of Senate acts to House committees the name of the committee will be repeated after the act, though there may be several acts referred to the same committee.]

COMMITTEE OF THE WHOLE HOUSE ON THE STATE OF THE UNION

WATER RESOURCES DEVELOPMENT ACT OF 2016

The SPEAKER pro tempore. Pursuant to House Resolution 897 and rule XVIII, the Chair declares the House in the Committee of the Whole House on the state of the Union for the further consideration of the bill, H.R. 5303.

Will the gentleman from Illinois (Mr. HULTGREN) kindly take the chair.

□ 1535

IN THE COMMITTEE OF THE WHOLE

Accordingly, the House resolved itself into the Committee of the Whole House on the state of the Union for the further consideration of the bill (H.R. 5303) to provide for improvements to the rivers and harbors of the United States, to provide for the conservation and development of water and related resources, and for other purposes, with Mr. HULTGREN (Acting Chair) in the chair.

The Clerk read the title of the bill.

The Acting CHAIR. When the Committee of the Whole rose earlier today, amendment No. 10 printed in House Report 114–790 offered by the gentleman from Louisiana (Mr. GRAVES) had been disposed of.

Pursuant to House Resolution 897, no further amendment to the amendment in the nature of a substitute referred to in House Resolution 892 shall be in order except those printed in House Report 114–794.

Each such further amendment shall be considered only in the order printed in the report, may be offered only by a Member designated in the report, shall be considered as read, shall be debatable for the time specified in the report equally divided and controlled by the proponent and an opponent, shall not be subject to amendment, and shall not be subject to a demand for division of the question.

AMENDMENT NO. 1 OFFERED BY MR. BYRNE

The Acting CHAIR. It is now in order to consider amendment No. 1 printed in House Report 114–794.

Mr. BYRNE. Mr. Chairman, I have an amendment at the desk.

The Acting CHAIR. The Clerk will designate the amendment.

The text of the amendment is as follows:

At the end of title I, add the following:

SEC. 11. GULF COAST OYSTER BED RECOVERY ASSESSMENT. . . .

(Voting occurs)

The amendment was agreed to.

The Acting CHAIR. Under the rule, the Committee rises.

Accordingly, the Committee rose; and the Speaker pro tempore (Mr. YODER) having assumed the chair, Mr. EMMER of Minnesota, Acting Chair of the Committee of the Whole House on the state of the Union, reported that that Committee, having had under consideration the bill (H.R. 5303) to provide for improvements to the rivers and harbors of the United States, to provide for the conservation and development of water and related resources, and for other purposes, and, pursuant to House Resolution 897, he reported the bill back to the House with an amendment adopted in the Committee of the Whole.

The SPEAKER pro tempore. Under the rule, the previous question is ordered.

Is a separate vote demanded on any amendment to the amendment reported from the Committee of the Whole?

If not, the question is on the amendment in the nature of a substitute, as amended.

The amendment was agreed to.

The SPEAKER pro tempore. The question is on the engrossment and third reading of the bill.

The bill was ordered to be engrossed and read a third time, and was read the third time.

So the bill was passed.

The result of the vote was announced as above recorded.

A motion to reconsider was laid on the table.

CONFERENCE REPORT AND STATEMENT

Conference reports and statements to be set in 7 point.

Use 3-point space before and after conference report and statement.

In the House the names of Members are to be first.

Follow manuscript literally in the report. Observe the form *Amendments numbered 1, 2, 3, etc.,* and, when the amendment is to make an independent paragraph, the phrase *And the Senate* [or *House*] *agree to the same* will be a paragraph by itself; otherwise it will be run in after the amendment with a semicolon. Examples of each are given in the report following.

In the statement change *numbered* to *No.,* as *amendment No. 1,* but do not supply *No.* or *amendment* if omitted in manuscript; otherwise regular style will prevail.

CONFERENCE REPORT (H. REPT. 114–669)

The committee of conference on the disagreeing votes of the two Houses on the amendments of the House do the bill (S. 524), to authorize the Attorney General to award grants to address the national epidemics of prescription opioid abuse and heroin use, having met, after full and free conference, have agreed to recommend and do recommend to their respective Houses as follows:

That the Senate recede from its disagreement to the amendment of the House to the text of the bill and agree to the same with an amendment as follows:

In lieu of the matter proposed to be inserted by the House amendment, insert the following:

SECTION 1. SHORT TITLE; TABLE OF CONTENTS.

(a) SHORT TITLE.–This act may be cited as the "Comprehensive Addiction and Recovery Act of 2016".

(b) TABLE OF CONTENTS.–The table of contents for this Act is as follows:

Sec. 1. Short title; table of contents.

Title 1–PREVENTION AND EDUCATION

Sec. 101. Task force on pain management.

Sec. 102. Awareness campaigns. . . .

In lieu of the matter proposed to be inserted by the House amendment to the title of the bill, insert the following: "An Act to authorize the Attorney General and Secretary of Health and Human Services to award grants to address the prescription opioid abuse and heroin use crisis, and for other purposes.".

And the House agree to the same.

For consideration of the Senate bill and the House amendments, and modifications committed to conference:

FRED UPTON,
JOSEPH R. PITTS,
LEONARD LANCE,
BRETT GUTHRIE,
ADAM KINZINGER,
LARRY BUCSHON,
SUSAN W. BROOKS,
BOB GOODLATTE,
F. JAMES
SENSENBRENNER, JR.,
LAMAR SMITH,
TOM MARINO,
DOUG COLLINS,
DAVID A. TROTT,
MIKE BISHOP,
KEVIN MCCARTHY,

From the Committee on Education and the Workforce, for consideration of title VII of the House amendment, and modifications committed to conference:

LOU BARLETTA,
EARL L. "BUDDY"
CARTER,

From the Committee on Veterans' Affairs, for consideration of title III of the House amendment, and modifications committed to conference:

GUS M. BILIRAKIS,
JACKIE WALORSKI,

From the Committee on Ways and Means, for consideration of sec. 705 of the Senate bill, and sec. 804 of the House amendment, and modifications committed to conference:

PATRICK MEEHAN,
ROBERT J. DOLD,

Managers on the Part of the House.
CHUCK GRASSLEY,
LAMAR ALEXANDER,
ORRIN G. HATCH,
JEFF SESSIONS,
Managers on the Part of the Senate.

JOINT EXPLANATORY STATEMENT OF THE COMMITTEE OF CONFERENCE

The managers on the part of the House and the Senate at the conference on the disagreeing votes of the two Houses on the amendments of the House to the bill (S. 524), to authorize the Attorney General to award grants to address the national epidemics of prescription opioid abuse and heroin use, submit the following joint statement to the House and the Senate in explanation of the effect of the action agreed upon by the managers and recommended in the accompanying conference report:

The House amendment to the text of the bill struck all of the Senate bill after the enacting clause and inserted a substitute text.

The Senate recedes from its disagreement to the amendment of the House with an amendment that is a substitute for the Senate bill and the House amendment. . . .

CONSTITUTIONAL STATEMENT OF AUTHORITY

Congress has the power to enact this legislation pursuant to the following: Article I, Section 8, Clause 3 of the United States Constitution.

For consideration of the Senate bill and the House amendments, and modifications committed to conference:
FRED UPTON,
JOSEPH R. PITTS,
LEONARD LANCE,
BRETT GUTHRIE,
ADAM KINZINGER,
LARRY BUCSHON,
SUSAN W. BROOKS,
BOB GOODLATTE,
F. JAMES
  SENSENBRENNER, JR.,
LAMAR SMITH,
TOM MARINO,
DOUG COLLINS,
DAVID A. TROTT,
MIKE BISHOP,
KEVIN MCCARTHY,

From the Committee on Education and the Workforce, for consideration of title VII of the House amendment, and modifications committed to conference:
LOU BARLETTA,
EARL L. "BUDDY"
  CARTER,

From the Committee on Veterans' Affairs, for consideration of title III of the House amendment, and modifications committed to conference:
GUS M. BILIRAKIS,
JACKIE WALORSKI,

From the Committee on Ways and Means, for consideration of sec. 705 of the Senate bill, and sec. 804 of the House amendment, and modifications committed to conference:
PATRICK MEEHAN,
ROBERT J. DOLD,
Managers on the Part of the House.
CHUCK GRASSLEY,
LAMAR ALEXANDER,
ORRIN G. HATCH,
JEFF SESSIONS,
Managers on the Part of the Senate.

Amendments
[As figures are used in bills to express sums of money, dates, paragraph numbers, etc., amendments involving such expressions must be set in figures thus: Strike out "$840" and insert "$1,000", etc. for other enumerations, etc., follow the manuscript as the data is picked up from the bill and used for the Record and then picked up from the Record and used for the report.]

EMANUEL F. LENKERSDORF

The Clerk called the bill (H.R. 2520) for the relief of Emanuel F. Lenkersdorf.

There being no objection, the Clerk read the bill as follows:

H.R. 2520

Be it enacted by the Senate and House of Representatives of the United States of America in Congress assembled, That for the purposes of the Immigration and Nationality Act, Emanuel F. Lenkersdorf shall be held and considered to have been lawfully admitted to the United States for permanent residence as of the date of the enactment of this Act, upon payment of the required visa fee. Upon the granting of permanent residence to such alien as provided for in this Act, the Secretary of State shall instruct the proper officer to deduct one number from the total number of immigrant visas and conditional entries which are made available to natives of the country of the alien's birth under paragraphs (1) through (8) of section 203(a) of the Immigration and Nationality Act.

With the following committee amendment:

On page 2, strike lines 4 through 6 and insert in lieu thereof: "which are made available to natives of the country of the alien's birth under section 203(a) of the Immigration and Nationality Act or, if applicable, from the total number of such visas which are made available to such natives under section 202(3) of such Act.".

The committee amendment was agreed to.

The bill was ordered to be engrossed and read a third time, was read the third time, and passed, and a motion to reconsider was laid on the table.

CONTESTED ELECTION, CARTER AGAINST LeCOMPTE—MESSAGE FROM THE CLERK OF THE HOUSE OF REPRESENTATIVES (H. DOC. NO. 235)

The SPEAKER laid before the House the following message from the Clerk of the House of Representatives, which was read and, with the accompanying papers, referred to the Committee on House Administration:

JULY 29, 2008.

The Honorable the SPEAKER,
House of Representatives.

SIR: *I have the honor to lay before the House of Representatives the contest for a seat in the House of Representatives from the Fourth Congressional District of the State of Iowa, Steven V. Carter against Karl M. LeCompte, notice of which has been filed in the office of the Clerk of the House; and also transmit herewith original testimony, papers, and documents relating thereto.*

LEAVE OF ABSENCE

By unanimous consent, leave of absence was granted to:

Mr. CONYERS (at the request of Mr. HOYER) for today on account of personal business.

Mr. ENGEL (at the request of Mr. HOYER) for today on account of a codel flight delay.

Mr. GENE GREEN of Texas (at the request of Mr. HOYER) for today on account of a doctor's appointment.

SPECIAL ORDERS GRANTED

By unanimous consent, permission to address the House, following the legislative program and any special orders heretofore entered, was granted to:

(The following Members (at the request of Ms. HAHN) to revise and extend their remarks and include extraneous material:)

Ms. HAHN, for 5 minutes, today.

Mr. DeFAZIO, for 5 minutes, today.

Ms. KAPTUR, for 5 minutes, today.

Mr. SIMPSON, for 5 minutes, today.

(The following Members (at the request of Mr. SMITH of Nebraska) to revise and extend their remarks and include extraneous material:)

Mr. POE, for 5 minutes, June 20, 23 and 24.

Mr. JONES of North Carolina, for 5 minutes, June 20, 23 and 24.

Mr. BISHOP of Utah, for 5 minutes, today and June 18.

Mr. McCAUL, for 5 minutes, June 19.

ADJOURNMENT

Mr. FORBES. Mr. Speaker, I move that the House do now adjourn.

The motion was agreed to; accordingly (at 9 o'clock and 56 minutes p.m.), under its previous order, the House adjourned until tomorrow, Wednesday, June 15, 2016, at 9:30 a.m.

RECESS

The SPEAKER pro tempore. Pursuant to clause 12(a) of rule I, the Chair declares the House in recess until 2 p.m. today.

Accordingly (at 12 o'clock and 50 minutes p.m.), the House stood in recess until 2 p.m.

□ 1400

AFTER RECESS

The recess having expired, the House was called to order by the Speaker pro tempore (Mr. BOST) at 2 p.m.

[Follow manuscript as to expressing time of adjournment as 6 o'clock and 25 minutes p.m., or 6:25 p.m.]

MOTION TO DISCHARGE COMMITTEE

MARCH 17, 2008.

TO THE CLERK OF THE HOUSE OF REPRESEN-
TATIVES:

Pursuant to clause 4 of rule XXVII, I, PERCY J. PRIEST, move to discharge the Committee on Banking and Currency from the consideration of the bill (H.R. 2887) entitled "A bill transferring certain functions of the Price Administrator, with respect to petroleum and petroleum products, to the petroleum Administrator for War," which was referred to said committee March 7, 2008, in support of which motion the undersigned Members of the House of Representatives affix their signatures, to wit:

1. Percy J. Priest.
2. Oren Harris. . . .
217. William E. Hess.
218. James G. Polk.

This motion was entered upon the Journal, entered in the CONGRESSIOAL RECORD with signatures thereto, and referred to the Calendar of Motions To Discharge Committees, February 29, 2008.

House briefs

[The briefs follow at end of day's proceedings, heads and dashes to be used as shown here. This data is supplied from the House and is printed as submitted.]

EXECUTIVE COMMUNICATIONS, ETC.

Under clause 2 of rule XIV, executive communications were taken from the Speaker's table and referred as follows:

6340. A letter from the Congressional Review Coordinator, Animal and Plant Health Inspection Service, Department of Agriculture, transmitting the Department's interim rule—Tuberculosis in Cattle and Bison; State and Zone Designations; California [Docket No.: APHIS-2016-0052] received August 8, 2016, pursuant to 5 U.S.C. 801(a)(1)(A); Public Law 104-121, Sec. 251; (110 Stat. 868); to the Committee on Agriculture.

6341. A letter from the Director, Issuances Staff, Department of Agriculture, transmitting the Department's final rule — Eligibility of Namibia To Export Meat Products to the United States [Docket No.: FSIS-2012-0028] (RIN: 0583-AD51) received July 28, 2016, pursuant to 5 U.S.C. 801(a)(1)(A); Public Law 104-121, Sec. 251; (110 Stat. 868); to the Committee on Agriculture.

[Use the following form if only one communication is submitted—8 point:]

7147. Under clause 8 of rule XII, a letter from the Director, Regulatory Management Division, Environmental Protection Agency, transmitting the Agency's final rule—(Z)-7,8-epoxy-2-methyloctadecane (Disparlure); Exemption from the Requirement of a Tolerance [EPA-HQ-OPP-2007-0596; FRL-8367-7] received June 9, 2016, pursuant to 5 U.S.C. 801(a)(1)(A), was taken from the Speaker's table, referred to the Committee on Agriculture, and ordered to be printed.

REPORTS OF COMMITTEES ON PUBLIC BILLS AND RESOLUTIONS

Under clause 2 of rule XIV, executive communications were taken from the Speaker's table and referred as follows:

6340. A letter from the Congressional Review Coordinator, Animal and Plant Health Inspection Service, Department of Agriculture, transmitting the Department's interim rule—Tuberculosis in Cattle and Bison; State and Zone Designations; California [Docket No.: APHIS-2016-0052] received August 8, 2016, pursuant to 5 U.S.C. 801(a)(1)(A); Public Law 104-121, Sec. 251; (110 Stat. 868); to the Committee on Agriculture.

REPORTS OF COMMITTEES ON PUBLIC BILLS AND RESOLUTIONS

Under clause 2 of rule XIII, reports of committees were delivered to the

Clerk for printing and reference to the proper calendar, as follows:

Mr. GOODLATTE: Committee on the Judiciary. H.R. 5578. A bill to establish certain rights for sexual assault survivors, and for other purposes (Rept. 114–707, Pt. 1). Referred to the Committee of the Whole House on the state of the Union.

Mr. MILLER of Florida: Committee on Veterans' Affairs. H.R. 3286. A bill to encourage effective, voluntary private sector investments to recruit, employ, and retain men and women who have served in the United States military with annual presidential awards to private sector employers recognizing such efforts, and for other purposes; with an amendment (Rept. 114–708). Referred to the Committee of the Whole House on the state of the Union.

[Use above form also when only one report is submitted.]

PUBLIC BILLS AND RESOLUTIONS

Under clause 2 of rule XII, public bills and resolutions of the following titles were introduced and severally referred, as follows:

By Mr. SHADEGG:

H.R. 6274. A bill to provide an equivalent to habeas corpus protection for persons held under military authority under that part of Cuba leased to the United States; to the Committee on the Judiciary, and in addition to the Committee on Armed Services, for a period to be subsequently determined by the Speaker, in each case for consideration of such provisions as fall within the jurisdiction of the committee concerned.

By Mr. ROYCE (for himself, Mr. ZELDIN, Ms. ROS-LEHTINEN, Mr. NUNES, Mr. MEADOWS, Mr. THORNBERRY, Mr. SESSIONS, Mr. DONOVAN, Mr. MCCAUL, Mr. DENT, Mr. CHAFFETZ, Mr. CONAWAY, Mr. ROHRABACHER, Mr. RIBBLE, Mr. TROTT, Mr. YOUNG of Iowa, Mr. DESJARLAIS, Mr. COOK, Mr. PITTENGER, Mr. DESANTIS, Mr. DUFFY, Mr. STIVERS, Mr. FITZPATRICK, Mr. YOHO, Mr. ROTHFUS, Mr. CHABOT, and Mr. WILLIAMS):

H.R. 5931. A bill to provide for the prohibition on cash payments to the Government of Iran, and for other purposes; to the Committee on Foreign Affairs.

By Ms. DUCKWORTH (for herself and Mr. ZELDIN):

H.R. 5932. A bill to amend title 38, United States Code, to eliminate copayments by

the Department of Veterans Affairs for medicines relating to preventive health services, and for other purposes; to the Committee on Veterans' Affairs.

[Use the following form when only one bill or resolution is submitted:]

Under clause 2 of rule XII:

Mr. FATTAH (for himself and Mr. WOLF): introduced a bill (H.R. 5158) to provide for the sealing or expungement of records relating to Federal nonviolent criminal offenses, and for other purposes; which was referred to the Committee on the Judiciary, and in addition to the Committees on Agriculture, and Ways and Means, for a period to be subsequently determined by the Speaker, in each case for consideration of such provisions as fall within the jurisdiction of the committee concerned.

MEMORIALS

Under clause 3 of rule XII, memorials were presented and referred as follows:

[Use the following form when submitted by the Speaker if *By the Speaker* is not in manuscript:]

296. The SPEAKER presented a memorial of the Senate of the State of California, relative to Senate Joint Resolution 26, calling upon the President of the United States to encourage the Secretary of the United States Department of Health and Human Services to adopt policies to repeal the current discriminatory donor suitability policies of the United States Food and Drug Administration (FDA) regarding blood donations by men who have had sex with another man and, instead, direct the FDA to develop science-based policies such as criteria based on risky behavior in lieu of sexual orientation; to the Committee on Energy and Commerce.

297. Also, a memorial of the Senate of the State of California, relative to Senate Joint Resolution 29, declaring unnecessary and unexplained increases in pharmaceutical pricing is a harm to our health care system that will no longer be tolerated because the system cannot sustain it; to the Committee on Energy and Commerce.

MEMORIALS

Under clause 3 of rule XII,

[Use the following form when only one memorial is submitted:]

326. The SPEAKER presented a memorial of the Legislature of the State of Louisiana, relative to Senate Concurrent Resolution No. 51 memorializing the Congress of the United States to establish a grant program to assist the seafood industry in St. Tammany, St. Bernard, Orleans, and Plaquemines parishes; to the Committee on Financial Services.

PRIVATE BILLS AND RESOLUTIONS

Under clause 3 of rule XII, private bills and resolutions of the following titles were introduced and severally referred, as follows:

By Mr. GROTHMAN:

H.R. 808. A bill to authorize the President to award the Medal of Honor to James Megellas, formerly of Fond du Lac, Wisconsin, and currently of Colleyville, Texas, for acts of valor on January 28, 1945, during the Battle of the Bulge in World War II; to the Committee on Armed Services.

By Mr. UPTON:

H.R. 809. A bill for the relief of Ibrahim Parlak; to the Committee on the Judiciary.

[Use the following form when only one bill or resolution is submitted:]

Under clause 3 of rule XII,

Mr. HUFFMAN introduced a bill (H.R. 6296) For the relief of Yeganeh Salehi Rezaian; which was referred to the Committee on the Judiciary.

ADDITIONAL SPONSORS

Under clause 7 of rule XII, sponsors were added to public bills and resolutions, as follows:

H.R. 27: Mr. RENACCI.

H.R. 169: Mr. REICHERT.

H.R. 213: Mrs. BEATTY and Mr. CONNOLLY.

H.R. 265: Ms. McCOLLUM.

H.R. 297: Ms. ROYBAL-ALLARD, Ms. KELLY of Illinois, Mr. FARR, Ms. EDDIE BERNICE JOHNSON of Texas, Mr. RYAN of Ohio, and Ms. WILSON of Florida.

[Note.—Set sponsors caps and Members caps and lower case.]

DISCHARGE PETITIONS

Under clause 2 of rule XV, the following discharge petitions were filed:

Petition 8, March 12, 2014, by Mr. BRADLEY S. SCHNEIDER on House Resolution 490, was signed by the following Members: Bradley S. Schneider, Steny H. Hoyer, James E. Clyburn, Sam Farr, Sanford D. Bishop, Jr., Joseph Crowley, Terri A. Sewell, Eddie Bernice Johnson, Adam B. Schiff, Sander M. Levin, Sheila Jackson Lee, Nydia M. Velazquez, Ruben Hinojosa, Zoe Lofgren, Janice D. Schakowsky, . . .

DISCHARGE PETITIONS— ADDITIONS OR DELETIONS

The following Members added their names to the following discharge petitions:

Petition 1 by Ms. DELAURO on the bill (H.R. 377): Katherine M. Clark.

Petition 9 by Mr. GARCIA on the bill (H.R. 15): Rosa L. DeLauro, David Scott, William L. Enyart, Bennie G. Thompson, John Conyers Jr., Allyson Y. Schwartz, Eliot L. Engel, Brad Sherman, Suzan K. DelBene, Donald M. Payne Jr., Carolyn McCarthy, Theodore E. Deutch, John B. Larson, Henry A. Waxman, Emanuel Cleaver, G.K. Butterfield, Andre Carson, William R. Keating, Terri A. Sewell, and Tim Ryan.

The following Member's name was deleted from the following discharge petition:

Petition 1 by Ms. DELAURO on H.R. 377: Edward J. Markey.

PETITIONS, ETC.

Under clause 3 of rule XII, petitions and papers were laid on the Clerk's desk and referred as follows:

19. The SPEAKER presented a petition of the City Commission of the City of Lauderhill, FL, relative to Resolution No. 15R-07-161, condemning the Dominican Republic's impending mass deportation of Haitian immigrants; to the Committee on Foreign Affairs.

20. Also, a petition of the Oakland County Board of Commissioners, Oakland County, MI, relative to Miscellaneous Resolution No. 15154, objecting to the development of a nuclear waste repository in close proximity to the Great Lakes; to the Committee on Foreign Affairs.

[Use the following form when only one petition is submitted:]

Under clause 1 of rule XXII,

139. The SPEAKER presented a petition of the Council of the District of Columbia, relative to the Council-adopted resolution entitled, "National Park Service-Georgetown Branch Rail Right-of-Way Acquisition Resolution of 1990"; which was referred to the Committee on the District of Columbia.

AMENDMENTS

Under clause 8 of rule XVIII, proposed amendments were submitted as follows:

H.R. 5303

OFFERED BY: MR. KILDEE

AMENDMENT No.: Add at the end the following:

TITLE V—DRINKING WATER

SEC. 501. DRINKING WATER INFRASTRUCTURE.

(a) DEFINITIONS.—In this section: . . . .

CONGRESSIONAL RECORD INDEX

General instructions
Set in 7 point on 8 point, Record measure (168 points, 14 picas).

Cap lines or italic lines are set flush left.

Entries are indented 1 em, with overs 2 ems.

Bill introductions are to be identified as to sponsor or cosponsor.

Bullet following page number in index identifies unspoken material.

Pages are identified as S (Senate), H (House), and E (Extensions).

Pages in bound Record index are entered numerically, without S, H, or E prefixes.

Abbreviations and acronyms—
(for use on notation of content line)

Abbreviations
Streets: St.; Ave.; Ct.; Dr.; Blvd.; Rd.; Sq.; Ter.
Names: Jr.; Sr.; II (etc.)
Businesses: Co.; Corp. (includes all Federal corporations); Inc.; Ltd.; Bros.
States: See rule 9.13.

Dept. of Agriculture	Sec. of Agriculture.
Dept. of Commerce	Sec. of Commerce.
Dept. of Defense	Sec. of Defense.
Dept. of Education	Sec. of Education.
Dept. of Energy	Sec. of Energy.
Dept. of Health and Human Services	Sec. of Health and . . .
Dept. of Homeland Security	Sec. of Homeland Security
Dept. of Housing and Urban Development	Sec. of Housing and . . .
Dept. of the Interior	Sec. of the Interior.
Dept. of Justice	Attorney General.
Dept. of Labor	Sec. of Labor.
Dept. of State	Sec. of State.
Dept. of Transportation	Sec. of Transportation.
Dept. of the Treasury	Sec. of the Treasury.
Dept. of Veterans Affairs	Sec. of Veterans Affairs.

Acronyms

Agency for International Development..AID
Acquired immunodeficiency syndrome ....AIDS
American Association of Retired Persons ....AARP
American Bar Association..ABA
American Civil Liberties Union ....ACLU
American Federation of Labor and Congress of Industrial Organizations......... AFL–CIO
American Medical Association..AMA
British Broadcasting Corp ....BBC
Bureau of Alcohol, Tobacco, Firearms and Explosives ....ATF
Bureau of Indian Affairs...BIA
Bureau of Land Management..BLM
Bureau of Labor Statistics...BLS
Cable News Network...CNN
Cable Satellite Public Affairs Network ....C–SPAN
Central Intelligence Agency ....CIA
Civil Service Retirement System...CSRS
Civilian Health and Medical Program of the Uniformed Services......CHAMPUS
Commodity Credit Corp..CCC
Commodity Futures Trading Commission..CFTC
Comprehensive Environmental Response, Compensation and Liability Act.....CERCLA
Congressional Budget Office ....CBO
Consolidated Omnibus Budget Reconciliation Act............................COBRA
Consumer Product Safety Commission...CPSC
Daughters of the American Revolution...DAR
Deoxyribonucleic acid ....DNA
Disabled American Veterans...DAV
Drug Enforcement Administration ....DEA
Employee Retirement Income Security Act ....ERISA
Environmental Protection Agency..EPA
Equal Employment Opportunity Commission......................................EEOC
Export-Import Bank of the United States..EXIM Bank
Federal Aviation Administration ....FAA
Federal Bureau of Investigation ....FBI
Federal Communications Commission ....FCC
Federal Crop Insurance Corp..FCIC
Federal Deposit Insurance Corp..FDIC
Federal Election Commission ....FEC
Federal Emergency Management Agency ....FEMA
Federal Employee Retirement System ....FERS
Federal Energy Regulatory Commission...FERC
Federal Housing Administration ....FHA
Federal Insurance Contributions Act..FICA

Federal National Mortgage Association..Fannie Mae
Federal Reserve System..FRS
Federal Trade Commission..FTC
Food and Drug Administration...FDA
General Agreement on Tariffs and Trade...GATT
General Services Administration...GSA
Government Accountability Office..GAO
Government Publishing Office...GPO
Gross national product..GNP
Health maintenance organization(s)..HMO(s)
Human immunodeficiency virus..HIV
Internal Revenue Service..IRS
International Business Machines Corp..IBM
International Monetary Fund..IMF
International Trade Commission..ITC
Legal Services Corp..LSC
Low-Income Home Energy Assistance Program...................................LIHEAP
Missing in action..MIA(s)
National Aeronautics and Space Administration..................................NASA
National Association for the Advancement of Colored People....................NAACP
National Broadcasting Co..NBC
National Collegiate Athletic Association..NCAA
National Institute of Standards and Technology...................................NIST
National Institutes of Health...NIH
National Labor Relations Board..NLRB
National Oceanic and Atmospheric Administration...............................NOAA
National Railroad Passenger Corp..Amtrak
National Rifle Association...NRA
National Security Council...NSC
National Science Foundation..NSF
National Transportation Safety Board...NTSB
North American Free Trade Agreement...NAFTA
North Atlantic Treaty Organization...NATO
Nuclear Regulatory Commission...NRC
Occupational Safety and Health Administration...................................OSHA
Office of Management and Budget...OMB
Office of Personnel Management...OPM
Organization of American States...OAS
Organization of Petroleum Exporting Countries...................................OPEC
Overseas Private Investment Corp...OPIC
Palestine Liberation Organization...PLO
Parent-Teachers Association..PTA
Prisoner of war...POW

Public Broadcasting Service	PBS
Racketeer Influenced Corrupt Organization Act	RICO
Reserve Officers' Training Corps	ROTC
Securities and Exchange Commission	SEC
Small Business Administration	SBA
Social Security Administration	SSA
Supplemental security income	SSI
Tennessee Valley Authority	TVA
Trans-Pacific Partnership	TPP
United Auto Workers	UAW
United Nations	U.N.
United Nations Children's Fund	UNICEF
United Nations Educational, Scientific, and Cultural Organization	UNESCO
Veterans of Foreign Wars	VFW
Voice of America	VOA
Women, Infants, and Children Program	WIC
World Health Organization	WHO
Young Men's Christian Association	YMCA
Young Women's Christian Association	YWCA

Spacing

Biweekly Record index folioed in upper right and left corner; no extra spacing.

Bound Record index folioed in upper right and left corner; no extra spacing.

History of Bills folioed in upper right and left corner using H.B. numbers; no extra spacing.

Bound History of Bills folioed in lower right and left corner, first folio numerically higher than the last folio of index; no extra spacing.

Capitalization

Capitalize principal words after these formats:

Addresses	Brochures
Analyses	Conference reports
Appendices	Descriptions
Articles and editorials	Documents
Biographies	Essays
Book reviews	Essays: Voice of Democracy
Booklets	Eulogies

Explanations
Factsheets
Forewords
Histories
Homilies
Hymns
Memorandums
Messages
Oaths of office
Pamphlets
Papers
Platforms
Poems
Prayers
Prayers by visitors
Prefaces

Press releases
Proclamations
Reports
Report filed
Resolutions of ratification
Résumés
Sermons
Songs
Statements
Studies
Summaries
Surveys
Synopses
Testimonies
Transcripts
Treaties

Lowercase after these formats:

Advertisements
Affidavits
Agenda
Agreements
Amendments
Announcements
Appointments
Awards
Bills and resolutions
Bills and resolutions cosponsored
Bills and resolutions introduced
Bills and resolutions relative to
Briefs
Briefings
Broadcasts
Bulletins
Certificates of election
Chronologies
Citations
Civilian
Cloture motions
Colloquies
Commentaries
Comments
Communications from

Communiques
Comparisons
Cost estimates
Court decisions
Court documents
Declarations
Dedications
Definitions
Descriptions
Designated acting Presidents pro tempore
Designated acting Speaker pro tempore
Digests
Dispatches
Examples
Excerpts
Executive orders
Financial statements
Granted
Granted in the House
Granted in the Senate
Guidelines
Hearings
Inscriptions
Interviews
Introductions

Invocations
Journals
Letters
Lists
Meetings
Military
Motions
Newsletters
Notices
Obituaries
Opinion polls
Orders
Outlines
Petitions
Petitions and memorials
Press conferences
Privilege of the floor
Programs
Projects
Proposals
Questionnaires
Questions
Questions and answers
Quotations

Recorded
Regulations
Remarks
Remarks in House
Remarks in House relative to
Remarks in Senate
Remarks in Senate relative to
Resignations
Resolutions by organizations
Results
Reviews
Rollcalls
Rosters
Rules
Rulings of the chair
Schedules
Subpoena notices
Subpoenas
Tables
Tests
Texts of
Transmittals
Tributes
Voting record

Punctuation

Comma precedes folio figures.

If numbers of several bills are given, use this form: (see S. 24, 25); (see H.R. 217, 218), etc.; that is, do not repeat S. or H.R. with each number.

In consecutive numbers (more than two) use an en dash to connect first with last: S46–S48, 518–520.

Quotes are used for book titles.

A 3-em dash is used as a ditto for word or words leading up to colon:

Taxation: capital gains rates
———earned income tax credit
———rates

Roman and italic
Use italic for Members of Congress descriptive data:
COCHRAN, THAD *(a Senator from Mississippi)*;
CONYERS, JOHN, Jr. *(a Representative from Michigan).*
Names of vessels in italic:
Brooklyn (U.S.S.);
Savannah (vessel);
Columbia (space shuttle).

Flush cap lines
All cap lines are separate entries. They are set flush with overs indented 2 ems:

LEAHY, PATRICK *(a Senator from Vermont)*

YOUNG, DON *(a Representative from Alaska)*

PRESIDENT OF THE UNITED STATES (Barack Obama)

VICE PRESIDENT OF THE UNITED STATES (Joseph R. Biden, Jr.)

COMMITTEE ON FOREIGN AFFAIRS (House)

COMMITTEE ON FOREIGN RELATIONS (Senate)

FARMERS *see* AGRICULTURE

SENATE *related term(s)* COMMITTEES OF THE SENATE; LEGISLATIVE BRANCH OF THE GOVERNMENT; MEMBERS OF CONGRESS; VOTES IN SENATE

DEPARTMENT OF THE INTERIOR *related term(s)* BUREAU OF LAND MANAGEMENT, BUREAU OF RECLAMATION

PRESIDENTIAL APPOINTMENTS

VOTES IN HOUSE

VOTES IN SENATE

No. XII

Congressional Record Index

PROCEEDINGS AND DEBATES OF THE 114th CONGRESS, SECOND SESSION

| *Vol. 162* | JULY 21 TO AUGUST 8, 2016 | *Nos. 119 to 132* |

NOTE.—For debate and action on bills and resolutions see "History of Bills and Resolutions" at end of Index, under numbers referred to in Index entry.

DATES, ISSUE NUMBERS, AND PAGES INCLUDED IN INDEX XII

July 21	No. 119	.... S6947–S6980	H6731–H6734	E1507–E1511	D919–D922
July 22	No. 120	.... S6981–S7088	H6735–H6826	E1513–E1527	D923–D930
July 23	No. 121	.... S7089–S7201	H6827–H7059	E1529–E1547	D931–D940
July 24	No. 122	.... S7203–S7434	H7061–H7166	E1549–E1554	D941–D948
July 25	No. 123	.... S7435–S7485		E1555–E1572	D950–D956
July 26	No. 124	.... S7487–S7537			D958–D960
July 27	No. 125	.... S7539			D961–D962
July 28	No. 126	.... S7541–S7578	H7167–H7169	E1573–E1577	D963–D966
July 29	No. 127	.... S7579–S7708	H7171–H7330	E1579–E1591	D968–D980
July 30	No. 128	.... S7709–S7804	H7331–H7631	E1593–E1625	D981–D994
July 31	No. 129	.... S7805–S7982	H7633–H7707	E1627–E1640	D996–D1008
July 31 (Pt. II)*	No. 129	....	H7709–H7790		D996–D1008
August 1	No. 130	.... S7983–S8079	H7791–H7810	E1641–E1703	D1009–D1016
August 5	No. 131	.... S8081			D1017–D1018
August 8	No. 132	.... S8083			D1019–D1020

*Continuation of proceedings

NOTE: Elements in brackets which follow page numbers in the Index refer to the dates of the Congressional Record in which those pages may be found. Unspoken material is indicated by a bullet (•).

AARP (ORGANIZATION)
Letters
Evaluate and extend the basic pilot program for employment eligibility confirmation and ensure protection of Social Security beneficiaries, H7592 [30JY]
Press releases
Medicare Trigger Ignores Real Problem-Skyrocketing Health Care Costs, H7125 [24JY]

ABERCROMBIE, NEIL (*a Representative from Hawaii*)
Bills and resolutions cosponsored
Armed Forces: tribute to the 28th Infantry Division (see H. Con. Res. 390), H7308 [29JY]
Bulgaria: independence anniversary (see H. Res. 1383), H7630 [30JY]
Bureau of Prisons: provide stab-resistant personal body armor to all correctional officers and require such officers to wear such armor while on duty (see H.R. 6462), H6734 [21JY]
Diseases: improve and enhance research and programs on cancer survivorship (see H.R. 4450), H7308 [29JY]
Education: strengthen communities through English literacy, civic education, and immigrant integration programs (see H.R. 6617), H7164 [24JY]
Medicare: ensure more timely access to home health services for beneficiaries (see H.R. 6826), H7808 [1AU]
————replace the prescription drug benefit with a revised and simplified program for all beneficiaries (see H.R. 6800), H7807 [1AU]
Motor vehicles: encourage increased production of

natural gas vehicles and provide tax incentives for natural gas vehicle infrastructure (see H.R. 6570), H7630 [30JY]
Palladio, Andrea: anniversary of birth (see H. Con. Res. 407), H7788 [31JY]
Power resources: open Outer Continental shelf areas to oil and gas leasing, curb excessive energy speculation, and require Strategic Petroleum Reserve sale and acquisitions of certain fuels (see H.R. 6670), H7628 [30JY]
————provide a comprehensive plan for greater energy independence (see H.R. 6709), H7785 [31JY]
U.S. Public Service Academy: establish (see H.R. 1671), H7789 [31JY]
Yunus, Muhammad: award Congressional Gold Medal (see H.R. 1801), H7629 [30JY]
Remarks
Pearl Harbor, HI: anniversary of the Pearl Harbor Naval Shipyard (H. Res. 1139), H6773, H6774 [22JY]

ABORTION
Remarks in House
China, People's Republic of: mandatory abortion and sterilization policies, H7344, H7345 [30JY]
Supreme Court: anniversary of Roe v. Wade decision, H7283 [29JY], H7611 [30JY], H7776 [31JY], E1545 [23JY], E1701 [1AU]
U.S. Leadership Against HIV/AIDS, Tuberculosis, and Malaria Act: prohibit use of funds for any organization or program which supports or participates in the management of coerced abortions or involuntary sterilization, H7116 [24JY]

Remarks in Senate
Dept. of HHS: proposed regulation to change the definition of abortion, S7141 [23JY]

**ACCESS, COMPARISON, CARE, AND
ETHICS FOR SERIOUSLY ILL PATIENTS
(ACCESS) ACT**
Remarks in Senate
Enact (S. 3046), S7620 [29JY], S8021 [1AU]

ACCESS FOR ALL AMERICA ACT
Bills and resolutions
Enact (see S. 3412, 3413), S7905 [31JY]
Remarks in Senate
Enact (S. 3413), S7971–S7973 [31JY]

ACHIEVING OUR IDEA ACT
Remarks in House
Enact (H.R. 1896), E1701 [1AU]

ACKERMAN, GARY L. (*a Representative from New
York*)
Bills and resolutions cosponsored
Bangladesh: elections (see H. Res. 1402), H7788
[31JY]
China, People's Republic of: call for end to human
rights abuses of citizens, cease repression of
Tibetan and Uyghur people, and end support for
Governments of Sudan and Burma (see H. Res.
1370), H7309 [29JY]
Dept. of the Treasury: establish a commemorative
quarter dollar coin program emblematic of promi-
nent civil rights leaders and important events
advancing civil rights (see H.R. 6701), H7809
[1AU]
Great Lakes-St. Lawrence River Basin Water
Resources Compact: grant congressional consent
and approval (see H.R. 6577), H7165 [24JY]
Human rights: defeat campaign by some members
of the Organization of the Islamic Conference to
divert the U.N. Durban Review Conference from
a review of problems in their own and other countries (see H. Res. 1361), H7059 [23JY]
Immigration: modify certain requirements with respect to H–1B nonimmigrants (see H.R. 5630),
H7629 [30JY]
New York, NY: extend and improve protections and
services to individuals directly impacted by the
terrorist attack (see H.R. 6594), H7630 [30JY]
Palladio, Andrea: anniversary of birth (see H. Con.
Res. 407), H7809 [1AU]
Religion: support spirit of peace and desire for unity
displayed in the letter from leading Muslim schol-
ars, and in the Pope Benedict XVI response (see H.
Con. Res. 374), H7165 [24JY]
Bills and resolutions introduced
Syria: express concern regarding continued viola-
tions of political, civil, and human rights and call
for release of prisoners of conscience and other political prisoners (see H. Res. 1398), H7788 [31JY]

ADAMS, MICHAEL F.
Letters
Higher Education Opportunity Act, S7854 [31JY]

ADERHOLT, ROBERT B. (*a Representative from
Alabama*)
Bills and resolutions cosponsored
Crime: provide for the use of information in the

National Directory of New Hires in enforcing sex
offender registration laws (see H.R. 6539), H7165
[24JY]
Dept. of the Interior: establish oil and gas leasing program for public lands within the Coastal Plain of
Alaska (see H.R. 6758), H7787 [31JY]
House of Representatives: prohibit adjournment until
approval of a bill to establish a comprehensive
national energy plan addressing energy conservation and expansion of renewable and conventional
energy sources (see H. Res. 1391), H7629 [30JY]
National Prostate Cancer Awareness Month: support
goals and ideals (see H. Res. 672), H7790 [31JY]
Power resources: expedite exploration and development of oil and gas from Federal lands (see H.R.
6379), H7629 [30JY]
——promote alternative and renewable fuels,
domestic energy production, conservation, and
efficiency, and increase energy independence (see
H.R. 6566), H6824 [22JY]
——provide a comprehensive plan for greater energy independence (see H.R. 6709), H7809 [1AU]
Schools: withhold Federal funds from schools that
permit or require the recitation of the Pledge of
Allegiance or the National Anthem in a language
other than English (see H.R. 6783), H7806 [1AU]
Social Security: extend funding for the State
Children's Health Insurance Program (see H.R.
6788), H7806 [1AU]
Bills and resolutions introduced
Power resources: enhance energy independence
through the usage of existing resources and technology (see H. Con. Res. 401), H7787 [31JY]

ADMINISTRATIVE OFFICE, U.S. COURTS *see*
COURTS

ADOPTION *see* **FAMILIES AND DOMESTIC RELATIONS**

ADRIAN, MI
Remarks in House
Sand Creek Telephone Co.: anniversary, E1703 [1AU]

ADVANCING AMERICA'S PRIORITIES ACT
Bills and resolutions
Enact (see S. 3297), S7030 [22JY]
Cloture motions
Enact (S. 3297): motion to proceed, S7509 [26JY],
S7551 [28JY]
Letters
Provisions: Lynne Zeitlin Hale, Nature Conservancy
(organization), S7548 [28JY]
——Molly McCammon, National Federation of
Regional Associations for Coastal and Ocean
Observing, S7547 [28JY]
——Peter R. Orszag, CBO, S7510 [26JY], S7543
[28JY]
——several ocean and coastal research, education,
and conservation organizations, S7547 [28JY]
Motions
Enact (S. 3297), S7509 [26JY]
Remarks in Senate
Appalachian Regional Development Act: reauthorize
and improve, S7545 [28JY], S7888 [31JY]
Chesapeake Bay Initiative Act: provide for con-
tinuing authorization of the Chesapeake Bay
Gateways.

In history of bills, sequence is: Senate bills, Senate joint resolutions, Senate concurrent resolutions, and Senate resolutions; then House bills, House joint resolutions, House concurrent resolutions, and House resolutions: S. 14, S.J. Res. 7, S. Con. Res. 26, S. Res. 5, H.R. 980, H.J. Res. 9, H. Con. Res. 16, and H. Res. 50.

History of Bills and Resolutions

DATES, ISSUE NUMBERS AND BILLS INTRODUCED IN INDEX VIII

May 12	No. 77	S. 3001–3009		S. Con. Res. 82	S. Res. 558–560
		H.R. 6021–6024			
May 13	No. 78	S. 3010–3014	S.J. Res. 32		S. Res. 561–563
		H.R. 6025–6046		H. Con. Res. 348	H. Res. 1187–1193
May 19	No. 82	S. 3030–3034			S. Res. 569–570
		H.R. 6083–6084		H. Con. Res. 354	H. Res. 1208–1209
May 21	No. 84	S. 3045–3047	S.J. Res. 33	S. Con. Res. 83	S. Res. 572–573
		H.R. 6104–6122	H.J. Res. 86–87	H. Con. Res. 360	H. Res. 1217–1219
May 22	No. 85	S. 3048–3073	S.J. Res. 34–36	S. Con. Res. 84–85	S. Res. 574–579
		H.R. 6123–6166	H.J. Res. 88–89	H. Con. Res. 361–365	H. Res. 1220–1232

Bills receiving legislative action during this Index period numerically precede new bills introduced.

SENATE BILLS

S. 11—A bill to provide liability protection to volunteer pilot nonprofit organizations that fly for public benefit and to the pilots and staff of such nonprofit organizations, and for other purposes; to the Committee on the Judiciary.
Cosponsors added, S4621 [21MY]

S. 2062—A bill to amend the Native American Housing Assistance and Self-Determination Act of 1996 to reauthorize that Act, and for other purposes; to the Committee on Indian Affairs.
Committee on Banking, Housing, and Urban Affairs discharged, S814 [8FE]
Amendments, S850 [11FE], S4836, S4839, S4844 [22MY]
Passed Senate amended, S4839 [22MY]

SENATE JOINT RESOLUTIONS

S.J. Res. 17—A joint resolution directing the United States to initiate international discussions and take necessary steps with other Nations to negotiate an agreement for managing migratory and transboundary fish stocks in the Arctic Ocean; to the Committee on Foreign Relations.
Debated, H4067 [19MY]
Text, H4067 [19MY]
Rules suspended. Passed House, H4402 [21MY]
Message from the House, S4790 [22MY]

S.J. Res. 28—A joint resolution disapproving the rule submitted by the Federal Communications Commission with respect to broadcast media ownership; to the Committee on Commerce, Science, and Transportation.
By Mr. DORGAN (for himself, Ms. Snowe, Mr. Kerry, Ms. Collins, Mr. Dodd, Mr. Obama, Mr. Harkin, Mrs. Clinton, Ms. Cantwell, Mr. Biden, Mr. Reed, Mrs. Feinstein, Mr. Sanders, Mr. Tester, and Mr. Stevens), S1597 [5MR]
Cosponsors added, S1704 [6MR], S1878 [11MR], S2136 [13MR], S2233 [31MR], S2348 [2AP], S2947 [10AP], S3081 [16AP], S3700 [1MY]
Reported (S. Rept. 110–334), S3975 [8MY]
Passed Senate amended, S4267 [15MY]
Text, S4270 [15MY]
Message from the Senate, H4065 [19MY]
Held at the desk, H4065 [19MY]

SENATE CONCURRENT RESOLUTIONS

S. Con. Res. 82—A concurrent resolution supporting the Local Radio Freedom Act; to the Committee on Commerce, Science, and Transportation.
By Mrs. LINCOLN (for herself, Mr. Wicker, Mr. Brownback, Mr. Allard, Mr. Nelson of Nebraska, Ms. Murkowski, and Mr. Webb), S4029 [12MY]

S. Con. Res. 85—A concurrent resolution authorizing the use of the rotunda of the Capitol to honor Frank W. Buckles, the last surviving United States veteran of the First World War.
By Mr. SPECTER (for himself, Mr. Byrd, Mrs. Dole, Mr. McCain, Mr. Warner, Mr. Lieberman, Mr. Rockefeller, and Mr. Burr), S4793 [22MY]

S. Con. Res. 85—Continued
Text, S4810, S4848 [22MY]
Agreed to in the Senate, S4848 [22MY]

SENATE RESOLUTIONS

S. Res. 496—A resolution honoring the 60th anniversary of the commencement of the carving of the Crazy Horse Memorial; to the Committee on the Judiciary.
By Mr. THUNE (for himself and Mr. Johnson), S2346 [2AP]
Text, S2362 [2AP], S4427 [20MY]
Committee discharged. Agreed to in the Senate, S4427 [20MY]

S. Res. 562—A resolution honoring Concerns of Police Survivors as the organization begins its 25th year of service to family members of law enforcement officers killed in the line of duty.
By Ms. MURKOWSKI (for herself, Mr. Biden, Mr. Brown, Mr. Menendez, Ms. Mikulski, Mr. Craig, Mr. Whitehouse, Mr. Baucus, Mr. Dodd, Mrs. Feinstein, Mr. Inouye, Mr. Lautenberg, Mrs. Lincoln, Mr. Nelson of Florida, Mr. Pryor, Mr. Smith, Ms. Stabenow, Mr. Stevens, Mr. Tester, and Mr. Thune), S4106 [13MY]
Text, S4114, S4121 [13MY]
Agreed to in the Senate, S4120 [13MY]

HOUSE BILLS

H.R. 158—A bill to direct the Secretary of the Treasury to mint coins in commemoration of the battlefields of the Revolutionary War and the War of 1812, and for other purposes; to the Committee on Financial Services.
Cosponsors added, H3108 [6MY], H4061 [15MY]

H.R. 503—A bill to amend the Horse Protection Act to prohibit the shipping, transporting, moving, delivering, receiving, possessing, purchasing, selling, or donation of horses and other equines to be slaughtered for human consumption, and for other purposes; to the Committees on Energy and Commerce; Agriculture.
By Ms. SCHAKOWSKY (for herself, Mr. Whitfield, Mr. Rahall, Mr. Spratt, Mr. Gallegly, Mr. Markey, Mr. Pallone, Mr. Nadler, Mr. Van Hollen, Ms. McCollum of Minnesota, Ms. Bordallo, Ms. Schwartz, Mr. Ackerman, Mr. Doyle, Ms. Lee, Mr. Cleaver, Mr. Serrano, Ms. Berkley, Mr. Shays, Mr. Jones of North Carolina, Mr. McCotter, Mr. Cummings, Ms. DeLauro, Mr. George Miller of California, Mr. Grijalva, Mrs. Capps, Ms. Bean, Ms. Matsui, Mr. King of New York, Mr. Burton of Indiana, Mr. Kildee, Ms. Kaptur, Mr. Dicks, Mr. Berman, Ms. Hirono, Mr. Chandler, Mr. Gerlach, Mr. Tierney, Mr. Bishop of New York, Mr. Frank of Massachusetts, Mr. Lynch, Mr. Kirk, Mr. Campbell of California, Mr. Wilson of South Carolina, Ms. Jackson-Lee of Texas, Mr. Sherman,

Mr. LaTourette, Mr. Larson of Connecticut, Mr. Israel, Ms. Woolsey, Mr. Brown of South Carolina, Ms. Eddie Bernice Johnson of Texas, Mr. Moore of Kansas, Mr. Moran of Virginia, Mr. McNulty, Mrs. Maloney of New York, Mr. Inslee, Mr. Wolf, Ms. Carson, Mr. Weiner, Mr. Ruppersberger, Mr. Smith of New Jersey, and Mr. Linder), H670 [17JA]
Cosponsors added, H1055 [30JA], H1153 [31JA], H1565 [13FE], H1668 [14FE], H1896 [16FE], H2165 [5MR], H2621 [15MR], H2821 [21MR], H3279 [28MR], H3363 [29MR], H3476 [17AP], H3724 [20AP], H4553 [7MY], H5054 [15MY], H5927 [24MY], H6181 [7JN], H6439, H6476 [14JN], H6828 [20JN], H7202 [26JN], H8121 [18JY], H8821 [27JY], H9656 [2AU], H10696 [20SE], H11028 [27SE]

H.R. 4841—A bill to approve, ratify, and confirm the settlement agreement entered into to resolve claims by the Soboba Band of Luiseno Indians relating to alleged interences with the water resources of the Tribe, to authorize and direct the Secretary of the Interior to execute and perform the Settlement Agreement and related waivers, and for other purposes; to the Committee on Natural Resources.
Cosponsors added, H390 [22JA], H480 [28JA], H558 [29JA]
Reported with amendment (H. Rept. 110–649), H4059 [15MY]
Debated, H4075 [19MY]
Text, H4075 [19MY]
Rules suspended. Passed House amended, H4401 [21MY]
Message from the House, S4790 [22MY]
Passed Senate, S7197 [23JY]

H.R. 6081—A bill to amend the Internal Revenue Code of 1986 to provide benefits for military personnel, and for other purposes; to the Committee on Ways and Means.
By Mr. RANGEL (for himself, Mr. Stark, Mr. McDermott, Mr. Lewis of Georgia, Mr. Neal of Massachusetts, Mr. Pomeroy, Mrs. Jones of Ohio, Mr. Larson of Connecticut, Mr. Emanuel, Mr. Blumenauer, Mr. Kind, Ms. Berkley, Mr. Crowley, Mr. Van Hollen, Mr. Meek of Florida, Mr. Altmire, Mrs. Boyda of Kansas, Mr. Cohen, Ms. DeLauro, Mr. Ellsworth, Mr. Loebsack, Ms. Tsongas, Mr. Welch of Vermont, Mr. Walz of Minnesota, Mr. Arcuri, Ms. Shea-Porter, Mr. Becerra, Mrs. Davis of California, and Mr. Doggett), H4064 [16MY]
Cosponsors added, H4151 [19MY]
Debated, H4160 [20MY]
Text, H4160 [20MY]
Rules suspended. Passed House amended, H4187 [20MY]
Message from the House, S4617 [21MY]
Passed Senate, S4772 [22MY]
Message from the Senate, H4821 [22MY]

H.R. 6166—A bill to impose certain limitations on the receipt of out-of-State municipal solid waste, and for other purposes; to the Committee on Energy and Commerce.
By Mr. WITTMAN of Virginia (for himself, Mr. Wolf, Mr. Moran of Virginia, and Mr. Donnelly),

20. Reports and Hearings

The data for these publications arrives at GPO from many different sources. Congressional committee staff members are responsible for gathering the information printed in these publications.

Report language is compiled and submitted along with the bill language to the clerks of the respective Houses. The clerks assign the report numbers, etc., and forward this information to GPO for typesetting and printing. In many instances the reports are camera-ready copy, needing only insertion of the assigned report number.

Likewise, hearings are also compiled by committee staff members. The data or captured keystrokes as submitted by the various reporting services are forwarded to GPO where the element identifier codes are programmatically inserted and galley or page output is accomplished without manual intervention. It is not cost effective to prepare the manuscript as per the GPO STYLE MANUAL as it is too time-consuming to update and change the data once it is already in type form. Therefore, these publications are to be FIC & punc., unless specifically requested otherwise by the committee. It is not necessary to stamp the copy. However, style as stated in the following rules will be followed.

Style and format of congressional reports

Below are rules that should be followed for the makeup of congressional numbered reports. In either Senate or House reports, follow bill style in extracts from bills. Report numbers run consecutively from first to second session:

1. All excerpts to be set in 10-point type, cut in 2 ems on each side, except as noted in paragraph 3 below. For ellipses in cut-in matter, lines of five asterisks are used.

2. Contempt proceedings to be considered as excerpts.

3. The following are to be set in 10-point type, but not cut in:

   (a) Letters that are readily identified as such by salutation and signature.

   (b) Appendixes and/or exhibits that have a heading readily identifying them as such; and

(c) Matter printed in compliance with the Ramseyer rule.[1]

4. All leaderwork and lists of more than six items to be set in 8-point type.

5. All tabular work to be set in 7-point gothic type.

6. An amendment in the nature of a substitute to be set in 8-point type, but quotations from such amendment later in the report to be treated as excerpts, but set full measure (see paragraph 10 below).

7. Any committee print having a report head indicated on original copy to be set in report type and style.

8. Committee prints not having a report head indicated on original copy to be set in committee print style; that is, excerpts to be set in 8 point, full measure.

9. If a committee print set as indicated in paragraph 8 is later submitted as a report or included in a report, and the type is available for pickup, such type shall be picked up and used as is in the report.

10. On matter that is cut in on the left only for purposes of breakdown, no space is used above and below, but on all matter that is cut in on both sides, 4 points are used above and below. Because of the indentions and the limited number of element identifiers, do not squeeze bills that are submitted as excerpts.

11. In reports of immigration cases, set memorandums in full measure unless preceded or followed directly by committee language. Memorandums are indented on both sides if followed by such language. Preparers should indicate the proper indention on copy.

12. Order of printing (Senate reports only): (1) Report, (2) minority or additional views, (3) the Cordon rule,[2] (4) appendix (if any).

---

[1] If a House report contains the "Changes in Existing Law" section (in compliance with the Ramseyer rule), all main heads within that report should be set in caps and small caps, with secondary heads set in all small caps.

[2] If a Senate report contains the "Changes in Existing Law" section (in compliance with the Cordon rule) with potential changes in law indicated, all main heads within that report should be set in caps and small caps, with secondary heads set in all small caps. However, if the "Changes in Existing Law" section consists of only an explanatory paragraph, all main heads within that report should be set in all small caps.

13. Minority or additional views will begin a new page with 10-point cap heading. In Senate reports, "Changes in Existing Law" begins a new page if following "views." In conference reports, "Joint Explanatory Statement" begins a new odd page.

14. Minority or additional views are printed only if they have been signed by the authoring congressperson.

[Sample of excerpt]

In *Palmer v. Mass.*, decided in 1939, which involved the reorganization of the New Haven Railroad, the Supreme Court said:

> The judicial processes in bankruptcy proceedings under section 77 are, as it were, brigaded with the administrative processes of the Commission.

[Sample of an excerpt with an added excerpt]

The Interstate Commerce Commission in its report dated February 29, 1956, which is attached hereto and made a part hereof, states that it has no objection to the enactment of S. 3025, and states, in part, as follows:

> The proposed amendment, however, should be considered together with the provisions of section 959(b), title 28, United States Code, which reads as follows:

> "A trustee, receiver, or manager appointed in any cause pending in any court of the United States," etc.

[Sample of amendment]

On page 6, line 3, strike the words "and the service", strike all of lines 4, 5, and 6, and insert in lieu thereof the following:

> and, notwithstanding any other provision of law, the service credit authorized by this clause 3 of rule XIII of the Rule of the House of Representatives, change shall not—

(A) be included in establishing eligibility for voluntary or involuntary retirement or separation from the service, under any provision of law;

[Sample of amendment]

The amendments are indicated in the bill as reported and are as follows:
On page 2, line 15, change the period to a colon and add the following:

Provided, That such approaches shall include only those necessary portions of streets, avenues, and boulevards, etc.

On page 3, line 12, after "operated", insert "free of tolls".

[Sample of amendment in the nature of a substitute]

The amendment is as follows:
Strike all after the enacting clause and insert the following:

That the second paragraph under the heading "National Park Service" in the Act of July 31, 1953 (67 Stat. 261, 271), is amended to read as follows: "The Secretary of the Interior shall hereafter report in detail all proposed awards of concessions leases and contracts involving a gross annual business of $100,000 or more, or of more than five years in duration, including renewals thereof, sixty days before such awards are made, to the President of the Senate and Speaker of the House of Representatives for transmission to the appropriate committees."

[Sample of letter inserted in report]

The Department of Defense recommends enactment of the proposed legislation and the Office of Management and Budget interposes no objection as indicated by the following attached letter, which is hereby made a part of this report:

March 21, 2008.

Hon. Nancy Pelosi,
Speaker of the House of Representatives,
Washington, DC.

My Dear Madam Speaker: There is forwarded herewith a draft of legislation to amend section 303 of the Career Compensation Act.

* * * * * * *

Sincerely yours,

Douglas A. Brook,☐☐☐☐☐
Assistant Secretary of the Navy☐☐☐
(Financial Management).☐

———————

[Sample of cut-in for purposes of breakdown; no spacing above or below]

Under uniform regulations prescribed by the Secretaries concerned, a member of the uniformed services who—

(1) is retired for physical disability or placed upon the temporary disability retired list; or

(2) is retired with pay for any other reason, or is discharged with severance pay, immediately following at least eight years of continuous active duty (no single break therein of more than ninety days);

may select his home for the purposes of the travel and transportation allowances payable under this subsection, etc.

———————

[Sample of leaderwork]

Among the 73 vessels mentioned above, 42 are classified as major combatant ships (aircraft carriers through escort vessels), in the following types:

Forrestal-class aircraft carriers	4
Destroyers	10
* * * * * * *	
Guided-missile submarine	1
Total	42

[Sample of sectional analysis]

SECTIONAL ANALYSIS

Section 1. Increase of 1 year in constructive service for promotion purposes

The principal purpose of the various subsections of section 1 is to provide a 1-year increase for medical and dental officers in . . .

*   *   *   *   *   *   *

Subsection 101(a) is in effect a restatement of the existing law

This subsection authorizes the President to make regular appointments in the grade of first lieutenant through . . .

*   *   *   *   *   *   *

[Sample of amendment under Ramseyer rule]

CHANGES IN EXISTING LAW

In compliance with clause 3 of rule XII of the Rules of the House of Representatives, changes in existing law made by the bill, as introduced, are shown as follows (existing law proposed to be omitted is enclosed in black brackets, new matter is printed in italic, existing law in which no change is proposed is shown in roman):

EXPORT CONTROL ACT OF 1949

*   *   *   *   *   *   *

TERMINATION DATE

SEC. 12. The authority granted herein shall terminate on June 30, [1956] *1959*, or upon any prior date which the Congress by concurrent resolution or the President may designate.

[The following examples are for sample purposes only]
[Sample of "Report" Skeleton]

| 114TH CONGRESS | HOUSE OF REPRESENTATIVES | REPORT |
| 2d Session | | 114–716 |

PROVIDING FOR STABILITY OF TITLE TO CERTAIN LANDS IN THE STATE OF LOUISIANA, AND FOR OTHER PURPOSES [1]

SEPTEMBER 6, 2016.—Committed to the Committee of the Whole House on the State of the Union and ordered to be printed [2]

Mr. BISHOP of Utah, from the Committee on Natural Resources, submitted the following

R E P O R T

together with

DISSENTING VIEWS

[To accompany H.R. 3342]

[Including cost estimate of the Congressional Budget Office]

The Committee on Natural Resources, to whom was referred the bill (H.R. 3342) to provide for stability of title to certain lands in the State of Louisiana, and for other purposes, having considered the same, report favorably thereon without amendment and recommend that the bill do pass. [3]

PURPOSE OF THE BILL [4]

The purpose of H.R. 3342 is to provide for the stability of title to certain lands in the State of Louisiana.

BACKGROUND AND NEED FOR LEGISLATION

In 1842, the U.S. government completed a survey of lands in Louisiana that included the area surrounding Lake Bistineau. Using the results of this survey, Louisiana delineated its ownership of lands under the Equal Footing Doctrine and transferred 7,000 acres of land around Lake Bistineau to the Commissioners of the Bossier Levee District in 1901. Three years later, the Commissioners of the Bossier Levee District conveyed this land to private ownership.

59–006

---

[1] If title makes more than three lines in 10-point caps, set in 8-point caps.

[2] Must be set as indicated in copy. If illustrations accompany copy and are not ordered to be printed, do not add *with illustrations*. Return copy to Production Manager.

[3] If the wording in this paragraph is prepared in the singular form, follow.

[4] For *Senate Committee on Finance* and *House Committee on Ways and Means*, heads are set in bold caps.

[Sample of "Report" Skeleton]

Calendar No. 584 [1]

114TH CONGRESS 2d Session	SENATE	REPORT 114–312

JOHN MUIR NATIONAL HISTORIC SITE EXPANSION ACT

AUGUST 30, 2016.—Ordered to be printed

Filed, under authority of the order of the Senate of July 14, 2016 [2]

Ms. MURKOWSKI, from the Committee on Energy and Natural
Resources, submitted the following

R E P O R T

[To accompany H.R. 1289]

The Committee on Energy and Natural Resources, to which was
referred the bill (H.R. 1289) to authorize the Secretary of the Interior to acquire approximately 44 acres of land in Martinez, California, and for other purposes, having considered the same, reports
favorably thereon without amendment and recommends that the
bill do pass.

PURPOSE

The purpose of H.R. 1289 is to acquire approximately 44 acres
of land in Martinez, California.

BACKGROUND AND NEED

The John Muir National Historic Site was established by Congress in 1964 (Public Law 88–547) and is located in the San Francisco Bay Area, in Martinez, California. The historic site preserves
the 14-room Italianate Victorian mansion where the naturalist and
writer John Muir lived, as well as a nearby 325-acre tract of native
oak woodlands and grasslands historically owned by the Muir family.
    The legislation would authorize the Department of the Interior
to acquire by donation approximately 44 acres for inclusion in the
John Muir National Historic Site. The 44 acres includes adjacent
lands from John Swett's historic estate, who was also a farmer,
friend, and neighbor of John Muir in the Alhambra Valley hills. Se-
curing this property would benefit the Muir site as it will help pro-

59–010

---

[1] Use this type and form only on Senate reports. There is only one calendar in the Senate.
[2] Style for filed line, if present.

[Sample of "Report" Skeleton]

114TH CONGRESS *2d Session*	HOUSE OF REPRESENTATIVES	REPORT 114–724

PROVIDING[1] FOR CONSIDERATION OF THE BILL (H.R. 5063) TO LIMIT DONA-
TIONS MADE PURSUANT TO SETTLEMENT AGREEMENTS TO WHICH THE
UNITED STATES IS A PARTY, AND FOR OTHER PURPOSES[2]

SEPTEMBER 6, 2016.—Referred to the House Calendar and ordered to be printed

Mr. COLLINS of Georgia, from the Committee on Rules,
submitted the following

R E P O R T

[To accompany H. Res. 843]

The Committee on Rules, having had under consideration House
Resolution 843, by a record vote of 9 to 2, report the same to the
House with the recommendation that the resolution be adopted.

SUMMARY OF PROVISIONS OF THE RESOLUTION

The resolution provides for consideration of H.R. 5063, the Stop
Settlement Slush Funds Act of 2016, under a structured rule. The
resolution waives all points of order against consideration of the
bill. The resolution provides one hour of general debate equally divided and controlled by the chair and ranking minority member of
the Committee on the Judiciary. The resolution makes in order as
original text for the purpose of amendment the amendment in the
nature of a substitute recommended by the Committee on the Judiciary now printed in the bill and provides that it shall be considered as read. The resolution waives all points of order against that
amendment in the nature of a substitute. The resolution makes in
order only those further amendments printed in this report. Each
such amendment may be offered only in the order printed in this
report, may be offered only by a Member designated in this report,
shall be considered as read, shall be debatable for the time specified in this report equally divided and controlled by the proponent
and an opponent, shall not be subject to amendment, and shall not
be subject to a demand for division of the question in the House
or in the Committee of the Whole. The resolution waives all points
of order against the amendments printed in this report. The resolution provides one motion to recommit with or without instructions.

59–008

[1] If copy reads "To make" change to "Making", "To provide" change to "Providing", "To amend"
change to "Amending".
[2] Sample of 8-point head.

114TH CONGRESS	HOUSE OF REPRESENTATIVES	REPORT
1st Session		114–376

TRADE FACILITATION AND TRADE ENFORCEMENT ACT OF 2015

DECEMBER 9, 2015.—Ordered to be printed

Mr. BRADY of Texas, from the committee of conference, submitted the following

CONFERENCE REPORT

[To accompany H.R. 644]

The committee of conference on the disagreeing votes of the two Houses on the amendment of the House to the amendment of the Senate to the bill (H.R. 644), to reauthorize trade facilitation and trade enforcement functions and activities, and for other purposes, having met, after full and free conference, have agreed to recommend and do recommend to their respective Houses as follows:

That the Senate recede from its disagreement to the amendment of the House to the amendment of the Senate and agree to the same with an amendment as follows:

In lieu of the matter proposed to be inserted by the House amendment, insert the following:

SECTION 1. SHORT TITLE; TABLE OF CONTENTS.

(a) SHORT TITLE.—*This Act may be cited as the "Trade Facilitation and Trade Enforcement Act of 2015".*

(b) TABLE OF CONTENTS.—*The table of contents for this Act is follows:*

Sec. 1. Short title; table of contents.
Sec. 2. Definitions.

TITLE I—TRADE FACILITATION AND TRADE ENFORCEMENT

Sec. 101. Improving partnership programs.
Sec. 102. Report on effectiveness of trade enforcement activities.
Sec. 103. Priorities and performance standards for customs modernization, trade facilitation, and trade enforcement functions and programs.
Sec. 104. Educational seminars to improve efforts to classify and appraise imported articles, to improve trade enforcement efforts, and to otherwise facilitate legitimate international trade.
Sec. 105. Joint strategic plan.
Sec. 106. Automated Commercial Environment.
Sec. 107. International Trade Data System.

97–818

JOINT EXPLANATORY STATEMENT OF THE COMMITTEE OF CONFERENCE

The managers on the part of the House and the Senate at the conference on the disagreeing votes of the two Houses on the amendment of the House to the amendment of the Senate to the bill (H.R. 644), to reauthorize trade facilitation and trade enforcement functions and activities, and for other purposes, submit the following joint statement to the House and the Senate in explanation of the effect of the action agreed upon by the managers and recommended in the accompanying conference report:

The Senate amendment struck all of the House bill after the enacting clause and inserted a substitute text.

The House amendment struck all of the Senate amendment after the enacting clause and inserted a substitute text.

The Senate recedes from its disagreement to the amendment of the House with an amendment that is a substitute for the House amendment and the Senate amendment. The differences between the Senate amendment, the House amendment, and the substitute agreed to in conference are noted below, except for clerical corrections, conforming changes made necessary by agreements reached by the conferees, and minor drafting and clarifying changes.

DIVISION A—TRADE FACILITATION AND TRADE ENFORCEMENT ACT OF 2015

TITLE I—TRADE FACILITATION AND TRADE ENFORCEMENT

SECTION 101. IMPROVING PARTNERSHIP PROGRAMS

Present Law

The Customs-Trade Partnership Against Terrorism (C–TPAT), codified in the Security and Accountability for Every Port Act (SAFE Port Act) of 2006 (6 U.S.C. 961 et seq.), is a voluntary trade partnership program in which Customs and Border Protection (CBP) and members of the trade community work together to secure and facilitate the movement of legitimate trade. Companies that are members of C–TPAT are considered low-risk, which expedites cargo clearance based on the company's security profile and compliance history.

House Amendment

Section 101 requires the Commissioner of CBP to work with the private sector and other Federal agencies to ensure that all CBP partnership programs provide trade benefits to participants. This would apply to partnership programs established before enactment of this bill, and any programs established after enactment. It establishes elements for the development and operation of any such partnership programs, which require the Commissioner to: 1) con-

103

EARMARK, LIMITED TAX BENEFITS, AND LIMITED TARIFF BENEFITS

In compliance with clause 9(e), 9(f), and 9(g) of Rule XXI of the Rules of the House of Representatives, the conference report and joint explanatory statement contain no earmarks, limited tax benefits, or limited tariff benefits.

CONSTITUTIONAL STATEMENT OF AUTHORITY

Congress has the power to enact this legislation pursuant to the following: Article I, Section 8, Clause 3 of the United States Constitution.

For consideration of the Senate bill and the House amendments, and modifications committed to conference:

FRED UPTON,
JOSEPH R. PITTS,
LEONARD LANCE,
BRETT GUTHRIE,
ADAM KINZINGER,
LARRY BUCSHON,
SUSAN W. BROOKS,
BOB GOODLATTE,
F. JAMES SENSENBRENNER, Jr.,
LAMAR SMITH,
TOM MARINO,
DOUG COLLINS,
DAVID A. TROTT,
MIKE BISHOP,
KEVIN MCCARTHY,

From the Committee on Education and the Workforce, for consideration of title VII of the House amendment, and modifications committed to conference:

LOU BARLETTA,
EARL L. "BUDDY" CARTER,

From the Committee on Veterans' Affairs, for consideration of title III of the House amendment, and modifications committed to conference:

GUS M. BILIRAKIS,
JACKIE WALORSKI,

From the Committee on Ways and Means, for consideration of sec. 705 of the Senate bill, and sec. 804 of the House amendment, and modifications committed to conference:

PATRICK MEEHAN,
ROBERT J. DOLD,
Managers on the Part of the House.

CHUCK GRASSLEY,
LAMAR ALEXANDER,
ORRIN G. HATCH,
JEFF SESSIONS,
Managers on the Part of the Senate.

○

FINANCIAL SERVICES AND GENERAL GOVERNMENT APPROPRIATIONS FOR 2016

HEARINGS

BEFORE A

SUBCOMMITTEE OF THE

COMMITTEE ON APPROPRIATIONS

HOUSE OF REPRESENTATIVES

ONE HUNDRED FOURTEENTH CONGRESS

FIRST SESSION

SUBCOMMITTEE ON FINANCIAL SERVICES AND GENERAL GOVERNMENT APPROPRIATIONS

ANDER CRENSHAW, Florida, *Chairman*

TOM GRAVES, Georgia
KEVIN YODER, Kansas
STEVE WOMACK, Arkansas
JAIME HERRERA BEUTLER, Washington
MARK E. AMODEI, Nevada
E. SCOTT RIGELL, Virginia

JOSÉ E. SERRANO, New York
MIKE QUIGLEY, Illinois
CHAKA FATTAH, Pennsylvania
SANFORD D. BISHOP, Jr., Georgia

NOTE: Under Committee Rules, Mr. Rogers, as Chairman of the Full Committee, and Mrs. Lowey, as Ranking Minority Member of the Full Committee, are authorized to sit as Members of all Subcommittees.

WINNIE CHANG, KELLY HITCHCOCK,
ARIANA SARAR, and AMY CUSHING,
Subcommittee Staff

PART 5

	Page
Oversight Hearing: Internal Revenue Service	1
Internal Revenue Service, FY 2016 Budget Request	123
Department of the Treasury	205

U.S. GOVERNMENT PUBLISHING OFFICE

96–927   WASHINGTON : 2015

COMMITTEE ON APPROPRIATIONS

HAROLD ROGERS, Kentucky, *Chairman*

RODNEY P. FRELINGHUYSEN, New Jersey
ROBERT B. ADERHOLT, Alabama
KAY GRANGER, Texas
MICHAEL K. SIMPSON, Idaho
JOHN ABNEY CULBERSON, Texas
ANDER CRENSHAW, Florida
JOHN R. CARTER, Texas
KEN CALVERT, California
TOM COLE, Oklahoma
MARIO DIAZ-BALART, Florida
CHARLES W. DENT, Pennsylvania
TOM GRAVES, Georgia
KEVIN YODER, Kansas
STEVE WOMACK, Arkansas
JEFF FORTENBERRY, Nebraska
THOMAS J. ROONEY, Florida
CHARLES J. FLEISCHMANN, Tennessee
JAIME HERRERA BEUTLER, Washington
DAVID P. JOYCE, Ohio
DAVID G. VALADAO, California
ANDY HARRIS, Maryland
MARTHA ROBY, Alabama
MARK E. AMODEI, Nevada
CHRIS STEWART, Utah
E. SCOTT RIGELL, Virginia
DAVID W. JOLLY, Florida
DAVID YOUNG, Iowa
EVAN H. JENKINS, West Virginia
STEVEN M. PALAZZO, Mississippi

NITA M. LOWEY, New York
MARCY KAPTUR, Ohio
PETER J. VISCLOSKY, Indiana
JOSÉ E. SERRANO, New York
ROSA L. DeLAURO, Connecticut
DAVID E. PRICE, North Carolina
LUCILLE ROYBAL-ALLARD, California
SAM FARR, California
CHAKA FATTAH, Pennsylvania
SANFORD D. BISHOP, JR., Georgia
BARBARA LEE, California
MICHAEL M. HONDA, California
BETTY McCOLLUM, Minnesota
STEVE ISRAEL, New York
TIM RYAN, Ohio
C. A. DUTCH RUPPERSBERGER, Maryland
DEBBIE WASSERMAN SCHULTZ, Florida
HENRY CUELLAR, Texas
CHELLIE PINGREE, Maine
MIKE QUIGLEY, Illinois
DEREK KILMER, Washington

WILLIAM E. SMITH, *Clerk and Staff Director*

(II)

[House Appropriation Hearing sample]

DEPARTMENT OF HOMELAND SECURITY APPROPRIATIONS FOR 2009

TUESDAY, FEBRUARY 26, 2008.

IMMIGRATION ENFORCEMENT: IDENTIFICATION AND REMOVAL OF CRIMINAL ALIENS, STUDENT AND EXCHANGE VISITOR PROGRAM FEE INCREASES

WITNESSES

CATHERYN COTTEN, DIRECTOR, INTERNATIONAL OFFICE, DUKE UNIVERSITY

JULIE L. MYERS, ASSISTANT SECRETARY, U.S. IMMIGRATION AND CUSTOMS ENFORCEMENT [ICE], DEPARTMENT OF HOMELAND SECURITY

Mr. PRICE. Subcommittee will come to order. Good morning, everyone. Today we will be discussing the wide variety of activities carried out by Immigration and Customs Enforcement, or ICE, and we will first focus on the Agency's Student and Exchange Visitor Program.

BALANCING SECURITY AND STUDENT NEEDS

Mr. PRICE. Thank you very much. We will put your entire statement in the record, which of course elaborates on the points you made and goes beyond them. Let me ask you first a rather broad question, and then I will zero in somewhat on the fee increases and the benefits that might accrue from an increased flow of fee revenue.

[Note style for questions and answers]

Question. What percentage of cases presented to prosecutors along the Southwest border are prosecuted? Provide by sector and/or state. What was the prosecution rate of criminals picked up off the street? (Culberson)

Answer. ICE does not track prosecutions, however, ICE works closely with U.S. Attorneys and state and local prosecutors nationwide on a wide variety of cases.

FY2007 SAC office	Criminal arrests	Indictments	Convictions*
El Paso, TX	2,435	1,882	1,704
Phoenix, AZ	1,641	623	770
San Antonio, TX	1,588	1,172	1,155
San Diego, CA	2,318	1,147	1,842
Fiscal Year Total	7,982	4,824	5,471

*Indictments and convictions may be comprised of arrests from previous years.

Mr. CULBERSON. Okay.

[Standard Hearing sample]

ORGANIZATIONAL MEETING ON ADOPTION OF COMMITTEE RULES; CONSIDERATION OF INTERIM REPORT; AND HEARING ON VOTING IN THE HOUSE OF REPRESENTATIVES

THURSDAY, SEPTEMBER 27, 2007

HOUSE OF REPRESENTATIVES,□□□□□□□
SELECT COMMITTEE TO INVESTIGATE THE VOTING□□□□□
IRREGULARITIES OF AUGUST 2, 2007,□□□
Washington, DC.□

The committee met, pursuant to call, at 9:11 a.m., in Room H–313, The Capitol, Hon. William D. Delahunt (Chairman of the committee) presiding.

Present: Representatives Delahunt, Davis, Herseth Sandlin, Pence, LaTourette and Hulshof.

The CHAIRMAN. A quorum being present, the select committee will come to order.

Today we are meeting to do three tasks: adopt our committee rules, adopt the internal report, and to hear for the first time—of what we expect to be multiple occasions—from the Office of the House Clerk. We will wait for the gentlelady from South Dakota, who was at her other select committee.

I now recognize myself for 5 minutes to make an opening statement, but before I do, let me note I will then go to Congressman Pence as the Ranking Member. And in subsequent hearings, it would be our hope that just he and I would make opening statements. But on this initial hearing, any member of the panel that wishes to make an opening statement is most welcome.

I would be remiss not to begin by thanking the Chair of the House Rules Committee, Louise Slaughter, and the Ranking Member, David Dreier, for making their hearing room available to the select committee.

I also want to welcome everyone to this initial meeting of the select committee that has been mandated by the House to review roll call No. 814. I would note that none of the Members sought this particular assignment, but each of us appreciates the role and the significance of the House in our unique constitutional order, and recognize that the integrity of the system by which we cast our votes on the House floor is essential to the confidence that the American people have in this institution, aptly described as the people's House.

Index

[Numbers in parentheses refer to rules; **bold** indicates chapter heading]

A

Abbreviations and Letter Symbols
(Chapter 9), 221–262
Addresses:
Correspondence (16.3, 16.9–16.16),
313, 315–317
Ordinals (12.10), 278
Signatures, lists of names (9.37, 16.3),
231, 313
Street (9.16–9.19, 13.6), 224–225, 285
Article, section (9.39), 232
Calendar divisions (9.44–9.46, 13.5), 233,
285
Closed up, with periods (9.7), 222
College degrees (9.32, 9.35–9.36), 230,
231
Comma before and after (8.39), 201
Company, etc. (9.25), 225–226
Not abbreviated (9.26), 226
Compass directionals (9.50), 235
Congressional terms (9.30, 9.41–9.43,
13.11), 230, 232–233, 286
Dates (9.44–9.46, 13.5), 233, 285
Et al., etc. (3.53, 8.59), 41, 205
Figure, not abbreviated (9.40), 232
Foreign countries (9.11), 223
Geographic terms (9.9–9.15), 222–224
Grammatical (7.13), 112
Information technology (9.64), 256
Land descriptions (9.20–9.22, 13.9), 225,
285
Latin (9.63, 11.3), 252–256, 269
Lists (9.61–9.64), 238–261
Measures, weights, etc. (9.5, 9.50–9.59),
221, 235–238
Metric (9.56–9.57), 236–237
Military titles, U.S., 226–230
Money (9.60, 12.9k), 238, 277
Foreign, 339–344
Numerals used with (9.5, 9.51, 13.4), 221,
236, 285

Organized bodies (9.8), 222
Parts of publications (9.38–9.40, 13.10),
231–232, 286
Period used (8.107–8.118), 212–214
Not used (8.119–8.127), 215–216
Preparing copy (2.42), 15
Provinces, etc. (9.13, 9.15), 223, 224
Senator, Representative (9.30), 230
States (9.12–9.13), 223–224
Tabular work (13.4–13.13), 285–286
Technology (9.64), 256–261
Territories and possessions (9.12–9.14),
223–224
Time zones (9.47), 234
Titles, civil and military, (9.25, 9.27, 9.29),
225–230
U.S.:
Before Government or Government
organization (9.9, 13.7), 222–223,
285
As adjective (9.10, 13.7), 223, 285
Vessels (9.27, 11.6–11.7), 226, 269–270
-able, words ending in (5.11, 6.30), 91–93,
105
About This Manual, v
Accents:
Anglicized and foreign words (3.15,
5.3–5.4), 30, 87–88
Geographic names (5.20–5.21), 95
Symbols (10.18), 262
Acronyms, initialisms, and coined words
(9.48, 9.61, 9.64), 234–235, 239–247,
256–261
Congressional Record (Ch. 19), 414–416
Plurals (8.11, 8.13), 195, 196
Act, 45
Adjectives (*see also* Compounding):
Capitalization (3.6–3.7), 28
Modifier (7.7), 111
Nationalities (demonyms) (5.22, Ch. 17),
95, 337–339

Administration, 45

Adverbs ending in -ly (6.20), 102

Advice to Authors and Editors (Chapter 1), 1–5

Air Force, 46, 226–230

Allmark (2.101–2.102, 2.110, 2.113), 22, 23

American National Standards Institute (ANSI) (2.2, 9.61), 7–9, 239

American Samoa (3.20, Ch. 4, 9.12–9.13, 9.47, Ch. 17), 33, 77, 223–224, 234, 334, 337, 339, 343, 354

Ampersand (&):

    Comma omitted before (8.60), 204

    Firm names (9.25), 225–226

    Index entries (15.27), 310

Anglicized foreign words (3.15, 5.3–5.4), 30, 87–88

ANSI (American National Standards Institute) (2.2, 9.61), 7–9, 239

Apostrophes and possessives (8.3–8.18), 193–197

    Abbreviations (8.11–8.12), 195–196

    Authentic form in names to be followed (8.6), 194

    Coined plurals (8.11), 195–196

    Contractions (8.11), 195–196

    Possessive (8.3–8.10), 193–195

    Pronouns (8.8–8.9), 194–195

    Spelled-out words (8.13), 196

Appendix:

    Abbreviation (9.38), 231

    Footnote numbering (15.2), 303

    Part of book (2.3n), 10

    Plural form (5.10), 90–91

Area:

    Abbreviations (9.56–9.58), 236–237

    Metric equivalents, 345–347

Army, 47–48, 227–230

Article:

    Abbreviation (9.38–9.39), 231–232

    Capitalization (3.12–3.13, 3.53), 29–30, 41

    Caps and small caps (9.39), 232

Assembly:

    Legislative, 66

United Nations (3.18), 31–32, 78

Association (9.25), 225–226

Asterisk(s):

    Ellipses (8.80–8.82), 208–209

    Footnote reference (13.67–13.68, 15.13–15.14, 15.17), 294, 308, 309

Astronomical:

    Bodies, capitalization (3.31), 36

    Time (12.9b), 275

Astrophysical abbreviations (9.59), 238

Atomic numbers (10.16), 264

B

Backstrips, run down (2.19), 12

Base lines and meridians, 352–353

Basin, 49, 62

B.C. (9.7, 9.61, 12.9c), 222, 238, 275

Bible, etc. (3.35), 37

Bibliography:

    Footnote numbering (15.2), 307

    Part of book (2.3m), 10

    References (2.128, 8.33, 8.62, 8.75), 25–26, 201, 205–206

Bill style (2.40), 15

Blank pages, avoid more than two (1.15), 2

Board on Geographic Names (5.20–5.21), 95

Boldface:

    Page numbers, contents (15.30), 311

    Punctuation (8.150), 220

Braces, equations (10.14), 264

Brackets (8.19–8.22, 10.14), 197–198, 264

    Dates abbreviated in (9.45), 233

    Emphasis added, etc. (8.19, 11.4), 197, 265

    Equations (8.21, 10.14), 198, 264

    Headnotes (13.87–13.88), 296

    More than one paragraph (8.22), 198

    Type (8.153), 220

Bylines in parentheses (8.101), 211

C

Calendar divisions:

    Abbreviations (9.44–9.46, 13.5), 233, 285

    Capitalization (3.24), 34, 50

Called, so-called (8.132), 216
Capacity:
    Abbreviations (9.56, 9.58), 236, 237
    Metric equivalents, 345–346
Capitalization Rules (Chapter 3), 27–43
    Addresses, salutations, and signatures (3.59, 16.2), 42, 313
    Articles, definite (3.12–3.13), 29, 30
    Calendar divisions (3.24), 34
    Common nouns and adjectives (3.6–3.11), 28–29
    Continued (13.37), 290
    Countries, domains (3.20–3.21), 32–33
    Firm names (Ch. 4), 60–61
    First words (3.44–3.49), 40–41
    Heads, center and side (3.50–3.58), 41–42
    Historic and documentary work (3.40), 39
    Historic events (3.33), 36
    Holidays, etc. (3.25), 34
    Interjections (3.60), 43
    Organized bodies (3.18–3.19), 31–32
    Particles (3.14–3.17), 30
    Proper names (3.3), 27
        Derivatives (3.4–3.5), 27
    Religious terms (3.35), 37
    Scientific names (3.27–3.32), 35–36
    Soil orders (3.30), 35
    Time zones (Ch. 4), 77
    Titles:
        Persons (3.36–3.39), 37–38
        Publications, etc. (3.40–3.43), 39
    Trade names and trademarks (3.26, Ch. 4), 35, 77
Capitalization Examples (Chapter 4), 45–80
Capitals, foreign (Ch. 17), 327–336
Capitals, U.S. (Ch. 17), 326, 354–374
Capitol (Ch. 4), 51
Caps and small caps:
    Abbreviation (1.22), 4–5, 239
    Article, section (9.39), 232
    Capitalization, in heads (3.50–3.58), 41–42

Congressional Record, (Ch. 19), 382–383
    Datelines, addresses, and signatures (9.37, 16.3), 231, 313
    Figure (2.71, 8.116), 18, 214
    Heads spaced with regular justification spaces (2.50), 16
    Names, surnames (3.51–3.52), 41
    Note (13.74), 294
    Quotation marks in (11.10), 271
    Use of in hearings (8.19), 197–198
    Vessel names (11.6–11.7), 269–270
-cede, -ceed, -sede (5.13), 93
Celsius (9.53, 9.62), 236, 248
Centerheads (*see* Heads, center and side).
Chair (3.34), 36, 51
Chairman (3.37), 38, 51
Chapter:
    Abbreviation (9.38), 231
    Alignment, in contents (15.28), 310
    Capitalization (3.10), 29
Chemical:
    Elements:
        Atomic numbers (10.16), 264–265
        Compounding (6.43), 108
        Numerals (6.43, 10.16), 108, 264–265
        Symbols (10.16), 264–265
    Formulas (6.44, 11.12, 12.15), 108, 271, 279
    Symbols:
        Preparing copy (2.34–2.35), 14
        Set in roman (10.16), 264–265
Church (3.35), 37
    And state (Ch. 4), 50
Ciphers:
    Leaderwork (14.7–14.8), 304
    Numerals (12.9d), 275
    Tabular work (13.29–13.36), 289–290
Citations:
    Abbreviations (9.42–9.43, 9.45), 232–233
    Biblical, etc. (8.32), 200
    Italic (11.3, 11.8), 269, 270
    Punctuation (8.100–8.101), 211
Civil and military titles:

Abbreviations (9.29–9.37), 226–231
Capitalization (3.34–3.37), 36–38
Plurals (5.8), 89–90
Coast (3.22), 33
Coast Guard (Chs. 4, 9), 45, 52, 226–230
Code (3.38), 39
Colon (3.44–3.45, 3.48, 8.23–8.37), 40,
   198–201
   Affecting use of numerals (12.8), 274
   After salutations (8.30, 16.14), 200, 316
   Biblical citations (8.32), 200
   Bibliographic citations (8.33), 201
   Bulleted or enumerated list (8.28),
      199–200
   Capitalization following (3.44–3.49,
      8.24), 40, 198
   Ratio (8.36–8.37), 201
   Subentries (8.29, 14.15), 200, 305
Combining forms (6.29–6.35), 104–106
Comma (8.38–8.63), 201–205
   Chemical formulas (6.44), 108
   Compound sentences (8.47), 203
   Omitted (8.54–8.63), 204–205
   Semicolon, used with (8.148), 219
Commandant (9.30), 230
Commander in Chief (3.37), 37–38
   Compounding (6.40), 107
   Plural (5.8), 89
Commission (3.18), 31–32
Committee (Ch. 4), 53
Company:
   Abbreviation (9.25–9.26), 225–226
   Ampersand with (9.25), 225–226
   List (Ch. 4), 54, 60
Compass directionals:
   Abbreviations (9.50), 235
   Capitalization (3.23), 34
   Compound words (6.14), 100
   Land tract description (9.20–9.21), 225
   Punctuation (6.14, 8.61, 9.17, 9.20–9.21,
      9.50–9.51), 100, 204, 224–225, 235
Compounding Examples (Chapter 7),
   111–192
Compounding Rules (Chapter 6), 97–109

Chemical terms (6.42–6.44), 108
Civil and military titles (6.40–6.41), 105
Fractions (6.38–6.39, 12.26–12.28), 107,
   283
General rules (6.4–6.7), 97–98
Improvised compounds (6.46–6.52),
   108–109
Numerical compounds (6.36–6.39,
   12.9o), 106–107, 278
Prefixes, suffixes, and combining forms
   (6.29–6.35), 104–106
   Short prefixes (6.7), 98
Scientific and technical terms (6.42–
   6.45), 108
Solid compounds (6.8–6.14), 98–100
Unit modifiers (6.15–6.28), 100–104
Units of measurement (6.45), 108
Congressional:
   Abbreviations (9.41–9.43, 13.11), 232–233,
      286
   Capitalization (3.18), 31–32
   Ordinals (12.10–12.11), 278–279
Congressional Record (Chapter 19),
   377–423
   Addresses and signatures, 389–390
   Call of the House, 388
   Capitalization, 379–380
   Caps and small caps, 382–383
   Committee of the Whole House on the
      state of the Union, 404–405
   Conference report and statement,
      406–407
   Credits, 390
   Extensions of Remarks, 392
   Extracts, 391–392
   Figures, 380
   Forms of titles, 388–389
   General rules, 377–378
   In gross or en gros, 382
   Italic, 380–381
   Miscellaneous, 381–382
   Parentheses and brackets, 384–385
   Poetry, 390–391
   Proceedings:

House, 400–404
  Senate, 393–399
  Punctuation, 383
  Samples, 382–412
  Speech heads, 392
  Tabular matter and leaderwork, 380
  Text headings, 392
  Title 44, U.S.C., iv, 377
  Voting:
    House and Committee of the Whole,
      385–387
    Pairs, 388
    Yeas and nays, 387–388
Congressional Record Index, 413–423
  Abbreviations and acronyms, 413–416
  Capitalization, 416–418
  Flush cap lines, 419
  General instructions, 413
  Punctuation, 418
  Roman and italic, 419
  Samples, 420–423
  Spacing, 416
Congressional work:
  Back title, 436, 438
  Cover and title pages, 431–434, 437,
    439–440
  Joint explanatory statement, 435
  Reports and hearings (2.39, Ch. 20), 15,
    425–440
Consonants:
  A, an, before (5.16–5.19), 94
  Doubled (5.14–5.15), 94
  Hyphen, to avoid tripling (6.7), 98
Contents (15.20–15.30), 309–311
  Part of book (2.3i, 2.12), 10, 11
  Type (15.28–15.30), 310–311
Contractions, apostrophe to indicate
  (8.11–8.12), 195–196
Copy (*see also* Preparing copy):
  Blank pages, avoid more than two (1.15),
    2
  Corrections marked (1.19–1.20), 2
  Covers to be indicated (1.13), 2
  Fold-ins, avoid use of (1.14), 2

Folioing looseleaf or perforated work
  (1.12), 2
Footnote references (1.7), 1
Illustrations:
  Instructions (1.8), 1
  Position (1.8), 1
  Separate sheets (1.8), 1
  Legible (1.2), 1
  Numbering (1.3), 1
  Paper stock (1.16), 2–3
  Paragraph, begin with (1.4), 1
  Proofreader's marks (1.22), 4–5
  Proper names, signatures, etc., plainly
    marked (1.5), 1
  Reprint, in duplicate (1.3), 1
  Style sheets furnished (1.11), 2
  Trim size (1.11, 1.17), 2
  Typewritten, one side only (1.3), 1
Cordon rule (Ch. 20), 426 fn.
Corrections:
  Author's (1.19–1.20), 2
  Proofreading (2.79–2.80), 19
Counties and geographic divisions,
  354–374
  Common misspellings, 374–375
Cover:
  Kind to be indicated (1.13, 2.5), 2, 11
  Report sample, 9
Crown (3.37, Ch. 4), 37–38, 56
Currency (*see also* Money), 339–344

D

Dagger (13.67–13.68, 15.14), 294, 308
Dash (8.64–8.79), 205–208
  Em dash (8.64–8.75), 205–206
  En dash (8.76–8.79), 207
    Figures, letters (8.76–8.77, 12.7), 207,
      274
    Not to be used for *and* (8.79), 208
    Not to be used for *to* (8.78, 13.110),
      208, 299
    Proportion (8.36), 201
Date columns (*see* Tabular work).

Datelines, Addresses, and Signatures
  (Chapter 16), 313–324
Dates:
  Abbreviations (9.44–9.46, 13.5), 233, 285
  A.D., B.C. (8.56, 12.9c), 204, 275
  Commas with (8.53, 8.56, 12.9c), 203,
    204, 275
  En dash (8.77–8.79, 12.9c), 207–208, 275
  Ordinals in (12.11), 278
  Roman numerals (12.29), 284
  Tabular work (13.5), 285
Days:
  Abbreviations (9.46), 233
  Holidays, etc. (3.25), 34
Decimal inches, converted to (Chapter 17),
    347
Decimals:
  Alignment (2.28, 13.31), 13, 289
  Ciphers with (13.29–13.33), 289
  Comma omitted (8.58), 204
  Used with numerals (12.9d), 275
Decorations, medals, etc. (Chapter 4), 56
Decree:
  Executive (Chapter 4), 60
  Royal (3.40), 39, 57
Degree mark:
  Repeated (10.6), 263
  Spacing (12.9f), 276
  With figures (9.50–9.51, 9.53, 10.6, 12.9f),
    235–236, 263, 270
Degrees (scholastic, etc.):
  Abbreviations (9.32, 9.33, 9.35–9.36), 230,
    231
  Capitalization (9.36), 231
  Closed up (9.7), 222
  Sequence of (9.35), 231
Deity, words denoting (3.35, Ch. 4), 37, 55
Demonyms (nationalities, American)
    (5.22–5.24, Ch. 17), 96–97, 337–339
Derivatives:
  Compounds (6.6), 98
  Proper names (3.4–3.5, Ch. 4), 27, 57
  Scientific names (3.27–3.29), 35
Devil, etc. (3.35), 37

Diacritical and writing marks (5.3–5.4,
    5.25), 87–88, 96
Dimensions (12.9j), 276–277
Diseases and related terms (3.32, Ch. 4),
    36, 58
Do. (ditto):
  Leaderwork (14.4, 14.6), 303–304
  Tabular work (13.41–13.50), 290–291
Dollar:
  Abbreviation (9.60, 10.6), 238, 263
  Leaderwork (14.7–14.8), 304
  Tabular work (13.51–13.56), 292
Dr. (9.29, 9.33), 226, 230
  Not used with other titles (9.33), 230

E

Earth (3.31), 36
Editorial marks (illustration) (1.22), 4–5
Editors and authors, suggestions (1.1–1.21),
    1–3
E.g. (9.7, 9.63), 222, 253
Ellipses (8.80–8.86), 208–209
Email, email (Ch. 4, 11.16), 59, 272
Emphasis, italic not used (11.2), 269
Emphasis added, etc. (11.4), 269
Equations (10.8–10.15), 264
Esq., abbreviation (8.43, 9.32–9.33, 9.37,
    16.3, 16.12, 16.19), 200, 230, 231, 313,
    316, 317
Et al. (9.63), 253
Et cetera, etc. (2.29, 9.63), 13, 253
Et seq. (9.63, 11.3), 252, 269
Even space after sentences (2.49), 16
Ex- (6.34), 105
Exclamation point (8.87–8.89), 209–210
Extracts:
  Footnotes (15.8), 307–308
  Quotation marks omitted (2.23), 12

F

Fahrenheit (9.53, Ch. 17), 235–236, 345
False title (2.3a), 10
Federated States of Micronesia (9.12, 9.13, Ch.
    17, Ch. 18), 223–224, 332, 338, 342, 356

FIC & punc. (2.29, 2.39, 2.41), 13, 15
Figure (2.70, 3.10), 18, 29
   Not abbreviated (9.40), 232
   Period not used at end (8.116), 214
Figures (*see* Numerals).
Firm names (*see also* Company) (Ch. 4), 60
First words capitalized (3.44–3.49), 40–41
Flush heads (*see* Heads, center and side).
Fol. lit. (2.39, 12.1), 15, 273
Fold-ins, oversize, avoided (1.14), 2
**Footnotes, Indexes, Contents, and
   Outlines** (Chapter 15), 307–312
   Footnotes and reference marks (15.1–
      15.19), 307–309
      Comma not used (8.54, 15.19), 204,
         309
      Follows punctuation (15.18), 309
      Footnote added (2.95), 21
      Footnote eliminated (2.94g), 21
      Run across (1.7, 13.71), 1, 294
      Sequence (15.14), 308
      Superior figures (13.67, 15.12), 294, 308
      Thin space (15.12), 308
   Indexes and tables of contents (15.20–
      15.30), 309–311
   Leaderwork (14.11–14.13), 305
   Outlines (15.31), 311–312
   Tabular work (13.65–13.84), 293–295
   Text (15.1–15.19), 307–309
Foreign:
   Countries:
      Abbreviations (9.11), 223
      Capital cities (Ch. 17), 327–336
      Currency (Ch. 17), 339–344
      Heads of state (Ch. 17), 327–336
      Money, abbreviations (9.60), 238
      Nationalities (demonyms) (Ch. 17),
         337–339
   Rivers (Ch. 18), 353
   Words:
      Accents (5.3–5.4), 87–88
      Compounding (6.24), 103
      Italic (11.2), 269
Foreword (2.3f), 10

Fort (Ch. 4), 62
   Not abbreviated (9.19), 225
   State name with (9.12), 223
Fractions (12.26–12.28), 283
   Comma omitted (8.58, 12.9e, 12.27), 204,
      276, 283
   Hyphen in (6.38–6.39, 12.27), 107, 283
   Land descriptions (9.20–9.22), 225
   Spelled out (6.38, 12.26), 107, 283
   Tabular work (13.85–13.86), 295–296
      Alignment (13.63), 293
Franking privilege (2.127), 25
Frontispiece (2.3b), 10
-ful, words ending in (5.9, 6.30), 90, 105

G

General Instructions (Chapter 2), 7–26
**Geologic Terms and Geographic
   Divisions** (Chapter 18), 349–375
   Geographic divisions, 352
   Geographic terms (Ch. 4), 62
   Geologic terms, 349
Gospel, etc. (3.35, Ch. 4), 37, 63
Government(s) (3.9, 3.21, Ch. 4), 28, 32–33,
   60
   Departments, capitalization (3.18), 31–32
   Foreign (Ch. 17), 327–336
Governor (3.36), 37
GPO's Digital Information Initiatives, ix
Gravity terms (9.53), 235–236
Guam (3.20, 4, 9.13–9.14, Ch. 17), 33, 77,
   223–224, 337, 341, 358

H

Halftitle:
   Imprint (2.115), 23
   Part of book (2.3j), 10
H-bomb, H-hour (Ch. 4, 6.51), 64, 109
Heads, center and side:
   Capitalization (2.31, 3.50–3.58), 14,
      41–42
   Tabular work (13.25–13.27), 288
Heads of state, foreign (Ch. 17), 327–336
Hearings (*see* Reports and Hearings).

Holidays, etc. (3.25), 34
Holy Scriptures, etc. (3.35, Ch. 4), 37, 62
Honorable, etc. (9.31), 230
House (Ch. 4), 64–65
Hyphen (*see also* Compounding Rules):
  Chemical formulas (6.43–6.44), 108
  Civil and military titles (5.8, 6.40), 89–90, 107
  Compass directionals (6.14), 100
  Division at end of line (8.91), 210
  Fractions (6.38–6.39, 12.26–12.28), 105, 283
  Numerical compounds (6.36–6.39, 12.9o), 106–107, 278
  Prefixes, suffixes, and combining forms (6.7, 6.29–6.35, 7.9–7.10), 98, 104–106, 112
  Scientific terms (6.42–6.44), 108
  State abbreviations (8.76, 9.12), 207, 223
  Unit modifiers (6.15–6.28), 100–104
    Not used when meaning is clear (6.16), 101

I

Ibid, id. (9.63, 11.3), 253, 269
-ible, words ending in (5.11, 6.30), 91–93, 105
i.e. (9.7, 9.63), 222, 253
Illustrations:
  Makeup (2.3i, 2.12, 2.18), 10, 11, 12
  Separate sheets (1.8), 1
Imprints (2.111–2.122), 23–24
  Signature marks (2.99–2.110), 22–23
Improvised compounds (6.46–6.52), 108–109
Inches, picas converted to (Ch. 17), 347
Indents (*see also* Overruns) (2.59–2.65), 17–18
  Datelines, addresses, and signatures (16.5–16.28), 313–324
  Do. (13.41–13.50), 290–291
  Extracts (2.23), 12
  Footnote tables (13.83), 295
  Hanging (2.62–2.63), 17
  Heads (2.64–2.65), 18

Paragraphs (2.59–2.60), 17
Index (15.20–15.30), 309–311
  Entries (15.27), 310
  Part of book (2.3o), 10
  Plural form (5.10), 90–91
  Roman numerals (15.22), 309
  See, see also (11.11, 15.20), 271, 309
Inferior figures and letters:
  Chemical elements (6.43), 108
  Chemical formulas (10.16, 11.12, 12.15), 264, 271, 279
  Equations (10.8), 264
  Italic (10.8, 11.12), 264, 271
  Precede superiors (10.15), 264
  Preparing (2.34), 14
Information technology acronyms (9.64), 256–261
Infra:
  Italic (11.3), 269
  Not abbreviated (9.49), 235
Integral sign (10.14), 264
Interjections:
  Capitalization (3.60), 43
  Exclamation point (8.87–8.89), 209–210
Internet, internet (Ch. 4), 65
Introduction (2.3f), 10
-ise, -ize, -yze (5.12), 93
Italic (Chapter 11), 269–272
  Aircraft (11.6), 269–270
  Ante, post (11.3), 269
  Continued from (11.11), 271
  Credit line (8.66), 205
  Datelines, addresses, and signatures (16.5–16.26), 313–323
  Emphasis (11.2), 269
  Equations (10.7–10.8, 11.12–11.13), 264, 271–272
  Fol. lit., etc. (2.39), 15
  Foreign words, etc. (11.2–11.3), 269
  Inferior letters (10.8, 11.12), 264, 271
  Infra, supra (11.3), 269
  Italic supplied, etc. (11.4), 269
  Legal cases (11.8), 270
  Legends (2.72, 11.14), 18, 272

*n*th degree (11.12), 267

Not used for (11.2), 269

Paragraphs and sections, indicating (11.15), 272

Provided, Resolved, etc. (3.49, 11.11), 40–41, 271

To be followed (11.5), 269

Publications, titles of (11.2), 269

Salutations (8.30, 16.14), 200, 316

Scientific names (11.9–11.10), 271

See, see also (11.11, 15.20), 271, 305

Symbols (2.73, 11.12–11.14), 18, 271–272

Tabular work (13.94–13.95), 297

Units of quantity (13.122, 14.14), 302, 305

v. (11.8), 270

Vessels (11.6–11.7, 13.94), 269–270, 297

x dollars (11.12), 271

-ize, -ise, -yze (5.12), 93

J

Journals (2.2), 8

Jr., Sr.:

Abbreviation (9.32, 9.34), 230

Index entries (15.27), 310

Punctuation (8.43, 9.34), 202, 230

Type (9.37, 16.3), 231, 313

K

King (3.36), 37

Known as (8.132), 216

L

Land area abbreviations (9.56), 236–237

Land descriptions (9.20–9.22, 12.9f), 225, 276

Latin abbreviations (9.63, 11.3), 252–256, 269

Latitude, longitude:

Abbreviated (9.51, 13.9), 235, 285

Division at end of line (9.52), 235

Spaces omitted (9.51, 12.9f), 235, 276

Law (3.40), 39

Leaders:

Abbreviation before (8.127, 13.13), 216, 286

Leaderwork (14.1), 303

Tabular work (13.96–13.100), 297–298

Leaderwork (Chapter 14) (*see also* Tabular Work), 303–306

Bearoff (14.2), 303

Clears (14.9), 304

Columns (14.3–14.4), 303–304

Continued heads (14.5), 304

Definition (14.1), 303

Do. (14.6), 304

Dollar mark and ciphers (14.7–14.8), 304

Double up (14.19), 306

Examples (14.15–14.20), 305–306

Flush items and subheads (14.9–14.10), 304

Footnotes (14.11–14.13), 305

Units of quantity (14.14–14.20), 305–306

Leading and spacing (2.47–2.58), 16–17

Leading:

Datelines, addresses, and signatures (16.4), 313

Extracts (2.53–2.56), 16–17

Footnotes (2.57), 17

Legends (2.57), 17

Line of stars (8.83), 209

Page, section, etc., over figure columns (15.21), 305

Tabular work, boxheads (13.18–13.21), 286

Tabular work, centerheads (13.25, 13.28), 288

Tabular work, footnotes (13.65–13.84), 293–295

Spacing:

Abbreviations with points (9.6), 221

Ampersand (9.7), 222

Article, section (9.39), 232

Citations (8.32), 200

Clock time (8.31, 12.9b), 200, 275

Colon (8.23–8.37), 198–201

Datelines, addresses, and signatures (16.4), 313

Degrees, academic (9.7, 9.32–9.33, 9.35–9.37), 222, 230, 231
Ellipses (8.80–8.86), 208–209
Footnote references (8.54, 15.12, 15.19), 204, 308–309
Footnote symbols (13.68, 15.12–15.13), 294, 304
Heads, center, side (2.50), 16
Initials, personal name (9.7), 222
Letters or figures in parentheses (2.39, 8.98), 15, 211
Mathematical signs (10.3), 263
Names, space after in small cap heads (3.14–3.17, 3.51–3.52), 30–31, 41
Particles (3.52), 41
Question mark (8.128–8.130), 216
Quotation marks (8.131–8.147), 216–219
Section mark (10.6), 263
Stars (8.83), 209
Symbols with figures (10.6), 263
Legal cases:
Capitalization (3.12), 29
Italic (11.8), 270
Legends (2.66–2.72), 18
Italic symbols (2.72, 11.14), 18, 272
Leading (2.57), 17
Makeup (2.67, 2.71, 2.94f), 18, 21
Punctuation (2.69, 8.116), 18, 214
Type (2.68), 18
Legislative bodies, foreign (Ch. 17), 327–336
Letter of transmittal (2.3e), 10
Looseleaf work, "blue" folios marked (1.12), 2
-ly, words ending in (6.20), 102

M

M., Mlle., etc. (9.29), 226
Magnification symbol (10.3), 263
Magnitudes (9.59), 238
Makeup (2.3–2.19), 10–12
Backstrips, run down (2.19), 12
Facing pages (2.7), 11
Fold-ins to be avoided (1.14), 2

Footnotes:
Leaderwork (14.11–14.13), 305
Tabular references repeated (2.13, 13.69), 11, 294
Tabular sample (14.15), 301
Tabular work (2.96), 21
Text (15.9–15.11), 308
Illustrations (2.66–2.72), 18
Parts of book (2.3), 10
Roman numerals (2.4), 11
Running heads and folios (2.9–2.10), 11
Signature marks, imprints, etc. (2.99–2.126), 22–25
Signatures, jobs over 4 pages (1.15), 2
Sink (2.8), 11
Title pages (2.5), 11
Widow lines (2.6), 11
Marine Corps (3.18, Ch. 4, Ch. 9), 31, 67, 226–230
Market grades (3.26), 35
Marshall Islands (9.12, 9.13, Ch. 17), 223–224, 332, 338, 342, 361
Mathematical equations (10.8–10.15), 264
Signs (10.2, 10.3, 10.18), 263, 266
Measurement:
Abbreviations (9.56–9.58), 236–238
Conversion table (Ch. 17), 347
Metric equivalents (Ch. 17), 345–347
Numerals (12.9j), 276–277
Symbols (9.62), 248–252
Medals (*see* Decorations).
Meridians and base lines (Ch. 18), 352–353
Messrs. (9.29), 226
Meteorology signs/symbols (10.18), 266–268
Metric:
Abbreviations (9.56–9.57), 236–237
Equivalents (Ch. 17), 345–346
Military:
Dates (8.56, 12.9c), 204, 275
Installations, State name with (9.12), 223
Time (12.9b, 12.14), 275, 279
Titles:
Abbreviations (Ch. 9), 226–230

Capitalization (3.36), 37
  Enlisted rank, 228–230
  Officer rank, 226–228
  Units, ordinals used (12.10), 278
Millimeters, converted to (Ch. 17), 341
Million, etc.:
  Roman numerals (12.29), 284
  Use of figures with (12.24), 282–283
Minute:
  Abbreviation (9.58), 238
  Latitude, longitude (9.51–9.52, 12.9f), 235, 276
  Time (12.9b, 12.9n), 275, 277
    Astronomical (9.59, 12.9b), 238, 275
Money:
  Abbreviations and symbols (9.60, 12.9k, Ch. 17), 238, 277, 339–344
  Decimals (12.9k), 277
  Fractions (12.26–12.28), 283
Months:
  Abbreviations (9.44–9.45, 13.5), 233, 285
    mo (9.58), 238
  Punctuation (8.53, 8.77–8.79, 12.9c), 203, 207, 275
Moon (3.31), 36
  Signs (10.18), 266–268
Mount, not abbreviated (9.19), 225
Mr., Mrs.:
  Abbreviation, when used (9.29), 226
  Type (9.37, 16.3), 231, 313
  With other abbreviations (9.33), 230
Mr. Chairman, etc. (3.37), 38

N

Names (*see* Personal names, Natives).
Nation, etc. (3.20–3.21), 32–33
Nationalities (*see* Demonyms).
Natives:
  Foreign countries (Ch. 17), 337–339
  States, U.S. (5.23–5.24), 95–96
Nature (3.34), 36
Navy, Naval, etc. (3.18, Ch. 4, Ch. 9), 31, 68–69, 226–230
Near East (3.22), 33

Newspapers:
  Capitalization (3.40), 39
  Datelines (16.8), 315
  Italic not used (11.2), 269
No., Nos. (9.38), 231
  Not abbreviated (13.22), 287
Northern Mariana Islands (9.12–9.13, Ch. 17), 223–224, 342, 367
Note (1.22, 8.111, 13.53, 13.74), 5, 213, 292, 294
Nouns:
  Capitalization (3.6–3.11, 3.50), 28–29, 41
  Compounding (6.8–6.11), 98–99
  Nationalities, foreign (Ch. 17), 337–339
  Plural forms (5.5–5.10), 88–91
  States, natives of (5.23), 95
*n*th degree (11.12), 271
Number:
  Abbreviation (*see* No.).
  Chemical elements (10.16), 264–265
  Mark (#) (10.6, 10.18, 15.15), 263, 266–268, 308
Numerals (Chapter 12), 273–284
  Age (12.9a), 274
  Beginning a sentence (12.16), 280
    Related numerals (12.25), 283
  Chemical elements (6.43, 10.16), 108, 264–265
  Chemical formulas (6.44, 12.15), 108, 279
  Clock time (9.54, 12.9b), 236, 275
  Colon affecting use (12.8), 274
  Compound (6.36–6.39), 106–107
  Dates (*see* Dates).
  Decimals (12.9d), 275
  Degrees (12.9f), 276
  Equations (10.8–10.15), 264
  Expressed in figures (12.4–12.13), 273–279
  Formal writing (12.19), 281
  Fractions (*see* Fractions).
  Game scores (12.9g), 276
  Hearings, etc. (12.17), 280
  Indefinite expressions (12.22), 281–282
  Land descriptions (9.21), 225

Large numbers (12.20, 12.24), 281–283
Market quotations (12.9h), 276
Mathematical expressions (12.9i), 276
Measurement and time (12.9a–12.9o),
    274–278
    In relation to other figures (12.6), 274
Money (9.60, 12.9k), 238, 277
Ordinals (*see* Ordinals).
Percentage (12.9l), 277
Proportion or ratio (12.9m), 277
Punctuation (8.52, 8.113–8.114, 12.14),
    203, 214, 279
Roman (*see* Roman numerals).
Serial (12.7), 274
Single:
    10 or more (12.4), 273
    Under 10 (12.23), 282
    Unit of measurement, etc. (12.6), 274
Spelled out (12.16–12.25), 276, 280–283
Tabular work (13.101), 298
Time (12.9n), 277
Unit modifiers (6.23, 6.36–6.37, 6.39,
    12.9o), 103, 106, 107, 278
Vitamins (12.9p), 278
With abbreviations (9.5, 13.4), 221, 285

O

O, Oh:
    Capitalization (3.60), 43
    Exclamation point (8.88–8.89), 209–210
-o, words ending in (5.5), 88
Occident, etc. (3.22–3.23), 33–34
O'clock (9.55, 12.9b), 236, 275
Office (3.18), 31–32, 69
Op. cit. (11.3), 222, 245, 254, 269
Order (3.40), 39
Ordered (3.49, 11.11), 41, 271
Ordinals (12.10–12.13, 13.101), 278–279, 298
    Beginning with 10th (12.13), 279
    In relation to other ordinals or numerals
        (12.11), 278–279
    Leaderwork (12.13), 279
    Military units (12.10), 278
    Street address (12.13, 13.6), 279, 285

Tabular work (12.13, 13.102), 279, 298
Outlines:
    Indents (15.31), 311–312
    Numbering sequence (15.31), 311–312
Overruns (*see also* Indents):
    Center, side heads (2.64–2.65), 18
    Datelines, addresses, and signatures
        (16.5, 16.26), 313–314, 320–324
    Hanging indents (2.61–2.62), 17
    Indexes (15.23–15.25), 309–310
    Leaderwork (14.4), 303–304
    Paragraphs (2.59–2.65), 17–18
    Tabular work (13.89–13.93), 296–297
        Total, mean, and average lines
            (13.91–13.93), 296–297

P

Pact (3.40), 39
Page (3.10), 29
    Abbreviation (9.38), 231
    Numbers (2.4, 15.22, 15.30), 11, 309, 311
Palau (9.12–9.13, Ch. 17, Ch. 18), 223–224,
    333, 338, 342, 368
Paper stock (1.16), 2–3
Paragraph (3.8), 29
    Abbreviation (9.38), 231
    Mark (¶) (10.6), 263
Paragraphs:
    Brackets, more than one paragraph
        (8.22), 198
    Indents (2.60–2.61), 17–18
        Overruns (2.61–2.62), 17
    Italic letters indicating (11.15), 272
    Numbering sequence (8.112), 213–214
Parentheses (8.95–8.106), 210–212
    Abbreviations in (9.2), 221
        Citations or references (9.45), 233
        Congressional (9.41–9.43), 232–233
        Latitude, longitude (9.51), 235
        Parts of publications (9.38), 231
        Steamships, railroads (9.27), 226
    Alignment in tables (13.59, 13.63), 293
    Byline (8.105), 212
    Chemical formulas (6.44), 108

Clauses (8.96), 210
Closed up (2.41, 8.98, 8.102), 15, 211
Column numbers or letters (13.23), 287
Enclose letters or figures (8.98), 211
Equations (10.14), 264
Explanatory word (8.97), 211
More than one paragraph (8.106), 212
Not part of main statement (8.95), 210
Paragraph sequence (8.112), 213–214
Type (8.153), 220
Verifying numbers (8.99, 12.18), 211, 280
With punctuation (8.100–8.102), 211–212
Part (3.9), 29
Abbreviation (9.38), 231
Particles (3.14–3.17), 30–31
Parts of books:
Abbreviations (9.38–9.40), 231–232
Capitalization (3.9, 3.40–341), 29, 39
Makeup (2.3), 10
Quotation marks (8.133), 217
Percent (5.2), 83
Mark (10.18, 15.15), 267, 304
Use of figures (12.9l), 277
Period (8.107–8.127), 212–216
Abbreviations (8.115, 9.6–9.7), 214, 221–222
After article, section, etc. (8.117), 214
Boxheads (8.119), 215
Decimals (8.113, 12.9d, 13.29–13.32), 214, 275, 285
Declarative sentence (8.107), 212
Ellipses (8.80–8.86), 208–209
Explanatory matter within parentheses (8.126), 215
Indirect question (8.108), 212
In lieu of parentheses (8.109), 213
Inside-outside quotation marks (8.138–8.139), 218
Legends (2.70, 8.116), 18, 214
Letters used as names (8.121), 215
Metric abbreviations (9.56–9.57), 236–237
Middle initial not abbreviation (8.122), 214

Multiplication (8.118), 214
Omitted (8.119–8.127, 9.3, 13.13, 15.23), 215–216, 221, 286, 309–310
Overruns, in indexes (15.23), 309–310
Roman numerals (8.124), 215
Run-in sideheads (8.111), 213
Short name not abbreviation (8.123, 9.23), 215, 225
Symbols (8.119), 215
To indicate thousands (8.114), 214
Words and incomplete statements (8.125), 215
Periodicals, titles of:
Capitalization (3.40–3.41, 3.43), 39
Italic not used (11.2), 269
Makeup (2.2–2.3), 7–10
Personal names:
Abbreviations followed (8.123, 9.23–9.24), 215, 225
Initials set without space (8.43, 9.7, 9.34), 202, 222, 230
Particles (3.14–3.17), 30–31
Variations (8.123, 9.23–9.24), 215, 225
Personification (3.34), 36
Physics, signs and symbols (10.18), 266–268
Physiographic regions (Ch. 18), 350–351
Pica conversion table (Ch. 17), 347
Pickup matter (2.32), 14
Correcting (2.44), 16
Place:
Abbreviation (9.16, 13.6), 224, 285
Ordinals (12.13, 13.6), 279, 285
Planets (3.31), 36
Plate (3.10), 29
Abbreviation (9.38), 231
Numbers aligned (15.28), 310
Plurals:
Apostrophe (8.7, 8.11), 194, 195–196
Coined (8.11), 195–196
Common noun as part of proper name (3.9), 29
Compound words (5.6–5.8), 87–88
Irregular (5.10), 90–91
Latin names (3.29), 35

Letters and figures (8.11), 195–196
Nouns ending in -ful (5.9), 90
Nouns ending in -o (5.5), 88
Word plurals (8.13), 196
Poetry:
Capitalization of titles (3.40), 39
Congressional Record (Ch. 19), 390–391
Credit line (8.70), 206
Quotation marks (3.40, 8.133), 39, 217
Point, not abbreviated (9.19), 225
Points, converted to (Ch. 17), 347
Political parties (3.18, Ch. 4), 31–32, 68
Adherents (3.19, Ch. 4), 32, 68
Port, not abbreviated (9.19), 225
Possessions, U.S. (9.12–9.14, Ch. 18),
223–224, 354–374
Possessives and apostrophes (see
Apostrophes and possessives).
Post (11.3), 269
Post Office (Ch. 4), 71
Box, as part of address (Ch. 4), 71
Directory of Post Offices (5.20), 95
ZIP Code numbers (8.55, 16.1), 204, 313
Pound mark (see Money, Number).
Preface (2.3g, 2.12), 10, 11
Prefixes (6.7, 6.29–6.35), 98, 104–106
Metric (9.56), 236–237
Preliminary pages (2.3–2.4), 10–11
Roman numerals for (2.4), 11
Preparing copy:
Abbreviations spelled out (2.42), 15
Bills (2.40), 15
Capitalization (2.26, 2.36), 13, 14
Copy kept clean (2.45), 16
Cut-in notes (2.33), 14
Datelines, addresses, and signatures
(2.27), 13
Addresses (16.9–16.16), 315–317
Datelines (16.5–16.8), 313–315
Signatures (16.17–16.28), 317–324
Decimals (2.28), 13
Et cetera, etc. (2.29), 13
Extracts (2.23), 12

FIC & punc., Fol. lit. (2.39–2.41), 15
Figures (2.25, 2.39), 13, 15
Folioing and stamping (2.30), 14
Footnotes and reference marks:
Tabular work (13.65–13.84), 293–295
Text (15.1–15.19), 307–309
Heads (2.31, 3.50–3.58), 14, 41–42
Instructions to be followed (2.41, 11.5),
15, 269
Italic (2.27, 2.39, Ch. 11), 13, 15, 269–272
Pickup (2.32), 14
Plurals (2.37, 8.13), 15, 196
Punctuation followed (2.39–2.41), 15
Sidenotes (2.33), 14
Signs, symbols, etc. (2.34–2.35), 14
Type to indicate shape (2.36–2.38), 14–15
Prepositions (3.53), 41–42
In compound nouns (6.47), 107
Presidents and Vice Presidents, U.S.,
325–326
Pronouns:
Compounding (6.12–6.13), 100
Possessive (8.8–8.9), 194–195
Proofreader's marks (1.22), 4–5
Proofreading (2.73–2.85), 18–19
Proofs:
Clean (2.45, 2.94a), 16, 20
Marking (1.18–1.20), 2
Proportion (8.36, 12.9m), 201, 277
Provided, etc.:
Capitalization following (3.49), 40–41
Italic (3.49, 11.11), 40–41, 271
Province (3.20), 32–33
Not abbreviated (9.15), 224
Public Law, etc. (3.40), 39
Not abbreviated (9.41, 9.43), 232, 233
Publications (see Periodicals):
GPO (1.21), 3
Puerto Rico (9.12–9.13), 223–224, 369
Punctuation (Chapter 8), 193–220
Abbreviations:
Omitted (8.127, 9.3, 13.13), 216, 221,
286

When used (8.43, 9.6), 202, 221
Apostrophe (8.3–8.18), 193–197
Brackets (8.19–8.22), 197–198
Colon (8.23–8.37), 198–201
Comma (8.38–8.63), 201–205
  Before and after abbreviations (8.43),
    202
  Omitted (8.54–8.63), 204–205
  Used (8.38–8.53), 201–203
Dash (3-em) (8.75), 206
Dash (em) (8.64–8.74), 205–206
  Not used (8.73–8.74), 206
  Used (8.64–8.72), 205–206
Dash (en) (8.76–8.79), 207–208
  Not used (8.78–8.79), 208
  Used (8.76–8.77), 207
Ellipses (8.80–8.86), 208–209
Exclamation point (8.87–8.89), 209–210
Function (8.1, 8.2), 193
Hyphen (8.90–8.94), 210
  Compounding (Ch. 6), 97–109
Legends (2.69, 8.116), 18, 214
Numerals (12.14), 279
Parentheses (8.95–8.106), 210–212
Period (8.107–8.127), 212–216
  Omitted (8.119–8.127), 215–216
  Used (8.107–8.118), 212–214
Question mark (8.128–8.130), 216
Quotation marks (8.131–8.147), 216–219
  Not used (8.142–8.147), 218–219
  Used (8.131–8.141), 216–218
Semicolon (8.148–8.151), 219–220
Sentence (2.49), 16
Single (8.128, 8.152), 216, 220

Q

Quantity (*see* Units of quantity).
Quart (9.58), 237–238
  Metric equivalent (Ch. 17), 345, 347
Quasi-, ex-, self- (6.34), 105
Queen (3.36–3.37), 37–38
Queries:
  Department must answer (1.20), 2

Not to be set (2.46), 16
Proofreading (2.74–2.76), 19
Question mark (8.128–8.130), 216
  Closed up (8.130), 216
  Direct query (8.45, 8.128), 202, 216
  Doubt (8.129–8.130), 216
  With quotation marks (8.138, 8.141), 218
Quotation marks (8.131–8.147), 216–219
  Addresses, books, etc. (8.133), 217
  Called, so-called, etc. (8.132), 216–217
  Direct quotations (8.131), 216
  Display initial with (8.147), 219
  Double, single, double (8.141), 218
  Entitled, marked, etc. (8.132), 216–217
  Extracts, omitted (2.23, 8.145), 12, 219
  Indirect quotations (8.146), 219
  Letters within a letter (8.135), 217
    Complete letter (8.144), 219
  Misnomers, slang, etc. (8.136), 217–218
  More than one paragraph (8.134), 217
  Precede footnote references (8.140), 218
  Punctuation with (8.51, 8.138–8.139),
    203, 218
  Scientific names (11.10), 267
  Spacing (8.137, 8.141), 218
  Tabular work (13.123), 298
  Thin space (8.137), 218
  Vessels (11.7, 11.8), 270
Quotations:
  Capitalization (3.44, 3.46), 40
  Comma before (8.39), 201
  Ellipses (8.80–8.86), 208–209

R

Railroads, abbreviated (9.27, 13.8), 226, 285
Ramseyer rule (Ch. 20), 426 fn.
Reference marks (*see* Footnotes and
  references).
Reference materials, GPO (1.21), 3
Region (3.10), 29
  Ordinals (12.10), 278
Regular, etc. (3.18, Ch. 4), 31, 48, 59, 69–79
Related numbers:

Group (12.5, 12.25), 273–274, 283
Ordinals (12.10–12.13), 278–279
Religious terms (3.35, Ch. 4), 37, 72
Report (3.40–3.41, Ch. 4), 39, 72
  With quotation marks (3.41, 8.133), 39,
    217
Reports and Hearings (Chapter 20),
  425–440
  Samples, 427–440
Representative (3.18), 32
  Not abbreviated (9.30), 230
Reprint:
  "All roman (no italic)" exceptions (11.5),
    269
  Dates (2.123–2.124), 25
  Pickup (2.32), 14
  Signature marks (2.124), 25
Republic (3.20), 32–33
Reservation (3.5), 27–28
  State name with (9.12), 223
Resolution (3.40), 39
  Abbreviation (9.42, 13.11), 232, 286
Resolved, etc. (3.49), 40
  Italic (3.49, 11.11), 40–41, 271
Reverend, etc. (9.31), 230
Revising (2.86–2.98), 20–22
  Galley (2.86–2.89), 20
  Page (2.90–2.96), 20–21
  Press (2.97–2.98), 21–22
Rivers (Ch. 18), 353
Road:
  Abbreviation (9.16, 13.6), 224, 285
  Ordinals (12.13, 13.6), 279, 285
Roman numerals:
  Army corps (12.10), 274
  Figure columns:
    Indexes and contents (15.22), 309
    Tabular work (13.62), 293
  List (12.29), 284
  Not preferred (12.3), 273
  Period:
    Aligned in contents (15.28), 310
    Not used after (8.124), 215

Preliminary pages (2.4), 11
Royal titles (3.36–3.37, 3.39), 37–38
Rules in tables (13.3), 285
Running heads:
  Copy for, supplied (1.19), 2
  Makeup (2.10–2.11), 11
  Period omitted (8.119), 215

S

Sales notices (2.125–2.126), 25
Salutation:
  Capitalization (3.59, 16.15), 42, 316
  Colon after (8.30, 16.15), 200, 316
  Italic (8.30, 16.14), 200, 316
Scientific terms:
  Abbreviations, punctuation omitted
    (9.3), 221
  Capitalization (3.27–3.32), 35–36
  Compounding (6.42–6.45), 108
  Italic (11.9–11.10, 13.95), 271, 297
  Quotation marks with (11.10), 271
  Set in roman (11.9), 271
Scriptures, etc. (3.33), 36
Seaboard (3.22), 33–34
Seal (16.27–16.28), 323–324
Seasons (3.23), 34
2d, 3d, etc.:
  Comma omitted before (8.43, 8.63, 9.32),
    202, 205, 230
  Ordinals (12.10–12.11), 278–279
  Type (9.32, 16.3), 230, 313
Secretary, etc. (3.35), 37–38, 74
  General, 74
    No hyphen (6.40), 107
    Plural form (5.8), 89–90
Section (3.10), 29, 74
  Abbreviation (9.38, 13.10), 231, 286
    Not abbreviated (9.39), 232
  Caps and small caps (9.39), 232
  Italic to indicate (11.15), 272
  Roman, over figure column (15.21), 309
Section mark (§):
  Footnote reference (15.14), 308

Space after (10.6), 263

-sede, -cede, -ceed (5.13), 93

See, see also:

   Italic (11.11, 15.20), 271, 309

   Roman (13.95), 297

See footnote, etc. (15.4), 307

Self-, ex-, quasi- (6.34), 105

Semicolon (8.148–8.151), 219–220

   Avoid, where comma will suffice (8.151), 220

   Before summarizing matter (8.150), 219

   Clauses containing commas (8.148), 219

Senate, 74

Senator, 74

   Not abbreviated (9.30), 230

Serial:

   Letter, italic (11.15), 272

      Parentheses (8.98), 211

   Numbers:

      Comma omitted (8.58, 12.14), 204, 279

      Figures used (12.7), 274

      Parentheses (8.98), 211

Session:

   Abbreviation (9.41, 13.11), 232, 286

   Ordinals (9.41, 13.11), 232, 286

Shape, letters used (2.36–2.38), 14–15

Shilling mark, in fractions (12.27), 283

   Sign (10.18), 266–268

Signature marks (2.99–2.110), 22–23

Signatures:

   Abbreviations (9.24, 16.19), 225, 317

   Capitalization (3.59, 16.2), 42, 313

   Caps and small caps (9.37), 231

   Examples (16.17–16.27), 317–323

   Preceded by dash (8.70, 16.17), 206, 317

   Preparation (2.27), 13

   Punctuation (16.23), 318

   Quoted matter (16.25), 320

Signed (8.132), 216

   In signatures (16.24), 318–321

Signs and Symbols (Chapter 10), 263–268

   Chemical:

      Elements (6.43, 10.16), 108, 264–265

Formulas (6.44, 10.15, 12.15), 108, 264, 279

Coined words and symbols (8.11, 8.76, 8.136, 9.48), 195–196, 207, 217, 234–235

Degree mark (9.50–9.51, 9.53, 9.56, 10.4, 12.9f), 235–237, 263, 276

Equations (10.8–10.15), 264

Footnote references (15.12–15.19), 308–309

   Sequence (15.14), 308

Foreign money (9.60, Ch. 17), 238, 339–344

Italic letters (2.72, 10.7–10.8, 11.12–11.15), 18, 264, 271–272

Legends (2.73), 18

List (10.18), 266–268

Mathematical signs (10.2–10.3), 263

Preparing copy (2.34–2.35), 14

Standardized (10.17), 266

Symbol columns (13.114–13.115), 299

$\times$, crossed with, magnification (10.3), 263

Single punctuation (8.128, 8.152), 216, 220

Sink (2.8), 11

Small caps:

   Etc., et al. (3.57), 42

   Heads spaced with regular justification spaces (2.50), 16

   Italic inferior letters (10.8), 264

   Proper names (3.51–3.52), 41

   Roman numerals (2.4, 15.22), 10, 309

   Seal (16.27–16.28), 323

   v., lowercase in legal cases (11.8), 270

Soil orders (3.30), 35

Spacing (*see* Leading and spacing).

Spelling (Chapter 5), 81–96

   Anglicized and foreign words (5.3–5.4), 87–88

   Apostrophes and possessives (8.3–8.18), 193–197

   -cede, -ceed, -sede (5.13), 93

   Doubled consonants (5.14–5.15), 94

   Geographic names (5.20–5.21), 95

   Idiomatic phrases (6.52), 109

   Indefinite articles, use of (5.16–5.19), 94

List (5.2), 81–87
Nationalities (5.22–5.24), 95–96
Native American words (5.25), 96
Plural forms (5.5–5.10), 88–91
Transliteration (5.26), 96
Square (Ch. 4, Ch. 7), 75, 175
Abbreviation (9.16, 13.6), 224, 285
Ordinals (12.13, 13.6), 278, 285
Stars (*see* Ellipses).
State, etc. (3.20, Ch. 4), 32, 75
Staten Island (9.14), 224
States (3.6, 3.20, 3.22, Ch. 7), 28, 32, 33, 75–76, 175
Abbreviations (8.76, 9.12–9.13), 207, 223–224
Capitals (Ch. 17, Ch. 18), 326, 354–374
Counties (Ch. 17), 354–374
Natives of (5.23), 95
Station (3.7, 3.10, Ch. 7), 28–29, 76, 175
State abbreviation with (9.12), 223
Statutes, etc. (3.40), 39
Abbreviations (9.43, 13.11), 233, 286
Street, 76
Abbreviation (9.16, 13.6), 224, 285
Ordinals (12.13, 13.6), 279, 285
Subentries (8.29, 13.89–13.90, 13.112, 14.15), 200, 296, 299, 305
Subheads:
Indexes and contents (15.29), 310
Leaderwork (14.10), 304
Suffixes (6.30–6.31), 105
Summation sign (10.14), 264
Sun (3.31), 36, 76
Sign (10.18), 266–268
Superior figures and letters:
Astrophysical matter (9.59), 238
Chemical elements (6.43), 108
Comma omitted (8.54), 204
Equations (10.8), 264
Follow inferiors (10.15), 264
Footnote references (13.66, 15.12, 15.17), 293, 308–309
Italic letters (8.54, 10.8, 11.12), 204, 264, 271

Preparing (2.33), 14
Type (8.153), 220
With punctuation (8.137), 218
Supra:
Italic (11.3), 269
Not abbreviated (9.49), 235
Survey (3.18), 31–32
Symbols (*see* Signs and Symbols)

T

Table (*see also* Useful Tables) (3.9, Ch. 4, Ch. 17), 29, 77, 325
Table of contents (*see* Contents).
Tabular Work (Chapter 13) (*see also* Leaderwork), 285–302
Abbreviations (13.4–13.13), 285–286
Bearoff (13.14–13.17), 286
Leaderwork (14.2–14.4), 303–304
Tables without rules (13.116, 13.119), 300, 301
Boxheads (13.18–13.23), 286–287
Horizontal (13.19–13.21), 286
Centerheads, flush entries, and subentries (13.25–13.28), 288
Ciphers (13.29–13.36), 289–290
Column numbers or letters (13.23), 287
Continued heads (13.37–13.38), 290
Dash instead of colon (13.26), 288
Dashes or rules (13.39–13.40), 290
To separate nonmoney groups (13.53), 292
Date column (13.28), 288
Decimals, alignment (13.29–13.36, 13.64), 289–290, 293
Ditto (Do.) (13.41–13.50), 290–291
Closing quotes (13.41), 290
Divide tables (13.103–13.108), 296
Dollar mark (13.51–13.56), 292
Figure columns (13.57–13.64), 293
Decimals (13.29–13.32, 13.63–13.64), 289, 293
Footnotes and references (13.66–13.84), 293–295
Fractions (13.85–13.86), 295–296

Hairline rules (13.3), 285
Headnotes (13.87–13.88, 13.103), 296, 298
Indents and overruns (13.89–13.93), 296
  Subentries (13.89–13.90), 296
  Total, mean, and average lines
    (13.91–13.93), 296
Italic (13.94–13.95), 297
Leaders (13.96–13.100), 297–298
Leading:
  Boxheads, solid in leaded tables
    (13.20), 286
  Notes (13.84), 295
Makeup (*see* Makeup)
No. (13.22), 287
None (13.33, 13.35, 13.45), 289–291
Numerals (13.101), 298
Parallel tables (13.102–13.108), 298
Quoted tables (13.123), 302
Reading columns (13.109–13.113), 299
See, see also (13.95), 297
Subentries (13.89–13.90, 13.112), 296, 299
Symbol columns (13.114–13.115), 299
Tables without rules (*see also*
  Leaderwork) (13.116–13.119), 300–302
Total, mean, and average lines (13.91–
  13.93), 296–297
Tracing figures (13.106, 13.108), 298
Type (2.23, 13.3), 12, 285
Units of quantity (13.120–13.122), 302
  Spacing (13.28), 288
  Years, spacing (13.28), 288
Technical terms (*see* Scientific terms).
Telephone numbers (8.58, 8.76, 12.7), 204,
  207, 274
Temperature, abbreviations (9.53), 235–236
Temperature conversion (Ch. 17), 345
Terrace:
  Abbreviation (9.16, 13.6), 224, 285
  Ordinals (12.13, 13.6), 279, 285
Territory, etc. (3.20, Ch. 4), 32, 77
Territories, U.S. (9.12–9.18), 223–224,
  354–374
Text footnotes (*see* Footnotes and
  references).

The:
  Part of speech (3.53), 41–42
  Title, part of (3.12–3.13, 9.31), 29–30, 230
Thin space:
  Footnotes (13.68, 15.12), 294, 308
  Names (3.51–3.52), 41
  Number mark, not used with (10.6), 263
  Paragraph mark (10.6), 263
  Quotation marks (8.137), 218
  Section mark (10.6), 263
Time:
  Abbreviations (9.54–9.55, 9.58, 9.59),
    236–238
  Astronomical (12.9b, 12.14), 275, 279
  Capitalization, 77
  Clock (12.9n), 277
  Geologic, 349
  Military (12.9b, 12.14), 275, 279
  Use of figures (9.59, 12.9b, 12.9n), 238,
    275, 277
  Zones (Ch. 4, 9.47), 77, 234
Title (3.10), 29, 77
Title page:
  Back of (2.3d), 10
  Congressional back title samples:
    Appropriations hearing, 438
    Conference report, 434
  Imprints, etc. (2.103, 2.111–2.122), 22–24
  Makeup (2.3–2.19), 10–12
  Part of book (2.3c), 10
  Period omitted at ends of lines (8.119),
    215
  U.S., not abbreviated (9.9), 222–223
Titles:
  Acts (3.42), 39
  Books, plays, songs, publications, papers,
    etc. (3.40–3.43, 8.133, 11.2), 39, 217, 265
  Civil and military:
    Abbreviations (9.25, 9.29–9.37),
      225–226, 226–231
    Compound (6.40–6.41), 107
    Plurals (5.8), 89–90
  Common nouns (3.37), 37–38
  Foreign books (3.43), 39

Heads of state, 327–336

Legal cases (3.40, 11.8), 39, 270

Persons (3.36–3.39), 37–38

Second person (3.39), 38

To, en dash for (8.78, 12.9c, 12.9m, 13.110), 208, 275, 277, 299

To Whom It May Concern (8.30, 16.14), 200, 316

Tracing figures (*see* Tabular work).

Trade names (3.26), 35, 77

Treasury, etc. (3.18), 31–32, 77

Treaty (3.10, 3.40), 29, 39, 77

Tribunal (3.18), 31–32, 78

Tunnel, 78

Type:

Boldface, punctuation in (8.153), 220

Brackets (8.153), 220

Illustrating shape and form (2.36–2.38), 14–15

Composition:

Correcting pickup (2.44), 16

Proofs, clean (2.45), 16

Dash (8.153), 220

Datelines, addresses, and signatures (16.2–16.3), 313

Extracts (2.23, 8.145), 12, 219

Footnotes (15.5), 307

Headnotes (2.14, 13.87–13.88), 11, 296

Headings (2.30, 3.50–3.58), 13, 41–42

Indexes and contents (15.20, 15.29–15.30), 309, 310–311

Italic (Ch. 11), 269–272

Vessels (11.6–11.7), 269–270

Jr., Sr. (9.37, 16.3), 231, 313

Leaderwork (14.1), 303

Legends (2.68), 18

Mr., Mrs., etc. (9.37, 16.3), 231, 313

Note (8.111, 13.53), 213, 292

Parentheses (8.153), 220

Picas converted to inches (Ch. 17), 347

Seal (16.27–16.28), 323–324

Signature marks (2.101), 22

Special typefaces (1.11), 2

Tabular work (2.23, 13.3), 12, 285

Text (2.23), 12

U

Under Secretary (*see also* Secretary) (Ch. 4), 78

Union (3.20), 32, 78

& in name (9.25), 225–226

Comma omitted between name and number (8.53), 203

Unit modifiers (*see* Compounding).

United Nations (3.18, Ch. 7), 31, 78

Units of quantity:

Leaderwork (14.14), 305

Numerals (12.6, 12.9), 274–278

Tabular work (13.120–13.122), 302

U.S. (*see* Possessions, Territories):

Abbreviation (9.9–9.10, 13.7), 222–223, 285

Closed up (9.7), 222

Spelled out (9.9–9.10), 222–223

Presidents and Vice Presidents (Ch. 17), 325–326

USD (9.60, Ch. 17), 238, 343

Useful Tables (Chapter 17), 325–347

Chemical elements (10.61), 264–265

Currency (Ch. 17), 340–344

Demonyms (nationalities) (Ch. 17), 337–339

Foreign countries, capitals, chiefs of state, etc. (Ch. 17), 327–336

Geologic time (Ch. 18), 349

Measures, metric, etc. (Ch. 17), 345–347

Meridians and base lines (Ch. 18), 352

Military titles (Ch. 9), 226–230

Physiographic regions, U.S. (Ch. 18), 350–351

Postal abbreviations (9.13), 224

Public land surveys (Ch. 18), 353

Rivers (Ch. 18), 353

Roman numerals (12.29), 284

Signs and symbols (10.18), 266–268

State populations and their capitals (Ch. 18), 326

Temperature conversion, 339

U.S. Presidents and Vice Presidents (Ch. 17), 325–326

V

v.:
  Italic (11.8, 13.94), 270, 297
  Roman (11.8), 270
Van, von (3.14–3.17), 30–31
Verbs:
  Adverb compounds (6.9), 98
  Capitalization (3.53), 41–42
    Infinitive (3.53, 3.56), 41–42
  Improvised (6.48), 109
Vessels:
  Abbreviations (9.27), 226
  Italic (11.6–11.7, 13.94), 269–270, 297
  Quotation marks (11.7–11.8), 270
Virgin Islands (9.12–9.13, Ch. 17), 223–224, 344, 372
Volume (3.10, Ch. 4), 29, 79
  Abbreviation (9.38), 231
    Metric (9.56), 236–237
Vowels:
  A, an, before (5.16–5.19), 94
  Hyphen, to avoid doubling (6.7), 98

W

War (3.31, Ch. 4), 36, 79

Ward (3.10, Ch. 4), 29, 79
Web (Ch. 4), 79
Website (Ch. 4, Ch. 7, 11.16), 79, 188, 272
Webster's Dictionary (5.1, 7.5), 81, 111
Weights:
  Abbreviations (9.56, 9.58), 236–238
  Metric (9.56–9.57), 236–237
  Metric equivalents (Ch. 17), 345–347
  Numerals (12.9j), 276–277
Widow lines (2.6), 11
Word division (8.91), 210
  Land descriptions (9.20–9.22), 225
  Latitude and longitude (9.50–9.52), 235
Words (see Spelling).
WWW (9.64), 261

X Y Z

x, dimension measurements (12.9j), 276–277
×, crossed with, magnification (10.3), 259
Yard (9.58), 237
  Metric equivalent (Ch. 17), 346–347
-yze, -ise, -ize (5.12), 93
Your Honor, etc. (3.39, Ch. 4), 38, 80
ZIP Code numbers (Ch. 4, 8.55, 9.61, 16.1), 53, 80, 247, 313